PUBLICATIONS OF THE NEW CHAUCER SOCIETY

THE NEW CHAUCER SOCIETY

Studies in the Age of Chaucer, the yearbook of The New Chaucer Society, is published annually. Each issue contains substantial articles on all aspects of Chaucer and his age, book reviews, and an annotated Chaucer bibliography. Manuscripts, in duplicate, accompanied by return postage, should follow the *Chicago Manual of Style,* 14th edition. Unsolicited reviews are not accepted. Authors receive free twenty offprints of articles and ten of reviews. All correspondence regarding manuscript submissions should be directed to the Editor, Frank Grady, Department of English, University of Missouri-St. Louis, 8001 Natural Bridge Road, St. Louis, MO 63121. Subscriptions to The New Chaucer Society and information about the Society's activities should be directed to David Lawton, Department of English, Washington University, CB 1122, One Brookings Drive, St. Louis, MO 63130. Back issues of the journal may be ordered from The University of Notre Dame Press, Chicago Distribution Center, 11030 South Langley Avenue, Chicago, IL 60628; phone: 800-621-2736; fax: 800-621-8476, from outside the United States: phone: 773-702-7000; fax: 773-702-7212.

Studies in the Age of Chaucer

Studies in the Age of Chaucer

Volume 27
2005

EDITOR
FRANK GRADY

PUBLISHED ANNUALLY BY THE NEW CHAUCER SOCIETY
WASHINGTON UNIVERSITY IN ST. LOUIS

The frontispiece design, showing the Pilgrims at the Tabard Inn, is adapted from the woodcut in Caxton's second edition of *The Canterbury Tales*.

ISBN 0-933784-29-5
ISSN 0190-2407

CONTENTS

CONTENTS

CONTENTS

CONTENTS

PRESIDENTIAL ADDRESS
The New Chaucer Society
Fourteenth International Congress
July 15th–19th, 2004
University of Glasgow

The Presidential Address

Chaucer and the European Tradition

Winthrop Wetherbee III
Cornell University

I WILL BEGIN BY APOLOGIZING for a title that might suggest absurdly grandiose ambitions. I remain dutifully subject to the authority of Charles Muscatine, E. R. Curtius, and the other "maisters soverayn" who have helped me think about literary tradition over the years, and, to this extent at least, I emulate the Chaucer I want to talk about. The Chaucer, that is, who was the one truly European poet of his place and time, yet whose unique appreciation of the larger view of poetic tradition that distinguished the writers of *trecento* Italy coexisted with a strong sense of his alien relation to this tradition. Despite the inspiration he drew from the example of Dante, and the deep affinity he came to feel with Boccaccio, he remained closer in spirit to the French tradition and above all to Jean de Meun. Chaucer *owned* the French tradition; his poetry is its finest flowering. But toward Italy he retained to the end something of the shyly self-deprecating attitude of the dreamer at the House of Fame. The assurance with which Dante and Boccaccio addressed the classical tradition, and the sense of the importance of poetry that their work expresses, seem to have made him keenly sensitive to the limitations of the Anglo-French poetic tradition to which he himself had been apprenticed.

I want to examine the ways in which this sense of limitations finds expression in Chaucer's work, how he both demonstrates an awareness of what poetry in the highest sense might be, and how, by design, and often to telling effect, he avoids a direct response to the challenge this knowledge represents. I will begin by considering a specific instance of challenge and response: Dante's and Chaucer's versions of the story of Ugolino of Pisa.

3

A brief essay by Jorge Luis Borges on *Inferno* 33, the canto of Count Ugolino, addresses the qualities in Ugolino's story that seem to me to have most impressed Chaucer. Borges's concern is with what he calls the "false problem" posed by line 75 of the canto, Ugolino's famous assertion that after days of starvation, during which he witnessed the deaths of four sons, "hunger proved more powerful than grief." Borges reviews the history of critical commentary on Ugolino's enigmatic declaration, and concludes that we *cannot* know whether Ugolino was driven to eat the flesh of the four victims or simply died of hunger after withstanding the effects of grief. To attempt to resolve this question, moreover, is to misread Dante's purpose, for the ambiguity is crucial to the effect of the scene: "To deny or affirm Ugolino's monstrous crime," says Borges, "is less horrifying than to be stunned by it."[1]

The one complex turn in Borges's generally straightforward argument occurs when he cites the earlier lines in which Ugolino's sons offer themselves to their father as food:

"tu ne vestisti
queste misere carne, e tu le spoglia."
(*Inferno* 33.62–63)

["you did clothe us
with this wretched flesh; and do you strip us of it."]

In the face of a hallowed critical tradition, Borges professes to find here "one of the very few falsehoods present in the *Commedia*": Dante, he says, "could not but feel its falseness, which is made more serious, without doubt, by the circumstance of the four children simultaneously toasting the ravenous banquet. Some will insinuate that we are dealing with a lie by Ugolino, concocted to justify (to suggest) the previous crime."

Borges's insistence on the falseness of the scene is based not just on the implausibility of Ugolino's depiction of his children's last hours but on its quality as art. There is a sense in which this narrative is unworthy of Ugolino—or, better, incommensurate with the power of Dante's con-

---

[1] "El falso problema de Ugolino," in *Nuevos ensayos dantescos* (Madrid: Espasa-Calpe, 1982), pp. 105–11; I quote from the English translation of the essay by Nicoletta Alegi in Giuseppe Mazzotta, ed., *Critical Essays on Dante* (Boston: G. K. Hall, 1991), pp. 185–88.

ception of him. Of all the damned souls in the *Inferno*, only Ugolino is assigned a punishment that consists in the perpetual avenging of the wrongs he claims to have undergone. The desire for vengeance that drives him to gnaw endlessly on the neck of Archbishop Ruggiero is of course insatiable, an eternal goad, but he is allowed to believe that he is causing eternal pain to his victim, and it is in order to inflict the further pain of infamy that he interrupts his labors to tell the story of Ruggiero's treachery. Dante goes so far as to hint at a kind of savage enthusiasm for the endless task when he compares Ugolino to a dog gnawing a bone (78).

It is as if the sheer force of Ugolino's obsession with his wrongs had placed on Dante's sense of justice a claim that could not be denied. Like Farinata, Ulysses, or Guido da Montefeltro, he compels our attention in ways to which the sin of which he stands condemned seems irrelevant, defying judgment and inviting a kind of admiring sympathy. On first seeing Ugolino, Dante himself raises the possibility that his rage against Ruggiero may be justified (*Inf.* 32.135–39), and he is given sole possession of the first seventy-five lines of his canto, a privilege elsewhere granted only to Justinian and Saint Bernard. Although Dante later concedes that Ugolino had been called a traitor (33.85–86), he does not confirm the charge, and the condemnation that follows is directed not against the Count but against his city. That this condemnation centers on the treatment of the children suggests a tacit sympathy with Ugolino's intense rage, and an unquestioning acceptance of his story—a story that only Dante has heard. But the focus of Dante's sympathy suggests as well the Pilgrim's vulnerability to the appeal of sentimental piety in Ugolino's narrative, an appeal that stands in unresolved contradiction to the colossal force of his pain and rage, his embodiment of the plight of "unaccommodated man,"[2] tragically at the mercy of his need for food, family, and vindication.

It is this strange, savage power that led Matthew Arnold to discover in Ugolino's colossal self-absorption, as in that of Milton's Satan, something monumental, almost a kind of heroism.[3] It is what makes the

---

[2] I borrow this apt citation of *Lear* from Robin Kirkpatrick's excellent discussion of Canto 33, *Dante's Inferno: Difficulty and Dead Poetry* (Cambridge: Cambridge University Press, 1987), pp. 415–27.

[3] In his essay "The Study of Poetry" (*Essays in Criticism: Second Series* [London, 1888], pp. 16–18), Arnold cites lines 49 and 50, in which Ugolino contrasts his own stony incapacity for grief with the weeping of his children. For Arnold, these lines exhibit "the very highest poetic quality."

pathos of his account of his sons' suffering, which many have seen as both strongly moving and spiritually profound,[4] ring false both for Borges and, I am quite sure, for Ugolino himself. The elaborate emotionalism of Ugolino's appeal aims at extorting grief and tears from the Pilgrim (40–42), but the experience he relates had left the speaker himself unmoved. We need not question Ugolino's account of how, being now blind, he had groped over his sons' bodies and called their names (72–74), but we must recognize also his inability to reach out to them while they were still alive. At no point does he express remorse for this failure, and, when at last, irredeemably cut off from any possibility of repentance or reparation, he acknowledges their suffering, the manner in which he does so amounts to an exploitation of their pain, an attempt to make of it grounds for his own vindication. It is a telling sign of his bad faith, and Dante's honesty, that the picture he offers is bad religious art, a narrative in which the poignancy of the young men's willingness to die, Christ-like, to ease their father's pain, makes a demand on our sensibilities that is finally outrageous.

Not only is the self-centered savagery of Ugolino impossibly distanced from the innocence and charity of the sons with whom he seeks to identify himself: the tale he tells is Kitsch, in the serious sense this quality can assume when it appears in a context that is in other respects truly serious. It is Kitsch of the sort that most of the world recognized instantly as the defining quality in Mel Gibson's cinematic treatment of the Passion of Christ, which dares us to keep our eyes fixed on its sadistic representation of sacred suffering, while at the same time inviting us to indulge in a kind of sentimental partisanship better suited to the Prioress's little clergioun, or Rocky Balboa. The same unholy coupling of extreme brutality with sentimental piety constitutes for Borges the falsehood of the narrative of Ugolino.

Chaucer of course knew Dante's Ugolino, and the version of his fall that appears in *The Monk's Tale*, perhaps influenced by Ugolino's brief but poignant appearance in Boccaccio's *De casibus virorum illustrium*,[5]

---

[4]The fullest treatment of the religious significance of the children's conduct—to which Ugolino himself is of course impervious—is that of John Freccero, "Bestial Sign and Bread of Angels, *Inferno* XXXII and XXXIII," *Yale Italian Studies* 1 (1977): 53–66; repr. in Freccero's *Dante: The Poetics of Conversion* (Cambridge, Mass.: Harvard University Press, 1986), pp. 152–66.

[5]*De casibus* 9, ed. P. G. Ricci and Vittoria Zaccaria (vol. 9 [1983] in *Tutte le Opere di Giovanni Boccaccio*, ed. Vittore Branca [Milan: Mondadori, 1965–]), p. 820: "Hugolinum Pisarum comitem vidi, amplissimo fletu ciuium suorum saeuitiam ac inediam qua cum filiis perierat deflentem."

distorts the story in a way that gives further point to Borges's reading of the Dantean episode. The Monk's Hugelyn is an apparently innocent victim, imprisoned on the "fals suggestioun" of Bishop Roger, and the Monk goes to great lengths to exploit the pathetic possibilities of his story.[6] Dante's Ugolino had taken pains to suggest that the children in his tale were small and helpless, but in fact two were grandsons, and even the younger of these, "little Anselmo" ("Anselmuccio," 50) was already in his teens at the time of their incarceration. The three sons of the Monk's Hugelyn have been explicitly reduced to little boys, and the youngest, a child of three, complains movingly of a starvation whose cause he cannot understand, before kissing his father as he dies. Ugolino, too, is altered. Where Dante's antihero describes himself as "turned inwardly to stone," unable to join his children in weeping, Hugelyn weeps freely as his children die around him, and this may suggest the community in suffering that is so strikingly absent in the *Inferno*. But in fact the selfishness of Hugelyn is as absolute as that of Ugolino, who sees in his children's faces only the reflection of his own suffering.[7] He shows emotion, but his feelings are only for himself. At the sound of the locking of the tower, he realizes that his enemies "wolde doon *hym* dyen."[8] It is for this that he weeps, and as he gnaws at his limbs he inveighs only against his own betrayal by Fortune (2445–46). The Monk has clearly let Ugolino himself dictate the tone and emphasis of his narrative. His tale aims to elicit sympathy for a bereaved parent, but the maudlin self-pity that it substitutes for the emotional void so starkly depicted in Dante's version provides instead a grotesque parallel to the artistic self-indulgence that is an ever-present danger for those who, like the Monk, practice the art of Gothic pathos.

The final line of the Monk's narrative of Hugelyn points to its limitations in another way: "From heigh estaat Fortune awey hym *carf*" (2457). The moral is utterly predictable in all but the curious verb, which reminds us that the story the Monk tells has itself been cut away,

---

[6] See Piero Boitani, What Dante Meant to Chaucer," in *Chaucer and the Italian Trecento*, ed. Boitani (Cambridge: Cambridge University Press, 1983), pp. 132–36, and the earlier discussions cited by Boitani; see also his *The Tragic and the Sublime in Medieval Literature* (Cambridge: Cambridge University Press, 1989), pp. 40–55.

[7] "e io scorsi / per quattro visi il mio aspetto stesso" (56–57).

[8] *The Monk's Tale*, 2428. All quotations of Chaucer are from Larry D. Benson, gen. ed., *The Riverside Chaucer*, 3rd ed. (Boston: Houghton Mifflin, 1987). Line references will be given in the text; those for the *Canterbury Tales* are given by numbered fragment and line.

excised both from the context of known Italian history that would render Ugolino's crisis intelligible and from the intricate structure of Dante's *Commedia*. Dante, the Monk says, can tell such a story "Fro point to point," in full detail; and for Chaucer, if not for the Monk, it was the continuity this implies, the ability to set his characters in a context of the fullest significance, spiritual and historical, that made Dante's poetry unique and revolutionary.

By the standard of Dante's seriousness, his constant awareness of fundamental social and religious issues, the Monk's very conception of "serious" literature stands condemned,[9] and his acknowledgment of Dante is a pathetic admission of failure; he gestures toward Dante's engagement with character and history as if toward another world. But this is only the most obvious of many points in *The Monk's Tale* at which we sense the inadequacy of his conception of tragedy. Repeatedly in the course of his string of exempla, he ignores or falsifies the contexts in which his tragic figures acted and suffered, and he responds to their several fates with the same undifferentiated "bewailing." All the Monk's heroes are pathetic in the same way, and the pathos of their stories is empty. As Aranye Fradenburg observes, *The Monk's Tale* is "sentimental about nothing," for the fortunes it chronicles render human character and values altogether meaningless.[10]

And of course *The Monk's Tale* is a failure not only by the standard of Dante, but by that of the *Canterbury Tales* themselves. Chaucer's pilgrims speak to us of lives lived in a dense social and psychological medium for which the self-revelations of Dante's great sinners offer the closest equivalent, and they have the same power to challenge and suspend our impulse to judge them. Dante's characters are fixed forever in the attitudes defined by their besetting sins, monumental in a way Chaucer's engaged actors cannot be, but the Pardoner, in his self-lacerating spiritual anxiety, or the Wife of Bath, endlessly at odds with a masculinist society from which she seeks validation even as she exposes its hypocrisy, are comparably trapped and goaded. *The Monk's Tale* reveals no such human crises, and despite its historical sweep it tells us nothing about history—nothing comparable, for example, to the disenchanted vision of the Knight, discovering in the histories of Thebes and

[9] See Jahan Ramazani, "Chaucer's Monk: The Poetics of Abbreviation, Aggression, and Tragedy," *ChauR* 27 (1993): 260–76.

[10] L. O. Aranye Fradenburg, *Sacrifice Your Love: Psychoanalysis, Historicism, Chaucer* (Minneapolis: University of Minnesota Press, 2002), p. 151.

Athens the same profound contradictions that beset the world of contemporary chivalry whose values his tale seeks to affirm. *The Clerk's Tale*, oscillating as it does between sentimentality and heroic idealism in its treatment of human suffering, might be seen as offering a comparably stunted perspective on its heroine, but there the contradiction is inherited from the Clerk's source, perhaps inherent in the story itself. The Monk's limitations are self-imposed, a refusal to acknowledge complexity rather than an inability to deal with it.

Nonetheless, the Monk can provide us with a certain insight into Chaucer's sense of literary possibilities, for his choice of subjects for his tragedies makes plain that Chaucer at least was able to see in the story of Ugolino, Hercules, Antiochus, or Samson the lineaments of "tragedy" of a more profound kind. Like Boccaccio, whose *De casibus* is the most likely model for *The Monk's Tale*, and seems to have furnished the title it often bears in the manuscripts,[11] Chaucer is aware that the tragic dimension of human experience is more complex than the repertory of themes and narrative patterns available to him can suggest, and *The Monk's Tale* gives a backhanded expression to this awareness. Richard Neuse has argued persuasively that the *Tale* can be seen as responding to the *Inferno* in its tragic aspect,[12] but the Monk's role resembles that of a sententious glossator, bent on extracting a simple lesson from each new story; his reductive summations provide a foil, rather than a key, to serious consideration of the lives he describes.

But the suppressions and omissions the Monk's narratives reveal when compared with their sources have a significance of their own. The tale is an experimental work, but the experiment is neither the serious, self-conscious exercise in quasi-classical tragedy that some have found in it nor the send-up of such strenuous neoclassicism that it has seemed to others. Chaucer's concern, I would argue, is with the light that an experiment in this newly reemergent form, defined with an exaggerated rigor for the occasion, could shed on more familiarly medieval narrative forms. From a range of sources, he draws stories whose character is inherently tragic, then deliberately dissipates their tragic power by contaminating it with arbitrary moralism, the pathos of popular religious

---

[11] See Thomas H. Bestul, "The Monk's Tale," in *Sources and Analogues of the Canterbury Tales*, ed. Robert Correale, Mary Hamel, vol. 1 (Cambridge: D. S. Brewer, 2002), pp. 410–11.

[12] *Chaucer's Dante* (Berkeley and Los Angeles: University of California Press, 1991), pp. 151–58.

literature, or the optimism and idealism of chivalric romance. The effect is to demonstrate how easily the process of *translatio* to these characteristic medieval modes can distort or obfuscate social and political reality.

In this respect *The Monk's Tale* is a particularly striking illustration of Chaucer's lifelong preoccupation with the status and value of his poetic projects. Worthiest of the heirs of Jean de Meun, he was keenly aware of the potentially revolutionary implications of Jean's challenge to the courtly tradition, and was inspired by the freedom with which he had incorporated classical poetry, contemporary history, science, and philosophy into his vast poem. From Jean, and still more from Dante and Boccaccio, Chaucer drew a sense of the capacities of literature that, as I have suggested, enabled him to see the French and English traditions in a larger, fully European perspective. But these traditions also made him keenly aware of their limited power to assimilate fully the great works of the classical tradition as Dante had or to emulate the modernity of Boccaccio's narratives.

It is possible, indeed, to read the evolution of Chaucer's poetry largely as a series of testings of the limits of his literary heritage. The preoccupation is already audible in his description of the volume of poetry with which the narrator of *The Book of the Duchess* attempts to put himself to sleep:

> And in this boke were written fables
> That clerkes had in olde tyme,
> And other poetes, put in rime
> To rede and for to be in minde,
> While men loved the lawe of kinde.
> (52–56)

If *The Book of the Duchess* is Chaucer's earliest surviving poem, then this is his first reference to books, poets, and reading. The name of "poet" is one that Chaucer will assign carefully in his later works; like Dante, he applies it almost exclusively to the ancient poets who wrote in Latin. Is "poet" used with the same precision here? If "clerkes" denotes a type of poet, and if "poets" write in rhyme, as the passage suggests, then the term must encompass vernacular writers in the tradition of *clergie*—the authors of *Le Roman de la Rose*, for example, or Guillaume de Machaut. And we should perhaps see the pairing of clerk and poet as hinting at the growing stature of the vernacular.

10

But we should also note how time is treated in this passage. That the clerks and other poets evoked wrote "in olde tyme" suggests a literary tradition more ancient and august than that defined by *Le Roman de la Rose*, scarcely a century old when Chaucer wrote, and still sufficiently "modern" to constitute the paradigm-text for makers of courtly verse. It is as if Chaucer had been prompted by his own reference to "olde tyme" to recognize that the "clerkly" tradition by itself was not really what he meant to invoke, and had added the more portentous term "poetes" as an almost involuntary gloss. But it is in the last two lines of the passage that our perspective is decisively broadened. Poetry is now the substance of thought and memory, an authoritative guide to the laws of nature. And perhaps here too we can see "olde tyme" becoming timeless. The phrase "While men loved the lawe of kinde" has seemed to some commentators to denote a time that is past, the pre-Christian era when pagans and their poets ordered their lives wholly in terms of vital necessity and cosmic process. Others have heard it as a periphrasis for the full span of natural human existence, historical time itself.

How does the tradition of the poets inform *The Book of the Duchess*? The poem falls into two main sections, the first centered around the legend of Ceyx and Alcyone, the second around the figure of the Man in Black. The two centers are intimately linked, and the connection expresses an underlying complementarity between vernacular rhyming and the work of the classical poets, between courtly idealism and the harsh inevitabilities of the "law of kind" embodied in ancient myth.

Chaucer's poem is recognizably a *dit amoureuse* in the tradition of Guillaume de Machaut, and it is from Machaut that he took the idea of making Ovid's Alcyone an emblem for the love-longing that is the proper concern of the *dit*. But the effect is very different. Machaut emphasizes the element of sentiment in the story of Alcyone, putting Ovid's narrative into the mouth of the lovelorn knight who is his counterpart to Chaucer's Man in Black, and who emphasizes Alcyone's loyalty and grief. Chaucer suppresses her raving grief and says nothing of the redeeming metamorphosis. He remains comically obtuse in the face of the self-pitying Man in Black, and reduces the elaborate lyric effusions of Machaut's courtiers to brief, often clumsy ejaculations of spontaneous feeling. Yet the poem is as sophisticated as its French models, and psychologically more profound. Its reading of Ovid is astute, and it shares with Ovid a serious insight into the experience of mourning. Even as it affirms Chaucer's right to a place in the French tradition, it shows him moving beyond this tradition and its preoccupation with "love-tidings." Chaucer has heard Ovid's voice as well as Machaut's, and the wisdom of the ancient poet has informed his use of the medieval poet's form and motifs. In taking up his book of fables, then, Chaucer is showing us what he sees as the most significant aspect of the work of his French predecessors, and, at the same time, as he quietly exposes the limitations of Guillaume de Machaut as an Ovidian poet, defining a possible program for his own poetry, nothing less than a marriage of the courtly and the classical traditions.

Troilus and Criseyde can be seen as a similar experiment on a larger scale. It relocates the urban intrigue of Boccaccio's *Filostrato* within the world of the *roman d'antiquité*, while making us constantly aware of the epic history that envelops its characters and menaces the decorum of the romance Chaucer's Trojans speak and act by the conventions of *courtoisie*, yet just out of view is a world as fated as Vergil's, and as modern as that of the *Decameron*, a world where cities are betrayed and heroes die in vain, where people count their money, sue one another, covet their brothers' wives, and make life-determining decisions on grounds that are not those of the courtly code. All the while, as Lee Patterson has shown, the story of Thebes lowers over Troy, a potential source of self-knowledge that surfaces repeatedly but that none can understand.[13]

Pandarus can be seen as an emblem of this complex project, at once wholly new, true to his origins in *Le Roman de la Rose*, and at times almost a tutelary spirit, a genius figure. In all of these ways he can be seen as a virtual complement to the Wife of Bath. The Wife, too, is a radically modern creation, yet subtly and solidly linked, both to the *Rose* and to the Latin tradition of Platonizing allegorical poetry that Jean de Meun had effectively undermined yet somehow kept alive. The Wife's obvious antecedent is La Vieille, but she is also a surrogate for Jean's goddess *Nature,* eloquently identifying herself with the forces that sustain universal life, yet garrulously bitter about their inability to fully inform the life of mankind. Like Nature's long plea for procreation, the Wife's *Prologue* displays prodigious intellectual and imaginative energy in affirming her sexual role, but for both figures sexual assertiveness is balanced by deep resentment and frustration at their inability to be "realized," possessed, and appreciated by a male sensibility commensu-

---

[13] Lee Patterson, *Chaucer and the Subject of History* (Madison: University of Wisconsin Press, 1991), pp. 128–36.

rate with their capacity for generous response. This is what Nature comes down to in the world of the *Canterbury Tales*, where no genius-figure exists to integrate human life with the larger natural order, and desire is the stuff of fiction.

In all these respects, Chaucer defines for himself a "subject" position vis-à-vis European literary tradition, "subject" in the sense in which he uses the term in the closing stanzas of *Troilus*. There, having imposed several unsatisfying conclusions on his love-story, he looks beyond, and defines its relation to "alle poesye"—poetry in the classical tradition, poetry with a capital P, poetry in the sense in which Dante uses the term—but declines to dignify his own work with this title as Dante does. And just as it is necessary to break through a series of formal barriers to attain this perspective and align his *roman d'antiquité* with the great tradition, so modernity will come to dominate the *Canterbury Tales* only by a similar breach of decorum. Here it is the decorum implied by the *Natureingang* of the General Prologue and the procession of portraits that follow, a decorum that is recognizably that of Guillaume de Lorris, but that gradually gives way to the anarchic energies of the world of Jean de Meun. Like its narrator, the poem frankly acknowledges its centrifugal tendency in various ways, while managing, through its mixed style and interplay of genres, to avoid any final capitulation to the social forces to which it gives rein.

The manner in which *The Monk's Tale* expresses Chaucer's oblique, "subjit" relation to the larger literary world, the world of Dante, Boccaccio, and the *poetae*, differs from the dialogic interplay of *Troilus* or the *Canterbury Tales* as a whole, in that Chaucer and his contemporaries only dimly recognized the aspect of the larger tradition to which it points. To a certain extent this limitation can be defined in terms of their limited understanding of what constituted tragedy. The standard definitions inherited from such sources as Boethius and Isidore associate it with public affairs, and define the tragic action wholly in terms of the unhappy ends of powerful and often wicked men. The Monk's remarks on tragic "storie" thus present the orthodox view, and the tales he tells conform to it, however reductively, both in their narrative trajectory and in their utter indifference to the particular situations of the heroes and rulers they depict.

The Monk's ignoring of the larger forces that shape his heroes' lives is all the more curious in that he is evidently aware of them. Thus he announces Samson, the subject of his first fully rendered story, as a man consecrated to God and "annunciat" by angelic prophecy, but then he focuses exclusively and repeatedly on Samson's inability to conceal secrets from his wives. The effect is to reduce the brief narrative to a tale of just deserts that ends appropriately with the hero blind and helpless at the mill. The Monk goes on to report Samson's destruction of the Philistine temple but offers no comment on the redemptive self-sacrifice that transforms his tragedy of fortune into a spiritual triumph, and instead ends with a final warning against confiding in one's wife. His stunted, philistine perspective recalls the recurring humiliation that dogged the hero in his life.

The story of the death of Hercules, which follows, has no moral at all beyond a pointless hint that the hero's acceptance of Deianira's gift of the poisoned garment of Nessus was a failure of self-knowledge. In place of the hero's agonized questioning of the justice of his fate, a memorable feature of the Ovidian version of this episode,[14] the Monk offers only bumbling remarks about the motive for Deianira's gift, and the story ends by focusing on Hercules' death throes for their own sake, with no hint of the meaning of his death for gods or mortals. This ignoring of larger implications is even more striking in the story of Antiochus, drawn from the second book of *Maccabees*. Much space is devoted to the literal details of the wounds with which Antiochus was afflicted by God for having thought to conquer Jerusalem. Antiochus finally acknowledges God's dominion, but the single line devoted to his repentance is all but lost amid repeated references to the "stink" of his wounds, and we hear nothing of the desperate attempts, so prominent in the the Monk's biblical source, to atone to God and make restitution to the Jews. In each of these three cases a story with the character of classical tragedy is robbed of its inherent power and rendered trivial.

As further evidence that this is a deliberate strategy, that Chaucer was aware of possible alternatives to his own "medievalizing" treatment of tragic material, I would like to consider passages from two other Chaucerian narratives that show him briefly contemplating tragic possibilities, only to decline the challenge they pose. The first is the account of the death of Hector in the fifth book of *Troilus and Criseyde*, an event singled out by Chaucer to illustrate the power of Fortune, as she effects the great "permutacioun" whereby *imperium* is tranferred from Troy to the Greeks (*Troilus* 5.1541–45). This characterization of Fortune is the

[14] *Metamorphoses* 9.134–272.

richest such passage in Chaucer, comparable to Dante's in its clarity and conciseness, and a reminder of what will be utterly lacking in *The Monk's Tale*. But having created this portentous setting, the narrator refuses to consider further the implications of Hector's death, and instead responds to it with chivalric rhetoric of an utterly conventional kind; it is an event

> For which me thynketh every manere wight
> That haunteth armes oughte to biwaille
> The deth of hym that was so noble a knyght;
>   (5.1555–57)

The grief of Troilus is reported in equally conventional terms. Within a bare two lines, the "sorwe" of Troilus the grieving fellow-warrior has been displaced by the pain and "unrest" of Troilus the jealous lover, and Hector is wholly forgotten. A pivotal event in world history has been effaced by the pathos of Troilus's loss of Criseyde. Here, as throughout the poem, the lesser hero, whose feats of arms are all for love, draws us away from larger, Homeric concerns. Much later, Homer will be invoked directly, in the lines that describe Troilus's final moments of heroism. This last stand is sonorously heralded as a display of "the wrath of Troilus," as if pathos had been left behind and a new and truly heroic phase of his career were opening. But in the event this *aristeia* runs its course in a single stanza, at the end of which romance in the person of Troilus is "dispitously" rendered subject to the more authentic wrath of Achilles, and epic at last regains the upper hand.

My second passage is the speech in which Saturn describes his all-encompassing influence on the human world of *The Knight's Tale*. The strange, somber figure of Saturn exists for the sole purpose of effecting worldly "permutacioun" by destructive means. He can hardly be called a god, and is perhaps best described in the terms used by Dante's Virgil to describe Fortune, as one of the *prime creature* (*Inferno* 7.95). He could almost be said to constitute an aspect of Fortune herself, and in him Chaucer has come as close as any medieval poet to giving that power a local habitation:

> I do vengeance and pleyn correccioun,
> Whil I dwelle in the signe of the leoun.
> Myn is the ruyne of the hye halles,
> The fallynge of the toures and of the walles

15

> Upon the mynour or the carpenter.
> I slow Sampsoun, shakynge the piler.
>
> (I.2461–66)

The feature I would call attention to in this passage is the reference to Samson in the last line. This is the central line of Saturn's speech, and thus locates Samson at the very center of the Knight's elaborately concentric universe. Samson's name constitutes the one nonpagan reference in a poem that otherwise preserves a resolutely pagan perspective on its action.

To imagine Chaucer as meditating a Samson Agonistes of his own devising would be wishfully anachronistic, but a poet who could set his medievalizings in the perspective attained in *The Monk's Tale* may perhaps be credited with special powers. What seems clear is that the very presence of Samson in a literally pivotal role poses the possibility of viewing human freedom in very different terms than those of the Knight's *Tale* or the Monk's. Fortune has been momentarily exposed as sheer stupid force, and the next stage would be a "translation," which would substitute for her meaningless dominion a demonstration that individual human experience is what matters, that the significance of political change is most truly expressed in the labor and sacrifice of the hero.

But Chaucer never makes a decisive move in this direction. Heroism in Chaucer, even when it can arguably be considered tragic, is never shown to bear an integral relation to larger events. The story of Troilus is a tragedy of *courtoisie,* as that of Arcite and Theseus in *The Knight's Tale* is a tragedy of chivalry. The inability of these masculine codes to confront their own inadequacies is the dilemma of "Thebanism," a blindness to the past that ensures its repetition, so that the passion and violence that assail the knightly hero assume the role of historical forces.[15] But Chaucer is curiously reluctant to pursue these implications. Even the explicit Thebanism of Cassandra's prophecy to Troilus remains enigmatic. Diomede may or may not be the agent of destiny, and Troilus never quite emerges as a microcosmic image of Troy.

The raising of such questions, though his poetry yields no answer to them, expresses a concern that Chaucer shares with his contemporaries.

[15] See Patterson, *Chaucer and the Subject of History*, pp. 129–31; Wetherbee, *Chaucer and the Poets: An Essay on "Troilus and Criseyde"* (Ithaca: Cornell University Press, 1984), pp. 130–31.

"The chief characters in Ricardian narrative," says John Burrow, "achieve little of public consequence"; questions of human freedom and responsibility are a central concern of the major poets of the period, but their view of humankind is unheroic, and they are at one in leaving these large questions conspicuously unresolved.[16] The Prologue to Gower's *Confessio Amantis*, largely a rehearsal of the themes of his earlier poems, wrestles with the question of how far humankind is to blame for the "division" that constantly threatens human institutions, and the poet broods on the uncertain relation of human and cosmic life. Both fortune and the chronic instability of the world are firmly linked to the unstable behavior of man, "Which of his propre governance / Fortuneth al the worldes chance"; yet the world, too, "of his propre kynde / Was evere untrewe,"[17] and the *Prologue* offers no assurance that human society is capable of withstanding its destabilizing power. Throughout the *Confessio* proper, the role of Amans is deliberately miniaturized, kept almost maddeningly out of touch with the political concerns that recur again and again in Genius's narratives. And in the end, question of responsibility and control are unresolved. Gower too has his European aspect, and at several points the *Confessio* becomes explicitly a mirror for princes in the continental mode, but the political and the social are never decisively brought together. That Apollonius, the hero of Gower's concluding narrative, triumphs over adversity is due mainly to his being a perfect gentleman, "well-grounded" as a husband and father, and he is never shown exercising political responsibility. The dreamer of *Piers Plowman,* on the other hand, struggles to establish a purposeful relation to a world that evades and confuses, where an endless series of voices contests his claim to legitimacy. What Anne Middleton says of Langland's project is true of Ricardian poetry in general: it is anti-Boethian, and expresses the situation of men who seek not to accept and transcend their alienation from the world but to reclaim possession of their identity and history as worldly beings.[18]

With the Ricardian qualities of Chaucer's poetry in mind, his peculiar

---

[16] J. A. Burrow, *Ricardian Poetry: Chaucer, Gower, Langland, and the* Gawain Poet (New Haven: Yale University Press, 1971), p. 100.

[17] *Confessio Amantis*, Prologue, lines 583–84, 535–36, in *The English Works of John Gower*, ed. G. C. Macaulay, EETS e.s. 81–82 (Oxford: Oxford University Press, 1900–1901).

[18] Anne Middleton, "Narration and the Invention of Experience: Episodic Form in *Piers Plowman*," in *The Wisdom of Poetry: Essays in Early English Literature in Honor of Morton W. Bloomfield* (Kalamazoo, Mich.: Medieval Institute Publications, 1982), p. 104.

17

blend of European vision with what can seem a willful provinciality, I would like to conclude by examining the view of poetry obliquely set forth in *The Nun's Priest's Tale*, which begins as an exercise in the humblest of genres and contains some of Chaucer's finest exercises in popular homiletics, yet manages also to invoke the classical tradition and raise serious questions about the social value of "serious" poetry. In the homeliness of its narrative vehicle and the loftiness of its allusions, it constitutes Chaucer's fullest statement about his relation to the European tradition.

The Nun's Priest's Tale, says Peter Travis, "is pure parody, and nothing else," its targets being Chaucer's own poetry and Western literature in general.[19] But while the tale can certainly be read this way, it is also studded with a remarkable number of references to tragic events, legendary and historical: the death of Hector (treated here with due solemnity); the treachery of Ganelon and Sinon; the deaths of two British kings; the capture of Troy; the burning of Carthage and Rome; and the murderous violence that accompanied the Uprising of 1381.

Chaucer harbored a deep distrust of religious enthusiasm, and of most forms of affective piety, and the narrative vehicles of his religious tales tend to complement, in their form and style, the flawed or distorted spirituality of the pilgrims who employ them. Emotive piety produces the Kitsch of *The Prioress's Tale*, and the kitschy moments in the Man of Law's, calculated invitations to vicarious involvement and the indulgence of false emotion. Striking features of *The Nun's Priest's Tale*, then, are its several examples of carefully controlled religious rhetoric, most notably the first mini-tale that Chauntecleer tells to Pertelote to illustrate the importance of dreams.

Two pilgrims are forced to take separate lodgings for the night, and one is visited with a series of dreams that report the murder of the other. Twice the dreamer fails to respond when his fellow pilgrim appears to announce his imminent death and appeal for aid. But when in a third dream his fellow, now dead, describes his murder and explains how it may be exposed, the dreamer finally acts. His loud appeal to the city magistrates stirs the crowd, the corpse is recovered, and the murderers are caught, tortured, and hanged.

[19] "Learning to Behold the Fox: Poetics and Epistemology in Chaucer's *Nun's Priest's Tale*," in Roland Hagenbüchle and Laura Skandera, eds., *Poetry and Epistemology: Turning Points in the History of Poetic Knowledge: Papers from the International Poetry Symposium, Eichstätt, 1983, Eichstätter Beiträge,* Band 20 (Regensburg: F. Pustet, 1986), pp. 30–32.

The brief story includes a small anthology of grim reminiscences of earlier tales. The face that appears to the sleeping pilgrim in his third dream, pitiful and pale of hue (VII.3023), is that of the condemned man invoked in the central stanza of *The Man of Law's Tale* as Custance stands trial (I.645–51), and the Christ-like aspect of both figures is reinforced in Chauntecleer's narrative when the dead man bids his friend "Bihoold my bloody woundes, depe and wyde" (VII.3015), exactly as Christ calls out from the Cross in many fourteenth-century hymns. The posture in which the friend envisions the corpse "gaping upright" (VII.3042) evokes the Knight's dark imagining of "colde deeth" in the Temple of Mars (I.2008). The dung-cart in which the murder victim is concealed recalls the Jewish privy of *The Prioress's Tale*, as the torture and hanging of the murderers recall the Provost's retaliation against the Jews.

On the whole, these allusions reinforce the power and efficiency of a story that is a textbook example of melodrama harnessed to homiletic purpose. A religious sensibility is provoked, first by warnings and then by a Christ-like apparition, and responds in a way that in turn provokes the community at large to collaborate in exposing evil and obtaining justice. To this extent the little tale is the efficacious exemplum par excellence. Whereas the pale face in *The Man of Law's Tale* is a gratuitous embellishment, irrelevant to the actual situation of Custance, the pale and bloody figure in Chaunticleer's exemplum plays a crucial admonitory role. And the echo of the Knight's grim panorama of the work of Mars in the lodger's horrific vision of the gaping corpse within the dung-heap lends added force to his appeal to the city fathers.

This appeal is worth examining more closely. It would seem to confirm the effectiveness of the vividly focused sequence of dreams, which finally elicit a uniquely efficacious response, as nightmare is abruptly translated into coherent political discourse:

> "I crye out on the ministres," quod he,
> "That sholden kepe and reulen this citee.
> Harrow! Allas! Heere lith my felawe slayn!"
>   (VII.3043–45)

But there is something implausible about a mode of vision this efficient. We can also hear in these lines an undertone of terror and near panic, and we should notice their larger effect, an explosion of mob violence that leads directly to the abrupt, brutal punishment of the murderers.[20] Are we finally edified or merely shocked by all this? Is the "intent" of the tale at this point fully in line with its homiletic pretensions? For Chaucer's purposes, the raising of such questions was primary. For Chauntecleer, meanwhile, the consciousness of having created an effect with the lurid details of his story, and the dramatic discovery that climaxes it, is an end in itself. Declaring his own dream an "avisioun," the highest type of prophetic dream, and making vivid the "adversitee" that threatens him becomes an occasion for striking a heroic pose, wholly unmindful of the obvious bearing of this and his other exempla on his own situation.

Chauntecleer's self-aggrandizing posture here mocks the world-historical and Dantean pretensions of the Monk, but his tale of the two pilgrims can be taken seriously, and recognizing its function can help us understand the relationship between Chauntecleer's situation and the frame of tragic history the Nun's Priest constructs around it. Despite its appeal to civic order, the Pilgrim's outcry on seeing the dung-cart is no more a political act than Chauntecleer's own "Cok! Cok!" at the sight of the fox. Its strange blend of fear, prayer, and advice to princes expresses a psychological need, an attempt to gain private stability by invoking public order. And the rhetoric of the later portions of *The Nun's Priest Tale*, for all its high comedy, responds to this same need, by suggesting how its humble story might be made to assume the dignity of tragedy.

The tact of the Nun's Priest's is flawless: it is never precisely his story or his hero that we take seriously, but he manages to convey the reality of our moral experience, and call attention to real dangers. High poetry is not spared his ironic and humbling scrutiny. When he notes that his story took place on Friday, and is then drawn to reflect on Friday as sacred to Venus, as the day on which King Richard Coeur-de-Lion was murdered, and therefore as the focus of the invective of the master-poet Geoffrey of Vinsauf, we are reminded of the limited power and potential foolishness of poetry, which can "do" nothing about the events it presumes to engage, and is all too apt to delude itself about its ability to interpret them. The distance between the particularity of fable and the aggrandizings of classical rhetoric may well seem unbridgeable.

---

[20] The pilgrim's outcry and the ensuing violence are not found in Chaucer's likely source, the *Super Sapientiam Salomonis* of Robert Holcot. See Thomas Bestul, "The Nun's Priest's Tale," in *Sources and Analogues of the Canterbury Tales*, ed. Correale and Hamel, 1.486–89.

But lurking amid the absurdity of the Nun's Priest's bewailings is a serious point. It *is* finally the business of poetry to engage with history, to give point to our own anxiety and sense of fatedness by focusing on the continuum of human experience, the precedents and likely consequences of our acts and follies, and the accidents we incur. As we move outward from hens bemoaning the plight of Chauntecleer to the desperate women of Carthage and Rome, we encounter the figure of Richard Lionheart, a king who was the stuff of legend, traditionally viewed through a haze of idealized chivalry and crusading piety, but whose historical presence here focuses and authenticates the poetic amplification of the story. And as the social world of the tale disintegrates into the pell-mell pursuit of the fox, a second historical allusion, this time to the disruption of the civic order of a modern city by a rioting mob, helps us bridge the gap between the barnyard world of the fable and the panorama of ancient cities destroyed by fire and the sword. *English* history, both the painfully fresh and the semilegendary, have become vital elements in an evocation of literary tradition in its fullest, most European sense.

A vision capable of comprehending these different social spheres and a depth of historical understanding sufficient to demonstrate the continuity among them—this is what Chaucer saw as the proper aspiration of serious poetry, what he saw being realized in the work of Dante and Boccaccio, what he sensed that tragedy, whatever tragedy was, might accomplish best of all.

THE BIENNIAL CHAUCER LECTURE

The New Chaucer Society
Fourteenth International Congress
July 15th–19th, 2004
University of Glasgow

The Biennial Chaucer Lecture

"I speke of folk in seculer estaat":

Vernacularity and Secularity in the Age of Chaucer

Alastair Minnis
The Ohio State University

ETWEEN 1934 AND 1946, Georges de Lagarde published a five-volume study entitled *La naissance de l'esprit laique*, wherein he tracks certain developments in the "secteur social de la scolastique," and places considerable emphasis on the political philosophy of Marsilius of Padua and William of Ockham, both of whom defended the interests of empire against those of the church.[1] From this material he amasses a substantial body of evidence for what he identifies as the growth and development of a "lay spirit" in the later Middle Ages. This study, considerably influential for at least three decades (it ran to three editions) may be criticized in respect of many of its details—or rather, the weight that Lagarde has them bear—and it too often suppresses or elides the religious frameworks that are indispensable for a comprehensive understanding of many of the developments that it identifies as crucial. But the ambition of Lagarde's study is quite stunning, and in my personal opinion its central thesis is fundamentally correct. It was supported by Walter Ullmann, albeit with different emphases, in his research on the development of political and social thought in the later Middle Ages, wherein the role of recently recovered Aristotelian texts, particularly the *Nicomachean Ethics* and the *Politics*, is seen as crucial for the growth of

---

[1] *La naissance de l'esprit laique*, 5 vols. (1934–46; 3rd ed. Louvain: Nauwelaerts, 1956–70).

secularity.[2] The past sixty years have seen the growth of a major tradition of studies in this crucial area, including (to name but a few) monographs by John W. Baldwin, Michael Wilks, J. A. Watt, Brian Tierney, and Joel Kaye.[3] Distinguished recent additions include Peter Biller's *The Measure of Multitude* and—a study of particular relevance for the present essay—Matthew Kempshall's *The Common Good in Late-Medieval Political Thought*.[4]

My aim here is to raise the possibility that research from such a perspective needs to be undertaken in respect of late medieval European literature. I will make the case with unapologetic reference to "high culture" texts produced in the fourteenth century in France and England, countries that were culturally close (insofar as they shared a corpus of crucial ideological sources) although politically divided. We have heard much recently of "vernacular theology," and of the special importance of "vernacularity" in religious culture. I have no desire whatever to criticize this trend, one of the most compelling in the past decade of Middle English Studies (and one that I myself have labored to promote). But surely it is high time that some sense of balance was restored by an examination of texts that are expressive of "vernacular social philosophy." Hence, betwixt earnest and game, I propose a new partner for that demanding term "vernacularity"—namely, "secularity." The playful element in my proposal is a means of admitting (initial) embarrass-

[2] See, for example, Ullmann's studies *The Origins of the Great Schism: A Study in Fourteenth-Century Ecclesiastical History* (London: Burns and Oates, 1948), *The Growth of Papal Government in the Middle Ages* (London: Methuen, 1955), and *Law and Politics in the Middle Ages* (Ithaca: Cornell University Press, 1975). Taking a different but crucially related tack, his younger contemporary Ernest Kantorowicz demonstrated the often-interwoven nature of medieval theological and political discourse, in *The King's Two Bodies: A Study in Mediaeval Political Theology* (Princeton: Princeton University Press, 1957).

[3] Baldwin, *The Medieval Theories of the Just Price* (Philadelphia: American Philosophical Society, 1959), *Masters, Princes, and Merchants: The Social Views of Peter the Chanter and His Circle* (Princeton: Princeton University Press, 1970), and *The Government of Philip Augustus: Foundations of French Royal Power in the Middle Ages* (Berkeley and Los Angeles: University of California Press, 1986); Wilks, *The Problem of Sovereignty in the Later Middle Ages* (Cambridge: Cambridge University Press, 1963); Watt, *The Theory of Papal Monarchy in the Thirteenth Century* (London: Burns and Oates, 1965); Tierney, *The Crisis of Church and State, 1050–1300* (Englewood Cliffs, N.J.: Prentice-Hall, 1980); Kaye, *Economy and Nature in the Fourteenth Century* (Cambridge: Cambridge University Press, 1998).

[4] Biller, *The Measure of Multitude: Population in Medieval Thought* (Oxford: Oxford University Press, 2000); Kempshall, *The Common Good in Late-Medieval Political Thought* (Oxford: Oxford University Press, 1999). Kempshall sharply questions the unique position that Lagarde assigned to Aristotle in the emergence of secular notions of the state and its citizens; see pages 56–57 below.

ment at the introduction of yet another piece of jargon into an already crowded lexicon. But the term is, I believe, useful as a means of calling attention to neglected textual territories.[5] And besides, it does have some genuine medieval warrant. In a Wycliffite text of 1395, "prelatis & curatis" are attacked for the "seculerte" whereby they take church profits for themselves and dispend it as they like, and a similar statement occurs in *Dives et Pauper* (c. 1410), during an explanation of Christ's aversion to anything that belongs to *seculerte* being sold in the temple.[6] The related noun *seculer(e)*, like its Latin and French counterparts, designates "a member of the laity as opposed to a cleric" (including a member of "the pagan laity as opposed to priests"), together with "a member of the clergy living in the world as opposed to living under a rule, a secular priest."[7] My interest here is in the first two of these definitions, which implicates (to adopt more phrases from the *MED*) a concern "with earthly life as opposed to spiritual or eternal life," "desire" and "behavior" that is "worldly" and "unspiritual," and matters "belonging to the laity as opposed to the clergy."[8] All these definitions set the "secular" in simple opposition to the "religious."[9] And one obvious advantage of the instatement of "secularity" is the fresh terms of engagement it offers to those "atheistic" readers of Chaucer implicated

[5] Of course, there have been substantial studies of secular ideologies and social practices in relation to Chaucer, including (to take just a few examples) Kenneth S. Cahn's article, "Chaucer's Merchants and the Foreign Exchange: An Introduction to Medieval Finance," *SAC* 2 (1980): 81–119, and (more directly relevant to my own discussion) Paul A. Olson's "*The Parlement of Foules:* Aristotle's *Politics* and the Foundations of Human Society," *SAC* 2 (1980): 53–69. An acknowledgment of the significance of the recovered *Politics* may be found in Paul Strohm's *Social Chaucer* (Cambridge, Mass.: Harvard University Press, 1989), but that is not his central interest. The same may be said of David Wallace's splendid *Chaucerian Polity* (Stanford: Stanford University Press, 1997), though many of the "associational forms" discussed therein are secular in nature. It remains true, I believe, that secularity in general has not been addressed as a distinctive cultural phenomenon in vernacular literature.

[6] *MED* s.v. *seculerte*. For a modern scholarly use of the term, see Derek Baker, ed., *Sanctity and Secularity: The Church and the World*, Studies in Church History, vol. 10 (Oxford: Blackwell, 1973). This wide-ranging collection of essays concerning "the proper relationship of the church to the world" poses the question: Can there "be a satisfactory accommodation of sanctity and secularity, or are they 'mutually exclusive?'" (p. xiii).

[7] *MED* s.v. *seculer(e)* (n.).

[8] *MED* s.v. *seculer(e)* (adj.).

[9] I use the term "religious" in its widest sense, as designating belief in and reverence for a divine ruling power, and the exercise of rites and observances that express this, rather than as specifically designating persons such as monks, nuns, and friars, who are bound by vow to a religious order (as distinguished from the secular clergy). See *OED* s.v. A.1a, 2a, B.1.a; *MED* s.v. *religious* (n.), 1 and *religious* (adj.), 1.

in Jill Mann's New Chaucer Society Presidential Address of 1994.[10] But a major caveat must be entered. Binary thinking can seriously damage the pursuit of *l'esprit laique*, as Lagarde's study makes all too clear. Competing interests there frequently were, but in many cases and circumstances the secular and the religious must be seen as complexly interwoven, operating in relationships of complementarity, mutual support, or even interdependence. If the late medieval reception of Aristotle gave princes and prince-pleasing clerics powerful discourses for self-promotion, it also provided the Christian Church with a means of justifying its monopoly over the spiritual welfare of the citizenry, with all the earthly consequences which that was made to entail. The Medieval Aristotle can be found both defending and denying the subordination of *ecclesia* to empire.

There is no ambiguity about the viewpoints of two of the major protagonists of Lagarde's grand narrative, Marsilius of Padua and William of Ockham, who sought the protection of the Holy Roman Emperor, Ludwig of Bavaria. These renegade clerics (both of whom were excommunicated) produced thoroughgoing affirmations of State over Church power. However, the production of discourses of lay hegemony was by no means limited to clerics who put themselves beyond the pale of orthodoxy. In late fourteenth-century France and England, where networks of secular patronage flourished, secular values were nourished, as may well be illustrated by the state-sponsored translations and vernacular hermeneutics patronized by King Charles V of France, to help consolidate the power and prestige of the new Valois dynasty.[11] Charles commissioned more than thirty translations of authoritative works, including such repositories of secular learning as the *De proprietatibus rerum* of Bartholomaeus Anglicus (by Jean Corbechon, 1372), Valerius Maximus (a translation of the first four books, by Simon de Hesdin, is extant; 1375), Giles of Rome's *De regimine principum* (by Jean Golein, 1379), and of course the Aristotle translations of Nicole Oresme, who provided erudite renderings of the *Politics, Nicomachean Ethics,* and *On the Heavens (De caelo),* along with the pseudo-Aristotelian *Economics.* Fol-

---

[10] "Chaucer and Atheism," *SAC* 17 (1995): 5–19.

[11] See C. R. Sherman, *Imaging Aristotle: Verbal and Visual Representation in Fourteenth-Century France* (Berkeley and Los Angeles: University of California Press, 1995), p. 6. On the development of "royal propaganda" in this period, see Gilbert Ouy, "Humanism and Nationalism in France at the Turn of the Fifteenth Century," in B. P. McGuire, ed., *The Birth of Identities: Denmark and Europe in the Middle Ages* (Copenhagen: Medieval Centre, Copenhagen University, 1996), pp. 107–25 (esp. p. 110).

lowing in Oresme's footsteps, the king's physician, Evrart de Conty (on whom more later) undertook a commentated translation of Aristotle's supposed medical treatise, the *Problemata*,[12] though this did not actually appear in the king's lifetime. Charles V's patronage was on a quite extraordinary scale, but he was following in the footsteps of several distinguished regal predecessors, who also had promoted the production (including the translation) of works deemed to serve the public good, or at least created an environment in which such texts could be produced.

Special mention may be made of two books made for King Philip IV "the Fair," whose reign is marked by an extraordinary triumph of State over Church. The king ruthlessly destroyed Boniface VIII's power base, subsequently securing the election of the pro-French pope Clement V; Philip's success was crowned with the relocation of the papacy to Avignon in 1309.[13] This was the ruler to whom Jean de Meun dedicated his translation of the *Consolatio philosophiae* of Boethius—a testament of philosophical rather than theological wisdom—which he made in the very early 1300s. Jean's prestigious prologue (which opens with Aristotle's statement—as found at the beginning of the *Politics*—that all things seek the good)[14] enjoyed an exceptional afterlife as the introduction to the anonymous verse-prose translation of Boethius, which became the most popular of all the vernacular *Consolations*. It was, however, Jean de Meun's original all-prose translation that Geoffrey Chaucer took as the basis of his Middle English *Boece*. This lacks a dedicatory preface—that being one of the most surprising features of the text. One can only speculate about which high-ranking recipient Chaucer originally had in mind, for no doubt he had one.

Returning to Philip "the Fair": Giles of Rome wrote for him the original (Latin) *De regimine principum* around 1280; a few years later it was

---

[12] An edition is being prepared by Michèle Goyens, Françoise Guichard-Tesson, and Joëlle Ducos.

[13] As R. W. Dyson has said, "It would be hard to overestimate the impact of [this] struggle upon the political shape of post-medieval Europe and upon the political fortunes of the papacy." Here one may detect intimations of the modern conception of the "consolidated nation state, intolerant of interference from without and willing to acknowledge no sovereign but its king." *Three Royalist Tracts, 1296–1302: "Antequam essent clerici," "Disputatio inter Clericum et Militem," "Quaestio in utramque partem,"* ed. R. W. Dyson (Bristol: Thoemmes, 1999), p. xi. On these momentous events and their significance, see G. A. L. Digard, *Philippe le Bel et le Saint Siège de 1285 à 1304* (Paris: Sirey, 1936); J. Rivière, *Le problème de l'église et de l'état au temps de Philippe le Bel* (Paris: Champion, 1926); and the studies by Watt and Tierney cited in note 3 above.

[14] *Politics* i.1 (1252a4).

translated into French by Henri de Gauchy, and in addition to the Jean Golein translation (already mentioned) one was prepared by an anonymous writer who seems to have been working for Guillaume de Beles Voies, a bourgeois of Orléans.[15] A Middle English translation of the *De regimine principum* appeared in the late fourteenth century. This text, of which substantial use will be made below, was probably the work of John Trevisa, working under the patronage of the Gloucestershire magnate Sir Thomas Berkeley (1352–1417).[16] Other texts produced within this network include Trevisa's translations of *De proprietatibus rerum*, Ralph Higden's *Polychronicon*, Richard FitzRalph's *Defensio curatorum*, and the Pseudo-Ockhamite *Dialogus inter militem et clericum*. The last of those was a quite radical choice, given that it promotes state power in terms similar to those that characterize the genuine treatises produced by Ockham in the interests of Ludwig of Bavaria. In fact, it dates from the years 1296–97 and was almost certainly written by a Frenchman in support of the interests of King Philip IV against those of Boniface VIII.[17] "Miles" presents himself as a "sleeping dog" who has been provoked to bark by "Clericus." "Because you do not know how to benefit from the humility and patience of princes," he adds, "I fear that after a just bark you will deservedly feel yourself bitten."[18] That humility and patience involves the defense and protection of the Church, and the maintenance of its privileges—which, however, may be revoked "if they subsequently become harmful to the commonwealth, or in case of harsh necessity, or for the commonwealth's benefit (*utilitate reipublicae*)."[19] Furthermore, if the Church does not act properly in spending what is necessary for "the pious relief of the poor and the miseries of the sick," the State may intervene to correct its mismanagement.[20] A deep bite indeed. The values in this *Dialogus* have been seen,[21] quite rightly I believe, as

[15] See Charles F. Briggs, *Giles of Rome's "De regimine principum": Reading and Writing Politics at Court and University, c. 1275–c. 1525* (Cambridge: Cambridge University Press, 1999), p. 76.

[16] *The Governance of Kings and Princes: John Trevisa's Translation of the "De regimine principum" of Aegidius Romanus*, ed. David C. Fowler, Charles F. Briggs, and Paul G. Remley (New York: Garland, 1997). For the Latin text, I consulted Aegidius Romanus, *De regimine principum libri III* (Rome, 1556; repr. Frankfurt: Minerva, 1968).

[17] Recently edited, under the title *Disputatio inter Clericum et Militem*, by R. W. Dyson, in *Three Royalist Tracts*, pp. 12–45. On authorship and date, see p. xviii. Trevisa's translation was edited by A. J. Perry, EETS 167 (London: Oxford University Press, 1925).

[18] *Disputatio*, ed. Dyson, pp. 28–29.

[19] Ibid., pp. 40–41.

[20] Ibid., pp. 30–31.

[21] By Ralph Hanna, "Sir Thomas Berkeley and His Patronage," *Speculum* 64 (1989): 878–916.

having something in common with those expressed in the longer of the two original prefaces that Trevisa prefixed to his English *Polychronicon*, which takes the form of a dialogue between a secular lord and a clerk, with the lord arguing persuasively in favor of translation.[22] According to the dialogue on translation, secular readers should have access to material hitherto confined within Latin; according to the Pseudo-Ockham dialogue, secular leaders should take property away from churchmen if the defense of the realm requires it, and interfere in Church affairs if clergymen are failing in their spiritual responsibilities. In short, secular lords are setting clerics right on matters relating to textual and temporal sovereignty, respectively.

Trevisa's dialogue on translation contains certain ideas deriving from, or at least reminiscent of, Oxford debates on Bible translation.[23] To offer this analogy is not tantamount to attributing (yet again) Lollard sympathies to Trevisa.[24] As Anne Hudson has argued, "In Oxford in 1401 it was still possible for men to urge the desirability of vernacular translations of the Bible without being suspected as heretics."[25] My point is simply that arguments of a kind that were bandied around by scholars such as William Butler, Thomas Palmer, and Richard Ullerston found their way into Trevisa's dialogue on translation. And yet, the fact that the Pseudo-Ockham treatise contains views that are akin to those of Wyclif must surely encourage further reflection. A similar point could be made about the virulently antimendicant *Defensio curatorum*.[26] Whatever Trevisa's own ideological position may have been, it seems reasonable to assume that, in his dialogue on translation and his rendering of

[22] See R. A. Waldron, "John Trevisa's Original Prefaces on Translation: A Critical Edition," in E. D. Kennedy, R. A. Waldron, and J. S. Wittig, eds., *Medieval English Studies Presented to George Kane* (Woodbridge, Suffolk: Boydell and Brewer, 1988), pp. 285–99.

[23] See Hanna, "Sir Thomas Berkeley," p. 896; see also Hanna, "The Difficulty of Ricardian Prose Translation: The Case of the Lollards," *MLQ* 51 (1990): 319–40 (p. 325). On the controversy, see, further, Anne Hudson, "The Debate on Bible Translation, Oxford 1401," in Hudson, *Lollards and Their Books* (London and Ronceverte: Hambledon, 1985), pp. 67–84, and Nicholas Watson, "Censorship and Cultural Change in Late Medieval England: Vernacular Theology, the Oxford Translation Debate, and Arundel's *Constitutions* of 1409," *Speculum* 70 (1996): 822–64.

[24] David C. Fowler recently reprised his argument (originally put forward at the beginning of the 1960s) that Trevisa was one of the translators of the Lollard Bible. See *The Life and Times of John Trevisa, Medieval Scholar* (Seattle: University of Washington Press, 1995), pp. 213–34.

[25] Anne Hudson, "Lollardy: The English Heresy?" in Hudson, *Lollards and Their Books,* pp. 141–63 (p. 150).

[26] For an account of the contents of this sermon, see Fowler, *John Trevisa*, pp. 164–76.

the Pseudo-Ockham *Dialogus*, the figure of the secular lord may be taken as a spokesman for views not dissimilar to those held by Trevisa's own lord, Thomas Berkeley.

Less can be assumed about the personal views of Sir Thomas's daughter, Elizabeth, for whom John Walton produced (in 1410) his all-verse English Boethius, a commentated translation that makes excellent use of Nicholas Trevet's Aristotelianizing commentary on the *Consolatio* as well as drawing on Chaucer's *Boece* (which in its turn had drawn on Trevet).[27] What is clear, however, is that the literary patronage of the Berkeley family stands out as most unusual for its time. If a direct comparison is made between the "court cultures" associated with the French kings I have just mentioned and King Richard II of England, the English evidence seems sparse, to say the least. But this is not the place to reopen the debate on Richard's artistic interests or lack thereof. Suffice it to identify myself as one who is to the left of the "Colston Symposium" collection of essays (which frequently subscribe to a reductively negative thesis) and to the right of Gervase Matthew and Michael Bennett (who take an excessively positive view),[28] though I would venture the thought that "international *lay* culture" is a far more appropriate and useful phrase than the one that has featured in this debate, viz. "international *court* culture."

Furthermore, my concern is not with the (admittedly substantial) differences between French and English textual communities and patronage networks in the late fourteenth century. It is rather with certain laicizing texts that they shared—treatises that define and promote secular values. And here the influence of Aristotle (along with various Pseudo-Aristotles) inevitably looms large. If we concentrate on those books that were deemed to be fit for kings and princes (whether or not actual kings or princes commissioned them), a quite remarkable consonance in respect of "practical philosophy" emerges, which—I sug-

---

[27] As I have demonstrated in my article "Aspects of the Medieval French and English Traditions of Boethius' *De Consolatione Philosophiae*," in M. T. Gibson, ed., *Boethius: His Life, Thought, and Influence* (Oxford: Blackwell, 1981), pp. 312–61 (pp. 343–47, 350–51). See, further, I. R. Johnson, "Walton's Sapient Orpheus," in A. J. Minnis, ed., *The Medieval Boethius: Studies in the Vernacular Translations of "De Consolatione Philosophiae"* (Woodbridge, Suffolk: Boydell and Brewer, 1987), pp. 139–68.

[28] V. J. Scattergood and J. W. Sherborne, eds., *English Court Culture in the Later Middle Ages* (London: Duckworth, 1983); Gervase Mathew, *The Court of Richard II* (London: Duckworth, 1968); Michael Bennett, "The Court of Richard II and the Promotion of Literature," in Barbara A. Hanawalt, ed., *Chaucer's England: Literature in Historical Context* (Minneapolis: University of Minnesota Press, 1992), pp. 3–20.

gest—is part and parcel of an emergent lay culture that was not circum-scribed by national boundaries.

Laicizing Philosophy: Revaluing the Active Life

When I speak of "practical philosophy" I have in mind Aristotle's defi-nition, which enjoyed an extraordinarily wide dissemination right across late medieval Europe. In the paraphrase of doctrines from the *Nicoma-chean Ethics*, which he incorporated into his *Livres dou Tresor* (c. 1260), Brunetto Latini—an Italian writing in French—explains that the practi-cal branch of philosophy teaches us what to do and what not to do. This can be done in three ways: in governing oneself, in governing "one's subordinates and household and possessions and inheritance," and in governing "peoples or kingdoms or a city, in war or in peace."

The first of these subjects is ethics (*etique*), which teaches us to govern ourselves first, to lead a moral life (*honeste vie*) and to do virtuous works and shun vice, for no one could live well or morally (*honestement*) or profitably in this world, for himself or for others, if he did not govern his own life and give himself direction according to the virtues. The second is economics (*yconomique*), which teaches us to govern our people and our sons as well, and thus does it teach us to protect and increase our possessions and our inheritance, and to have mov-able goods and chattel to use or retain as the times change. The third is politics (*politique*), and without a doubt this is the highest wisdom (*science*) and most noble profession there is among men, for it teaches us to govern others, in a kingdom or a city or a group of people or a commune, in peace and in war, according to reason and justice.[29]

Brunetto's version of this classification was followed directly by the En-glish poet John Gower in his *Confessio Amantis*; specifically, in the sev-enth book of this poem, where a condensed "Regiment of Princes" is offered.

> Practique stant upon thre thinges
> Toward the governance of kinges;
> Wherof the ferst Etique is named,

[29] *Li Livres dou Tresor*, I.i, ed. Francis J. Carmody (Berkeley and Los Angeles: Univer-sity of California Press, 1948), pp. 20–21; trans. Paul Barrette and Spurgeon Baldwin, *Brunetto Latini: The Book of the Treasure* (New York: Garland, 1993), p. 4.

> The whos science stant proclamed
> To teche of vertu thilke reule,
> Hou that a king himself schal reule
> Of his moral condicion
> With worthi disposicion
> Of good livinge in his persone,
> Which is the chief of his corone.
>
> . . . .
>
> That other point which that Practique
> Belongeth is Iconomique,
> Which techeth thilke honeste
> Thurgh which a king in his degree
> His wif and child schal reule and guie,
> So forth with al the companie
> Which in his houshold schal abyde,
> And his astat on every side
> In such manere forto lede,
> That he his houshold ne mislede.
> Practique hath yit the thridde aprise,
> Which techeth hou and in what wise
> Thurgh hih pourveied ordinance
> A king schal sette in governance
> His Realme, and that is Policie . . .
>
> (VII.1649–83)[30]

This Aristotelian interrelationship between ethics, economics, and politics is at the very heart of Gower's conception of his *Confessio Amantis* as a whole,[31] and Gower would have read about it in sources apart from the *Tresor,* most obviously Giles of Rome's *De regimine principum,* wherein it forms the basis of this text's tripartite structure. It is crucial to note that such texts do *not* direct their doctrine exclusively at princes; their ethics-centered practical philosophy is meant for mankind in general. As Gower says,

> To every man behoveth lore,
> Bot to noman belongeth more

[30] All Gower quotations are from *John Gower: The English Works*, ed. G. C. Macaulay, EETS e.s. 81–82 (London: Oxford University Press, 1900–1901).

[31] As has been well demonstrated by Elizabeth Porter, "Gower's Ethical Microcosm and Political Macrocosm," in A. J. Minnis, ed., *Gower's Confessio Amantis: Responses and Reassessments* (Cambridge: D. S. Brewer, 1983), pp. 135–62.

> Than to a king, which hath to lede
> The people . . .
>
> (VII.1711–14)

And at the outset, Giles of Rome makes it quite clear that though his treatise is entitled "Concerning the education of Princes," *everyone* should be instructed by it,[32] for (as John Trevisa puts it in his translation of this passage) although not "eueriche man may be kyng oþer prince, ȝit eueriche man schulde desire besiliche to make himself worthi to be a kyng oþer a prince."[33] Each and every man ought to conduct himself in such a way that he may be fit to rule. Here, then, is one of the essential characteristics of a secular ideology of virtue that late medieval philosophers and poets deduced from Aristotle.

At its center is a vision of the active life as the virtuous life of man in society, following the philosopher's description of man as a social animal (or "compaynable beste," as John Trevisa puts it, rendering Giles's *animal sociale*) who wishes to live his life in association with others—parents, wife, and children (see *Nicomachean Ethics* I.7, also *Politics* I.2).[34] In early medieval monastic theology, the *activa vita* was often denigrated in the process of aggrandizing the contemplative life; thanks largely to Aristotle, in the later period it could enjoy a much more positive valuation. Excellent examples of such a valuation are afforded by a late fourteenth-century French poem, the *Eschez amoureux*,[35] and the extensive commentary written on it (also in French) by Evrart de Conty, already mentioned as one of the scholarly translators associated with the court

---

[32] *De regimine principum*, I.i.1, fols. 2v–3r.

[33] *Governance*, ed. Fowler, Briggs, and Remley, p. 7.

[34] "Homme est par nature ordené a vivre civilement et en communité," to quote Nicole Oresme's translation; *Le Livre de Éthiques d'Aristote*, ed. A. D. Menut (New York: Stechert, 1940), p. 118. See the gloss in his version of the *Politics:* "Home est naturelement chose civile, ce est a dire qu'il est ordené de nature a vivre en communité civile." And the husband and wife together form a "communité." *Le Livre de Politiques d'Aristote*, ed. A. D. Menut (Philadelphia: American Philosophical Society, 1970), p. 48. See also *De regimine principum* I.i.4 and II.ii.1, in *Governance*, ed. Fowler, Briggs, and Remley, pp. 13, 161–62.

[35] An edition of the first part of the *Eschez amoureux* has been published by Gianmario Raimondi, "Les *Eschés amoureux*, Studio preparatorio e edizione (I v.1–3662)," *Pluteus*, 8–9 (1990–98), pp. 67–241. Raimondi's work is replacing the edition by Christine Kraft, *Die Liebesgarten-Allegorie der "Échecs amoureux": Kritische Ausgabe und Kommentar* (Frankfurt-am-Main: Lang, 1977), which ignores the damaged but usable Dresden manuscript of the poem.

of Charles V.[36] (It has recently been argued, by Caroline Boucher, that Evrart wrote the poem as well as the commentary on it.)[37] Both texts are imbued with the spirit of Aristotelian learning, Giles of Rome's *De regimine principum* being a major source. Evrart de Conty also draws heavily on the moralized *Metamorphoses*, which formed part of the vast *Reductorium morale* of Pierre Bersuire—but quite selectively, with the material that refers to prelates or prelatical theology being systematically reduced, and Bersuire's heavy use of biblical quotations severely curtailed. Hence Evrart's most astute modern reader, Françoise Guichard-Tesson, has identified a "tendance laïque" in his use of Bersuire, and this is also a feature of his use of other mythographic sources.[38] A similar conclusion could easily be reached concerning the adaptation of mythography in Chaucer's *Parliament of Fowls* and Gower's *Confessio Amantis.*

But for the moment, let us stay with Evrart de Conty. Allegorizing the story of the Judgment of Paris (wherein this representative young man has to choose between the goddesses Pallas, Juno, and Venus), Evrart interprets the *troiz manieres de vies,* which they represent as the *contemplative,* the *active,* and the *voluptueuse,* deriving his categories from Book 1, chapter 5 of the *Nicomachean Ethics.*[39] Thus he is able to take a very positive view of the *vie active* while not calling in question the ultimate supremacy of the *vie contemplative,* in marked contrast to the mythography of Fulgentius, another major influence here. Contemplatives, Evrart explains, are "angelic" or "demigods" and therefore better than

[36] For the identification of Evrart as author of the commentary, see F. Guichard-Tesson, "Evrart de Conty, auteur de la *Glose des Echecs amoureux,*" *Le Moyen français* 8–9 (1981): 111–48. This treatise has been edited by Françoise Guichard-Tesson and Bruno Roy as *Le Livre des Eschez amoureux moralisés,* Bibliothèque du moyen français, vol. 2 (Montreal: CERES, 1993).

[37] Caroline Boucher, "Des problèmes pour exercer l'entendement du lecteur: Evrart de Conty, Nicole Oresme et la recherche de la Nouveauté," forthcoming in *Aristotle's "Problemata" in Different Times and Tongues,* ed. Michèle Goyens and Pieter De Leemans (Leuven).

[38] "La *Glose des Echecs amoureux:* Un savoir à tendance laïque: comment l'interpreter?" *FCS* 10 (1984): 229–60

[39] Oresme distinguishes between the *vie voluptuose,* the *vie civile et active,* and the *vie contemplative*; *Le Livre de Éthiques,* ed. Menut, p. 110. See Giles of Rome, *De regimine principum,* I.i.4, fols. 7r–9r. In John Trevisa's translation, the "þre maners of leuyng" are described as the *voluptuouse, pollitic,* and *contemplative*; *Governance,* ed. Fowler, Briggs, and Remley, p. 12. Brunetto Latini, explicitly paraphrasing the *Ethics,* contrasts the life of concupiscence and covetousness (*concupiscense et covoitise*), the life of sense, prowess, and honor (i.e., the civic life, *vie citeine*), and the life of contemplation (*contemplative*): *Tresor,* II.4, ed. Carmody, p. 177; trans. Barrette and Baldwin, p. 147.

men.[40] However, those who live in human society by following the path of virtue and reason are properly men, and should properly be called men, for the active life, "ordered by reason, is the life which is right, proper and natural to man."[41] Here the influence of Aristotle (perhaps as interpreted in Giles of Rome's *De regimine principum*) is evident, as it is in the subsequent statement that, by nature, mankind does not like to lead a solitary life, but rather wants to live "en compaignie . . . et en communication."[42] And because such association is necessary to the continuation of our human species, marriages are appropriate to the active life.[43] Evrart reassures his readers he is not claiming that, since the active life is more proper and suitable to man insofar as he is man, it is therefore the best life. Rather, one could say that, while in absolute terms gold is worth more than iron, in a battle an iron sword is worth more than a gold one.[44] It would seem that Evrart is writing for those engaged in the battles of the active life, for whom "iron" values and mores—marriage included—are of more use than the higher virtues of the contemplative life. The young aristocrats who are his target audience[45] are advised to love honorably, avoiding excesses of carnal delight that cause damage to both body and soul. One of the things they need to know, according to Evrart, is that "great love" can exist between man and woman, and marriage is the best state in which it may flourish. And in making this claim, he turns to Aristotle as an authority on marriage—successful marriage being seen as an aspect of good economics.

[40] See *Nicomachean Ethics* X.7 and *Politics* I.2; see also *De regimine principum*, I.i.4 and II.i.1, fols. 7v–9r, 130r–v.

[41] *Eschez amour. moral.*, ed. Guichard-Tesson and Roy, p. 350.

[42] In a similar vein, Brunetto declares that "it is a natural thing for a man to be a citizen and to live among men," and "it would be against nature to live alone in the desert where no people live, because man naturally delights in company ("l'ome se delite naturelement en compaignie"). In contrast, beatitude (*beatitude*) is complete in itself and needs nothing outside itself, therefore it is deemed "the highest and best of all good things." *Li Livres dou Tresor*, II.5, ed. Carmody, p. 178; trans. Barrette and Baldwin, p. 147.

[43] *Eschez amour. moral.*, ed. Guichard-Tesson and Roy, p. 353. By contrast, Evrart continues, the voluptuous life is mad (*fole*) and unreasonable, more suited to beasts than to men (p. 354).

[44] *Eschez amour. moral.*, ed. Guichard-Tesson and Roy, p. 356.

[45] Guichard-Tesson and Roy emphasize the didactic purpose of the *Eschez amoureux* poem, which they see as designed to occasion the "initiation érotique, éthique et scientifique" of a young nobleman, a purpose that is further pursued in Evrart de Conty's commentary; *Eschez amour. moral.*, ed. Guichard-Tesson and Roy, p. lxii. A similar claim could be made for Gower's *Confessio Amantis*.

Honest Love: Aristotle as Authority on Marriage

In the Pseudo-Aristotelian *Economics*,[46] the family is defined as the basic economic unit, with a good relationship between husband and wife being seen as essential to its proper operation. "Nothing is more natural than the tie between female and male," and in the case of mankind (in contrast with beasts) this association aims "not merely at existence, but at a happy existence."[47] In his commentated translation of the *Economics*, Nicole Oresme emphasizes the companionate aspect of marriage, confidently asserting that "two young people" can love each other in a manner that involves both joy and reasonableness. Such a relationship is described as a "friendship" that "comprises at once the good of usefulness, the good of pleasure, and the good of virtue and double enjoyment—that is, both the carnal and the virtuous or the sensual and the intellectual pleasures."[48] In Evrart de Conty's more elaborate treatment, Aristotle—actually the Pseudo-Aristotle of the *Economics*—is cited in support of the assertion that marriage to an "honest and good wife" provides the best social situation for the engendering of descendants:

"A respectable man should desire a good wife, and should take pains to see that he has one", as Aristotle says, "for she is the one he has chosen for life to be his companion and for so important an end as the act of generation, for there cannot be a more divine or worthy thing in the estate of marriage than

---

[46] For a recent discussion of the complicated textual tradition of this work, at least part of which may reflect the genuine teaching of Aristotle, see the introduction to *Aristote: Économique*, ed. B. A. van Groningen and A. Wartelle (Paris: Société d'édition Les Belles Lettres, 1968).

[47] *Oeconomica*, I.iii.1, in *Aristotle: Metaphysics Books X–XIV, Oeconomica, Magna Moralia*, ed. and trans. H. Tredennick and C. Cyril Armstrong (Cambridge, Mass.: Harvard University Press, 1935), p. 331. Nicole Oresme's gloss lists the six "conditions" that exist in the union between man and wife more than in any other domestic relationship (*communication domestique*). It is more "naturele, raisonnable, amiable, profectable [i.e., profitable], divine et convenable [i.e., in keeping with social conventions]"; *Le Livre de Yconomique d'Aristote*, ed. A. D. Menut (Philadelphia: American Philosophical Society, 1957), p. 811.

[48] *Le Livre de Yconomique*, ed. Menut, p. 813. For discussion of this passage, see Sherman, *Imaging Aristotle*, pp. 286–91, 297–301, who believes that Oresme "makes a genuine contribution to humane concepts of the marriage relationship" (pp. 290–91). See the genuine Aristotle's own statements in *Nicomachean Ethics* VIII.12: "human beings cohabit not only to get children but to provide what is necessary to a fully lived life," there being "general agreement that conjugal affection combines the useful with the pleasant" (trans. J. A. K. Thomson [Harmondsworth: Penguin, 1955], pp. 251–52).

to engender descendants in an honest and good wife (*fame honeste et bonne*)", as he says, for "by engendering his kind a man becomes immortal and divine."[49]

Evrart explains the purpose of Venus, or human desire, with reference to Nature's wish to ensure the survival of the species. A special kind of love exists between man and woman, which is "above all else natural and marvellous, by which it often happens that from a thousand women a man chooses a single one, whom he loves and desires so singularly that no separation can be made and he would not wish to desire any other."[50] But Evrart—as a medical man (physician to King Charles V of France, no less, and expositor of the *Problemata*)—is fully aware of the ways in which love can damage an aristocrat's health.[51] Taking special pleasure

[49] *Eschez amour. moral.*, ed. Guichard-Tesson and Roy, p. 583. The *Economics* declares that the husband should treat justly and honorably the wife who has entered "his household as a companion in the procreation of children and as a partner in his life (*compaigne de vie*)." Marriage is a *chose saincte et divine*. "What could a man of healthy mind do that is more sacred or holy than to father the children of a good and precious wife?" Furthermore, a husband should remain faithful to his wife, approaching her with "grande honesté et modestie" and avoiding roughness, dirty talk, and dissolute behavior (*sans verconde et oveques paroles deshonnestes et en maniere dissolue*). *Livre de Yconomique*, ed. Menut, pp. 830, 832, 835–36; see p. 837. The man should be sure to give the woman a sufficiency of sexual pleasure—but not too much, lest she cannot contain herself if he is ill or has to go away from home (p. 816). Pseudo-Aristotle praises strong-souled women who show their mettle when misfortunes befall their husbands—like Alceste and Penelope (see *Oeconomica* III.1; ed. Armstrong, pp. 404–5).

[50] See Oresme's gloss: "it often happens that two young people, man and woman, love each other by special choice from a feeling of joy in their hearts (*en especial par election et plaisance de cuer*), with a love that is accompanied by reason, even though it may sometimes happen to be without correct reason." Married friendship (*amisté de marriage*) "includes all the causes and kinds of friendship" as stated in the *Ethics*, 8.17. (Here Oresme appropriates discourse of friendship that, in Aristotle, relates primarily to male friendship rather than to heterosexual relationships.) "Nature accorded the human species" carnal pleasure "not only for reproduction of its kind but also to enhance and maintain friendship (*amisté*) between man and woman." Pliny says that "no female, after she has become pregnant, seeks sexual union, except woman only" (see *Natural History* 8.5), "and this greater unity is a cause of greater friendship." *Le Livre de Yconomique*, ed. Menut, pp. 812, 813.

[51] The Arabic texts that were the sources of much Western medical lore do not mention a particular social class as more susceptible to the lovers' malady, but, as Mary Frances Wack explains, the medieval medical profession labeled "love as an occupational hazard of the nobility. It became another mark of precedence, like wealth and leisure." The *Viaticum* of Constantine the African (who died c.1087 at Montecassino), which became an important textbook in university faculties of medicine, explains that "if erotic lovers are not helped so that their thought is lifted and their spirits lightened, they inevitably fall into a melancholic disease." If untreated or unchecked, this could prove terminal. Cures recommended by Constantine include actual consummation of one's love (or, failing that, therapeutic sex with another woman!), recreational activities with friends, and the enjoyment of music, poetry, and beautiful gardens. In his *Viaticum* commentary, Gerard of Berry (writing in the late twelfth century) includes in his list of

in one single woman can induce melancholy, and therefore Raison, in *Le Roman de la Rose*, defines love as a mental illness, and the wise philosophers agree—here Evrart's main authority is Andreas Capellanus, simply referred to an "an ancient sage."

Andreas causes Evrart considerable problems, not least when he introduces his doctrine that love *par amours* is a different kind of love from that which exists in marriage, "wherein the people are obligated to each other"—but love should lack such mastery, the partners being equal and free. "And therefore an ancient wise man (*un sages ancien*, i.e., Andreas) says that love and lordship do not accord well and are not suitable together."[52] Evrart does not contradict this troublesome "ancient sage" outright; he simply chooses to concentrate elsewhere on the positive aspects of *amour delitable*, identifying marriage as its best possible outlet. Venus's daughter Hymen can be understood as representing all kinds of harmony, especially that which exists between a man and a woman who "liberally, without refusing anything, reciprocally accord with each other." It would seem, then, that marriage, far from being in conflict with personal and mutual pleasure (that being the reason why Andreas had reacted against it), actually allows and promotes an abundance of it. Hymen, explains Evrart, "signifies the delight that is in marriage, where the people are by the ordinance of the law legally joined together, and this delight, as they say, is the greatest of them all and the least

---

treatments "consorting with and embracing girls, sleeping with them repeatedly, and switching various ones," that is, changing partners regularly. See Wack, *Lovesickness in the Middle Ages: The "Viaticum" and Its Commentaries* (Philadelphia: University of Pennsylvania Press, 1990), pp. 61, 188–89, 202–3. Unsurprisingly, Christian *medici* found some of this doctrine difficult to support. It may be identified as a site for secular expertise that could conflict with the "cure of souls" as preached and practiced by medieval clergymen. See, further, Alastair Minnis, *Magister Amoris: The "Roman de la Rose" and Vernacular Hermeneutics* (Oxford: Oxford University Press, 2001), pp. 53–55, 60–62, 266–67, 303, and (with special reference to the issue of abortion) Monica Green, "Constantinus Africanus and the Conflict Between Religion and Science," in G. R. Dunstan, ed., *The Human Embryo: Aristotle and the Arabic and European Traditions* (Exeter: Exeter University Press, 1990), pp. 47–69.

[52] *Eschez amour. moral.*, ed. Guichard-Tesson and Roy, p. 546. Andreas attributes to the Countess of Champagne the view that "love cannot extend its sway over a married couple. Lovers bestow all they have on each other freely, and without the compulsion of any consideration of necessity, whereas married partners are forced to comply with each other's desires as an obligation, and under no circumstances to refuse their persons to each other." *Andreas Capellanus on Love*, ed. and trans. P. G. Walsh (London: Duckworth, 1982), pp. 156–57. See pp. 146–47, where it is argued: "Love is nothing other than an uncontrolled desire to obtain the sensual gratification of a stealthy and secret embrace," which cannot take place between married couples, "since they are acknowledged to possess each other."

intermingled with sorrow, because [in marriage] one can accomplish better, more freely and more legally (*plus franchement et plus licitement*), all the abovementioned pleasures."[53]

A similar solution to the perennial problem of how—within the active life—desire and reason may be reconciled is offered in the seventh book of John Gower's *Confessio Amantis*. And Aristotle once again is cited as a major authority, though in fact this is (yet another) Pseudo-Aristotle, the author of the letter of advice to the emperor Alexander that was known as the *Secretum secretorum*. Gower takes the five points of "policie" recommended therein—Liberality, Wisdom, Chastity, Mercy, Truth, and Justice—and makes them the basis of an arrangement that is much firmer than what is found in the *Secretum* itself. When Gower gets to the "point" of Chastity, a series of *exempla* that illustrate ways in which men are led astray by love is prefaced with the ideal solution to the problem of how not to "excede" the "mesure" of "fleisshly lust" (4235–37). The male is made for the female, but Nature does not force a man to desire many women.[54] A husband should be content with the embraces of his "honeste" wife:

> For whan a man mai redy finde
> His oghne wif, what scholde he seche
> In strange places to beseche
> To borwe an other mannes plouh,
> Whan he hath geere good ynouh
> Affaited at his oghne heste,
> And is to him wel more honeste
> Than other thing which is unknowe?
> (VII.4218–25)

Since man is naturally disposed to wedlock, it follows that "fornicacioun þat is contrarie to wedlock schuld be forsake of al citeseyns," says Giles

---

[53] *Eschez amour. moral.*, ed. Guichard-Tesson and Roy, p. 537. For further discussion of these passages, see Minnis, *Magister amoris*, pp. 304–12. In his version of the *Economics*, Oresme remarks that sometimes human love "is chaste and prepares for marriage and if there is sin in it, it is a human sin. But to approach anyone at all with no desire other than the fulfillment of one's sexual urge (*sa concupiscence*), this is a bestial sin." *Le Livre de Yconomique*, ed. Menut, p. 812. Obviously, this stands in stark opposition to the views of Andreas.

[54] Oresme, developing the doctrine of the *Economics*, asserts that "according to natural reason, a man should possess only one woman and vice-versa," drawing attention to book seven of the *Politics* (chap. 15). *Le Livre de Yconomique*, ed. Menut, p. 812.

of Rome (as translated by John Trevisa); "þe housebonde mot hold hym onlich to his wif" in a relationship of "trewe faith and frendschipe."[55] Gower evidently shares these Aristotelian opinions.

Giles/Trevisa also asserts that, since it is seemly for kings and princes to surpass other men in goodness, "þe more þei scholde forsake fornicacioun and al vnlaweful vse of lecherie."[56] But for Gower (like his French contemporary Evrart de Conty), the moral choice was not that simple or straightforward. He reveals himself as being fully aware of the fashionable status of the doctrine of love *par amours*—

> Among the gentil nacion
> Love is an occupacion,
> Which forto kepe his lustes save
> Scholde every gentil herte have
> (IV.1451–54)

—and indeed of its (quite relative, of course) moral advantages, inasmuch as it contains desire within love for one woman rather than for many. Here in the *Confessio Amantis*, as Gower's character Genius reacts to the story of Rosiphilee, a princess who sought to avoid human love altogether, it is freely admitted that women who serve Venus may follow "Cupides lawe" through the love "of paramours" (1470–71). But this is seen as very much an inferior form of love, seldom conducive to peace, always riven with "janglinge" and "fals Envie," and often intermixed with "disese" (1472–75). Marriage, then, is by far the best option:

> Bot thilke love is wel at ese,
> Which set is upon mariage
> (IV.1476–77)

As Evrart de Conty put it, in marriage "one can accomplish better, more freely and more legally" all the pleasures of love.

Indeed, Gower's Genius finds it utterly surprising that a maiden should hold back from hastening to the feast of honest, married love:

[55] *De regimine principum*, II.i.7 and 8, in *Governance*, ed. Fowler, Briggs, and Remley, pp. 177, 178. See the material from Oresme's *Livre de Yconomique* quoted in note 54 above.

[56] *De regimine principum*, II.i.7, in *Governance*, ed. Fowler, Briggs, and Remley, pp. 177–78.

> A gret mervaile it is forthi
> How that a Maiden wolde lette,
> That sche hir time ne besette
> To haste unto that ilke feste,
> Wherof the love is al honeste.
>
> (IV.1480–84)

Her inexperienced desires ("lustes greene," 1491) will come to full maturity in marriage, and in a few years she will take on the crucial duty ("charge") of bearing children, without which the world "scholde faile" (1447). One is reminded of Evrart's assertion that "there cannot be a more divine or worthy thing in the estate of marriage than to engender descendants in an honest and good wife." Gower's narrative is very much a tale of the active life, as revalued by Aristotelian social philosophy; the contemplative life is simply not an option for Rosiphilee—Gower is not telling that kind of tale. There is no evidence whatever that she is one of those special people who would "lyve in contemplacioun and in Goddis seruyse" and therefore wants to choose "a lyf þat is aboue a man and is as it were a god" (to borrow more phrases from Trevisa).[57] And so, she may rightly be criticized for her reluctance to contribute to the economic success (in Aristotelian terms) of some noble family, to commit to a relationship that is at once useful and pleasurable, and (as Oresme remarked) offers "the good of double enjoyment," the enjoyment of virtue together with the enjoyment of each other's bodies.

At moments like this, the warring goddesses who officiate over the writings of Evrart de Conty and John Gower, namely, Pallas, Juno, and Venus, seem to have attained some measure of reconciliation—but of course many tensions remain. This is admitted in the Latin glosses that Gower himself seems to have written to accompany his English poem. The remark (quoted above) that love is an "occupacion" that every "gentil herte" should have is accompanied with the health warning, "Non quia sic se habet veritas, set opinio Amantum"—this is not true in itself but is rather the opinion of a lover. Indeed, at the beginning of the first book of the *Confessio*, Gower takes pains to distinguish between the moral *auctor* identified by the scholar who lives in his manuscript margins and the love-obsessed characters who inhabit the vernacular text: "Here as it were in the person of other people (*quasi in persona*

---

[57] Ibid., p. 78.

aliorum), who are held fast by love, the author, feigning himself to be a lover (*fingens se auctor esse Amantem*), proposes to write of their various passions one by one in the various distinctions of this book."[58] In a similar vein, Evrart de Conty explains that the author of the *Eschez amoureux* (perhaps Evrart himself?) has feigned and introduced several characters (*personnes*; cf. the Latin term *personae*), each of whom speaks in his turn as is appropriate to his nature, in the "manner of feigning" (*la maniere qu'il est faint*) used in *Le Roman de la Rose*. "And no doubt one can sometimes feign and speak figuratively and in fable in a way which is beneficial and to a good end."[59] That "good end" is spelled out at the end of Evrart's commentary as we have it. Here we are assured that the author was not really "maddened and overcome by love"; rather, he feigned this poem "to take the occasion for speaking of love better, more pleasantly, and more beautifully." And his principal intention "and the end of his book" was to reprehend and blame these who are foolish in love as acting "contrary to reason."[60] But this allows much room for a quite positive doctrine of reasonable love, which Evrart spends much time elaborating, as we have seen. And he seems to have no doubt that love is a subject that may be spoken of pleasantly and beautifully.

Boethius in Love: The Laicizing of Consolation in Machaut and Chaucer

Anicius Manlius Severinus Boethius was not interested in speaking pleasantly and beautifully of human love. His concern in *De consolatione philosophiae* was rather with the many and various ways in which men act contrary to reason, and love affords many opportunities for doing just that. *Prima facie*, the *Consolatio*—another of those texts that was regarded as an appropriate gift for princes and princely readers—was far harder to assimilate to the literature of noble lay education, given its critique of so much that (according to the practical philosophy nurtured by the Medieval Aristotle) was normative to the "active life," providing of course due moderation was exercised. Here I have in mind the "inferior goods," as Boethius identified them, of material wealth, honor, power, fame, and bodily pleasure. However, a quite extraordinary measure of assimilation was indeed achieved, as I now will argue with the

[58] *English Works*, ed. Macaulay, I.37.
[59] *Eschez amour. moral.*, ed. Guichard-Tesson and Roy, p. 22.
[60] Ibid., pp. 764–66.

help of works by Chaucer and Guillaume de Machaut (c. 1300–1377), a figure who enjoyed substantial patronage from members of the French high nobility, including John of Luxembourg, King of Bohemia (his first patron), Charles, King of Navarre, and John, Duke of Berry. Both writers brought Boethius within the bounds of their love poetry.

"Boethius in love"? A deliberately provocative praise—but susceptible of some justification. At the most obvious and uncontentious level (but let us recognize how extraordinary this is in itself), the *Consolatio* furnished source material for vernacular poetry of human love. What about the values that, in Boethius, imbued that material; did they transmit along with it? Only partially, I believe. They did not inevitably gain ideological control of the new contexts into which they had been introduced. Indeed, some of them were subjected to radical reappraisal, of a kind indicative of the different priorities of an emergent lay culture.

All of this is in evidence in Machaut's *Remede de Fortune* (c. 1340).[61] Here the ups and downs of love are positioned in relation to the ever-turning wheel of Fortune, with much material being taken over from the *Consolatio* and reconfigured to suit the new situation. Part of this process involves the placing of love's trials in a wider moral perspective; the lover's changing fortunes are seen as symptomatic of the insecurities of human beings in general. Now, it is true that in *Le Roman de la Rose* Boethian ideas on fortune had featured prominently; the *Consolatio* was one of Jean de Meun's favorite sources (and he predicted his own future translation of it). However, the *Rose* lacks a clear didactic purpose and educational vision; as Christine de Pizan tartly remarked, it fails to conclude unequivocally "in favour of the moral way of life."[62] Many of Jean de Meun's successors sought to remedy that perceived failure— including Machaut, who seems always in the business of offering models for moral self-fashioning and illustrating how noble people actually should conduct their lives.[63] In the *Remede*, amatory discourse is amplified even as room is made within ethical discourse (of a kind that owes much to Boethius) for the trials and tribulations of lovers. In his *Confessio*

---

[61] *Le Jugement du Roy de Behaigne* and *Remede de Fortune*, ed. and trans. James I. Wimsatt and William W. Kibler (Athens: University of Georgia Press, 1988).

[62] *Le débat sur le Roman de la Rose*, ed. Eric Hicks (Paris: Champion, 1977), p. 135; trans. Joseph L. Baird and John R. Kane, *La Querelle de la Rose: Letters and Documents*, North Carolina Studies in the Romance Languages and Literatures, 199 (Chapel Hill: University of North Carolina Press, 1978), p. 132.

[63] On the debt of Middle French poets to the *Rose*, see especially P.-Y. Badel, *Le "Roman de la Rose" au XIVe siècle: Étude de la réception de l'œuvre* (Geneva: Droz, 1980).

Amantis, John Gower would pursue this experiment even further, with mixed results.

A more complicated case is presented by Machaut's *Jugement du Roy de Behaigne* (composed shortly before 1342), which features a debate between a bereaved woman and a knight whose lover has left him. Here (highly negative) Boethian notions of human affection serve the argument that the woman's suffering is less than the man's because earthly love cannot survive death. According to the jilted knight, "when the soul has left the body and the body is interred beneath the gravestone," it is "soon forgotten, although it may be mourned." He has "seen no man nor woman weep so long that he'd not found joy again before the year was out, no matter how true his love" (1109–22).[64] Now, one would expect the knight to say this: it is part and parcel of his strategy of affirming the superiority of his suffering, as a rejected suitor, to that of the recently widowed woman. We are presumably on firmer ground with the words of Reason, who acts as an adviser to the text's aristocratic authority-figure, the King of Bohemia. Reason is even more ruthless than the knight in identifying the love of men and women as essentially a thing of the flesh and concluding that therefore it cannot survive the grave. "Love comes from carnal affection, and its desires and essence all incline to pleasure" (1709–11).[65] Therefore the love of the lady who has been widowed shall diminish "from day to day," and "in like measure is her sorrow diminishing" (1717–23).[66] This is reminiscent of the Boethian categorization of bodily pleasure as one of those "false goods" that lead men astray from the pursuit of *beatitudo* or true happiness, the supreme good that contains all the inferior goods within itself (*DCP* pr. 2 10–15).[67] The longing for bodily pleasure is full of anxiety and its satisfaction is full of repentance (III pr. 7, 1–3). Moreover, the human body is subject to change and decay: "How brief is the brightness of beauty, how swiftly passing, more quickly fleeting than the changing loveliness of spring flowers" (III pr. 7, 21–22). But—and here is the major difference—in the *Behaigne* there is no advocacy of true happiness, no injunction to seek the *summum bonum,* and certainly no hint of the

[64] *Behaigne,* trans. Wimsatt and Kibler, pp. 114, 116.
[65] Ibid., p. 147.
[66] Ibid.
[67] All references are to *The Theological Tractates and "The Consolation of Philosophy,"* ed. H. F. Stewart, E. K. Rand, and S. J. Tester (Cambridge, Mass.: Harvard University Press, 1973).

consolations of religion. The human body in all its beauty, and the love that it inspires, may be ephemeral, but it is the poem's central concern. Dead is dead; the living are left to love as best they can while they can.

This is not Machaut's last word on the matter; indeed, Machaut does not offer any single "last word." A new authority-figure features in his later *Jugement dou Roy de Navarre* (1349), where the poet-persona's procedure in the *Behaigne* is criticized, albeit in a way that leaves his dignity intact and his earlier point of view still valid. Death in a larger and more horrifying aspect is confronted in the *Navarre*'s initial evocation of the horrors of plague, to which are opposed the joys of aristocratic life— represented here first by hunting (described as a noble, pleasurable and improving occupation and an honorable recreation) and, second, by love-debate (described as a pleasant task and seen as affording joyful entertainment).[68] The superlative nature of women's love, and particularly the value of female suffering, is affirmed through a series of forceful *exempla*. Furthermore, in *Le Lay de plour*, a poem written from the point of view of the bereaved lady in the *Behaigne* and originally appended to the *Navarre*, Machaut profoundly reconsiders the strength of human recollection in matters of the heart.[69] The values remain rigorously secular, but now more optimism is allowed. With extraordinary delicacy and telling simplicity, the suggestion is put that love can indeed survive the grave, thanks to the memory's ability to conserve the best that human life has offered us.[70] "Whoever loves well forgets slowly"—and the better the love, it would seem, the slower the forgetting. The poem ends with the speaker beseeching God that, before her own life ends, their love may find life in a book (lines 206–10). This prayer has clearly been granted, inasmuch as the *Lay de plour* is itself that very "book." But God

---

[68] On Machaut's appeal to secular pleasures in this poem (and their therapeutic value), see Alastair Minnis, *Oxford Guides to Chaucer: The Shorter Poems* (Oxford: Oxford University Press, 1995), pp. 103, 149–53.

[69] An edition and translation (which I have drawn on here) is included in *Guillaume de Machaut: The Judgment of the King of Navarre*, ed. R. Burton Palmer (New York: Garland, 1988), pp. 190–213.

[70] The theory of memory in use here owes much to Aristotle's attack on Plato's vision of the disjunction between body and soul. Knowledge arises not from recollection of past knowledge of the Forms but from human experience as gained in the empirical world: hence the soul must inevitably use "phantasms" or images in its thinking, these being the work of the imagination (the soul cannot think without an image, as the *De anima* taught its many readers). And such images are stored in the treasury of the memory. This is one of the many ways in which the rediscovered *libri naturales* of Aristotle, as interpreted in the later Middle Ages, helped the human faculties and the human perception to gain a new dignity.

has been assigned no significant role in the poem; the only afterlife envisioned is textual.

Chaucer's most profound renegotiations of Boethian matter and meaning occur in three poems that are set in pagan antiquity, a locus that afforded Chaucer excellent opportunities for exploration of the strengths—and limitations—of secular culture. In *The Knight's Tale, The Franklin's Tale*, and *Troilus and Criseyde*, the Boethius-persona's protestations about the apparent unfairness of human existence are metamorphosed, respectively, into Palamon's lament about that cruel "prescience" that torments guiltless innocence (I[A], 1313–14), Dorigen's anguished questioning of the divine purpose behind those "grisly feendly rokkes blake" (seemingly created "in ydel") that have resulted in the deaths of "An hundred thousand bodyes of mankynde" (V[F], 865–80), and of course Troilus's disputation with himself about the workings of that "necessitee" which seems to have predestined the departure of Criseyde (IV.956–66). In the *Consolatio*, the Boethius-persona is subsequently put right by Dame Philosophy, who leads him to true understanding of the relationship between God's infallible knowledge and man's freedom of will. In the above-mentioned Chaucer poems, there is no such explicit instruction; we are simply, painfully, left with the problems,[71] though the ending of *Troilus* has been seen as offering a "solution" that is "precisely that furnished by Boethius, who also bids mankind to lift its eyes to the contemplation of eternal values." The author of those words,

---

[71] In contrast, Bridget of Sweden was able to get definite answers from Christ Himself to a wide range of questions, including two of particular concern to Chaucer's anguished heathen. First, why do the just suffer? Because it is in their best interest to suffer tribulations for a time; here God acts like a mother who rebukes her children, that they might be "drawn away from wrongdoing and . . . become accustomed to discipline and good behaviour." Besides, God stands by them in their trouble. It is true that the wicked sometimes have greater prosperity in the world than the good; "this is an indication" of God's "great patience and charity and a testing for the just." Second, why have so many useless things (like fiendish black rocks, one may imagine) been created? "Nothing," Christ retorts, "has been made without a cause or a use, not the highest mountains, nor the desert, nor the lakes; not the beasts, nor even the venomous reptiles. I provide for the usefulness of all creatures as well as of mankind." All things have been arranged "in a rational manner"—some "for man's use and delight, some to be refuges for animals and birds, some for the training and bridling of human cupidity, some for the harmony of the elements, some for the admiration of my work [i.e., God may be known and honored by mankind out of admiration for the many creatures He has made], some for the punishment of sin and for the harmony of things higher and lower, some for a cause known and reserved to me alone." For this, and much more, see *Revelationes*, vol. 5, trans. A. R. Kezel, *Birgitta of Sweden: Life and Selected Revelations* (New York: Paulist Press, 1990), pp. 108–9, 138, 143–44.

Howard R. Patch, freely admits that there is no specific "verbal influence" involved here; his argument is rather that *Troilus* is imbued with "the spirit of the *Consolatio*"; "its hymns are taken over in various parts of the poem, its philosophy quoted here and there, and the final moral is the same."[72] In the foundational literary criticism concerning Troilus's double sorrow—which retains considerable influence today—the progression of the protagonist's love affair came to be read as "an exemplum of the lesson which the *Consolatio* promulgated."[73] Or, as D. W. Robertson famously put it, Chaucer's character was a victim of idolatrous lust.[74] And the *Consolatio* provided the moral values against which Troilus's behavior was to be measured and found wanting. According to Robertson, "The Boethian elements in *Troilus* and their implications were . . . easily recognizable to the members of Chaucer's audience," who could not possibly have regarded "passionate love for a fickle woman with anything but disfavor."[75] The conclusions of the *Consolatio* are, then, *implicit* in this and Chaucer's other ventures into the *roman antique* genre; they hang over the texts like some avenging angel, offering superior Christian wisdom to those "members of Chaucer's audience" who have ears to hear.

Little wonder, then, that the most radical appropriation of a Boethian passage which Chaucer ever attempted—the hymn to "Love, that of erthe and se hath governaunce" placed near the end of Book 3 of *Troilus*—was read as a blatant confusion of cupidinous and charitable love, this being the poet's method of revealing the absurdity of elevating sexual passion to a metaphysical, even mystical, plane. This misses the poet's point, I think—which is rather that Troilus's feelings, as part and parcel of a now-requited love that cannot be reduced to "vnlaweful vse of lecherie" (as condemned by Giles/Trevisa and the Medieval Aristotle in general), have actually helped this virtuous heathen rise to the highest

[72] Howard R. Patch, "Troilus on Determinism" (1929), repr. in R. J. Schoeck and Jerome Taylor, eds., *Chaucer Criticism, vol. II: Troilus and Criseyde and the Minor Poems* (Notre Dame: University of Notre Dame Press, 1961), pp. 71–85 (p. 83).
[73] Theodore A. Stroud, "Boethius' Influence on Chaucer's *Troilus*" (1951), repr. in Schoeck and Taylor, *Chaucer Criticism, vol. II,* pp. 122–35 (p. 127). See J. L. Shanley's comment, "The ultimate reason for Troilus's woe was not that he trusted in a woman but that . . . he placed his hope for perfect happiness in that which by its nature was temporary, imperfect, and inevitably insufficient." "The *Troilus* and Christian Love" (1939), repr. in Schoeck and Taylor, *Chaucer Criticism, vol. II,* pp. 136–46 (p. 137).
[74] D. W. Robertson Jr., *A Preface to Chaucer: Studies in Medieval Perspectives* (Princeton: Princeton University Press, 1962), pp. 491–502.
[75] Robertson, *Preface to Chaucer,* p. 472.

of his philosophical achievements. In the direct source of Troilus's hymn, Book 2, meter 8 of the *Consolatio philosophiae*, Chaucer found what he reconstructed as the fullest possible vision of that love which may be attained through secular, philosophical wisdom, without recourse to the love of Him who "starf" on the cross "oure soules for to beye" (see *Troilus and Criseyde*, V.1844–45). This served well the poet's project of depicting enlightened pagans who are innocent of Christian love, in itself a striking instance of his valorization of the secular. And he adapted the text to fit his love story by emphasizing the original's (somewhat minimal) reference to the bond of heterosexual love, in contrast to its praise of virtuous friendship, that being what particularly interested Nicholas Trevet (whose commentary on the *Consolatio* was well known to Chaucer, as already mentioned).[76] But far more radical than any specific alteration is the profound shift of meaning that is effected by Chaucer's positioning of this Boethian text. For it comes after the physical consummation of his love for Criseyde, and its philosophical insight seems to have been prompted by the joy of that experience.

In having his distant (and distancing) pagan protagonist voice the most fascinating piece of postcoital philosophy to have survived from the Middle Ages (only the quasi-eucharistic passion of Gottfried von Strassburg's Tristan and Isolde gets anywhere close), Chaucer went far beyond anything that medieval scholars derived from their philosophical *auctores*. I would contend, however, that he built quite specifically on their doctrines. Hence in Troilus's hymn to love, *coitus* is tacitly yet decisively implicated in the process, as described by Aristotle, whereby mankind seeks the good.[77] Like Evrart de Conty and John Gower, Chaucer

---

[76] See Alastair Minnis, *Chaucer and Pagan Antiquity* (Woodbridge, Suffolk: Boydell and Brewer, 1982), pp. 99–101.

[77] Here I have in mind the Aristotelian dictum that there is an elaborate hierarchy of superior and inferior goods or "ends" with the *summum bonum* at the very top. That is the ultimate end toward which all things tend, but this does not mean that the lesser goods or ends are necessarily to be condemned or despised (that being a tendency in early medieval Boethius commentary). Each has its own value, and each has its part to play in a chain of causation that leads to the supreme good and ultimate end. To find a succinct formulation of this doctrine, Chaucer had to look no further than the preface to Jean de Meun's Boethius translation, and inevitably it permeates Trevet's Aristotelianizing Boethius commentary. For example, commenting on Book IV, metre 6, Trevet explains that the "love common to all things" (this being the kind of love which Boethius also has in mind in Book II, metre 8) should be understood as the general appetite of all creation that tends toward, as to its ultimate end, the chief good, that is, the Creator who "sits on high, and ruling the universe guides its reins" (*DCP* IV met. 6, 44, 34–35). For a fuller discussion, see Minnis, *Chaucer and Pagan Antiquity*, p. 99.

had to contend with the discourses of love *par amours* then fashionable among the "gentil nacion" in a way in which the scholarly interpreters of Aristotle and Boethius had not, or chose not to.[78]

There is no reason to suppose that Chaucer, as the author of *Troilus and Criseyde*, swallowed Boethius whole, the parts we cannot see as well as the parts we can see—particularly given the well-established tradition of negotiation and occasional transformation of Boethian doctrine that may easily be illustrated from Middle French poetry. Machaut and his contemporaries quarried the *Consolatio*, extracting large pieces of material that they shaped for their own purposes, purposes that were not necessarily those of the original author, who had written more than eight hundred years previously for a very different interpretive community. The audience addressed by Machaut and Chaucer comprised, along with the inevitable clerics, aristocrats (including women) of various ranks together with members of the merchant class, people whose distinctive social situations meant that they pursued lifestyles unlike those of the clerics. For them, marriage, child-rearing, and household management (all aspects of economics, according to Aristotle) were regular courses of action; within their lay culture, sexuality was constructed somewhat differently from what appertained in the clerical world without women. It is therefore quite possible to read Troilus's hymn to love as a daring expression of that "lay spirit" so persuasively evoked by Georges de Lagarde. The fact that the love of Troilus and Criseyde comes to nothing does not retrospectively render valueless that extraordinary discourse at the end of Book III, anymore than the love of the Man and Black and his "Fair White" is demeaned by the fact that it is brought to a premature material end with the lady's death. At the very least, it may be claimed—to borrow a phrase from Walter Clyde Curry—that Chaucer "has bestowed dignity upon ephemeral human relationships by linking them up with the processes of cosmic forces."[79] Ephemeral relationships are, after all, part and parcel of the active life, men and women of secular estate inevitably being subject to the vagar-

[78] Nicole Oresme, in explaining the difference between the irrational lusts of beasts and the rational love of man and woman (which, however, "may sometimes happen to be without correct reason"), disingenuously adds, "accordingly, Ovid wrote a book on the art of this kind of love, which does not exist between dumb animals." *Le Livre de Yconomique*, ed. Menut, p. 812. No attempt is made to reconcile the *Ars amatoria* with the *Economics*.

[79] *Chaucer and the Medieval Sciences*, 2nd ed. (New York: Barnes and Noble, 1960), p. 267.

ies of the "false worldes brotelnesse" (*Troilus and Criseyde*, V.1832). The One who "nyl falsen no wight . . . / That wol his herte al holly on hym leye" (1845–46) does offer certainty and security. But, for the most part, that is not Chaucer's concern in his poems of pagan antiquity—and secularity.[80]

Those Magnificent Men . . . from Aristotle to Chaucer

In the space remaining to me, I would like to consider vernacular realization of a virtue that, although discussed in the *Nicomachean Ethics*, had considerable economic and political import—namely, magnificence. Giles of Rome, drawing heavily on the fourth book of the *Ethics*, explains that *magnificencia* "stondeþ in greet spendyng and cost," in contrast to liberality, which consists in moderate spending and cost.[81] This virtue "hath þe name of workes and of *facio*, makynge. *Magnificus* is cleped as it were *magna faciens*, makynge and doynge grete thinges."[82] Given that it is "semeliche for a kyng to be *magnificus*," Giles illustrates what "grete workes and dedes" are appropriate. In brief, the king should perform magnificent works in respect of God, of the common good of his state, of special persons "þat ben worthi worschep," and of himself and his family.

The first of these works involves the construction of temples to the glory of God—"For he is heed of þe regne and þerby he hath þe liknesse of God þat is heed and prince of alle [*gerit in hoc dei vestigium, qui est caput & princeps vniuersi*], it is most semelich þat he bere hymsilf as *magnificus* schulde in makyng holy temples and ordinaunce and araye of seruice and worschip of God."[83] The last entails the maintenance of a splendid home, paying for splendid weddings for his family members, and attracting great chivalry to his court: "it longeth to a kyng to haue hymself as *magnificus* schulde to his owne persone and to oþer persones þat bien aboute hym as to his wif and children and oþere maynye; hauyng worschepful place to dwelle inne; and makyng semeliche festes of

---

[80] We are in need of research on the Stoical traditions that underlie the pagan values simulated by Chaucer. The way forward has been shown by Marcia Colish, though unfortunately (for Chaucerians) her work ends with the sixth century: *The Stoic Tradition from Antiquity to the Early Middle Ages*, rev. ed. (Leiden and New York: Brill, 1990).

[81] *De regimine principum*, I.ii.19, in *Governance*, ed. Fowler, Briggs, and Remley, p. 79.

[82] Ibid., p. 80.

[83] *De regimine principum*, I.ii.20, fol. 67r; *Governance*, ed. Fowler, Briggs, and Remley, p. 83. See *Le Livre de Éthiques*, ed. Menut, p. 246.

mariage; and drawynge to hym wonderfullich cheualrie [*faciendo nuptias decentes, exercendo militias admirabiles*]." Similarly, Brunetto Latini says that magnificence is a virtue "in which wealth is displayed through great spending and large houses," the magnificent person being "by nature eager to have his business carried out with great honor and at great expense (*grant despens*) rather than small."[84] This virtue is concerned "with great, marvelous things," he continues, "such as building temples and churches and other lofty undertakings for the honor of Our lord, and likewise with lavish weddings and providing people with luxurious lodgings, expensive foods and great presents." Brunetto adds that wealth alone does not make one magnificent; for a person to excel in this virtue he "must know how to spend it and arrange things in a suitable (*covenable*) way." Magnificence is not just a matter of spending great amounts of money, as Nicole Oresme makes clear in his *Livre de Éthiques*; it also involves spending wisely and prudently, *sagement et prudenment*, and doing what is *honeste et convenable*, in respect of major projects (*grans choses*).[85] All these interpreters of Aristotle emphasize that the magnificent man will act in a way that is appropriate and proportionate (*avenant et correspondant*), when excellent opportunities "pour la chose publique et pour le bien commun" present themselves.[86]

[84] *Tresor*, II.22, ed. Carmody, p. 193; trans. Barrette and Baldwin, p. 162.

[85] *Le Livre de Éthiques*, ed. Menut, pp. 243, 245.

[86] Here I deploy more phrases from Oresme, *Le Livre de Éthiques*, ed. Menut, p. 244. Similarly, Thomas Aquinas, commenting on the *Ethics,* explains that magnificence deals only in great and princely expenditures (*magnas expensas*), disbursed in keeping with what is becoming. "The work must be worth the cost, and the cost equal to or in excess of the work." The magnificent man "can judge rightly (*decens*) and spend great sums prudently (*prudenter*)," hence he needs to possess all the moral virtues. *Apirocolia* (bad taste) must be avoided, that is, spending beyond what right reason dictates, in the wrong circumstances, and in a merely ostentatious manner. *In decem libros ethicorum Aristotelis ad Nicomachum expositio*, IV lec. 6, ed. R. M. Spiazzi, 3rd ed. (Turin: Marietti, 1964), pp. 198–99; trans. C. I. Litzinger (Chicago: Regnery, 1964), 1:309–12. A more extensive account is provided in the *Ethics* commentary of the English secular master Walter Burley (c. 1275–c.1344), one of the distinguished group of natural philosophers at Merton College, Oxford, who went on to study theology at Paris, and enjoyed close associations with high-ranking members of the English aristocracy. (He was the Black Prince's tutor, and in 1336 became a clerk in the king's household.) Burley explains that the magnificent man is chiefly concerned with honors (which are lavished on those who enjoy good fortune), disinterested in empty display, and does not remember past evils and slights (for such things are not worthy to be remembered); magnificence is difficult to attain, since it is consequent on the other virtues. *Expositio super decem libros ethicorum Aristotelis*, IV tract. 2 (Venice, 1500), fols. 65r–69v. For an introduction to Burley's brilliant commentary on the *Politics*, see S. H. Thompson, "Walter Burley's Commentary on the *Politics* of Aristotle," *Mélanges Auguste Pelzer* (Louvain: Bibliothèque de l'Université, 1947), pp. 557–78.

Chaucer's philosopher-ruler Duke Theseus certainly rises to those exceptional occasions that are "selde ido in a mannes lif tyme, as festes of mariage and of weddyng and of knyʒthode."[87] In the first instance, he does much to promote "wonderfullich cheualrie." Whereas Boccaccio in his *Teseida* had the great tournament take place in an already-existing amphitheater, Chaucer's Theseus commands that a new structure be built—and on the very site where he had discovered the young lovers secretly and illegally fighting over Emily (see I[A], 1862).[88] Thus he seeks to bring order out of chaos, civilization out of strife, and to replace potential destruction with actual construction. Theseus, then, operates as the great maker (as well as the "first mover") of the human world of *The Knight's Tale*; he richly merits the accolade *magna faciens*.

According to the rationale of magnificence, a great enterprise justifies great cost. Chaucer's Knight draws attention to the expenditure ("dispence") "of Theseus, that gooth so bisily / To maken up the lystes roially" and build a vast "noble theatre"—a mile in circumference, "walled of stoon, and dyched al withoute" (1881–87). There was no painter or sculptor who was not employed on this splendid project, all available artists being provided with "mete and wages / The theatre for to maken and devyse" (1900–901). If Richard II was reluctant to lavish patronage on major public works, Theseus more than makes up for any such deficiency. (He could be deemed Chaucer's fantasy patron.) The duke also makes "greet spendyng and cost" in "worschep of God"—or rather, in his case, of the gods. The "oratories" of Venus, Diana, and Mars, in which Palamon, Emily, and Arcite pray to their respective deities, are all new constructions, richly adorned with "noble kervyng" and "portreitures" (1915, cf. 1938, 1968, etc.), which the Knight spends much time describing and commending. The depiction of Diana earns special praise; he is impressed by both the craftsmanship and the cost of the materials used:

> Wel koude he peynten lifly that it wroghte;
> With many a floryn he the hewes boughte.
>
> (1 [A], 2087–88)

---

[87] Plato's advocacy of philosopher-rulers was well known, not least through Boethius's reference to it in *De consolatione philosophiae*, I pr. 4, 18–25. For discussion of the concept by English "classicizing friars," see Minnis, *Chaucer and Pagan Antiquity*, pp. 142–43, 182.

[88] Walter Burley explains that the magnificent man acts in an open (*manifeste*) rather than a secret manner; *Expositio*, IV tract. 2, fol. 67r.

The Knight's account concludes with an allusion to the "greet spendyng and cost" (to echo one of Trevisa's phrases) necessitated by such an awe-inspiring venture:

> Now been thise lystes maad, and Theseus,
> That *at his grete cost* arrayed thus
> The temples and the theatre every deel,
> Whan it was doon, hym lyked wonder weel.
> (2089–92; italics mine)

Theseus looks upon his creation and finds it good. His good taste is obviously impeccable, but we are never allowed to forget that he has footed the bill. Indeed, within the Knight's "magnificent" discourse, stylish spending is inseparable from expensive style.

The duke's magnificent "big spending" does not end when his buildings have been completed. For he provides lavish hospitality for all the knights who have gathered "for love and for encrees of chivalrye" (2184). They are honourably housed and fed ("inned" and "fested"; 2192–93; see the "greet . . . feeste" described in line 2483), and entertained with much "mynstralcye" and dancing. When the battle's lost and won, the combatants enjoy a further feast of three days' duration (2736), and Theseus, ever the great maker, casts his mind to how Arcite's sepulcher "may best ymaked be" (2855). The description of the elaborate "funeral servyse" that follows leaves us in no doubt that he has spent a pretty penny on this exceptional event, which is worthy of exceptional expenditure. And, of course, the tale ends with a wedding— though at this point Chaucer gives priority to Theseus's Boethian philosophy rather than his magnificence. However, an Aristotelianized deity features in the duke's speech about the "faire cheyne of love" that maintains the harmony of the universe—a more comprehensive, and certainly more mature, version of Troilus's hymn to love—when "Juppiter, the kyng" is described not only as "heed and prince of alle" (to echo a phrase from Trevisa) but also as the "firste," "stable," and "eterne" "Moevere" who is "cause of alle thyng" (2986, 2994, 3004, 3036). It is pointless to fight against the way in which this Prime Mover has organized the corruptible world (with the "speces of thynges" surviving "by successiouns," as individual members of each species are born and die); however, men are free to meet the inevitable with dignity and honor, thus making virtue of necessity. Rarely has secularity received more eloquent expression.

And yet: in the very midst of this fine evocation of the "lay spirit," we find a subtle reminder of its limitations. For Theseus claims that "it is best, as for a worthy fame," for a man to die "whan that he is best of name" (3055–56). It was a commonplace of late medieval classicism that even the best of the virtuous heathen could be too concerned with public reputation and merely earthly glory, and that seems to be the case here. Theseus is paying insufficient attention to the religious dimension, despite all the good work he had initiated earlier in the text by ordering the construction of "holy temples and ordinaunce and araye of seruice and worschip of God"—though to be fair to the Duke, he does go on propose that the Athenians should thank "Juppiter of al his grace" (as they move from a time of sorrow to a time of joy, 3067–69). Giles of Rome was in no doubt that a king should "sette his felicite in God"; the higher a person's position, the more he needs divine grace, for the good of his subjects as well as for his own good.[89] And Nicole Oresme found much support in holy Scripture for his Aristotelian philosophy of marriage, even describing Jacob as having "served seven years"—shades of the love-service mandated by *fin amor*—"for the love of Rachel and the time seemed short because of the greatness of his love" (see Genesis 29:18).

These thoughts bring us full circle to the very beginning of this paper, where I sought to distance myself from the binary thinking that hindered Lagarde's search for a "lay spirit." Fourteenth-century secularity had its own proper concerns (as I have sought to show), but it did not *necessarily* operate in opposition to religious considerations; the relationship between the competing discourses was far more complicated than that. Paradoxically enough, Aristotle's account of ethics, economics, and politics could be, and often was, enlisted in support of the church's status and authority in moral matters. The fact that "The Philosopher" had identified virtue as the defining goal of the political community made it difficult "to argue that temporal authority could be independent from the jurisdiction of the church."[90] Indeed, Matthew Kempshall has argued that, rather than seeing "Aristotle's political philosophy as a radical alternative framework," we should pay more attention to "the integration of certain aspects of the *Ethics* and the *Politics* with existing patristic and Biblical authorities." Hence it could be said

[89] *De regimine principum*, I.i.12 and I.i.3, in *Governance*, ed. Fowler, Briggs, and Remley, pp. 30, 11.
[90] Kempshall, *Common Good*, p. 353.

that "the truly radical texts in scholastic political thought were provided, not by Aristotle, but by Augustine and the Bible."[91] In a manner of speaking, that is quite true—but I myself would add the caveat that it was in large measure due to the impetus provided by the "New Aristotle" that the relevant *auctoritates* from Augustine and the Bible were marshaled in the service of a secular theory of the state and of the individual citizen.

One final proof of the often-paradoxical nature of the relationship between secularity and religiosity, this time specific to fourteenth-century England, must suffice. John Wyclif was perfectly willing to serve as an "expert witness cum political spin-doctor"[92] in support of John of Gaunt's interests during the Parliament of 1378, when he attacked ecclesiastical privileges in general and the rights of sanctuary in particular. Indeed, Michael Wilks has gone so far as to claim that "after 1370 virtually all of Wyclif's enormous output was intended either directly or indirectly for the benefit of the monarchy, and in particular John of Gaunt."[93] An overstatement, I believe, but there is much truth in it. It is indubitable that in his *De ecclesia*, Wyclif developed the view that the state should police the church, acting to curb its excesses and punish its transgressions. Furthermore, Wyclif's Donatism—the doctrine that an officeholder (whether priest, pope, or king) must be predestined to glory in order to perform rightly the duties associated with his office—loses much force in the case of kingship, when Wyclif insists that subjects should obey their sovereign and not presume to judge his character.[94] He might well have played the role of Ockham to the

[91] Ibid., p. 362.

[92] To borrow a phrase from Ralph Hanna, *London Literature, 1300–1380* (Cambridge: Cambridge University Press, 2005), p. 235.

[93] Michael Wilks, "Royal Patronage and Anti-Papalism from Ockham to Wyclif," in Anne Hudson and Michael Wilks, eds., *From Ockham to Wyclif*, Studies in Church History, Subsidia 5 (Oxford: Blackwell, 1987), pp. 135–63 (p. 136). Wilks argues that Wyclif set about proving "an historical basis for the regalian rights which the king had over ecclesiastical property," denying any notion of "a double or divided jurisdiction" (pp. 156, 163). See, further, E. C. Tatnall, "John Wyclif and *Ecclesia Anglicana*," *Journal of Ecclesiastical History* 20 (1969): 19–43, and the comprehensive treatment by William Farr in *John Wyclif as Legal Reformer* (Leiden: Brill, 1974).

[94] Here I follow the judgment of Malcolm Lambert, *Medieval Heresy: Popular Movements from the Gregorian Reform to the Reformation*, 2nd ed. (Oxford: Blackwell, 1992), p. 259. It should be noted, however, that on occasion Wyclif recognizes the difficulty of knowing whether *any* officeholder is predestined to eternal salvation or "foreseen" to eternal damnation. But there is no doubt of his desire to view kingship in the best possible light.

duke's Ludwig of Bavaria, had not Gaunt taken fright at his protégé's dangerous views on the Eucharist. In the age of Richard II, at least some brands and branches of Lollardy were set fair to ally with state interests, many Wycliffite clerics being well placed to become champions of secular power—and this may help explain the attraction of Wycliffism to the so-called Lollard Knights. Earthly as well as heavenly advantage was on offer. But such an alliance was not to be. And in Lancastrian England, church and state joined together to crush a narrowly defined and hereticated version of Lollardy; the contrast could hardly be more blatant. Here, then, is the paradox: secularity and fourteenth-century "vernacular theology" (at least of the kind generated by Wyclif) had a closer association than hitherto has been admitted. Had Wyclif listened to the Duke of Lancaster's advice, it could have been closer still.

In Search of Secularity

In Chaucer's *Parliament of Fowls*, a man of great authority, Scipio Africanus, pushes the Chaucer-persona into a garden of love, but he does not enter himself. In many other vernacular poems, however, the philosophers have gained access to that very garden. They bustle about with furrowed brows, offering rationalizations of at least some of its values, seeking to accommodate desire within the framework of "practical philosophy"—and eager to have the last word. Other manifestations of the same lay spirit may be found in other types of "princely" literature, by which I mean literature fit for princes, if not specifically made for princes, and/or for the princely (because rational) part of mankind in general. The dissemination of Aristotelian notions of the magnificent man affords an excellent case in point. These are only a few examples among many of the challenging presence of laicizing tendencies in vernacular literature. A greater respect for secular culture in fourteenth-century literature holds out new possibilities for reading poems by Chaucer, Gower, and their French contemporaries in terms of a secularity that is allowed its own space and special valence, even as its relationship with (or disjunction from) religious interests is brought into sharp focus. And so, we should learn to listen more carefully when Chaucer *cum suis* speaks "of folk in seculer estaat." Let the search for vernacular secularity begin in earnest.

Lydgate's Literary History:

Chaucer, Gower, and Canacee

Maura Nolan
University of California, Berkeley

T HE *FALL OF PRINCES* has traditionally been seen as Lydgate's least inspired work, a monotonous translation of Laurent de Premierfait's translation of Boccaccio's *De casibus virorum illustrium*, undertaken during his long retirement at the behest of Humphrey of Gloucester and showing signs that even he found the endeavor tiresome. Indeed, it *is* long (36,000 lines), repetitive, sprawling, and disorderly. Unlike another famous compilation, the *Canterbury Tales*, the *Fall of Princes* does not contain "God's plenty" (in Dryden's felicitous phrase) but rather limits itself to the ceaseless reenactment of a single basic narrative: the fall of a great man. It is true that there are many lengthy sections of the poem in which nothing much happens, in which the eye of the critic—trained to seek out the oddity, the poetic swerve, the contradictory or inexplicable detail—slides helplessly over the smooth and impenetrable surface of the text. But as I will show, Lydgate used the poem to grapple with the most serious literary and aesthetic questions known to him, questions with which he engaged many times over the course of his career and which came to fruition in his last work. In particular, he was concerned to explore the vexed relations among the classical and vernacular models of writing history that he had inherited from such figures as Ovid, Boethius, Boccaccio, Chaucer, and Gower, and put to the test in a variety of genres and historical contexts, from the early days of the Lancastrian era, through its zenith during the reign of Henry V, and culminating in the "laureate" years of Henry VI's mi-

Many thanks to Andrew Cole, Jill Mann, and Paul Strohm, who read and commented on this essay in an earlier form, and to James Simpson and the anonymous reader for *SAC* for their comments and suggestions.

nority.[1] These include the Boethian understanding of Fortune, an Ovidian model of complaint or elegy found in *The Legend of Good Women*, and the clerkly practice of moralization, exemplified for Lydgate by the *Confessio Amantis*.

The only way to cope with the immense size of the *Fall of Princes* is to narrow one's focus and examine it in parts; I will concentrate here on Book One, itself a substantial poetic intervention in the literary tradition inaugurated by Chaucer and Gower. In it, I will argue, Lydgate remakes as he translates the text he inherited from Laurent de Premierfait and Boccaccio, mining an essential ambiguity—its uncertainty regarding worldly causality—by exaggerating available understandings of Fortune and stressing their ultimate incompatibility. On the one hand, as several critics have noted, Lydgate makes the explicit claim, over and over, that sin, not chance, causes the falls of great men, a claim latent in Boccaccio's *De casibus*, and articulated more fully in Laurent's version of the text but most forcefully asserted here.[2] However, as I will show, he also makes room for a notion of Fortune as radical contingency, as a force that operates in the world without regard for right and wrong, morality and immorality. This latter vision of Fortune is hardly dominant. But it does surface at critical moments in the *Fall of Princes*, posing a serious challenge to the moralism that otherwise pervades the text, and demanding from readers a far more nuanced reading than the poem typically receives. Indeed, I will argue that Fortune functions as a kind of "vernacular philosophy" in the *Fall of Princes*, a mode of engagement with history and with the aesthetic that emerges from the sheer intensity of Lydgate's relationship to his predecessors—especially, of course, his connection to Chaucer, but also his little-noticed (but crucial) use of Gower's *Confessio Amantis*. These relationships become critical in the exemplum that concludes book one, the story of Canacee, and it is on that story that I will focus here.

---

[1] The tag "laureate" is Derek Pearsall's; see his *John Lydgate* (London: Routledge and Kegan Paul, 1970), pp. 161–91. I discuss the years of the minority in my book *John Lydgate and the Making of Public Culture*, forthcoming from Cambridge University Press.

[2] Pearsall, *John Lydgate*, pp. 241–42 (though Pearsall also notes that there are other ideas about Fortune at work in the text overall, including a "fatalistic" notion in which Fortune is "fickle and arbitrary" and Lydgate's "half-articulate admiration for Roman attitudes [about admirable deaths]"; see also Lois Ebin, *John Lydgate* (Boston: Twayne Publishers, 1985), pp. 66–68. As Paul Strohm has argued, "Rather than follow their predecessors in recommending caution in the face of erratic Fortune, Premierfait and Lydgate recommend precautionary action" (*"Politique": Language and Statecraft from Chaucer to Shakespeare* [Notre Dame, Ind.: University of Notre Dame Press, 2005], p. 96).

Like the *Fall of Princes* more generally, book one is structured along Boccaccian lines, beginning with Adam and Eve, moving through the major foundational narratives of Thebes and Troy, and culminating with an excursus on the malice of women, complete with examples. Although he substantially expanded Boccaccio's text, and added relevant French stories, Laurent hewed very closely to this general order.[3] Not so Lydgate. Most of book one dutifully replicates Boccaccio and Laurent's works, but he makes several critical changes to the text, including the expansion of a major exemplum to conclude the book, the story of the incestuous love of Canacee and Machaire. This episode is of course familiar to all readers of late medieval poetry as a notorious point of imaginary contention between Chaucer and Gower; the Man of Law's famous assertion about Chaucer, that "No word ne writeth he / Of thilke wikke ensample of Canacee," coupled with Gower's thorough retelling of the story in the *Confessio Amantis*, has firmly linked incest ("wikke" sexuality) to poetry and poetic competition in the eyes of readers and critics.[4] Lydgate is clearly familiar with both Chaucer and Gower's representations of Canacee, and his choice of the story to conclude book one brings to the fore his relationship to the English vernacular tradition, demanding that readers engage not only with the overtly moral reading of the exemplum but also with a notion of literary history produced by the intersection of his source texts. The easiest way of accounting for this choice is simply to assert that, like Gower, he so thoroughly believes in the sheer power of moralization to adapt any story, no matter how "wikke," to a didactic end that he uses the incest tale to flex his poetic muscles and demonstrate his skill. No doubt there is an element of the anxiety of influence here. But reducing both Lydgate and Gower to unreflective moralists does neither of them justice—and as I will show, Lydgate's evocation of Canacee is part of a far more complex poetic strategy, one he employs throughout book one.

Gower's Canacee

The idea of adding the story of Canacee to Boccaccio's text was not original to Lydgate. Laurent before him had included the exemplum,

[3] See Patricia May Gathercole's discussion of Laurent's alterations to Boccaccio, in her edition of Book 1 of his text, *Laurent de Premierfait's "Des Cas Des Nobles Hommes et Femmes, Book 1, Translated from Boccaccio: A Critical Edition Based on Six Manuscripts"* (Chapel Hill: University of North Carolina Press, 1968), pp. 17–33.
[4] See, for example, Carolyn Dinshaw, *Chaucer's Sexual Poetics* (Madison: University of Wisconsin Press, 1989), pp. 88–112, and Elizabeth Scala, "Canacee and the Chaucer Canon: Incest and Other Unnarratables," *ChauR* 30 (1995): 15–39.

but his version was very short, describing only the bare outlines of the narrative and emphasizing the sinfulness of the main characters, their "horrible pecchie."[5] But as an English writer, Lydgate would already have known the story of Canacee well and recognized it as a contested and controversial narrative; no reader of Chaucer and Gower could fail to note the significance of the Man of Law's critique of the "wikke ensaumple" or ignore Genius's description of Canacee's defeat by "kinde" and Eolus's wrathful and excessive response.

Gower's *Confessio Amantis* is a lurking presence throughout book one of the *Fall of Princes*, particularly in its Ovidian narratives, and the Canacee story provides a signal example of Lydgate's assimilation and modification of Gower's particular brand of moralism. There can be no doubt that Gower was the primary source for the Canacee episode; Lydgate follows the text of the *Confessio Amantis* very closely, incorporating elements unique to Gower even as he expands and abbreviates the text. When Gower revised the story from Ovid's *Heroides*, he added vivid details and images that accentuated the pathos of Canacee's plight, a practice that Lydgate continued, and indeed amplified. Two examples will suffice to demonstrate the close link between the two Middle English texts. First, when Gower's Canacee writes to her brother, she tells him that she writes with "ink and tears": "Now at this time, as thou shalt wite, / With teres and with enke write / This lettre I have in cares colde: / In my riht hond my Penne I hold, / And in my left the swerd I kepe, / And in my barm ther lith to wepe / Thi child and myn which sobbeth faste."[6] In the *Heroides*, Canacee's epistle opens by describing her holding a pen in her right hand, a blade in her left, and the letter itself in her lap, "dextra tenet calamum, strictum tenet altera ferrum, et

---

[5] The passage from Laurent reads: "Cestui Machareus filz du roy Eolus ama deshonnestement sa suer Canaces. Ceste suer conceut de son frere et enfanta un filz. Comme Machareus par une nourrice envoyast l'enfant pour estre nourry hors de l'ostel royal, l'enfant comme maleureux brahy et cria si hault que le roy Eolus l'entendi, et in courroucié pour le desloyal fait commenda que l'enfant feust donné aux chiens pour estre devouré. Le roy aussi par un varlet envoya une espee a sa fille Canaces, afin que elle feist de soy ce que elle avoit desservi. Mais les histoires taisent se elle se occit. Toutevoies Machareus sentant son horrible pecchie et le courroux de son pere s'enfouy, et comme dict est devint prestre ou temple de Appollo en la cité Delphos" (Gathercole, *Laurent de Premierfait's "Des Cas Des Nobles Hommes et Femmes,"* p. 220)

[6] *Confessio Amantis*, book 3, lines 297–303, in *The Complete Works of John Gower*, ed. G. C. Macaulay, 4 vols. (Oxford: Clarendon Press, 1899–1902), 2:234. Subsequent references are given in the text by book and line number.

iacet in gremio charta soluta meo."[7] Gower's addition of the infant to the scene exaggerates the pitiful quality of Canacee's situation by turning the reader's attention to her innocent son[8]—and when Lydgate retells the story, he retains both this *mise en scène* and the striking image of ink mingled with tears:

> The salt[e] teris from hir eyen cleere,
> With pitous sobbyng, fet from hir hertis brynke,
> Distillyng doun to tempre with hir ynke.[9]
>
> Writyng hir lettir, awappid al in dreede,
> In hir riht hand hir penne gan to quake;
> And a sharp suerd to make hir herte bleede
> In his lefft hand, hir fader hath hir take.
> And most hir sorwe was for hir childes sake,
> Vpon whos face in hir barm slepyng
> Ful many a teer she wept in compleynyng.
>
> (1.7022–28)

In taking these images from Gower, Lydgate divides and expands them, producing an even more pathetic portrait of Canacee and her son—and as we shall see, drawing the reader further into the emotional ambit of the story. The second (though by no means the last) detail that Lydgate appropriates from Gower is the famous image of Canacee's son bathing in her blood:

> The child lay bathende in hir blod
> Out rolled fro the moder barm,
> And for the blod was hot and warm,
> He basketh him aboute thrinne.
> (*Confessio Amantis*, 3.312–15)

---

[7] Ovid, *Heroides and Amores*, trans. Grant Showerman (Cambridge, Mass.: Harvard University Press, 1977), epistle 11, lines 3–4. Subsequent references are given in the text by epistle and line number.

[8] A. C. Spearing notes this substitution as well, arguing that Gower "has chosen to exclude from his poem, at least on any explicit level, the problematic of female authorship into which Ovid plunged at the outset"; see his "Canace and Machaire," *Mediaevalia* 16 (1993): 211–21 (p. 219).

[9] *Lydgate's Fall of Princes*, ed. Henry Bergen, 4 vols., EETS e.s. 121–24 (London: Oxford University Press, 1924–27), book one, lines 6879–81; subsequent references are given in the text by book and line number.

Lydgate's version is similarly vivid, designed to arouse the reader's pity for the helpless child: "Hir child fill doun, which myht[e] nat asterte, / Hauyng non helpe to socoure hym nor saue, / But in hir blood the silff began to bathe" (1.7033–35). It would not be an exaggeration to say that the Canacee story in the *Fall of Princes* reads as if it had been written with the *Confessio Amantis* immediately to hand, and, as such, the changes that Lydgate makes to Gower's version assume an even greater significance. The two versions of the story are approximately the same length; Gower narrates it in 217 lines, Lydgate in 237. But Lydgate dramatically alters the emphasis of his source text by compressing the plot— which takes up 127 lines in the *Confessio Amantis*—into a mere 48 lines in *Fall of Princes*, and by expanding Canacee's letter to Machaire from 27 lines to 139. These changes, coupled with Lydgate's excision of Gower's asides concerning "kynde," incest, and wrath, turn our attention away from the philosophical and moral focus of Gower's version and toward (as we shall see) the relationship between love and Fortune, between amatory complaint and Boethian Stoicism.

In the Canacee story, Gower focuses his moralizing energies on the dominant male character, King Eolus, rather than on the notorious female figure at the center of the exemplum. His version of the exemplum works as an illustration of the destructiveness of wrath, the sin with which Book Three of the *Confessio Amantis* is especially concerned, and a good deal of critical ink has been spilled on the question of his perspective on the sexual sin of incest.[10] What Gower's amatory narrator, Ge-

---

[10] The most comprehensive discussion of medieval incest can be found in Elizabeth Archibald's *Incest and the Medieval Imagination* (Oxford: Clarendon Press, 2001); for her comments on Gower, see pp. 25–26 and 80–84. C. David Benson, "Incest and Moral Poetry in Gower's *Confessio Amantis*," *ChauR* 19 (1984): 100–109, argues that "incest . . . is the extreme example of the dangers of sexual passion and is therefore neither honest nor truly human" (105). Larry Scanlon, "The Riddle of Incest," in *Re-Visioning Gower,* ed. Robert Yeager (Asheville, N.C.: Pegasus Press, 1998), pp. 93–127, suggests that, for Gower, sexuality was an "autonomous force that must be governed from within history" and that incest became "a nearly intractable problem implicating the mechanisms of social order in their most basic operations" (pp. 111, 127). Alastair Minnis points out that in describing Canacee and Machaire's love as natural, but *illicitus*, Gower was entirely consistent with medieval commentators on *Heroides* 11, who did not condemn the lovers as unnatural; see his "John Gower: Sapiens in Ethics and Politics," in *Gower's "Confessio Amantis": A Critical Anthology,* ed. Peter Nicholson (Cambridge: D. S. Brewer, 1991), pp. 158–80, esp. 165–66. Georgiana Donavin, *Incest Narratives and the Structure of Gower's "Confessio Amantis"* (Victoria: University of Victoria Press, 1993), sees the story of Canacee as ironic, revealing "the incompleteness of Genius's moral development" by presenting incestuous love as natural; see pp. 33–39. Thomas Hatton similarly argues that Genius's articulation of natural law is not Gower's own, noting

nius, says on the subject is perfectly clear; he argues that Canacee and Machaire could not help themselves because they were subject to the law of "kinde":

> Whan kinde assaileth the corage
> With love and doth him forto bowe,
> That he no reson can allowe,
> Bot halt the lawes of nature:
> For whom that love hath under cure,
> As he is blind himself, riht so
> He makth his client blind also.
>
> And so it fell hem ate laste,
> That this Machaire with Canace
> Whan thei were in a prive place,
> Cupide bad hem ferst to kesse,
> And after sche which is Maistresse
> In kinde and techeth every lif
> Withoute lawe positif,
> Of which sche takth nomaner charge,
> Bot kepth hire lawes al at large,
> Nature, tok hem into lore
> And tawht hem so, that overmore
> Sche hath hem in such wise daunted,
> That thei were, as who seith, enchaunted.
> (3.154–60, 166–78)

Here, Gower takes up the Ovidian account of Canacee's desire—in which she describes herself as helplessly subject to the invading force of love ("ipsa quoque incalui, qualemque audire solebam, nescio quem sensi corde tepente deum" [epistle XI, lines 25–26])—and embeds it within a broader consideration of the relationship between "kinde," de-

that in the *Mirour de L'Omme*, Gower strongly condemns incest; see "John Gower's Use of Ovid in Book III of the *Confessio Amantis*," *Mediaevalia* 13 (1987): 257–74, 261. María Bullón Fernández, in contrast, argues that Gower's primary attitude toward Canacee is one of sympathy for her subjection to a tyrannical father; see her *Fathers and Daughters in Gower's "Confessio Amantis"* (Cambridge: D. S. Brewer, 2000), pp. 158–72. For discussions of the Canacee story in relation to the Man of Law, see Winthrop Wetherbee, "Constance and the World in Chaucer and Gower," in *John Gower: Recent Readings*, ed. R. F. Yeager (Kalamazoo, Mich.: Medieval Institute Publications, 1989), pp. 65–93, and Elizabeth Allen, "Chaucer Answers Gower: Constance and the Trouble with Reading," *ELH* 64 (1997): 627–55.

sire, and positive law. These were by no means settled relationships in medieval theology or poetry; as Elizabeth Archibald has shown, both Augustine and Aquinas confronted the problem of incest among the patriarchs in the Old Testament and "acknowledged that the supposedly natural and universal law prohibiting incest was in fact socially constructed, and thus open to interpretation and alteration by Church authorities."[11] Gower, too, begins Book Eight of the *Confessio Amantis* with a long discussion of the laws of marriage that describes how in the First Age sibling incest was accepted as a means of populating the earth—and though it is clear that Canacee and Machaire do not fall under this exception, it is also the case that Gower recognizes the naturalness of their lust.[12]

The lesson that Lydgate learns from Gower's account, however, is less theological or moral, and more formal: he appropriates the Ovidian affectivity of the story and makes it the centerpiece of his own version. In fact, Lydgate's description of Canacee and Machaire's incest directly contradicts Gower's in moral terms:

> Afftir this Pirrus cam Canace the faire,
> With teres distillyng from hir eyen tweyne,
> And hir brother, that callid was Machaire;
> And bothe thei gan ful pitousli compleyne,
> That Fortune gan at hem so disdeyne,
> Hyndryng ther fate be woful auenture
> Touchyng ther loue, which was ageyn nature.

> He was hir brother and hir loue also,
> As the story pleynli doth declare;
> And in a bed thei lay eek bothe too,
> Resoun was non whi thei sholde spare:
> But loue that causith wo and eek weelfare,
> Gan *ageyn kynde* so straungeli deuise,
> That he hir wombe made sodenli tarise.
> (1.6833–46; emphasis added)

[11] Archibald, *Incest and the Medieval Imagination*, p. 26.

[12] Archibald notes that "[Gower] does not share Augustine's optimistic view that there is natural respect for the incest taboo" (p. 25); she bases this statement on Genius's assertion that many ignore incest laws, which of course suggests that it cannot unequivocally be attributed to Gower himself. However, my point is simply that Gower was interested in the story of Canacee and Machaire as part of a very complex set of philosophical and theological questions—an interest that Lydgate shared in a very different way.

Love here works "ageyn kynde" to produce Canacee's pregnancy, which is rendered as a "straunge" and "soden" occurrence rather than as the natural effect of a natural act. Indeed, Canacee herself begs Machaire not to let "kynde" make him forget her and her son:

> "I holde hym streihtli atwen myn armys tweyne,
> Thou and nature leide on me this charge;
> He gilt[e]les with me mut suffre peyne.
> And sithe thou art at fredam and at large,
> Lat kynd[e]nesse our loue nat so discharge,
> But haue a mynde, where-euer that thou be,
> Onys a day vpon my child and me.
>
> (1.6917–23)

It would seem that, though Nature has produced Canacee's child, "kyndenesse" works against incestuous love and promises to erase Machaire's feelings for his son and sister—precisely the opposite understanding of "kynde" that we find in Gower's version of the story.[13]

In thus wedding Gower to Chaucer, Lydgate not only tackles the problem of the Man of Law's moralizing judgment of the *Confessio Amantis*—a crucial subtext for his use of Ovid here—but he also sets in opposition the two formal poetic modes of didactic exemplarity and amatory complaint. He does so by appropriating a Gowerian (and Dantean, for that matter) poetic trick, by which the reader's emotion (pity, sorrow) is solicited by an inappropriate object of identification—in this case, Canacee. What Lydgate eliminates from Gower's account is not the moralization—he follows Gower in condemning Eolus's wrath—but rather the infrastructure of the world that Gower has imagined, a world in which events occur as the result of human action and agency, driven by human characteristics like "kynde." For Gower, even the love of Canacee and Machaire is the particular and inevitable result of a specific human act: the siblings were housed in the same room throughout their childhood—"Whil thei be yonge, of comun wone / In chambre thei togedre wone, / And as thei scholden pleide hem ofte, / Til thei be growen up alofte / Into the youth of lusti age" (3.149–53)—a detail he adds to Ovid's version.[14] Lydgate removes this explanation for Canacee

[13] Archibald, *Incest and the Medieval Imagination*, p. 84, notes this difference as well.
[14] Judith Shaw, "The Role of the Shared Bed in John Gower's *Tales of Incest*," *ELN* 26 (1989): 4–8, notes this addition, as well as Gower's similar revision of his source in his

and Machaire's sin, merely stating that, "in a bed thei lay eek bothe too" (1.6842), and replaces Gower's discourse of causality with his extended version of Canacee's complaint. In other words, Lydgate is more interested in Gower's Ovidianism, his tendency to invoke the subjective language of the *Heroides*, than in his philosophical meditations, and he alters the story accordingly. As we will see, Canacee becomes in Lydgate's hands an Ovidian heroine in Chaucerian style; most of the additions he makes to Gower's text are Chaucerian interpolations that recall various pitiful heroines from the *Canterbury Tales*, *The Legend of Good Women*, and the *House of Fame*. But while the reader of the *Confessio Amantis* is gradually being led through a complex process of education, in which he or she is asked to ponder some very fine points of moral theology (the role of "kynde," for example), the reader of the *Fall of Princes* is merely stymied by the apparent contradiction between the logic of virtue that guides the enterprise as a whole (sin causes falls) and the affective principle of pity that the story of Canacee so insistently enforces. As a closer examination of the exemplum will show, this latter principle is taken directly from Chaucer and deployed in such a way that the poetic questions raised by the Man of Law—what constitutes moral poetry? How should Chaucer's poetic career be defined?—are reanimated and made to signify in a new context. At issue of course is the problem of literary authority. The Canacee story stands at the intersection of several competing authorities in Lydgate's poetic world: Ovid, Laurent, Gower, Chaucer, and inevitably, Humphrey of Gloucester, a figure who looms over the *Fall of Princes* in a decidedly material and embodied way.[15] It is Humphrey who dictates the moral logic of the text as a whole; as Lydgate tells us in the Prologue to Book Two, his

---

account of Antiochus's rape of his daughter in book 8 of the *Confessio*; in that case, while the Latin *Historia Apollonii Regis Tyri* merely states that King Antiochus invades his daughter's chamber, Gower's version has him allowing her to sleep in *his* chamber, which leads to his incestuous lust. Again, we see the implication that incestuous desire is natural, albeit sinful and wrong.

[15] Throughout the text, Lydgate refers to Humphrey's influence, not only his editorial control over the text (Lydgate describes himself "Undir the wyngis off his correcioun" [1.436]) but also his response to Lydgate's pleas for money. See *Fall of Princes*, book three, lines 64–91, where Lydgate describes the approach of Poverty and the relief that Humphrey's "bounteuous largesse" provides; book three, lines 3837–71, where Lydgate complains again of his poverty and describes the dependence of poets such as "Daunt," "Virgile," "Petrak," and "prudent Chaucer" on patronage; and book nine, lines 3303–86, the envoy to the poem as a whole, in which Lydgate self-deprecatingly describes his own "rudnesse" and pleads for his lord's favor. For discussion of these passages, see Pearsall, *John Lydgate*, pp. 227–30.

patron demands that he add envoys to each exemplum that will explain how princes can learn to resist Fortune, so that "Bi othres fallyng [thei myht] themsilff correcte" (2.154)—a vision of human agency that the Canacee story distinctly undermines.[16] Lydgate's articulation of the contradictory demands of such authorities demonstrates—in a way he may not have predicted—that power does not derive only from patrons and *auctors* but also, and more forcefully, from poetic modes, genres, and discourses themselves: in short, from form.

Canacee's Complaint

A close look at Lydgate's version of the Canacee story reveals this formal complexity at work. It begins with an evocation of Fortune:

> Afftir this Pirrus cam Canace the faire,
> With teres distillyng from hir eyen tweyne,
> And hir brother, that callid was Machaire;
> And bothe thei gan ful pitousli compleyne,
> That Fortune gan at hem so disdeyne,
> Hyndryng ther fate be woful auenture
> Touchyng ther loue, which was ageyn nature.
>
> (1.6833–39)

Here we see the two sinners failing to recognize their own responsibility for their fall, tearfully blaming Fortune for "hyndryng ther fate," and fitting nicely into the moral paradigm demanded by Humphrey; according to its logic, their lack of self-awareness merely opens a space for the moralizing work of the text and the education of the princely reader. But as Lydgate follows Gower's account, we quickly find this moralizing energy fragmenting, carrying the story in almost the opposite direction and exerting a powerful pull on the reader's imagination rather than her conscience. Lest we think that the pity aroused by Canacee's plight is merely an authorial ploy designed to demonstrate the moral inadequacy of our emotional response to the story—a potential reading, perhaps, of Canacee's letter, which is self-interested and thus unreliable—Lydgate

---

[16] See book two, lines 1–126; as Lydgate explains, "It is nat she [Fortune] that pryncis gaff the fall, / But vicious lyuyng, pleynli to endite" (lines 45–46). This vision of Fortune underlies Humphrey's demand for a "remedie" for each exemplum, an envoy that will show how to avoid falls.

both interjects his own response to the story and compares his heroine to two well-known Chaucerian figures:

> But, o alas! his suster muste abide,
> Merciles, for ther hatful trespace
> Suffre deth; ther was non other grace.

> First hir fader a sharp suerd to hir sente
> In tokne off deth for a remembraunce,
> And whan she wiste pleynli what he mente
> And conceyued his rigerous ordenaunce,
> With hool purpos tobeien his plesaunce,
> She gruchchith nat, but lowli of entente
> Lich a meek douhter to his desir assente.

> But or she died she caste for to write
> A litil lettre to hir brother deere,
> A dedli compleynt compleyne & endite
> With pale face and a mortal cheere,
> The salt[e] teris from hir eyen cleere,
> With pitous sobbyng, fet from hir hertis brynke,
> Distillyng doun to tempre with hir ynke.
> (1.6865–81)

Unlike Gower or Chaucer, Lydgate has no mediating narrator, no Genius or Man of Law whose subjectivity can be presumed to intrude into the tale-telling; his "o alas!" instead points to his *own* empathic involvement with the story. This effect is further enhanced by two details of his description of Canacee's behavior, "she gruchchith nat" and "with a pale face," both drawn from Chaucer's depictions of the pitiful and saintly Griselda and Custance. "Gruchchith," in fact, is a loaded word in the *Canterbury Tales*; it appears in a secular register in *The Knight's Tale* and *The Clerk's Tale*, and in the religious discourse of *The Parson's Tale*, and always refers to the relationship of an individual to adverse worldly circumstances.[17] When Walter describes to Griselda the nature of their

---

[17] Thus, Theseus consoles the Athenians for Arcite's death by telling them that "whoso gruccheth ought, he dooth folye" (I.3045) in light of the providential actions of the First Mover. In *The Parson's Tale,* "gruchchyng" is a species of Envy, and it "spryngeth of inpacience agayns God, and somtyme agayns man" (X.498); as the Parson explains, "gruchching" entails complaining about almost any worldly circumstance: "Agayn God it is whan a man grucheth agayn the peyne of helle, or agayns poverte, or los of catel, or agayn reyn or tempest; or elles grucheth that shrewes han prosperitee, or elles for that goode men han adversitee./ And alle thise thynges sholde man suffre

marriage contract, he requires not only obedience but *uncomplaining* obedience (IV. 351–56; emphasis added):

> I seye this: be ye redy with good herte
> To al my lust, and that I frely may,
> As me best thynketh, do yow laughe or smerte,
> And nevere ye to *grucche* it, nyght ne day?
> And eek whan I sey "ye," ne sey nat "nay,"
> Neither by word ne frownyng contenaunce?

And Griselda resolutely does not "grucche" until Walter has revealed the nature of his tyrannical plan, and even then she does not directly accuse him. But Canacee, also a female figure subject to a tyrannical ruler, does in fact "grucche" in her letter to Machaire, a behavior in which she is preceded by yet another Chaucerian heroine, Custance. Like Custance, Canacee is described as having a "pale face"; the Man of Law asks his readers rhetorically, "Have ye nat seyn somtyme a pale face, / Among a prees, of hym that hath be lad / Toward his deeth" (II.645–47), as Custance is led before Alla's court to face the accusation of murder. Canacee of course *does* face certain death, and her choice of affective complaint in answer to her plight is first and foremost an Ovidian response to adversity. Like the other epistolary heroines of the *Heroides*, she turns to the highly subjective discursive mode of first-person narrative. But her "pale face" reminds us as well that pagan heroines are not the only "pleynyng" women to be found in Chaucer; Custance famously laments her plight at several junctures in *The Man of Law's Tale*, both at the very beginning, when she complains that "Allas, unto the Barbre nacioun / I moste anoon" (II.281–82), and after she has been cast out to sea by Donegild, when she prays to the Virgin Mary about her son:

> O litel child, allas! What is thy gilt,
> That nevere wroghtest synne as yet, pardee?
> Why wil thyn harde fader han thee spilt?
> (II.855–57)

---

paciently, for they comen by the rightful juggement and ordinaunce of God" (X.499–500). And it should be noted that one of the demands Walter makes of his subjects is that they should not "grucche" against his choice of a wife (IV.170), suggesting further the link between tyranny and "grucching"; see my discussion of Canacee and Eolus above.

All quotations from Chaucer are drawn from *The Riverside Chaucer*, gen. ed. Larry D. Benson, 3rd ed. (Boston: Houghton Mifflin, 1987); subsequent references are given in the text by tale and line number.

This latter prayer is echoed by Canacee, who exclaims:

> O thou, my fader, to cruel is thi wreche,
> Hardere off herte than tigre or leoun,
> To slen a child that lith withoute speche,
> Void off al mercy and remissioun.
> And on his mooder hast no compassioun,
> His youthe considred, with lippis softe as silk,
> Which at my brest lith still & souketh mylk.
>
> (1.6938–44)

Here we see that Lydgate has imagined Canacee imagining herself as a saintly, Chaucerian, Custance-like figure, the victim of tyranny, with a legitimate right to "grucche" or "pleyne." In part, of course, this is a literary joke: Lydgate describes the very figure anathematized by the Man of Law in the terms that the tale-teller uses for his own virtuous heroine, modeling himself as a narrator after Chaucer's Sergeant, an effect enhanced by such interjections as "o alas!" which recall the lawyer's frequent apostrophes and bits of commentary on Custance's fate. Lydgate is most certainly playing the game of literary one-upsmanship here, presenting himself in the *Prologue* with the same air of humility as the Man of Law, and then proceeding to repeat the "wikke ensaumple" that so distressed that upright pilgrim—and he does so in the very poetic style for which the Man of Law is renowned. It is a poetic gesture, moreover, that triangulates the competition between "maistere" and acolyte by inserting Gower as the missing third term in what is too often imagined as a one-to-one equation between Lydgate and Chaucer. But Canacee stands at the nexus of a far more complex set of influences than anxiety of influence can explain. First, the implicit comparison of Griselda and Custance contrasts two markedly different modes of relation to the world, the former a Boethian Stoicism characterized by silence, and the latter an affective piety that constructs a space for, and imagines the efficacy of, complaint. As Jill Mann has argued, Griselda's plight resembles nothing so much as that of the victim of Fortune described in Chaucer's *Boece*, in a passage in which Fortune herself explicitly questions the value of "pleynyng":[18] "Now it liketh me to withdrawe myn hand.

---

[18] Jill Mann, *Feminizing Chaucer* (Cambridge: D. S. Brewer, 2002), p. 120. Mann's readings of Griselda and Custance are linked, in that she sees both as figures through whom "the human subjection to God's 'purveiaunce' is focussed and explored"; Lydgate

Thow has had grace as he that hath used of foreyne goodes; thow hast no ryght to pleyne the, as though thou haddest outrely forlorn alle thy thynges. Why pleynestow thanne? I have doon the no wrong" (bk. II, pr. 2, lines 23–28). The proper response to Fortune, in this model, is quiet acceptance, *contemptus mundi*, a rejection of the world and worldly things. Here we see the image of Fortune (as an arbitrary and relentless force in the world) that Humphrey's envoys specifically reject, with their emphasis on virtue and reward, sin and punishment. This tension between a Stoic philosophy that counsels passive acceptance and an opposing ideology of active virtue is mirrored in the contrast between the Chaucerian heroines to whom Lydgate alludes, with Griselda standing as an oppositional figure for Humphrey's philosophy of action and agency in relation to the world.[19] Lydgate's canny pairing of Griselda and Custance, then, enforces a reading of Custance that emphasizes precisely her ability to act—a quality rarely associated with the Man of Law's heroine, usually seen as a passive and helpless figure.[20] Further, by linking Canacee's complaint with Custance's prayer, Lydgate exposes the formal similarity between Ovidian "pleynyng" and affective piety, both modes that imply a certain performativity of discourse; the former seeking to arouse pity in the reader, the latter pleading for the intervention of the divine.

He also, however, uses Griselda and Custance to set in opposition the two understandings of Fortune that have riven Book One of the *Fall of Princes* from the beginning, an idea of radical contingency and arbitrariness, and a notion of linear causes and effects, virtues and rewards. In Chaucer's Christian tales, that opposition is hidden by the presence of a

---

would have agreed. Another possible intertext for Lydgate's use of Chaucer's complaining women is, of course, as Frank Grady reminds me, *The Physician's Tale*, in which Virginia asks for "a litel space" "for to compleyne" (VI.239); significantly, Harry Bailly understands her story to be a tragedy of Fortune ("Wherfore I seye al day that men may see / That yiftes of Fortune and of Nature / Been cause of deeth to many a creature" [VI.294–96]).

[19] This "philosophy of action" is described by Paul Strohm in "*Politique*": *Languages of Statecraft*. My reading differs slightly from his in emphasis, in that I see Lydgate as sustaining a tension between this philosophy and a notion of unpredictable contingency—of Fortune—that threatens human agency.

[20] Custance's passivity is of course the dominant reading of the text; Chaucer's own revisions of his sources reveal him to have eliminated many active characteristics of the heroine and to have emphasized her helplessness. The classic discussion of Chaucer's use of Trivet remains Edward A. Block's "Originality, Controlling Purpose, and Craftsmanship in Chaucer's *Man of Law's Tale*," *PMLA* 68 (1953): 572–616. Lydgate, in contrast, suggests an alternative way of seeing Custance in relation to Griselda.

providential God, embodied in the narrative effect of the happy ending, "joye after wo," as the Man of Law would say. But Lydgate's Ovidian tragedy wears this opposition on its sleeve, relentlessly exposing the contradictions at work in Humphrey's vision of remediable Fortune and his ideology of virtue. Two further examples from the Canacee story illustrate this process at work. First, when Canacee ventriloquizes Custance's Marian prayer, she simultaneously alludes to yet another Chaucerian image of victimized innocence, the Prioress's "litel clergeoun":

> Our yonge child in his pur innocence
> Shal ageyn riht suffre dethis violence,
> Tendre of lymes, God wot, ful gilt[e]les,
> The goodli faire that lith heere specheles.
>
> A mouth he hath, but woordis hath he noone,
> Cannat compleyne, alas, for non outrage,
> Nor gruchith nat, but lith heer al a-loone,
> Stille as a lamb, most meek off his visage.
> What herte off steel coude doon to hym damage,
> Or suffre hym deie, beholdyng the maneer
> And look benygne off his tweyne eyen cleer?
>
> (1.6927–37)

Not only do we recall the "clergeoun"—another male child subjected to irrational violence—but we also, and more vividly, remember the Prioress's own poetic self-authorization:

> My konnyng is so wayk, O blisful Queene,
> For to declare thy grete worthynesse
> That I ne may the weighte nat susteene;
> But as a child of twelf month oold, or lesse,
> That kan unnethes any word expresse,
> Right so fare I, and therfore I yow preye,
> Gydeth my song that I shal of yow seye.
>
> (lines 481–87)

And we remember as well her description of praising God, "by the mouth of children thy bountee / Parfourned is, for on the brest soukynge / Somtyme shewen they thyn heriynge" (lines 457–59). In both cases, innocence is associated with speechlessness, with a prelapsarian image of pure communication, the miraculous *Alma Redemptoris*

Mater. The "litel clergeoun," of course, is distinguished precisely by his capacity to speak even after his tormenters have attempted to silence him by cutting his throat; just as the Prioress claims to be speechless but continues to tell her story, so too the young victim miraculously continues to praise the Blessed Virgin until the "greyn" is removed from his mouth. Canacee's baby, in contrast, represents the literalization of the Prioress's claim to be like "a childe of twelf month oold, or lesse," the material embodiment of her analogy; he cannot "grucche" or "pleyne," and no divine intervention comes to his aid. As such, Canacee's baby presents the ultimate stumbling block to Humphrey's logic of Fortune: *men* may make their own fates, but babies do not. If *The Prioress's Tale* had imagined a world in which the miraculous interference of the divine could transform an act of aggression into an occasion for poetic praise (*Alma Redemptoris Mater*), if *The Man of Law's Tale* had similarly understood outraged innocence as an incitement to prayer and lament, to action of a sort for its usually passive heroine—and if, in both cases, speech had proven entirely efficacious in producing a happy ending—the story of Canacee and her baby represents the futility of complaint in a world of tyranny. Whether she speaks or not, whether he is guilty or not, her son *will* be rent and devoured by dogs. The baby thus signals the blind spot inherent in the causal logic of the *Fall of Princes* as a whole. He is neither susceptible to the essentially comic sensibility of Chaucer's *Man of Law's Tale*, *Clerk's Tale*, and *Prioress's Tale*, nor can he be assimilated by the generic form of the tragedy as Lydgate has defined it here: the downfall of a great but sinful man. He is, in a sense, the perfect Boethian Stoic, better even than Griselda at remaining silent in the fact of injustice. As I will show, however, Lydgate not only uses the baby's silence as a way of undermining his patron's insistence on human agency in the world, but he also rejects the idea that such silence—such Stoicism—constitutes the proper response to adversity and tyranny.

Mute Innocence: "Pleynyng" and Poetic Function

If Lydgate's opposition between Griselda and Custance signaled the division in the *Fall of Princes* between competing notions of Fortune, and if the parallel between Custance and Canacee highlighted the similarity between Ovidian complaint and Christian prayer, then Lydgate's elaboration of the baby's speechlessness marks the limit point of all forms of agency, and the relentless intrusion of the arbitrary and contingent into the world of causality demanded by Humphrey and the providential universe sketched by Chaucer. The silence of the baby represents a point of negotiation between the conflicting poetic models (which we might call "innocent" and "guilty") Lydgate found anatomized by the Man of Law. Because Canacee is an *Ovidian* heroine, she brings to the *Fall of Princes* the discursive potential of the private and subjective world of emotion and feeling as it is expressed in the first-person narratives of the *Heroides.* Ovid of course is content to let the guilt of his heroines stand. But when Chaucer takes up the Ovidian model, he insists upon the innocence of his heroines—an insistence that the Man of Law acknowledges and appreciates.[21] This link between innocence and emotion—between saintliness and Ovidian "pleynyng"—is countered, in the Man of Law's estimation, by Gower's version of the Canacee story, in which sinners are allowed to speak. The brilliance of Lydgate's response to these conflicting poetic models lies in his capacity to contain *both* Chaucer and Gower's moral visions in the figure of mother and child. The sinner speaks; the innocent baby is silent—an effect made more powerful by the fact that it is Lydgate's innovation. In Gower's version of the story, the baby is crying (he "sobbeth faste") as Canacee writes her letter.

But the key to understanding the baby's silence is ultimately to be found in Ovid himself. Not only does Canacee's son weep in the *Heroides,* but his weeping has potential *content:* "vagitus dedit ille miser—sensisse putares—quaque suum poterat voce rogabat avum" ("the hapless babe broke forth in wailings—you would have thought he understood—and with what utterance he could entreat his grandsire") (XI, lines 85–86). In contrast, when Lydgate silences the baby, he not only invokes such Chaucerian children as Maurice and the "litel clergeoun," but he rewrites their fates, turning from a world in which complaint *functions*—has real effects in that world—to a world in which "grucching" and "pleynyng" do no good whatsoever. This world is even bleaker than Griselda's; we recall, for example, that Walter actually responded to the complaints of his people that he needed a wife. Griselda's silence is a dignified Boethian *choice,* as Jill Mann astutely points out.[22]

---

[21] For a discussion of Chaucer's relationship to Ovid, and specifically to the question of morality and Ovid, see Michael Calabrese, *Chaucer's Ovidian Arts of Love* (Gainesville: University of Florida Press, 1994), particularly his treatment of books three through five of *Troilus and Criseyde* (pp. 51–80), in which he argues that Chaucer sees Ovidan poetry as creating "moral dangers" (p. 79).

[22] Mann, *Feminizing Chaucer,* p. 114. As Mann argues, "Griselda's unquestioning obedience to her husband is not the simple result of her marriage vow, but something that she takes upon herself with the unique promise that is the special condition of her marriage."

It would seem, then, that Lydgate sought to evoke the terrifying and cruel world of absolutism, a world in which princes like Eolus operate unchecked by morality and, driven by unlimited emotion (wrath), commit terrible crimes against the innocent. In this reading, the story functions as a cautionary tale about tyranny. But it is a tale whose logic simply does not fit any of the models we have seen operating so far. It does not work as a form of *contemptus mundi*, a retreat from the world and from history. It does not embody a forward-looking idea of human agency and action in the world. And it provides the single greatest challenge to Humphrey's moralism that can be articulated: innocence is no guarantee against the fall of this little prince.[23] If we see this challenge in the light of the inevitable parallel between Lydgate's commission to write the *Fall of Princes* and Chaucer's famous portrait in *The Legend of Good Women* of poet and patron—a comparison made more pressing by the fact that both the Canacee story and Chaucer's tales of good women are Ovidian texts—then it becomes possible to see this portrait of Eolus's unchecked absolutism as a form of resistance to the tyranny of Humphrey's ideology of culpability. In this sense, Lydgate would seem to align himself with the critique of tyrannical male authority we see in the Prologue to *The Legend of Good Women*, a critique that James Simpson has recently argued represents a form of Ovidianism distinct to the late fourteenth century, to Chaucer and Gower.[24]

[23] Elsewhere, following Chaucer's *Boece* and *Monk's Tale*, Lydgate calls this view of Fortune the "unwar strook"—the bolt of lightening that descends randomly and suddenly to destroy the innocent and guilty alike. For Chaucer's use of the phrase, see *Boece*, book two, prose 2, line 78, and *The Monk's Tale*, VII.2764. For Lydgate's use of it, see *Serpent of Division*, 51, line 19, as well as *Fall of Princes*, book one, line 2019 (in which Lydgate uses the phrase to refer to the fate of Semele at the hands of Juno), and line 3792 (where it refers to death, specifically Jocasta's death), and book eight, line 1862 (where Lydgate is describing the falls of Maximus and Andragracian as the result of Fortune's "vnwar strok"). Another "little prince" described by Lydgate appears in *Siege of Thebes*, when the nurse Ipsiphyle fails to watch King Lycurgus's son and he is fatally bitten by a snake. As James Simpson points out, this inspires a speech of consolation by the Greek Adrastus, one that explicitly recalls Theseus's "Prime Mover" speech in *The Knight's Tale*, but one that fails to give the same comfort: "This is a very limited and unconvincing form of consolation—it is as if the optimistic Theseus had been transformed into the grim Egeus" ("'Dysemol daies and fatal houres': Lydgate's *Destruction of Thebes* and Chaucer's *Knight's Tale*," in *The Long Fifteenth Century: Essays for Douglas Gray*, ed. Helen Cooper and Sally Mapstone [Oxford: Clarendon Press, 1997], pp. 15–33 (p. 30)). The ultimately optimistic vision of Humphrey of agency in the world is, in this episode of the *Siege of Thebes*, thoroughly undermined.

[24] See James Simpson, *Reform and Cultural Revolution* (Oxford: Oxford University Press, 2002), pp. 171–75, in which he discusses the "tyrannical discursive environment governed by Cupid" (p. 175) in the *Prologue* to *The Legend of Good Women*, linking it specifically to an "Ovidian dialectic of history and the self" (p. 161); I discuss the Ovidianism of *Fall of Princes,* and Simpson's reading of fourteenth-century Ovidianism,

But the story is by no means this simple. The innocence of the baby is of course paired with the guilt of his mother—a guilt, further, that Lydgate anatomizes in detail despite Chaucer's explicit rejection of the "wikke ensaumple" of Canacee. In other words, the one-upsmanship I described earlier constitutes a parallel form of resistance to authority— this time, literary authority—to the challenge posed by Lydgate to Humphrey. The dyad of mother and son, guilt and innocence, allows Lydgate to engage in a double, and contradictory, oppositional game, in which each of his "maisteres," Chaucer and Gloucester, undermines the other, the former by insisting on the unspeakability of certain stories, the latter by demanding that Lydgate speak. Lydgate negotiates this opposition by engaging in one of his favorite poetic practices: mixing and mingling source texts to create a new story that is nevertheless riven by old faultlines. Thus, for example, the "pleynyng" of Canacee's baby echoes loudly from the *Confessio Amantis*, providing the inevitable counter to Lydgate's shockingly brutal picture of the helpless, unnaturally mute child ripped apart at the behest of his grandfather. I suggested earlier that in Gower's version of the story we saw a tension between didactic exemplarity and amatory complaint, in which the reader's pity is aroused by the sinful figure of Canacee and a moment of extreme contradiction occurs. Faithful to the principles outlined in his own Prologue—in which he described the task of the translator as the "prolongation" of virtuous texts—Lydgate has "prolonged" this Gowerian moment to such an extent that he has created a *series* of incoherences and incompatibilities.[25]

What, then, is the function, or purpose, of such prolongation? Let me suggest that the extreme polarities we find in the Canacee story come about as the result of a double poetic causality. On the surface, as I have shown, we see a picture of a poet stitching together a story from

in the companion piece to this essay, " 'Now wo, now gladnesse': Ovidianism in the *Fall of Princes*," *ELH* 71 (2004): 531–58.

[25] The passage reads:

> And he [Laurent] seith eek, that his entencioun
> Is to a-menden, correcten and declare;
> Nat to condempne off no presumpcioun,
> But to supporte, pleynli, and to spare
> Thyng touchid shortly off the story bare,
> Vndir a stile breeff and compendious,
> Hem to *prolonge* whan thei be vertuous.
>
> (*Prologue*, lines 85–91; emphasis added)

various disparate threads—Ovidian complaint, Gowerian moralism, Boethian Stoicism, Chaucerian pietism (itself a bit of a contradiction)—in such a way that the internal contradictions in each are thrown into relief. Less evident is the way in which those narrative threads also form parts of broader stories about the growth and change of a literary or philosophical tradition. Such stories always propose a relationship between the aesthetic and history in which each shapes and informs the other—a relationship we see dramatized, in a sense, by Lydgate's staging of the encounter of a real, embodied authority (Humphrey) with its textual counterparts (Ovid, Boccaccio, Chaucer, Gower) and its fictions (tyrants like Eolus). I have suggested that the nodal point for the Canacee story—the locus of all of the intersecting stories, genres, and narratives we have encountered thus far—is the silence of the baby, the interpretive stumbling block inassimilable by either moralism or complaint. It is tempting to read this silence metonymically, as the particular instance of a larger "uneasiness" within the very idea of poetic tradition as Lydgate understood it, an uneasiness produced by a desire to synthesize the extreme contradictions he found in his sources. But the very fact of contradiction itself points to a set of larger aesthetic questions at play in the *Fall of Princes*. It is crucial to recognize here that the aesthetic works as a mode of formal organization that is both specific and universalizing at the very same time. Thus, for example, Ovidianism means something distinct in the late fourteenth century, in the fifteenth century, and the sixteenth and beyond, all the way up to and including the translations of Ted Hughes. These are the historical meanings of aesthetic form. But all of those Ovidianisms *share* certain characteristics, and, indeed, each builds on its predecessors to create a variegated and layered discourse in which multiple histories are sedimented and occasionally, anachronistically, rise to the surface. This effect of "sedimentation"—the layering of a whole range of meanings within a single story—is not caused by "literary history," in an old-fashioned sense. Rather, it is a characteristic of textuality itself, one that, under the right circumstances, creates a distinctive aesthetic trajectory in which poetic forms and contexts can be traced over time and made to conform to a diachronic logic.

In the case we are discussing here, the effect of "sedimentation" reveals itself particularly strongly in Lydgate's answer to the muteness of the baby he has so carefully inserted into the exemplum. Lydgate is a poet of dichotomies, who tends to structure heterogeneity by confining it within binary oppositions, which themselves often multiply and escape his control. The oppositions between notions of Fortune—as chance or punishment—between genres (didacticism and complaint), between poets (Chaucer and Gower), between modes of "pleynyng" (amatory and Christian), and between forms of *auctoritee* (the patron versus the literary *auctor*) are cases in point. The baby's muteness is no exception to this rule. As I will show, it is coupled with a notion of ventriloquized speaking that complements the subjective, feeling-laden Ovidian complaint and begins to lead us out of the quagmire of contradictions the story has churned up. As she "pleynes," Canacee clearly understands herself to be speaking *for* her son, to be "grucching" because he cannot. She further understands her letter and her story to have a literary future. In a long passage that Lydgate adds to Gower, she articulates a series of relationships between Fortune and fame, Fortune and Cupid, and complaint and memorialization that begin to suggest how we might understand the Canacee episode in relation to broader aesthetic and historical questions raised by the *Fall of Princes*. In particular, as I will show, Lydgate turns away from the Chaucerian models he deploys at the beginning of the story—images of saintly women—and toward the more vexed figures of Dido and Criseyde, posing the problem of Fortune in a new and more pressing way. If Canacee had seemed early on to accept blame for her sin—"On the and me dependith the trespace / Touchyng our gilte and our gret offence" (1.6924–25)—she soon turns away from this penitential rhetoric and toward the discourse of secular love:

> But love and Fortune ha[ue] turned up-so-doun
> Our grace, alas, our welfare & our fame,
> Hard to recure, so sclaundrid is our name.
>
> Spot of diffamyng is hard to wasshe away,
> Whan noise and rumour abrod do folk manace;
> To hyndre a man ther may be no delay:
> For hatful fame fleeth ferr in ful short space.
> But off vs tweyne ther is non othir grace
> Sauff onli deth, and afftir deth, alas,
> Eternal sclaundre off vs; thus stant the cas.
>
> Whom shal we blame, or whom shal we atwite
> Our gret offence, sithe we may it nat hide?

For our excus reportis to respite
Mene is ther non, except the god Cupide.
And thouh that he wolde for vs prouide,
In this mateer to been our cheeff refuge,
Poetis seyn he is blynd to been a iuge.

He is depeynt[e] lich a blynd archer,
To marke ariht failyng discrecioun,
Holdyng no meseur, nouther ferr nor neer;
But lik Fortunys disposicioun,
Al upon happ, void off al resoun,
As a blynd archer with arwes sharp[e] grounde
Off auenture yeueth many a mortal wounde.

(1.6970–93)

We are reminded in these lines, of course, of a Chaucerian heroine similarly aware of her own literary future; as Criseyde complains (V.1058–64),

Allas, of me, unto the worldes ende,
Shal neyther ben ywriten nor ysonge
No good word, for thise bokes wol me shende.
O, rolled shal I ben on many a tonge!
Thorughout the world my belle shal be ronge!
And wommen moost wol haten me of alle.
Allas, that swich a cas me sholde falle!

Like Criseyde, Canacee blames Fortune for her woes *even as* she acknowledges her fault. As any reader of the *Troilus* knows, the link between the arbitrary God of Love and the turning of Fortune's wheel was explicitly articulated throughout the literature of love. Indeed, as Howard Patch showed long ago, Fortune and Venus are often indistinguishable in pictorial and literary representations.[26] The effect of this turn to the discourse of love is simultaneously to sharpen the contrast between the innocent child and his guilty amorous mother, and to dissolve further the distinction between the pious lament and the Ovidian complaint. Canacee's letter serves both purposes at once, ventriloquizing the legitimate "grucching" of her son while asserting her own self-justifying

---

[26] Howard Patch, *The Goddess Fortuna in Medieval Literature* (Cambridge, Mass.: Harvard University Press, 1927), pp. 90–98.

81

logic. The notion of speaking for another, of soliciting readers on another's behalf, plays a critical role in understanding what so fascinated Lydgate about the Canacee story. As I have said, though the initial incitement to telling the tale may have come from poetic competitiveness—doing Chaucer one better, or prioritizing Gower over Chaucer—its significance, indicated by the sheer density of its allusions and its concluding position in Book One, is clearly linked to the broader questions undergirding Lydgate's poetic project as a whole, and cannot be limited to the narrow, judgmental logic of the Man of Law, who sees poetry simply as an opportunity for moralization and competition (recall his allusion to the "Pierides").[27] When Canacee begins to present herself as the *object* of stories ("sclaundrid" by fame), she articulates precisely the opposite moral question from that posed by the Man of Law. The issue is not, "is it right to recount a 'wikke ensaumple' lest readers be led astray?" but rather "is it *ethical* to 'sclaundre' Canacee?" This shift in perspective, from Canacee as negative exemplar to Canacee as victim of Fame, is further enhanced as she continues her plaint:

> At the and me he wrongli dede marke,
> Felli to hyndre our fatal auentures,
> As ferr as Phebus shynyth in his arke,
> To make us refus to alle creatures,
> Callid us tweyne onto the woful lures
> Off diffame, which will departe neuere,
> Be newe report the noise encresyng euere.
>
> Odious fame with swifft wengis fleeth,
> But al good fame envie doth restreyne;
> Ech man off other the diffautis seeth,
> Yit on his owne no man will compleyne.
> But al the world out crieth on vs tweyne,
> Whos hatful ire bi us may nat be queemyd;
> For I mut deie, my fader hath so deemyd.
> (1.6994–7007)

---

[27] The Man of Law mistakenly refers to the "Muses that men clepe Pierides" (II.92), making an Ovidian slip; the "Pierides" are the daughters of King Pierus, known for contending with the Muses in a singing contest and being changed into magpies (see *Metamorphoses*, 5.293–678). His interest in the idea of a poetic contest is evident; immediately after this reference, he refers to himself humbly as coming after Chaucer with "hawebake" and turning to prose as a result. Of course, he goes on to tell a story in verse.

These lines recall another Chaucerian figure and text, this time Dido in the *House of Fame*, who laments (345–52),

> O wel-away that I was born!
> For thorgh yow is my name lorn,
> And alle my actes red and songe
> Over al thys lond, on every tonge.
> O wikke Fame!—for ther nys
> Nothing so swift, lo, as she is!
> O soth ys, every thing ys wyst,
> Though hit be kevered with the myst.

At one level, it would seem that we have been brought full circle, back to a relatively simple model of "pleynyng" that would suggest Canacee's complaint be seen as the subjective utterance of yet another victim of love and passion. But Lydgate's evocation of the *House of Fame* (and especially of Dido) necessarily turns our attention to the kind of meta-poetic questions that Chaucer persistently raises, not only in the *House of Fame*—where he poses the problem of poetry and reputation—but also in *The Legend of Good Women*, where his retelling of the Dido story forms part of a pseudo-ethical maneuver based on the fiction of poetic judgment outlined in the *Prologue*, where Cupid condemns Chaucer's *Troilus and Criseyde*. If Canacee, like Criseyde and Dido, sees herself as the victim of fame, stained by a proleptic historical notoriety, then Lydgate's retelling of her story—like the *Troilus*, in Cupid's view— inevitably contributes to that "sclaundre," both concretely (by impugn- ing Canacee specifically) and in the abstract (by thus impugning women as a whole). This effect becomes even more pronounced in light of the long excursus on the "malis of wommen" that Lydgate translates from Laurent just prior to telling the Canacee story, in which he somewhat ineffectually disclaims responsibility for "Bochas'" sentiments: "And treu[e]li it doth my witt appall / Off this mateer to make rehersaile; / It is no resoun tatwiten women all, / Thouh on or too whilom dede faile" (1.6644–47). By the time we have finished reading the exemplum of Canacee and Machaire, Boccaccio's comments on women retrospectively appear, in light of *The Legend of Good Women*, as violations of the law of love. In other words, Lydgate animates a discourse of literary criticism from the *Legend* that counters the overwhelming moral logics of both his patron (Humphrey) and his source (Boccaccio/Laurent), each of whom, in different but complementary ways, proposes a distinctive and powerful mode of poetic judgment that relies on a specifically Christian rhetoric of sin. What the shift in perspective—from Canacee as object of blame, to Canacee as subject of "sclaundre"—allows is the articulation of an alternative rhetoric, one that still relies on the *concept* of sin, but that redefines transgression according to the Ovidian logic of *The Legend of Good Women*.

It further links that logic to the work of conceptualizing the purpose of poetry itself. There would seem to be no doubt of course about Humphrey's notion of the proper function of poetry: its job is to teach princes about the wages of sin and the rewards of virtue by way of negative examples. Nor does Chaucer's Cupid allow for any confusion about *his* understanding of the purpose of tale-telling, to honor women as a means of furthering his own end of promoting a kind of ethical love. How then, does the Canacee story fit these models? Unsurprisingly, the answer is, not very well. It works neither as a warning about the dangers of incest (our identification with Canacee is too strong) nor, for obvious reasons, as a positive illustration of the virtues of women or love. In other words, it is not a good exemplar. And because the story fits neither Humphrey nor Cupid's model, it exposes their essential similarity: both depend upon a notion of exemplarity in which narratives submit to abstraction and poetry's function is to further the rule of law, be it the law of Christian morality or the law of love. But Canacee herself has a very different understanding of the purpose of writing. As she explains:

> Now farweel, brother, to me it doth suffise
> To deie allone for our bothe sake.
> And in my moste feithful humble wise,
> Onto my dethward thouh I tremble & quake,
> Off the for euere now my leue I take.
> And onys a yeer, forget nat, but take heed,
> Mi fatal day this lettre for to reed.
>
> So shaltow han on me sum remembraunce,
> Mi name enprentid in thi kalender,
> Bi rehersaile off my dedli greuaunce;
> Were blak that day, & mak a doolful cheer.
> And whan thou comest & shalt approche neer
> Mi sepulture, I pray the nat disdeyne
> Vpon my graue summe teris for to reyne.
>
> (1.7008–21)

Lydgate has taken his cue from Gower, whose Canacee asks that her son be buried with her "so schalt thou have / Upon ous bothe remembrance" (lines 294–95), but he has greatly extrapolated upon the idea of "remembrance" by making the letter itself a memorial object. Canacee asks that the letter be read and reread as a means of "enprenting" her memory on Machaire's "kalender"—not as a warning to sinners (amatory or otherwise) but as an incitement to emotional display: "wer blak that day & mak a doolful cheer." Here we find the counter to the exemplary notion of poetry underwritten by Humphrey and Cupid: poetry both arouses emotions and furthers remembrance. It memorializes the dead by inciting feeling, and that subjective emotion constitutes an end *in itself.*

One might object that such a reading relies all to heavily on the warped "pleynyng" of an outrageous sinner to have any validity within the broader logic of the *Fall of Princes* as a whole. It is certainly true that readers of the text are in no doubt as to the moral purpose of Lydgate's poetry. But the fact remains that in his envoy—the feature of the poem designed explicitly for moralization—he refuses to make the obvious judgment about Canacee's sin:

> Whan surquedie oppressid hath pite,
> And meeknesse is with tirannie bor doun
> Ageyn al riht, & hasti cruelte
> To be vengable maketh no dilacioun,
> What folweth theroff?—be cleer inspeccioun,
> Seeth an exaumple how Pirrus in his teene
> Off hatful ire slouh yonge Polliceene
>
> King Eolus to rigerous was, parde,
> And to vengable in his entencioun
> Ageyn his childre Machaire & Canace,
> So inportable was his punycioun,
> Off haste procedyng to ther destruccioun;
> Wers in his ire, as it was weel seene,
> Than cruel Pirrus, which slouh Polliceene.
>
> (1.7057–63)

The pairing of Pirrus, who kills an innocent girl, and Eolus, who is "to rigerous" to Canacee and Machaire, obliterates the difference between the two stories and enforces an explicitly political reading, in which "meeknesse" is oppressed by "tirannie" and "surquedie" suppresses "pite." In this reading, it would seem that "pleynyng" has a distinct efficacy in the world, that it "makes a difference" by soliciting the pity of princely readers and enjoining them to temper their justice with mercy. But the mathematical simplicity of this cause-and-effect logic (poetry makes something happen) belies the fundamental problematic at work in representing tyranny in a moralizing poem. Tyranny is tyranny *precisely because* it refuses moralization; it punishes the innocent along with the guilty. It is tyranny that creates the impossible conundrum of Canacee's mute baby, the innocent who falls despite his sinlessness; it is tyranny itself that issues the most profound challenge to Humphrey's (tyrannical) moralizing logic, and ultimately to the very idea that human agency can have material effects in this world. By making the implicit critique of tyranny staged by Chaucer in *The Legend of Good Women* explicit—by naming "tirannie" and confronting it directly—Lydgate ultimately produces a far bleaker picture of the world than his "maistere." In the Canacee story, tyranny goes unchecked and unpunished; Eolus acts with impunity and without fetters—and though he is censured by Lydgate, he does not "fall" like the other sinners in the text. He stands as a pure example of absolutist power; like the innocent baby, his opposite number, he cannot be assimilated to the logic of moralization.

Lydgate is not satisfied, however, with this uncompromising narrative of tyrannical impunity. In what seems like a quixotic and futile gesture, he insists in the envoy that the story function as an efficacious narrative, one that can curb the tyrannical impulses of princes: "Noble Pryncis, prudent and attempre / Differrith vengaunce, off hih discrecioun; / Til your ire sumwhat asuagid be / Doth neuer off doom non execucioun" (1.7063–67). The "pite" that readers feel, then, is supposed to prevent them from acting vengefully and induce them to behave mercifully; like Theseus in *The Knight's Tale*, Lydgate's ideal prince is moved by that noble emotion to eschew tyranny and act with kindness. But not only does the failure to punish Eolus lend the envoy an air of impotence, but the affective demand of the text—that readers feel "pite"—also contradicts the moralism of the *Fall of Princes* as a whole. Here we return to the central difficulty of the Canacee story: were Lydgate's princes to feel "pite" upon reading the narrative, they would be being moved by the plight of a sinner—and not just any sinner, but a particularly egregious violator of the laws of God and Nature. It is this paradox upon which the entire apparatus of *Fall of Princes* stumbles, a stumble, I will argue, that ultimately allows Lydgate to produce something new, a new way of thinking about poetry and a new means of approaching the problem of Fortune.

"Vernacular Philosophy" and the Aesthetic: Poetry and Fortune

I have traced, bit by bit, the series of contradictions and impasses that permeate the Canacee story as a way of showing how Lydgate's obsessive engagement with Chaucer and Gower leads him to construct a series of oppositions and tensions that cannot be resolved. Having now seen the care and sophistication with which Lydgate has created this story, with its allusions, cross references, contradictions, and competing demands on its readers, we can see further how this episode functions in relation to the *Fall of Princes* as a whole, both poetically and historically. It is intimately bound up with the question of Fortune, partly because it is Fortune that forms the major philosophical subject of *Fall of Princes*, and partly because Fortune was the most serious poetic question posed by Chaucer and Gower; indeed, one might even say that meditations on Fortune form a kind of "vernacular philosophy" in the late fourteenth and fifteenth centuries. Fortune becomes a poetic question not simply because the idea provides aristocrats with a secular notion through which they can justify their own mode of living (while poetry about Fortune provides them with affirmation), as Larry Scanlon has argued, but also because thinking about Fortune poses the problem of poetic *function*.[28] What, in a world governed by Fortune, is poetry *for?* Does it lament? "Grucche"? Instruct by moralizing? Give pleasure? Each of these possibilities proposes a different relationship of the aesthetic to history, of poetry to Fortune (which we might in some sense say is another way of describing the mass of unprocessed data that constitutes "history" in its rawest guise). If, for example, poetry is meant to moralize, then at root it is a way of *acting in the world*—a way of imposing order, on, and in, history. Even if the message of that moralization is simply that one should embrace virtue and let Fortune work as she

---

[28] Larry Scanlon, "Sweet Persuasion: The Subject of Fortune in *Troilus and Criseyde*," in *Chaucer's* Troilus and Criseyde: *"Subgit to alle Poesye,"* *Essays in Criticism*, ed. R. A. Shoaf (Binghamton: Medieval and Renaissance Texts and Studies, 1992), pp. 211–23; as Scanlon states, "In the figure of Fortune an aristocratic class can at once recognize the flux of historical existence, and affirm its own privilege as a locus of stability beyond such flux" (p. 217).

will, the implication of didactic poetry is that writing is fundamentally efficacious, with tangible results. This model of efficacy constitutes the explicit self-understanding of the *Fall of Princes*. But when Lydgate deploys other discourses, he also activates alternative notions of Fortune. "Pleynyng" or "grucching" is a case in point. At one level, "pleynyng" fits the moralizing model, in that it assists in the didactic mission of the text by arousing pity. But in another way, complaint is the quintessential genre of helplessness, a mode of discourse articulated by Fortune's victims that is useless as a way of imposing human will upon the world. "Pleynyng," as Boethius tells us, is what human beings do when afflicted with bad Fortune, and it is a fruitless and foolish indulgence, a paradigmatic example of wasted speech. Far better to model oneself on Griselda, the Boethian Stoic, than to "grucche" about the implacability of Fortune, which in this model is a principle of irresistible historical causation that is utterly exterior to the human subject. According to such logic, the aesthetic—of which "pleynyng" is a type—is stripped of agency and meaning, made not only impotent but surplus to requirements.

These two notions of Fortune (the idea of a remediable negative force and an efficacious poetry versus the fearsome thought of arbitrary contingency and the uselessness of speech) are the twin poles between which Lydgate suspends the Canacee story. Jumbled together in this episode we find precisely these opposing epistemologies, the former a model in which the world is saturated with a single meaning and the latter a paradigm that evacuates the human world of all significance and silences all speech. History is both subject to logic—available to hermeneutics—and utterly excessive and irrational at the same time. Lydgate knows this, in the sense that he knows that his sources fundamentally conflict—that Ovid, Boccaccio, Chaucer, and Gower each propose a different solution to the basic problem of finding meaning in history. His instinctive response to these conflicts—a response utterly characteristic of him—is to seek some kind of synthesis. Ultimately, Canacee and her son represent ideal subjects for the kind of "vernacular philosophy" that permeates the *Fall of Princes*, precisely because they expose the structural contradictions at work in the historical models for human life in the world that Lydgate inherited from his predecessors. Neither Boethian Stoicism (Griselda) nor Christian complaint (Custance) functions in the universe of moral ambiguity described by the Canacee story, a world in which exemplars contain more than one kind of sin (incest, tyranny) and solicit deeply ambivalent responses (pity, horror). In the end, Lydgate asks us to choose between a morally compromised aesthetic mode— "pleynyng"—and a pure, and purely doomed, form of human living: an impossible, mute innocence. But of course, the choice he offers is no choice at all. We are implicated in Canacee's "pleynyng" simply by virtue of having read it. Nor does Humphrey's moral vision of poetry provide a way out of the dilemma Lydgate articulates. Not only does the indictment of tyranny ultimately implicate Humphrey himself, but the very purposiveness of poetry he demands is countered by the "pleynyng" of guilty Canacee. Recall that Canacee herself understands her letter as a means to an end *in itself*, as a form of memorialization, nothing more. This vision of "pleynyng" obtrudes as a third term between Griselda's *contempus mundi* and Custance's belief in efficacious prayer— and it is a vision, in the end, of the aesthetic, of a pointless, functionless mode of discourse with no purpose external to itself.[29] Contra Boethius, in a world ruled by arbitrary Fortune, "pleynyng" saves us from both silence and moralism, from the despair of impotence and the impossible fantasy of agency.

Lydgate is not, however, presenting a kind of "middle way," a "solution" to the contradictions the Canacee story has exposed. He is rather making a very minor claim for the value of an aesthetic engagement with the world. It is not a value conferred by an ethos of salvation or moral improvement, but instead is a simple assertion that speaking (writing) is better than silence, even in the face of imminent destruction. Fortune, in this reading, constitutes a flexible way of imagining the world in which either contingency or causality, chance or sin, may be operating at any given moment; it is a "vernacular philosophy" with its own discursive mode: "pleynyng." And it is precisely because "pleynyng" lacks purpose ("Why pleynestow?" asks Fortune) that it becomes, for Lydgate, a model for the aesthetic.

[29] Lee Patterson, in his "Writing Amorous Wrongs: Chaucer and the Order of Complaint," in *The Idea of Medieval Literature: New Essays on Chaucer and Medieval Culture in Honor of Donald R. Howard*, ed. James M. Dean and Christian Zacher (Newark: University of Delaware Press, 1992), pp. 55–71, makes a similar point about the relationship between complaint as a genre and the problem of poetic function, arguing that in complaint "uselessness is programmatic"; "the claim it lays upon the world is virtually always self-cancelling" (p. 56). More broadly, he suggests that the lyric voice in Chaucer functions as a kind of radically ahistorical and unassimilable voice that calls into question that stability of authorized discourses (pp. 66–67). Lydgate certainly recognizes this capacity of the complaint to challenge and destabilize authority, as his resistance to Humphrey's causal model shows.

It might fairly be noted that in an argument that hinges on an idea about history—Fortune in all its variations—I have said almost nothing about "history" as it is usually understood, nothing about the 1430s, nothing about the Lancastrians, nothing about Lydgate's own biography, and I have made only the briefest mention of Humphrey's historical role. This is not because such matters are irrelevant; indeed, much work remains to be done on the *Fall of Princes* and its historical, political, and social contexts and resonances. Rather, I have focused so closely on textual matters because this particular text is determinedly anti-topical. Apart from its references to Humphrey of Gloucester, it includes only two references to recent English history, the first a bit of praise and memorialization for Henry V, and the second a revision of Boccaccio's account of King John of France's English imprisonment.[30] Of course, as has been amply demonstrated over the past fifteen years, historicity is not the same as topicality, and an analysis of the *Fall of Princes* as a poem of its moment (with regard to questions of governance and sovereignty, for example) has much to teach us about Lydgate and about the status of poetry and patronage during the reign of Henry VI. But the paradox of the *Fall of Princes* is that any attempt to locate it diachronically, as part of a broader literary or cultural history stretching from medieval to renaissance depends upon its *anti*-historical qualities, its tendency to assert its transhistorical relevance, its resistance to local temporality. Ultimately, it is the final poetic move we see in book one—the articulation of the extreme moral ambiguity of "pleynyng"—that constitutes the bedrock of historicity in the *Fall of Princes*. It is a special kind of historicity, however, one in which the past is rendered through the mingling of the forms, genres, and modes of articulation in which various histories are sedimented and layered, only to be transported from time to time, past to present to future, and reused and remade in strikingly new ways.

If it is true that the curious effect of retreat from history proper of the *Fall of Princes* (through the privileging of form, including exemplarity) is in the end a *return* to historicity—if, that is, the very fact that a mode of discourse like "pleynyng" resists local contextualization constitutes the ultimate historical meaning of the text—what are the implications

---

[30] See *Fall of Princes*, book one, lines 5951–85; Lydgate is describing how Henry V commissioned the *Troy Book*. In book nine, Lydgate transforms Boccaccio's story of the fall of King John of France into praise for the Black Prince ("Prince Edward"), noting Boccaccio's partiality ("ful narwe he gan hym thinke, / Lefft spere and sheeld[e], fauht with penne & inke" [lines 3167–68]); see lines 3134–203.

of this assertion for our understanding of Lydgate's place in literary history?[31] It should be clear by now that the old assumption that he is a quintessentially "medieval" poet no longer works as a way of accounting for the complexity of Lydgate's engagement with the plethora of texts and stories available to him.[32] That is, as Lydgate negotiates the contradictory and conflicting sources to which he has dedicated his loyalties, he is forced to make a series of editorial choices that lead inevitably to the birth of something new, if only because he delights so thoroughly in pitting one authority against another, Chaucer against Gower, Humphrey against Chaucer. This poetic habit leads Lydgate away from the historical—understood as the concatenation of local practices, politics, and events—and into the seemingly more rarefied world of the aesthetic, a fantasy world like Dante's Elysian fields, in which *auctors* communicate with other *auctors* and history rages on outside the text. But the aesthetic does not work in this way. The very opposition between an ahistorical realm of literary form and a secular realm of events is itself a phenomenon with a history; neither fully "medieval" (in which we would see a different kind of retreat from history) nor entirely "modern" (which would demand a level of secularization not possible for Lydgate), the aesthetic of "pleynyng" that emerges in book one represents a small piece of a much larger historical development. For Lydgate to open the space for "pleynyng" to emerge as a viable human behavior *in spite of* its seeming purposelessness constitutes an assertion, however unintentional, of the value of a certain form of the aesthetic.[33] And despite the

---

[31] The *Fall of Princes* stands at a critical juncture between the late fourteenth century and the sixteenth century, with its "humanist" revival of figures like Ovid and genres like tragedy. In discussions that lie outside the scope of this essay, both James Simpson and Paul Strohm, in different ways, have recently made arguments regarding the transition from "medieval" to "renaissance" in literary terms, Simpson (in part) in relation to Ovidianism, and Strohm in connection to tragedy through his comparison of *Fall of Princes* with *A Mirror For Magistrates*; see Simpson's *Reform and Cultural Revolution* (especially chapter 4—"The Elegiac"—and the "Envoi") and Strohm's *"Politique": Languages of Statecraft*.

[32] The notion that Lydgate "medievalized" the texts with which he came in contact is expressed most thoroughly by Derek Pearsall in his *John Lydgate*; for example, he states that "every mask [Lydgate] puts on is a well-worn medieval one" (p. 2), and argues that Lydgate is "perfectly representative of the Middle Ages" (p. 14).

[33] My thinking about "uselessness" has been influenced by a talk given by Aranye Fradenburg at Princeton University in 2003, a version of which has been published as her "Simply Marvelous," *SAC* 26 (2004): 1–27. She argues, among other things, that "all forms of creative activity and consumption, including economic ones, are directly functions of enjoyment, usefulness being a part of this field rather than its cause or foundation" (p. 10).

fact that this form seems imbued with a certain "modernity" (early or late), the *Fall of Princes* does not constitute a way station along a progressive road to the future; in fact, "pleynyng" is what Ovid's heroines have been doing since long before Lydgate dreamed of writing poetry. The Canacee story, with its multiple sources and contradictory lessons, constitutes an idea of mingling and mixing—of sedimentation—that embodies the capacity of the aesthetic to be historical while steadfastly resisting the historicity of facts and lessons. This aesthetic asserts the stubborn persistence of the human (of "pleynyng") in the face of both moralism and radical contingency—and, as we have come to understand in this post-human age, that persistence has its own troubled history. It is nevertheless worth preserving a place in our own rationalized world for "pleynyng," for the fantasy of an escape from cause and effect—for uselessness.

"T'assaye in thee thy wommanheede":
Griselda Chosen, Translated, and Tried

Tara Williams
Oregon State University

SCHOLARLY VIEWS of Chaucer's Griselda remain split. More traditional readings stress her passivity or submission in support of *The Clerk's Tale*'s allegorical or exemplary significance.[1] Newer feminist or historicist interpretations stress her assertiveness, even if only ironically.[2] In this fuller picture Griselda's identity itself becomes a crucial focus of Chaucer's interest. As Carolyn Dinshaw suggests, the interpretive puzzle of the relationship between Walter and Griselda raises "the question of the feminine."[3] This essay will suggest that for Chaucer the question of the feminine is literally a question of *wommanheede*. Chaucer coins the word and, in a significant revision to his sources, introduces the concept the word signifies to the tale. I will argue Chaucer offers Griselda as a mediating figure: in an essentially ironic strategy, he intensifies the extremes already present in the tale in order to intensify her mediation.[4]

I would like to thank Larry Scanlon, Frank Grady, and the anonymous *SAC* readers for their useful comments on earlier versions of this essay.

[1] See, for example, Deborah S. Ellis, "Domestic Treachery in the *Clerk's Tale*," in *Ambiguous Realities: Women in the Middle Ages and Renaissance,* ed. Carole Levin and Jeanie Watson (Detroit: Wayne State University Press, 1987), pp. 99–113; Michaela Paasche Grudin, "Chaucer's *Clerk's Tale* as Political Paradox," *SAC* 11 (1989): 63–92; and Charlotte C. Morse, "The Exemplary Griselda," *SAC* 7 (1985): 51–86.

[2] See, for example, Elaine Tuttle Hansen, *Chaucer and the Fictions of Gender* (Berkeley and Los Angeles: University of California Press, 1992), chap. 7; Jill Mann, *Feminizing Chaucer* (1991 as *Geoffrey Chaucer;* Rochester: D. S. Brewer, 2002), pp. 114–25; and Carolynn Van Dyke, "The Clerk's and the Franklin's Subjected Subjects," *SAC* 17 (1995): 45–68.

[3] Carolyn Dinshaw, *Chaucer's Sexual Poetics* (Madison: University of Wisconsin Press, 1989), p. 133.

[4] David Wallace has argued that Chaucer exploited the contradictions in Petrarch's version of the story in order to critique the tyranny Chaucer associated with Petrarch; here I read some of the same aspects of the tale as allowing Chaucer's examination of the category of womanhood. Wallace, *Chaucerian Polity: Absolutist Lineages and Associational Forms in England and Italy* (Stanford: Stanford University Press, 1997), chap. 10.

Walter, largely a cipher in most previous accounts of the tale, plays a central role in Chaucer's irony.[5] However inexplicable his cruelty or mysterious his motives, in testing Griselda he seeks to answer the same question as Chaucer: Can her femininity successfully combine apparently contradictory elements (such as her incompatible duties as wife and mother: to submit to her husband and, in doing so, allow the killing of her children)? As we shall see, Chaucer's morally ambiguous deployment of Walter also enables him to project the question of Griselda's womanhood onto a larger scale, as a juxtaposition of the courtly and the hagiographical.

This essay begins with an overview of the linguistic and intellectual background to Chaucer's concept of womanhood. Then we move to the tale itself and womanhood's close relation to Griselda's "translation" and her trials, two issues that have occupied so much previous scholarship. The word *womanhood* appears twice in *The Clerk's Tale:* when Walter first sees Griselda and when he ends the tests and offers an explanation. The concept is also significant in several other passages where Chaucer does not directly invoke the term, including the marriage contract, Griselda's "translation" and its subsequent reversal, and the three trials.

Inventing Womanhood

Womanhood was something that Chaucer both "found" in the rhetorical sense of *inventio*—by responding to the social and intellectual trends

[5] Hansen and, to a lesser extent, Dinshaw and Wallace see Walter as primarily a reactionary, while those who focus on the marquis and his possible motivations, such as Kathryn L. Lynch, "Despoiling Griselda: Chaucer's Walter and the Problem of Knowledge in *The Clerk's Tale*," *SAC* 10 (1988): 41–70; Andrew Sprung, "'If it youre wille be': Coercion and Compliance in Chaucer's *Clerk's Tale*," *Exemplaria* 7.2 (1995): 345–69; and Thomas A. Van, "Walter at the Stake: A Reading of Chaucer's *Clerk's Tale*," *ChauR* 22.3 (1988): 214–24, tend to flatten out the complexities in Chaucer's portrayal of Griselda. Many of these readings have been influenced by Robert O. Payne's early interpretation of the tale as a "sentimental experiment" in which Chaucer seems to be "working toward a . . . moral statement which will be immediately apprehensible emotionally and nearly incomprehensible by any rational or intellectual faculty." In such a reading, there is no need to seek intelligibility in either Walter or Griselda. Payne, *The Key of Remembrance: A Study of Chaucer's Poetics* (New Haven: Yale University Press, 1963), p. 164. By contrast, I will argue that Walter plays a vital role in the construction of Griselda's exemplary womanhood; if Griselda is a mediating figure, then Walter necessarily becomes slightly more rational or at least intelligible. Chaucer also employs the term "womanhood" in *The Man of Law's Tale*, which might be read as presenting a similar "sentimental experiment," but there the term applies to the Virgin Mary rather

of the late fourteenth century—and "created," by coining the term and others related to it.[6] These coinages raise issues crucial to recent work on language in Chaucer. In *The Making of Chaucer's English*, Christopher Cannon argues against an older but still prevalent view that Chaucer created or refined the English language for literature, contending that "Chaucer's English is not 'new' but generally 'traditional.'"[7] Taking Chaucer's words as specific and historicized objects of study, Cannon examines first uses (in Chaucer and in the Middle English written record), number of uses in Chaucer's works, and number of Chaucerian works in which a word appears. While ultimately claiming that Chaucer does create new vocabulary, Cannon sees this practice as common to Middle English writers, who worked to connect English to the literary languages of Latin and French by adopting words from them and thereby created a textual tradition in which "the very novelty of borrowings" was "constitutive of Middle English literature."[8] In support of his larger claim, Cannon presents three points that are pertinent here: first, that Chaucer invents words by borrowing from French or Latin and by combining extant English elements;[9] second, that this borrowing, often

than Constance. Hence, while Constance represents a similar combination of the courtly and the hagiographical, the mediating function of womanhood remains primarily implicit in that tale.

[6] Although he does not discuss the issue of Chaucer's coinages, John M. Fyler does present an interesting examination of the ways in which Chaucer plays on the words "man" and "woman"; see Fyler, "Man, Men, and Women in Chaucer's Poetry," *The Olde Daunce: Love, Friendship, Sex, and Marriage in the Medieval World*, ed. Robert R. Edwards and Stephen Spector (Albany: State University of New York Press, 1991), pp. 154–76.

[7] Christopher Cannon, *The Making of Chaucer's English: A Study of Words* (Cambridge: Cambridge University Press, 1998), p. 4.

[8] Ibid., p. 77. Cannon defines that tradition and Chaucer's relation to it carefully:

Chaucer's language is not traditional by virtue of an interlocking line of influence . . . but by virtue of the set of common linguistic procedures employed by Chaucer and earlier Middle English writers. The connection is circumstantial, not patrimonial; the coercive force is not the strong example of earlier excellence but the common linguistic constraints of writing in the same language at roughly the same time. Chaucer employed the traditional procedures he did, not *because* they were employed in earlier texts, but because he found before him the same linguistic possibilities that made those procedures essential to Middle English literary making. (55, emphasis in original)

[9] David Burnley identifies more precisely "two primary methods of word formation": compounding and derivation. The former involves "the combination of free morphemes" and the latter "the addition of affixes to a base." David Burnley, "Lexis and Semantics," in *The Cambridge History of the English Language*, 6 vols., ed. Norman Blake (New York: Cambridge University Press, 1992–2001), 2:440. Originally a distinct noun, "hood" survived as a suffix and, by the time of Chaucer, the invention of "wom-

inspired by sources, was common poetic practice for Middle English writers; and third, that Chaucer discarded words as he replaced them with new ones, resulting in a working vocabulary of stable size but varying content.[10]

Substantiated with careful counts and tables of word occurrences, Cannon's case is undoubtedly persuasive as regards Chaucer's general poetic practice. Nevertheless, Ralph Hanna has raised a cogent objection to Cannon's method, one that is particularly relevant to my argument. As Hanna notes, Cannon's approach "tends to argue for the absence of any Chaucerian uniqueness." The claim that Chaucer's "lexical novelty" was produced by the conditions of writing in Middle English (and hence not evidence for poetic genius) suggests that nothing distinguishes Chaucer's language from that of any other Middle English writer. Chaucer's poetic achievement is distinct from his relatively banal linguistic innovation. Hanna argues that the object of study needs to be broadened: he calls for a consideration of usage in addition to lexicon, contending, "Lists [such as Cannon's appendices or the *Middle English Dictionary*] define only possibility, not the performance that constitutes usage."[11] There are many instances in which Chaucer's linguistic inven-

---

anhood" would be a derivation. "Hood," *Oxford English Dictionary Online*, 2003, Rutgers University Libraries, March 10, 2003: <http://dictionary.oed.com>. All subsequent references to the *OED Online* will be to this date and version unless otherwise noted.

[10] Borrowing from French or Latin sources was the first source of new vocabulary for Middle English writers. Eventually, however, "the practical need for new Romance words to meet the exigencies of translation was finally so habitual that even where French and Latin words were not immediately at issue lexical novelty became a formal attribute of Middle English poetics" (*Making of Chaucer's English*, p. 77). "Lexical novelty" could be created by anglicizing words (preserving the sense or rhyme of the source) or by placing English elements into new combinations. This practice was characteristic of Chaucer as well as other Middle English writers; as Cannon summarizes, "lexical invention constituted Chaucer's English because lexical invention constituted Middle English literary culture" (ibid., p. 90). Within Chaucer's body of work, however, this continuing "lexical invention" does not create a progressively larger vocabulary. Cannon emphasizes that "Chaucer's vocabulary *did not grow more dense*. . . . Chaucer did not use more words in later texts than he had in earlier texts, even though . . . the novelty of his vocabulary increased significantly with almost every successive text" (ibid., p. 120). So what happened to these words? "Chaucer simply threw them away . . . his lexical procedures got rid of words he had already used precisely because new words were entering his vocabulary to take their place." In other words, "Chaucer's vocabulary may have been shrinking at exactly the same rate it was growing: it may have been *only* iteratively novel" (ibid.).

[11] Ralph Hanna, "Chaucer and the Future of Language Study," *SAC* 24 (2002): 309–15, at 312–13. In the same volume, Wendy Scase more generally identifies the "next step" in language study as "analyzing linguistic practice (of Chaucer and of other authors) in light of the linguistic system as a whole, and in light of what the users and shapers of that system knew about its meanings and its implications as a social practice."

tions *are* related specifically to performance, and *womanhood* provides a particularly striking example.

Chaucer first coins the term to use in *Anelida and Arcite* and "A Complaint to His Lady." He continues to use the term throughout his career, in "Womanly Noblesse," *Troilus and Criseyde*, *The Legend of Good Women*, and in the *Canterbury Tales*, where, in addition to *The Clerk's Tale* and *The Man of Law's Tale*, it also occurs in one of the collection's earliest tales, *The Knight's Tale*, and in one of the latest, *The Canon's Yeoman's Tale*. The word tends to appear at moments where Chaucer is departing from his sources and interpolating moments or episodes of his own invention rather than in response to those texts. In *The Knight's Tale*, for instance, the word appears during the intercession of the queen and other women for Arcite and Palamon, a moment that does not appear in the *Teseida*. In almost every case, Chaucer is motivated by an interest in the spiritual conditions and qualities of femaleness. As he brings this interest to the Griselda story, the term *womanhood* and its concept alter his Latin and French sources considerably. Because he is not adapting the term from his sources and because he never discards it, *womanhood* represents a departure from Chaucer's habit of invention as Cannon describes it. As Chaucer continues to use the word, it continues to accrue resonance and complexity.

Moreover, *womanhood* is one of several related terms Chaucer devises, including *wifehood, femininity,* and *wifely.*[12] Although one sense of *wifehood* can be found in Anglo-Saxon, where *wife* could mean *woman,* he distinguishes that term from *womanhood* by associating the former specifically with female married virtue.[13] Wifehood is an aspect of womanhood—and one that he also explores—but the two are not synonymous for Chaucer.[14] His invention and use of these words suggests that he

---

Wendy Scase, "Tolkien, Philology, and *The Reeve's Tale*: Toward the Cultural Move in Middle English Studies," *SAC* 24 (2002): 325–34, at 328).

[12] "Wifhode," "femininite," and "wifli," *Middle English Dictionary* (*Middle English Compendium*), January 2002, Rutgers University Libraries, March 10, 2003: <http://ets.umdl.umich.edu/m/med>. All subsequent references to the *MED* (*MEC*) will be to this date and version unless otherwise noted.

[13] Most of its appearances (six) are in *The Legend of Good Women.* See "wifhod" in Larry D. Benson, *A Glossarial Concordance to the Riverside Chaucer*, 2 vols. (New York: Garland, 1993), 1:977. Gower's usage follows the same distinction. Interestingly, the *OED* attributes the form "wifehead" to Chaucer but "wifehood" (the form that ultimately survives) to Gower. See "wifehood" and "wifehead," *OED Online.*

[14] Perhaps the most interesting moment is in *The Wife of Bath's Prologue*, when she declares, "In wyfhod I wol use myn instrument / As frely as my Makere hath it sent. / If I be daungerous, God yeve me sorwe!" (III.149–51). Clearly this is not a typical reference to married virtue; the Wife recasts what the condition of wifehood entails and

had a noteworthy interest in representing women, particularly in representing them as a gendered group. Chaucer created abstractions that allowed him to describe—and to imagine—feminine qualities and the condition of being a woman in a new way. John Gower also experiments with these notions, and both Chaucer's and Gower's experimentation influence later writers, including Thomas Hoccleve, John Lydgate, and Robert Henryson; these later writers' usage of the terms Chaucer coined confirms that these abstractions were both productive and useful. Specific denotations developed within the specific texts of these writers, but a general sense of experimentation prevailed throughout. Because *womanhood* and its related terms—and the ideas behind them—were new, each time one appeared its meaning was in question and had to be established within the context of that usage, within the parameters of that text as a whole, within the context of the author's canon, and within the representations of women circulating in contemporary society. Every usage of *womanhood* affected what it would come to denote and connote in general usage.

Although its usage was distinctive, the invention of *womanhood* combines a familiar root with a familiar suffix. New words with the *–hood* or *–head* suffix emerged fairly steadily throughout the span of Middle English; more than twenty words with those suffixes occur in Chaucer and five appear ten times or more: *knighthode* (10 uses), *maidenhede* (20), *manhede* (10), *wifhod* (11), and *wommanhode* (15). Of these five, only the last two are original to Chaucer.[15] Both *–hood* and *–head* designated quality or condition and, as I have argued, Chaucer's invention and use of these words (and the related *femininity*) suggest a corresponding interest in representing the qualities and condition of women.[16] Because he was thinking about them in a new way (outside the extant categories of maidenhood, motherhood, and widowhood—all words that were al-

---

permits. All Chaucer quotations are drawn from Larry D. Benson, gen. ed, *The Riverside Chaucer*, 3rd ed. (Boston: Houghton Mifflin, 1987).

[15] In total, nine words with the "-head" or "-hood" suffix are coined by Chaucer: *chapmanhede, godlihede, liklihode, lustihede, mistihede, semelihede, wifhod, wilfulhede,* and *wommanhode*. (Although the *MED* [*MEC*] cites an earlier appearance of *womanhood*, this is because of its practice of sorting texts by date of manuscript rather than date of composition.) The words used but not originated by Chaucer include *brotherhede, childhod, falshede, godhead, grenehede, knighthode, maidenhede, manhede, presthede, unmanhede, widwehod,* and *yonghede*.

[16] The first is from Old English, the second a development of Middle English; writers used them indiscriminately. See "-hood" and "-head" in *OED Online* and "-hede" in *MED* (*MEC*).

ready in use),[17] new abstractions were required. *Womanhood* is the center of this phenomenon, the focal manifestation of what appears to be Chaucer's more general preoccupation with how to represent women and with what qualities or virtues women as a whole should or could have.[18] As David Burnley has recently explained, linguists use the term "lexical gap" to describe that sociolinguistic condition wherein "radical alterations to [a] society and to its communicative needs . . . may leave a language lacking words for the new circumstances."[19] Chaucer's usage and invention of related terms suggest that *womanhood* filled just such a "lexical gap" in Middle English.

A number of important intellectual and social developments in the later fourteenth century may have prompted Chaucer to bring *womanhood* and its constellation of associated terms into the language. Composed of vernacular parts, *womanhood* was made from and born into a language that was considered more available to women and associated with them strongly enough that it had "the potential to feminize its male audience by aligning them with non-Latin-literate women."[20] Contemporary with Chaucer, the anonymous translator of *The Knowing of Woman's Kind in Childing* writes in English "because whomen of oure tonge cunne bettyre rede and undyrstande thys langage than eny other [and so that] every whoman lettyrde [may] rede hit to other unlettyrd and help hem and conceyle hem in here maledyes withowtyn sheuynge here dysese to man."[21] This imagined female reading community—one

---

[17] As Burnley points out, there is a relationship between language and perception specifically associated with these three female roles: "The triplet *maiden, wife, widow,* which is a frequent collocation in the works of Chaucer and Gower, became a collocational set from frequent repetition in discourse reflecting contemporary Christian perceptions of the role of women" ("Lexis and Semantics," p. 452).

[18] This interest is also apparent in the theme of *The Wife of Bath's Tale.* The question of what "wommen moost desiren" (III.905) requires an answer that is true for all women; in other words, the knight must discover something that is common among women as a gender. This is similar to the conceptual problem explored through the word "womanhood."

[19] Burnley goes on to note: "The same situation may, however, arise more slowly as the product of cultural evolution, and in either case, if the deficit occurs in some highly structured area of the lexis, it is often referred to as a 'lexical gap' " ("Lexis and Semantics," p. 489).

[20] "Addressing and Positioning the Audience," in Jocelyn Wogan-Browne, Nicholas Watson, Andrew Taylor, and Ruth Evans, eds., *The Idea of the Vernacular: An Anthology of Middle English Literary Theory, 1280–1520* (University Park: The Pennsylvania State University Press, 1999), pp. 121–22.

[21] "The Knowing of Woman's Kind in Childing: Translator's Prologue," in *Idea of the Vernacular*, p. 158.

that can circumvent male involvement—necessitates a vernacular text. Chaucer did not have the same interest in an ideal, exclusively female community. Nevertheless, as a brief examination of *The Man of Law's Tale* will demonstrate, he did use *womanhood* to designate a spiritual purchase on social life that was specifically female and specifically vernacular. *The Man of Law's Tale* contains the single instance of another of Chaucer's inventions, *femininity*. This word is broadly similar to *womanhood* but of French and Latin extraction, and Chaucer's single usage offers very negative connotations. The Man of Law apostrophizes the Sultan's mother, Constance's first evil mother-in-law: "O serpent under femynynytee, / Lik to the serpent depe in helle ybounde!" (360–61). By contrast, Constance will address Mary, the Virgin Mother, as "thow glorie of wommanhede" and ask her to have pity on her son (851). The quality of mercy or pity would come to be associated with womanhood (a facet drawn out in *The Knight's Tale*), as would motherhood and beauty (important features for Griselda in *The Clerk's Tale*). All of these qualities are present in this scene. However, what is most significant about this association of the Virgin with womanhood is the word's secular origins. Unlike several similar terms—including *manhood*, *fatherhood*, and *motherhood*—*womanhood* did not originate as an explicitly sacred term. By the time that Chaucer was writing, *manhood* had been in recorded use for about two hundred years. Its earliest uses seem to have been theological: it described the humanity of Christ, as opposed to the *godhood* or *godhead*.[22] *Motherhood* and *fatherhood* came into use later, originating in the fourteenth century (although neither of these occurs in Chaucer's work).[23] In both cases, the earliest uses of the terms were religious: *fatherhood* described God's relationship to man or the relationship of male religious authority figures to those for whom they were responsible, while *motherhood* applied only to descriptions of Mary. In short, medieval writers initially imagined both *motherhood* and *fatherhood* as spiritual conditions involving a spiritual connection. More secular uses of *motherhood* (for example, uses that involve human women) appear either contemporaneously with or after Chaucer.[24] In this linguistic context, *womanhood* is unusual because Chaucer conceived it as a human

---

[22] "Manhede," *MED* (*MEC*).

[23] "Moderhede" and "faderhod," *MED* (*MEC*).

[24] Gower, for instance, uses the term in his *Confessio Amantis*; see 2.1073 and 5.5893 in G. C. Macaulay, ed., *The English Works of John Gower*, 2 vols. (1901; London: Oxford University Press, 1957).

condition that, while it might include spiritual virtues, was not overtly sacred. Its connection to Mary, the paragon of womanhood, is based on her human nature and characteristics.

As a term mediating between the secular and the sacred, *womanhood*'s appearance in *The Clerk's Tale* may draw on two contemporary, if divergent, versions of female sanctity: the maternal martyr and the virgin saint. Barbara Newman has identified the "hagiographic ideal [of] the maternal martyr" as an important hagiographical tradition.[25] This motif was popular in the thirteenth and fourteenth centuries and used child-sacrifice plots as a strategy by which mothers could become saints. A woman who gave up her children "no longer did so to attain a virile or gender-neutral state of equality with men. By a peculiar paradox, it was precisely this renunciation of her children that set a holy seal on her motherhood, reconciling it as far as possible with the ideal of sexless, sacrificial maternity embodied in the Virgin."[26] Griselda does not become a saint, but she does achieve this superior form of motherhood by sacrificing her children; then, by relinquishing her husband, she achieves a similarly superior kind of wifehood. What is ultimately validated in both cases, however, is her womanhood: it is the ground on which these priorities play out (wifehood over motherhood), and it remains when these other roles have been stripped away. Newman compares the maternal martyrs of hagiography to the "cruel mothers" of romance (among whom she numbers Griselda) and argues that the rising popularity of child-sacrifice plots in the later fourteenth century "seems to be correlated with a shift toward the alternative consensual model of marriage . . . [in which] the indissoluble loyalty of the wedded pair . . . takes precedence over their fertility."[27] If Newman is right, then this change could have provided another impetus for Chaucer's interest in womanhood.[28]

[25] Barbara Newman, *From Virile Woman to WomanChrist: Studies in Medieval Religion and Literature* (1995; Philadelphia: University of Pennsylvania Press, 1997), p. 93.

[26] Ibid., p. 84.

[27] Ibid., p. 97.

[28] Nor should we overlook the influence of the economic. After the Black Death, employment opportunities for women expanded as the labor force decreased and women gained greater financial independence and had the option of delaying or forgoing marriage. As economic recession set in, a backlash occurred and women were excluded from occupations in order to protect men's opportunities. Ideas about women, about the kind of work that was appropriate for them to do, and about when and whether they should marry underwent a serious expansion and subsequent restriction within a relatively short span of time. Economic change created social change, affecting marriage customs, and this in turn affected other identities for women that were dependent upon their marital status. Jeremy Goldberg posits this as a three-stage process; see P. J. P. Goldberg,

We can illustrate the richness Chaucer found in the notion of woman-hood by briefly comparing Griselda and her mixed spirituality with Ce-celia, a virgin saint and his one authentic hagiographic protagonist. Noting that "virgin martyr legends of the fourteenth century focus on conflict and emphasize the saint's antisocial behavior," Karen Winstead goes on to argue that such legends "distanced the saints from the rank-and-file faithful by emphasizing their miraculous powers, their virginity, and their contempt for the institutions of marriage, family, and state."[29] As the author of *The Second Nun's Tale*, Chaucer actively participated in this trend.[30] He presents Cecilia not as a passive sufferer but as a power-ful figure who controls and changes her circumstances. However, even here he also demonstrates his interest in Cecilia as a woman. Rephrasing his sources, he makes Almachius's first question to her, "What maner womman artow?" (424). The sources make the question more simply about Cecilia's condition,[31] and Chaucer allows her answer to retain that simpler focus: she answers by identifying her class status as a woman. Still, the question itself points to a deeper concern with the nature of women and how they can behave. What kind of woman acts as Cecilia does and how are her actions womanly?

As the author of *The Clerk's Tale*, Chaucer appears less interested in the hagiographic trend described by Winstead. Instead, he seems to want to determine the relationship between these aggressive female saints and other narrative characterizations of women. Griselda's charac-ter (submissive but powerful) and her situation (suffering followed by

---

Women, Work, and Life Cycle: Women in York and Yorkshire, c. 1300–1520 (Oxford: Claren-don Press, 1992), pp. 336–37. Judith Bennett traces the economic opportunities for women in brewing in *Ale, Beer, and Brewsters in England: Women's Work in a Changing World, 1300–1600* (New York: Oxford University Press, 1996) and concludes that they were sharply limited. However, these two theses are not incompatible; it is likely that women were hampered by their lack of capital even under Goldberg's model. Bennett's example of brewing was affected by social changes (the move to beer from ale) and technological advances (equipment that women could not afford); these reasons are specific to that occupation and caution should be used in generalizing from this ex-ample.

[29] Karen A. Winstead, ed. and trans., *Chaste Passions: Medieval English Virgin Martyr Legends* (Ithaca: Cornell University Press, 2000), p. 4, and *Virgin Martyrs: Legends of Sainthood in Late Medieval England* (Ithaca: Cornell University Press, 1997), p. 14.

[30] Winstead, *Virgin Martyrs*, esp. pp. 83 and 85.

[31] "Cujus condicionis es?" in the *Legenda Aurea* and "Cuius conditionis es?" in *In Festo Sancte Cecilie Virginis et Martyris* in Sherry L. Reames, ed., *"The Second Nun's Prologue and Tale," Sources and Analogues of the Canterbury Tales*, ed. Robert M. Correale and Mary Hamel, vol. 1 (Cambridge: D. S. Brewer, 2002), pp. 515 and 523. Chaucer amends both the question and the answer to include "woman."

triumph) provide a basis for this investigation. Some critics have read Griselda as the antithesis of the Wife of Bath and an attempt at rehabilitating antifeminist ideas.[32] I would argue instead that Chaucer is exploring the antifeminist archetype to see whether some of its elements could be productively recuperated. He experiments with the related unruly female saint figure by combining some of its characteristics with the virtuous feminine model, which Griselda often represented and was used to exemplify in conduct books.[33] Can a woman be both powerful and virtuous, both articulate and submissive? If Cecilia and the Wife of Bath are near one end of the spectrum of womanhood and Constance and the Virgin Mary are at the other, is there a middle ground? In other words, what do you get when you mix Jankyn's *Book of Wikked Wyves* with *Le Ménagier de Paris*?

Using the Griselda story to explore these questions was a departure from its literary origins and from other contemporary versions. Griselda is a twofold exemplar, modeling for wives as well as Christians, but no other writer exploited this status to consider the divergent representations of women in courtly and religious texts. Most writers who used the exemplum acknowledged its dual significance, but the Clerk's multiple morals amplify this divided tradition rather than attempting to reconcile it. At the conclusion of the tale, he tells us that the story is "nat for . . . wyves" but for "every wight" (1142, 1145); in the envoy, he reworks his advice for "noble wyves" and "archewyves" (1183, 1195; the latter term is another invention of Chaucer's). Some scholars have read the Clerk as hedging between Chaucer's sources: Petrarch's version, which asserts the universal moral of the exemplum, and the anonymous French prose translation *Le Livre Griseldis*, which directs its message toward "des femmes mariees."[34] Such interpretations assume that the broader

---

[32] For example, Morse observes that Chaucer was "the first to set her [Griselda] against the antifeminist type of woman, perhaps in the translation itself, certainly in the responses he invents to the tale at its end" ("The Exemplary Griselda," p. 55).

[33] In her recent book, Susan Crane observes that "Griselda's imagined performance of marriage articulates social understandings of wifehood" and that "Chaucer's version sharply interrogates women's place in marriage. Chaucer took that cue from the French versions of the tale, which are particularly concerned to model conduct for women." Crane, *The Performance of Self: Ritual, Clothing, and Identity During the Hundred Years War* (Philadelphia: University of Pennsylvania Press, 2002), p. 29. I agree, but would add that Chaucer also takes his cue from contemporary hagiography, from which the tale draws.

[34] See the preface of *Le Livre Griseldis* in J. Burke Severs, *The Literary Relationships of Chaucer's Clerkes Tale* (New Haven: Yale University Press, 1942; Hamden, Conn.: Archon Books, 1972), p. 255, and in Amy W. Goodwin and Thomas J. Farrell, eds., *"The Clerk's Tale," Sources and Analogues* I, p. 141.

Petrarchan moral is unusual. But this view is too narrow. It is true that like *Le Livre Griseldis*, Boccaccio's *Decameron*, Philippe de Mézières's *Livre de la Vertue du Sacrement de Mariage*, *Le Ménagier de Paris*, and the play *Estoire de Griseldis en rimes et par personages* (based on de Mézières's *Livre*) all seem to stress the specifically female nature of Griselda's virtue, and, indeed, that the French versions explicitly address wives.[35] Nevertheless, each of these fourteenth-century versions also acknowledges Griselda as a human exemplar, as well as a womanly one. Even Petrarch himself describes her virtue not as inimitable but as capable of being imitated only with difficulty ("vix imitabilis") by women and exhorts his readers to emulate what he specifies as her feminine or womanly constancy ("femine constanciam").[36]

Thus, Griselda's identity as a woman is a significant feature of every medieval version of the tale.[37] However, by introducing the concept of womanhood, Chaucer makes this feature a focus of investigation. The adaptation of the story in different genres (conduct book, drama, religious exemplum, etc.) and languages (literary Latin as well as various vernaculars) suggests its potential for this kind of use. As Judith Bronfman points out in her history of the Griselda story, "In less than 50 years, Griselda had appeared in virtually all the dominant literary genres of the [fourteenth] century: she had been in a prose cycle tale, an independent prose tale, an epistolary tale, an exemplary tale, a drama, a

[35] For the history of the tale, see Judith Bronfman, *Chaucer's "Clerk's Tale": The Griselda Story Received, Rewritten, Illustrated* (New York: Garland, 1994); Farrell and Goodwin, *"The Clerk's Tale"*; Dudley David Griffith, *The Origin of the Griselda Story* (Seattle: University of Washington Press, 1931); and Severs, *Literary Relationships*.

[36] Petrarch, *Epistola*, in Severs, *Literary Relationships*, p. 288; for an alternate version, see Farrell, *"The Clerk's Tale,"* p. 129 and 26n. In the *Decameron*, the story is addressed to women but has a mixed audience and is on the topic of governance; Mézières follows Petrarch in offering Griselda as a female and human model; *Le Ménagier* presents the story in a conduct book for a young wife, but the writer asks his wife not to take it as an example for herself (Severs, *Literary Relationships*, p. 22); the play is written "in order that people can use [it] as a mirror, and in order that those ladies who are visited by adversity can bear it with patience" (Brownlee p. 876; see full reference below). Note that all the French versions rely (directly or indirectly) on Petrarch rather than on Boccaccio. For a discussion of the differences between some of these versions, see Kevin Brownlee, "Commentary and the Rhetoric of Exemplarity: Griseldis in Petrarch, Philippe de Mézières, and the *Estoire*," *SAQ* 91 (Fall 1992).

[37] This is particularly interesting because one possible antecedent of the tale, the Cupid and Psyche group of folktales, could involve human protagonists of either sex or gender. However, this proposed precursor (Griffith's) is no longer widely accepted; William E. Bettridge and Francis L. Utley suggest "The Patience of a Princess" as an antecedent, which does depend on a female protagonist. Bettridge and Utley, "New Light on the Origin of the Griselda Story," *TSLL* 13:2 (1971): 153–208.

poetry cycle tale, an independent poem."[38] The Griselda story was adaptable for all of these genres by all of these authors for the same reasons that it was appropriate for Chaucer's examination of womanhood: it provided the basis for multiple interpretations, it was relevant to ideas about and representations of medieval women, and, most significantly, Griselda herself was a nexus of power and submission. As the suffering heroine, Griselda could be cast as exercising a female form of power or enduring in the face of capricious male authority.[39] She could be the submissive, virtuous, and lovely ideal of courtly poetry or the unpredictable and independent saint of contemporary hagiography. The nature of the story and its main character lent themselves to an exploration of what otherwise seemed to be irreconcilable representations of women; Chaucer's addition of *womanhood* to the story introduced the possibility that these representations were not irreconcilable but instead could be combined through the new abstraction. *Womanhood* designated a concept that could mediate between these conflicting roles and represented femaleness as a comprehensive spiritual quality.

At First Sight

Griselda is an unlikely paragon of feminine behavior. She transgresses or exceeds the major categories in narrative and social ideals of medieval femininity: maidenhood, wifehood, motherhood, and widowhood. How could a model maiden mortgage her virginity against an upwardly mobile future, presenting it as her dowry in compensation for her peasant status? How could a model mother agree to her children's murders? And how could a model wife be "widowed" not by her husband's death but by his replacement of her with a younger, prettier, and nobler version of herself? Chaucer mobilizes these paradoxes in order to investigate the ideas of womanliness underlying them. The word "wommanhede" first occurs with Walter's first sight of Griselda and it contravenes an important poetic convention (232–41):

> Upon Grisilde, this povre creature,
> Ful ofte sithe this markys sette his ye

[38] Bronfman, *Chaucer's "Clerk's Tale,"* p. 17.

[39] See, for example, Mann: "the most obvious testimony to Griselda's strength is the tale's ending. . . . For it is not Griselda who gives way under the pressures of her trial, but Walter. . . . [T]he story does not simply illustrate the virtue of patience; it shows that patience *conquers*" (*Feminizing Chaucer*, p. 119).

> As he on huntyng rood paraventure;
> And whan it fil that he myghte hire espye,
> He noght with wantown lookyng of folye
> His eyen caste on hire, but in sad wyse
> Upon hir chiere he wolde hym ofte avyse,
>
> Commendynge in his herte hir wommanhede,
> And eek hir vertu, passynge any wight
> Of so yong age, as wel in chiere as dede.

This passage actually rewrites one of the most celebrated *topoi* in medieval literature: the first sight of the beloved. In most first sightings, the lover is struck powerfully by the woman's image and wounded by love. When Dante first sees Beatrice in *La Vita Nuova*, he describes her appearance and then its effect on him: "At that moment I say truly that the spirit of life, which dwells in the most secret chamber of the heart, began to tremble so strongly that it appeared terrifying in its smallest veins; and trembling it said these words: 'Behold a god more powerful than I, who comes to rule over me.'"[40] Petrarch describes the onset of his love for Laura as being "taken," and explains, "I did not defend myself against it, / for your lovely eyes, Lady, bound me."[41] In Boccaccio's *Teseida*, Palemone sees in Emilia's eyes the god of love, fitting an arrow to his bow.[42] In *Troilus and Criseyde*, Chaucer offers his magisterial version of the *topos*. Troilus has "scorned hem that Loves peynes dryen" but "sodeynly hym thoughte he felte dyen, / Right with hire look, the spirit in his herte" (I, 303 and 306–7). When he first sets eyes on Criseyde, his heart speeds up and he appreciates her appearance, including her "wommanhod" (I, 283). In this scene from the *Troilus*, Chaucer uses "wommanhod" in purely erotic terms, associating it with her "lymes" and "the pure wise of hire mevynge" (I, 282 and 285); in *The Clerk's Tale* scene, Chaucer makes "wommanhede" the pivotal term in his an-

---

[40] Dante, *La Vita Nuova*, ed. and trans. Dino S. Cervigni and Edward Vasta (Notre Dame: University of Notre Dame Press, 1995), pp. 46–47: "In quello punto dico veracemente che lo spirito de la vita, lo quale dimora ne la secretissima camera de lo cuore, cominciò a tremare sì fortemente, che apparia ne li menimi polsi orribilmente; e tremando disse queste parole: 'Ecce deus fortior me, qui veniens dominabitur michi.'"

[41] Robert M. Durling, ed. and trans., *Petrarch's Lyric Poems: The Rime sparse and Other Lyrics* (Cambridge, Mass.: Harvard University Press, 1976), pp. 38–39: "i' fui preso, et non me ne guardai, / ché I be' vostr' occhi, Donna, mi legaro."

[42] N. R. Havely, *Chaucer's Boccaccio: Sources for Troilus and the Knight's and Franklin's Tales: Translations from the Filostrato, Teseida, and Filocolo* (Cambridge: D. S. Brewer, 1980), p. 113.

nexation of the hagiographic to the erotic. Walter does commend Griselda "in his herte" and, like many objects of courtly love, Griselda is gazed upon but does not respond or appear aware of her effect. There is no mention of love, however. The encounter should be an erotic connection; instead, Walter is struck by her sanctity. He looks "upon hir chiere," but there is no description of her beauty or even her physical appearance beyond the mention of her womanhood. The attraction is about how Griselda looks—since Walter has no other information—but not in the expected way.

The emphasis is on Griselda's "wommanhede, / And eek hir vertu." The Clerk has already enumerated the unseen virtues that he associates with Griselda's womanhood here; the signal virtue is submission, which is characteristic of womanhood. Her first virtuous quality is that "no likerous lust was thurgh hire herte yronne" (214). This establishes that sensual desire does not motivate her any more than it purportedly does Walter's notice of her. Griselda also drinks little, knows no idleness, and exhibits "rype and sad corage" (220). Her exemplary respect and care for her father, however, overshadow her other virtues. The Clerk explains, "in greet reverence and charitee / Hir olde povre fader fostred shee" (221–22). He reiterates the point more strongly later: "And ay she kepte hir fadres lyf on-lofte / With everich obeisaunce and diligence / That child may doon to fadres reverence" (229–31). In other words, Griselda sustains her father's very existence through her marvelous reverence and obedience to his will. The people also notice this virtue in Griselda: "And wondred hem in how honest manere / And tentifly she kepte hir fader deere" (333–34). These virtues, involving submission to male authority, are specific to womanhood. Patience, the virtue of Griselda's that most readings emphasize, is a form of this chief virtue of womanhood, although critics have not directly connected the two.[43]

Chaucer refigures this scene by making Walter's attraction to Griselda an attraction to her womanhood. Chaucer clearly links "wommanhede" with Griselda's physical appearance, indicating that the condition is at least partially visible in a woman's body. The implied connection builds on one made some lines earlier between virtue and physical beauty. Griselda is "fair ynogh to sighte" (209) while not a remarkable beauty until her virtue is taken into account: "But for to

---

[43] See esp. Morse, "Exemplary Griselda."

speke of vertuous beautee, / Thanne was she oon the faireste under sonne" (211–12). Although the relationship is largely metaphorical, these lines establish an association between beauty and virtue that prepares the way for the hint that Griselda's womanhood manifests in her body and catches Walter's eye. Walter's reaction to Griselda is unusual no less by the standards of his established personality than by the tradition of first meeting scenes. The physical nature of her womanhood has attracted Walter's attention but not "with wantown lookyng of folye." Instead, she is the object of his "sad" admiration. This seems out of character for the marquis since one of the first things we learn about him is that "on his lust present was al his thoght" (80). His passion for hunting demonstrates this temperament and he is engaging in that very activity when he sees Griselda. If he has noticed this peasant girl for ostensibly virtuous reasons, his fascination would seem an exception to his general preoccupation with his own desire.

Chaucer's version of this scene amplifies a more implicit feature of Boccaccio's original treatment that Petrarch definitively eliminated. In the *Decameron*, Gualtieri finds Griselda "very beautiful" and thinks "a life with her would have much to commend it."[44] He concludes the marriage contract and then gives a speech to his followers, reiterating that he is marrying not because he wants to but because they have requested that he do so; he explains, without identifying Griselda, that he has "found a girl after my own heart" and plans to marry her.[45] Petrarch's account omits this second speech, as do *Le Livre Griseldis* and *The Clerk's Tale*. More crucially, Petrarch also anticipates the scene with the comment that "a mature, manly spirit lay hidden in her virginal breast" and explains the virtue that Walter sees in her as "excellent beyond her age and gender."[46] In Boccaccio, Gualtieri realizes he must marry, remembers the pretty peasant girl he has noticed, and decides they would have a good marriage. In Petrarch and those texts derived

---

[44] Giovanni Boccaccio, *The Decameron*, trans. G. H. McWilliam (New York: Penguin, 1972), p. 785. "[E] parendogli bella assai, estimò che con costei dovesse potere aver vita assai consolata." Giovanni Boccaccio, *Il Decamerone*, ed. Angelo Ottolini (Milan: Ulrico Hoepli, [1948]), p. 665. The *Decameron* is now being more seriously considered as an influence, if not a direct source, for Chaucer's *Clerk's Tale*. See Helen Cooper, "The Frame," *Sources & Analogues* I.

[45] McWilliam, *Decameron*, p. 785. "Io ho trovata una giovane secondo il cuor mio, assai presso di qui." Ottolini, *Il Decamerone*, p. 666.

[46] Petrarch, *Epistola*, in Farrell and Goodwin, "*The Clerk's Tale*," pp. 114–15: "virilis senilisque animus virgineo latebat in pectore" and "virtutem eximiam supra sexum supraque etatem."

from him, Walter sees Griselda and, knowing that he needs a wife, makes a practical choice to marry her based on her virtue, which proceeds from her mature, virile spirit. Chaucer's revision makes Griselda a figure of womanhood, both beautiful peasant, as in Boccaccio, and virtuous exemplar, as in Petrarch. Seeing Griselda as an object of love or a notably beautiful woman places her within the particular tradition of female representation associated with romance and courtly poetry. Depicting her as an embodiment of virtue locates her in a different tradition of saints' lives and exempla. In *The Clerk's Tale*, Griselda is both beautiful and virtuous, but the focus of Walter's desire will become her womanhood. By exploiting the peculiar nature of the first sight scene and shifting the focus to Griselda's womanhood, Chaucer opens a space between narrative traditions.

From Maid to Wife: Womanhood as Translation

Chaucer's exploration of the concept in the rest of the tale is no less narrative. On the one hand, Griselda's exemplarity is all excess, ambiguity, and paradox. On the other hand, Chaucer's exposition of this narrative continually returns to the political realities of her gender and class, but only through the refractive fictions of her relation to Walter. The trials of Griselda's womanhood are generally taken to begin with the birth of her first child. In fact, they begin with the marriage contract that sets the terms for her wifehood and motherhood. Although apparently an agreement between the couple to marry, the contract does not focus on whether Griselda will be Walter's wife but on how she will perform that role. This is her first trial and, by engaging in an unusual kind of negotiation, Griselda gives initial proof of her womanhood. Most critical interpretations of the contract focus on the promise of submission that Walter requires; if he is concerned with safeguarding his freedom, then it seems logical for him to seek verbal assurance from Griselda on that issue. He asks her to be "redy . . . to al my lust" (351–52), echoing the narrator's description of Walter's concern with "his lust present" (80). Walter makes it clear that he addresses Griselda not to seek her assent to the marriage—"As I suppose, ye wol that it so be," he says confidently (347), having already set the date and ordered clothes and jewels made for her (253–60)—but to present his "demandes" regarding her behavior (348). The question is not whether Griselda will consent to marriage; it is about the additional terms on which Walter predicates *his* agreement to marry.

The marriage agreement begins as an exchange between men, father and prospective husband. Walter speaks to Janicula, asking "if that thou wolt unto that purpos drawe, / To take me as for thy sone-in-lawe" (314–15). Janicula replies, "I wol no thyng, ye be my lord so deere; / Right as yow lust, governeth this mateere" (321–22). Walter's superior social status and his power over Janicula complicate their relationship; Walter is in a position to dictate the terms of the marriage agreement. Still, the agreement is contractual and couched in terms of negotiation: they have a "collacioun" and "tretys" (325, 331). A structure now exists for Griselda to move from being under her father's authority to Walter's. When this happens, Walter can reasonably expect that Griselda will accord him an obedience and reverence similar to that she showed her father.

When Walter approaches Griselda, he makes it clear that an agreement exists between himself and Janicula to which they expect her to accede: "It liketh to youre fader and to me / That I yow wedde" (345–46). Without pausing to hear Griselda's response, Walter gives the provisions of the agreement (351–57):

> I seye this: be ye redy with good herte
> To al my lust, and that I frely may,
> As me best thynketh, do yow laughe or smerte,
> And nevere ye to grucche it, nyght ne day?
> And eek when I sey 'ye,' ne sey nat 'nay,'
> Neither by word ne frownyng contenance?
> Swere this, and heere I swere oure alliance.

Although Walter presents these provisions as questions, they are clearly the only terms under which he is prepared to conclude the marriage. An impressive amount of patriarchal authority backs them: Janicula's authority as Griselda's father and Walter's authority both as her prospective husband and as the marquis who rules father and daughter as his subjects. Under these circumstances, a refusal is virtually impossible, especially from a woman whose submission to male authority has already been established. The conditions Walter offers Griselda are the first test to which he subjects her, preceding the more frequently recognized trials during the marriage. In all of these tests, her womanhood is at issue; she must agree to (and later demonstrate) its characteristic virtue: submission.[47]

Although the contract is a set of requirements, it is put into effect only by Griselda's consent. Walter constructs a model of behavior that she must agree to emulate (or not); however, this model was predetermined. Before seeing Griselda, the Clerk tells us, Walter sat in his "paleys honurable" and "shoop his mariage," considering the kind of wedded life he desired and, presumably, how to achieve it (197–98). Walter's complete ideal is not yet clear to the audience, but Griselda goes beyond the question of consent by reshaping the model he has proposed. Her reaction to his offer highlights the importance of her role in the contract by refiguring the terms of the deal: her promise to submit exceeds his request. She swears, "nevere willyngly, / In werk ne thoght, I nyl yow disobeye" (362–63). The remarkable pledge of obedience in thought as well as deed is a testament to her womanhood. Even by raising the demands on herself, Griselda exercises a certain degree of control in the exchange, and this, too, is a function of her womanhood. Chaucer uses Griselda's character to explore the contradictions of womanly behavior: she is articulate and exercises a kind of feminine power while not only retaining but even heightening her virtuous submission.

After Walter and Griselda agree to marry, but before he gives her the ring, she is "translated." This "translation" renders her transformation from maiden to wife and potential mother in visible and material terms; although it has been a focus of several contemporary studies, most consider the linguistic or literal significance of the phrase rather than the means by which that change is completed.[48] The translation must later be undone (as far as possible) when Walter pretends to dissolve the marriage. As Griselda returns Walter's gifts of clothing and ornaments—the material of her translation—she also describes the dowry gifts she gave, including her "maydenhede" (836, 866). Along with its indispensable complements, sexual availability and submission, Griselda's maidenhead forms an important part of her womanhood, which

---

[47] Walter's first sight of Griselda seemed to validate her "wommanhede," since it was the basis of his choice. However, he insists on excessive submission from her as a condition of their marriage, which suggests that her behavior may be in doubt.

[48] For instance, Dinshaw grounds her entire reading in the trope of *translatio,* even titling the relevant chapter "Griselda Translated" (*Sexual Poetics*, chap. 5). Wallace also makes important use of the trope in his reading of the tale (*Chaucerian Polity*, chap. 10). Crane is an exception; in *The Performance of Self*, she investigates Griselda's clothing as a material expression of identity and its role in the ritual of marriage (pp. 29–37).

serves as a priceless (and irrecoverable) counter-gift in the exchange with Walter.

After she agrees to the marriage terms, Walter presents Griselda to the crowd outside and a group of women "dispoillen hire right theere" (374); they comb her hair, dress her in new clothes, and adorn her with ornaments. The improvement is dramatic: "Unnethe the peple hir knew for hire fairnesse / Whan she translated was in swich richesse" (384–85). She is "another creature" (406). It is only after Walter sees that the translation was successful that he "hire spoused with a ryng" (386). And it is only now that Griselda is loved as she was not upon first sight; everyone "hire lovede that looked on hir face" (413). This change of clothes renders Griselda's womanhood visible to all, whereas before only Walter's keen eye discerned it. His ability to identify this quality in a lower-class maiden distinguishes him from his people, who "have no greet insight / In vertu" (242–43). It is within Walter's power not only to recognize Griselda's womanhood but also to make it apparent to his people through her translation. At the same time, this change of clothes signifies a change in her womanhood. Griselda's finery renders her sexuality visible, transforming her from the object of Walter's admiration to the legitimate object of his sexual desire. In Italy, the setting for the tale, a husband's gift of clothing to his wife in the Middle Ages functioned as "proof of the carnal consummation of the marriage," a sign that the wife was honoring the conjugal debt.[49] Similarly, Griselda's change of clothes signifies simultaneously her change of social status and her new sexual availability to Walter. This in turn is an expression of her womanhood, a state in which the sexual act plays such a large role.

The change of clothes also transforms Griselda from a maiden into a wife and potential mother, two important states of womanhood. Christiane Klapisch-Zuber explains that gifts of clothing were customary in medieval Italy: "During the days or months preceding the marriage and within the year following, the husband provided what was in effect a wardrobe for his wife, a kind of countertrousseau." These gifts were "indispensable symbolic agents in the integration of the wife into another household and another lineage."[50] Susan Crane reads clothing as

---

[49] Christiane Klapisch-Zuber, "The Griselda Complex: Dowry and Marriage Gifts in the Quattrocento," *Women, Family, and Ritual in Renaissance Italy*, trans. Lydia Cochrane (Chicago: University of Chicago Press, 1985), p. 245. Consciously or not, Chaucer's emphasis on clothing and dowry echoes some of the issues in medieval Italian wedding customs, which are appropriate to the story's Italian setting and provenance.

[50] Ibid., pp. 219 and 224.

an important signifier in literary terms as well, arguing that Griselda's "reclothing accomplishes her absorption into Walter's household and her subordination to him in marriage."[51] Walter's translation of Griselda is an acceptance of her into his household and, perhaps most important, as the mother of his lineage. Because she is his wife, her appearance functions as a symbol of his wealth and power. He effects the transformation in public so that his people will recognize Griselda as the legitimate mother of his heirs. Making good on the earlier suggestion that womanhood is physical and visible, Griselda's body is the site where her incompatible roles—peasant and marchioness, maiden and wife—are reconciled.

Griselda's translation must be undone when the marriage dissolves. The clothing Walter provided—the mechanism of her metamorphosis—was a marriage gift that she now returns. Although the exchange of gifts originally seemed unequal, the reversal of the translation reveals that it was a mutual exchange involving somewhat unusual commodities. When Walter orders Griselda to return to her father's house, she catalogs both of their contributions: "To yow broghte I noght elles, out of drede, / But feith, and nakednesse, and maydenhede; / And heere agayn your clothyng I restoore, / And eek your weddyng ryng, for everemore" (865–68). Walter's gifts, clothing and a wedding ring, were visible and valuable in economic terms. Klapisch-Zuber identifies such gifts as a counterbalance to the wife's dowry in medieval Italian marriage customs.[52] But while Walter's gifts are fairly straightforward and typical, Griselda's are not. Because of her lower-class origins, she does not bring the customary cash dowry. She did not come to the marriage empty-handed, however; she brought her husband "feith, and nakednesse, and maydenhede." Klapisch-Zuber carefully notes, "An analysis of the dowry cannot be confined to its economic terms alone."[53] Walter cannot measure Griselda's dowry in economic terms, but her womanhood is undeniably valuable to him. She makes the connection between maidenhead and wifehood, saying that she will henceforth live as a widow: "For sith I yaf to yow my maydenhede, / And am youre trewe wyf, it is no drede, / God shilde swich a lordes wyf to take / Another man to housbonde or to make" (837–40). "Maydenhede" was the

---

[51] Crane goes on to argue that this reclothing "leaves visible a residual self that remains unincorporated" (*Performance of Self*, p. 33).

[52] Klapisch-Zuber, "Griselda Complex," pp. 218–24.

[53] Ibid., p. 224.

dowry she brought as a "trewe wyf" and, having given it, she cannot "take / Another man to housbonde". In Chaucer's usage, maidenhead is part of (though not synonymous with) womanhood, and Griselda's maidenhead is an important part of both her womanhood and the dowry she brings to Walter.

Griselda returns to the importance of her "maydenhede," pointing out that Walter cannot restore it to her as she has restored his dowry gifts. In its place, she requests a "smok" (883–88)

> in gerdon of my maydenhede,
> Which that I broghte, and noght agayn I bere,
> As voucheth sauf to yeve me, to my meede,
> But swich a smok as I was wont to were,
> That I therwith may wrye the wombe of here
> That was youre wyf.

Griselda asks for "a smok" like that she wore before her translation, conflating to some extent her "maydenhede" with her clothing. The smock is symbolic of her former sexual condition in addition to being a sign of her former social condition. Griselda also discloses the purpose behind her request; she wishes to "wrye the wombe of here / That was youre wyf." She associates the fine clothing with her role as a wife and with her womb, or ability to bear children, which we have already seen to be a critical element of womanhood. This second change of clothing is an attempt on Griselda's part to reclaim her former sexual status, at least partially, and she represents this attempt in sartorial terms.[54]

Womanhood is generally a virtuous condition of being, but within the system of gift and counter-gift that comprised marriage, Griselda's womanhood is also a valuable commodity. While the socioeconomic importance of the dowry is undeniable, Griselda brings the most critical elements to marriage in her sexuality and submission. These two related components of womanhood become Griselda's dowry. Her sexuality is made available to her husband through her submission. Marital intercourse is more than a site for the exercise of masculine authority; it justifies the existence of such authority. The sexual act, with its ramifications for noble lineage and inheritance, is perhaps the most important

---

[54] The undoing of the translation does not work; as she walks home, her father tries to cover her with her old coat: "But on hire body myghte he it nat brynge, / For rude was the clooth, and moore of age / By dayes fele than at hire mariage" (lines 915–17).

reason for a man to have authority over his wife. Submission to the husband ensured that a wife would render the conjugal debt, remain sexually faithful, and continue to bear and raise children in spite of the physical danger that such rigorous maternity represented in the Middle Ages. The ability to produce suitable or legitimate offspring can thus be seen as a defining feature of womanhood, important enough to the husband to justify murder in his mind, as the stories of several female martyrs attest. Sexual submission is also important synecdochically; if a wife did not submit to her husband sexually, her submission in other areas was irrelevant. Apart from practical considerations of heritability, sexual submission was significant symbolically to the husband and to others outside the marriage. Women were most valuable as the producers of heirs and motherhood was the most critical facet of womanhood. Other feminine virtues relate, directly or indirectly, to this vital role.

Womanhood on Trial

Walter tests Griselda's submission, the focus of her marriage promise and an important component of the womanhood that she brought as her dowry, by pretending to murder her children and take a new wife. These trials are the heart of *The Clerk's Tale* and the focus of the Griselda story in every medieval version; they have inspired a corresponding amount of scholarly interest (and bewilderment). Why does Walter test his wife and why, having begun, does he cease? Elaine Tuttle Hansen suggests that Walter tries Griselda because she demonstrates threatening masculine virtues by ruling well in her husband's absence.[55] Kathryn Lynch argues that Walter is trying to gain knowledge of Griselda empirically since he cannot completely trust his intuitive sense of her virtue.[56] Andrew Sprung, apparently unable to discern any viable motivation for the trials, claims that Griselda is simply a figure of male fantasy.[57] Each of these readings, however, oversimplifies Chaucer's depiction of either Walter or Griselda. Walter's testing is crucial to Griselda's model virtue; his extreme demands create the necessary environment for her to demonstrate convincingly the mediating power of womanhood, but through this demonstration she exceeds his ideal of womanhood as complete sub-

[55] Hansen, *Fictions of Gender*, chap. 7.
[56] Lynch, "Despoiling Griselda," passim.
[57] Sprung, "Coercion and Compliance," passim.

mission. Thus both Griselda and her husband contribute to her exemplarity.

The trials demonstrate Griselda's virtue by putting her womanhood doubly at stake. Walter is nervous about Griselda's ability to produce suitable and legitimate heirs (which, for him, means heirs that his people will accept), a major function of womanhood. Her lower-class origins give the lineage she mothers questionable status in his mind and he projects this anxiety onto his people, even though they evidence little concern on this point. This is a corollary, however, to Walter's concern about Griselda's suitability as a wife, specifically within the context of the marriage terms he has set. Because he designed those terms to ensure his own authority and freedom within the marriage, Griselda must display that chief virtue of noble womanhood, submission. The anxiety of his people over the lack of heirs motivated Walter's decision to wed, but his own anxiety over marriage as an institution ill-suited for a marquis focused on his present pleasure determined his choice of wife. As a result, it is critical that Griselda's womanhood be tested and proven in both these ways. Having commended her "wommanhede" at first sight, Walter ends the trials by proclaiming that he has tested Griselda "For no malice, ne for no crueltee, / But for t'assaye in thee thy wommanheede" (1074–75). These two moments frame the tale.

The close association of the trials with the children demonstrates their importance in the tests of Griselda's womanhood. Before the birth of their first child, the couple "in Goddes pees lyveth ful esily" (423) and Griselda "koude al the feet of wyfly hoomlinesse" (429). Her excellence extends to governance: "The commune profit koude she redresse. / Ther nas discord, rancour, ne hevynesse / In al that land that she ne koude apese" (431–33). Negotiation, mediation, and "juggementz of so greet equitee" are also within the realm of womanhood for Griselda (439). In this early phase of their marriage, Walter shows no inclination to test Griselda; in fact, he congratulates himself on choosing wisely (425–26). Before long, however, their daughter is born and this birth initiates Walter's desire to test his wife. Although the narrative does not present the two events in a causal relationship, their connection is evident in the action of the story: "Whan that this child had souked but a throwe, / This markys in his herte longeth so / To tempte his wyf" (450–52). The association between the birth of the child and the onset of the testing is also apparent in their close juxtaposition in the text. The daughter's birth occurs in the final stanza of the second section and the third section opens by referring to the child and then immediately describing Walter's wish to test Griselda.

The birth of a daughter is an important proof of Griselda's womanhood because it attests to her fertility and ability to bear children; that is, her ability to fulfill her responsibility as a wife. However, this proof is not completely satisfactory, as the reaction of the people reveals (445–48):

> Glad was this markys and the folk therfore,
> For though a mayde child coome al bifore,
> She may unto a knave child atteyne
> By liklihede, syn she nys nat bareyne.

The birth of a daughter is an encouraging sign that Griselda "nys nat bareyne" and the primary connotations of this passage are hopeful. However, for the first time in the tale, there is a hint that Griselda may be less than perfect: she has not yet proven that she can produce an heir to perpetuate the line. The Clerk's condemnation of Walter's testing as "nedelees" (455) follows this passage. The Clerk seems satisfied with Griselda's virtue, saying that Walter "hadde assayed hire ynogh bifore, / And foond hire evere good" (456–57). It is not, however, Griselda's goodness that is at issue but her womanhood and specifically her ability to provide an heir. Griselda herself seems to have internalized this perspective; she would "levere have born a knave child" (444). For Griselda, as well as Walter and his people, the birth of a daughter is a positive sign of her fertility but does not finally resolve the issue of the ruling lineage.

Up to this point, Griselda's lower-class origins have not been manifested in any negative way, but Walter may see the threat of this possibility in the birth of his daughter. The reason he offers for the first trial intimates this: "They [the people] seyn, to hem it is greet shame and wo / For to be subgetz and been in servage / To thee, that born art of a smal village" (481–83). He offers the daughter's birth as the explanation behind the complaints of his people and proposes her death as the only solution. Walter manufactures this excuse, with no apparent basis in reality. The fact that he chooses this fiction, when he need not have offered any explanation at all—when not providing an explanation might have better served to prove his dominance and authority—is notable and reflects his own anxiety over Griselda's womanhood and lower class.

Four years pass between the removal of the daughter and the birth of their second child, a son. Walter has given Griselda no other trials in this interval. But after the birth of this second child, his yearning to test her returns: "Whan it was two yeer old, and fro the brest / Departed of his norice, on a day / This markys caughte yet another lest / To tempte his wyf yet ofter, if he may" (617–20). Here again, the onset of a trial is closely associated with a child. In this case, it is not immediately after the child's birth but at another milestone in his early development, the day of his weaning, that Walter desires to test the mother. The birth of a son testifies to Griselda's womanhood and her ability to provide her husband with an heir. As such, it would seem sufficient to end the doubts inspired by the birth of a daughter. Walter does not stop the trials, however, indicating that this proof is inadequate. Griselda's womanhood has been proven because she has produced an heir, but, because of her lower-class origins, the suitability of this heir is still in question for Walter. Womanhood is not simply a question of fecundity; if the people do not accept the line mothered by Griselda, her function as a wife and a woman is unfulfilled. Walter articulates this concern in the justification he offers for the second trial, the apparent murder of their son (625–27, 631–34):

> My peple sikly berth oure mariage;
> And namely sith my sone yboren is,
> Now is it worse than evere in al oure age.
>
> . . . .
>
> Now sey they thus: 'Whan Walter is agon,
> Thanne shal the blood of Janicle succede
> And been oure lord, for oother have we noon.'
> Swiche wordes seith my peple, out of drede.

Again, Walter crafts the excuse without basis, but his choice of fictions is significant; although his people have the heir they wanted, he remains uneasy about the larger question of the children's acceptability. He has also constructed an excuse that would seem particularly plausible to Griselda. Her concerns closely resemble the fictional concerns of the people, as demonstrated by her sense of her own lower-class status and her desire for a "knave child."

After the sergeant takes the son, the Clerk interrupts the tale briefly to ask "of wommen" whether this is not enough: "What koude a sturdy housbonde moore devyse / To preeve hir wyfhod and hir stedefastnesse?" (698–99). The birth of her children verified Griselda's motherhood; their simulated murder has tested Griselda's "wyfhod" by requiring her to subjugate her motherly feelings to her wifely loyalty. In fact, her perfect submission does cause Walter a moment of doubt about her motherhood, and "if that he / Ne hadde soothly knowen therbifoore / That parfitly hir children loved she," he would have had grave suspicions (688–90). As the final test, the sham marriage will confirm Griselda's womanhood by demonstrating both the nobility of her children (and thus the viability of her motherhood) and her enduring devotion to serving her husband's "lust" (757, 962) even when she is no longer his wife (and thus the perfection of her wifehood).[58] The sham marriage planned by Walter requires the participation of his children. This choice is more than simply arbitrary or convenient in terms of plot. In addition to being another test of Griselda's submission and, by extension, womanhood, the sham marriage is a demonstration of Walter's control over his daughter and a test of her womanhood. This final piece of evidence—the daughter's womanhood—also proves Griselda's womanhood and thus brings the testing to an end.

Timing is as important a consideration for the sham marriage as it was in the two prior trials. Five years have passed since the second test and, once again, the interval between tests has passed peacefully.[59] Walter begins preparations "whan that his doghter twelve yeer was of age" (736). This is "the age at which a woman allegedly achieved the majority that supposedly corresponded to puberty and marriageability."[60] For practical reasons, Walter could not have carried out his plan until his daughter reached marriageable age. He might have pretended to marry someone else at any point, but he has waited until his daughter was of an age to play her part. The involvement of the daughter in the charade makes it a double test of Griselda (her motherhood and her wifehood) and a double test of womanhood (Griselda's and her daughter's).

[58] "Lust" is reiterated as the term for Walter's self-interested desires; Griselda is grieved to leave her husband but does so, "abidynge evere his lust and his plesance" (line 757), and when she returns to prepare for the new wife, Walter directs Griselda to array the chambers "in ordinaunce / After my lust" (lines 961–62).
[59] The son was two years old when he was taken away (line 617) and is seven when he returns (line 780).
[60] Dyan Elliott, *Spiritual Marriage: Sexual Abstinence in Medieval Wedlock* (Princeton: Princeton University Press, 1993), p. 220.

Walter's justification for the third test is the same as for the others: the fictitious complaints of his people about Griselda's lower-class background. He explains that he chose her based on his own desires, but that now he must consider what his people want (792–801):

> Certes, Grisilde, I hadde ynogh plesance
> To han yow to my wyf for youre goodnesse,
> As for youre trouthe and for youre obeisance,
> Noght for youre lynage, ne for youre richesse;
> But now knowe I in verray soothfastnesse
> That in greet lordshipe, if I wel avyse,
> Ther is greet servitute in sondry wise.
>
> I may nat doon as every plowman may.
> My peple me constreyneth for to take
> Another wyf, and crien day by day.

"Lynage" and "richesse," Walter implies, are what his people would prefer in a marchioness; in choosing Griselda for other reasons, he acted like a "plowman." He suggests that Griselda's class has tainted his own and perhaps endangered his position as ruler. The irony of course is that while Walter equates lower status with greater freedom, Griselda's lower class has not allowed her to act more freely; she has experienced "greet servitute" in both of the social classes that she has inhabited. While Walter is again inventing this excuse, it is true enough that his people have begun to talk about his marriage; rather than speaking against Griselda, however, "the sclaundre of his diffame / Made hem that they hym hatede therfore" (730–31).

The opinion of the people quickly changes when they see the proposed new wife, unaware that she is the daughter of Walter and Griselda. The daughter's submission to her father's plan gives initial evidence of her womanhood, but the people's reaction to her as the prospective wife of their marquis is the crucial validation. The concerns of the people led to the first marriage and were used by Walter to explain each of the tests; now the opinion of the people helps to end the trials even as it seems to undermine Griselda's position.[61] They admire the daughter at first sight (985–91):

---

[61] Morse sees the people not as a crucial part of Griselda's testing, as I argue, but as themselves subject to a similar test: "The testing of Griselda proves to be also the testing of the people, which shows the people less strong in their faith to Walter than Griselda is." Morse, "Griselda Reads Philippa de Coucy," in *Speaking Images: Essays in Honor of V. A. Kolve*, ed. R. F. Yeager and Charlotte C. Morse (Asheville, N.C.: Pegasus,

> And thanne at erst amonges hem they seye
> That Walter was no fool, thogh that hym leste
> To chaunge his wyf, for it was for the beste.
>
> For she is fairer, as they deemen alle,
> Than is Grisilde, and moore tendre of age,
> And fairer fruyt bitwene hem sholde falle,
> And moore plesant, for hire heigh lynage.

The people focus on the daughter's beauty and her potential motherhood. It is the daughter's perceived superior womanhood, in both those senses, that reconciles the people to Walter's ill treatment of his current wife and the murders of his children (for which they previously "hatede" him). Although this reversal leads to a lamentation on the people's inconstancy, it is not their fickleness that is important here but their perception of the daughter. Walter's anxiety over the suitability of the children borne by Griselda can be soothed only by his people's acceptance of them. Thus it is absolutely vital that the people recognize and confirm the nobility of the children. Their opinion is later substantiated when Walter marries off his daughter "richely," giving her "unto a lord, / oon of the worthieste / Of al Ytaille" (1130, 1131–32).

The people's reaction to the daughter includes the first explicit reference to the importance of motherhood. Walter did not mention it when he first saw Griselda or in the marriage contract and, although the people noted Griselda's "fairnesse" (384) after her translation, they did not remark on the "fruyt" that might result from that marriage. Within the narrative, this silence about Griselda's motherhood allows Walter to fabricate the reaction of his people to his children. It also heightens the dramatic effect of this scene: the people unconsciously affirm Griselda's motherhood in the act of disparaging it. Still, the people's desire to avoid a "straunge successour" inspired them to ask Walter to marry and continue his line and so the absence of any earlier mention of motherhood seems odd (138). Perhaps the passage of time has made them more anxious on this point, or perhaps Walter's rejection of the children has made his people question their suitability. Most notably, this absence

---

2001), pp. 352–53. Lynn Staley also argues that Chaucer places particular emphasis on the role of the people in his version of the tale. Staley, "Chaucer and the Postures of Sanctity," in *The Powers of the Holy: Religion, Politics, and Gender in Late Medieval Culture*, ed. David Aers and Lynn Staley (University Park: The Pennsylvania State University Press, 1996), pp. 233–57.

underscores the effectiveness of Walter's translation of Griselda and the effect of its undoing. The translation completely convinced the people, if not Walter himself, of Griselda's potential motherhood; the retranslation of her womanhood leaves her in an indeterminate space between maidenhood and widowhood, undercutting her motherhood. The crowd's reaction to the daughter hints that they did not anticipate such beauty and nobility from Griselda's offspring; the daughter herself is "fairer fruyt" than they expected.

The establishment of the daughter's womanhood is also partial evidence of Griselda's womanhood because it speaks to the suitability of the children she has produced. The crowd's recognition of the son as noble completes the proof of the mother's womanhood by legitimating him as an heir. The people credit Walter's good governance for bringing these noble children into his family: "Hir brother eek so fair was of visage / That hem to seen the peple hath caught plesaunce, / Commendynge now the markys governaunce" (992–94). The word "commendynge" recalls Walter's original sighting and valuation of Griselda and her virtues. The trials have vindicated Griselda's womanhood: she has demonstrated submission, the salient virtue of womanhood; given birth to two legitimate children, including an heir to perpetuate the line of the marquis; and established her wifehood by relinquishing it. Through the translation, its reversal, and its (forthcoming) reinstatement, her womanhood persists.

Once Griselda's womanhood has been proven, the trials can end. I have already noted that the text explicitly offers this justification for Walter's cruelty. Walter was drawn to Griselda because of her womanhood and then successfully tested it within their marriage through three trials, all associated with their children and her submission of them to his will. When Walter reveals the sham of the third trial and stops testing Griselda, he says to her (1065–75):

> This is thy doghter, which thou hast supposed
> To be my wyf; that oother feithfully
> Shal be myn heir, as I have ay disposed;
> Thou bare hym in thy body trewely . . .
> Taak hem agayn, for now maystow nat seye
> That thou hast lorn noon of thy children tweye.
>
> And folk that ootherweys han seyd of me,
> I warne hem wel that I have doon this deede

For no malice, ne for no crueltee,
But for t'assaye in thee thy wommanheede.

This passage openly identifies Walter's motivation for testing Griselda: "t'assaye in thee thy wommanheede."[62] Now that it has been proven, the roles of mother and wife that were stripped from her are restored. Walter identifies the son as "myn heir," accepting him as noble and suitable to carry on the line and stressing Griselda's role as mother of the heir. The explanation Chaucer offers is an interpolation; in his sources, Walter states, tautologically, that the trials were to test his wife.[63] Here he accompanies his justification with a less credible claim: he has not tried Griselda out of "malice" or "crueltee." The tale contradicts this, and the Clerk has bluntly condemned Walter's actions as "yvele" (460). His behavior, however, was necessary for two reasons. First, it is the malicious and cruel nature of his demands upon Griselda that prove his sovereignty in marriage. Second, his malice and cruelty are what allow Griselda to prove her womanhood completely and effectively.

Walter's concern that he might lose sovereignty through marriage has permeated the tale. In their initial request that he marry, his people

---

[62] Alcuin Blamires, the only other critic to have paid substantial attention to this phrase, reads the meaning of "wommanheede" in this scene differently:

> Womanhood remains unexplained here and seems at first sight peculiar. In conventional Middle English, a test of someone's manhode would signify a test of his courage. There was no broadly agreed complementary significance for wommanheede. However, from a question asked at 698–9, about what more a stern husband could do "to preeve hir wyfhod and hir stedefastnesse," it seems that in The Clerk's Tale Griselda's "wifehood" and her "steadfastness" are symbiotic: one might conjecture that her womanhood and her steadfastness are similarly meant to be symbiotic in this tale. That is to say, in "assaying" (investigating the quality of) Griselda's womanhood, Walter is investigating the degree of stabilitas in her, he is determining the level of unchangeability in her because this was the supreme criterion for assessing women in a culture obsessed with feminine "weakness."

Blamires, The Case for Women in Medieval Culture (Oxford: Oxford University Press, 1998), pp. 167–68. The question of Griselda's womanhood is broader, however; it is not simply about her stabilitas, but about her ability to combine different models of femininity while maintaining appropriate feminine virtues to an exemplary degree.

[63] "Let those who believed the opposite know me painstaking and testing, not impious. I have proved my wife rather than condemning her [Sciant qui contrarium crediderunt me curiosum atque experientem esse, non [impium]; probasse coniugem, non dampnasse] and "I did what I did only to test and try you [moy avoir fait ce que j'ay fait pour toy approuver et essaier tant seulement]" (Farrell and Goodwin, "The Clerk's Tale," pp. 128–29 and 164–65). See also Severs, Literary Relationships, pp. 286 and 287.

ask, "Boweth youre nekke under that blisful yok / Of soveraynetee, noght of servyse, / Which that men clepe spousaille or wedlok" (113–15). As a ruler whose mind is always on his own "lust," however, no "yok" is amenable to Walter. He responds to their petition by saying, "I me rejoysed of my liberte, / That seelde tyme is founde in mariage; / Ther I was free, I moot been in servage" (145–47). His choice of Griselda (when his people asked for a marchioness "born of the gentilleste and of the meeste / Of al this land" (131–32)), his unreasonable demands within the marriage contract, and his trials of her demonstrate that his "soveraynetee" remains intact. It is rather Griselda who is "bisy in servyse" (603) and "mooste servysable of alle" (979). Walter continues to explain his rationale for the trials by asserting that he took away the children "to kepe hem pryvely and stille, / Til I thy purpos knewe and al thy wille" (1077–78). In truth, however, the trials have taught him nothing about his wife's individual "purpos" and "wille" but instead have reassured him that she has none beyond what he imposes. Only tests excessive in their malice and cruelty could definitively establish—to Walter and his people—that he is not "in servage" but is instead served by the unusual marriage he has constructed.

Perversely, his cruelty also creates the environment necessary for Griselda to prove herself an exemplar of womanhood. Like the spouses themselves, the two qualities—cruelty and perfect womanliness—are interdependent: womanhood is most apparent (and possibly most meaningful) in the context of unreasonably demanding male authority, while only that kind of authority would require the type of exemplary womanhood Griselda exhibits. Walter's malice sets up in sharp contrast the conflicts and categories that she must mediate. The need to provide a male heir and specifically one that is suitable (a need played upon and exaggerated by Walter) heightens the ordinary demands of motherhood for Griselda as a former peasant. However, the demands of wifehood on her are also greater because of the promise of obedience that is the basis of her marriage, inspired by Walter's desire to preserve his sovereignty to the greatest degree. He pits her wifehood against her motherhood and raises the stakes of each. In addition, his malicious demands require excessive virtue to endure, which creates the impression of Griselda's patience as Job-like and saintly, bringing undertones of hagiography to the secular context of the tale. Enduring the cruel trials also requires great love, however, which Griselda also demonstrates. She refers to her love as she reiterates her excessive marriage pledge (and even ups the ante further) in response to the testing (857 and 973). This cultivates the sense of Griselda as a figure of romance; "Deth," she says, "may noght make no comparisoun / Unto youre love" (666–67). Hence Walter sets up the conflicts Griselda must mediate (between the social roles of wifehood and motherhood and the literary categories of hagiography and romance) and it is the "malice" and "crueltee" he denies that make the conflicts extreme enough to warrant and witness an extraordinary response. Walter stages the trials for his own ends but becomes, almost in spite of himself, a crucial participant in the construction of Griselda's exemplary womanhood.

Walter's revelation is followed by a third translation: Griselda is again stripped and reclothed, this time with a "clooth of gold" and a "coroune" (1117, 1118). Finally "she was honured as hire oghte" (1120). This honor, however, is due as much to her husband's agency as her own—both have contributed to this realization of her excellent womanhood. The moment Walter first admires Griselda's womanhood and the moment he ends the trials bracket the tale, providing answers to the puzzling questions of why Walter chooses Griselda and why, having chosen her, he tests her so excessively. However, the ideal of womanhood that Griselda ultimately displays—which exceeds Walter's predetermined model—marks a new conception of what is womanly.

This new conception is admittedly extreme: in order to pass Walter's tests, Griselda must prove herself to be possessed of a womanhood that becomes threatening through its endurance and ultimate triumph. The Clerk concludes the tale with several assurances that most (if not all) women would fail such tests. Womanhood may have the potential to combine these different ideals of womanhood, but most women would have less of the steadfast saint in their combination. In other words, Griselda's womanhood is so exemplary that it may mark the limit of the mediating power of womanhood. Chaucer employs a two-part strategy at the tale's conclusion to allay any discomfort that might be caused by this new conception: first, he draws on Petrarch to universalize Griselda's example and, second, he reminds the reader of more familiar images of powerful women as manipulative wives rather than secular saints.[64]

[64] These multiple endings of the tales have invited multiple interpretations. Many critics have discussed the envoy in response to Charles Muscatine's view of it as a comic strategy (*Chaucer and the French Tradition* [Berkeley and Los Angeles: University of California Press, 1957], p. 197). For the connections to (and distinctions from) Petrarch that Chaucer constructs, see Wallace, *Chaucerian Polity*, p. 293, and Emma Campbell, "Sexual Poetics and the Politics of Translation in the Tale of Griselda," *CL* 55.3 (2003):

This recharacterization of womanly power undermines Griselda's authority while, at the same time, preserving the possibility that there are multiple forms of feminine power.

Immediately after ending the story, the Clerk offers the Petrarchan moral (1142–48):

> This storie is seyd nat for that wyves sholde
> Folwen Grisilde as in humylitee,
> For it were inportable, though they wolde,
> But for that every wight, in his degree,
> Sholde be constant in adversitee
> As was Grisilde; therfore Petrak writeth
> This storie, which with heigh stile he enditeth.

Chaucer redirects us to the allegorical level of the poem: Griselda's womanhood is important insofar as it stands in for subjecthood, and so the tale is not for "wyves" but for "every wight." This interpretation makes the "storie" not about Griselda's powerful submission—her "humylytee"—but about the human ability to endure suffering and "be constant in adversitee." Walter's cruelty is muted somewhat, but we are left with serious gaps between his allegorical likeness to God and his behavior as Chaucer represented it and the Clerk judged it.

After invoking and summarizing Petrarch, the Clerk signals a shift in perspective by offering "o word . . . er I go" (1163). This "word" turns out to be the envoy, which, apparently unlike the tale itself, is meant specifically for wives; he addresses it to the Wife of Bath and "al hire secte" (1171).[65] Such women are nearly anti-Griseldas: unable to combine different models of womanhood as successfully as she did, they resemble the traditional overbearing wife of the fabliau. While Walter's excessive exercise of authority enables Griselda's exemplarity to exceed

---

191–216, esp. pp. 211–14. The multiple endings have also produced divergent interpretations on the issue of the tale's treatment of women (and specifically Griselda). Dinshaw suggests that the Clerk "addresses himself, finally, not to another man—he does not pass his text on from clerk to clerk—but to women" (*Sexual Poetics*, p. 152), while Hansen argues that "the Clerk's humorous ending deflates rather than protects Griselda's virtue . . . [he] devalues and dismisses the feminine powers of silence without liberating women from the complementary myths of absence or excess" (*Fictions of Gender*, p. 205).

[65] We might read "secte" as "sex" or as a more exclusive subset of that sex. The latter reading is best supported by the text and by the later address to "archewyves," another Chaucerian coining that seems to describe a particular group of women (line 1195).

his own ideal, these women are comfortably comic because they can be powerful only in a vacuum, when husbands cannot or do not know how to exercise their own masculine and marital authority.

In the end, Chaucer may be retreating from the new and anxiety-producing model of womanhood that Griselda represents into conventional images of more limited feminine authority, returning the readers to the kind of female characters that can be recognized and enjoyed more easily. Chaucer renames these stereotypes, however, calling such women "archewyves" (1195). In the context of Griselda's story, we might read these stereotypes from a different perspective: as an alternative and more accessible (if less effective or comprehensive) form of feminine authority. In a distinct and fundamental departure from Petrarch, Chaucer uses the tale to question and ultimately to broaden the idea of what is womanly and how women can exercise power, creating womanhood as a category that can encompass "archewyves" as well as Patient Griselda. The addition of womanhood reshapes the story and allows Chaucer to use *The Clerk's Tale* to explore his new concept and examine new ways of representing women that sought their similarities as a gender beyond traditional social roles or generic archetypes.

Jews and Saracens in Chaucer's England:

A Review of the Evidence

Henry Ansgar Kelly
University of California, Los Angeles

MUCH ATTENTION HAS BEEN GIVEN to Chaucer's treat-
ment of Jews in *The Prioress's Tale* and to Chaucer's own attitudes toward
Jews and the attitudes of others of his time and place.[1] But it would
profit us, in my view, to expand our focus beyond Jews to other non-
Christians,[2] and beyond literary influences to the actual presence of "in-

---

I observe the following procedures in my citations: I use modern punctuation and
capitalization; regularize *u/v, i/j,* and *i/y;* and I convert *edh, thorn,* and *yogh* into modern
values. I treat medieval Latin like the vernacular of the author of each passage (which
is the way the author spelled and pronounced it); and in citing classicized editions, I
convert *ae* and *oe* to their medieval form (namely, *e*). This is in keeping with my mani-
festo, "Uniformity and Sense in Editing and Citing Medieval Texts," published in the
Medieval Academy News, Spring 2004, and my supplementary letter in the Spring 2005
issue.

[1] For a review of bibliography, including older works, see Larry D. Benson's edition
of Chaucer's *Canterbury Tales* (Boston: Houghton Mifflin, 2000), p. 438. Among recent
noteworthy studies are: Lawrence Besserman, "Chaucer, Spain, and the Prioress's Anti-
semitism," *Viator* 35 (2004): 329–53; Jeffrey J. Cohen, "The Flow of Blood in Medieval
Norwich," *Speculum* 79 (2004): 26–65; Roger Dahood, "The Punishment of the Jews,
Hugh of Lincoln, and the Question of Satire in Chaucer's *Prioress's Tale,*" *Viator* 36
(2005); the various articles in Sheila Delany, ed., *Chaucer and the Jews: Sources, Contexts,
Meanings* (New York: Routledge, 2002); Denise Despres, "Cultic Anti-Judaism and
Chaucer's Litel Clergeon," *MP* 91 (1993–94): 413–27 (Despres's "The Protean Jew in
the Vernon Manuscript" is in Delany, pp. 145–64); Elisa Narin van Court, "Socially
Marginal, Culturally Central: Representing Jews in Late Medieval English Literature,"
Exemplaria 2 (2000): 293–326; Lee Patterson, "'The Living Witnesses of Our Redemp-
tion': Martyrdom and Imitation in Chaucer's *Prioress's Tale,*" *JMEMSt* 31 (2001):
507–60; Sylvia Tomasch, "Postcolonial Chaucer and the Virtual Jew," *The Postcolonial
Middle Ages,* ed. Jeffrey J. Cohen (New York: St. Martin's, 2000), pp. 243–60 (repr. in
Delany, pp. 69–85).

[2] Brenda Deen Schildgen, *Pagans, Tartars, Moslems, and Jews in Chaucer's Canterbury
Tales* (Gainesville: University Press of Florida, 2001), has made a good start in this
direction; and see Gila Aloni and Shirley Sharon-Zisser, "Geoffrey Chaucer's 'Lyne Oriental': Mediterranean and Oriental Languages in the *Treatise on the Astrolabe,*" *Mediterranean Historical Review* 16:2 (December 2001): 69–77; and Sheila Delany, "Chaucer's
Prioress, the Jews, and the Muslims," in Delany, *Chaucer and the Jews,* pp. 43–57.

fidels" or ex-infidels in England. Most of us, I think, have assumed that there were laws against allowing non-Christians, especially Jews, into England, and that such laws were successfully enforced. We sometimes see it argued that the absence of Jews from England made an important difference to Chaucer's understanding of the tale told by the Prioress. Not many Chaucerians, it seems, are aware of the presence of the Domus Conversorum in London or of its history, even though the basic facts have long been available. However, some of the alleged facts need to be corrected, and new data concerning not only Jews but also Muslims and northern pagans need to be added. Hence my present review of documentary evidence for the presence of non-Christians and ex-non-Christians (converts) in England. At the end of it, I hope that we will be in a better position to assess all proximate and remote influences upon beliefs and prejudices in Chaucer's day.

The House of (Jewish) Converts

I will begin with the Jews and will focus on the Domus Conversorum, or House of Converts, in London. The only thorough account of it is that of Michael Adler in 1939,[3] and before him the most informative discussion of the institution is in the first volume of the *Victoria History of London*, by an author who signs herself modestly as M. Reddan.[4] The Domus Conversorum was established in 1232 by King Henry III on New Street, which by the time of Chaucer's birth had come to be called Chancellor's Lane,[5] as a "hospital" or hospice for converted Jews. When the Jews were expelled in 1290,[6] it was assumed that the hospice would eventually come to an end. In 1292, there were ninety-seven members,

[3] Michael Adler, *Jews of Medieval England* (London: Jewish Historical Society, 1939).
[4] M. Reddan, "Domus Conversorum," *The Victoria History of London*, ed. William Page, vol. 1 (London 1909, repr. London: Dawsons, 1974), pp. 551–54.
[5] Eilert Ekwall, *Street-Names of the City of London* (Oxford: Clarendon, 1954), p. 118. It is the present Chancery Lane.
[6] For a recent account of the expulsion, and the circumstances of Jews before the expulsion, see Robin R. Mundill, *England's Jewish Solution: Experiment and Expulsion, 1262–1290* (Cambridge: Cambridge University Press, 1998); he gives a summary account in "Medieval Anglo-Jewry: Expulsion and Exodus," *Judenvertreibungen in Mittelalter und früher Neuzeit*, ed. Friedhelm Burgard et al. (Hannover: Hahn, 1999), pp. 75–97. The official decree of expulsion was issued on 18 July 1290; it has since been lost (p. 92). See also Mundill's essay, "Edward I and the Final Phase of Anglo-Jewry," *The Jews in Medieval Britain: Historical, Literary, and Archaeological Perspectives*, ed. Patricia Skinner (Cambridge: Boydell and Brewer, 2003), pp. 55–70. See also note 118 below.

and in 1308 the membership was down to fifty-two, according to Reddan,[7] though Adler finds ninety-six in 1280 and fifty in 1308.[8] But the Domus was given new life under Edward III, who assigned to it some children of converts. We know of two in 1336, another two in 1337, and one in 1344, and we hear of another in 1349.[9]

By the last dates, the Keeper was a prominent priest, John St.-Paul ("Seynpol," "Seintpol," "Seintpoul," etc.), who received his life-interest in the Domus in 1339.[10] His surname (in Latin, "de Sancto Paulo") is identical to that of certain converts. Eleanor St.-Paul was sponsored before the expulsion, in 1289, by Edward I's eldest daughter, Eleanor (1264–97).[11] Then there was Isabel St.-Paul, probably to be identified with the Isabel la Converse who was baptized in France in the presence of Edward II's queen (widow), Isabel, who thereby became her godmother, and who granted her a pension.[12] Isabel St.-Paul and Eleanor St.-Paul (possibly, though just barely, the same as the earlier one) are among the converts living in the House in 1344 and 1345.[13] However, though John St.-Paul himself has rashly been called a convert,[14] he seems to have been born after the expulsion, around 1295, to a Yorkshire family, which probably came originally from Guienne, and which

---

[7] Reddan, "Domus Conversorum," p. 552.

[8] Adler, *Jews of Medieval England*, p. 308.

[9] Reddan, "Domus Conversorum," p. 552 n. 25.

[10] *Calendar of Patent Rolls* (CPR), 1338–40, p. 256: 7 June 1339: "Grant for life to John de Sancto Paulo, king's clerk, keeper of the Chancery Rolls, of the custody of the *Domus Conversorum*, London." See *Calendar of Close Rolls* (CCR), 1339–41, p. 313 (entry of 20 April 1344), where it·is stated that the king granted St.-Paul the keepership of the House of Converts for life on 7 June in his fourteenth year (i.e., 1340); but in the entry for 14 January 1345 (p. 489) it is stated as having been in the thirteenth year (1339).

[11] *CCR*, 1288–96, p. 27: 8 November 1289: "Eleanor de Sancto Paulo, formerly a Jew of London, now converted to the Catholic faith, is to have restored to her all the goods she possessed on the day of her conversion, by order of the king at the instance of his daughter Eleanor." See Adler, *Jews of Medieval England*, pp. 300, 309.

[12] *CPR* 1330–34, p. 122: 13 April 1331, Pont Ste. Maxence: "Confirmation of a grant for life by Queen Isabella to Isabella la Converse, her god-daughter, of a daily allowance of 8 pence of Paris out of the issues of Ponthieu, payable half-yearly." See Adler, *Jews of Medieval England*, p. 309. Queen Isabel deposed her husband Edward II in 1327 and acted as regent of her son Edward III until she was arrested in 1330; she lived in semiretirement until her death in 1358.

[13] In the *CCR* entries cited above, note 11, and see also the entry for 14 April 1345, pp. 559–60.

[14] By E. J. Burford, *Bawds and Lodgings: A History of the London Bankside Brothels, c. 100–1665* (London: Owen, 1976), p. 71. Burford's work is filled with erroneous conclusions.

shows no signs of having been Jewish.[15] But one of the early Keepers who had a similar name, John St.-Denis (appointed in 1270),[16] may have been a convert. There were, in fact, convert priests, but they may have been fairly rare, and they are difficult to trace, because they would have been thoroughly integrated into the general clergy. They were, however, sought after for the Domus. In 1280 provision was made to hire a suitable convert priest to assist the priest who served as proctor for the Domus.[17]

The position of Keeper of the House of Converts, as well as being a secular appointment in the gift of the king, may have entailed an ecclesiastical benefice of some sort, since St.-Paul relinquished the post just before becoming archbishop of Dublin in February 1350. The same thing had happened in 1325, when the current Keeper, William Ayermin, was made a bishop.[18] While St.-Paul was Keeper, he was an especially generous benefactor of the Priory of St. Leonard at Stratford-at-Bow, the monastery associated with Chaucer's Prioress, to whom Chaucer gave the tale of the little boy killed by Jews.[19]

We have seen that Isabel St.-Paul was a foreign convert, and others appear later: Edward of Brussels, a Jewish convert, in 1339,[20] Janettus of Spain in 1344,[21] and Theobald of Turkey in 1348.[22] Since the latter

---

[15] E. I. Carlyle, "St. Paul, John de (1295?–1362)," *Dictionary of National Biography* (*DNB*). The entry by Philomena Connolly in the *Oxford Dictionary of National Biography* (2004) is much less informative. See also A. B. Emden, *A Biographical Register of the University of Oxford to A.D. 1500*, 3 vols. (Oxford: Oxford University Press, 1957–59), 3:1629–30: "Saint-Pol, John of."

[16] Reddan, "Domus Conversorum," p. 553 n. 48.

[17] Adler, *Jews of Medieval England*, p. 349. See Robert Stacey, "The Conversion of Jews to Christianity in Thirteenth-Century England," *Speculum* 67 (1992): 263–83, who says that he has not been able to trace any convert priests (p. 276).

[18] Reddan, "Domus Conversorum," p. 553 n. 60.

[19] H. A. Kelly, "A Neo-Revisionist Look at Chaucer's Nuns," *ChauR* 31 (1996–97): 115–32 at 123–24, and "Bishop, Prioress, and Bawd in the Stews of Southwark," *Speculum* 75 (2000): 342–88 at 350–51. It is suggested in these articles that St.-Paul may have kept his position until his death in 1362, but this was not the case, since his successor, Henry Ingleby, was appointed Keeper for life, succeeding St.-Paul on 28 January 1350. See *CPR 1348–50*, p. 475.

[20] Adler, *Jews of Medieval England*, pp. 317–18; see *CPR 1338–40*, p. 400: 3 December 1339

[21] Reddan, "Domus Conversorum," p. 552 n. 26: *CPR 1343–45*, p. 190: 28 January 1344.

[22] PRO C66/225 m. 43 (cf. *CPR 1348–50*, p. 87: 24 April 1348): "Rex omnibus ad quos, etc., Salutem. Volentes Theobaldo de Turkie, qui ad fidem catholicam conversus et baptizatus existet et non habet unde vivat nec scit se ipsum juvare aliunde de sustentacione congrua providere, de gracia nostra speciali et caritatis intuitu concessimus ei

two converts are not identified as having been Jews, could they have been Muslims? Janettus is specifically assigned to the Domus Conversorum, while Theobald is not; he is, however, included in the foundation that King Henry made for "our converts in London," the provisions of which seem rather lavish, referring to houses in the plural and not only wages from the Exchequer but also rents, revenues, and "other things."[23] If this means that he was assigned to the Domus, and if the Domus was restricted only to Jewish converts, as seems to have been the case, then he was of course definitely Jewish. The same can be said of Thomas de Acres, mentioned below, who, if he came from Acre in the Holy Land, could have been either Jewish or Muslim.

Even in Chaucer's time, the House of Converts was still known as having been established for the maintenance of converts "from Jewish depravity," *de Judaica pravitate*. This is stated in the account, dated 14 January 1388, of the suit between the present Keeper, John Burton, and John Brampton, parson of the parish church of Saint Dunstan in the West, which, Burton says, had been assigned with its revenues by Henry III to the Domus.[24] It is confirmed in later patents that the Domus was only for Jews: the payments specified are like those paid "to other converted Jews" ("as autres Jues conversez") in the House.[25] The Burton-Brampton dispute is also important for explaining the function of the Domus: the converts could come and go at their pleasure, "but

---

tales statum et sustentacionem quales unus de conversis nostris in civitate nostra Londoniis commorantibus, et de fundacione clare memorie domini Henrici quondam Regis Anglie progenitoris nostre existentibus, habet et percipit ibidem, ut in domibus pro inhabitacione sua et vadiis ad Scaccarium nostrum percipiendum ac redditibus et proficuis et aliis rebus quibuscumque ad totam vitam prefati Theobaldi" ("The king to all to whom, etc., Good health. Wishing to provide for Theobald of Turkey, who now is converted to the Catholic faith and baptized and has not the wherewithal to live and knows not how to help himself from elsewhere for his fitting sustenance, we have granted of our special grace and charitable intent such state and sustenance as one of our converts living in our city of London and existing from the foundation of Lord Henry of illustrious memory, sometime King of England, our progenitor, has and receives there, as in houses for his habitation and wages to be received from our Exchequer, and rents and revenues and other things whatsoever for the whole life of the said Theobald").

[23] See the record cited in note 22.
[24] *CPR* 1385–89, pp. 397–98.
[25] PRO E101/251/15 m. 2; Adler, *Jews of Medieval England*, p. 369 (16 December 1413); see also E101/251/11 m. 12 (11 Henry IV, 22 April 1410): "grantez a William de seint Jakes nadgaurs Ju . . . coms sont acustumez a ester paiez a autres Jues convers qont este receuz illoeques" ("granted to William of St. James, recently Jew . . . as are wont to be paid to other converted Jews who are received there").

their maintenance was at the expense of the funds of the Domus, whether they lived within the walls of the institution or not."[26]

The records of the Domus are missing from 1359 to 1386, but Adler has been able to find records of converts from other sources. For instance, on February 25, 1368, a grant was made by Edward III to John of St. Mary "in Ispanum," recently a Jew, because he is now converted to the Christian faith, "of having such wages and houses for his sustenance and dwelling in our House of Converts in London as other such converts in the same House before this time have had by our grant, along with the profits of the gardens and other commodities and easements pertaining to such a convert according to the foundation of the said House of Converts from our alms for the whole life of the said John."[27] Adler over-reads this grant to infer that John was appointed the gardener of the Domus, whereas it clearly states that all of the converts of the House were to share in the proceeds of the gardens. He also says that his name was "John the Convert of the Annunciation of St. Mary" and that he was baptized in London in 1371.[28] But he would have to have been baptized before February 1368, and there is no indication whether he was baptized in England or Spain. The *Calendar of Patent Rolls* takes the addendum to his name, *in Ispanum*, for *in Ispania*, perhaps on the assumption that he received his name from a Spanish church named Santa Maria. But it may simply be the equivalent of "from Spain," as with Thomas Levyn, who appears briefly in the records of the Domus in 1393, identified as recently a Jew "from the parts of Spain," "de partibus Ispanum."[29] Here it is clear that *Ispanum* is an indeclinable noun for *Ispania*.

Adler calculates from later records that John of St. Mary was at the Domus for a total of thirty-four years[30]—which presumably should be

---

[26] Adler, *Jews of Medieval England*, p. 322, commenting on *CPR* 1385–89, pp. 397–98.

[27] This letter of Edward III survives only in the confirmation given to it by Richard II, 18 January 1384: PRO C66/317 m. 337 (cf. *CPR* 1381–85, p. 366). The pertinent part of Edward's grant reads: "Sciatis quod de gracia nostra speciali concessimus Johanni de Sancta Maria in Ispanum, nuper Judeo, nam ad fidem Christianum converso, talia vadia et domos pro sustentacione et inhabitacione suis in Domo nostro Conversorum Londoniis qualia alii hujusmodi conversi in eadem Domo ante hec tempora ex concessione nostra habuerunt habendi, una cum proficuis de gardinis et aliis commoditatibus et aisiamentis ad hujusmodi conversum juxta fundacionem dicte Domus Conversorum pertinentibus de elemosina nostra ad totam vitam ipsius Johannis."

[28] Adler, *Jews of Medieval England*, p. 321.

[29] PRO E101/251/1, text in Adler, *Jews of Medieval England*, p. 366.

[30] Ibid.

recalculated to thirty-seven years, starting with 1368 rather than 1371. From other sources he finds a total of six arrivals during the gap in the record, including John: "John of St. Mary, a Spaniard; Laurence of St. Martin, probably also of Spain; John of Kingston, Thomas of Acre, Edmund, and Peter."[31] Both John St.-Mary and Laurence St.-Martin were already present in the Domus when "John de Kyngeston" and "Thomas de Acres" arrived on March 22, 1380.[32]

John St-Paul's successor as Keeper of the Domus was Henry Ingleby, who resigned in 1371. He was followed by William Burstall (1371–81) and John Waltham (1381–86). John Burton took over in 1386, and was followed by John Scarle in 1394 and Thomas Stanley in 1397; the latter was reappointed in 1399 by the new king, Henry IV.[33] St.-Paul had been appointed Keeper of the Rolls of Chancery two years before his appointment as Keeper of the House of Converts, and the two posts normally went together. Then, under Burstall, just two months before the death of Edward III, the Keepership of the Domus was formally annexed to the Keepership of the Rolls.[34] Burstall was still in charge of the Rolls when Cecily Champain enrolled her release of Chaucer from any further action concerning her rape, on 4 May 1380.[35] And, of course, any business that Chaucer himself had at the Chancery would have brought him into close proximity of the House of Converts and, perhaps, any inmates who were there at any given time, like John "Seintmarie," who may or may not have worked the gardens as well as sharing in their profits.

Burstall's successor, John Waltham, who was appointed not for life but at the king's pleasure, sought and received a confirmation of this juncture of offices in 1383. As Keeper of the Rolls of Chancery, he extended the jurisdiction of the Court of Chancery by introducing the writ of subpoena. After becoming archdeacon of Richmond early in 1385, he was given leave to exercise his Rolls office by deputy when he visited his

---

[31] Adler, *Jews of Medieval England*, p. 320.

[32] PRO C54/220 m. 33 (cf. *CCR* 1377–81, p. 409): 5 October 1380, referring to the previous 22 March.

[33] Reddan, "Domus Conversorum," p. 554.

[34] W. J. Hardy, "The Rolls House and Chapel," *Middlesex and Hertfordshire Notes and Queries* 2 (1896): 49–68 at pp. 58–59 (date of 11 April 1377).

[35] Martin M. Crow and Clair C. Olson, *Chaucer Life-Records* (Oxford: Oxford University Press, 1966), p. 343. See my "Meanings and Uses of *Raptus* in Chaucer's Time," *SAC* 20 (1998): 101–65, repr. in *Inquisitions and Other Trial Procedures in the Medieval West* (Aldershot: Ashfield, 2001), chap. 10, esp. pp. 102–3, 115–18, 142.

archdeaconry, but he resigned his joint offices on October 24, 1386. Two years later, he became bishop of Salisbury.[36]

John St.-Mary was alone in the *Domus Conversorum* when he was joined in 1386 by a pair of French Jewish converts, Aseti Brianti and his wife Perota. Then, in 1393, as mentioned above, there appeared a man named Thomas Levyn, recently a Jew in Spain ("nuper Judeus de partibus Ispanum"), and now, it was claimed ("et jam, ut dicitur") a convert of the Christian faith. But after drawing the convert stipend for a month, he disappeared.[37] Other converts of Chaucer's time show no signs of being foreign, as far as the extant records are concerned, for they are referred to only by their baptismal names, like Edmund and Peter in Adler's list,[38] or by their new name and a local toponymic surname, like John Kingston.

The next convert to appear in the Domus Conversorum was a woman named Elizabeth, who entered in 1399. The most intriguing thing about her is her father, who is identified as Rabbi Moses, Bishop of the Jews. A grant of 1403 in her favor was printed long ago by Thomas Rymer:

Rex omnibus, ad quos, etc., Salutem.

Sciatis quod, de gratia nostra speciali, concessimus Elizabethe, filie Rabi Moyses, episcopi Judeorum, converse, unum denarium per diem, ultra unum denarium quem eadem Elizabeth, ut una Judeorum ad fidem Christianorum conversa, per manus custodis Domus Conversorum Londoni[is], de summa pro hujusmodi conversis ad Scaccarium percipienda assignata, singulis diebus percipit; habendum et percipiendum dictum denarium diurnum per nos eidem Elizabethe tenore presentium concessum, una cum dicto altero denario diurno quem, ut est dictum, percipit de dicta summa predictis conversis assignata, per manus custodis domus predicte pro tempore existentis ad totam vitam ipsius Elizabethe.

In cujus, etc. Teste Rege apud Westmonasterium, decimo die Aprilis. Per ipsum Regem.[39]

---

[36] Hardy, "The Rolls House and Chapel," pp. 59–60; Mary Tout, "Waltham, John," *DNB*.
[37] Adler, *Jews of Medieval England*, pp. 321–22, 366.
[38] See *CPR* 1381–85, p. 491, 7 December 1384: "Peter the Convert," "Edmund the Convert."
[39] Thomas Rymer, *Foedera*, 2nd ed. (London: Tonson, 1726–35), 8:299; 3rd ed. (The Hague: Neaulme, 1739–45), 4:1:44.

(The King to all those to whom, etc.: Good health.

Know that of our special grace we have conceded to Elizabeth, daughter of Rabbi Moses, bishop of the Jews, a convert, one penny a day, in addition to the penny that the same Elizabeth, as one of the Jews converted to the Christian faith, receives every day from the hands of the Keeper of the House of Converts, from the sum to be paid at the Exchequer assigned to such converts. This daily penny, conceded by us to the said Elizabeth by the tenor of these present letters, is to be had and received along with the other daily penny, which, as was said, she receives from the said sum assigned to the said converts by the hands of the Keeper of the aforesaid House, from the present time through the whole life of the said Elizabeth.

In whose, etc. Witnessed by the King at Westminster, the tenth day of April. By the King himself.)

When Elizabeth first arrived, four years earlier, she received the usual stipend of a penny a day, and it was doubled in 1403 by the above-cited grant. Later on, her stipend fell in arrears, and in 1410 it was ordered to be paid up.[40] The stipend was confirmed in 1413, when Henry V took over from his father.[41] From 1409 on, she identified herself as "Elizabeth Pole, convert, wife of David Pole," who was a London tailor. She continued to draw her income for the next seven years, and Adler assumes that she remained an inmate of the Domus during that time; but her receipts only specify that she received her stipend from the Keeper, not that she lived there.[42]

We will discuss Elizabeth's father, Rabbi Moses, after we finish our survey of the Domus. Two years after Elizabeth first came to the House of Converts, there arrived, in 1401, another convert, who, though he was known by an English name, William (of) Leicester, signed his first two receipts in Hebrew characters that identify him as Spanish. He stayed a total of sixteen years.[43]

In 1409 King Henry IV sent to the House of Converts two converts from Dartmouth, a mother and daughter named Joan and Alice, who do not seem to have been recent arrivals in England. At any rate, they

[40] PRO E101/251/11 m. 7, given in Adler, *Jews of Medieval England*, pp. 368–69.
[41] PRO E101/251/15 m. 2; Adler, *Jews of Medieval England*, p. 369 (16 December 1413).
[42] Adler, *Jews of Medieval England*, pp. 323, 370.
[43] Ibid., pp. 323–24. For one of the two receipts signed in Hebrew, see p. 367, with a photo opposite p. 374; on both pages, however, the date is mistakenly given as "1410" instead of "1401."

were definitely not baptized abroad but in Dartmouth itself, as testified by letters sealed by the mayor and burgesses of the city, after they had yielded up all of their goods and chattels on arriving "en port de notre dite ville"—the gate (or, possibly, the port) of Dartmouth. Forfeiture to the king of all possessions by converts was the law, or at least the practice, of the land since at least the time of King John (1199–1216), one not designed to encourage conversions. This procedure was in direct violation of church law, ever since the Third Lateran Council of 1179. Eventually, beginning with Edward I after 1280, converts were allowed to keep half of their property.[44] It is noteworthy that the rule of total forfeiture was the one being enforced in the fifteenth century. In this case, since the king was informed that they did not have the wherewithal to support themselves (a normal consequence of giving up all of one's goods!), he ordered them to be received into the House of Converts and the usual convert stipend paid to them for the rest of their lives.[45]

[44] For the English practice, see Stacey, "Conversion of Jews," pp. 266, 279. According to the Third Lateran decree, *Judei sive Saraceni*, confiscation of possessions is strictly prohibited, "since converts to the faith should enjoy better conditions afterwards than they had before they received the faith"; and all rulers are ordered to make full restoration of all such property, under pain of excommunication. The decree was incorporated into the *Decretales Gregorii IX* (= *Liber Extra* = X) of 1234, 5.6.5 (book 5, title 6, chap. 6): *Corpus iuris canonici*, ed. Emil Friedberg, 2 vols. (Leipzig: Tauchnitz, 1879–81), 2:773. According to the Ordinary Gloss to this decree, even when the goods are ill-gotten through usury, they are to be sold and the money paid out in restitution: *Corpus juris canonici* [*CJC*], 3 vols. (Rome, 1582; repr. Lyons, 1606), 2:1657, v. *a possessionibus*.

[45] Adler, *Jews of Medieval England*, pp. 370–71, from PRO E 101/251/11 m. 13: "Henri par la grace de Dieu Roy d'Engleterre et de France et Seignur d'Irland. A notre tres cher clerc Johan Wakeryng, Gardein de notre Maison de Convers en la Suburbe de Londres, saluz. Come noz bien amees Johanne, conversse de notre ville de Dertemuth, et Alice sa fille, nadgairs esteantes Juwesses mescreantes, et desirantes d'estre de la secte Christiene, refuserent touz lour bons et chateulx que eles avoient et arriverent en port de notre dite ville et y feurent convertees et baptisees, sicome par lettres testimoniales eut faces et sealees desouz les sealx de Maire et autres Burgeys de mesme la ville il poet assez apparon; et, n'aient les dites Johanne et Alice dont lour mesmes susteigner ne gouner, sicome nous avons entenduz, si nous, aiantz a ce consideracion a la reverence de Dieu, volons et vous mandons que les dites Johanne et Alice facez admittre et recevire en ycelle Maison pur terme de leur vies, donnant et ministrant a eles, et a chacune de eles antieux, vivre et sustinance come autres femmes de leur condicion ont eues et prinses en mesme notre Maison par les mains du Gardein d'ycelle pur le temps esteant avant ces heures."

(Henry, by the grace of God King of England and France and Lord of Ireland, to our most dear clerk John Wakering, Warden of our House of Converts in the Suburb of London, good health. Since our well beloved Joan, convert of our city of Dartmouth, and her daughter Alice, recently being unbelieving Jewesses, and desiring to be of the Christian sect, yielded up all of the goods and chattels that they possessed and presented themselves at the gate of our said city, and there they were converted and baptized, as can sufficiently appear from letters made and sealed under the seals of the Mayor and

This turned out to be forty more years for the mother and forty-five for the daughter.[46] The stipend by now seems to have been a penny and a half a day, since another arrival of 1409, a recent convert (*nuper conversus*) named William St.-Jakes, was given an extra halfpenny a day in addition to the usual penny and a half for a convert from the Jews.[47]

Three converts who arrived in 1413, Henry Woodstock and his sons Martin and Peter, were definitely foreigners, since Henry and Peter were allowed to return to their country of origin. Martin, however, stayed, for fifty-five years.[48]

Finally, let me take note of Henry Stratford, whom King Henry V identifies as the godson of his father, Henry IV ("Henri de Stratford, convers, filiol a notre treschier seignur et pere le Roy"). Stratford's baptism must have taken place near the end of the king's life (he died on March 20, 1413), and it seems to have fallen to Henry V to establish the pension of 1 1/2d a day at the House of Converts—making it probable that Stratford was Jewish (we will read below of non-Jewish converts sponsored by Henry IV before he became king).

Henry V made good on his obligation to his father's godson on January 29, 1416, a few months after returning from his victory at Agincourt. Henry rehearses this history in a further letter of January 19, 1422, in which he orders the Keeper of the Domus, Simon Gaunsted (appointed 1415, died 1423), to pay the said pension, which was in arrears.[49] It is probable that the Stratford from which the convert took his name was not Stratford-at-Bow in Middlesex, but rather Stratford Abbey in Essex, a bit farther out from London, where Henry sometimes stayed during the last year of his life.[50]

No other converts are mentioned in the records for the reign of Henry

---

other Burgesses of the same city; and, the same Joan and Alice not having wherewithal to sustain and clothe themselves, as we have heard, therefore we, having in this matter regard to the reverence of God, desire and command you to admit and receive the said Joan and Alice in that House for the rest of their lives, giving and ministering to them, and to each of them together, living and sustenance, as other women of their condition have had and received in that same House of ours by the hands of its Warden during the time before the present day.)

[46] Adler, *Jews of Medieval England*, pp. 324, 370–71.
[47] Ibid., pp. 325, 371. Adler makes the total 2 1/2 d rather than 2d.
[48] Adler, *Jews of Medieval England*, pp. 325–26.
[49] Ibid., pp. 326, 373–74. Adler misreads the order to say that the convert was Henry V's own godson.
[50] James Hamilton Wylie, *History of England under Henry the Fourth*, 4 vols. (London: Longmans, 1884–98), 2:403 n. 2.

V, and not much is known about the handful recorded in the subsequent reigns of the fifteenth century.[51]

Now, then, back to Rabbi Moses. Who could he have been? There is clear evidence that the Latin "Episcopus" and French "L'Eveske" were used to translate the Hebrew surname *Cohen* of a prominent Jewish family in thirteenth-century England. H. P. Stokes is of the opinion that by this time the term did not designate an office (if it ever did), but only the surname. However, there is a deed dating to the time of Henry III witnessed by a series of Jews, beginning with Benedict, bishop of the Jews (*episcopus Judeorum*), followed by Joceus, priest (*presbiter*), Manser, cleric (*clericus*), and others, including Benedict Crispin.[52] But the title given to the head of the English Jews by the Exchequer of the Jews was not "Bishop" but "Priest"—*Presbyter Judeorum*, who was said to hold "the Presbyterate of all of the Jews of all of England."[53] But this was a secular title imposed by the English officials, not a religious office of the Jews themselves.

So it may be that Elizabeth's father really was a bishop of the Jews, that is, the religious head of a congregation of Jews. None of the early records of payments to his daughter Elizabeth make any further elaboration upon the identity of her father. It is only when her grant is confirmed in the first year of the reign of Henry V that we find any speculation about him. Elizabeth is called the "daughter of a Rabbi Moses, the bishop of the Jews of France and Germany" ("file dun Raby Moyses, l'evesque des Jues de France et d'Almaigne"). But the accompanying Latin record refers to her only as "the daughter of a certain Rabbi Moses" ("Elisabeth filie cujusdam Raby Moyses").[54] Adler is clearly justified in thinking that the writer of the patent was only improvising.[55]

[51] Adler, *Jews of Medieval England*, pp. 326–27.

[52] *A Descriptive Catalogue of Ancient Deeds in the Public Record Office*, 6 vols. (London: H.M. Stationery Office, 1890–1915), 5:509, no. A 13423. This deed is undated, but the previous deed, A 13422, says that Benedict Crispin died between 1250 and 1252. For a later Benedict L'Eveske, see note 74.

[53] See, for example, the appointment of Elias L'Eveske in 1243 by Henry III: "Sciatis nos concessisse et presenti carta nostra confirmasse Elye Episcopo, Judeo Londiniensi, Presbiteratum omnium Judeorum totius Anglie habendum et tenendum quamdiu vixerit" ("Know that we have granted and by this present charter have confirmed to Elias L'Eveske, Jew of London, the Presbyterate of all of the Jews of all England, to have and to hold for the rest of his life"); H. P. Stokes, *Studies in Anglo-Jewish History* (Edinburgh: Jewish Historical Society of England, 1913), p. 245; cf. pp. 30–33. The title of "Arch Presbyter," which even Stokes uses, was invented by modern historians.

[54] PRO E101/251/15 m. 1.

[55] Adler, *Jews of Medieval England*, pp. 323, 369: PRO E101/251/15 m. 2.

But it is also clear that there was no memory of who he actually was. If in fact he had been a resident of England and in charge of a community of Jews living there, it would seem rather unlikely that this fact would not be known in 1413. On the other hand, it is possible that he was French, and that he came to England from France when the Jews were expelled from there in 1394.[56] We will hear below of a Spanish rabbi who spent some time in England in 1388–89.

An Alleged Jewish Convert, and Sundry Visitors

A man who claimed to be a convert from Judaism was John Berkyng or Barking, not mentioned by Adler and not recorded as associated with the House of Converts. He fell afoul of the Mayor and other authorities of the City of London in 1390.[57] On Tuesday, March 1, "John Berkyng, who was lately a Jew, as he said, was attached to make answer as well to the Mayor and Commonalty of the City of London as to William Shedewater, serjeant of the Duke of York, in a plea of falsehood and deceit." Shedewater complained that on the previous Friday Barking had been consulted by the Council of the Duke of York about a pair of silver dishes that had been stolen from the duke some weeks earlier, on February 2. Barking claimed to be an expert in magical arts and incantations, and by these alleged means he falsely accused Shedewater of the theft, whereupon Shedewater "was arrested and imprisoned, and in his body much injured, and on the point of being forced to swear that he would never come within ten leagues of the hostels" of the king and the dukes of York and Gloucester. But somehow (we are not told how) Shedewater managed to get his complaint to the Mayor. Then another complaint was made against Barking, by Robert Mysdene and John Geyte; they said that, after a furred mantle had been stolen from Lady

---

[56] See Roger Kohn, *Les Juifs de la France du Nord dans la seconde moitié du XIVe siècle* (Louvain: Peeters, 1988), pp. 251–75; William Chester Jordan, *The French Monarchy and the Jews: From Philip Augustus to the Last Capetians* (Philadelphia: University of Pennsylvania Press, 1989), pp. 248–50; Gilbert Dahan, ed., *L'expulsion des Juifs de France, 1394* (Paris: Cerf, 2004). All the recorded destinations of the exiled Jews lay to the east and south of France. Delany, "Chaucer's Prioress, the Jews, and the Muslims" (n. 3 above), p. 51, thinks that Chaucer would have known of the expulsion, and she promises (57 n. 42) a study suggesting that Chaucer was influenced by the case of Jews condemned to death by the Provost of Paris in 1395 for trying the persuade a convert, Denis Machaut, to return to Judaism. This incident may have been a factor in precipitating the expulsion of the Jews. See Kohn, *Les Juifs de la France du Nord*, pp. 253–59.

[57] The whole entry is translated from the Latin original by Henry Thomas Riley, *Memorials of London and London Life* (London: Longmans, 1868), pp. 518–19.

Despencer on January 18, they were falsely accused of the theft by Barking, and, being arrested, they received the same injurious treatment as Shedewater. Barking pleaded guilty to the charges of malicious defamation, and, on March 4, because "such soothsaying, art magic, and falsities are manifestly against the doctrine of Holy Writ and a scandal and disgrace to the whole Commonalty of the City," he was sentenced to an hour on the pillory, with the reasons for the punishment posted. He was then brought back to remain in prison until the Mayor and Aldermen gave order for his release. They did so on March 19, making him swear never to return to the liberty of the City, and to forswear all future soothsaying.

We note that John Barking claimed to be a converted Jew, but it may be that his claim was false, made only to enhance his reputation as a diviner (on the supposition that Jews possessed the sort of occult knowledge that would assist in the magic arts). He did not, it seems, make a claim for the convert pension to which he would have been entitled. Even if he had done so, he still could have been faking his Jewishness and conversion, and this may likewise have been the case with Thomas Levyn a few years later, who, as we saw, was also only "said" to be a convert. We have seen from the case of Joan and Alice of Dartmouth that at least some converts carried sealed testimonies of their conversion.

Another convert in England during this time who avoided contact with the House of Converts was Charles Converse (Charles the Convert), who was not a charlatan but, it seems, an acknowledged practitioner of both medical and surgical arts. On June 11, 1391, he was given a five-year special protection for himself, his servants, and his goods, to practice his arts and gain a livelihood. He did not arrange for such protection beforehand, but only after his arrival in England, and the permit took no notice of his being a convert, apart from the fact that he called himself such, without specifying what religion he was converted from.[58]

[58] PRO C66/332 m. 4 (*CPR 1388–92*, p. 430), 11 June 1391: "Sciatis quod cum Karolus le Convers, phisicus et sururgicus, regnum nostrum Anglie ad dicta artificia sua inibi exercendi et sustentacionem suam pro exercicio hujusmodi artificiorum suorum ibidem lucrandam sit ingressus, suscepimus ipsum Karolum in eodem regno nostro jam existentem infra dictum regnum morando et hujusmodi artificia sua exercendo necnon servientes et bona sua quecumque" ("Know that since Charles Converse, physician and surgeon, has entered our kingdom of England for the exercise of the said arts and for earning his sustenance here for the exercise of such arts, we have received the said Charles, already present in our said realm, to stay in the said realm and to exercise these arts of his, and also his servants and all his goods whatsoever"). The patent goes on to

A few years before this, in 1388, an unconverted Jew arrived in England, namely, Solomon ha-Levi, the chief rabbi of Burgos in Castile. While he was there, in February 1389, he wrote a humorous letter bewailing the lack of wine for celebrating the feast of Purim.[59] It is likely that he came to London as one of the sixty-some hostages sent to guarantee the payment of 600,000 French francs to John of Gaunt, Duke of Lancaster, as part of the settlement for Gaunt's relinquishing of his claim to the Spanish throne.[60] They were given safe-conduct for a year in England by Richard II on August 26, 1388.[61] Gaunt's claim of course came through his marriage to Constance of Castile, for whom Chaucer's

---

say that he will be in the king's protection for the next five years. Noted by Cecil Roth, "The Middle Period of Anglo-Jewish History (1290–1655) Reconsidered," *Jewish Historical Society of England Transactions* 19 (1960): 1–12 at 2 n. 7.

[59] For an English translation of the Purim letter, see Judith Gale Krieger, "Pablo de Santa María: His Epoch, Life, and Hebrew and Spanish Literary Production" (Ph.D. diss., UCLA, 1988), pp. 245–61, and see pp. 43–47 for a commentary. Krieger accompanies her translation with a Hebrew text that does not mark the line and stanza divisions of the verse sections; these can be found in the edition of I. Abrahams, "Paul of Burgos in London," *Jewish Quarterly Review* 12 (1900): 255–63.

[60] Francisco Cantera, "Selomó ha-Leví, rehén en Inglaterra en 1389," *Homenaje a Millás-Vallicrosa*, 2 vols. (Barcelona: Consejo Superior de Investigaciones Científicos,1954–56), 1:301–7; Roth, "Middle Period," p. 2. See the account of Pero López de Ayala's history of King Juan I, year 10 (1388), chap. 2, *Crónicas de los reyes de Castilla*, ed. Cayetano Rosell, 3 vols., Biblioteca de Autores Españoles 66, 68, 70 (Madrid: De Sancha, 1875–78), 2:118–20; *Crónicas,* ed. José-Luís Martín (Barcelona: Planeta, 1991), pp. 634–39. While the hostages were in England, Ayala himself was serving as King Juan's ambassador to Gaunt in Bayonne, around the end of February 1389. See P. E. Russell, *The English Intervention in Spain and Portugal in the Time of Edward III and Richard II* (Oxford: Clarendon, 1955), pp. 522–23. Among the hostages that López names is Juan Rodríguez/Ruiz de Cisneros. For a discussion of an attempt to identify the author of the *Libro de buen amor* with an earlier Juan Ruiz de Cisneros, see H. A. Kelly, *Canon Law and the Archpriest of Hita* (Binghamton: MRTS, 1984), pp. 68–70, 119–20. If the *Libro* was composed later in the fourteenth century, as suggested here, the younger Cisneros (the 1388–89 hostage) would be in the running for authorship. But more likely, perhaps, is the Juan Ruiz/Rodríguez of Salamanca, doctor of laws, who was Juan I's ambassador to the pope in Avignon in 1389, or his son of the same name, a student in canon law at Salamanca, for whom Dr. Ruiz asked a benefice at this time. See Vicente Beltrán de Heredia, *Bulario de la Universidad de Salamanca (1219–1549),* 3 vols. (Salamanca: Universidad de Salamanca, 1966–67), 1:472–73; H. A. Kelly, "A Juan Ruiz Directory for 1380–1382," *Mester* 17 (Fall 1988): 69–93 at pp. 87–88. Both father and son were active during the first two decades of the fifteenth century, when the Salamanca manuscript of the *Libro* was copied.

[61] Rymer, *Foedera,* 2nd ed., 7:603; 3rd ed., 3:4:31; reproduced in Cantera, "Selomó ha-Leví, rehén en Inglaterra en 1389," pp. 304–5. Safe-conducts were also required for the sixty or so persons charged with escorting the money; see Edouard Perroy, *L'Angleterre et le grand schisme d'Occident: Etude sur la politique religieuse de l'Angleterre sous Richard II (1378–1399)* (Paris: Monnier, 1933), p. 256.

wife, Philippa, was a lady-in-waiting (she may have died in 1387); Chaucer's son, Thomas, was also a member of this Spanish entourage.[62] Rabbi Solomon in the next year, 1390, back in Burgos, converted to the Christian faith and took the name of Paul of St. Mary, and he was eventually appointed bishop of Burgos. His learned super-commentary on Nicholas of Lyre's biblical commentaries became part of the ordinary apparatus of the Latin Bible.

We do not hear of another Jewish visitor until 1409, when there arrived in England, by the invitation of the celebrated merchant and civic leader Richard Whittington, a Jewish doctor, who, unlike Dr. Charles in 1391, was not a convert. Whittington received permission from King Henry IV to invite Master Samson of Mirabeau to attend on his ailing wife. Dr. Samson's place of origin was probably the Mirabeau located in Vaucluse, in the southeast of present-day France.[63] Later on, in 1417, Samson is found to be practicing in Northern Italy.[64]

In the next year, 1410, Henry IV himself summoned a celebrated Jewish doctor to attend to his own ills. He gave a safe-conduct for two years to Dr. Elias Sabot and his large entourage (ten mounted servants) to practice his science or *mistera* anywhere in the kingdom. He is identified as "Magister Helias Sabot, Hebrewe de Boleyne la Crase, doctor in artibus medicinarum."[65] The Boleyne in question is Bologna, called *Crassa* or *Grassa* from the fertility of its soil.[66] It has been suggested that Elias took such a large number of persons with him to provide "a private *minyan*," that is, "the number of adult males requisite for public worship."[67] He remained only a year in England, after which he returned to

[62] Derek Pearsall, *The Life of Geoffrey Chaucer: A Critical Biography* (London: Blackwell, 1992), pp. 142–43.

[63] A. Weiner, "A Note on Jewish Doctors in England in the Reign of Henry IV," *Jewish Quarterly Review* 18 (1906):141–45 at p. 145. Whether this Mirabeau was under the control of the King of France at the time is not clear, but we do know that Jewish doctors were still to be found in France after the expulsion of 1394. See Kohn, *Juifs de la France du Nord*, pp. 273–74.

[64] Roth, "Middle Period," p. 2.

[65] Rymer, *Foedera*, 2nd ed., 8:667 (3rd ed., 4:1:184); not calendared in *CPR*. His full name was Elijah Be'er ben Sabbetai. He was the son of Sabato of Fermo. See A. Milano, "Beer, Elia," *Dizionario biografico degli Italiani* 7 (1965): 526–28.

[66] Wylie, *History of England under Henry IV*, 3:231 n. 5.

[67] Weiner, "A Note on Jewish Doctors," pp. 142–43; cf. Cecil Roth, *A History of the Jews in England*, 3rd ed. (Oxford: Clarendon, 1964), p. 133; and Roth, "Middle Period," p. 2. Another imported physician, David de Nigarellis of Lucca, who attended on Henry IV in 1412, is conjectured by Weiner to have been a Jew, but Roth says that there is no evidence for it except his biblical name (*History*, p. 133 n. 4). Weiner admits that he is relying on Wylie, who calls him a Jew without further ado, and who says that Henry made him Warden of the Mint in 1408 (Wylie, 3:231 n. 7).

Italy. In 1417 he was named the chief physician of the new pope, Martin V, and it is thought that he inspired the pope's bull in favor of the Jews, dated February 20, 1422.[68]

Saracens and Saracen Converts

Whether or not there were in fact any Muslims or ex-Muslims in London, in or out of the Domus Conversorum, it is beyond a doubt that there was a suspicion that Saracens as well as Jews were living in England under false pretenses. In the "Good Parliament" of 1376, the Commons asserted that some of the alleged Lombards living in England were really Jews and Saracens and privy spies, who had recently introduced into the country a dreadful unmentionable vice:

The Commons petition that all of the Lombards who have no other occupation than that of broker be made to quit the land within a short time, since evil usury and all sorts of subtle plottings connected with it are practiced and maintained by them; understanding, most noble Lords, that there is in the land a much greater multitude of Lombard brokers than merchants, who do nothing but mischief, and many of those who are held to be Lombards are Jews and Saracens and secret spies, and they have recently brought to the land a very horrible vice that is not to be named, through which the Kingdom cannot fail to be destroyed within a short time if strict corrective measures be not quickly taken.[69]

Why the covert non-Christians in England were suspected of practicing sodomy is not known, though Saracens were associated with the vice in canon law, both as perpetrators and punishers.[70] As for the allegation

---

[68] Milano, "Beer, Elia," p. 527.

[69] *Rotuli Parliamentorum*, 6 vols. (London, 1767–83), 2:332 no. 58: "Item, supplie la Commune, qe touz les Lombardz queux ne usent autre mestier fors cele de brokours, q'ils soint deinz brief faitz voider la terre; issint come male usure et touz les subtils ymaginations d'icell sont par eux compassez et meyntenuz. Entendantz, tres nobles Seigneurs, q'il i ad deins la terre moult greindre multitude de Lombardz brokours qe marchantz, ne ne servent de rien fors de malfaire. Issint come plusours de eux qi sont tenuz Lombards sont Juys et Sarazins, et privees espies, et ont ore tard menez deins la terre un trop horrible vice qe ne fait pas a nomer. Par quoi le Roialme ne poet failler d'estre en brief destruyte, si redde corrigement ne soit sur icell hastivement ordeignez." The Commons have other complaints against Lombards and other foreigners, especially the French. See below at notes 72, 121, and 122.

[70] In a decretal of Alexander III to the archbishop of Palermo, *In archiepiscopatu*, X 5.31.4 (Friedberg, 2:809), he tells him how to deal with the Saracen rapists who abuse Christian women and boys (they can be fined and flogged). The Ordinary Gloss to this

that Italian usurers were harboring Jews and Saracens in their midst, Cecil Roth comments, "Though religious toleration was not conspicuous in the Italian mercantile centers at this period, there may have been some justification for the statement."[71] I should note that in another petition the Commons compare foreign Christians unfavorably to Jews and Saracens,[72] and they consider some Englishmen to be as bad as the Jews who crucified Christ.[73]

As an example of a Lombard who might have aroused the Commons' suspicions, let me cite the vintner Benedict Zachary, who had a given name much in favor with the Jews[74] and a patronymic more suggestive of the Old Testament prophet than the father of John the Baptist. When he received London citizenship in 1365, his place of origin was given simply as "parts of Lombardy."[75] He acted as a broker,[76] and he was in the business of lending money.[77] Whether or not his activity

---

decretal, *CJC*, 2:1728, v. *abuti*, cites another connection, in which Saracens were sent as a divine punishment of sodomy: in Gratian's canon *Si gens Anglorum, Decretum* D. 56 c. 10 (Friedberg 1:222), Saint Boniface warns the king of England about reports that the English are indulging in sexual vices like the Sodomites ("ad instar gentis Sodomitice"), noting that God punished similar behavior in Spain, Provence, and Burgundy by allowing the savage invasion of the Saracens.

[71] Roth, *History*, p. 133.

[72] *Rot. Parl.* 2:337–38 nos. 96–97: Benefices are in the control of brokers in the sinful city of Avignon, and aliens, enemies of our country, have rich benefices but never fulfill their spiritual duties; such bad Christians do more harm than all of the Jews and Saracens of the world. Cf. p. 338, no. 104: The Papal Collector, a French subject, and many other open enemies and spies of English secrets live continually in London, and they and their English and Lombard proctors and "explorers" constantly report on vacant benefices to the Court of Rome and the cardinals, mainly enemies of the English, so that they can purchase the benefices from the pope.

[73] Ibid., 2:338, no. 99: Lay patrons of churches, imitating the greed and simony of the clergy, sell their churches to people who destroy them, just as God was sold to the Jews, who put him to death.

[74] See the discussion of Benedict, Bishop of the Jews, and Benedict Crispin, at note 52 above. In one document of 1297, *CCR* 1296–302, p. 27, there is reference to three Jewish Benedicts of Oxford: Benedict Levesqe, Benedict Caus, and Benedict of Winchester (Benedict Levesk is mentioned again on p. 343), and in 1301 we hear of another Benedict, who used to live in Lincoln (p. 482). The form "Bennet" is also found: *Cal. Ancient Deeds* 2:511, C 2362: Bennet son of Master Elias, Jew of London.

[75] Alice Beardwood, *Alien Merchants in England, 1350 to 1377: Their Legal and Economic Position* (Cambridge, Mass.: Medieval Academy, 1931), pp. 66–67, 185, 199.

[76] *Calendar of Plea and Memoranda Rolls Preserved among the Archives of the Corporation of the City of London at the Guild-Hall*, ed. A. H. Thomas, 6 vols. (Cambridge: Cambridge University Press, 1926–61), 2:103: 18 August 1369, "Letter of Attorney from William de Nerny, merchant of Genoa, to William de Strete and Benedict Zacarie, vintners."

[77] *CCR* 1364–68, p. 290: 11 July 1366; *CCR* 1369–74, pp. 477–78: 12 November 1372; *CPR* 1370–74, p. 229: 14 December 1372.

constituted "evil usury," we should remember that, even though usury might be deemed sinful, if one agrees to it one is obliged to pay up.[78]

A possible candidate for an Italian—in fact, Sicilian—Muslim in England is to be had in the 1380s in the person of Richard of Sicily, who was baptized by Robert Braybrooke, bishop of London, at the manor of Langley in the presence of King Richard II. The king obviously served as sponsor, that is, godfather, for him and gave him his baptismal name. He has been brought to the attention of medievalists in recent years, notably by Lee Patterson.[79] But Patterson is misled by Adler, who in turn was misled by Frederick Devon, the editor of the Exchequer calendar, in identifying him as a Jew.[80] Adler also has him baptized in 1390, whereas the baptism must have occurred in 1386. The Exchequer record, dated December 14, 1389, states that at the time of his baptism he was granted an annuity of £10, which was in arrears, to the amount of 50 marks, which comes to more than £33. The king orders this sum to be paid to him, and he authorizes the convert to trade "Catholically" with certain Christians outside the realm of England.[81] The entry on the

---

[78] This is brought out in the standard papal crusader-letter exempting crusaders from usuries otherwise due, such as that issued to John of Gaunt by Pope Urban VI in 1383 to take arms against the schismatics (those who sided with the Avignonese pope, Clement VII). He does not have to pay interest ("usuries") to money-lenders, and, if the lenders are Jewish, the principal does not have to be repaid until he has died or returned home. Shlomo Simonsohn, *The Apostolic See and the Jews*, 7 vols. (Toronto: PIMS, 1988–91), vol. 1 (*Documents: 492–1404*), no. 437 (Urban VI to John of Gaunt, 8 April 1383, pp. 464–65). For a fuller text of a crusader privilege, with explanation, see Simonsohn, no. 143 (Gregory IX, 13 April 1235, pp. 153–54): "Creditors of the crusaders, including Jews, are to free them from their oaths, desist from the exaction of interest, and return that already collected. Crusaders who are unable at present to pay their debts to Jews shall not incur interest until their death or return is known. Jews are to add to the principal the income from the pawn, after deduction of expenses." Christian creditors are to be constrained by ecclesiastical censure (excommunication), and Jews by threat of being shunned (subtracting the communion of the faithful from them).

[79] Lee Patterson, "Living Witnesses" (note 2 above), p. 541.

[80] Adler, *Jews of Medieval England*, pp. 322–23, citing Frederick Devon, *Issues of the Exchequer . . . from King Henry III to King Henry VI* (London: Murray, 1837), p. 242, the Issue Roll for Michaelmas, 13 Richard II, 14 December 1389). Devon's summary reads: "To Richard de Cicilia, a converted Jew, baptized by the Venerable Father Robert, Bishop of London, at the manor of Langeley, in the presence of the Lord the King, on account of which the said Lord the King granted to the said Richard a certain annuity of £10, to be received at the Exchequer for term of his life in aid of his support. In money paid to him by assignment made this day in discharge of 50 marks which the said Lord the King commanded to be paid him as a reward, because that, as yet, the aforesaid Richard had received nothing of the annuity aforesaid, and also to qualify him as a Catholic to traffic with certain Christians out of England. By writ, etc., £33 6s 8d."

[81] London, Public Record Office, E 403/527 m. 12 (14 December 1389): "*Ricardus de Cicilia, conversus. Ricardo de Cicilia converso, jam raro per venerabilem patrem Robertum Episcopum Londoniensem apud manerium de Langeley in presencia Domini Regis bap-*

Patent Rolls, which was made a month before this, on 14 November 1389, is a notification to all and sundry that Richard of Sicily, having recently received baptism at Langley from the bishop of London in the presence of the king, now proposes to go abroad and engage in Catholic trading with other Christians, and the king wishes to broadcast these circumstances in order to allay any "sinister suspicion" that might arise concerning the convert.[82]

On the face of it, it would seem strange for a Sicilian of any sort to be in England, and stranger still for him to be either a Jew or a Muslim. There were plenty of Jews in Sicily, but their businesses and trading were mainly internal, and they appear only rarely in maritime trade; and the only Muslims or other non-Christians in Sicily at this time in any significant numbers were slaves purchased in the slave market.[83]

---

tisato, ob quam quidem causam dictus Dominus Rex concessit dicto Ricardo quandam annuetatem decem librarum ad Scaccarium ad terminum vite sue in auxilium sustentacionis sue. In denariis etc. liberatis per assignationem etc. factam isto die in persolucionem L marcarum, quas predictus dominus Rex etc. liberare mandavit, in recompensacionem, et pro eo quod hucusque predictus Ricardus nichil receperit de annuetate predicta. Et ipsum disponit ad Catholice mercandisandum cum quibusdam Christianis extra partes Anglie," etc. ("*Richard of Sicily, convert.* To Richard of Sicily, convert, now recently (?) baptized by the venerable father Robert, Bishop of London, at the manor of Langley, in the presence of the Lord King, for which reason the said Lord King granted to the said Richard a certain annuity of £10 at the Exchequer for the term of his life to aid in his sustenance. In pence, etc., delivered by assignment, etc., made this day in payment of 50 marks, which the foresaid Lord King ordered in recompense, and because up until this time the foresaid Richard had received nothing of the foresaid annuity. And he disposes him to trade in Catholic fashion with certain Christians outside the parts of England").

[82] PRO C66/329 m. 29 (*CPR* 1388–92, p. 158: 14 November 1389): "*Pro Ricardo de Cicile, converso.* Rex omnibus ad quos, etc., Salutem. Quia Ricardus de Cicile, conversus, nuper in presentia nostra apud manerium nostrum de Langeley recepit sacramentum baptismi per venerabilem in Christo patrem, carissimum consangineum nostrum, episcopum Londoniensem, et est in proposito proficiscendi ad diversas partes ad mercandisandum Catholice cum aliis Christianis, ut dicit, nos, ob reverentiam Dei, ne de prefato Ricardo sinistra suspicio futuris temporibus habeatur, vobis omnibus et singulis hoc innotescimus per presentes" ("*For Richard of Sicily, convert.* The King to all to whom, etc., Good health. Because Richard of Sicily, convert, recently in our presence received the sacrament of baptism through the venerable father in Christ, our dear kinsman, the bishop of London, and because he proposes to go to various parts to merchandise Catholically with other Christians, as he says, we, out of reverence for God, make this known to you, all and singular, by these present letters, lest sinister suspicion be had concerning the aforesaid Richard in future times"). The CPR calendarer, wrongly assuming that Richard is wishing to conduct such trade within England itself, paraphrases the text thus: "he proposes to go to divers parts [of the country] to trade *catholice* with other Christians."

[83] My informant here is Professor David Abulafia, Professor of Mediterranean History at Cambridge University, and author of *Italy, Sicily, and the Mediterranean, 1100–1400* (London: Variorum Reprints, 1987).

Even the Jews who ventured onto the waters seem to have restricted themselves, like other traders, mainly to Mediterranean ports.[84] The slave trade at this time was in the "Tartar cycle," roughly 1360–1400.[85] The Tartar slaves came mainly from the Crimea (the northern shores of the Black Sea).[86] Only a third of the Tartar slaves in Sicily in the period 1370–1400 were men, and most of them seem to have been baptized.[87] Nevertheless, in spite of the small number of available candidates, it seems no more unlikely that Richard of Sicily was a manumitted slave[88] than a Jewish mariner, and, since the Genoese were the most active traders in importing slaves from the Black Sea,[89] and since the Genoese regularly visited England, he may have hired on as a seaman or merchant apprentice on one of their ships and arrived in London in that way.[90]

All that we really know about Richard of Sicily is that he received the high honor of being adopted as Richard II's godson and was baptized by the bishop of London at one of the king's manors and given a lavish annuity. But three years later he returned with a complaint, or perhaps

[84] See Henri Bresc, *Arabes de langue, Juifs de religion: L'evolution du Judaisme sicilien dans l'environement latin, XII–Xve siècles* (Paris: Bouchène, 2001), esp. pp. 228 (Jews on a Catalan galley go to Syria, 1448), pp. 245–46 (products come from Alexandria, Turkey, Genoa, Catalonia, Naples, Gaeta, Amalfi, and Saracen countries), p. 253 (trade in the fourteenth century with Majorca, Catalonia, even Cyprus), p. 255 (trade with Tunisia).

[85] Ibid., p. 257. Earlier there was the Saracen cycle, 1280–1310, and the Romanian Greek cycle, 1310–60, while the subsequent cycle, 1400–1440, was of Blacks and unbaptized Saracens. See also Bresc's paper, "Une société esclavagiste médiévale: L'exemple de la Sicile," *Sardegna, Mediterraneo e Atlantico tra Medioevo ed etè moderna: Studi storici in memoria di Alberto Boscolo*, ed. Luisa d'Arienzo, 2 vols. (Rome: Bulzoni, 1993), 2:297–314.

[86] To judge from the slave trade in Florence at this time, "Tartar" had quite a wide range of meaning, since the slaves, so designated, were classified as being in six different colors. Of a group of 242, 2 are black, 18 brown, 161 olive, 11 blond (*flavus*), 5 reddish, and 45 white. See Steven A. Epstein, *Speaking of Slavery: Color, Ethnicity, and Human Bondage in Italy* (Ithaca: Cornell University Press, 2001), p. 108.

[87] Out of a series of deeds concerning 78 slaves listed by a notary in Palermo between 1378 and 1384, 29 are male and 49 female; for 7 of the males and 9 of the females, there is no indication about whether they are baptized, but of the 22 males for which the information is given, only two are unbaptized. See Charles Verlinden, *L'esclavage dans l'Europe médiévale*, 2 vols. (Ghent: Rijksuniversiteit te Gent, 1955–77), 2:179–83, 239, 1017.

[88] For formulas of manumission, see Matteo Gaudioso, *La schiavitù domestica in Sicilia dopo i Normanni: Legislazione, dottrina, formule* (Catania: Galàtola, 1926), pp. 115–30: "Il formulario degli atti de manomissione."

[89] Verlinden, *L'esclavage dans l'Europe médiévale*, 2:184.

[90] Verlinden gives examples of a freed Black who obtained a job in 1360 as a muleteer, and a freed Bulgarian in the same year who worked as a household handyman (2:246).

two complaints, and a request. In the first place, his annuity had never been paid. In the second place, he was concerned about his ability to engage in trade as a Christian abroad, fearing that other Christians would suspect him of not really being a Christian. Perhaps he had already experienced such a reaction, whether because of his foreign appearance (dark skin?) or for other reasons. The Commons of 1376 of course would have also suspected him of fostering sodomy.

Another likely Muslim convert is William Piers, to whom a payment was made on January 9, 1393, in keeping with a grant of two pence a day made by Richard II in the previous May, because he had been "converted to the Christian faith and recently baptized in our law." Once again, he is identified in the modern Exchequer calendar as a Jew,[91] but not in the original enrollment.[92] This convert undoubtedly came from the Iberian peninsula; there were Portuguese and Spanish shipmen and merchants in England of this name, which also appears as Peres, Perez, Peritz, Periz, Pers, Perytz, and Pieres.[93] A prominent example was Lope Piers, knight of Spain (*Lupus Piers, miles Ispannie*), one of John of Gaunt's Castilian retainers, who in 1386 was given a grant to pay off his debts in London.[94] As claimant to the Spanish throne, Gaunt maintained a chancery and had a large following in England, not only numerous knights and their retinues, but also "a number of Castilians of lesser rank and of various trades and professions. . . . Among them were Cas-

[91] Devon, *Issues*, p. 250: Issue Roll, Michaelmas, 16 Richard II, 9 January (1393): "To William Piers, a converted Jew to whom the present Lord the King by his letters patent granted 2d daily, to be received during his life at the Exchequer, etc., because the same William was converted to the Christian faith and lately baptized into our law. In money paid to him, viz., to his own hands, in discharge of £1 10s 4d, etc., for 182 days, etc., by writ, etc., £1 10s 4d."

[92] PRO E 403 / 541 m. 11 (9 January 1393): "*Willielmus Piers conversus*. Willielmo Piers, converso, cui Dominus Rex memoratus secundo die Maii proximo preterito ii d. denarios [*sic*] ad Scaccarium ad totam vitam suam ad terminos sancti Michaelis et Pasche per equales porciones percipiendos, pro eo quod idem Willielmus ad fidem Christianam conversus et in lege nostro nuper baptizatus fuit, per has litteras patentes conceditur. In denariis sibi liberatis, videlicet per manus proprias in persolucionem xxxx iiiid sibi liberandorum [. . .] videlicet pro rato a secundo die Maii proximo preterito usque ultimum diem Octobris termino proximo sequentem, per C iiii-xx ii [= 182] dies utroque die computato," etc. (Devon's entry in the previous note gives an adequate translation except for calling William a Jew).

[93] *Index of Ancient Petitions of the Chancery and the Exchequer Preserved in the Public Record Office*, rev. ed., Public Record Office, Lists and Indexes, no. 1 (New York: Kraus, 1966), p. 244. One of the persons listed here, John Piers de Saruspe, is a shipmaster from Berneo in the Bay of Biscay, near Bilbao. See the *CCR* entries for 16 June 1384 (1381–85, p. 381) and 21 November 1385 (1385–89, p. 92).

[94] Russell, *English Intervention*, p. 414 n. 3.

tilian sea-captains, sailors and merchants, friars, and a variety of nonde-script persons, including agents from Castile, about whom we know nothing more than their Peninsular names."[95] One of the latter is Martin Piers, said to be exiled from Castile by "le Batard" (Henry of Trastamara, that is, Enrique II) because of his loyalty to Gaunt.[96]

"Perez" is usually to be taken as the Christian patronymic, meaning "of Peter."[97] If that was the case with William Piers, it would mean that he adopted it along with his Christian baptismal name, or, even more likely, that he had adopted it before his conversion, since it was customary for Castilian Jews and Moors to use Christian names.[98] Given these naming practices in Spain, therefore, it is not evident from Martin Piers's Christian name whether he was Christian, Jewish, or Muslim, or an ex-Jewish or ex-Muslim Christian. As discussed above, the fact that neither Richard of Sicily nor William Piers were to be paid by the Keeper of the House of Converts may be an indication that they were not Jews, but rather Muslims.[99]

[95] Ibid., pp. 176–84, esp. 182.

[96] Ibid., p. 182 n. 4, citing PRO Chancery Warrants (Signets): C81/1730, no. 59. The name appears as "Martin Piers" in the French text of the warrant, which Russell simply gives as "Martín Pérez."

[97] Another possibility to be considered is that William Piers's name was the Hebrew name Perez or Peretz, from Genesis 38.29, but I have as yet found no sign of its use in Iberia. My UCLA colleague Herbert Davidson informs me that the given name Peretz was used in the Middle Ages and into modern times among the Ashkenazic Jews, and that Peretz as a family name appears after European Jews took surnames—e.g., Y. Peretz, a celebrated Yiddish writer, who lived in Warsaw in the late nineteenth and early twentieth centuries. Shimeon Peres has a different name, with an "s," not a "tz."

[98] Shortly after the downfall of King Pedro ("the Cruel") in 1369, which Chaucer describes as the tragedy of "Petro, glorie of Spaine" (The Monk's Tale, 2375), the new king, Enrique II, in the Cortes of 1371 ordered that the Jews, who were Peter's "warm supporters," could no longer use Christian names (Russell, 165 n. 1). But, in fact, Enrique was responding to a petition of the nobles and proctors against the power exercised by "the enemies of the faith, especially the Jews." The complaint about taking Christian names came at the end, and the king in his answer took it up first, saying that neither Jews nor Moors were to have names of Christians: Cortes de los antiguos reinos de León y de Castilla, vol. 2 (Madrid: Rivadeneyra, 1863), Córtes de Toro, 1371, petition 2, pp. 203–4.

[99] Another Spanish retainer of Gaunt's who was to receive an income of two pence a day from the duke's great wardrobe, by an order of 10 December 1374, might strike us as having a Jewish name: Emanuel of Spain. See Sydney Armitage-Smith, ed., John of Gaunt's Register, 2 vols., Camden Society 3.20–21 (London 1911), 2:274 no. 1591, and Besserman, "Chaucer, Spain, and the Prioress's Antisemitism," pp. 346–47. But Emanuel, or Manuel, seems to have been only a Christian name in this era; it was first used by the Greeks and then became popular in Spain and Portugal; so E. G. Withycombe, The Oxford Dictionary of English Christian Names, 3rd ed. (Oxford: Oxford University Press, 1977), p. 102.

When we look at the entry on the Patent Rolls, made at the time of the original grant (May 2, 1392) to William, we find an interesting reason given for action: the grant of two pence a day to William Piers, described as in the later entry as "a convert to the Christian faith and recently baptized in our law," was made in order "to attract and induce the unbelieving to accept the Catholic Faith."[100] This sounds very much as if there are other "infidels" living in England who are expected to take note of the pension awaiting them if they convert; and, additionally (or, alternatively), it can be seen as an invitation for other non-Christians to come to England and convert.

A convert who was certainly an ex-Muslim was a godson of Henry Bolingbroke, Earl of Derby, whom he doubtless brought back with him from Rhodes on his return trip from the Holy Land. He probably arrived with him in England at the end of June 1393. He is variously called "the baptized Henry," "Henry of Rhodes," "Henry the Turk," and "Henry the Saracen."[101] But just as we should be alert to the possibility that "Lombards" refers to all Italians or all bankers, so too we should remember that under the name of "Saracens" it was common at this time to include all non-Jewish non-Christians. I need only refer to the *Middle English Dictionary* entries "Sarasin," "Sarasine," and so on. In other words, "pagan," "heathen," and "Saracen" were often interchangeable words designating infidels, and Saracens of various sorts had long been the enemy in romances.[102] We should also recall that the followers of Mahomet were readily classed with heathens and idolators

---

[100] PRO C66/334 m. 15 (*CPR 1391–96*, p. 50: 2 May 1392): "*Pro Willielmo Piers, converso.* "Rex omnibus ad quos, etc., Salutem. Sciatis quod de gracia nostra speciali, ac eciam ad incredulos ad fidem catholicam trahendos et inducendos, concessimus Willielmo Piers, ad fidem Christianam converso et in lege nostra nuper baptizato, duos denarios per diem percipiendos singulis annis ad Scaccarium nostrum pro termino vite sue ad terminos sancti Michaelis et Pasche per equales porciones" (*For William Piers, convert.* The King to all to whom, etc., Good health. Know that, of our special grace, and also for the purpose of attracting and inducing the unbelieving to the Catholic faith, we have conceded to William Piers, a convert to the Christian faith and recently baptized in our law, two pence per day to be drawn every year at our Exchequer for the term of his life, at the terms of St. Michael and Easter, in equal portions").

[101] Lucy Toulmin Smith, ed., *Expeditions to Prussia and the Holy Land Made by Henry Earl of Derby (Afterwards King Henry IV) in the Years 1390–1 and 1392–3; Being the Accounts Kept by His Treasurer During Two Years*, Camden new series 52 ([London] 1894), pp. lxvi, 230, and 254 ("Henricus baptizatus"), 233 ("Henricus Turk"), 240 and 284 ("Henricus de Rodez"), 287 ("Henricus Sarasin").

[102] See Diane Speed, "The Saracens of *King Horn*," *Speculum* 65 (1990): 564–95, and Dorothee Metlitzki, *The Matter of Araby in Medieval England* (New Haven: Yale, 1977), esp. chap. 6, "History and Romance," pp. 117–219.

(see the *MED* entries on "maumet" and "maumetrie"). Chaucer does this in *The Parson's Tale* (749–50), though not in *The Man of Law's Tale*, where it is recognized that "Makomete" claimed to be a messenger of God (MLT 333).[103]

From his reading of Nicholas Trevet's *Chroniques*, Chaucer learned of the "pagan merchants from the Great Saracen" ("marchantz paens hors de la grande Sarazine") who came to the court of the Roman emperor; they were converted to the Christian faith through the preaching of the emperor's daughter Constance, and when they went home to their own land and revealed their faith to their Saracen neighbors and relatives, they were brought before the high sultan.[104] The Man of Law claims to have heard this story from a merchant (ProlMLT 132–33), and Chaucer may have been thinking of similar foreign merchants in his own day who were not Jewish but pagans of the Mohammedan variety, like, presumably, the "Lord of Palatie," for whom the Knight fought in Turkey against "another hethen" (GP 65–66).

The Heathens of the North

What about pagans of the polytheistic variety encountered in the Knight's other forays into "hethenesse"? We are told (GP.54–56),

> Ful ofte time he hadde the bord bigonne
> Aboven alle nacions in Pruce;
> In Lettow hadde he reised and in Ruce,

referring to Prussia, Lithuania, and Russia. One well-publicized foray of English knights into Prussia was led by Henry of Grosmont, Earl of Derby, and Duke of Lancaster, in 1351.[105] According to John Capgrave's *Liber de illustribus Henricis*, Henry was accompanied by a number

---

[103] My citations of Chaucer are from *The Canterbury Tales*, ed. Larry D. Benson, and, for his other works, from *The Riverside Chaucer*, gen. ed. Larry D. Benson (Boston: Houghton Mifflin, 1987).

[104] Nicholas Trevet, history of Constance in *Les Chroniques ecrites pour Marie d'Angleterre*, ed. Margaret Schlauch, *Sources and Analogues of Chaucer's Canterbury Tales*, ed. W. F. Bryan and Germaine Dempster (Chicago: University of Chicago Press, 1941), pp. 165–81, at 165.

[105] Toulmin Smith, *Expeditions to Prussia and the Holy Land*, pp. xv, xvii; Kenneth Fowler, *The King's Lieutenant: Henry of Grosmont, First Duke of Lancaster, 1310–1361* (New York: Barnes and Noble, 1969), pp. 105–6.

of other earls: Northampton, Suffolk, Salisbury, and Stafford.[106] A late fifteenth-century report says that yet another English earl, Thomas of Warwick, not only went to Prussia but captured the son of the king of Lettow and brought him back to London to be baptized with his own name, Thomas.[107] Warwick's sojourn in Prussia is not mentioned by English writers, but the Prussian chronicler Wigand of Marburg tells us of his presence there in 1365, and his account allows us to conclude that his Lithuanian godson was a prince named Surwillo. Surwillo later returned to Prussia (if it is true that he was taken to England to be baptized), and, as Thomas Surwillo, joined the Teutonic Knights and was among the forces launched against the Lithuanians in 1390.[108]

The terms of the conflict should have been very different in 1390, since the Lithuanians had converted en masse to Catholic Christianity in 1387. But, as is evident from the reports of the chroniclers, not only Wigand in Prussia but also Thomas Walsingham in England, the allies of the Teutonic Knights in the 1390 campaign were under the impression that the Lithuanians were still pagan. This was also the report of the biographer of the celebrated French knight Boucicaut, who calls the adversaries Saracens.[109] Walsingham at this point calls them simply *pagani*,[110] but when he reports on the battle of Tannenberg twenty years later, he too refers to the infidels of the area as Saracens. But now, at this point, in 1410, Walsingham knows that the Lithuanians are neophyte Christians, but he believes that they were only recently converted.[111]

One of the English knights who participated in the 1390 campaign against the Lithuanians was Henry Bolingbroke, who purchased and cared for several Lithuanian boys, one of them called Henry Lettowe. Lucy Toulmin Smith assumes, no doubt rightly, that Henry's purpose

---

[106] Theodor Hirsch in his edition of Wigand of Marburg, *Cronaca nova prutenica*, in *Scriptores rerum Prussicarum*, vol. 2, ed. Hirsch et al. (Leipzig 1863, repr. Frankfurt: Minerva, 1965), pp. 429–800, collects the reports of Prussian campaigns in English sources in appendix 9, pp. 788–96 (the account of Capgrave referred to is on p. 794; he gives Scottish reports in appendix 10, pp. 796–800).

[107] *Pageant of the Birth, Life, and Death of Richard Beauchamp, Earl of Warwick, K.G., 1389–1439*, ed. Viscount Dillon and W. H. St. John Hope (London: Longmans, 1914), pp. 43–44.

[108] Wigand, chap. 61 (p. 549); chap. 63a (pp. 550–51); chap. 149 (p. 640).

[109] *Le livre des fais du bon messire Jehan le Maingre, dit Bouciquaut, mareschal de France et gouverneur de Jennes*, ed. Denis Lalande (Geneva: Droz, 1985), 1.11, p. 40.

[110] Thomas Walsingham, Oxford, MS Bodl. 462, fol. 203v (an unpublished section of his early abbreviated chronicle).

[111] Walsingham, *Historia anglicana*, ed. Henry Thomas Riley, 2 vols., Rolls Series 28.1 (London: Longman, Green, Longman, Roberts, and Green, 1863–64), 2:284 .

was to make Christians out of the boys, and that he was the godfather of young Henry; but Toulmin Smith's assumption is based partly on a misreading of Thomas Walsingham's report of the siege, to say that eight Lithuanians were captured and converted, whereas he should be read to say 8,000.[112]

Probably, then, Bolingbroke had the boys baptized, whether or not they had been baptized before, either not knowing about their christening or accepting the word of the Teutonic Knights that the Lithuanian conversion was bogus. As with his Rhodian godson a bit later, it is likely that he brought these converts back to England with him,[113] and the same may have been true of other Englishmen who served in the area, as Chaucer's Knight was said to have done.

In 1393, shortly after Bolingbroke's return from his second foreign tour, which started out in the summer of 1392 in Prussia, we hear of a Prussian convert, Peter Prus, to whom a Londoner named Paul Salesbury was licensed to give an annual income for life of forty shillings. The income is to come from Salesbury's properties, but the grant makes it sound as if the king is doing him a favor ("by our special grace to Paul he can pay Peter").[114] What Salesbury's involvement with the con-

---

[112] Toulmin Smith, *Expeditions to Prussia and the Holy Land*, p. xix, citing Walsingham, *Historia anglicana*, 2:197–98: "Facti sunt Christiani de gente de Lettow octo, et Magister de Lifland duxit secum in suam patriam tria, millia prisonum." This is the long version of Walsingham's chronicle. The abbreviated version makes the meaning clear: "De gente de Lettowe octo millia Christianitatis ritum susceperunt, preter eos quos Magister de Lyfland secum duxit in patriam, ad tria millia captivorum" (loc. cit. MS Bodl. 462). I treat these matters more fully in another essay, "Chaucer's Knight and the 'Northern Crusades': The Example of Henry Bolingbroke," in *Medieval Cultural Studies in Honor of Stephen Knight*, ed. Helen Fulton, David Matthews, and Ruth Evans (Cardiff: University of Wales Press, 2005, forthcoming).

[113] Toulmin Smith, *Expeditions to Prussia and the Holy Land*, p. xxxi.

[114] *CPR 1391–96*, p. 323, 22 October 1393. The record reads (PRO C66/338 m. 18): "Sciatis quod de gratia nostra speciali concessimus et licenciam dedimus dilecto nobis Paulo Salesbury quod ipse dare possit et concedere Petro Prus, converso, quendam annuum redditum quadraginta solidorum percipiendorum de terris et tenementis prefati Pauli in Civitate nostra Londoniense ad totam vitam ipsius Petri" ("Know that we of our special grace have granted to our beloved Paul Salesbury that he can give and grant to Peter Prus, convert, an annual income of forty shillings to be received from the lands and tenements of the said Paul in our city of London for the said Peter's whole life"). The text of the king's warrant to the chancellor throws no further light on the matter: PRO C81/543 no. 9051: "Richard, par la grace de Dieu Roy d'Engleterre et de France et Seigneur d'Irlande, a l'onnrable Piere en Dieu, nostre treschere cousin, l'Ercevesque d'Everwyk, Primat d'Engleterre, nostre Chanceller, saluz. Come de notre grace especiale eous [sic] grantez et donez congie a nostre bien ame Paul Salesbury qil puisse doner et granter a Petir Prus, convers, un annuele rent de quarante soldz a prendre des terres et tenementz du dit Paul en nostre Citee de Londres a toute la vie du dit Petir, vous

vert was is not known. He owned a quay near the Tower, and during the uprising of 1381 he had tried to take advantage of the tumult to get back some properties that had eluded his hands.[115] It is possible that Peter Prus was not a "prize of war" but rather a Baltic seaman or merchant.

Summary: The Documentary Evidence

Enough has been said to put Chaucer's lifetime into context, and to indicate the sort of direct knowledge of Jews, Muslims, and other "Saracens," including those from the Baltic regions, that could have been available to him in his own country. Of course, we must suppose that Chaucer would have encountered non-Christians and converts on his trips outside England, especially Jews and Muslims in Spain in 1366 and Tartar slaves in Italy, particularly in Genoa.

If the above evidence does not justify our concluding that the general attitude of Chaucer's time was one of easy toleration of non-Christians, attended by the hope of converting the unbelievers to the true faith, we should at least be able at this stage to modify the opinion of Nigel Saul: "Exceptionally among English rulers, [Richard II] was vigorous in sponsoring the conversion of unbelievers: on two occasions he was present when Jews were received into the faith in the chapel of his manor at King's Langley."[116] He is referring to Richard of Sicily and William Piers, but, as explained above, they were probably both Muslims, and only the former was baptized before the king at Langley. Moreover, as we have seen, both Richard's immediate predecessor, Edward III, and his immediate successor, Henry IV, were active in supporting converts; Henry in fact had pagan, Muslim, and Jewish godchildren. Furthermore, we must be wary of W. D. Rubenstein's assessment that "medie-

---

mandons qe sur ce facez faire noz lettres desous nostre grand seal en due forme. Dousouz nostre prive seal a Westm. le xxii jour d'Octobre, l'an de nostre regne dys et septisme" ("Richard, by the grace of God King of England and France and Lord of Ireland, to the honorable Father in God, our most dear cousin, the Archbishop of York, Primate of England, our Chancellor, good health. Since of our special grace we have granted leave to our well loved Paul Salesbury that he can give and grant to Peter Prus, convert, an annual rent of forty shillings to be taken from the lands and tenements of the said Paul in our City of London, for the whole life of the said Peter, we order you to have our letters made on this matter under our great seal in due form. Under our privy seal at Westminster, the 22nd day of October, the year of our reign ten and seventh").
[115] CPR 1381–85, p. 30, pardon to Paul Salesbury, 22 July 1381. See pp. 149, 299.
[116] Nigel Saul, *Richard II* (New Haven: Yale University Press, 1997), p. 449.

val England was among the least tolerant and most anti-semitic of European states of the day, even by the standards then prevailing."[117]

It is absolutely certain that Richard of Sicily was in England in 1386 as a non-Christian, since he was baptized at Langley. It is probable, too, that William Piers, recently baptized in 1392, was also in England before his conversion (especially since his pension was given as an example to other infidels to convert), and the same is definitely true of the ex-Jews Joan and Alice, baptized at Dartmouth in the next decade. There appears to have been, then, at least a transient population of non-Christians in the realm, and possibly even a permanent community of resident Jews who were attended by "bishops" like Rabbi Moses.

It may have been common knowledge that pensions were available for converts. To judge from that data we have seen, the going rate for a Jewish convert was a penny a day, to be received at the House of Converts. It seems to have been decided in 1392 to make conversion more attractive for non-Jews, by promising a pension of 2 pence a day, beginning with William Piers. That came to 60s a year, far less of course than the pension of 200s (£10) a year received by the king's godson, Richard of Sicily in 1386, but more than the 40s per annum that Peter Prus was awarded in 1393. The rate for Jews was still a penny a day (about 30s) when Rabbi Moses's daughter Elizabeth entered in 1399. As a special concession to her, it was doubled in 1403 to 60s, and then, a few years later, the stipend was increased for all Jewish converts to a penny and a half a day (45s).

By the latter part of the fourteenth century, there seems to have been no call to renew the old expulsion order of 1290 against the Jews. This expulsion did not take the form of a statute in the first place but was simply an *ad hoc* measure dictated by a temporary crisis.[118] Although there were some place names that recalled the previous Jewish population, as with London's Old Jewry,[119] and occasional references to the

[117] W. D. Rubinstein, *A History of the Jews in the English Speaking World: Great Britain* (London, 1940; repr. New York: St. Martin's, 1996), p. 40.
[118] See Stacey, "Conversion of Jews," p. 282: "Officially, the expulsion was justified as punishment for the Jews because they allegedly had continued to lend money at interest despite the prohibitions pronounced in the king's 1275 Statute of Jewry [citing *CCR*, 1288–96, p. 109]. In fact, the expulsion was the unpremeditated outcome of a four-month-long parliamentary negotiation in which the financially indebted Edward sought permission to raise a tax from his Christian subjects without being able to claim any ongoing military necessities that would have justified one. He was therefore compelled to bargain, and in the bargaining that followed the king was forced to concede a variety of legal and administrative reforms as well as the expulsion of the Jews."
[119] See below, pages 164–5.

expulsion in regard to property once owned by the Jews,[120] there is no sign of regarding Jewish exclusion as a continuing policy. *A fortiori*, there was never an articulated policy about keeping out Muslims and polytheists. In fact, it is hard to imagine how such a policy could have been put into effect. There could hardly have been a faith-based interrogation (Christian? Jewish? Other?) administered to all hands and passengers on every vessel entering English ports. We note that the Commons in their effort to rid the realm of infiltrated Jews and Saracens did not refer to any such kind of passport controls, or suggest a rounding up of suspects for grilling, but instead came up with a new expulsion plan: cut short the visits of all Lombards who are not gainfully employed. In the same Parliament of 1376, the Commons also wished to have all Frenchmen ejected while hostilities with France continued, but this petition was summarily rejected by the king.[121] Their complaint against foreigners' staying as long as they pleased in England, holding hostels, acting as brokers, and selling retail met with a bland response.[122] However, their further petition to deny all Church benefices to foreigners received a pledge of action; and, sure enough, six years later, in the Parliament of 1383, a statute was passed prohibiting all present and future holding of benefices by aliens.[123] So, of all the concerns of the Commons in 1376, it was not non-Christian foreigners or Frenchmen that the government was most concerned about, but rather foreign clergymen who were taking over benefices. I should note that earlier on, in 1369, the Commons

[120] See, for instance, two patents of Henry IV, issued in 1402 and 1406. The first, calendared in *CPR 1401–5*, pp. 90–91: 2 April 1402, is a grant for life to one William Wyghtman of 29s yearly from the issues of certain lands, specified thus (in the calendar summary): "the citizens of Canterbury owe to the king 10s yearly from the houses late of the Friars of the Sack in Canterbury which the king recovered as escheat in the eyre of Henry [*lege* Hervey] de Staunton; they owe 10s yearly from a house in the city late of John Bord who abjured the realm, which the king recovered as escheat in the said eyre; the bailiffs of Canterbury owe 8d of rent of houses late of the Jews in the city," and so on. The Eyre of Kent was held by Justice Staunton in 1313–14: *Year Books of Edward II: The Eyre of Kent, 6 and 7 Edward II, A.D. 1313–1314*, ed. Frederic William Maitland et al., 3 vols., Selden Society 24, 27, 29 (London, 1910–13). The second patent, calendared in *CPR 1405–8*, p. 281, 23 November 1406, is a grant to king's clerk Richard Gabriell "of all lands late of Nicholas de Wodegrave in the town of Chellesward *alias* Chollesworthy, in the king's hands by the exile of the Jews," and so on.

[121] *Rot. Parl.* 2:343 no. 128 (1376).

[122] Ibid., 2:347 no. 143.

[123] Ibid., 3:162: 7 Richard II (1383) no. 49; *The Statutes of the Realm*, 12 vols. (London 1810–28, repr. London: Dawsons, 1963; Buffalo: Hein, 1993), 2:34–35. See Keechang Kim, *Aliens in Medieval Law: The Origins of Modern Citizenship* (Cambridge: Cambridge University Press, 2000), p. 83. Kim thinks that the statute was never enforced (pp. 85–86).

intervened to kill a fact-finding mission concerning foreigners living in England: "After commissioners had been appointed to make a census of aliens living in the country, they were recalled at the request of the Commons, because they were annoying to the foreigners."[124]

If there was any likely time to revive an official anti-Jewish stance, it might seem to have been during the later years of Chaucer's life, when there was increasing concern over the Wycliffite threat to orthodox religion, which culminated in the statute *Contra Lollardos* (which modern historians wrongly call *De heretico comburendo*) in 1401.[125] The statute was made at the request of the clergy, and the language of their petition was incorporated into it.[126] The present king's progenitors are praised for their zeal in preventing any perverse doctrines from gaining ground, and the bishops now appeal for royal help in combating the new sect that has arisen against the faith.

Would this not have been a good opportunity to increase vigilance against anti-Christian religions as well? The standard term for heresy was *heretica pravitas*, and we have seen that the Jewish religion was referred to as *Judaica pravitas*. It is quite clear that there had been laxity in the recent past, especially concerning the latter depravity. There is, however, no indication that any such reaction was to be found. Moreover, it is unlikely that any visiting or resident non-Christians would have been bound to wear distinctive garb, though the Fourth Lateran requirement to do so was still on the canonical books.[127] Spanish Jews

[124] Alice Beardwood, *Alien Merchants in England, 1350 to 1377: Their Legal and Economic Position* (Cambridge, Mass.: Medieval Academy, 1931), p. 39.

[125] *Statutes of the Realm*, 2:125–28: *Contra Lollardos*. The rubric *De heretico comburendo*, if it can be found at all, would be applicable to the writ that authorized the burning of specific heretics. The first such writ, issued against William Sawtrey just before the passing of the statute, is titled (as usual, in the left margin), *De comburendo Willielmum Sautre, capellanum*. PRO C54/247 m. 6. This title for the writ is not recorded in *Rotuli Parliamentorum* 3:459, or in Rymer, *Foedera*, 8:178 (3rd ed., 3:4:197), or in *CCR* 1401–5, p. 265: 26 February 1401.

[126] A. K. McHardy, "*De heretico comburendo*, 1401," *Lollardy and the Gentry in the Later Middle Ages*, ed. Margaret Aston and Colin Richmond (New York: St. Martin's, 1997), pp. 112–26.

[127] Innocent III, *In nonnullis*, canon 68 of the Fourth Lateran Council (1215), *X* 5.6.15, Friedberg 2:776–77: noting that in some provinces diversity of dress distinguishes Jews and Saracens from Christians, the pope orders a similar practice to be instituted everywhere, for both sexes. This obligation is to be enforced by the secular princes of each region, to prevent inadvertent sexual mixing. Raymund of Pennafort in editing this decree for *X* left out the pope's explanation that this policy was also enjoined by Moses in the Old Testament. The Ordinary Gloss explains that such miscegenation is condemned because there can be no marriage between Jew and Christian: *CJC* 2:1665 v. *commixtionis*. The *Casus* to this decree explains *commiscentur* ("they mingle [with women]") as *carnaliter commiscentur* ("they mingle sexually") (ibid.).

and Moors were supposed to wear a yellow or red circle on their breasts, but exemptions seem to have been relatively numerous, at least until Enrique II attempted to enforce the law in Castile in 1371.[128] However, it would hardly have been observed outside the realm. Thus, there is no reason to think that, when Rabbi Solomon of Burgos came to England in 1388, he was wearing anything that would single him out as a Jew or Moor. And he seems to have been able to practice his religion without trouble, except for the matter of finding adequate wine for Purim. Was Rabbi Moses in a similar situation?

Rich and Poor Jews in London?

Let us move to different kinds of evidence that may indicate the presence of unconverted non-Christians, specifically Jews, in the London in Chaucer's day.

First, we will consider two sermons of Thomas Brinton, Bishop of Rochester from 1373 to 1389, in which he speaks to the English clergy as if there were a wealthy community of Jews living in England at this time.[129] Brinton is well known to students of *Piers Plowman* for having introduced the fable of the rats into his sermon to Convocation during

[128] Ulysse Robert, *Les signes d'infamie au Moyen Age* (Paris: Champion, 1891), pp. 58–65. The reference is to the Cortes of 1371, mentioned above, in which both Jews and Moors were ordered not to use Christian names ("que los Judios nin los Moros non ayan nonbres de Christianos"). He responded to the other request by speaking of "los dichos Judios," but this expression seems to have done service for "los dichos Judios e Moros." The purpose is to be able to recognize them among Christians ("porque se conozean entre los Christianos"), and so they are to wear the signs that he commands them to wear ("e plaze nos que anden senalados de la sennal que nos acordaremos e mandaremos que trayan"). He does not refer to past laws commanding this, but when he goes on to conclude his response, he says that, as regards the other points in their petition, all these matters are to continue as they did in the time of his predecessors and his father King Alfonso: Cortes de Toro (1371), petition 2 (*Cortes*, 2:203–4). Petition 18 addresses privileges that have been given to "los Judios e Moros," and the king responds by speaking of "los dichos Judios" (p. 210). In 1385 Enrique II's son Juan (who was to marry Gaunt's daughter in 1388) in the Cortes of Valladolid responded to a petition to prohibit Christian men and women from living with Moors and Jews ("con los Moros e con los Judios") by only prohibiting Christian women from living with Jews and Moors ("Mandamos a todas las christianas que non bivan con los Judios nin con los Moros") or nursing their children: Córtes de Valladolid (1385), petition 3 (p. 322). Among the much stricter laws of 1387 given by the king in the Cortes of Briviesca (see Russell, p. 497) is one that prohibits all Christians from having nonslave Jews or Moors in their houses, and Jews and Moors likewise are not to live with Christians, or have their office, or have them living in their households: Cortes de Briviesca (1387), law 3.1 (p. 369).
[129] See Emden, *Bio. Reg. Oxford*, 1:208–9.

the Good Parliament of 1376.[130] We recall that during that Parliament there was a complaint on the part of the Commons that Jews and Saracens were surreptitiously living in England under the guise of Italian brokers. However, their petition expressed no sign of worry about false religion, but only concern about the introduction of the unnamable vice into England. The government's reply paid no attention to this aspect of the complaint and only indirectly addressed the main charge of troublesome brokering: "As for the brokers of foreign countries, there is a partial response in the bill concerning the liberty of London."[131]

Brinton said nothing about Jews and Saracens in his sermon on that occasion, but he did in other sermons. Often his comments do not concern England, but listen to what he says in Sermon 91, one of the sermons he preached on the feast of the Translation of Saint Thomas of Canterbury (July 7), perhaps in 1375 or 1377.[132] He begins with the tradition that Thomas's mother was a non-Christian princess; after telling of her arrival in London, and her baptism and marriage to Thomas's father, he moves on to the following:

Why in this glorious city, in which a firm faith should flourish the stronger, are so many "faithless Jews" favorably permitted? And why are they not "translated" from their errors to the faith of Christ by the persuasions and doctrines of so many holy fathers, so many prelates, so many doctors? The opinion commonly preached is clearly that many Jews would very willingly become Christians, if they did not fear the dispersal or loss of their wealth after their conversion.

But far be it that the Roman Church, the ruler and teacher of other churches, should boil with such avarice that the pursuit of money would shine forth more readily and avidly than zeal for souls! But if this were true, I would be inclined to declare that those by whom the Jews should be converted will, in the age to come, be found deserving to die as many deaths as precious souls have been lost because of their negligence, souls that had been redeemed by the blood of Christ.

[130] Thomas Brinton, *The Sermons of Thomas Brinton, Bishop of Rochester, 1373–1389*, ed. Sister Mary Aquinas Devlin, 2 vols., Camden 3rd ser. 85–86 (London 1954), Sermon 69, 2:317–21, esp. 317, and see 1:xxiv–xxv. Much of Sermon 69 is translated in Francis Aidan Gasquet's study of Brinton, "A Forgotten English Preacher," in *The Old English Bible and Other Essays* (London: Nimmo, 1897), pp. 63–101, on pp. 71–78.
[131] *Rot. Parl.* 2:332: "*Responsio:* Quant a les brokours d'estraunge pays, est en partie responduz en la bille touchant la fraunchise de Londres."
[132] Devlin dates it 7 July 1375 (p. xxxvii), while it is dated 7 July 1377 by Eleanor H. Kellogg, "Bishop Brunton and the Fable of the Rats," *PMLA* 50 (1935): 57–68, p. 62.

Therefore, let them meditate, and meditate again, my fathers, you who are the salt of the earth and the light of the world, that, since the band of Apostles went forth into the whole world so that infidels, even those far away, might publicly confess the faith of Christ, how much more should those who have "come up to the place of the Apostles" labor with one mind in their own neighborhoods, in order that our enemies the Jews might be translated by the doctrines of the faith "into the kingdom of the Son of God," so that the words of Job might be verified of each of them, "A rock is moved from its place" (likening the Jew to a very hard rock), when a Jew is converted.[133]

He has a similar but shorter treatment in Sermon 84, preached *ad cleros* in honor of Saint Louis, Bishop of Toulouse, canonized in 1317. His feast day was established on the date of his death, August 19, and Brinton may have ordered it observed in his diocese.[134] He says:

Moreover, this saint taught the saving knowledge so ardently that, once he was made bishop of Toulouse (out of obedience to the pope), he was girded round

[133] Brinton, Sermon 91, pp. 413–14:

Cur in hac civitate gloriosa, in qua debet florere forcius fides firma, tot "perfidi Judei" favorabiliter sunt permissi, nec persuasionibus vel doctrinis tot patrum sanctorum, tot prelatorum, tot doctorum ad fidem Christi a suis erroribus transferuntur? Cum tamen vulgaris opinio predicet evidenter quod multi Judei libentissime fierent Cristiani, si post conversionem non timerent diviciarum suarum dispendium vel jacturam.

Set absit quod Romana ecclesia, aliarum ecclesiarum domina et magistra, tanta avaricia estuaret quod questum pecuniarum pocius quam zelum animarum et avidius auclaret [sic]. Quod si esset verum, forte dicerem quod ipsi per quos Judei essent convertendi, in futuro tot mortibus digni erunt quot preciose anime per Christi sanguinem redempte eorum negligencia perierunt.

Cogitent igitur et recogitent, patres mei, sal terre et lux mundi, quod si turba apostolica in omnem terram exivit ut infideles, et longe positi, faterentur publice fidem Christi, quanto magis ipsi qui "loco apostolorum surrexerunt" (D. 22, *In Novo*), laborarent unanimiter in vicino, ut hostes nostri Judei per documenta fidei transferentur "in regnum filii" Dei (ad Col. 1), ut de unoquoque eorum, Judeum, tamquam saxum durissimum, convertente, verificetur quod scribetur, Job 14, "Saxum transfer[tur] de loco."

He is quoting Gratian's canon *In Novo Testamento, Decretum* D. 21 c. 2 (Friedberg 1:69–70: "in locum eorum surrexerunt episcopi"); Colossians 1.13 ("Transtulit in regnum filii dilectionis sue"), and Job 14.18 ("Et saxum transfertur de loco suo"), and also referring to the prayer for the Jews in the liturgy for Good Friday: "Oremus et pro perfidis Judeis, ut Deus et Dominus noster auferat velamen de cordibus eorum, ut et ipsi agnoscant Jesum Christum Dominum nostrum" ("Let us pray also for the faithless Jews, that our God and Lord may lift away the veil from their hearts, so that they too may acknowledge Jesus Christ our Lord"): *Missale ad usum insignis et praeclarae ecclesiae Sarum*, ed. Francis Henry Dickinson (Burnt Island; Oxford, 1861–63), col. 327.

[134] Kellogg, p. 62, assigns it to 1377, probably on August 19.

with such great zeal and fervor for the faith that by sound doctrine he sedulously induced Jews and Gentiles, who abounded at that time in those parts, towards baptism, and baptized many of them, remembering the words that our Savior said, "Go and teach all Nations," and so on. But, saving the due favor of whomever, no little wonder impels me to ask why, in this glorious city, in which a firm faith should flourish the stronger, are so many "faithless Jews" favorably permitted? And why are they not converted from their errors to the faith of Christ by the persuasions and doctrines of so many holy fathers, so many prelates, so many doctors?

I dare say that if any of us in his own degree were as diligent and intent on instructing and saving souls as for multiplying benefices and assembling riches, he would immediately and effectually fulfill the words of the Psalmist, "Lord, I will teach the wicked your ways, and the impious will be converted to you."

Therefore, let them meditate, and meditate again, my fathers, you who are the salt of the earth and the light of the world, that, since the band of Apostles went out into the whole world, so that infidels, even those far away, might publicly confess the faith of Christ, how much more should those who have "come up to the place of the Apostles" labor with one mind in their own neighborhoods, in order that our enemies the Jews might be converted to the faith of Christ, "instructed in the words of faith and doctrine"?[135]

What are we to make of this? Brinton had been appointed a papal penitentiary in 1362, two years before he received his doctorate in canon

---

[135] Brinton, Sermon 84, pp. 383–84:

Immo scienciam salutarem iste sanctus docuit tam ardenter quod, ex obediencia papale factus episcopus Tholosanus, tanto zelo et fervore fidei est accinctus quod Judeos et Gentiles, qui pro tunc in illis partibus habundabant, per sanam doctrinam inducabat sedule ad baptismum et plurimos baptizabat, recolens Salvatoris sentenciam sic dicentis, "Ite et docete omnes gentes, baptizantes eos," etc. [Matt. 28.19]. Sed salva pace debita cujuscumque, admiracio non modica me percellit cur in hac civitate gloriosa, in qua debet florere forcius fides firma, cur "perfidi Judei" tot favorabiliter sunt permissi, nec persuasionibus vel doctrinis tot patrum sanctorum, tot prelatorum, tot doctorum, a suis erroribus convertuntur.

Audeo dicere quod si quilibet nostrum in gradu suo esset ita diligens et intentus pro animabus doctrinandis et salvandis sicut est pro beneficiis multiplicandis et pecuniis congregandis, statim impleret effectualiter illud Psalmiste dicentis, "Domine, docebo iniquos vias tuas, et impii ad te convertentur" [Ps. 50.15].

Igitur cogitent, immo recogitent, patres nostri, sal terre et lux mundi, quod si tu[r]ba apostolica in omnem terram exivit, ut infideles, eciam longe positi, faterentur publice legem Christi, quanto magis illi qui "in loco apostolorum surrexerunt" (D. 22, *In Novo*) debent laborare unanimiter in vicino, ut hostes nostri Judei converterentur ad fidem Christi, "Eruditi verbis fidei et doctrine" (1 ad Tim. 4[.6: "Enutritus verbis fidei et bone doctrine"])?

law at Oxford, and by 1366 he was at the pope's court in Avignon, and he probably accompanied Urban V to Rome in 1368 and stayed there until he was appointed bishop of Rochester in January 1372, or even until he was consecrated bishop in March 1373. At one time there was extant a volume of the sermons that he gave before the pope, which is presumed lost.[136] It seems likely that the "glorious city" passages in the two Rochester-era sermons cited above are a relic of his papal sermons and originally referred to Rome.[137] However, it is significant that he does not think it incongruous to preach it to the English clergy, where it would be natural to apply it to London. But in England, of course, the danger to converts' wealth came not from the Church but from the Crown, with its uncanonical practice of confiscation, noted above.

If we cannot conclude, on the basis of Brinton's words, that there really were some wealthy Jews living openly in London at this time, we can nevertheless take his words as aimed at inculcating a positive attitude toward non-Christians, which would be important in itself.

We look now at a different kind of evidence, namely, that of proper toponyms. The district where the Jews had congregated before the expulsion was called "Jewry," *Judaismus* in Latin. It was a large area in Cheap Ward and Coleman Street Ward, and it extended as far west as St. Lawrence Parish—"St. Lawrence Jewry." After the Jews were expelled, it came to be called "Old Jewry" (*Vetus Judaismus*), meaning "The District formerly held by the Jews." In 1327–28 there is reference to the church of St. Olave in "Olde Jiuwerie"—referring to the street between Poultry and Gresham Street. In 1336 it is called "Elde Jurie."[138]

---

[136] Devlin, *Sermons of Thomas Brinton*, 1:xii–xiv. In conjecturing the date of Sermon 92, which was on a feast of Saint Thomas's translation (7 July) that fell on a Sunday, which happened in 1370, 1381, and 1387, Devlin chooses 1370 as the most likely (1:xxxvii, 2:420); but that would be before he became bishop and before he presumably returned from Rome.

[137] Later on in Sermon 91, Brinton contrasts the virtuous practices of England in former times with those of the current papal court. He tells the story of an abbot who tried to expedite a case in the curia of Saint Thomas by handing out money, but, to his edification, all gifts were refused. This is in great contrast, Brinton says, to what happens in the Roman Curia. Sermon 91, p. 417; see Devlin's translation of the second part, dealing with the Roman Curia, 1:xxii. Brinton introduces the story of the abbot by citing the decretal *Etsi questiones*, X 5.3.18 (Friedberg 2:754–55); why he does so is not clear, but the decretal does say that the *Romana ecclesia* does not consider certain gifts by recipients of benefices to be simoniacal.

[138] Ekwall, *Street-Names of the City of London*, p. 201. I should note, by the way, that when names appear in Latin documents preceded by *la* or *le* or *les*, as with "la elde Jurie" here, or "le Jeu," and so on, it is not a sign that the text is breaking into French and using the definite article ("the Old Jewry," "the Jew," etc.). Rather, the particles *le*

There was, however, another district where Jews lived in London, which is first heard of in the fourteenth century, namely, "Poor Jewry," or *Pauper Judaismus*. In the will of William Stanford in 1349, he describes his tenement and shops, which he had acquired from his father, Thomas Beldstede, as located in Poor Jewry (*apud Pauperum Judaismum*) in the Parish of St. Olave near the Crutched Friars.[139] This parish, with its church on Hart Street, is to be distinguished from that of St. Olave Old Jewry.[140] Henry Harben says that "the Jews after their return to the country seem to have congregated in this eastern portion of the City and not to have returned to the western portion, 'the Old Jewry,' from which they were expelled temp. Ed. I,"[141] and he may be right. He is, of course, thinking about the return of the Jews in the seventeenth century, but it may be that they started to come back earlier, since the name first appears some sixty years after the expulsion. Harben, however, believes that the Jewish settlement there was earlier. He says, speaking of "The Jewry": "It would seem that the Jews not only had quarters in and around the present Old Jewry, but also further east in and about recent Jewry Street, Aldgate, as well as within the precincts of the Tower Liberties and St. Katherine's. They do not seem to have re-established themselves in the western quarter after they were banished from the land by Edward I, but upon their return to have congregated more in the eastern districts, as at the present time."[142]

In 1366, we find that a specific lane is called "Pore Jewerie." It is described as being in the Parish of Holy Trinity by "Algate."[143] It was

---

etc. are a signal that what follows is in English. It is the medieval equivalent of italicizing. See my "Bishop, Prioress, and Bawd," p. 351.

[139] Ekwall, loc. cit.; *Calendar of Wills Proved and Enrolled in the Court of Husting, London, A.D. 1258–A.D. 1688*, ed. Richard R. Sharpe, 2 vols. (London: Francis, 1889–90), 1:553.

[140] See the map of the parishes of London, ca. 1520, in *The City of London from Prehistoric Times to c. 1520*, gen. ed. Mary D. Lobel, mapping ed. W. H. John, The British Atlas of Historic Towns, vol. 3 (Oxford: Oxford University Press, 1989). There is another map showing the wards of London, as well as a series of four maps showing the streets (referred to below). Chapter 6, "The Later Middle Ages: 1270–1520," is by Caroline Barron, pp. 42–56.

[141] Henry A. Harben, *A Dictionary of London: Being Notes Topographical and Historical Relating to the Streets and Principal Buildings in the City of London*, ed. I. I. Greaves (London: Jenkins, 1918), p. 322.

[142] Ibid., p. 321.

[143] *Catalogue of Ancient Deeds* (note 53 above), 2:31: A 2047. The reference is doubtless to Holy Trinity Priory (Austin Canons) on Alegate Street, which was in the parish of St. Katharine Cree, as was most of the present Jewry Street. The first modern synagogue was established in 1656 in Cree Church Lane, to the west of the priory precincts, and the first permanent synagogue was built on nearby Bevis Marks, in 1701.

the road that paralleled the city wall, coming from Crutched Friars' Street on the south and merging into Alegate (modern Aldgate) Street at the Gate on the north.[144] We recall that Chaucer lived above the Gate from 1374 to 1386. The name continued to be associated with the road, though in modern times it was shortened to "Jewry Street."[145]

However, there is a record of 1390 that identifies a district in this same area not as Poor Jewry but as "Little Jewry," *Parvus Judaismus*. It mentions four messuages in Little Jewry in Alegate Street.[146] The name might be taken as supporting the idea that this Jewry was contrasted with the main Jewry, and that it too goes back to the time before the expulsion. We cannot stake too much on the fact that it is not referred to as "Old Poor Jewry." We see Old Jewry Street in 1348 being called "Jewerie Lane," with the "Old" omitted.[147] Another pre-expulsion Jewish site shows up in London about the same time without an "Old" designation, namely, "Jews' Garden," in St. Giles (Cripplegate Ward Without): "Jeues Gardyn," 1341; "Jewes Gardin," 1349; "Jewen Gardyn," 1405–6, and so on.[148] The garden took its name from the site of the former Jewish cemetery.[149]

Conclusion

Much has been made in the past of the absence of the Jews from England in the fourteenth century. H. G. Richardson says, "As their mem-

[144] See this street in the *City of London* series of large maps, Map 4. These maps are laid out with coordinates in Caroline M. Barron, *London in the Later Middle Ages: Government and People, 1200–1500* (Oxford: Oxford University Press, 2004), pp. 399–430. For The Poore Jurie, see 25 C4.

[145] John Stow, *A Survey of London, Reprinted from the Text of 1603*, ed. Charles Lethbridge Kingsford, 2 vols. (Oxford: Clarendon Press, 1908), 1:149, does not associate the name with the road, which he leaves nameless, but with buildings on it: "At the east [1598 ed.: west] end of this lane ["a lane that leadeth downe by Northumberland House towards the Crossed Friers"], in the way from Aldgate toward the Crossed Friers, of old time were certaine tenements called the Poore Jurie, of Jewes dwelling there."

[146] PRO C66/332 m. 11: "quatuor messuagia cum pertinenciis in parvo Judaismo in Algatestrete in eadem civitate." See *CPR*, 1388–92, p. 417: 14 February 1391.

[147] *Calendar of Wills*, 1:653; so Ekwall, *Street-Names of the City of London*, p. 201. Harben, *A Dictionary of London*, p. 322, identifies this street as referring to Poor Jewery, but there is nothing to indicate that this is so.

[148] Ekwall, *Street-Names of the City of London*, p. 18 n. 1.

[149] Sharpe, *Calendar of Wills*, 1:452 n. 1, identifies it as "a plot of ground formerly appointed for a burial-ground for Jews, and continued to be so used until their expulsion, when it was [in the words of Stow] 'turned into fair garden plots and summer houses for pleasure.'" In 1349 the garden is said to be owned by Reymundy Burdeaux (*Calendar of Wills*, 1:620).

ory faded from the minds of Englishmen, they became an evil thing, unknown, dreaded and accursed." But the only indication he can cite for this attitude is the parliamentary complaint of 1376 about disguised Jews and Saracens.[150] In fact, there was an abundance of positive characterizations of Jews in the realm, as well as negative ones. As well as being denigrated, Jews, like Saracens, were often praised as having morals and characters superior those those of Christians. These latter themes are particularly evident in the sermons of Bishop Brinton, and his lessons, and also his zeal for converting the infidel, undoubtedly influenced William Langland.[151] "Good" and "bad" themes (showing Jews and Saracens as moral and well intentioned, on the one hand, and as evil and deserving of death, on the other) are often found mixed together in the same works or in the same collections—for instance, miracles of the Virgin.[152]

Bishop Brinton's exhortations to the clergy raise the possibility that not only were there some Jews and Saracens residing in England without being recognized as such, but also that there were other Jews who lived there openly as Jews. We can definitely say that English churchmen

[150] H. G. Richardson, *English Jewry under Angevin Kings* (London: Methuen, 1960), p. 232.

[151] I take these matters up in "The Prioress's Tale in Context: Good and Bad Reports of Non-Christians in Fourteenth-Century England," *Studies in Medieval and Renaissance History*, New Series, vol. 3: *Nation, Ethnicity, and Identity in Medieval and Renaissance Europe* (forthcoming, 2006). Good work has been done by Denise Despres ("The Protean Jew in the Vernon Manuscript") and Elisa Narin van Court ("Socially Marginal, Culturally Central: Representing Jews in Late Medieval English Literature"); see note 2 above. Narin van Court also deals with the topic in "The Hermeneutics of Supersession: The Revision of the Jews from the B to the C Text of *Piers Plowman*," YLS 10 (1996) 43–87. In this article she shows that the C text adds a reference to the enmity of Jews and Saracens to Christianity. But though the B text passage in which the Jews are praised as being more charitable to each other than Christians are (B 9.80–88) is omitted in C, in both B and C texts Jews and Saracens are characterized as being predisposed for conversion, if only Christians would preach the Trinity to them.

[152] Other combinations can be found. For instance, in *L'Apparicion maistre Jehan de Meun* by Honorat Bovet (formerly known as Bonet), composed in 1398, Jews are bad, but not as bad as Christians, whereas Saracens are cast in an altogether favorable light. The first interlocutor of the spectral Jean de Meun, a "false Jew," is asked how he dares to return, after the wicked and useless Jews were expelled by the king. He responds that he has been sent there secretly by the Jews to negotiate a return, on the guarantee that their practice of usury will be more moderate than the outrageous form practiced by Christians since they left. The next interlocutor, a "Saracen black as coal," is an accomplished ambassador who travels openly through France on his way to Spain. He wishes to study the *mores* of the French, and he describes their failings at great length. See Michael Hanly, *Medieval Muslims, Jews, and Christians in Dialogue: The APPARICION MAISTRE JEHAN DE MEUN of Honorat Bovet. A Critical Edition and English Translation* (Tempe, Ariz.: Medieval and Renaissance Texts and Studies, 2005).

were encouraged to be on the lookout for potential converts. And perhaps some of Brinton's listeners took the cue and welcomed Rabbi Solomon of Burgos, the future Bishop of Burgos, when he arrived in 1388, and prepared the way for his conversion, which took place in 1390, just a year after he returned home from England. Perhaps others accorded a similar treatment to Bishop Moses and any congregants that he had in England; if so, they succeeded at least with his daughter Elizabeth.

Lee Patterson has taken note of the crusade expeditions of Henry Bolingbroke and others in the 1390s, which we have dealt with above to some extent, and he thinks that "there are signs of an interest in making sure England was *Judenfreie.*" But his evidence is not convincing, especially as it concerns crusading efforts.[153] Such efforts would of course be directed against the Saracens of the East and the "Saracens" of the North, and not against the Jews.[154] But I can partially agree with his statement that Richard II's sponsoring of Richard of Sicily "suggests a response to the demand that he extend the borders of Christendom in a world that was in fact fast becoming far more heterogeneous, and far more dangerous to Christians, than ever before."[155] That is, this sponsorship indicates to me that Richard II, like his cousin-german Henry Bolingbroke, was interested in welcoming non-Christians into the Christian fold. The fact that a Sicilian merchant (whom I believe to have been, as I argued above, not a Jew but a manumitted Tartar Muslim) was baptized in England and that the king stood as his godfather, and that Bolingbroke's multiple and ecumenical proselytizing—adopting a Northern pagan, Henry Lettowe, an Eastern Muslim, Henry Turk, and, later on, as king, a Jewish convert, Henry Stratford—show that this

[153] Patterson, "Living Witnesses," p. 540. His evidence is as follows: the chronicle of Gloucester Abbey, compiled between 1382 and 1412, tells of the martyred boy Harold; relics of two of the Holy Innocents were brought to England in 1396; and in the 1420s Lydgate wrote a poem about the martyred Robert of Bury. Moreover, Richard II in the winter of 1385–86 gave a huge pension to King Leo of Armenia, who had been driven from his kingdom by the Turks, and who tried to interest Richard in crusading; the Wilton Diptych may have been a "crusading icon"; Richard and Anne were devoted to Lincoln cathedral, and in 1387 they enrolled in its confraternity; and Richard sponsored the conversion of Richard of Sicily (pp. 540–41).

[154] Delany, "Chaucer's Prioress," notes the "constant appeals to the English government for support of anti-Islamic crusades, to which appeals English knights and nobles flocked in response, despite the reservations of their government" (p. 46), at a time when John of Gaunt was attempting to make alliances with the Muslim rulers of Granada (pp. 45–46). Gaunt had committed to a crusade against the schismatic Christians of Spain (see note 78 above), and he was enlisting Moorish support for it.

[155] Patterson, "Living Witnesses," p. 541.

approach was encouraged by the highest secular authorities, and the actions and words of bishops Braybrooke and Brinton show the backing of the ecclesiastical establishment.

There was a widespread belief in Chaucer's day that Saint Thomas Becket was half-Saracen—we saw that Bishop Brinton told the story in one of the sermons cited above[156]—and it is obvious that having a pagan princess for a mother only enhanced his appeal. In a more disreputable way, a claim to Jewishness must have enhanced the reputation of the thief-finder John Barking, until he was sent packing by the London authorities. But he was in no way punished for being Jewish. The exotic may of course give rise to suspicions of unspeakable sins, but sometimes it may also, especially when present in small doses, banish prejudice and leave only fascination.

As for Chaucer, at the very least we can conclude that he could have laid eyes with some regularity on one or other converted Jew on his visits to Chancery, which was next door to the Domus Conversorum, and he may even have found Jews living at his own doorstep, in Poor Jewry. If there were no longer Jews living there, the name of the area would still of course have reminded him the Jews used to live there, Jews that were impoverished rather than grown wealthy from "foule usure and lucre of vileynye," as with the Jewry among Christian folks in the great city of Asia described by the Prioress. It is highly likely that he could have encountered other converted and unconverted non-Christians elsewhere in the city, whether knowing it or not, what with the crews of trading vessels on shore leave and the troops of piepowders ("dusty-footed" traveling salesmen) in the streets and at fairs. Such probable or possible encounters must be taken into consideration in our own attempts to understand Chaucer in his time and place.

---

[156] Brinton, Sermon 91, p. 413. He treats it also in Sermon 4, pp. 3–4. I discuss it fully in my "Prioress's Tale in Context."

Radical Historiography:

Langland, Trevisa, and the *Polychronicon*

Emily Steiner
University of Pennsylvania

"Takeþ hire landes, ye lordes, and leteþ hem lyue by dymes"
—*Piers Plowman* B 15.564[1]

T HE 1370S AT QUEEN'S COLLEGE, Oxford, were heady years in academic life, especially for the intellectual circle that might have included the likes of Nicholas Hereford, William Middleworth, John Trevisa, and John Wyclif.[2] We imagine these scholars pondering dominion, contemplating translation, and angling for the kind of patron who could extend academic life to practical politics.[3] The evidence for such a circle may lie in the transmission of shared ideas and texts. David Fowler

Versions of this essay were delivered at the University of Pennsylvania Borders seminar, the Delaware Valley Medieval Association, and the Yale English Department Medieval-Renaissance seminar. I thank Frank Grady, Ralph Hanna III, Steven Justice, Sarah McNamer, Maura Nolan, Lee Patterson, and an anonymous reader for their helpful comments on earlier drafts and Cristina Pangilinan for her invaluable research assistance.

[1] All citations of the *Piers Plowman* B-text are to *Piers Plowman: The B Version*, ed. George Kane and E. Talbot Donaldson (London: Athlone Press, 1975). Subsequent citations will follow the quotation in the main text with passus and line numbers.

[2] Hereford, Middleworth, and Trevisa were admitted there between 1369 and 1372, after Trevisa and Middleworth had been expelled from Exeter College. Middleworth, in 1369, had also been expelled from Canterbury College because of his ties to Wyclif. Wyclif rented a room in Queen's from 1374 to 1381. For a description of Wycliffite Oxford and the scholars who may or may not have been associated with it, see David C. Fowler, *The Life and Times of John Trevisa, Medieval Scholar* (Seattle: University of Washington Press, 1995), pp. 221–30; and Anne Hudson, *The Premature Reformation: Wycliffite Texts and Lollard History* (Oxford: Clarendon Press, 1988), pp. 394–95.

[3] On Berkeley's patronage of Trevisa, see note 31 below. For Gaunt's patronage of Wyclif, see John Dahmus, *The Prosecution of John Wyclif* (New Haven: Yale University Press, 1952); K. B. McFarlane, *Lancastrian Kings and Lollard Knights* (Oxford: Clarendon Press, 1972); Peter McNiven, *Heresy and Politics in the Reign of Henry IV: The Burning of John Badby* (Woodbridge, Suffolk: Boydell, 1987), pp. 19–21; and Steven Justice, "Lollardy," in David Wallace, ed., *The Cambridge History of Medieval English Literature* (Cambridge: Cambridge University Press, 1999), pp. 663–64, 670–73.

maintains that Trevisa's ties to Wyclif are evidenced by his translation of Ranulph Higden's Latin universal history, the *Polychronicon* (1330s–60s).[4] Between 1377 and 1380, Trevisa and other scholars left Queen's, taking with them a number of books and liturgical objects, including a copy of the *Polychronicon*. According to Fowler, the theft of the *Polychronicon* connects Trevisa at once to biblical translation at Oxford in the late 1370s and to Trevisa's translation of Higden a decade later.[5]

The significance of the stolen *Polychronicon*, however, is not limited to identifying the members of a coterie or establishing links between controversial thought and vernacular translation. As Anne Hudson has shown, Fowler's *Polychronicon* evidence is circumstantial at best: Trevisa possibly knew Wyclif at Queen's; a decade or so later he translated the *Polychronicon*, among other Latin works; the "collaborative Wycliffite enterprise" of translating the Bible probably took place later than 1377, after Trevisa had left Queen's.[6] But Fowler was surely hinting at other questions when he called Higden "Wyclif's favorite historian": what exactly would it mean for a medieval writer to have a favorite historian, and what does the reception of a chronicle have to do with its capacity to represent ideas that it does not explicitly support?[7] In this essay I

---

[4] For a survey of arguments about biblical authorship, see Hudson, *The Premature Reformation*, pp. 238–47. The only medieval evidence that Trevisa translated the Bible is Caxton's attribution in his preface to the *Polychronicon*, which John Bale influentially repeats in his *Catalogue of Illustrious British Writers* (1557). For Bale, the value of medieval historical writing—and by extension, the value of an English literary tradition—depended upon its incidental connections to a Reformist program, just as the textual evidence for that program, the English Bible, is supported in part by the vernacularization of a national history. For a fascinating recent discussion of Bale's *Catalogue* and the relationship that it posits between Britishness and literary history, see James Simpson, *The Oxford English Literary History, vol. 2, 1350–1547: Reform and Cultural Revolution* (Oxford: Oxford University Press, 2002), pp. 23–43.

[5] Fowler, *The Life and Times of John Trevisa*, pp. 228–30; this argument is a restatement of the one that he makes in *The Bible in Early English Literature* (Seattle: University of Washington Press, 1976). Fowler does cite other books on the list that were of interest both to Trevisa and to later Lollard writers, including works by Nicholas Lyre and Richard FitzRalph. He regards the *Polychronicon*, however, as the most important connection between Wyclif and Trevisa, based upon Trevisa's comments on possessioners in his translation of the *Polychronicon* (6.465–67, among other examples), the *Dialogue*'s defense of vernacular translation, and Caxton's claim that Trevisa translated the Bible.

[6] Hudson, *The Premature Reformation*, pp. 394–98.

[7] Several scholars repeat Fowler's phrase even while disputing his central claim, because it suggests the processes by which ideas attach themselves to texts. See Hudson's reformulation of Fowler's phrase in *The Premature Reformation*, p. 397 ("the *Polychronicon* may be described as Wyclif's favourite history book, and later Lollard writing shared his taste"); and Galloway's in "Writing History in England," in *The Cambridge History of Medieval English Literature*, ed. David Wallace, p. 277. ("Trevisa may have first en-

argue that the *Polychronicon* captured the political imagination of four-teenth-century writers, and that its reception in medieval England at-tests to the profound historiographical investments—what I call the "radical historiography"—of polemicists, preachers, translators, and poets. Medieval English writers discovered in the universal history an innovative way of theorizing political issues, especially those pertaining to the institutional Church. Civil dominion, clerical disendowment, and lay learning were hot topics in the late fourteenth century, topics that transcended academic Wycliffism.[8] As we shall see, it was the vernacular and literary appropriation of Latin historiography that helped to give such topics a discursive heft and complexity. Yet the term "radical histo-riography" does not imply simply that literary writers borrowed pas-sages from Higden in order to develop opinions disseminated from the schools; rather, it proposes that these writers, in grappling with the idea of *Polychronicon* as a *whole work* or even as a *master genre*, were able to theorize relations between clergy and laity in the particular ways in which they did. In this view, radical historiography leads to radical eccle-siology, but only insofar as genre becomes a locus for the political imagi-nary. Thus the *Polychronicon* does not merely organize or represent a set of ideas. It brings to light a literary project—a project exemplified by Trevisa's *Dialogue Between a Lord and a Clerk* and William Langland's *Piers Plowman*—that runs parallel to, but by no means reproduces, the dissemination of Wycliffite thought.[9] In short, the medieval reception

---

countered the *Polychronicon* in Wyclif's circle at Queen's College, Oxford, for Wyclif was said to have thought it his favorite history.")

[8] Hudson importantly demonstrates that Wycliffite issues were neither confined to the schools nor necessarily classified as Wycliffite in nonacademic and nonpolemical texts. See her chapter, "Vernacular Wycliffism," in *The Premature Reformation*, and "A Lollard Compilation and the Dissemination of Wycliffite Thought," in *Lollards and Their Books* (London: Hambledon, 1985), pp. 13–29, in which she describes the dissemination of Wycliffite thought from university scholars to those outside.

[9] At the end of *Piers Plowman* B. 15, Langland calls for lay disendowment of the clergy, if the clergy do not properly reform. As Hudson observes, the concept of disen-dowment had long provided fodder for earlier political theorists, such as William Ock-ham and Marsilius of Padua, who championed royal over papal sovereignty; there is no need to argue, in other words, that Langland is specifically promoting a Wycliffite agenda because he may be tapping into an older rhetoric of clerical reform. Moreover, argues Hudson, Langland never fully embraces those positions that make Wycliffism distinctive, such as the idea that disendowment might be a viable solution, or that an erring cleric is one who accepts more than is strictly necessary for survival, or that judgment of clerical error rests in the individual layman. See Hudson, *The Premature Reformation*, pp. 330–37, 343. See also Pamela Gradon, "Langland and the Ideology of Dissent," *Proceedings of the British Academy* 66 (1980): 179–205; and Margaret Aston, "'Caim's Castles': Poverty, Politics, and Disendowment," in R. B. Dobson, ed., *The Church, Politics, and Patronage in the Fifteenth Century* (New York: St. Martin's, 1984), pp.

of the *Polychronicon* suggests a different way of writing intellectual history as literary history: not as the transmission of a theme or idea, but as the search for the formal properties of political discourse.

The Reception of the *Polychronicon* in Late Medieval England

To understand how the *Polychronicon* became a locus of formal invention with implications for political theory, we must first examine its extraordinary currency in late medieval England. Composed by a Benedictine monk of St. Werburgh's Abbey, Chester, and extant in approximately 120 manuscripts, the *Polychronicon* was the most commonly cited chronicle in late medieval England, and it quickly displaced the earlier histories that it contains.[10] Like Orosius's influential *History against the Pagans* (early fifth century), divided into the seven ages of man, the *Polychronicon* was composed in seven books, a symbolically fitting number for a Christian universal history. Unlike Orosius's history, however, the *Polychronicon* is not universal because it is polemical or apocalyptic, but rather because it claims totality within a specifically English context. It synthesizes all histories, periods, and genres, and drives them resolutely toward the English present, toward English localities, conquests, and lineages, and even to the deeds of the Chester nobility: Book 1 describes the geography of the world, following Vincent Beauvais's *Speculum historiale* (1245); book 2 records biblical history from Creation to Nebuchadnezzar (the first four ages); the third book is devoted to the life of Christ (the fifth age); and the fourth through seventh books recount the history of England from the Saxons to Edward III, liberally interspersed with the history of the medieval papacy, legends of saints and martyrs, the history of Islam, the life of Charlemagne, and the fortunes of the crusaders.[11] Significantly, the totality that the *Polychronicon* represents is simul-

45–81. On the question of endowment in court circles and the schools before Wycliffe, see J. I. Catto, "Wyclif and Wycliffism at Oxford, 1356–1430," in J. I. Catto and Ralph Evans, eds., *History of the University of Oxford, vol. 2, Late Medieval Oxford* (Oxford: Oxford University Press, 1992), pp. 202–12.

[10] On the circulation of the *Polychronicon* in monastic libraries, see Antonia Gransden, *Historical Writing in England I: c. 1307 to the Early Sixteenth Century* (Ithaca: Cornell University Press, 1982), p. 55; and John Taylor, *English Historical Literature in the Fourteenth Century* (Oxford: Clarendon Press, 1987), pp. 55–56, 101–3.

[11] Higden uses the three conquests of England as a "continuous structuring principle" (Galloway, "Writing History in England," p. 276), and he discusses the three branches of the English language (*Polychronicon* 2.158). Text in Rev. Joseph Rawson Lumby, ed., *Polychronicon Ranulphi Higden monachi Cestrensis, together with the English translations of John Trevisa and of an unknown writer of the fifteenth-century*, 9 vols., Rolls Series 41 (Her Majes-

taneously encyclopedic and linear: it includes all sorts of ethnographic details, set pieces, exempla and prodigies, while following an obvious narrative course. The *Polychronicon*'s double claim to totality, then—its conception of a supra-history or master genre within an English framework, and its subordination of encyclopedia to linear narrative—is what makes it special, even while it appears, for the same reason, to be a quintessentially medieval history.[12]

Like the *Brut,* the *Polychronicon*'s structure invited continuations, but the *Polychronicon* soon surpassed even the *Brut* in popularity. By the beginning of the fifteenth century, more than a dozen continuations had been added to the *Polychronicon*.[13] Most notable among these is John Trevisa's translation of the entire work, which survives in fourteen manuscripts, and which Trevisa completed between 1385 and 1387 at the request of his patron, Sir Thomas Berkeley. William Caxton printed and modernized Trevisa's translation in 1482, adding his own continuation, and Wynkyn de Worde reprinted Caxton's edition in 1495.[14] Another fifteenth-century translation of the *Polychronicon* appeared sometime between 1432 and 1450.[15]

The *Polychronicon* became something of a sensation immediately following its publication. From the 1360s it was used as a model of historical writing, as well as a standard authority for exempla collections, versified Bible redactions, and legendaries. Thomas Brinton, bishop of Rochester, frequently paraphrases the *Polychronicon* in his Latin sermons, and the sermon-writer John Mirk ransacks Higden for the kind of stories that he could just as easily find elsewhere, in exempla collections or

---

ty's Stationers Office, 1882; Kraus Reprint, 1964). All subsequent citations of Higden's Latin text and Trevisa's translation are to this edition. Citations refer to Higden's book and chapter numbers and to the page numbers of the printed volume.

[12] For descriptions of the *Polychronicon* and its relation to earlier universal histories, see John Taylor, *The Universal Chronicle of Ranulf Higden* (Oxford: Clarendon Press, 1966), pp. 33–55; and Fowler, *The Bible in Early English, Literature*, pp. 194–246.

[13] See A. S. G. Edwards, "The Influence and Audience of the *Polychronicon:* Some Observations," *Proceedings of the Leeds Philosophical and Literary Society: Literary and Historical Section* 17, pt. 6 (1980): 113–19; and Galloway, "Writing History in England," pp. 275–79. Continuations of the *Polychronicon* in the fourteenth and fifteenth centuries, such as the *Vita Edwardi Secundi* and the chronicle of Adam Usk, tend to be interested in contemporary politics.

[14] On Caxton's transmission (and authorship) of the *Brut* and the *Polychronicon,* see Lister Matheson, "Printer and Scribe: Caxton, the *Polychronicon,* and the *Brut," Speculum* 60.3 (1985): 593–614.

[15] Edwards, "The Influence and Audience of the *Polychronicon"*; Gransden, *Historical Writing in England,* pp. 43–57; Taylor, *English Historical Literature,* pp. 134–47.

legendaries. As late as 1513, Henry Bradshaw, a monk from Higden's own abbey in Chester, was citing the *Polychronicon* in his *Life of St. Werburgh* to argue for the regality of the kingdom of Mercia.[16] The *Stanzaic Life of Christ*, another Chester production, uses the *Polychronicon,* along with the *Legenda aurea*, as the source for its expanded and apocryphal account of Christ's life.[17] In turn, the *Stanzaic Life of Christ* probably contributed materials to the Chester cycle plays, which the post-Reformation Banns ascribe to Ranulph Higden.

In the context of these texts, the *Polychronicon* emerges not only as a handy sourcebook but also as part of a long trend of historicized scriptures or diversified bibles. As David Lawton observes, "Englishing" the Bible in the Middle Ages refers to a "spectrum of linguistic activity from translation through paraphrase to different kinds of imaginative substitution and of social process whereby sacred texts are made accessible to vernacularity."[18] This spectrum of activity, which ranged from the English biblical chronicle, the *Cursor mundi* (c. 1300), to collections of saints' lives, to the Corpus Christi cycle plays, offered a range of vernacular texts that were regarded as adjunct or supplementary to scripture, in part because they were never meant to produce a single authoritative text. These texts tend to be concerned more with narrative than with theology, and they tend to seek authority in comprehensiveness rather than in sacredness or canonicity. The Latin *Polychronicon,* along with its English translations, helped to produce biblical redactions and devotional texts in English by assembling in one place an enormous number of historical narratives, exempla, anecdotes, and "background" information. These narratives were pressed into to the service of religious education—they were used to flesh out gospel stories and saints' lives—while at the same time tailoring that education to English-speaking audiences.

It was thus in its capacity as a supra-history, as a massive collection of stories and subjects laid out chronologically, that the *Polychronicon* served the narrative ambitions of vernacular piety. The *Stanzaic Life of*

[16] Henry Bradshaw, *The Life of St. Werburghe of Chester*, ed. Carl Horstmann (London: N. Trubner & Co., 1881), pp. 253–55, 259, 386. For Thomas Walsingham's debts to Higden, see James G. Clark, "Thomas Walsingham Reconsidered: Books and Learning at Late-Medieval St. Albans," *Speculum* 77.3 (2002): 854–55.

[17] Kennneth Muir, "Translations and Paraphrases of the Bible and Commentaries," in J. Burke Severs, ed., *A Manual of the Writings in Middle English, 1050–1500,* vol. 2 (Hamden, Conn.: Archon Books, 1970), pp. 381–409.

[18] David Lawton, "Englishing the Bible," in *The Cambridge History of Medieval English Literature*, pp. 454–82, (455).

Christ draws on Higden for its New Testament redaction, but it also includes, as historical markers for Christ's life, stories tangential to the gospels, for example, stories about Tiberius's witty retorts and Ovid's punishment and repentance.[19] In this instance, the *Polychronicon* helped to produce an English version of the gospels by providing exempla from classical history. In a similar fashion, Thomas Usk in the *Testament of Love* plunders the Roman sections of the *Polychronicon* for examples of political truths (for example, how the bad will reverse themselves and be praised; how the law rewards those who support those in power), but he claims that these examples illustrate the lives of Christian saints.[20] The *Polychronicon*'s bid to narrative totality also made it an imaginative substitute for biblical commentary. Vernacular writers frequently cast Higden in the role of *auctor*, whose authority was not interpretative in exegetical or empirical senses, but rather in the sense that he could verify the existence of a story. Higden carefully shields his authorship by citing other *auctores*, at the same time that he registers himself as a compilator by marking his own opinions with a capital R.[21] Later authors, however, use Higden's stance as a compilator to turn him into an *auctor* proper within vernacular scriptural traditions. To take just one example, John Mirk suppresses both his and Higden's sources, ascribing exempla to "Rondylf Hyldon, monke of Chestyr" who "tellyþe yn hys cronyclys anoþyr myracull . . . etc," as if Higden, merely by rehearsing these stories within his chronicles, might take responsibility for them.[22]

Finally, it was the *Polychronicon*'s bid to narrative totality, which first had to be made by a Latin history subsuming other Latin histories, that would help link vernacularity to English identity. The Chester post-

---

[19] Francis Foster, ed., *A Stanzaic Life of Christ* (London, Oxford University Press, 1926), lines 5173–216 (*Polychronicon*, 4.4.316).

[20] *Testament of Love*, ed. Gary W. Shawver (Toronto: University of Toronto Press, 2002), Book I, chap. 6, lines 38–45. Shawver explains in his introduction that Usk draws from Higden's Latin original and Trevisa's translation, even though the latter must have been unfinished, as Trevisa claimed to finish it in 1387 (34).

[21] On Higden's self-inscriptions, see Alistair Minnis, *Medieval Theory of Authorship: Scholastic Literary Attitudes in the Late Middle Ages*, 2nd ed. (Philadelphia: University of Pennsylvania Press, 1988 [1984]), pp. 193–200; and Galloway, "Writing History in England," p. 276.

[22] *Mirk's Festial*, ed. Theodor Erbe, EETS e.s. 96 (London: K. Paul Trench, Trubner, & Co., 1905), p. 81. Likewise the author of the *Stanzaic Life of Christ*, while not mentioning Higden specifically, nonetheless cites Higden's sources in the passages he borrows from the *Polychronicon*. In the prologue, he actually imitates Higden, explaining that he has carefully followed his *auctores*, lest clerks complain that a fool wrote these "newe fables" (line 32).

Reformation Banns praise Higden, who, despite the institutional pressures and shortcomings of monkhood, tried to educate laymen by spreading the Bible "in a common Englishe tonge never reade nor harde."[23] As Clopper and Mills point out, the *Polychronicon* may have been better known by its expanded or offshoot versions, such as the *Stanzaic Life of Christ*, and it was possibly this notion of the *Polychronicon* that reinforced Higden's connection to the Chester cycle. The *Stanzaic Life of Christ*, however, never names Higden or the *Polychronicon* specifically, and it seems unlikely either that the Banns would "know" an author that earlier readers never identified, or that they would be aware of the *Polychronicon*'s transmission history. It seems more likely that the authors of the Banns, by attributing the cycle to Higden, recognized the peculiar double claim of the *Polychronicon*: narrative totality in the service of English identity, and the subordination of compendium or encyclopedia to linear narrative.[24] This claim was attractive to anyone trying to write an expanded scriptural narrative, and in the context of Protestant literary history, it was a claim that served the Chester cycle especially well.[25]

When we consider the currency of the *Polychronicon* in medieval England, it comes as no surprise that Higden was also Wyclif's "favorite historian." But whereas for writers of vernacular religious texts, the *Polychronicon* served as a narrative authority for extra-scriptural writing, for Wyclif it constituted both the materials and the method with which to

---

[23] Text is found in "The Late Banns: Rogers' Breviary in Chester City Archives," in R. M. Lumiansky and David Mills, eds., *The Chester Mystery Cycle: Essays and Documents* (Chapel Hill: University of North Carolina Press, 1983), pp. 285–95, at line 22. According to the Banns, Sir John Arneway, the Chester mayor who staged the plays, "contented himselfe to sett out in playe / the devise of one Rondall, moncke of Chester Abbaye" (lines 6–7). This is an unlikely chronology. The authors of Banns clearly hoped to defend the legitimacy of the plays by attributing them to the collaboration of civic and religious authorities (Arneway and Higden were two of Chester's most famous residents), just as they hoped to ascribe the cycle's archaisms and apocrypha to a medieval monk.

[24] Lawrence Clopper, "Arnewaye, Higden, and the Origin of the Chester Play," *Records of Early English Drama Newsletter* (1983): 4–11, at 7; David Mills, *Recycling the Cycle: the City of Chester and Its Whitsun Plays* (Toronto: University of Toronto Press, 1998), p. 46. As Mills points out, moreover, from the perspective of the Reformers, Trevisa's purported authorship of the English Bible, along with his translation of the *Polychronicon*, may have helped to give Higden Lollard credentials. For further discussion off the Late Banns and the relationship they demonstrate between lay piety and clerical authority, see Clopper, *Drama, Play, and Game: English Festive Culture in the Medieval and Early Modern Period* (Chicago: University of Chicago Press, 2001), pp. 204–31.

[25] The *Polychronicon*, after all, was known as an English as well as a Latin chronicle.

construct a polemical Church history.[26] For one thing, Wycliffite ecclesiology tends to be as interested in political history as it is in political theory. Wyclif was deeply skeptical of institutional Church history, which, in his opinion, was a fabricated history authorizing "new" corruptive practices such as clerical temporalities, the Franciscan order, and papal sovereignty. For Wyclif and many of his followers, the *Polychronicon* offered a source for an alternative Church history, a source that, in Wyclif's use of it, approximates traditional exegesis. In *De potestate pape*, for example, Wyclif transforms Higden from being a source for patristic commentary to a quasi-patristic authority. According to Higden, at the Donation of Constantine an angel announced that poison had now infiltrated the Church. Higden's account includes a supportive statement from Jerome, which Wyclif cites as part of Higden's text and not as a separate authority on papal corruption. Wyclif concludes that papal heresy resulted from Constantine's Donation, because, in the *Polychronicon*, Higden follows the story of the Donation with an account of Julius and other early popes who supported the wrong side of theological controversies (*Polychronicon*, 4.27). In this case, historiography substitutes imaginatively for ecclesiology, at the same time that history substitutes imaginatively for exegesis (for example, "in cronicis autem Cestrensis [of Chester] narravi," "narrat idem Cestrensis," "ut patet ex cronicis predictus," etc.).[27] In *De officio regis*, Wyclif refers to the same chapters in the *Polychronicon* to prove that if a pope has deposed an emperor or taught others to do the same, nevertheless an emperor has also deposed popes for their blasphemy, as Higden makes clear.[28] We often find

---

[26] Monastic histories were long considered to be sources of political counsel, and it is interesting, in this respect, that Higden was summoned along with his chronicles to the king's council on August 21, 1352. The purpose of the summons is not known, although presumably it had to do with Higden's expertise as a historian. See Gransden, *Historical Writing in England*, p. 43; and Taylor, *Universal Chronicle*, p. 1.

[27] *Tractatus de potestate pape,* ed. Johann Loserth, with notes by F. D. Matthew (London: Wyclif Society, 1907), pp. 198–99 (see *Polychronicon*, 4.26.128–32; 4.27.160–62), In some versions of the story, the voice is that of the devil.

[28] This may be Wyclif's deliberate misreading of 4.27, in which popes are deposed precisely because they do not subscribe to Arianism. *Tractatus de officio regis*, ed. Alfred W. Pollard and Charles Sayle (London: Wyclif Society, 1882), pp. 128–29. Following Wyclif's example, an early Wycliffite polemicist, arguing that Christ never confirmed tithes in the New Law, attributes the institution of tithes to Pope Gregory VI, but he cites the *Polychronicon* as evidence for this papal error. See *The English Works of Wyclif*, ed. F. D. Matthew (London: Oxford University Press, 1880), p. 391. Similarly, the author of the "long Luke" version of the Glossed Gospels uses Higden to condemn Innocent III's edicts on oral confession. See Hudson, *The Premature Reformation*, p. 258.

Wyclif in dialogue with the *Polychronicon*, as if Higden was an oft-cited commentator and the universal history the primary source of canonical truth and error. In *De potestate pape*, for example, Wyclif takes Higden to task for perpetuating the error of the pope's two names ("in qua material credendum est cronicis"). Higden mistakenly reports that the *pontifex* is called "pape" because the bishop of Rome is the chief father over other bishops, just as the Roman emperor is above all kings.[29] According to Wyclif, the pope is called *pontifex* because he must be elected both in his human nature (by the cardinals) and his divine nature (insofar as he has divorced himself from worldly things).

Wyclif's citations further demonstrate the currency of the *Polychronicon* in later medieval writing, and especially the way that experiments in historiography might help shape narrative into polemic. In this view, Wycliffite ecclesiology could even be said to be a function of radical historiography and not *vice versa*. Indeed, if we move from Wycliffite polemic to two literary texts, Trevisa's *Dialogue Between a Lord and Clerk* and *Piers Plowman*, we see how the literary engagement with historical writing, and specifically with Higden's universal history, generated new ways of describing the institutional Church. But where Wyclif uses the *Polychronicon* to write a polemical Church history, Trevisa's and Langland's projects represent a bolder and much more speculative encounter with historical writing. These two authors look to Higden not for the sources and exempla of history but for the modes of exemplarity that the universal history enjoins. They are interested, in other words, not in the stories that might be culled from the *Polychronicon* to justify an idea or develop a theme, but in the theories *about* narrative and example that drive the universal history as a *genre*. And it is precisely their interest in the formal properties of the universal history, in the principles that govern its composition, that leads them to conclusions at once surprisingly radical and seemingly inconsistent with the general tenor of their works.

It is in the service of literary history, finally, that we must read backwards from Trevisa to Langland. The historiographical sensibility found in Trevisa's *Dialogue Between a Lord and a Clerk* (c. 1387) and in *Piers Plowman* (c. 1377) does not correspond to the usual markers of persons, events, or reigns. Rather, it corresponds to the life of the *Polychronicon* in English poetry and intellectual prose, for Langland's generation and for Trevisa's. Further, as we shall see, radical historiography produces a the-

---

[29] *De potestate pape*, pp. 177–78.

ory of clerical exemplarity that may be more coherently traced in Trevisa than in Langland. This theory, for which Trevisa's *Dialogue* holds the key, allows us to read both forward and backwards the politics of late medieval literature.

Trevisa's Historiography

John Trevisa's *Dialogue Between a Lord and a Clerk* is appended to five of the fourteen extant manuscripts of Trevisa's translation of the *Polychronicon* (c. 1385–87), and it was printed as a preliminary to Caxton's edition of the *Polychronicon* in 1482.[30] In the *Dialogue*, the Lord deftly argues for the value of translating the *Polychronicon* into English: he cites the importance of informing all Englishmen about the "loore of deeds"; he notes the pervasiveness of translation in preaching; and he reminds the Clerk of the network of patronage that has always sustained translation. The Clerk, in his turn, argues for the sufficiency of Latin, weakly refutes arguments to the contrary, and finally, bested by the Lord, turns the conversation to questions of style.

The *Dialogue*, if a cheerfully implausible representation of a debate between a lord and his clerk, is surely meant to be a fictionalized exchange between Trevisa and his patron, Sir Thomas Berkeley. Berkeley, lord of the family estates in Gloucester from 1368 to his death in 1417, allied himself through marriage to some of England's most powerful players, and he used his abundant capital and leisure to support a stable of clerical dependents, including several chaplains.[31] The activities of these chaplains chiefly included estates administration and religious services, but they also included, more unusually, the translation of Latin chronicles, classical political theory, and advice-to-princes treatises, as well as the production of luxury manuscripts.[32] Trevisa, sometime vicar

[30] Ronald Waldron, "Trevisa's Original Prefaces on Translation: A Critical Edition," in *Medieval English Studies Presented to George Kane*, ed. Edward Donald Kennedy, Ronald Waldron, and Joseph S. Wittig (Wolfeboro, N.H.: D. S. Brewer, 1988), pp. 285–89.

[31] On Berkeley's political clout and extensive patronage, see Ralph Hanna III, "Sir Thomas Berkeley and His Patronage," *Speculum* 64 (1989): 878–916.

[32] On the circulation of manuscripts and printed editions of Trevisa's translation of the *Polychronicon*, see Edwards, "The Influence and Audience of the *Polychronicon*." See also Steven Justice and Kathryn Kerby-Fulton, "Langlandian Reading Circles and the Civil Service in London and Dublin, 1380–1427," in Wendy Scase, Rita Copeland, and David Lawton, eds., *New Medieval Literatures* 1 (Oxford: Oxford University Press, 1997), pp. 59–84; and "Scribe D and the Marketing of Ricardian Literature," in Kathryn Kerby-Fulton and Maidie Hilmo, eds., *The Medieval Professional Reader at Work: Evidence from Manuscripts of Chaucer, Langland, Kempe, and Gower* (Victoria: University of Victoria Press, 2001), pp. 217–37.

of Berkeley, benefited greatly from Sir Thomas's support. Berkeley probably sponsored Trevisa's education at Oxford, and while in Berkeley's service, Trevisa translated five voluminous Latin works in addition to the *Polychronicon:* Bartholomeus Anglicus's *De proprietatibus rerum,* Giles of Rome's *De regime principum,* Richard FitzRalph's *Defensio curatorum,* the *Gospel of Nicodemus,* and the pseudo-Ockham *Dialogus inter clericum et militem.* These translations molded the tastes of the English aristocracy well into the fifteenth century and helped set the stage for an English prose tradition as well.[33]

The *Dialogue* has attracted critical attention in the last decade because of the kinds of arguments it makes for vernacular translation, and the implications of those arguments for biblical translation and for medieval clerical-lay relations. As the authors of *The Idea of the Vernacular* explain, by rehearsing traditional arguments for Bible translation in the *Dialogue,* Trevisa seems to be arguing for universal access to scripture through the vernacular, even if he projects this access through the desires of a lay lord.[34] Similarly, Fiona Somerset shows that the *Dialogue* shares concerns with *Piers Plowman* and Wycliffite texts because it imagines its potential audience to be made up of "the whole of the lay population," even if it is not explicitly calling for the education of the entire laity.[35] In such texts, translation does not just fulfill one patron's demand; it also drives an audience it to seek its own spiritual education. Somerset rightly asks, however, why Berkeley needed to commission a translation of the *Polychronicon,* which was already available to clerks and lords in Latin, and therefore, what purpose the *Dialogue* actually served.[36] She proposes that, for the Lord, to argue for translation is to acquire intellectual capital by broadening the base "of what had traditionally been clerical 'in-

---

[33] Concerning the historical tastes of the English aristocracy, see Richard Firth Green, *Poets and Princepleasers: Literature and the English Court in the Later Middle Ages* (Toronto: University of Toronto Press, 1980), pp. 135–67, esp. pp. 135–38 on the usefulness of historical writing and p. 154 on translation activities at Berkeley Castle. As Green puts it, "A list of [Trevisa and Walton's] translations reads almost like a prospectus of works essential for the formation of a basic aristocratic library" (p. 154).

[34] Jocelyn Wogan-Browne, Nicholas Watson, Andrew Taylor, and Ruth Evans, eds., *The Idea of the Vernacular: An Anthology of Middle English Literary Theory, 1280–1520* (University Park: The Pennsylvania State University Press, 1999), pp. 130–31.

[35] Fiona Somerset, "The 'Publyschyng' of 'Informacion': John Trevisa, Sir Thomas Berkeley, and their project of 'Englysch translacion,'" in *Clerical Discourse and Lay Audience in Late Medieval England* (Cambridge: Cambridge University Press, 1998), pp. 62–100, at 65–66.

[36] Ibid., p. 66.

formacion.' "[37] By commissioning a translation and presenting arguments on its behalf, the Lord might appropriate the Clerk's proper function at the same time that he asserts the prerogatives of the aristocratic patron. Along the same lines, Rita Copeland influentially argues, with respect to Gower but with implications for Trevisa, that the appropriation of lay learning was a status symbol for the aristocracy.[38]

As this brief summary suggests, what perplexes critics about the *Dialogue* is that the *Polychronicon* seems to warrant neither a translation nor the kind of apology for translation found in the *Dialogue*. In fact, Trevisa discloses his project (his translation of Higden) in ways that appear counter to his purpose: he invokes the trope of universal access found in texts dealing with lay spiritual education, and he enlists academic arguments for biblical translation. Even if larger sociopolitical forces must partly account for the discrepancy between rhetoric and subject, the *Dialogue*'s ideological work remains only obliquely related to its rhetorical form. If, however, we take the *Polychronicon* to be the subject of, and not simply the occasion for, the *Dialogue*, we find that it provides an argument for translation in and of itself. In Trevisa's reading of the *Polychronicon*, the universal history offers its own "sovereign" hermeneutics, by which I mean first, the interpretation of a text through the exercise of lay sovereignty, according to the way that lords judge need and distribute profit; and second, an interpretation of a text that values historical precedent and genealogical descent, the cultural foundations of lay lordship. Thus, in Trevisa's view, the universal history makes a very specific argument for translation because its structure inherently expresses the values of lay lordship; it is in making this argument, for Trevisa, that the *Polychronicon* posits a secular and aristocratic notion of English identity.

The Universal History and the Subject of Need

The Lord begins the dialogue by lamenting the communication crisis that has befallen humankind since the Tower of Babel. Since that unhappy event, people of different countries have not been able to understand each other, even though they "have grete nede of informacioun

---

[37] Ibid.

[38] Rita Copeland, *Rhetoric, Hermeneutics, and Translation in the Middle Ages: Academic Translations and Vernacular Texts* (Cambridge: Cambridge University Press, 1991), p. 224.

and of lore, of talking and of speche."[39] Fortunately clerks, out of their "godenesse and curtesie" (line 18), have addressed the crisis by cultivating a *lingua franca*, Latin, through which information may be universally shared "in diverse naciouns ond londes" (line 19). Higden's *Polychronicon*, which describes "the world about in lengthe and in brede," which reckons the years between Creation and the Last Judgment, and which records all sorts "of doynges and of dedes, of mervails and of wondres," exemplifies this goal to disseminate in Latin "noble and greet informacioun and lore" (lines 21–24). The *Polychronicon*'s encyclopedic bid to universality, its claim to encompass all useful information, in some way mirrors the remedial purpose of the language in which it is written. Consequently, concludes the Lord, the *Polychronicon* should be translated into English, so that even "moo men shuld hem [the chronicles] understonde and have thereof kunnyng, informacioun and lore" (lines 26–27). English furthers the purpose of Latin as modeled by Higden's *Polychronicon*: if the Latin *Polychronicon* remedies history by spreading useful information, then it will continue to do so by being disseminated to "moo men." According to the Lord, the totality represented by the *Polychronicon* defines the universality of translation; translation realizes linguistically the *Polychronicon*'s generic claims.

The Clerk protests that Latin is a true *lingua franca*, not a common language. Its virtue resides in the fact that it is "so wide iused and iknowe" (line 33) and not in the numbers it reaches. In fact, says the Clerk, if universality is defined as breadth, Latin is less exclusive than English, which is "nought iused and iknowe but of Englisshe men al oon [alone]" (lines 33–34). The Lord insists that what is finally at stake is the dissemination of profitable information to those who need it. Translation would increase the numbers of those who understood the *Polychronicon*, period.

Here the Clerk makes his first tactical mistake: he shifts the definition of need from the need to comprehend to the need to know, or from skill to profit. First, he tries to locate need in the Lord alone, arguing that if the Lord understands Latin, then "it nedeth not to have siche an Englisshe translacioun" (lines 38–39). The Lord objects that his own—and the Clerk's—Latin is imperfect (Latinity is relative), and besides, "though it were not nedeful for me, it is nedeful for other men that understondeth

---

[39] *The Idea of the Vernacular*, p. 132, lines 1–10. All subsequent citations of the *Dialogue between a Lord and a Clerk* are to this edition and will follow the quotations in the text with line numbers.

no Latyn" (lines 43–44). All sorts of obstacles stand in the way of those who would learn Latin, says the Lord: time, old age, stupidity, finances, and various other hindrances (lines 46–48). To which objections the Clerk tersely remarks, "hit nedeth not that alle siche know the cronicles" (line 49), that is, those who do not know Latin do not need to know the chronicles in the first place. Language not only facilitates education but also fixes the social contexts of learning. The Lord promptly admonishes the Clerk, informing him that it is he, the Lord, who decides what need is, who represents it, and how it should be addressed. "Speke not to straitliche [importunately] of thing that nedeth," he exclaims. "Straitliche" [strictly speaking], there is only one needful thing, God, because God cannot fail. The second category of need comprises only those things that sustain life, such as food and drink. But, says the Lord, if need is defined as "al that is profitable" (line 57), then "alle men nedith to knowe the cronicles" (line 58).

If the ostensible subject of this exchange is vernacular translation, its real subject, embodied in the word "need," is the reciprocal relation between the universal history and the expression of lay lordship. By lordship, I mean, in the first place, the will to magnanimity, the way that the Lord praises the "godeness and curteisie" of clerks like Higden who use Latin to disseminate "informacioun and lore" to the entire community. Again, this magnanimous desire to address "grete nede" through a positive good—communicating useful information—is modeled by the *Polychronicon*, a Latin compendium that ultimately extends, like the Lord's definition of universality, to England itself. Its very comprehensiveness is an argument, not for an international community of clerks, but to nobility, the remedy of history, whose benefits should extend to as many men as possible. Likewise, just as the *Polychronicon* extends romantically toward the English present, so Latin should extend from the historical reversal of Babel to fourteenth-century England, the time and place of the present Lord. In sum, the courteous act of translating the *Polychronicon* exposes the aristocratic lay values underwriting translation in the first place.

By lordship, second, I mean the will to rule, the authority to judge the profit of a realm, as when the Lord lists the obstacles to learning Latin, or, in a different way, when he enumerates the categories of need. The Clerk, by defining need as the lack of profit (in the Lord's words, "alle men nedith to knowe the chronicles," line 58), rather than the lack of skill (in the Clerk's words, "hit nedith to have an Englisshe translacioun," lines 66–67), allows the Lord to redefine translation in his own person, not as the rhetorical inclusion of the disenfranchised, but as the exercise of sovereignty, under which the profit of the entire laity is subsumed. Once again, it is the universal history that supplies the rhetorical and ideological materials for him to do so: the *Polychronicon* implicitly transforms the problem of translation into the problem of lay profit and lay need. The *Polychronicon*, as an exhaustive source of information, represents that third category of need—profitability—the category that belongs to and is defined by lordship. And as the Lord makes clear, profitable information is not a generalized knowledge but rather knowledge as generalized by the *Polychronicon*.

Historical Exemplarity and the "Loore of Deeds"

So far we have seen that the universal history, the very subject of the *Dialogue*, sets the terms by which an argument about translation can take place. Vernacular translation, insofar as it concerns the *Polychronicon*, is about the exercise of lordship: the determination of need and the dissemination of profit. In the second half of the *Dialogue*, the Clerk changes tactics once again, arguing that Latin is "gode and fayre" in itself, and therefore "hit nedith not to have an Englisshe translation" (lines 66–67). The Clerk may be intimating either that Latin is sufficient to the task or that it is essentially untranslatable, that its very goodness proscribes translation. The Lord, outraged by this statement, counters the Clerk by citing a number of patristic translators, who translated the Bible into Greek and Latin, and who, on account of their translations, "bith highliche ypreysed of al Holy Chyrche" (lines 79–80). To say that Latin is "gode and fayre" in itself (line 66) is to imply that the early Church fathers were "lewdeliche occupied" by rendering the "gode and fayre" (lines 78–79) language of scripture into their own vernaculars. The only "lewde dede" (line 84), says the Lord, would be if a clerk should happen to preach in Latin to a mixed audience, failing to take into account the spiritual profit of the laity.

To this the Clerk cryptically replies that "a grete dele of these bokes [that is, the patristic translations] stondith myche by holy writ, by holy doctours, and by philosophie; than these bokes shuld not be translated into Englisshe" (lines 91–93). In other words, the kinds of patristic translations to which the Lord refers belong to a tradition of texts canonized by and through a community of clerics. Consequently, to translate the Vulgate into English is to take it out of its signifying context, thus committing an impropriety with respect to sacred scripture.

The Lord responds to the Clerk by arguing that patristic translations set historical precedents for translation, just as they establish continuity between translators of the past and present. He argues, in other words, for a genealogical rather than intertextual context for translation, and, to this end, he recites a new genealogy of translators, only some of them, strictly speaking, biblical translators, and all of whom happen to be described in the *Polychronicon*.[40] He begins with Latin translations of Aristotle rendered from the Greek. He then proceeds from the classical to the medieval, to the French king Charles the Bald, at whose request John Scotus Erigena translated works by Pseudo-Dionysius.[41] From there he moves from the Continent to England, citing the scholarly labors of King Alfred the Great, who, the Lord, slyly remarks, "founded the Universite of Oxenford" (where Trevisa was trained), who translated "the best lawes into the Englisshe tonge, and a grete del of the Sauter out of Latyn into Englisshe," and who ordered Werfirth, bishop of Worcester, to translate the *Dialogues* of Saint Gregory the Great (a collection of saints' lives) (lines 100–103).[42] The Lord continues with two Anglo-Saxon luminaries, Caedmon, who turned much of the Bible into "[wonde]r poysies in Englisshe" (line 105), and Bede, who apparently translated the Gospel of Saint John. Finally, the Lord concludes by inscribing himself materially and locally into this illustrious company of translators, alluding to the translations painted on the interior walls of his own Berkeley Chapel: "Also, thou wost whare the Apocalips is ywrite in the walles and roof of a chapel bothe in Latyn and in Frensshe" (lines 106–7).

By reciting this second translation genealogy, the Lord once again projects traditional arguments for translation through the lens of the universal history. What is most striking about this last exchange is that

[40] Compare Trevisa's description of Alfred in this passage with his description in the *Polychronicon*: "þerfore by counsail of Neotus þe abbot, whom he visited ful ofte, he was þe firste þat ordeyned comyn scole at Oxenforde of dyverse artes and sciens . . . he tornede [Higden, *convertit*] þe beste lawes into Englissh tonge. At þe laste he auntred hym to torne [Higden, *transferre*] þe psauter in to Englisshe. But he tornede unneþe þe firste party to fore his ende day" (*Polychronicon* 6.1.355–57).
[41] Trevisa, like many medieval authors, mistakes Pseudo-Dionysius for Saint Denis, patron saint of France.
[42] Higden was the first to claim Alfred as the founder of the University of Oxford. See Fowler, *The Bible in Early English Literature*, p. 238.

it revolves around arguments for biblical translation, when clearly the *Polychronicon* is not sacred scripture, but an admixture of apocryphal, hagiographical, cosmographical, ecclesiastical, and secular chronicles. Indeed, the discrepancy between the *Polychronicon* and the Bible, along with the Clerk's refusal to name his impropriety, suggests that their debate is nothing more than an apologist's sleight of hand. Yet significantly, the Lord's second genealogy *recapitulates* the universal history, moving as it does from the classical to the medieval, and from the Continent to England, and it includes translators who are by no means biblical translators. As discussed above, the *Polychronicon* provided content for redactions of the Bible, biblical commentary, and polemical Church histories.[43] In charting his so-called history of biblical translation, the Lord re-envisions the *Polychronicon* not as a vernacular bible but as an alternative tradition, supplementary to scripture, from which a new translation theory can be drawn.[44]

[43] The author of the *Determination*, what was probably a Lollard translation of Richard Ullerston's pro-translation tract in the Oxford translation debate of 1401, follows Trevisa's *Dialogue*, both the translations of the *Polychronicon* in the *Dialogue*, and the *Dialogue*'s historiographical argument for vernacular translation. His description of King Alfred the Great follows Trevisa's description in the *Dialogue* almost to the letter, even though he cites Higden (following the Latin): "Also Cistrence in his sext book þe Ic., seiþ þat Al[f]rede the kynge ordined opene scolis of diverse artes in Oxenforde; and he turnede the best lawes in-to his modor tunge, & þe sawter also" (lines 146–50). For the text, see C. F. Buhler, "A Lollard Tract: On Translating the Bible into English," *MÆ* 7 (1938): 167–83. He likewise uses the *Polychronicon* as a stand-in for traditional exegesis, and specifically for arguments for biblical translation. Like Trevisa, he begins with traditionally cited biblical translators, such as Origin and Jerome, continues with early English translators, such as Oswald king of Northumberland, Alfred, and Bede, for which he explicitly cites Higden, interspersed with some recent English examples, such as a London man named Wyring, who supposedly possessed a Bible in a Northern dialect, which appeared to be two hundred years old. The Lollard translator concludes with a number of Lollard English favorites, including Grosseteste, Rolle, and Thoresby. Unlike Trevisa, however, Ullerston and his translator are interested more in the sheer proliferation of historical examples than they are in any purposeful genealogy, probably because they are more interested in lay education than they are in aristocratic patronage. On Ullerston's authorship of this treatise, and the relationship between the Latin version and its English translation, see Hudson, "The Debate on Bible Translation, Oxford 1401," in *Lollards and Their Books*, pp. 67–84. Hudson notes in this essay that the English text depends upon the authorities cited in the Latin version, but it introduces a new, more controversial frame, abbreviates much of the Latin, and adds details such as Wyring with his English Bible, pp. 70–71. I thank Kantik Ghosh and Anne Hudson for sharing with me a passage from their transcription of the Latin manuscript.

[44] It is interesting to compare the Lord's translation theory here with Ullerston's understanding of biblical translation as paraphrase. See Nicholas Watson, "Censorship and Cultural Exchange in Late-Medieval England: Vernacular Theology, the Oxford Translation Debate, and Arundel's Constitutions of 1409," *Speculum* 70 (1995): 822–64, esp. 841–45.

Specifically, it is by making the *Polychronicon* the source for an alternative tradition that the Lord is able to justify vernacular translation in terms of what I shall call historical exemplarity. The examples of Charles the Bald and especially Alfred the Great suggest that to translate the *Polychronicon* is to participate in a lay aristocratic approach to the past based on the emulation of deeds and the logic of descent. From the perspective of the universal history, the act of translation and the defense of translation are one and the same. Indeed, from the perspective of the universal history, translation *is* descent: it is the continuous act of generation through the imitation of preceding acts. Crucially, the Lord is arguing not for the essential translatability of texts (the possibility of access) but rather for the idea that translation refers to great deeds reproduced over time, an idea that upholds the values of lay lordship but is framed by the Lord's "reading" of the *Polychronicon*.[45] The Lord is generally interested in the *Polychronicon* as a source of "noble and greet informacioun and lore" (lines 23–24), yet for him that information consists most profitably of "doynges and of dedes, of mervails and of wondres" (line 22). As the Lord reminds the Clerk, the ignorant man has no idea what he needs to know, "nameliche of loore of dedes that come never in his mynde" (line 62). By commissioning a translation of the *Polychronicon*, the Lord addresses this cultural need—he recalls to the ignorant man the "doynges and dedes" of the past. He demonstrates in the process, however, that translation, as a noble deed, is part of the cultural apparatus of lordship, just as lordship is the theoretical justifi-

---

[45] It is telling, in this respect, that Trevisa, in his translation of Higden's prologue, tends to emphasize the deeds of great men recorded *in* history over the deeds of those who *recorded* history. For example, Higden writes that we should praise those wise authors of the past who took the time to acquire knowledge, because it was their mixing together of sweetness and profit that left to posterity written accounts of the excellent deeds of men preceding ("qui magnifica priscorum gesta beneficio scripturae posteris derivarunt"). Trevisa's version, by contrast, stresses the greatness of the deeds performed rather than the greatness of the acts of writing: we should praise those, says Trevisa, "þat write and left vs write meruailles and wondres, greet berynge and dedes of oure forme fadres, of stalworthe wyt, wise and worthy, and of dyuerse manere men þat were in olde tyme" (*Polychronicon*, 1.1.2–3). Likewise, Higden asks, who alive today would know about emperors, marvel at philosophers, and follow the apostles, if the acts of writers had not distinguished ("insignirent") such figures? ("Quis, quaeso, Caesares hodie sciret, philosophos miraretur, apostolos sequeretur, nisi eos insignirent momumenta scriptorum?"). Trevisa's translation, by contrast, shifts the import of "insignerere" (to distinguish, to make notable) from the written testimony of *auctores* to the deeds that they record: "I praye who schulde now knowe emperours, wonder of philosofres, oþer folwe þe apostles, but hir noble dedes and hir wonder werkes were i-write in stories and so i-kept in mynde?" (*Polychronicon*, 1.1.4–7).

cation for translation. If need and profit are the routine expressions of lay sovereignty, historical exemplarity is sovereignty's foundation. To imagine oneself within a history of translation is to assume one's rightful place in the (English) present. Thus the Lord imagines himself at the end of translation and at the end of the *Polychronicon* by citing his own chapel in Gloucestershire, whose roof and walls are painted with the text of the Apocalypse.[46]

The Lord's genealogy suggests further that it is patronage that produces a workable theory of translation, because it is patronage that incorporates translation into the historical relations of time and place. The movement from Greek to Latin to French to English; from classical antiquity to medieval Europe; from the Continent to England; and from the English past of King Alfred to the English present, as represented materially by Berkeley Chapel: all these *translationes* are motivated by the complementary labors of lord and clerk. This dynamic between lord and clerk is represented historically by the collaborations of King Charles and John Scotus Erigena, and of King Alfred and Werfrith, and biographically, by the Lord's references to Oxford University and Berkeley Chapel, the two poles of Trevisa's career. This is not just to say that *translatio studii* depends upon and is enabled by *translatio imperii*. It is to say that translation acquires meaning and purpose within the history of aristocratic generation and possession, within a history, which, for the Lord, is a history of Englishness itself.

The Lord's genealogy reminds the Clerk that academic labor is a consequence of lay dispensation. More seriously, however, it implies that a clerk must embrace the values of the universal history if he hopes to write himself into patronage, and by extension, into Englishness. Ultimately, what is at stake in the *Dialogue* is not so much the exclusivity of clerks but the possibility of their exclusion, from patronage and from history.[47] As the Lord's reading of the *Polychronicon* suggests, historical exemplarity, by its very nature, incorporates the clergy into relations of

---

[46] According to Fowler, these verses are inscribed on the roof and timbers of the Chapel to Saint Mary the Virgin in Berkeley Chapel. Fowler speculates that the verses (the ones surviving are in Norman French) were probably written by one of Trevisa's predecessors in the mid-fourteenth century. *The Life and Times of John Trevisa*, pp. 116–17.

[47] As Ralph Hanna observes about the *Dialogue*, "The clerical hope of retaining secular power, of keeping Ranulph Higden's history the exclusive property of a Latinate community, is routed by the Lord's insistence upon the rights of secular readership." "Sir Thomas Berkeley and His Patronage," p. 895.

lay sovereignty: the distribution of needful things and the continual performance of deeds from one generation to another. Lay sovereignty, in turn, situates history in the present of aristocratic possession, those things that pertain to or belong to Englishness, such as the walls of the chapel in Gloucestershire. (With the example of Berkeley Chapel, moreover, the Lord shows that Englishness is constituted not by the English *language*, as distinct from French, but by the dynamic between vernacular translation and lordship.) Thus to practice a hermeneutics informed by the *Polychronicon* is first, to conceive of translation as genealogy, that is, as a history of sovereignty, and second, to direct arguments for translation to the local instantiations of English possession. The Clerk proposes the existence of a clerical community that is by its very nature ahistorical: its exemplarity consists of its nonproductivity. But, by participating in the Lord's genealogy, he is included in the translation from history to nation.[48]

Langland's Historiography

Like Trevisa, Langland makes the universal history a theoretical experiment in lordship at the expense of traditional clerical arguments. Like Trevisa, too, he reproduces the form of Higden's *Polychronicon* without naming it outright, and in doing so, he transforms the universal history into a commentary on clerical-lay relations. Yet for Langland, writing in the late 1370s, a decade before Trevisa completed the *Polychronicon*, the political implications of historical writing are considerably different. For Trevisa, the universal history helped fashion arguments for translation sympathetic to the values of lay patronage. In *Piers Plowman*, Trevisa's "sovereign hermeneutics" culminates in fantasies of disendowment, as in the lines, "Takeþ hire landes, ye lordes, and leteþ hem lyue be dymes. / If possession be poison and inparfite hem make" [Take away their lands, you lords, and let them live by tithes, if possession becomes poison and makes them imperfect] (15.564–65). This is not, as might be assumed, because Langland could channel radical ecclesiology in the 1370s in a way that Trevisa could not do in the post-Wyclif 1380s, or because he somehow let his material get away from him. Rather, Lang-

---

[48] For a cogent recent study of monastic historians' contributions to theories of English national identity, see Andrew Galloway, "Latin England," in Kathryn Lavezzo, ed., *Imagining a Medieval English Community* (Minneapolis: University of Minnesota Press, 2004), pp. 41–95.

land's historiography is headier, more ambitious, and more diffuse, first, because it is his style to exploit the ideological assumptions of any literary form, and second, because he is writing deep inside a historiographical project that began with the publication of Higden's Latin text in the 1350s and ended, for the time being, with Trevisa's English translation in the late 1380s.[49] To translate the *Polychronicon* into English is already to think outside of it. So whereas Trevisa's *Dialogue* coolly reflects upon a project already complete, Langland enacts the project at the moment of its conception, when it is still operating at the level of discourse, rather than as a unified or even identifiable text.

As we shall see, Langland waxes polemical where Trevisa remains reflective, precisely because the poem's fifth vision is composed of those materials that have become the *Dialogue*'s occasion and subject. Consequently, Anima's speech in B.15 is more controversial, not exactly because it *can* be controversial (Trevisa's choice of translation thus being a safer topic than disendowment), but rather because it is caught up in the nascent and inchoate idea of the *Polychronicon*. Whereas Trevisa uses the *Polychronicon* to rethink translation through the values of aristocratic patronage, Langland adopts the universal history as the very discourse of clerical reform. And whereas, in the *Dialogue*, the conditions of English identity are provisional, circumscribed by an exchange between clerical dependent and lay patron, in *Piers Plowman* they are extreme because Langland pushes the universal history to its logical conclusions, and beyond the bounds of patronage. Trevisa argues in the *Dialogue* that clerks may participate in Englishness by submitting themselves to historical exemplarity: the demands of lay profit, and the commitment to precedent and descent. In B.15, not only must reformed clerks embrace historical exemplarity, but in doing so they give up Englishness altogether.

Historical Exemplarity and the Search for England

The last four passus of *Piers Plowman* enact a dramatic shift from an academic disputation (passus 8–14) to a romance of sacred history (passus 16–20), a vernacular bible set to the tempo of chivalric ro-

---

[49] In general, Langland is less likely than Trevisa to offer radical solutions or target particular religious organizations. He tends to be approving of monks, for example, whereas Trevisa is happy to sacrifice them in the name of other forms of clerical service (*Polychronicon*, 6.9.465). For discussions of this passage, see Somerset, *Clerical Discourse and Lay Audience*, p. 67; and Fowler, *The Life and Times of John Trevisa*, p. 189.

mance.[50] Passus 15 anticipates the poem's turn to history by investigating historical writing and particularly the historiographical model represented by the *Polychronicon*. Rather than placing the dreamer within the experience of history, it shows how history provides examples with which to evaluate charity, which in this passus refers to the conduct of the contemporary English clergy.[51]

Throughout *Piers Plowman*, Langland is interested in exemplarity and its implications for individual salvation and clerical reform; passus 15 is a virtual treatise on the subject. As will become clearer below, the *Polychronicon* provided Langland with new ways of thinking about exemplarity, with startling implications for clerical-lay relations. Langland's radical engagement with the universal history leads him to the conclusion that true moral reform depends upon the emulation of historical precedent. Historical exemplarity, as elaborated by Trevisa's Lord, can be summarized as the following: our forefathers acted in the past, and we read and imitate their actions in the present. In this view, the past is a romance or chronicle; it provides examples of behavior that should be imitated literally, because history itself is a record of generation and descent, culminating in the English present.[52] For Trevisa, then, as for Langland, historical exemplarity is a critical method that reveals a mode of being and becoming, a critical method that implicitly supports the

[50]James Simpson has identified this section as a historical quest of the self. "The central problem of the poem," he writes, "is now being broached from an historical perspective. . . . Langland's representation of the Incarnation answers to the problem of justice from both an historical and moral perspective. Beyond both these frames, the Incarnation is also represented as a psychological act." Simpson, *Piers Plowman: An Introduction to the B-Text* (London: Longman, 1990), p. 190.

[51]I am building here on Steven Justice's seminal essay on generic authority in *Piers Plowman*, in which he argues that throughout the *Visio* (which, he argues, can be taken as a model for the poem as a whole) Langland moves through genres to search for "the literary form that is as little literary, as little dependent upon human authority, as possible" ("The Genres of *Piers Plowman*," *Viator* 19 [1988]: 291–306 [292]).

[52]Historical exemplarity has obvious similarities to Franciscan imitation, a concept frequently evoked in *Piers Plowman*. The difference between the two has to do with their relationship to history: whereas Franciscanism demands imitation *despite* history, historical exemplarity demands imitation *as a consequence of* history. Whereas Franciscanism renews the past in the present, historical exemplarity maintains a narrative continuum between past and present. As we will see below, Anima cites Saint Francis as an example of a charitable clerk but then suggests that contemporary clerks fail to imitate Saint Francis because they do not subscribe to a larger historical narrative culminating in the English present. Lawrence Clopper discusses the ecclesiology of this passus in some detail with reference to the friars, arguing that Langland sees the friars, rather than bishops, as the true heirs to the apostles. See *"Songes of Rechelesnesse": Langland and the Franciscans* (Ann Arbor: University of Michigan Press, 1997).

values of lay lordship. Toward the beginning of passus 15, the speaker, Anima, declares that true charity is knowable neither through study nor observation, but only through Piers the Plowman, who perceives everyone's true intention ("Therfore by colour ne by clergie knowe shaltow hym nevere, / Neither thorugh wordes ne werkes, but thorugh wil oone, / And that knoweth no clerk ne creature on erthe / But Piers the Plowman—*Petrus, id est Christus*" (lines 209–12). Yet he proceeds to show that historiography offers a critical discourse with which lords may judge and reform clerks. As such, the universal history offers what Anima calls a "long bible" (line 89), a collection of examples that sheds light on the behavior of the English clergy at the same that it narrates the history of the world.

From "*Petrus, id est christus*" until the end of the passus 15, Langland recounts a universal history that loosely traces the order and interests of the *Polychronicon*, re-creating the scope and texture of the original through the very process of interpreting it. The following is an outline of the last 400 lines of the passus:

1. English royal saints Edward and Edmund
2. Saint Francis
3. Desert fathers Anthony and Egidius
4. Saint Paul, the apostles, and Mary Magdalene
5. Muhammad and the origins of Islam
6. Monastic founders, saints Dominick, Francis, Benedict, and Bernard
7. Saint Augustine of Canterbury and the conversion of the English
8. The unconverted Saracens and Jews (or Greeks)
9. References to Nazareth, Nineveh, Neptalym, and Damascus
10. References to India, Alexandria, Armenia, and Spain
11. The martyrdom of Saint Thomas of Canterbury
12. The dissolution of the Order of the Knights Templar
13. Constantine's Donation
14. The unconverted Saracens and Jews

As this outline suggests, passus 15 consists primarily of ecclesiastical history and saints' lives, but, like the *Polychronicon*, it is resolutely directed toward English history: English martyr-kings, Augustine of Canterbury's conversion of Britain, and the murder of Thomas Becket,

England's most problematic saint.[53] Notably, the word "Engelond," which appears only four times in the B-text, is used twice in passus 15 alone. Langland's historiography also addresses English history through the peculiar conditions of its narration: it is told by a speaker addressing a lay audience invested in contemporary English affairs. In theory, the speaker is still Anima, but he poses alternately as fulminating preacher and clerical dependent catering to the tastes of a silent patron. Throughout *Piers Plowman*, Langland imagines an ignorant lay audience, entirely unaware of the poem, whose members could not translate Latin to save their lives (literally) and therefore could never put into practice the poem's cagey, often Latinate anticlericalism: if "lewed [ledes]" could only read Latin, says Anima earlier in the passus, they would see to it that clerics exchanged swords and jewelry for rosaries and prayerbooks (15.119–22). The dramatic absence of this audience suggests that the poem is an "in-house" clerical production, while still maintaining the fiction of a wider dissemination. But in passus 15 this absent audience is joined by a proximate group of Lord Berkeleys who pay laborers, maintain dependents, bequeath property, and invent policy. This new audience makes Langland's history English by reading it into the holdings and policies of the present. Just as the *Polychronicon* itself directs different histories toward the English present, and even to Higden's own Chester, so this audience realizes interpretatively what the *Polychronicon* realizes chronologically; it translates ecclesiastical history into contemporary ecclesiology.[54]

[53] The *South English Legendary*, which in many ways anticipates the *Polychronicon* and which was no doubt one of Langland's sources for passus 15, is also partial to English history and figures in recent critical discussions of English nationalism (see note 65 below). For example, it relates the life of Saint Wulfstan as an Arthurian figure pitted against William the Conqueror and his Norman ecclesiastics. It also makes a number of connections between early Christian history and English history, as, for example, the story about Saint Edward the Confessor and Saint John the Evangelist. Most conspicuously, it devotes more than 2,500 lines to the life of Saint Thomas of Canterbury. As mentioned below, however, a crucial difference between the *South English Legendary* and the *Polychronicon* is that the former does not demand literal imitation: it is not about the realization of the past in the present. Similarly, its sense of Englishness, while taking the form of patriotism, does not require immediate or urgent action.

[54] Anima addresses other groups as well. As Somerset observes about Anima, he "addresses himself beyond Will to a broadly inclusive audience", which includes friars, bishops, lettered folk, ignorant folk, lords and ladies, and rich people of all classes (*Clerical Discourse and Lay Audience*, p. 51). Somerset goes on to argue that Anima is more uncomfortable about spreading information about clerical misbehavior than he is about offering suggestions for pastoral care. His anxieties about translating Latin reflect this discomfort (pp. 52–53). What is so striking about this passus, though, is that it addresses a wealthy lay audience as if that audience has the capacity to implement change,

Throughout this passus, Langland follows the trajectory of the universal history and in doing so shows how it posits a lay theory of exemplarism that is fundamentally anticlerical. For one thing, as we saw with Trevisa, it is the universal history that makes historical writing the proper commentary of the aristocratic reader and the means by which clerical reform may be expressed in terms of lay profit. Toward the beginning of the "historical" section of passus 15, for example, Anima lists a number of early saints who subsisted on meager rations, such as Saint Anthony, fed by the birds in the desert, Saint Paul, who made baskets, Mary Magdalene, who lived on roots, and various other saints, who were nourished by the gentler members of the animal kingdom. Anima interprets these stories to mean that righteous laymen should provide for the deserving religious, but even more surprisingly, that laymen should not provide for professional religious at the expense of tenants or heirs. Anima urges the nobility to pay their tenants before funding friars (lines 309–12) and refrain from alienating their lands to possessioners, who probably do not need them anyway:

> If lewed men knewe þis latyn þei wolde loke whom þei yeue,
> And auisen hem bifore a fyue dayes or sixe
> Er þei amortisede to monkes or [monyales] hir rente[s].
> Allas, lordes and ladies, lewed counseil haue ye
> To ʒyue from youre heires þat youre Aiels yow lefte,
> And [bisette] to bidde for yow to swiche þat ben riche,
> And ben founded and feffed ek to bidde for oþere.
>
> (lines 319–25)

[If ignorant men could understand this Latin, they would look to whom they gave, and seek counsel for five or six days before they turned their rents over to monks or nuns. Allas, lords and ladies, you have been poorly counseled, you who deprive your heirs of their patrimonies, and who arrange for those to pray for you who are already rich enough and have been adequately endowed to pray for others!]

Where one would expect this gloss to promote clerical values such as poverty, faith, or almsgiving, instead it addresses lay lords and ladies, advising them to ensure the inalienability of their own lands. The his-

---

and as if the discourse of clerical reform explored in the passus might translate into a program sympathetic to lay interests.

tory of early asceticism, in this example, is not merely a reproof to the medieval clergy but also an exhortation to lay lordship at the expense of the professional religious. Earlier in the passus, Anima warns priests that unless they exemplify the morals they preach, their congregants (if they only knew Latin) would make them give up their swords and brooches (lines 119–22). Here he makes a similar point by subjecting moral exemplarity to a "sovereign hermeneutics," or the interpretation of a text according to the values of lay lordship: magnanimity and profit, generation and descent. Indeed, as will become clearer below, the threat of disendowment hinted in these lines and stated outright by the end of the passus has everything to do with radical historiography. By making historiography a discourse of clerical reform, Langland inherently appeals to the corrective hand of lay lords, for whom examples from the past bear directly upon the locations and possessions of the present.

Langland further transforms the universal history into a lay discourse of clerical reform in his peculiar reference to Muhammad.[55] According to medieval legend, Muhammad was born a Christian, but, because he could not be elected pope, he traveled to pagan Syria, where he won a number of adherents using the following trick. He acquired a dove and fed her night and day by placing grain in his ear. Whenever he preached to a crowd, the dove would alight on his shoulder looking for food, appearing to onlookers to be speaking in his ear. Muhammad swore that the dove had been sent from God in heaven, and he won over many people accordingly. Langland glosses this story in the following manner:

> And siþþe oure Saueour suffred þe Sarȝens so bigiled
> Thoruȝ a cristene clerk acorsed in his soule—
> [Ac] for drede of þe deeþ I dar noȝt telle truþe,
> How englisshe clerkes a coluere fede þat coueitise hiȝte
> And ben mannered after Makometh þat no man vseþ trouþe.

> (lines 412–16)

[55] Higden tells two versions of this story in the *Polychronicon*. According to the first version, there was once a monk named Sergius who was exiled because he had fallen into Nestorius's heresy. He traveled to Arabia and taught the orphan Muhammad, who spent the rest of his life learning the customs of Christians and Jews, witchcraft and necromancy. Muhammad forbade idolatry, adopted circumcision, and legalized polygamy. Most accounts of this story, such as the one in Matthew of Paris's *Chronica majora* (1259), focus on its sensational "ethnography." Trevisa insists that this ethnographic version is more authentic than the second "exemplum" version, reiterated in *Piers Plowman* and attributed by Higden to Steven of Canterbury and Gerald of Wales (*Polychronicon* 5.14.18–21).

[And in this way our Savior allowed the Saracens to be beguiled by a Christian clerk cursed in his soul. But for fear of death I dare not tell the truth, how English clerks feed a dove called Covetousness, and take after Muhammad, with the result that no one acts justly]

This story teaches us, Anima nervously concludes, that English clerks, rather than being inspired by the Holy Spirit, are inspired by the spirit of covetousness, figured by Muhammad's well-trained "colvere."

This gloss first appears to be an example of traditional clerical exegesis: it extracts from the literal narrative a moral value or doctrinal truth that should be exemplified in the lives of the present-day clergy. In fact, however, it ushers in a more radical phase of Langland's historiography. In this phase, he does not just deduce from illustrations how the clergy should act and the laity react; he also measures clerical behavior by the standards of historical exemplarity. Indeed, as passus 15 suggests, if historical writing is the stuff of medieval preaching, its exemplary mode is both antihomiletic and, when pushed to its logical conclusions, anticlerical. To ask ecclesiastics to conform to historical exemplarity is to suggest that they are entitled to privilege or distinction, not because they preach, or because they practice what they preach, but because their actions are prefigured by the apostolic "doynges and dedes" of the past. In this way, a universal history such as the *Polychronicon*, which charts a history from Creation to Christ to the most recent English king, offers the clergy something like a cultural genealogy of conversion, miracle, and martyrdom. Anima explains that Christ both made his life a compendium of examples (he performed them in deed) and offered parables and maxims ("*verbi gracia*," for example) to teach others how to do the same.[56] But whereas this latter form of exemplarity depends upon exegesis, historical exemplarity depends upon precedent. It depends, that is, on whether or not contemporary people embody history through lineage or by imitating literally the great deeds recorded in chronicles.

Technically, ecclesiastical distinction depends not on exemplarity but on ordination, which is based on a *metaphor* of lineage. As Anima tells

[56] God suffered for us, says Anima, "In ensample we sholde do so, and take no vengeaunce . . . he suffrede in ensample þat we sholde suffren also,/And seide to swiche þat suffre wolde,/ '*Pacientes Vincunt verbi gracia*,': and [verred] ensaumples manye" (lines 260, 266–68) [(God suffered) as an example that we should do the same and take no vengeance . . . he suffered as an example that we should also suffer, and he said to those who would suffer, "Patience will overcome," i.e., for example, and many true (or possibly "offered many") examples].

the dreamer, *"Petrus, id est, christus"*: Christ awarded to Saint Peter and his "descendents" the authority to bind and loose, and hence all bishops are justified through an unbroken "succession" from the prince of the apostles. Like all legal precedent, however, ordination is based neither on real succession nor on a cultural genealogy of deeds, but on a symbolic representation of lay descent. In this way, historical exemplarity exposes the metaphoricity of ordination, while at the same time implying that ecclesiastical distinction depends on the literal embodiment of history, the realization of metaphorical lineage through apostolic imitation.

It is in this respect that the Muhammad gloss effects a transition from a clerical to a lay interpretative system: the gloss suggests that clerks, and English clerks in particular, fail to fulfill the cultural genealogy expressed by the universal history. Their figurative resemblance to Muhammad is both a moral condemnation of greed and a historical reproach: Saracens still exist in the world because English clerks no longer follow the apostles literally by converting the infidel. Sure enough, the Muhammad gloss is followed by successive glosses on the gloss. As the passus progresses, Anima repeatedly urges bishops to become evangelists and convert the Saracens and Jews: "And so may Sarȝens be saued, Scribes and [Grekes or Iewes] / Allas, þanne, but oure looresmen lyue as þei leren vs, / And for hir lyuynge þat lewed men be þe loþer god agulten. / For Sarȝens han somwhat semynge to oure bileue" (lines 390–93) [And so may Saracens be saved, Scribes and (Greeks or Jews). Allas! It is a shame that our teachers do not practice what they preach, and on account of their good living make ignorant men reluctant to go against God. After all, the Saracens already possess something similar to our belief]; "Allas þat men so longe [sholde bileue on Makometh]! / So manye prelates to preche as þe Pope makeþ" (lines 492–93) [It is a shame that people have believed in Muhammad for so long when the pope has ordained so many bishops]; "And siþen þat þe Sarȝens and also þe Iews / Konne þe firste clause of our bileue. . . . Prelates of cristene prouinces sholde preue if þei myȝte / Lere hem litlum and litlum" (lines 607–10) [And since the Saracens and Jews already know the first clause of the Apostles Creed (that is, "I believe in God the Father") . . . prelates of Christian provinces should try to teach them little by little].[57]

---

[57] Simpson points out that in passus 15 the historical limits of Christianity (the Jews) underline the contemporary limits of Christianity (converting the Jews and Muslims). *Piers Plowman*, p. 178.

Further, Langland extracts from the universal history not simply a critical method with which to evaluate the clergy, but also a definition of Englishness that is at once fundamentally anticlerical and exclusively lay. This definition of Englishness, hinted at in the Muhammad gloss ("englisshe clerkes"), has to do with the relation of social estate to geographical place, and it emerges precisely when historiography becomes a discourse of clerical reform. For one thing, while ostensibly presenting models of behavior for the medieval clergy, Langland's historiography banishes clerical exemplarity to the dark recesses of the Christian—and English—past. The passus as a whole is informed by a sense of ecclesiastical history at once chronologically removed and deliberately anachronistic, suggesting that history offers both a necessary measure of, and *impossible conditions* for, the present clergy. For example, in answer to the dreamer's question, "where is charity?" (the question that launches the "historical" section of the passus) Anima immediately refers him to two early English royal saints, Edmund the martyr (d. 869) and Edward the Confessor (d. 1066): "Edmond and Edward, [eiþer] were kynges / And seintes yset; [stille] charite hem folwede" (lines 223–24).[58] He then continues with the example of Saint Francis, whom he contrasts favorably to fourteenth-century friars: "And in a freres frokke [Charity] was yfounden ones, / Ac it is *fern [and fele yeer* in] Fraunceis tyme; / In þat secte *sippe to selde* haþ he ben [knowe]" (lines 230–32, emphasis mine). Medieval writers tend to have a remarkably expansive sense of the past, and in the whole scheme of things, "Ac it is fern [and fele yeer in]," is an odd line, considering that Francis's death in 1226 occurred only a century before Langland was born and Higden began to write the *Polychronicon*. At the very least, Edmund and Edward belong to a different past than Saint Francis. The clearest sense of the line is that fourteenth-century friars are morally distanced from their illustrious forbears. But by invoking royal English saints, this line also suggests that the lost virtue of the fraternal orders is a historiographical problem, and not merely a failure to adhere to the Rule. It points to a critical distance from the English past, a past framed by saintly English kings.

More telling, perhaps, Langland repeatedly holds up early missionaries as examples for the contemporary English clergy. Good preachers and popes, like "goddes salt" (line 442), should preserve the souls of

men, but in the world of the universal history pastoral care means proselytizing to the unconverted, just as Augustine of Canterbury converted
the heathen English and Welsh back in the sixth century:

> Al was hethynesse som tyme Engelond and Walis
> Til Gregory garte clerkes to go here and preche.
> Austyn [þe kyng cristnede at Caunterbury],
> And þoruӡ miracles, as men mow rede, al þat marche he tornede
> To crist and to cristendom, and cros to honoure,
> And follede folk faste, and þe feiþ tauӡte
> Moore þoruӡ miracles þan þoruӡ muche prechynge;
> As wel þoruӡ hise werkes as wiþ hise holy wordes
> [Enfourmed] hem what fullynge and feiþ was to mene.
>
> (lines 443–51)

[England and Wales at one time were totally heathen, until Pope Gregory sent
clerics here to preach. Augustine converted the king at Canterbury, and
through miracles, as men may read, he converted that whole region to Christ
and to Christendom, and to the worship of the cross. And he baptized people
firmly, and he taught the faith, more through miracles than through a lot of
preaching, and as well through works as through holy words. He instructed
them as to the meaning of baptism and faith.]

The example of Augustine of Canterbury suggests that clerical exemplarity belongs to the ecclesiastical origins of English historiography, the
period in which the English were heathens, kings converted, and preaching was a brave deed in itself. Augustine, says Langland, taught "moore
þoruӡ miracles þan þoruӡ muche prechynge" (line 449), and ideally, all
clerks should perform their duties, not by explaining parables, but by
converting the heathen. From a historiographical perspective, good examples are not principally parables but banners, or emblems, or heroes
who take to the highway. Unhappy is the soul, says Anima, "þat seeþ
no goo[d] ensampl[e] / Of hem of holi chirche þat þe heighe wey sholde
teche / And be gide and go bifore as a good Banyer, / And hardie hem
þat bihynde ben, and ӡyve hem good euidence" (lines 434–37) [that
sees no good example from those representatives of Holy Church, who
should teach the high way and be guides and go in front like a good
banner, and strengthen those who are behind and responsibly bear wit-

ness].[59] It is true that English historiography begins with the enterprising acts of clerks, such as the Venerable Bede. From the Anglo-Saxon epic to the *South English Legendary*, moreover, the romanticizing of conversion ("the gospel was his shield," "he carried the cross as his banner") was a way of making Christian "heroics" meaningful to lay readers accustomed to secular romance.[60] But in Langland's historiography, which directs ecclesiastical history insistently toward the English present, Christian heroics—proselytizing and crusading—are the literal measure of clerical exemplarity.[61] Significantly, if Langland's universal history sometimes resembles a *legenda sanctorum* (cf. 15.269: "in *legenda sanctorum*, þe lif of holy seintes," etc.), a staple of homiletic discourse, it differs significantly in the mode of exemplarity that it proposes. Collections of saints' lives, however much directed toward English interests, do not demand literal imitation from their readers and listeners; instead they attest to the continual manifestation of divine grace, and they call upon their audiences to recognize the power of faith exhibited by exceptional people at various times and in different places. By contrast, the universal

[59] For example, see the *South English Legendary*'s account of Augustine's mission to the English, in which the English king invites Augustine to deliver his message, and Augustine and his followers prepare themselves as if for battle. Charlotte D'Evelyn and Anna J. Mills, eds., *The South English Legendary*, 2 vols. (Oxford: Oxford University Press, 1956–59), p. 215, lines 39–46.

[60] For example, the *Banna Sanctorum*, the prologue to the *South English Legendary*, portrays Christian history as a martial procession: the "trompours" and "al blasters" are the prophets and patriarchs, Saint John the Baptist was Christ's "baneour and is baner bar byvore" (line 49), and the apostles and martyrs, the subject of the *South English Legendary*, are the rearguard. This version of Christian history is explicitly opposed to secular romances ("þat muchedel is lesynge"), not because such romances glorify arms over Christ, but more spectacularly because their warrior kings and hardy knights are not on par with the apostles and martyrs "þat hardy kniZtes were" (*South English Legendary*, lines 59–63). In this view, hagiography is the true history of Christian prowess, and as such is as much pro-Crusade as it is antiromance. See Catherine Sanok, "The Geography of Genre in the *Physician's Tale* and *Pearl*," *New Medieval Literatures* 5 (2002): 177–201.

[61] As Thorlac Turville-Petre points out, the thirteenth century produced a number of texts that bridge the gap between clergy and laity by appealing to a sense of national pride. See *England the Nation: Langland, Literature, and National Identity, 1290–1340* (Oxford: Clarendon Press, 1996), p. 27. The *South English Legendary* was clearly one of these texts, as was the *Cursor mundi*, a long narrative of scriptural history with a "supranational scope," which expresses pride in England the nation but does not give any account of England from an ecclesiological or political perspective (*England the Nation*, p. 41). Diane Speed attributes the "true beginning of national literature to the rise of the romance" in the thirteenth century, and especially to the *South English Legendary*. See "The Construction of the Nation in Medieval English Romance," in Carol Meale, ed., *Readings in Medieval English Literature* (Woodbridge, Suffolk: D. S. Brewer, 1991), pp. 135–57, at 157.

history, in Langland's reading of it, directs the lives of saints typologically toward the English present, demanding both literal imitation and continual generation.

As the examples of Augustine and Muhammad suggest, however, insular evangelism is strictly a phenomenon of the past: for an English cleric to write himself into the universal history is to convert the heathen abroad. Thus Langland centers his critique on the "hard case" of metropolitan bishops, because these bishops represent the possibility of imitating the apostles literally, that is, through proselytizing feats in the Holy Land. Although at the beginning of passus 15, Langland is concerned with the quality of local preaching and the benefits of clerical poverty, by the end of the passus he is nearly entirely focused on the negligence of metropolitans. Certain clerics, complains Anima, have been ordained to sees abroad, but they choose to stay home in England. He points out that the pope has ordained many prelates in the Middle East "of Naʒareth, of Nynyue, of Neptalym and Damaske" (line 494),[62] but few of these prelates, though they desire the name of pastor, are willing to do more than preach the verse, "the good shepherd gives his life for his sheep" (John 10:1; *Piers Plowman* 15. 496a). In these lines, Anima is referring in a general way to those areas of the world that no longer welcome Christians, but in a specific and stranger way to titular sees whose occupants are in no way expected to take up residency. In this sense, the failure of all clergy to perform their duties at home can be understood in terms of the meaningless titles of metropolitan bishops. He exclaims, "What pope or prelat now parfourneþ þat crist highte, / *Ite in vniuersum mundum & predicate, &c. . . .* ?" (lines 491–491a) [What pope or prelate performs now what Christ commanded: "Go into the whole world and preach, etc."]. Whereas bishops ought to emulate the saints who preached and died in foreign countries, "in ynde, in alisaundre, in ermonye and spayne, / In dolful deþ deyeden for hir faith" (lines 521–22), they are content to remain bishops in name only. Christ wrought miracles "in ensaumple" of Christian belief, namely, he "bicam man of a maide and *metropolitanus*" (line 516); he assumed humanity in a community of non-Christians. He did so to illustrate the lesson that metropolitan bishops of "Bethleem and Babiloigne" (line 510) should

---

[62] "Neptalym" probably refers to "Naphtali," a region in the Galilee, rather than to any metropolitan see. Its purpose in the passage is probably simply to complete the alliterative meter with an exotic-sounding name. Langland likely knew the name either from medieval cosmographies or from the Book of Tobias.

expend their energies converting the Saracens in the cities to which they are assigned.[63]

Of course, by the 1370s the conversion of the infidel and the recovery of the Latin Kingdom of Jerusalem were projects largely confined to the dustbins of history, even if they endured for some time at the borders of Europe (the Baltic regions and Spain, as opposed to Syria-Palestine), in fantasies about Jewish conversion, in *Mandeville's Travels* (c. 1371), and in the pages of Middle English romance.[64] By insisting that clerical ex-emplarity is exemplified by metropolitan bishops, that it belongs to an outdated, impracticable, or exceptional ecclesiology, or to the military dreams of the fourteenth-century gentry, Langland implies that the clergy acquire Englishness only in that textual moment in which ecclesi-astical history becomes English history and in that liminal period when preaching had dire consequences. In this sense, the English clerks con-demned in the Muhammad gloss are a contradiction in terms: medieval clerks are justified as clerks and as English only at boundaries of English historiography and English identity, when England was the *terra incog-nita*, and the clergy were all apostles among the heathen. For the re-formed clerk, the English present is a perpetually elusive imperative. But Langland further implies that to be an exemplary English clerk

[63] Here Anima evokes the dreamer's "naming" joke about ecclesiastical titles at the beginning of the passus. In that earlier passage, the dreamer meets Anima, who intro-duces himself as a list of Latin names: *ratio, memoria, conscientia,* i.e., the cognitive aspects of the soul (lines 23–39). The dreamer jokingly responds that Anima must be a bishop because bishops also assume "names an heep" (line 43) as it profits them in different situations: *presul, pontifex, metropolitanus, episcopus, pastor* (lines 40–43). The thrust of this joke, presumably, is that it is as difficult to recognize an honest bishop as it is to name one's own soul, so variable and expedient are today's ecclesiastical titles (*Piers Plowman,* p. 183).

[64] On the crusading fantasies of Middle English alliterative romances, see Christine Chism, *Alliterative Revivals* (Philadelphia: University of Pennsylvania Press, 2002), pp. 125–30, 151–54. Iain Higgins argues about *Mandeville's Travels,* a work that purports to be the memoir of an English Knight, that it appealed emotionally "to those for whom the crusades was not yet a dim memory" (*Writing East: The "Travels" of Sir John Mandeville* [Philadelphia: University of Pennsylvania Press, 1997], pp. 7–8, 30–31), and more specifically, it entertains the continued possibility of Saracen conversion. As Higgins explains about Mandeville's dialogue with a Sultan, because the Koran contains the principle articles of Christianity, "overseas missionary work" remains a useful com-plement to crusading, pp. 114–15. See also Gransden's discussion of Trevisa's mappa-mundi and its peculiar illustration of the spread of Christendom (*Historical Writing in England,* p. 55). For a study of alliterative romance and cultural fantasy, see chap. 5, "Warring Against Modernity," in Geraldine Heng, *Empire of Magic: Medieval Romance and the Politics of Cultural Fantasy* (New York: Columbia University Press, 2003), pp. 116–79.

today is not to be in England at all: it is to forfeit preaching for proselytizing, and local benefices for campaigns abroad. The gloss on Muhammad proposes missionary activity as an antidote to clerical greed, but it also opposes it to the localness of possession, or that which pertains materially and geographically to Englishness. To put this idea a different way, Langland's historiography reframes the conventional issue of clerical greed as the more contentious issue of clerical possession by equating time and place, historical difference and physical dislocation. From the perspective of history, the English clergy justify themselves as clergy and as English by claiming an identity and purpose outside England itself.[65]

Disendowing Saint Thomas

Although Langland is surely more interested in clerical reform than he is in defining Englishness, by making the universal history speak to clerical reform, he eventually arrives at a notion of English identity intrinsically tied to clerical disendowment. He has intimated earlier in the passus that clerical reform is bound up in questions of lay profit. But the link between historical exemplarity and clerical disendowment is forged in the peculiar allusion to Saint Thomas of Canterbury near the end of the passus, an allusion followed by pleas to the clergy to convert the infidel, and to the laity to strip corrupt clergy of their possessions.

> Many a seint syþen haþ suffred to deye
> Al for to enforme þe faith; in fele countrees deyeden,
> In ynde, in alisaundre, in ermonye and spayne,
> In dolful deþ deyeden for hir faith.

[65] On the relationship between border writing, national identities, and Arthurian historiography, see Michelle Warren, *History on the Edge: Excalibur and the Borders of Britain, 1100–1300* (Minneapolis: University of Minnesota Press, 2000). On frontier writing and national identity, see Kathy Lavezzo, "Beyond Rome: Mapping Gender and Justice in *The Man of Law's Tale*," *SAC* 24 (2002): 149–80. Examples of recent medievalist work on national identity in the Middle Ages include Simon Forde, Lesley Johnson, and Alan Murray, eds., *Concepts of National Identity in the Middle Ages*, Leeds Texts and Monographs, n.s. 14 (Leeds: University of Leeds Printing Services, 1995); and Kathleen Davis, "National Writing in the Ninth Century: A Reminder for Postcolonial Thinking about the Nation," *JMEMSt* 28.3 (1998): 611–37. See also Susan Reynolds's discussion of the nation in *Kingdom and Communities in Western Europe, 900–1300*, 2nd ed. (Oxford: Clarendon Press, 1997), and Patricia Ingham's response in *Sovereign Fantasies: Arthurian Romance and the Making of Britain* (Philadelphia: University of Pennsylvania Press, 2001).

In sauacion of [mannes soule] seint [Thomas] was ymartired;
Amonges vnkynde cristene for cristes loue he deyede,
And for þe riȝt of al this reume and alle reumes cristene.
Holy chirche is honoured heiȝliche þoruȝ his deying;
He is a forbisene to alle bisshopes and a briȝt myrour,
And souereynliche to swiche þat of surrye bereþ þe name],
[And nauȝt to] huppe aboute in Engelond to halwe mannes Auteres
And crepe [in] amonges curatours, confessen ageyn þe lawe.

(lines 519–30)

[And many saints have endured death since. They all died to teach the faith in many countries: in India, Alexandria, Armenia, and Spain. In sorrowful death they died for their faith. For the salvation of men's souls Saint Thomas was martyred; among unnatural Christians he died for Christ's love and for the right of this whole realm and for all Christian realms. Holy Church is highly honored through his death. He is an example and bright mirror to all bishops, especially to those bishops who bear the name of Syria, and he is an example to them not to hop around England sanctifying men's altars or to creep in among parish priests and hear confession illegally.]

This is a mystifying passage for all sorts of reasons. Most obviously, the twelfth-century archbishop Thomas Becket died in his own cathedral at the hands of the king's henchmen, not in Outremer preaching to the Saracens (as Langland seems to suggest when he places Thomas in the company of preaching martyrs and calls him an example to Syrian bishops). He died, moreover, defending papal sovereignty in England. And paradoxically, of course, it is Becket, that consummate English saint, whose shrine would become the target of reformist antipilgrimage sentiment, and whose campaign to defend ecclesiastical privilege would become the epitome of clerical abuse.[66] How has it happened, then, that in B.15, a passus that defines clerical exemplarity as proselytizing abroad, Saint Thomas exemplifies the ideal English clerk? The simple irony is that a prospective martyr need not embrace a suffering ministry: he can be martyred perfectly well at home. But the larger irony sug-

[66] Medieval chroniclers never uniformly supported Becket's policies, even if they regarded him unequivocally as a saint. In his English *Chronicle* (c. 1300), for example, Robert Mannyng of Brunne sympathizes with Henry II, explaining that Thomas wanted to ensure that if any man complained against a cleric, the cleric would be judged by an ecclesiastical rather than a lay court. Mannyng believes that Henry was justly upset by Thomas's policies, because today's clerks are so quick to abuse their privileges. *The Chronicle*, p. 570, Part II, lines 3210, 3220–21.

gested by this passage and borne out by the passus as a whole is that proper execution of clerical duties at home can be described only in terms of proselytizing abroad. So how then does Thomas come to represent the missionary ideal with which English clerks may justify, however hypothetically, their very existence?

Ranulph Higden tells us surprisingly little about Thomas's martyrdom in the *Polychronicon*, but he spends quite a bit of time recounting the life of Henry II. He describes Henry's charismatic leadership, the many warnings the king ignored about his future, and his eventual moral and political downfall. Much of this account has to do with the delicate balance between leadership at home and abroad, which Henry failed to strike. It was this struggle for balance, moreover, that linked the fates of England and Jerusalem. At his coronation, Higden tells us, Henry swore to defend Holy Church and exile the Jews from England, neither of which he did. Another time, he swore to liberate the Holy Land, but he put off taking the cross, swearing instead that he would found abbeys in England. Later, Higden revisits Henry's crusading dilemma in the story he tells about the visit from the Patriarch of Jerusalem, Heraclius. The Patriarch comes to England to ask Henry to lead the crusades. Henry responds that he does not want to leave his land without a guardian, but he would be happy to fund any men who wanted to go. The Patriarch insists that the crusaders need a prince, and he warns the king that he will rule badly in the future, should he refuse this request. Just think, says the Patriarch to Henry, "how þou were false to þe kyng of Fraunce and slouȝ seynt Thomas, and now þou forsakest the defens and protectioun of Cristene men." When the king becomes angry, the Patriarch meekly offers him his own head, saying, "Do by me ryȝt as þou dedest by Thomas, for me is as leef by y-slawe of þe in Engelond as of Sarsyns in Siria, for þou art wors þan eny Sarsyn" [Do to me what you did to Thomas, because I would just as well be slain by you in England as by Saracens in Syria, because you are worse than any Saracen].[67]

What is immediately arresting about this account is that it figures the tension between the king who guards his kingdom and the king who leads the crusades as the tension between royal and papal sovereignty.

---

[67] The king protests that his own sons would rise up against him should he leave England. After his ill-fated meeting with the Patriarch, the king sends Prince John to Ireland with little success, and the Saracens take Jerusalem and bear away the holy cross. This story can be found in the *Polychronicon* 7.24.69–75.

Remarkably, too, in this account Saint Thomas becomes the figure through which the institutional English church is allied with crusading interests abroad: Henry, by refusing to lead the crusades, is "wors than eny Sarsyn," as evidenced by the murder of Saint Thomas, as well as by the Patriarch's invitation to Henry to behead him. Whatever the logic of Henry's defense, Thomas becomes an English saint through Henry's reluctance to support the crusades. Rather than losing his life in a fight against English royal interests, interests portrayed here as the preservation of lands and throne, Thomas becomes an English saint by embodying the interests of international Christendom, by dying at the hands of a royal "Sarsyn."

If the Patriarch's crusading rhetoric metaphorically turns Henry into a Saracen and Thomas into an English saint, later medieval writers tried to literalize the metaphor by awarding Thomas a Saracen lineage and a spiritual connection to the Holy Land. Both Thomas Brinton in his *Sermons* (c. 1373–89) and the author of the *South English Legendary* tell the story of Thomas's father, Gilbert, who languished in chains in Jerusalem, won the heart of a Saracen princess (Thomas's mother), converted her to Christianity, and married her back in England.[68] John Mirk tells a similar story for the feast of Saint Thomas, in which Gilbert, a London sheriff, travels to the Holy Land, rescues a woman in distress (Thomas's mother), and later marries her in Saint Paul's Cathedral. Later Mirk reports that the day Thomas was martyred, a monk in Jerusalem also lay at the point of death. After his death he appeared to his abbot, telling him that on the day he died he went to heaven where he saw a bishop (Saint Thomas) arrive with a huge company of angels and saints, his head dripping blood. God set a crown of burning gold on the bishop's head, saying, "as much joy as I have given Saint Peter, I give to you." Mirk reports that this story was originally told by the Patriarch of Jerusalem, while he was recruiting crusaders in England.[69] These ac-

[68] Turville-Petre points out that the *South English Legendary* also turns Thomas into an English saint by making him the "people's champion" against the king (*England the Nation*, pp. 64–65). As Lawrence Warner has discovered, Langland alludes to Brinton's gloss on this story in B.15: like Langland, Brinton exhorts the clergy, whom he calls the salt of the earth, to convert the Jews, just as the apostles converted the infidels. Lawrence Warner, "Becket and the Hopping Bishops" *YLS* 17 (2003): 107–34. Warner argues that Langland can sincerely praise Becket, even within a discussion of disendowment, because of Becket's "sermonic, legendary, and liturgical associations, often wholly unconnected with the historical circumstances of the murder in the cathedral."

[69] Mirk, *Festial*, p. 38, lines 11–33.

counts helped make Thomas an English saint by linking him both spiritually and genealogically to the Holy Land.

Langland draws upon this apologetic hagiography in his allusion to Saint Thomas, but he does so by reading twelfth-century history into fourteenth-century historiography, a move implicitly advertised by the *Polychronicon* itself. Langland perversely literalizes Thomas's link to the crusades—here, Thomas is practically a crusading bishop himself—suggesting that the ideal English clerk severs his connections to England in favor of a missionary career abroad. He suggests, moreover, that if the story of Saint Thomas might be used to argue for royal or papal privilege, it can now be read through the universal history as a distinction between clerical and lay sovereignty. Like the Patriarch of Jerusalem, Langland associates Thomas with "crusading" martyrs—"Many a seynt syþen haþ suffred to deye / Al for to enforme þe faith in fele countrees deyeden" (lines 519–20)—even though he knows perfectly well that Thomas was killed by Christians in England. Like the Patriarch, too, he plays with the relationship between unnatural and alien behavior: just as the Patriarch calls Henry "wors than eny Sarsyn," so Langland uses the word "unkynde" (unnatural, foreign) to connect Thomas's death to the crusades. "In sauacion of [mannes soule] seint [Thomas] was ymartired; / Amonges vnkynde cristene for cristes loue he deyede, / And for þe riȝt of al this reume and alle reumes cristene" (lines 523–25). He was killed by those Christians who were unnatural in their murderous rage, but who are also foreign "Saracen-types." But whereas Higden constructs English sainthood within the complex of papal-royal relations, Langland makes Saint Thomas a literal mirror, an example or "forbisne," for English clerks, as imagined through metropolitan bishops. Langland complains earlier in the passus that clergy are not fulfilling their pastoral duties: they are ignorant, abstruse, or corrupt. They "ouerhuppen" (skip over passages), for example, in "office and in houres" (line 386). Throughout the passus, however, he increasingly ties clerical negligence, not to pastoral incompetence but to the failure to fulfill the historical imperative, to imitate the "doynges and dedes" of the ecclesiastical past, of which Thomas becomes an unlikely, even cautionary, example. From Thomas's supposed example, bishops should learn that they should neither "huppe aboute in Engelond" to sanctify men's altars, nor should they "crepe [in] amonges curatours, confessen ageyn þe lawe" (lines 529–30). From the perspective of history, the problem is not so much that clergy neglect their duties ("overhuppen"), but that they are solicitous of profit, as evidenced by their insistence on remaining local, on hopping about England, from one lucrative benefice to another, rather than leaving England to convert the heathen. To send Saint Thomas packing, however, and to force him to be a historical exemplar for today's clergy, is to redirect English clerks to an alliterative fantasyland of missionary outposts, "of Naȝareth, of Nynyve, of Neptalym and Damaske."

It is finally, then, through the universal history that the passus moves from lay endowment ("Allas, lordes and ladies, lewed counseil haue ye / To ȝyue from youre heires þat youre Aiels yow lefte" [lines 322–23]) to clerical disendowment ("Takeþ hire landes, ye lordes, and leteþ hem lyue by dymes" [line 564]). Directly after his allusion to Thomas Becket, Langland turns to the example of the Knights Templar, warning English clerks that they might soon suffer the same fate on account of their greed: "For coueitise of þat [gold] cros [clerkes] of holy kirke / Shul [ouer]torne as templers dide; þe tyme approcheþ faste" (lines 546–47).[70] He then threatens bishops that they will lose their "lordshipe of londes" entirely should the two lay estates—"knyghthod and kynde wit and þe commune [and] conscience"—band together and love each other loyally (lines 553–55). In the end, lords should remedy the effects of the Donation of Constantine by disendowing corrupt clergy of their lands: "Takeþ hire landes, ye lordes, and leteþ hem lyue be dymes. / If possession be poison and inparfite hem make / Charite were to deschargen hem for holy chirches sake, / And purgen hem of poison er more peril falle" (lines 564–67).

The story of Thomas Becket helps us to see that disendowment, Langland's final statement, is simultaneously a polemical position and the formal extension of the universal history. If converting the infidel is the way that English clergy become exemplary religious and exemplary English, disendowment, divorcing the clergy from profit, or from the material locations of England, is the flip side to proselytizing. By forcing the clergy to fulfill the historical imperative, and by compelling them to be latter-day apostles, disendowment restores the clergy to Englishness at the same time that it institutes clerical reform. In fact, within the genre of historical writing, exemplified by Higden's *Polychronicon*, it is the duty of lordship to make clerks embody the past, even if that means imaginatively expelling them from England or actually divesting

[70] For Higden's account of the fall of Templars, see the *Polychronicon*, 7.16.464–66.

them from possession. It is unlikely that Langland wanted corrupt clergy to be stripped of land or benefice; rather, he was looking for new approaches to clerical reform. But in Langland's radical historiography, the universal history, when pushed to its logical conclusions, leads inevitably to clerical disendowment. It reveals the failure of the contemporary clergy to participate in the cultural genealogy of doings and deeds, and to translate past histories into present. At the same time, it shows that for clerks to subscribe to historical exemplarity, to define themselves as English clerics according to the terms of the universal history, is to eschew Englishness entirely, or at least that definition of Englishness that pertains to the lay aristocracy—the material locations of the present. Disendowment, in short, is the outcome of a hermeneutics that the universal history enjoins.

In conclusion, Trevisa's and Langland's encounters with historiography suggest ways of thinking about literary dissent, not just as a set of propositions, which transcends the bounds of academe, or as a literary style interchangeable with polemic, but as a widespread generic experiment. When we ask how Langland could possibly write the lines, "Takeþ hire landes, ye lordes, and leteþ hem lyue by dymes" (B.15.564), we are suggesting that the history of literary politics is primarily a history of ideas, ideas that were, in their respective contexts, mainstream, conservative, or revolutionary. From a different perspective, however, the same question might reveal a parallel history, a history that has to do with the literary invention of political discourse.

Jacob's Well and Penitential Pedagogy

Moira Fitzgibbons
Marist College

Freres and fele oþere maistres þat to þe lewed folk prechen,
Ye moeuen materes vnmesurable to tellen of þe Trinite
That lome þe lewed peple of hir bileue doute.
Bettre it were by manye doctours to bileuen swich techyng
And tellen men of þe ten comaundementȝ, and touchen þe seuene synnes,
And of þe braunches þat burione of hem and bryngen men to helle,
And how þat folk in folies hir fyue wittes mysspenden . . .
                        —*Piers Plowman* XV:73–76[1]

*J*ACOB'S WELL, a sermon cycle composed in the late fourteenth or early fifteenth century, in many ways fulfills Anima's vision of a positive educational plan for the laity. Using the metaphor of the human soul as a foul, stinking well badly in need of cleansing and repair, the unnamed *Well* writer—who was almost certainly a parish cleric writing for an audience primarily composed of lay men and women—places basic Christian precepts like the Seven Deadly Sins and the Ten Commandments at the center of his text.[2]

---

[1] *Piers Plowman, The B-Version*, ed. George Kane and E. Talbot Donaldson (London: Athlone Press, 1975), p. 538.

[2] *Jacob's Well* survives in one manuscript, MS Salisbury Cathedral 103. In print, the work is available in two parts. The first fifty sermons are edited within *Jacob's Well: An English Treatise on the Cleansing of Man's Conscience*, ed. Arthur Brandeis, EETS 115 (London: Kegan Paul, Trench, Trübner & Co., 1900). The last forty-five sermons have been edited by Clinton Atchley in "The 'Wose' of *Jacob's Well:* Text and Context" Ph.D. diss., University of Washington, 1998). I have silently regularized Brandeis's and Atchley's use of italics and brackets, respectively, to indicate omitted or abbreviated letters in the manuscript. My citations use "i" and "ii" to distinguish between these two editions. Citations are by page number.
  For the dating and authorship of *Jacob's Well*, see Brandeis, *Jacob's Well*, pp. x–xiii; Robert Raymo, "*Jacob's Well*," in *A Manual of Writings in Middle English, 1050–1500*, ed. Albert E. Hartung (New Haven: Connecticut Academy of Arts and Sciences, 1972), p. 2262; and Leo Carruthers, "Where Did *Jacob's Well* Come From? The Provenance and Dialect of MS Salisbury Cathedral 103," *ES* 71 (1990): 335–40. These studies date the original composition of *Jacob's Well* to the first two decades of the fifteenth century.
  The uncertainty surrounding the text's exact dating makes it impossible to state conclusively whether the *Well* writer is writing before or after Archbishop Thomas Arundel's Constitutions of 1407–9, which set strict limits on the content and scope of vernac-

While this decision allows the *Well* writer to avoid the abstruse speculative theology criticized by Anima in the epigraph above, it does not
provide him with a straightforward answer to vexing questions concerning the kinds of knowledge that should be taught to lay Christians. As
this essay will demonstrate, teaching the fundamentals of the faith is
anything but simple for the *Well* writer. The "fals techyng" of the Lollards represents one danger to his flock, but other challenges loom just
as large: he wrestles with the recalcitrance of his own congregation, the
guidelines imposed upon preachers by ecclesiastical authorities, and the
self-interested activities of the fraternal orders, whose authority he both
mocks and cites.

In many portions of his text, the *Well* writer addresses these problems
by adopting a rigidly hierarchical pedagogical stance toward his listeners. Particularly in the early parts of *Jacob's Well*, he urges his listeners
to focus exclusively on repairing their own sinful souls and to value
childlike compliance above all other virtues. As the work progresses,
however, this mode of instruction begins to break down. New metaphors involving childhood and learning emerge, and the separation between individual examinations of conscience and wider forms of
intellectual inquiry proves impossible for the *Well* writer to maintain. In
the text's final exemplum, he not only urges his audience to embark on
a search for truth but also makes clear that their efforts must include
questioning ecclesiastical institutions as well as themselves.

For the *Well* writer, then, working closely with traditional elements

---

ular writing and preaching. (For the text of Arundel's Constitutions, see *Concilia Magnae
Britanniae et Hiberniae*, ed. David Wilkins, 4 vols. [London, 1737], 3.314–19.) In his
seminal essay, "Censorship and Cultural Change in Late-Medieval England: Vernacular
Theology, the Oxford Translation Debate, and Arundel's Constitutions of 1409" (*Speculum* 70 [1995]: 822–64), Nicholas Watson implicitly associates *Jacob's Well* with the
post-Arundel era when he briefly asserts that the work adheres to the guidelines set by
Archbishop Pecham in *Ignorantia Sacerdotum*, the thirteenth-century legislation
praised by Arundel in his Constitutions. (For the text of Pecham's decrees, see Wilkins,
2.51–61). The work's presence in a single manuscript, as well as its ambivalence regarding lay learning, supports the idea that it was produced in a more constrained climate
than texts of the late fourteenth century. As the following argument should make clear,
however, its content cannot be said to function as a straightforward extension of Arundel's assumptions and goals.

Detailed analyses of Arundel's legislation and its effects can be found in Anne Hud-
son's *The Premature Reformation: Wycliffite Texts and Lollard History* (Oxford: Clarendon
Press, 1988), pp. 390–445, and in H. Leith Spencer's *English Preaching in the Late Middle
Ages* (Oxford: Clarendon Press, 1993), pp. 163–88.

of the pastoral syllabus raises more questions than it answers. Even as he acknowledges that his parish should be a locus for learning (not just for obedience or blind faith), he seems uncertain about the exact contours this community should have. Ultimately, he resists conventional teacher-student relationships in favor of a more collaborative model. Having instructed his audience in the fundamentals of the faith, he tells them that there are some truths they will need to figure out for themselves.

In its very willingness to revise and reflect upon pastoral instruction, *Jacob's Well* enriches our understanding of late medieval vernacular theology.[3] Specifically, it demonstrates the ongoing interest in pedagogical innovation within pastoral literature of the late fourteenth and early fifteenth centuries, even within texts that might initially seem to take a reactionary stance toward questions of lay learning. Moreover, the *Well* writer was not alone in his responsiveness to increasingly intense controversies and pressures: *Dives and Pauper*, for example, uses its dialogic structure to propose new definitions of "lerned" and "lewed."[4] These texts suggest that relatively late-stage examples of vernacular theology might offer particularly rich reflections on the process of religious instruction. Organized around a particular body of knowledge—the "curriculum" set forth in the pastoral syllabus promulgated in Lateran IV

[3] My use of the phrase "vernacular theology" derives, of course, from Watson's definition of the term in "Censorship"; in *The Idea of the Vernacular: An Anthology of Middle English Literary Theory, 1280–1520,* ed. Jocelyn Wogan-Browne, Nicholas Watson, Andrew Taylor, and Ruth Evans (University Park: The Pennsylvania State University Press, 1999); and in "The Middle English Mystics," in *The Cambridge History of Medieval Literature,* ed. David Wallace (Cambridge: Cambridge University Press), pp. 539–65.
Bernard McGinn sets forth an analogous application of the phrase in his introduction to the third volume of his history of Western mysticism, *The Flowering of Mysticism: Men and Women in the New Mysticism, 1200–1350* (New York: The Crossroad Publishing Company, 1998), pp. 1–30.

[4] *Dives and Pauper,* ed. Priscilla Heath Barnum, EETS o.s. 275, 280, and 323 (New York: Oxford University Press, 1976, 1980, 2005). For considerations of *Dives and Pauper* in light of fifteenth-century religious debates, see Hudson, *Premature Reformation,* p. 419; Watson, "Censorship," pp. 850 and 855; and *Idea of the Vernacular,* pp. 249–52, which presents an excerpt from the text itself. Connections between *Jacob's Well* and *Dives and Pauper* are briefly explored in Marjorie Curry Woods and Rita Copeland, "Classroom and Confession," in Wallace, pp. 399–400, and in Leo Carruthers, " 'Know Thyself': Criticism, Reform, and the Audience of *Jacob's Well,*" *Medieval Sermons and Society: Cloisters, City, University,* ed. J. Hamesse, B. M. Kienzle, D. L. Stoudt, and A. T. Thayer (Louvain-la-Neuve, F.I.D.E.M., 1998), pp. 238–40. For a discussion of other work by the author of *Dives and Pauper,* see Hudson and H. L. Spencer, "Old Author, New Work: The Sermons of MS. Longleat 4," *MÆ* 53 (1984): 220–38.

and beyond—their writers could not afford to overlook the link between teaching strategies and belief itself.[5]

As Rita Copeland's recent study of heterodox pedagogy has made clear, this connection was of paramount importance to Lollard writers.[6] In Copeland's account, new modes of instruction—specifically, those resisting the infantilization of lay people, and upholding the value of literal interpretation—constituted an essential part of Lollard thought. *Jacob's Well* complicates this picture by reminding us that Lollard writers were not the only ones to resist, or revise, what Copeland has called "pastoral condescension" toward lay learners.[7] To be sure, the *Well* writer's competing responsibilities do not allow him to develop a fully realized alternative pedagogy like the Lollards': he never, for example, tells his audience to seek God's truth in texts, scriptural or otherwise. He does, however, uphold the value of critical inquiry at the end of his text, and implies that this must go on outside the confines of the mind or the parish. These aspects of *Jacob's Well* indicate a crucial area of shading within the "grey area" between orthodoxy and heterodoxy described by Anne Hudson.[8] Even—or, perhaps, especially—in the shadow of Arundel's restrictions on teaching and preaching, writers of various stripes shared a commitment to envisioning new communities of knowledge.

Moreover, this conversation was not confined to sermon literature. As the analysis below will indicate, writers like Langland and the poet of *Mum and the Sothsegger* approach questions of lay learning, useful knowledge, and discernible truth with much the same blend of vehemence and perplexity displayed by the *Well* writer.

Structure and Sources

The questions posed by *Jacob's Well* are particularly striking given the disciplined metaphorical framework within which they emerge. Confronted with a potentially unwieldy list of precepts—including, among other things, the articles of excommunication, the gifts of the Holy

---

[5] For the promulgation of these decrees in England, see H. Leith Spencer, *English Preaching in the Late Middle Ages* (Oxford: Clarendon Press, 1993), 196–227, and Thomas Heffernan, *The Popular Literature of Medieval England* (Knoxville: University of Tennessee Press, 1985).

[6] Copeland, *Pedagogy, Intellectuals, and Dissent in the Later Middle Ages: Lollardy and Ideas of Learning* (Cambridge: Cambridge University Press, 2001).

[7] Ibid., p. 140.

[8] Hudson, *Premature Reformation*, p. 411.

Spirit, and the virtues and vices—the *Well* writer carefully associates Christian precepts to the structure of each person's individual "well." Gravel and ooze within the pit correspond to deadly sins; shovels represent confessional practices; the rungs of the ladder to heaven stand in for the Ten Commandments. Every Christian tenet connects to a particular material object, and the writer regularly reminds his audience of the parts of the project that have been completed or remain unfinished. The work's structure has a temporal dimension as well: it is divided into ninety-five distinct sermons. Noting that this is the precise length of time between Ash Wednesday and Pentecost on the Christian liturgical calendar, and that the sermon corresponding to Easter on this time frame is particularly extended and affirmative, Leo Carruthers has persuasively argued that the *Well* writer designed his work to cover the Easter Cycle as a whole.[9]

Drawing from a wide variety of sources gave the *Well* writer plenty of material for this plan. A great deal of the text's theological material derives from *Speculum Vitae*, the fourteenth-century verse treatise by William of Nassyngton, which places an encyclopedic amount of doctrinal information into an intricate schema linking the petitions of the Lord's Prayer to the vices, virtues, and other elements of the faith.[10] (The *Vitae* derives from the *Somme le Roi*, Friar Lorens of Orleans' thirteenth-century treatise, which was the progenitor for the fourteenth-century *Aʒenbite of Inwit* and *Book of Vices and Virtues*.) Another crucial source for the *Well* writer was the Latin *Alphabetum Narrationum*, compiled in the fourteenth century by the Dominican Arnold of Liège: this provided the *Well* writer with the majority of the illustrative narratives with which he concludes each day's sermon.[11] Close correspondences

[9] See Carruthers, "Allegory and Bible Interpretation: The Narrative Structure of a Middle English Sermon Cycle," *L&T* 4 (1990): 1–14, and "The Liturgical Setting of *Jacob's Well*," *ELN* 24 (1987): 12–24. Atchley (pp. 40–66) suggests some plausible revisions to Carruthers's schema for the work's sermons.

[10] For the connections between *Jacob's Well* and *Speculum Vitae*, see Edna Stover, "*A Myrour to Lewde Men and Wymmen*, edited from MS Harley 45" (Ph.D. diss., University of Pennsylvania, 1951), and Venetia Nelson, *A Myrour to Lewde Men and Wymmen: A Prose Version of the Speculum Vitae, ed. from B.L. MS Harley 45* (Heidelberg, MET, 1981). *Speculum Vitae* is not in print, but it has been edited within John W. Smeltz's "*Speculum Vitae*: An Edition of British Museum MS Royal 17C.viii" (Ph.D. diss., Duquesne University, 1977). Carruthers succinctly summarizes the relationship of *Jacob's Well* to several of its sources in "Liturgical Setting," pp. 12–13.

[11] Joan Young Gregg persuasively establishes this connection in "The Exempla of *Jacob's Well*: A Study in the Transmission of Medieval Sermon Stories," *Traditio* 33 (1977): 359–80. See also Gregg's dissertation, "The Narrative Exempla of *Jacob's Well*:

between portions of *Jacob's Well* and two other texts—Richard Lavynham's *A Lityl Tretys on the Dedly Synnes*, and the late fourteenth- /early
fifteenth-century compilation *Pore Caitif*—suggest that the *Well* writer
drew upon these works as well.[12]

The *Well* writer's use of such sources supports Clinton Atchley's assessment of him as "an educated man with a respectable knowledge of
Latin"; beyond this, however, little is known about the work's authorship or date of origin.[13] The sole manuscript of the work, MS Salisbury
Cathedral 103, appears to date from the 1440s, but it is not from the
author's hand.[14] Nothing in the source material or work itself contradicts the suggestion of Arthur Brandeis, who edited the work's first fifty
sermons in 1900, that the text dates from approximately the first quarter of the fifteenth century.[15] Evidence regarding the location of the
work's original composition is also tentative: Carruthers's dialect study
leads him to locate the manuscript's scribe in Suffolk, but he cannot
confirm anything about the *Well* writer himself.[16] Building upon this
suggestion as well as internal evidence, Atchley suggests Bury St. Ed-
munds as a likely location or the *Well* writer's community of listeners.[17]
Again, however, scholars at this point must still confine themselves to
speculation: as Carruthers concedes, current evidence does not even confirm whether the text ever "saw the light of day outside the scriptorium."[18]

The *Well* writer's references to his audience do, however, make clear
that he intended his work to function within a congregation made up

A Source Study with an Index for *Jacob's Well* to *Index Exemplorum"* (Ph.d. diss., New
York University, 1973). The *Alphabetum Narrationum* is not in print; quotations below
are drawn from B.M. MS Harley 268. Readers could also consult *"An Alphabet of Tales:"*
An English 15th Century Translation of the "Alphabetum Narrationum," ed. Mary MacLeod
Banks, EETS o.s. 126–27 (London: Kegan Paul, Trench, Trübner & Co., 1904–5).

[12] For the connections between *Jacob's Well* and Lavynham's treatise, see Carruthers,
"*Jacob's Well*: Études d'un sermonnaire pénitentiel anglais du Xve siècle" (Thèse d'Etat,
University of Paris–Sorbonne, 1987), esp. pp. 348–50. Having discovered that the
treatment of the Ten Commandments in *Jacob's Well* (as well as other passages) corre-
sponds closely with passages in *Pore Caitif*, I hope to say more about this relationship in
future work. *Pore Caitif* is edited within Sister Mary Teresa Brady's dissertation, *"The
Pore Caitif*, Edited from MS Harley 2336 with Notes and Introduction" (Ph.D. diss.,
Fordham University, 1954).

[13] Atchley, "The 'Wose' of *Jacob's Well*," p. 21.

[14] Carruthers, "Provenance," p. 336.

[15] Brandeis, *Jacob's Well*, pp. x–xiii.

[16] Carruthers, "Provenance," p. 338–40.

[17] Atchley, "The 'Wose' of *Jacob's Well*," p. 30.

[18] Carruthers, "Liturgical Setting," p. 24.

of lay men, lay women, and even other clerics. Writing with Marjorie Woods, Copeland has pointed out that *Jacob's Well* "achieve[s] such rhetorical complexity as to challenge the generic distinction between instructions to priests and guides to lay persons."[19] After carefully exploring various modes of address within the text, Carruthers suggests that the audience for the work was probably lay people of fairly substantial wealth and education.[20] But the text's working-man metaphors and concern for farming regulations lead Atchley to speculate that at least some of the work's listeners might have been lower-class and rural.[21]

Whatever his audience's social class, the *Well* writer directly addresses lay people throughout the text, and often characterizes them as deficient in their knowledge of penance and other aspects of the faith. What is more, they risk being led astray by the ideas of wrongheaded instructors. In his few direct references to the Lollards, for example, the *Well* writer highlights the movement's educational and intellectual dimensions. The sin of "euyll tunge," he writes, involves people "þat wyln noȝt lerne for techyng, but fallyn in erroure, in heresye, in lollardrye" (i.156). Elsewhere, he castigates Lollards for pretending to be holy so that they "myȝt þerby dysseyue þe peple be [their] fals techyng" (i.164).[22] The *Well* writer's choice of words here merits our attention, since fifteenth-century writers used many different terms when condemning the Lollards. Reginald Pecock often hones in on their tendency to "vndirnyme" (rebuke) and "blame," for example, while Nicholas Love frequently highlights their connection to the Antichrist.[23] As Alexander Patschovsky has written, allegations of heresy often reveal less about the ideas of the "heretics" themselves than about anxieties and contradictions operating within the accusing culture or institution.[24] On a small scale, the *Well* writer's emphasis on the Lollards as resistant learners and deceptive teachers demonstrates his preoccupation with the pedagogical dimension of Christian penitential practices.

[19] Woods and Copeland, "Classroom and Confession," p. 399.
[20] Carruthers, "Know Thyself," pp. 227–33.
[21] Atchley, "The 'Wose' of *Jacob's Well*," p. 28.
[22] The *Well* writer also takes care to point out that "alle wycches, & heretykes, & lollardys, & alle þat beleuyn on here heresye" will be excommunicated (i.59).
[23] See, for example, Reginald Pecock, *The Repressor of Over Much Blaming of the Clergy*, ed. Churchill Babington (London: Longman, Green, Longman, and Roberts, 1860), p. 2, and Nicholas Love, *The Mirror of the Blessed Life of Jesus Christ: A Reading Text*, ed. Michael Sargent (Exeter: University of Exeter Press, 2004), pp. 236–37.
[24] Alexander Patschovsky, "Heresy and Society: On the Political Function of Heresy in the Medieval World," in *Texts and the Repression of Medieval Heresy*, ed. Caterina Bruschi and Peter Biller (York: York Medieval Press, 2003), esp. pp. 32–33.

Moreover, Lollards are not the only bad teachers and learners at issue for the *Well* writer; as we shall see, poor instruction *within* the Church becomes his primary target by the end of the text. In response, the *Well* writer ultimately offers his listeners a conception of parish life defined by shared intellectual engagement. While he does not want his listeners to become scholars per se, he does afford them the opportunity to regard themselves as thinkers.

Juveniles and Delinquents: The *Well* Writer's Audience

Exploring the *Well* writer's initial characterizations of his audience reveals parallels between his own descriptions of lay people and those employed by other writers in the wake of Archbishop Thomas Arundel's Constitutions of 1407–9. Of particular interest are passages where he likens lay believers to children. As Copeland has argued, analogies in which "the association of laity with unlearned simplicity could be conflated with the intellectual limitations of childhood" were politically useful for those interested in maintaining lay people's subordinate position within the Church, and were strongly resisted by the Lollards.[25] A noteworthy example of this trope emerges in Love's *Mirror of the Blessed Life of Jesus Christ*, which argues that lay men and women "hauen nede to be fedde with mylke of lyȝte doctryne & not with sadde mete of grete clargye & of hye contemplacion."[26] As we shall see below, the *Well* writer sets forth similar ideas in some portions of his text. As the work progresses, however, he implies that lay listeners' duties involve much more than consuming "pious pabulum."[27]

Initially the *Well* writer characterizes his audience as dangerously ignorant and his own mission as clear-cut and urgent. After an introduction sketching out the plan for the work, the second sermon begins to explain the articles of excommunication. Presenting this material is crucial, the writer declares to his audience, because "þou art blynde in ignoraunce, & seest noȝt, ne knowyst noȝt þe watyr of þis pytt, þat is for to saye, þou art a layman, & knowyst noȝt þe artycles of þe sentencys, & art falle þere-in, & seest noȝt þe peryles, but schuldest perysche in soule

---

[25] Copeland, *Pedagogy*, p. 7.

[26] Love, *Mirror*, p. 10. See Watson's quotation and discussion of this passage in *Idea of the Vernacular*, p. 345; for analysis of a similar metaphor in Alan of Lille's *Art of Preaching*, see Copeland, *Pedagogy*, p. 99.

[27] The phrase is Spencer's (*English Preaching*, p. 188).

220

endlesly in deth of helle" (i.7–8). In an almost offhand manner ("þat is for to saye"), the writer associates lay status with ignorance, blindness, and possible damnation. He goes on to promise his listeners that they may overcome their spiritual degradation through repentance and shrift. But even this transformation has its limits. The writer promises that penitents will move "fro curs to blysse, fro synne to grace, fro peyne to ioye" (i.13), but he refrains from saying whether believers will progress from ignorance to knowledge, or even from blindness to sight. Similarly, his claim that after confession his listeners "schalt . . . be goddys chyld, þere before þou were þe deuelys chyld" (i.11) relegates even virtuous lay people to the position of dependents within the Christian "family." Through such statements, the *Well* writer seems to divorce intellectual development from the process of religious instruction. His listeners' potential for salvation goes hand in hand with their willingness to see themselves as reliant upon God's mercy and clerics' guidance.

Within this very sermon, however, the writer acknowledges his listeners' ability to make their own decisions. Immediately after pointing out the ignorance of lay people, the priest addresses their potential response to him: "þou awȝtyst noȝt to hatyn þi curate, but þou awȝtyst for to louyn hym al þi lyif"(i.8). He subsequently reiterates this in more personal terms: "whanne I schewe to ȝou an-oþer day þe artycles of þe sentencys, beeth noȝt euyll payed wyth me, but beth glad to here hem" (i.8). The writer recognizes that he is not speaking into a vacuum: his listeners will actively react to his words, either with love or with hate. His listeners may lack knowledge, but they do have choices. Their agency influences not just the relationship between priest and parishioners but also the sermon-giving situation itself. As both Carruthers and Atchley have noted, the writer feels compelled to remind his listeners that they should "go noȝt out of þe cherche" while his discussion of the articles takes place (i.11).[28] The *Well* writer's dilemma is unenviable: he needs his listeners to stay in church so that he can explain to them the grounds on which ecclesiastical officials might exclude them. Such paradoxes emerge repeatedly within *Jacob's Well*. Even as the *Well* writer tells his audience that they need the mediation of the Church, he recognizes that his parish's viability—and his own authority as a speaker—are contingent upon his listeners' goodwill.

[28] Atchley, "The 'Wose' of *Jacob's Well*," p. 27; Carruthers, "Liturgical Setting," p. 14.

Conflicts specifically related to knowledge emerge when the writer turns to the virtue of humility. The meek must love God, he writes, and they should do so unquestioningly: "loue þi god, & worschipp in þi feyth. ȝif þou be symple of kunnyng, trowe & beleue þe woord of god, wyth-oute sekyng of resouns how it myȝt be so, as a ȝung chyld trowyth it sooth þat men sayn. loue & honoure þi god wyth symple mood" (i.245). Although the writer leaves open the possibility that some lay listeners could approach belief in a sophisticated manner (i.e., the more educated, who are presumably not "symple of kunnyng"), he urges other adults to embrace childish credulousness, and implies that their "symple" state is a permanent one. The *Well* writer is not alone in this idea of course: in many ways, his recommendations here parallel those in Passus X of *Piers Plowman*, in which Will extols the "pure bileue" evinced by "lewed [laborers]" and others "of litel knowing" (B.X.470, 478).

But the *Well* writer is no more satisfied with this solution than is Langland. As the *Well* writer elaborates upon the value of humble prayer, he offers a simile focusing on a different aspect of childhood. He exhorts his listeners to "thynk þi-self vnworthy & pray to god wyth terys, felyng þi-self badde & bare of goodnes, as a chyld þat kan noȝt his lessoun, stant nakyd a-forn hys mayster, dredyng, knelyth doun ful hertyly praying" (i.245). The writer again likens his audience to children—this time without any qualification—and encourages them to adopt an attitude of fearful submission. But the analogy works differently this time. Whereas the first passage advocates belief over learning, the second one encourages listeners to envision themselves as delinquent students. The connection between sin and ignorance overlooked by the first passage emerges forcefully here, and the vulnerability attendant to a lack of knowledge is graphically depicted (or even erotically charged). Once again, lay people occupy a position of puerile inferiority. By evoking the schoolroom scenario, however, the *Well* writer complicates his previous advocacy of simple piety and implies that his listeners should see themselves as students, not just as believers. Knowledge remains a requirement, even if it is one that goes unfulfilled: good Christians know that they do not know everything they should.

The *Well* writer's analogy between a penitent's interaction with God and a student's relationship to a master raises particularly interesting questions for the people in his audience excluded from formal schooling by virtue of their gender, social status, or geographic location. As Jo

Ann Moran has demonstrated, elementary schooling was increasing, but by no means was it widely available, in the first half of the fifteenth century: rural areas often had trouble procuring or retaining the services of qualified teachers, and girls' education was still largely a private and isolated phenomenon.[29] Given that the curriculum for elementary education in many cases seems to have closely followed the syllabi for lay instruction set forth by later medieval bishops—one fourteenth-century primer described by Moran contains the Creed, the deadly sins, the bodily and spiritual works of mercy, and so on—the *Well* writer may perceive that his own preaching provides listeners with a form of cultural literacy that would otherwise be unavailable to them.[30] However negative, his image of the unprepared child makes the schoolroom setting available to listeners without distinction, and implies that all Christians possess the potential to better themselves through diligent study.

Academic learning emerges as an even more crucial issue later in the text, when the writer describes the gift of knowledge provided by the Holy Spirit to those of goodwill. In this case, the writer cannot simply characterize his audience as ignorant and fearful. Recognizing the ways in which this grace might increase lay people's sense of spiritual authority, the writer takes great care to inform his listeners about the narrow realm in which they should apply their knowledge. As part of this argument, he extols the laity's ability to achieve *sapientia*, or the wisdom attainable through emotional meditation upon God. At the same time, he struggles with the proper way to present *scientia*, and offers an extended narrative that both resists and upholds the relationship between intellectual inquiry and faith.[31]

Knowledge: A Dangerous Blessing

The seven graces of the Holy Spirit—deriving ultimately from Isaiah 11:2–3, and expounded upon by scholastic theologians during the High

[29] See Jo Ann Moran, *The Growth of English Schooling, 1340–1548* (Princeton: Princeton University Press, 1985), pp. 75–82. Further explorations of schooling for medieval children can be found in William J. Courtenay, *Schools and Scholars in Fourteenth-Century England* (Princeton: Princeton University Press, 1987), pp. 15–20, and Nicholas Orme, *English Schools in the Middle Ages* (London: Methuen, 1973), pp. 59–79.

[30] Moran, *The Growth of English Schooling*, p. 43.

[31] For discussions of this distinction, see James Simpson, "From Reason to Affective Knowledge: Modes of Thought and Poetic Form in *Piers Plowman*," *MÆ* 55 (1986): 1–23; Kantik Ghosh, *The Wycliffite Heresy: Authority and the Interpretation of Texts* (Cambridge: Cambridge University Press, 2002), pp. 60–66; Fiona Somerset, *Clerical Discourse and Lay Audience in Late Medieval England* (Cambridge: Cambridge University Press, 1998), pp. 43–44; and Watson, "Politics," p. 339.

Middle Ages—form a crucial part of the *Well* writer's scheme.[32] The well-digging he describes will, ideally, allow the "watyrs of grace" to spring up within each human soul. As with so much of the doctrinal material found in *Jacob's Well*, the writer's analysis of knowledge draws heavily from *Speculum Vitae*. A brief excursion into the treatment of knowledge within *Speculum Vitae* allows us to see the *Well* writer's specific preoccupations: the earlier text primarily focuses on emphasizing the benefits of knowledge, rather than on striving to define its proper scope.

As mentioned previously, *Speculum Vitae* possesses a complicated structure of its own, in which each petition of the Pater Noster corresponds to a particular gift of the Holy Spirit, to one of the deadly sins, to a virtue, and to a component of the Beatitudes.[33] Its author, William of Nassyngton, links the gift of knowledge to the "first askyng" of the prayer—"Forgive us our debts"—and defines it as the ability to perceive one's own spiritual status:

> Þe gyft of knawyng shewys vs right
> What we er and what ys our myght
> And in what perille we er alle,
> And wyns we come and weþer we shalle,
> And what folys þat we haue done,
> And makys vs for sak our syn son.
>
> (256)

According to *Speculum Vitae*, this gift proves especially helpful in eradicating the sin of ire. After explaining this vice at length, Nassyngton declares that "þis syne of ire with outyn doute / Þe gyft of knawyng puttes out" (259). He asserts that knowledge replaces anger with the virtue of equity (the capacity to place one's reason in accord with one's will), lists the seven branches of this virtue, and links knowledge to the mourning described in the Beatitudes. Nassyngton concludes the section by repeating that equity "commes of þe gyft of knawyng" (269).

In several places, the discussion of knowledge found in *Jacob's Well* follows *Speculum Vitae* almost word for word. The *Well* writer incorpo-

---

[32] For example, Thomas Aquinas deals with the gifts extensively in I.II, Question 68 of the *Summa Theologica* (New York: Benziger Brothers, 1947), pp. 877–85.

[33] See Smeltz, *Speculum Vitae*, pp. 37–66, for a summary of the text's structure. Citations from his edition of the text are by page number.

rates the Beatitudes into his chosen metaphorical framework, for example, describing mourning as the "watyr of terys" within the well (i.275). In other places, however, he tailors his source to his own ends. Most conspicuous are the *Well* writer's efforts to attach limitations and caveats to the topic of knowledge. He introduces the subject by describing this gift as the ability to "seest þi-self wel wrecchyd & synfull" (i.275). While this definition closely parallels that found in *Speculum Vitae*, the latter text simply alludes to "knawyng" in subsequent references, while the *Well* priest goes out of his way to stipulate that he speaks of self-knowledge. He makes this point at both the beginning and the end of his analysis of weeping: "þis ȝyfte of grace, þat is, knowyng þe-self, makyth þe to wepyn in vj. maners . . . þise vj. maners wepyng of terys spryngeth in þi welle þe ȝyfte of knowyng, ȝif þou, thruȝ grace, kanst knowe þi-self" (i.275). A similar specificity prevails when he contrasts sinners' spiritual blindness with "þe grace of knowyng to knowe þe-self" (i.275).

The *Well* priest does not, however, manage to confine knowledge exclusively to the realm of the individual soul. After yet another reference to "a knowyng of þe-self," he delineates the parameters of this gift:

vnderstondyth þanne weel what þis knowyng is! it techyth þe to lyven ryȝtfully a-monge euyll lyuerys, & to teche ryȝtly, & to defende þi feyth wyth resouns fro inpugnyng of heretykes; It techyth how þou schalt absteyne fro synne & wyckydnesse, and how þou schalt medefully mynystryn, expendyn, dyposyn, þi temperall godys; It techyth þe be resoun to redresse þi werkys lyckly to be conformyd to þi feyth; It techyth þe þat wyckydnesse may noȝt ben hyd to þe vndyr coloure of goodnesse. be þis ȝyfte of kunnyng þou knowyst þi-self what þou art, wher-of þou art, what þou schalt be. It techytz þi conscyens what þou schalt do, & what þou schalt bydden oþere do in resoun and equyte. (i.276)

Within this passage, which has no analogue in *Speculum Vitae*, the *Well* writer engages explicitly with the social import of *scientia* for his audience. While the passage disparages heretics, it also reveals the impossibility of knowledge's remaining an internal phenomenon. Instead of functioning exclusively as self-examiners, the *Well* writer's listeners should teach and correct others. Even as he primarily presents this instruction as a defensive activity against sinners and heretics, his repeated references to reason lend credence to lay people's interpretive abilities. The *Well* writer here describes his pedagogical project in a new way: his listerers' primary teacher is not a cleric, but their own store of "knowyng." Moreover, there are other places in the text where the *Well* writer refers to teaching in a surprisingly open-ended manner: "þou þat hast connyng teche it to þe peple," he commands in his discussion of pity (i.250), without qualifying the recommendation by considering questions of clerical learning or status. While there are numerous passages in *Jacob's Well* where the writer reminds his listeners to accept the tenets set forth by priests and the Holy Church,[34] he also remains open to intellectual and pedagogical activity on the part of lay people themselves.

With this openness, however, comes a large measure of anxiety. The *Well* writer's subsequent treatment of the gift of knowledge suggests that he is troubled by the possibility that lay people will interpret the blessing too broadly. Immediately following his definition of the gift and its uses, the *Well* priest departs from his source once again, in order to distinguish between certain kinds of knowledge and the Holy Spirit's gift: "þis ȝyfte of kunnyng techyth þe noȝt of þe sterrys, ne of oþer sotyltes of þe vij. scyencys; but it techyth þe to kun knowe þe-self, whanne þou art synfull, & whanne þou art ryȝtfull, and how þou schalt gouerne þe to saue þi soule" (i.276). *Speculum Vitae* and many other instructional texts remain silent on the distinction between the gift of knowledge and academic education. The prologue to the popular fourteenth-century work *The Prick of Conscience*, for example, comments extensively on the need for man to "knaw himself with-inne," without setting that self-knowledge against scholarly pursuits.[35]

Nevertheless, texts outside *Jacob's Well*'s immediate circle of sources and analogues ponder this problem extensively. *Piers Plowman* is probably the most prominent example. Most readers tend to share Andrew Galloway's sense that "Will's temptations, anxieties, and uncertainties about learning" are central to the poem, but critical opinions vary widely on Langland's actual argument regarding the relationship of intellectual knowledge and Christian salvation.[36] Texts within the mystical

---

[34] When explaining the fourth commandment, for example, the *Well* writer tells his listeners to "worshepe" and "obeye" their curates (ii.439); they should also "beleuyst alle thyng as holy cherche beleuyth," even in difficult circumstances (ii.376).

[35] See *The Pricke of Conscience*, ed. Richard Morris (Berlin: A. Asher & Co., 1863; reissued 1973), p. 5.

[36] See Andrew Galloway, "*Piers Plowman* and the Schools," YLS 6 (1992): 89–107. Daniel Murtaugh (*"Piers Plowman" and the Image of God* [Gainesville: University Press of Florida, 1978]) argues that Langland insists upon the connection between intellect and salvation, while Nicolette Zeeman contends that Langland feels knowledge must be combined with grace ("'Studying' in the Middle Ages—and in *Piers Plowman*," *New Medieval Literatures* 3 [1999]: 185–212). Simpson perceives a movement from *scientia* to

tradition addressed this question as well: Dame Studie's condemnation of learned men who "haue [God] muche in [hire] mouþ" but not in their heart (B.X. 71) is echoed within *The Cloud of Unknowing*, which castigates those displaying a "proude, corious witte" instead of genuine belief.[37] From a political perspective, *Mum and the Sothsegger* turns this insight into an allegorized journey: the poem's speaker's search for truth leads him to seek "alle the vij sciences," but they neither they nor the fraternal orders can give him useful information.[38]

Questions of excessive and inappropriate knowledge also emerge in the polemic surrounding Lollardy. Pecock sarcastically notes that knowledge of "narraciouns and parabolis and lijknessis" may enable a cleric to "preche ful gloriosely," but it does not allow for the best kind of reasonable discourse.[39] Surprising parallels can emerge in opposing texts' treatment of this question: when Nicholas Love argues that Christians need to "leue hir owne witte & kyndely reson" at the door, so to speak, he recalls Lollard sermonizers' own deprecations of "worldly wyt."[40] While the former writer emphasizes the primacy of the Church's teachings and the latter the practice of "knowyng of God"[41] through textual analysis, both texts evince a common distrust for intellectual activity ungoverned by spiritual priorities.

The *Well* writer shares these concerns, and has an even more difficult time resolving them. In the remainder of his treatment of the gift of knowledge, the *Well* writer offers two exempla that reveal herculean efforts on his part to define clearly the relationship between scholarly learning and spiritual well-being.

The first narrative concerns a devil worshiped as a god within a town. When a man asks him the best route to heaven, the fiend gives him an unequivocal answer—"knowe þi-self"—and repeats the *Well* priest's negative definition of proper knowledge: "To knowe sterrys, & oþer scyens, þat kunnyng comyth of stodye; but to knowe þe-self comyth of

---

sapientia in the work; by contrast, Somerset feels the text's ideas regarding knowledge remain unresolved.

[37] *The Cloud of Unknowing and The Book of Privy Counselling*, ed. Phyllis Hodgson, EETS o.s. no. 218 (London: Oxford University Press, 1944), p. 22.

[38] See *Richard the Redeless and Mum and the Sothsegger*, ed. James M. Dean (Kalamazoo: Medieval Institute Publications, 2000), p. 93.

[39] Pecock, *Repressor*, p. 89.

[40] See Love, *Mirror*, p. 235, and *English Wycliffite Sermons*, vol. 1, ed. Anne Hudson (Oxford: Clarendon Press, 1983), p. 511.

[41] Hudson, *English Wycliffite Sermons*, p. 511.

no skole, ne of no clergye, ne of no letterure" (i.276). The fiend takes the *Well* priest's argument a step further, by ridiculing the learning possessed by the well educated. According to the fiend, some of these "doctourys of lawe & of dyuynyte, & maystrys of oþere scyence . . . knowe noȝt hem-self, ne wyll noȝt knowyn hem-self, to gouerne hem fro synne to ryȝtwysnesse" (i.276). In fact, he argues, "summe lay-men kun bettyr knowyn hem-self in gouernaunce fro synne þan summe grete clerkys . . . þys ȝyfte of knowynge comyth of þe holy gost, & noȝt of skole" (i.276). Not satisfied with this declaration, the *Well* priest elucidates the distinction between spiritual and scholarly knowledge one more time, in his own voice. The trappings of learning—"furryd tabbardys, hodys, chymerys, & pylyouns"—mean nothing to the Holy Spirit; instead, the spirit bestows knowledge "to leryd & lewyd þat arn in þe grounde of obedyence in ful equyte. to hem springeth þe holy gost þis watyr of grace to knowe hem-self, & to gouerne hem-self in goodnesse" (i.277). As a coda to the narrative, the writer describes how Christ at the Ascencion gave all people "his ȝyfte of kunnynge for to knowe þe-self to gouerne þe in vertuys," and exhorts his listeners to behave "as chyldrin in obedyens," so that they themselves may someday reach heaven (i.277).

Carruthers, who includes this exemplum within his analysis of *Jacob's Well*'s audience and social message, cites it as evidence of the writer's tendency to criticize people from all walks of life, including university "maystrys."[42] I think we might say even more about the social implications of the narrative, particularly since the writer apparently went out of his way to incorporate the story: as Gregg has shown, this narrative constitutes one of only three occasions in the first fifty sermons where the *Well* priest recounts an exemplum not found in the Latin *Alphabetum Narrationum*. Although he does cite a source for the story ("Alysander in cronicis libro viij"), a close analogue has never been found, and Gregg perceives "a uniquely purposeful manner which suggests some invention" on the part of the *Well* priest.[43] In several ways, the story recalls the writer's earlier statements regarding lay people's role within Christianity. Arguing against differences in social status even as he vividly depicts them (indeed, his references to "furryd tabbardys" and the like may suggest that he shares his listeners' resentment of such trappings),

[42] Carruthers, "Know Thyself," p. 239.
[43] Gregg, "The Narrative Exempla of *Jacob's Well*," pp. 374–76.

the writer upholds lay people's spiritual equality to clerics. But this parity applies to an individual's obedience, at the expense of his or her intellectual abilities. As in his discussion of humility, the writer encourages his listeners to see themselves as children: his references to obedience in this passage evoke both the simple acceptance he attributes to young children and the delinquent student's fear before the schoolmaster. According to the exemplum, other kinds of knowledge—including schooling and "letterure"—only clutter the soul, detracting from its ability to receive the Holy Spirit's gift.

Of course, the *Well* writer's own methods belie this assertion. His disparagement of academic learning conveniently overlooks, for example, the fact that his own sermons expose the laity to the learning and rhetoric of the friars.[44] But this is not mere hypocrisy on the *Well* writer's part. His text will alter fraternal scholarship by anchoring it to the context of parish life. Instead of functioning as an accoutrement of prestige, the Christian knowledge set forth by the *Well* writer ideally will facilitate conversation, remonstrance, and genuine contrition within his community.

This possibility emerges even more forcefully in the section's other illustrative narrative, which both evokes and resists the connection between book learning and devout religious belief. Although the *Well* priest draws this narrative from the *Alphabetum Narrationum*, his initial description of the exemplum's protagonist reveals his willingness to alter his source to reflect his own preoccupations. The story concerns John of Damascus, the monk and saint, and his betrayal at the hands (literally) of his student.[45] The *Alphabetum* describes John as a person who combines piety with learning. Chaste and devoted to the Blessed Virgin, he is also well versed in Greek letters and the liberal arts, and skilled "in scribendo in dictando and cantando" (in writing, composing, and singing).[46] The *Well* writer begins the story with a different emphasis, asserting that John was so "full of pes" and "obedyent" that he receives the ability to "knowyn hym-self, & kowde gouerne hym-self in thou3t, in

[44] I am grateful to Larry Scanlon for bringing this contradiction to my attention.

[45] This narrative is listed under the rubric "Hand restored to virgin" in Frederic C. Tubach, *Index Exemplorum: A Handbook of Medieval Religious Tales* (Helsinki: Suomalainen Tiedeakatemia, 1969), p. 191. For the relationship between this tale and a closely related one involving Pope Leo, see Brian S. Lee, " 'This is no fable': Historical Residues in Two Medieval *Exempla*," *Speculum* 56 (1981): 728–60, esp. 730–43.

[46] The "John of Damascus" narrative occurs on folios 129v and 130r of B.M. Harley 268.

woord, in dede, in pes, in obedyens, [and] in grace" (i.277). Only after
setting these terms does the *Well* writer follow his source in stressing
John's great learning. Even then, the writer chooses his words carefully:
his protagonist has mastered "scyens of clergye" (277) rather than all of
the liberal arts.

The *Well* priest stays close to his source when he describes the events
befalling the monk. Having been taken prisoner by the Saracens, John
is put to work instructing a lord's son "in wrytyng, & in endyȝtyng, in
letture, & oþer kunnyng of clergye" (i.278). Eventually, the lord's son
gains the ability to write and speak exactly like his master. Becoming
envious of John's position at court, he writes a treasonous letter in his
master's handwriting. When the emperor finds "þis cursed lettere," he
summons John, who admits that it "is lych myn hand & lyche myn
endyȝtynge," but swears that he did not write it (i.278). The disbeliev-
ing emperor orders John's right hand to be cut off; as an additional
punishment, the hand is suspended near an image of the Blessed Mother
in John's priory. John returns home, exposes his wounded arm to the
image, and mournfully asks her what he has done to deserve this suffering. That night, Mary appears to him and restores the hand. When the
emperor and the court see his "arme & hand hool" the next morning,
they realize their mistake and beg for John's forgiveness (i.279).

The *Well* writer departs from the *Alphabetum* in order to highlight
John's obedience. When Mary appears to John in the *Alphabetum*, she
calls him "puer meus fidelissime" (my most faithful boy); in *Jacob's Well*,
she refers to him as "my chyld, trewe, meke, & obedyent in equyte to
my sone & to me" (i.279). Even more striking is the writer's decision at
the end of the narrative. The *Alphabetum*'s exemplum concludes with the
revelation of the truth—"rei veritas diligentius inquisita innotuit" (the
truth of the matter, inquired into more carefully, became known)—and
with a celebration of "mariam virginem et fidelitatem et patientiam et
credulitatem" (the Virgin Mary and faith and patience and trust). By
contrast, the narrative in *Jacob's Well* ends with an execution: "Þanne þe
emperour putte þat lordys sone to a schamefull deth" (i.279).

These alterations, combined with the material in the preceding exemplum, give John's story a much different meaning in *Jacob's Well* than it
has in the *Alphabetum Narrationum*. The latter text offers the narrative
as an example of "infamia": John loses his reputation through treachery
and regains it with the help of the Virgin Mary. Within the context of
Jacob's Well, the story provides another opportunity for the *Well* writer

to interrogate the problems raised by Christian knowledge. By depicting the punishment of the traitorous pupil, the *Well* writer presents education as a risky undertaking, for students as well as teachers: the lord's son's learning stirs him to envy, facilitates his forgery, and leads him to an ignoble and violent end.[47] The *Well* writer's added emphasis on John's obedience further suggests that he wants his audience to value submissiveness over academic training.

But these interpellations cannot cancel out the fact of John's embodiment of a complementary relationship between learning and virtue: he continues to think and act throughout the story, rather than simply retreating into silent compliance. When he stands before the image of Mary, he demands that she explain (if not justify) his situation; when he receives the gift of a restored hand, he regains the ability to write songs and letters, not just to pray. While the picture of Mary and the restored hand are nonverbal signs that avoid the complications inherent in letter-writing, they represent conversation and literary creation, not simply pious meditation. Despite its negative portrayal of an educational scenario, then, the exemplum does not attempt to replace thought with blind faith. As we shall see, other parts of *Jacob's Well*—particularly its analysis of truth—also leave room for active lay inquiry and critique, even as they stop short of advocating book learning for all people.

The Pursuit of Truth

In his analysis of changing conceptualizations of truth in late fourteenth-century England, R. F. Green writes that in their works "Chaucer, Langland, and the *Gawain*-poet appear to have been wrestling with the meaning of a word [that is, truth] that also preoccupied many of their less prominent contemporaries."[48] Certainly, truth is a problematic concept in *Jacob's Well*. Another gift of the Holy Spirit, understanding, brings this uncertainty to the forefront. Once again confronted with a grace affording a large measure of credit to all believers' intellectual abilities, the *Well* writer first defines understanding broadly as a "lyȝt of grace [that enables people] gostly to knowyn god. & to vnderstonde

---

[47] The nature of the pupil's crime also parallels Arundel's characterizations of the Lollards as liars and forgers in his introduction to the Constitutions (Wilkins, *Concilia*, p. 315).

[48] R. F. Green, *A Crisis of Truth: Literature and Law in Ricardian England* (Philadelphia: University of Pennsylvania Press, 1999), p. 5.

scripture and to haue vndyrstondyng in creaturys of god . . . þus vnderstondyng of þe holy gost makyth vs to se god gostly in scripture and in his creaturis. & to sen oure self & oure defawtys" (ii.105). These references to Scripture are particularly provocative. Though the *Well* writer does not specify that this comprehension would come through *reading* God's word, he nevertheless upholds the importance of holy writ and implies that its ideas can be comprehensible to all believers. But he follows up this passage by linking the gift of understanding to a heavy burden of self-restraint and obedience: "holde þou mesure in vnderstondyng. þat is in alle artycles of þe feyth wythoute musyng aboue mannys wytt & resoun. ffor seynt Poule seyth Be no man wysere þan ryȝt wyle. but lede he his wytt in sobyrnesse. after þe mesure of truthe and desyre he noȝt to se resoun þere non may be. but holde he þe truthe þat holy cherche techyth. & seke he no ferthere" (ii.107). Having conceded that lay people possess the ability to know God and to understand Scripture, the *Well* priest explicitly rejects active inquiry into theological matters. Christians should forgo rational inquiry in favor of accepting "þe truthe þat holy cherche techyth."

While this might seem to resolve the question, the *Well* writer later depicts the church's own teachings as fraught with deception. Preaching is a particular problem, both in its delivery and its reception. People are happy to listen to criticisms of "prelatys & . . . oþere grete men," the *Well* writer complains, but react angrily against remarks that hit too close to home: "whan þe preest comyth ny hem. & towchyth hem trewly & plentyously of here defawȝtes. þei turnyn awey wrothly fro þe preest herte & defendyn here dyffawȝtys wyth false colourys & excusyn & turnyn to tellyn talys. & iapys & to depraue þe preest & þe woord of trowthe" (ii.226–7). In addition to reflecting badly on the congregation's morals, these responses taint the actions of priests themselves: "prechourys hye and lowe arn a feryd to sey þe trouthe. bothe seculere & relygious and stodyin how in here sermouns þey mown wyth flateryng colourys symylacyouns & fals excusacyouns fauouryn & plesyn þe peple grete & smale. leryd and lewyd in here synne. & to excusyn here vyces. wrongys & here falsnesse" (ii.227). As he did when he asked his listeners not to hate or walk out on him, the writer demonstrates an awareness of the preacher-audience relationship as a two-way encounter, risky for both speaker and listeners. The institutional edifice indicated by the writer's earlier reference to "holy church's" truth reveals itself to be composed of individuals who are fallible and dishonest themselves.

The *Well* writer does not stop there. He develops his critique of priests and other members of the higher social orders ("Iustyses. iuges. prelatys doctourys and clerkys preestys & alle men of holy cherche") by calling them the unfaithful husbands of truth (ii.228). When their wives give birth to ugly "children"—that is, to "rowe woordys and foule bacbytynges. foule lesynges. in hate of þe peple for þou seyst trouthe"—they conceive a hate for truth itself, and take on the "lemman" of flattery (ii.229).

The writer does not say which role he himself occupies within the troubled family he describes. Switching metaphors, he describes truth as the language of heaven. At this point, however, he evokes a schoolroom scene that offers yet another formulation of the relationship between learning and spiritual well-being: "ȝyf a gramaryan speke his owyn langwage in scole. englysche. he schal be smit with a pawmere on þe hand or scouryd or taken be þe cheke or be þe ere. and he schal be tawȝt to speke latyn or frensche. Ryȝt so in þis world. who so speke his owyn langwage þat is truthe he schal be chastysed & betyn in his body or in his good þat wo is hym & he schal be tawȝt to lye" (ii.230). For modern readers, the most striking aspect of this passage might well be its vivid portrayal of student vulnerability. As Nicholas Orme, Copeland, and others have noted, corporal punishment was so common in the later Middle Ages that whips and canes almost invariably constitute part of visual representations of schooling.[49] This passage is perhaps made even more evocative by its reference to actual physical contact (not just "smiting," but actual grabbing of the face or ear).

The analogy certainly explains the terror felt by the delinquent student "who kan noȝt his lessoun" described elsewhere in *Jacob's Well*. Within that passage, the *Well* writer implied that Christians should debase themselves before God, in recognition of their sinfulness: his reference to the child did not question the need to learn lessons in the first place. In this discussion, however, the writer places education itself on

---

[49] For discussions of corporal punishment in medieval grammar and elementary schools, see Orme, *English Schools in the Middle Ages*, pp. 123–28; Copeland, "Introduction: Dissenting Critical Practices," *Criticism and Dissent in the Middle Ages*, ed. Rita Copeland (Cambridge: Cambridge University Press, 1996), pp. 6–14; Jody Enders, "Rhetoric, Coercion, and the Memory of Violence," in *Criticism and Dissent*, esp. pp. 36–42; and Ralph Hanna, "School and Scorn: Gender and *Piers Plowman*," *New Medieval Literatures* 3 (1999): 220–23. For its use in medieval song-schools, see Bruce Holsinger, "Pedagogy, Violence, and the Subject of Music: Chaucer's *Prioress' Tale* and the Ideologies of 'Song,'" *New Medieval Literatures* 1 (1997): 157–92.

the side of flattery and deception: people are "taw3t" to tell lies, just as they are instructed in Latin and French. Far from functioning neutrally, then, the physical violence in this passage mirrors the brutality of those who deny or obscure the truth.

Even more important, the *Well* writer makes clear that the student already possesses knowledge—the pupil speaks English, his "owyn langwage." This idea represents a crucial revision of characterizations of scholarly learning within the "gift of knowledge" section of *Jacob's Well*. In the tale depicting the devil and his recommendations, education emerges as a useless distraction from the necessary business of achieving self-knowledge. The John of Damascus story, for its part, presents knowledge both negatively (in the hands of the forger) and positively (when coupled with John's virtue). But the logic of this grammarian simile adds a crucial new dimension to the *Well* writer's analysis of schooling, and to his depiction of lay people in general. Although it disparages education, it posits a positive alternative that goes beyond penitential self-examination. People should seek to speak their "owyn langwage"—the truths they possess before being influenced by worldly considerations. In a work whose major metaphor depicts individual Christians as foul-smelling wells, the recognition of an essential goodness represents a substantial development.

Moreover, because he has stated so emphatically that people of all stations are "taw3t to lye"—indeed, he has stressed that preachers are particularly susceptible to this instruction—the *Well* writer departs from the hierarchies at work in some of his earlier statements. When the writer concludes his discussion by telling his listeners to "putte falsnesse & lesynges owt 3our mowth. & seye truthe" (ii.230), he implies that all people should return to a childlike state—not one of blindness, submissiveness, or ignorance, but of honesty and authenticity.[50] In addition, the *Well* writer argues that his audience should not merely ponder the truth but should take on the authority of speaking it aloud. Despite his disenchantment with the preaching of his peers, he remains committed to outward conversation, as opposed to inner meditation or scholarly dispute.[51]

---

[50] *Mum and the Sothsegger* makes a similar point when it likens truth-tellers to a "barn un-ylerid" who "bablith fourth bustusely" (50), though it does not specifically link the uneducated child's words to a community of English-speakers.

[51] Pecock, for example, privileged academic teaching and disputation over preaching; for analysis of this argument, and his contemporaries' reactions to it, see R. M. Ball, "The Opponents of Bishop Pecock," *Journal of Ecclesiastical History* 48 (1997): 230–62, esp. 230–34.

By suggesting that people should speak out their "owyn langwage," the writer seems to be feeling his way toward a collaborative model for community interaction: not one in which the "lered" instruct the "lewde," but in which people come together in a shared effort to remove themselves from rampant societal dishonesty. This passage's anticlerical statements and association of the vernacular with truth suggest links between his ideas and Wycliffite views. The *Well* writer implies that his own preaching allows the truth to be spoken and heard, and his text involves an effort to communicate with people in their own language. In effect, his text functions as an alternative form of education—one well removed from the violence of actual schools. While he does not include textual study in the model he proposes, he does raise the possibility of lay people's assuming new forms of authority, based on his recognition of their existing interpretive skills and of the need to repair crucial problems within conventional Christian communities.

At the very end of his text, the *Well* writer affirms these ideas even more resoundingly. Having recapitulated the schema of the text as a whole, the writer asserts that those who adhere to Christian principles will enjoy the benefits of truth, charity, and mercy. To illustrate these virtues, he tells of a "peddere in a markett" who has six baskets full of fish to sell (ii.545).[52] He sets three of them, named God's curse, sin, and falseness, out for immediate sale; they are quickly bought up by the rich. Meanwhile, he hides the other three—truth, charity, and mercy—in his stall in an effort to save these more precious baskets for later. Unfortunately, the latter three baskets are stolen while peddler is busy selling the first three. Desperate to sell them to the poor customers at his stall, "þe peddere ran abowtyn to enqueryn after his 3. panyerys of fyshe" (ii.546). Recalling the narrator's pursuit of the truth-teller in *Mum and the Sothsegger*, the fishmonger's journey takes him to every segment of society. He travels to "þe Popys paleys. and . . . þe Paleysis of cardyna-lys, Erschebysschopys & bysschopys," to the households of vicars and secular priests, and on to the abbeys of the monastic orders (ii.546). Everywhere the result is the same: when he asks if they have heard or seen truth, charity, or mercy, the reply comes back that the inhabitants "knewe non swyche" (ii.546). When he reaches the friars, the response is slightly different: "þe frerys seyden þat þei haddyn þe savere of hem.

---

[52] Carruthers edits and briefly discusses this narrative in "'And What Schall Be þe Ende': An Edition of the Final Chapter of *Jacob's Well*," *MÆ* 61 (1992): 289–97.

but it smellyd so strong on hem. þat þey leetyn all 3 panyers truth
charyte and mercy pacyn forth by here gate. but non of hem thre abode
þere ne koom in amongis hem" (ii.547). Turning to the nonclerical
world, he asks everyone from emperors to squires and beyond—
"ryche & pore and . . . alle þe comouns"—but all deny that these baskets are among them (ii.547).

The exemplum remains open-ended: no divine force of aid or retribution intervenes to aid the peddler. Instead, the *Well* writer addresses his
audience directly:

þerwhyle is stolyn awey out of oure welle þe fysche þat is. delyȝt & desyir of
truthe charyte & mercy. þat I drede me sore þowȝ we sekyn þere aftyr in ony
astate of holy cherche or of temporalte. eythir in heyȝ or lowe. poore or ryche
grete or smale. it is wol hard to fyndyn hem. ffor þe fysche of truthe of charyte
and of mercy smellyn so stronge vp on vs. þat we mowe noȝt sufferyn þe sauour
þer of. but puttyn hem awey fro vs. But ȝif I wyste where þat I myȝte fynde
þis fysch of truthe charyte & mercy. I wolde gladlyche byggen þerof. And be
my counseyl enquyreth and aspyeth þerafter. ȝyf ȝe mowe wyte where it is.
byeth þerof. (ii.548)

If truth, charity, and mercy are found, the writer advises in the last lines
of his text, they need to be incorporated into the well (as stonework,
parts of the ladder to God, and so on) so that the well-builder may
partake of the "watyr of grace" (ii.549).

To Carruthers, the narrative is lively and humorous, but it also reflects the writer's "deep-seated pessimism about human nature," attrib-
utable to "long years of hearing confessions."[53] I would argue, however,
that the exemplum directly links examinations of conscience to a larger
societal context. The narrative suggests that people cannot, after all,
simply generate tools and building materials from within the self: they
need to search the world for them. The *Well* writer tells his listeners to
look outward rather than inward, and states very specifically that their
questions will not be resolved by clerical authorities. His invitation to
his listeners—"enquyreth and aspyeth þerafter"—manifests a trust in
his audience: instead of just scrutinizing their own sins, they should
interpret the world for themselves. Although elsewhere he downplays
the connection between belief and book learning, here he suggests that
his listeners should take the world as a kind of text, and should read

[53] Carruthers, "Ende," p. 291.

236

it critically. The fact that such analysis would also involve a sensory activity—one could "follow one's nose" to the fish, as well as knocking on doors—recalls the image and the hand within the John of Damascus exemplum, in that they all involve interpretation and investigation, while remaining outside the textual practices rendered suspect by the Lollards, or the academic sophistries of the friars.

As in his discussion of the English-speaking grammarian, the *Well* writer stops short of advocating a program for change specifically focused on widespread literacy and preaching. Even so, the *Well* writer's willingness to end his concluding narrative with a series of "ȝyfs" suggests that he seeks to teach his audience modes of questioning and analysis, not just pieces of information to be swallowed and internalized. Indeed, the story implies that confident self-assertion is essential to an honest Christian life. The *Well* writer never suggests that the baskets will become fragrant when found, and the friars' refusal to admit them into their community bodes ill for anyone carrying them. In this concluding narrative, as well as in the image of the abuses suffered by the grammarian, the *Well* writer characterizes resilience in response to society's hostility, disdain, and physical violence as an essential component of piety.[54]

Simultaneously hopeless and determined, the *Well* writer's attitude recalls that of Conscience at the end of *Piers Plowman,* who sets out on a truth-seeking quest of his own. *Jacob's Well* of course is no dream vision: the imperatives the *Well* writer sets for himself involve a specific body of knowledge, not the "determined indeterminacy"[55] that so many readers find operating in Langland's text. The list of precepts is finite, as is the time period of his preaching. At the same time, however, he implies that the information he conveys will provide a stimulus for thought and discussion, rather than a conclusion to it. Like *Dives and Pauper,* which builds a vigorous debate between a mendicant and a layman of sophisticated understanding around an exposition of the Ten Commandments, *Jacob's Well* demonstrates that a syllabus can organize instruction without confining it. The *Well* writer acknowledges that his listeners' process of education will extend far beyond the parameters of his own text, or indeed of his own pastoral authority.

[54] The *Well* writer's interest in the social dimension of individual belief leads him to conclusions quite similar to those set forth within the explicitly political *Mum and the Sothsegger.* Even as *Mum* emphasizes the "scorn oþer scathe" suffered by truth-tellers (ranging from sorrow to imprisonment or even death), it also affirms that "trouthe is so tough" that it will never be completely eliminated from the earth (165–92).

[55] Somerset, *Clerical Discourse and Lay Audience,* p. 23.

Colloquium: Administrative Perspectives on Chaucer Studies

The State of Medieval Studies:

A Tale of Two Universities

Martin Camargo
University of Illinois

MY ADMINISTRATIVE EXPERIENCES as department chair may not have provided me with any unique insights into the current state of medieval studies. If anything, the many tasks that go into leading a large department have absorbed so much of my attention that I almost certainly have spent less time reflecting on the specific concerns facing medievalists during my four years as an administrator than during any comparable period of my twenty-six-year career as a practicing medievalist. Where I hope I might have something unique to contribute is in my experience as a medievalist who has both thought about and experienced the state of medieval studies at two different universities. Indeed, my perspective on those experiences may have been colored more than I realize by my having served as chair of English at each of those universities.

Two years ago I made the most important and in some ways the most difficult decision of my professional career when I left my position as Professor and Chair of English at the University of Missouri at Columbia, where I had spent the previous twenty-three years, to become Professor and Head of English at the University of Illinois at Urbana-Champaign. I had great affection for my colleagues at Missouri, who had just elected me to a second three-year term as department chair by a unanimous vote, and considerable loyalty to the institution that had fostered my development as a scholar and teacher of medieval literature. Nonetheless, I decided to accept the offer from Illinois for a variety of reasons, some of them obvious—the opportunity to lead a nationally ranked department, the superb research library, a significantly higher salary—others less so. As the university where I had done my doctoral work, Illinois also had claims to my loyalty and affection, but not least among my reasons for moving were the present state and future prospects of medieval studies at the two institutions.

When I think of the present state of Chaucer studies or, as I prefer to do, of medieval studies more broadly, I do so not only from the perspective of both scholar-teacher and administrator but also, more fundamentally, in the context of the two institutions where I have spent most of my professional life. At first glance, the University of Missouri at Columbia and the University of Illinois at Urbana-Champaign have much in common. Both are research-intensive, land-grant universities. They are the flagship campuses of multicampus, public-university systems in contiguous states in the center of the country. Each is located in a small urban area surrounded by farmland and several hours' drive from the major metropolitan areas that provide a majority of its undergraduate students. Each has struggled to compensate for declining state contributions as a share of its total operating budget, declines that have shifted from steady to precipitous in recent years. Nonetheless, despite these and other similarities, the position of medieval studies at Missouri is in many respects weaker now than it was when I first arrived there twenty-six years ago, while at Illinois it has become stronger over the same period. At least some of the causes of those contrasting trajectories illustrate the threats and opportunities that currently face medieval studies at all public research universities.

The greatest threat to the future of medieval studies is the loss of tenure-track faculty positions, usually through the nonreplacement of a retired or departing faculty member. Such losses may be strictly related to budget constraints. Medievalist positions cut for budgetary reasons are often regarded as temporary losses. The assumption is that, when and if the budget situation improves, the vacancy will be filled, presumably with another medievalist, though probably at a lower rank and hence a lower salary. While losses of this sort sometimes prove in practice to be permanent, they are not the chief threat to faculty strength in medieval studies. More common, at least in my experience in large research universities, are permanent losses due to reclassification of vacant positions. In other words, departments increasingly choose to replace departing medievalists with specialists in something other than medieval studies.

Such decisions are sometimes made in response to directives from the higher administration. At Missouri, for example, a former chancellor required each academic department to identify its "niche," that is, the area in which it would stake its claim to national preeminence, before he would authorize resources for new hires. In responding to that directive, departments had to show how "replacement" hires as well as new hires would strengthen that niche. Subfields that could not be related directly to the niche would be allowed to languish and, if necessary, to disappear through attrition. In other words, niche planning was yet another way to put a positive spin on a chronic shortage of resources that made strength across the board impossible to achieve. As many a jaded faculty member observed, the new road to "excellence" promised to leave most of a department's academic programs stranded in mediocrity or worse.

Just as often, the pressure to reduce or even eliminate traditional specializations comes from within a department in response to developments within the discipline. In language and literature departments, the erosion of the traditional canon has reduced the obligation to cover the historical periods, while the emergence of new focuses of interest has created different curricular needs. The simultaneous decline in linguistics, philology, and close reading as components of both undergraduate and graduate training has further weakened the position of medieval literature and other specializations that have traditionally been associated with them. With no immediate prospects of increasing the overall number of faculty, an English department might face a choice between maintaining its complement of medievalists and using the retirement of its Chaucerian or—still more likely—its Anglo-Saxonist as an opportunity to add a specialist in Postcolonial or Queer Theory or in African American, Asian American, Latino, or Native American literature.

If medieval studies is disproportionately vulnerable to such attrition by disciplinary redefinition, that is only in part because the newest developments in literary studies disproportionately favor the most recent historical periods. I have heard tales of English departments in which the critical theorists directly targeted the medievalists in their efforts to modernize the curriculum. In my own experience, however, I have found that the place of medieval studies in the English curriculum is called into question far less frequently than that of more career-oriented subfields, such as business and technical writing. In most English departments at large research universities, the great majority of the faculty consider themselves specialists in some area of English or American literature and thus feel a greater affinity for a Chaucerian than for, say, a composition specialist, even one who is working on material that is chronologically closer to the subject of their own research and teaching.

When a department cuts medieval studies to make way for other, newer areas of study, the key factor often turns out to be as banal as the number of medievalists in the department. By contrast with gunnery practice, in academic reallocations the smaller the target, the easier it is to hit. If a department's only medievalist leaves, especially at a time of program reevaluation and stagnant resources, there is less chance that the arguments for hiring another medievalist will be made (and heard) than if another medievalist is already there to make them. When I arrived in Columbia twenty-six years ago, the University of Missouri had one medievalist each in French, German, Italian, and Spanish. Over the years, efforts were made to maintain those numbers: when the medievalist in German took a position elsewhere, she was replaced by a Renaissance specialist who also taught medieval language and literature; when the Hispanist retired, he was replaced by another medievalist; when the Italianist resigned, she was replaced by a nonmedievalist, but when a second position in Italian was created, the first person hired to fill it was a medievalist. With the advent of niche-planning, however, the solitary medievalists in the foreign-language departments provided irresistible targets of opportunity. Within the space of a few years, the medievalist in Italian took a position elsewhere, the one in German died unexpectedly, and the one in French retired: none was replaced by another medievalist. During that same time span, the History department, which already had two medievalists, was able to add a third, and though not without debate, the English department recently replaced a retired medievalist and me, to maintain its long-standing complement of three medievalists. In neither of these larger departments was medieval studies part of a niche, but in both the number of medievalists was sufficient to preserve the succession or even stimulate growth.

One way of creating a larger target is to forge links across departments. This strategy has always made sense for medieval studies, a field in which the best scholarship is inherently interdisciplinary. It makes even more sense in the current climate, in which "interdisciplinarity" has become a shibboleth among higher-education administrators. As medievalists, we are well positioned to benefit when scarce resources are tied to interdisciplinary initiatives, as they increasingly are, and we don't even have to stretch the truth in order to get our share.

Before interdisciplinarity had become so fashionable, indeed before I had joined the profession, the University of Missouri at Columbia had recognized and institutionalized the authentic interdisciplinarity of medieval studies by establishing a graduate concentration in Medieval and Renaissance Studies. By combining forces, the faculty in the two areas were able to muster substantial numbers—around twenty, before attrition in both areas reduced the total to the present fifteen—but the goals and the resources were always rather modest. A committee, with an annual budget of $600, met as needed to conduct business that consisted of approving individual programs of study for the doctoral minor in Medieval or Renaissance Studies, planning an annual sponsored lecture by a visiting scholar, awarding one or two small grants to support graduate students traveling to professional conferences, and encouraging faculty to consider teaching the interdisciplinary seminar that remained on the books but was rarely offered. Except for the annual lecture, the committee's activities probably had less impact on interdisciplinary collaboration than the graduate school's requirement that one member of every doctoral committee come from outside the candidate's major department. It was not surprising when even the modest annual budget fell victim to the recent cuts. What is true within departments is true of interdisciplinary programs: smaller targets are easiest to hit.

Although created more recently than the one at Missouri, the Program in Medieval Studies at the University of Illinois has been more successful in weathering the current fiscal crisis and benefiting the constituent departments. To an important degree, this must be because medieval studies was already a significant presence on the Urbana-Champaign campus before the formal program was created. With more than twenty medievalists on the faculty, a convincing case could be made for providing additional resources to develop an existing strength. Without the dean's strong support for humanities and for interdisciplinary work, the resources would never have materialized, and the arrival of a new chancellor, whose commitment to the arts and humanities was equally strong, shielded the new program from the round of severe budget cuts that began at the end of its first year of existence. The ambitious agenda and commitment of resources made it possible in turn to attract a major scholar to serve as the first director, and his enthusiasm and creativity have helped build momentum. One clear sign of that momentum was the decision to shift the focus of the *Journal of English and Germanic Philology* exclusively to medieval studies. Another is the fact that Illinois has hired four medievalists in the past two years, three of them at the full-professor rank and all of them to fill new positions. The English department now has more medievalists (four) than it did when I began my graduate studies there in 1972, even though faculty strength as a whole has declined by about a third since then.

The point of my study in contrasts is not simply that bigger is better. Even when one is talking exclusively about the financial bottom line, size is not in itself sufficient guarantee of continued prosperity. State appropriations for the University of Missouri have increased this year (2003–04), after two years of cuts, while those for the University of Illinois have been cut for the third year in a row. At the same time, the chancellor, whose support has been so crucial to the flourishing of the humanities at Illinois, has departed for the presidency of another university and the original director of the Program in Medieval Studies has relinquished his administrative position after three years in order to pursue his own research. It may well be that medieval studies at Missouri will experience an upswing in the next few years, while medieval studies at Illinois will grow more slowly or even stabilize at its present level until the funding picture brightens.

Bigger is definitely not better when it comes to balancing one's contributions as a teacher and scholar of medieval literature with one's contributions as an administrator. At Missouri, where I was chair of a somewhat smaller and significantly less complex department, I taught twice as much as I do at Illinois but still had considerably more time available for conducting research. Even at Missouri, I had to make adjustments in my research program: I suspended work on an argument-driven historical analysis and shifted to a critical edition and translation of a medieval rhetorical treatise. That was a perfect project for the kind of research opportunities my schedule provided, which were fairly frequent but unpredictable and highly variable in length. During my first two years as department chair, I was able to make steady progress on the edition, devoting a certain amount of time to it nearly every week. If that progress slowed during my third year, that was due to unforeseen, extra demands on my time and not to the match between my normal administrative schedule and the requirements of the project. At Illinois, the gaps in my schedule during which I can do research are fewer and more widely separated but seem to last longer. They favor smaller, more discrete projects with definite deadlines rather than the easily picked-up and put-down sort with open deadlines that best fit my schedule at Missouri. Accordingly, most of the scholarship I have done since becoming head at Illinois has taken the form of conference papers and solicited articles like this one. To survive as a scholar-administrator in my current position, I have had to become more of a hare than a tortoise. Perhaps as I grow more familiar with the routines of my new job, I will be able to return to working on the edition and translation. The more complicated book will have to wait until my next sabbatical.

What I hope to have shown so far is that generalizations about the state of Chaucer studies or the state of medieval studies can be difficult to substantiate, whether one comes to them from the perspective of an administrator, a scholar, a teacher, or, as I do, all three. I won't go so far as to say that the "corporatization" of the university poses no threat to medieval studies, though I will say that it does not pose a special threat. As medievalists, we face the same challenges from that quarter as those who teach in other areas of the humanities. Increased reliance on the cheap labor provided by adjunct faculty, for example, jeopardizes the future of all doctoral candidates in English, not just or even especially those whose interest happens to be in Chaucer. If some developments in literary studies marginalize our subject matter as excessively esoteric or insufficiently diverse, others, such as the valorizing of interdisciplinarity and the equally pronounced swing from theory to history, work very much in our favor. One could even argue that there is a bias in favor of medieval studies among members of grant-review panels, judging from the disproportionately high rate of success applications in the area seem to enjoy.

As the English major is made more consumer-friendly, through the reduction or even the elimination of historical distribution requirements, some are concerned that decreased enrollment in courses on medieval literature will endanger the future of the field. My own experience at Missouri and Illinois suggests that undergraduate demand for such courses persists despite a more laissez-faire model for the major, though that demand frequently is driven more by the cultural products of medievalism—such as Tolkien's *Lord of the Rings*—than by those of the Middle Ages. Many of us have responded to this state of affairs by developing courses that incorporate or even focus on pseudo-medieval texts and films on medieval topics. Such products of popular culture of course may be studied in their own right, even as we use them to draw students into classes where we can create a taste for the "real thing." Because of the decreasing emphasis on language study in the English major, however, the "real thing" is taught increasingly in translation. Students continue to find Chaucer compelling as a storyteller and social commentator, but I wonder how much longer I can go on teaching him as a poet, while pretending that even the very best of my students are regularly reading his works in the original Middle English.

The day may come—perhaps it already has—when Chaucer, like *Beowulf,* is usually taught to undergraduates in modern English translation and only to graduate students in the original language. Such a development, while regrettable, can at least be justified on practical grounds as one way of increasing the number of undergraduate students who will be exposed to medieval literature in some form. Harder to justify, though not to explain, is a growing tendency in some graduate programs to produce Middle English specialists who have no training in Old English. With all the emphasis on interdisciplinarity and theoretical sophistication, it is easy to see how study of the earlier stage in the language might come to be regarded as optional: there is only so much space in one's program of study, after all. Since I am supposed to offer an administrator's perspective, I'll skip the intellectual arguments to be made against this attitude and confine myself to mentioning two practical disadvantages of acting on it. The long-standing assumption that any medievalist fresh from graduate school can step right into teaching courses on the history of the English language is predicated on a requirement that all medievalists-in-training study both Old and Middle English. Medievalists who have not received such training are at a disadvantage in the job market, especially when competing for positions at smaller schools that need to replace the full range of teaching done by their retired medievalist. If Old English is studied only by future Anglo-Saxonists, moreover, Anglo-Saxonists become that much more susceptible to decline through attrition. If medievalists as a group often present a small target, their chances of survival diminish still further if they are subdivided into two distinct groups. The Anglo-Saxonists may be the first to go, but once they are gone, the Chaucerians have fewer allies to secure their positions.

Whatever else they may be, successful administrators are pragmatic and persistent. In this sense, to ensure a bright future for medieval studies medievalists would do well to act more like administrators. We need to think pragmatically when making the case for resources, especially for recruiting new faculty, when choosing which job candidates to hire, and in training the graduate students who will make up the next generation of medievalists. Besides making connections with each other across disciplines, we need to find ways of connecting with other members of our own departments, through our research and our teaching. When hiring new colleagues, we need to seek out not only outstanding scholars but also innovative teachers who will attract undergraduate students to courses on medieval literature. We need to model such teaching for our own graduate students, even as we encourage them to develop the expertise in areas other than medieval literature—whether philology and historical linguistics, early modern literature, gender studies, rhetoric, or film studies—that will maximize their potential contributions to the department that will hire them. In all these activities we must be open to compromises that will preserve the long-term health of medieval studies without seriously weakening its integrity. At the same time, we need to be persistent in making the case for the inherent value and disciplinary centrality of medieval literature, by making certain that we are represented on the various committees and task forces that decide the shape of the curriculum, the mix of graduate students admitted, and the priorities in hiring new faculty. Such tireless advocacy is essential to the preservation of medieval studies but carries certain risks for the advocate: if you are sufficiently effective at it, you just might end up an administrator yourself.

Searching for a Medievalist:

Some (Generally Positive) News About the State of Chaucer Studies

Sylvia Tomasch
Hunter College, City University of New York

W HEN HE SENT HIS invitation to contribute to this colloquium, Frank Grady, the editor of *Studies in the Age of Chaucer*, said he
was trying "to cast a wide net and include people working in schools
that are rich and poor, large and small, public and private, North American and British."[1] Writing as the chair of a poor, large, public, North
American English department—at Hunter College of the City University of New York—I will, nonetheless, *not* be here bewailing what is
often seen as a crisis in higher education (with a concomitant crisis in
medieval studies). While not denying for a moment that there is much
to bewail—including, as Professor Grady writes, "the apparently inexo-
rable spread of business-oriented, bottom-line corporate models designed to rationalize the operation of colleges and universities"—the
narrow view from this chair's chair is somewhat, and perhaps surprising,
different.

In fact, for a medievalist teaching in and chairing a large, diverse
department with a thriving undergraduate major and a healthy M.A.
program, rumors of the demise of medieval studies (not to mention
Chaucer studies, or the ideals of the university) seem greatly exaggerated. Increasingly corporatized and financially constrained as we are,
and as heavily burdened as our mostly first-generation college students
are, our faculty is nonetheless faced with a continual demand for literature, creative writing, and linguistics courses, which we are often hard

I wish to thank Steven Kruger and the Medieval Club of New York for inviting me
to present my initial findings as part of a panel on "The Future of Medieval Studies". I
also thank my colleague, Nico Israel, for his helpful comments on a draft of this essay.
[1] Frank Grady, letter of September 25, 2003.

put to satisfy. It may well be that my own department and school are anomalous, yet here, at least, medieval studies, including Chaucer studies, is not faring badly at all.[2] With more than 1,300 English majors, we cannot keep up with the demand for all our upper-level courses, including multiple sections of Chaucer and medieval literature every semester, even with the help that is on the way in the form of a new medievalist.

Of course, I am writing as someone delighted and relieved to have successfully completed a search for a medievalist—a *second* medievalist, that is—after having spent more than a dozen years as the one-and-only. For most of the hundred or so years of its existence, our English department traditionally had three medievalists, but by 1992 the state of medieval studies at Hunter was so reduced that my predecessor as chair was forced to draw upon what I call "the medieval mystique" (which says that medieval studies is so arcane that only specialists can understand it, let alone teach it) in order to save the last position. Thankfully for me, he was able to keep the line and make the hire. In contrast, in 2003 I did not have to draw upon the mystique to make that argument or, for that matter, make much of an argument at all. The executive committee of my department recognized the need, and my dean (an anthropologist) was already well aware of the excitement and the quality of the work being undertaken in medieval studies.

To the question of what occurred in the eleven intervening years to bring about a situation in which hiring a medievalist now made good sense to everyone, I can only offer some speculations. While some of these conditions are likely specific to CUNY, I would expect that similar factors prevail at other academic institutions, both public and private, large and small. At CUNY, first, the removal of virtually all remediation to the community colleges opened space at the senior colleges for the development of more specialized and more academically advanced programs. Second, in the last seven years, considerable CUNY-wide hiring has taken place, in part to compensate for years of retrenchments. In my own department during this period, we have hired twelve new

---

[2] Hunter College is one of the eighteen units of the loose confederation of senior and community colleges and professional schools known as the City University of New York. Hunter is one of the most senior of the senior colleges, along with City, Brooklyn, and Queens colleges, having been founded in 1870 as a normal school for women. English is the largest department at Hunter, with more than 1,300 undergraduate majors, and 38 full-time and 100 or so part-time faculty.

faculty members, whose presence and example of vital scholarship have been wonderfully revitalizing. Third, within the last three years, we have been joined at Hunter by a completely new set of administrators. Our new president, new provost, new dean, et al., have shown their support—albeit within very real budgetary constraints—for what they understand to be the most innovative and promising fields of scholarship. They recognize medieval studies as one of these fields.[3] (While valuing their support, I also wonder if it doesn't derive, at least in part, from other aspects of the medieval mystique that perceives medieval studies to be an historically based, traditional discipline on the "hard" end of the spectrum of the humanities, in contrast to what are seen as suspiciously undisciplined fields like cultural studies). Fourth, these changes at Hunter and in CUNY are undoubtedly related to wider cultural swings that periodically shift the fortunes of the Middle Ages.[4] For medievalism (if not always medieval studies), the present shift has been a boon, so that in popular culture the *Star Wars*, *Lord of the Rings*, and *Harry Potter* romances are in full swing, while Chaucer himself gets naked in the movies.[5]

As I review the results of the search that resulted from all of these

[3] In addition to the position in English, our Philosophy and Classics departments also successfully searched for a medievalist as part of a CUNY hiring cluster in Hebrew/Arabic/Spanish medieval culture.

[4] It is outside the scope of this essay to speculate as to the causes of such pendulum swings, but Gerald Graff, in *Professing Literature: An Institutional History* (Chicago: University of Chicago Press, 1987), and David R. Shumway, in *Creating American Civilization: A Genealogy of American Literature as an Academic Discipline* (Minneapolis: University of Minnesota Press, 1994), have delineated the growth of English departments and American universities, within which we can see the rise and fall of medieval studies. Along with Sealy Gilles, I discuss Chaucer's place in the newly professionalized research universities in "Professionalizing Chaucer: John Matthews Manly, Edith Rickert, and the *Canterbury Tales* as Cultural Capital," in *Reading Medieval Culture: Essays in Honor of Robert W. Hanning on His 65th Birthday*, ed. Robert M. Stein and Sandra Pierson Prior (University of Notre Dame Press, forthcoming). For the long view of Chaucer's place in the wider culture, see Thomas A. Prendergast, *Chaucer's Dead Body: From Corpse to Corpus* (New York: Routledge, 2004); Prendergast and Barbara Kline, eds., *Rewriting Chaucer: Culture, Authority, and the Idea of the Authentic Text, 1400–1602* (Columbus: Ohio State University Press, 1999); and Lee Patterson, *Negotiating the Past: The Historical Understanding of Medieval Literature* (Madison: University of Wisconsin Press, 1987).

[5] As purposely anachronistic as the 2003 film *A Knight's Tale* is, its most interesting and unusual feature is the character Geoffrey Chaucer, who loses his clothes gambling but introduces himself as the author of *The Book of the Duchess*: all of which adds up to an unexpectedly fresh portrait of a medieval artist. For another perspective on this film, within an extended consideration of modern uses of the Middle Ages, see Angela Jane Weisl, *The Persistence of Medievalism: Narrative Adventures in Contemporary Culture* (New York: Palgrave, 2003).

factors, it seems that something positive is happening in more places than just Hunter College. In fact, 2003 was a banner year for medieval literature positions, with more than thirty positions posted in the October 2003 MLA Job List alone, including many at the top schools in the country. Initially, we were concerned that highly credentialed candidates might pass up the opportunity to apply for our position, for like most institutions we offer both advantages and disadvantages, including a great location *and* a high cost of living, immense research opportunities *and* an inadequate library, wonderfully diverse students *and* pedagogical challenges. As it turned out, our ad—which read in part: "Fields of specialization should include some combination of the following: medieval cultural or ethnic studies, Middle English, Anglo-Saxon, or Anglo-Norman literature, and Chaucer"—attracted more than 150 applications, most of them from extremely well-qualified candidates with strong publication and teaching records. About one-third were from graduate students just finishing their degrees, half from those who had completed their degrees within three years of applying, with the remaining one-sixth coming from applicants already in tenure-track (or even tenured) positions. An informal survey of other chairs in departments hiring medievalists suggests that their applicants were similar in terms of types and backgrounds; in terms of numbers, we seem to have been near the upper end of the pool. These informal conversations also led me to believe that there was relatively little overlap in departmental short lists, either at the MLA or the campus interview stage—a fact that may be heartening to job seekers, as it suggests that departments are very individual in terms of their own needs and expectations and therefore will seek to hire candidates of varied accomplishments and backgrounds.

The scholarly interests of the 150 (plus) job candidates, as stated in their initial letters of application, are listed in each of the four tables below, according to authors, texts, topics, and approaches.[6] These counts are, in many instances, duplicative or omissive. For example, if an applicant mentioned Chaucer *and* the *Canterbury Tales and* a specific tale *and* a period *and* a theoretical approach, each item would show up separately, in different categories. (Thus, while Chaucer was cited at least 43 times, individual Chaucerian texts were cited more than 64

---

[6] Applicants' privacy has been maintained by excluding all personally identifying characteristics.

times; since these tables are meant to provide an overview rather than serve as a rigorous study, no attempt has been made to reconcile such differences.) In addition, each table concludes with a list of other items mentioned only once; these are examples only and not meant to constitute a definitive list.

Tables 1 and 2 show the distribution of authors and texts specified by applicants in their initial letters of inquiry.

From Tables 1 and 2, it appears that Chaucer studies remains quite healthy, as Chaucer and his works are cited far more frequently than any other author or text. Of course it is possible that this dominance is an artificial consequence of our own advertisement. By presenting a long list of possible fields of expertise, we meant to indicate that while we were not looking primarily for a Chaucerian, we were, like many other departments, I suspect, seeking someone prepared to teach, periodically at least, the *Canterbury Tales*. Most applicants seemed to have inferred this, and they almost universally mentioned Chaucer as among their

Table 1. Named Authors

Chaucer	43
Langland	13
Kempe	10
Gower	8
Julian of Norwich	7
Pearl-poet	6
Bede	4
Hoccleve	4
Malory	4
Henryson	3
Lydgate	3
Aelfric	2
Boccaccio	2
Caxton	2
Cynewulf	2
Geoffrey of Monmouth	2
Shakespeare	2
Wace	2

Authors/writers mentioned only once include: Alfred, Arundel, Arnaut Daniel, Dante, Gildas, Hadewich, Hilton, Gervase of Tilbury, Isidore of Seville, John of Howden, Love, Mannyng, Marie de France, John Pecham, Petrarch, Spenser, Trevisa, Walter of Wimborne, William of Rubruck, Wulfstan, and Wyclif.

Table 2. Named Texts

Canterbury Tales (as a general category)	11
"Wife of Bath's Prologue" and/or "Tale"	8
"Clerk's Tale"	5
"Knight's Tale"	3
"Physician's Tale"	3
"Franklin's Tale"	2
"Merchant's Tale"	2
"Second Nun's Tale"	2
Troilus and Criseyde	8
Book of the Duchess	4
Legend of Good Women	3
House of Fame	2

Chaucerian texts mentioned only once include: *Parliament of Fowls,* "Man of Law's Tale," "Miller's Tale," "Monk's Tale," "Pardoner's Tale," "Prioress's Tale," "Reeve's Tale," "Shipman's Tale," and "Summoner's Tale."

Beowulf	8
Mandeville's Travels	3
Battle of Maldon	2
Bayeux Tapestry	2
Exodus	2
Genesis B	2

Texts mentioned only once include: *Ancrene Wisse, Andreas, Battle of Brunanburh, Castle of Perseverance, Chanson de Roland, Christ I* and *II, Cursor Mundi, Deor, Dream of the Rood, Floire and Blancheflor, Maxims I, The Owl and the Nightingale, Siege of Jerusalem, Sir Orfeo, Solomon and Saturn, Wanderer, Widsith, William of Palerne, Wonders of the East.*

primary teaching interests (these counts are not included here). In terms of their research, the works of Chaucer were also mentioned by the largest number of applicants, but often only as a corollary, rather than the main, field of scholarly interest.

It is also possible that the results have little to do with our particular ad and more with candidates' pragmatism, that is, with knowing what gets taught in English departments and considering how they therefore needed to present themselves. And of course it is entirely possible that Chaucer is simply what most literary medievalists do—at least those applying for jobs in English departments—so the counts may in fact accurately reflect applicants' true interests. Whatever the explanation for the predominance of Chaucer as a field of study, we can also note that more than fifty other authors and texts, from Alfred to Wace and from *Ancrene Wisse* to *Wonders of the East*, were cited as of primary scholarly interest. Such diversity suggests that whatever the state of Chaucer studies, medieval literary studies as a whole is a burgeoning field.

Table 3 shows the range of topics specified by the applicants; these necessarily overlap with the items in Tables 1 and 2. For example, someone interested in Chaucer might *also* express an interest in Middle English culture *and* orientalism *and* cartography *and* drama.

The results in Table 3 were somewhat surprising: given the dominant interest in Chaucer, we would expect larger numbers of applicants to cite Middle English literature, language, and culture as a discrete item. In contrast, Anglo-Saxon literature, language, and culture is cited much more frequently, suggesting that an interest in Anglo-Saxon studies remains quite strong, with a wide range of texts, from the literary to the religious, being subject to analysis and interpretation. (It is also possible merely that it remains an important part of the graduate education of certain doctoral institutions.) Especially among Anglo-Saxonists, an interest in the history of the English language and philology also remains vigorous.

The results also suggest that fifteenth-century studies is a growing field, especially in such related topic clusters as printing and print culture, manuscripts and scribal culture, and textuality, hypertextuality, e-texts, and editing. Even so, only five applicants were actually editing texts, though many more were interested in theories and histories of editing practices. These concerns were also related to a growing sense of the importance of text and image and visual culture, seen in such topics as crosses and such texts as maps and tapestries. These interests also indicated an expanded concern with material culture, for example, clothing and fashion, and broadened definitions of textuality.

One of the strongest clusters of interest connects cartography, space, and travel writing, colonialism, nationalism, and national identity, orientalism and postcolonial theory, and such specific topics as Prester John and Wales. Also integral to this cluster was an interest in race, otherness, and ethnicity, Jews, Muslims, monsters and monstrosity, Africans, cannibals, and werewolves. In addition, East-West relations were often (though far from universally) evinced in discussions of romances and other chivalric texts as well as crusade and pilgrimage narratives.

A specific interest in women (though only one applicant chose to characterize her work with the telling phrase "feminist") has been supplemented—if not yet entirely supplanted—by the popularity of gen-

Table 3. Topics

Anglo-Saxon literature/language/culture	24
fifteenth-century literature/culture	16
Middle English literature/language/culture	8
Anglo-Norman literature/culture	5

Literary cultures mentioned only once include: Cymro-Latin, Greco-Byzantine, Hebrew, and Norse.

mysticism/mystical literature/female mysticism	12
romances (courtly/crusade)/chivalric (Arthurian) literature	12
history of the English language/philology	11
manuscript/scribal culture	10
reading (esp. devotional)	10
cartography/space/travel writing	8
colonialism/nationalism/national identity	7
crosses (Anglo-Saxon, Irish, late medieval, stone)	7
drama	7
race/otherness/ethnicity	7
chronicles/histories/historiography	6
medieval use of pagan culture/Latin antiquity	6
printing/print culture	4
Jews/Judaism/anti-Semitism	5
text and image/visual culture	5
hagiography/sainthood	4
medievalism	4
Muslims	4
courtly culture	3
devotional literature/religious writing	3
dream poems	3
love/courtly love	3
chess	2
clothing/fashion	2
East-West relations	2
monsters/monstrosity	2
pedagogy	2
politics	2
vernacularity	2

Topics mentioned only once include: Africans, blood, canon formation, cannibalism, cosmology, crusades, death, the devil, fashion, Germanic afterlife, incarnational poetics, infancy narratives, lay piety, material culture, masculinity, memory systems, patronage, penitential literature, pilgrimage literature, popular religion, prayer, Prester John, poverty, preaching, scholasticism, Troy, Wales, and werewolves.

der, sexuality, and homosexuality studies, with masculinity and queer studies mentioned as well. Research on mysticism, particularly female mysticism and devotional practices, remains strong and was often related to a more traditional interest in devotional literature and religious writing, as well as hagiography and sainthood.

Despite their specifying particular topics, most applicants did not specify a theoretical approach. As Table 4 shows, fewer than 60 of the more than 150 writers presented themselves in this fashion. (While on occasion it might have been possible to derive specific approaches from applicants' descriptions of their scholarly interests, I did not attempt to do so.)

There are at least two possible explanations for the low numbers in Table 4. First, theoretical interests are by now so completely integrated into medieval literary studies that it simply does not occur to most applicants to specify an approach. Second, applicants' methodologies are, for the most part, so eclectic that having to identify just one or even two simply makes no sense to them. Rather, in their letters job candidates typically borrowed ideas and terminology from a multiplicity of theoretical schools, without stopping to name them. Thus, in this sample at least, "post-theory" is manifesting itself not in ignorance or resistance but in fully integrated acceptance. I can only conclude that in this respect medieval literary studies has at long last come of age.

If this sample reveals to us, at least partly, the current state of Chaucer studies, what can it tell us about the future? One prediction I would venture is that, for the near future at least, Chaucer studies will remain politically tinged. For instance, an interest in gender studies will likely remain strong, with masculinity and queer studies utilized increasingly often. Theories of the body and embodiment will also probably continue

Table 4. Approaches

gender/sexuality/homosexuality/masculinity/queer studies	15
textuality/hypertextuality/e-texts/editing	14
women/feminism	10
critical theory	5
philology	5
orientalism/postcolonial theory	4
psychoanalytic theory/Lacan	2

Approaches mentioned only once include: reception theory, and rhetoric and poetics.

to grow, as seen in the current interest in blood, infancy narratives, incarnational poetics, lay piety, and popular religion—but as these relate to the politics of identity (as in the race, cartography, and colonialism clusters) rather than to traditional hagiography. The lack of interest in the lyric (an unfortunate lack, in my view) will also likely continue—but only until more scholars notice that it has as much potential for politicized analysis as do the more obvious forms of chronicle, sermon, and romance. Yet until that happens, certain traditional medieval literary topics, such as courtly love, will not be of major concern.[7]

At the same time, there is one way in which this sample does not reflect the future, which is already upon us. While medievalism is of some interest to these job applicants, only one or two of the most advanced candidates are writing the kinds of institutional or personal histories (particularly of early female medievalists) that are increasingly being published by scholars in the field. It could be that graduate students have not yet absorbed this interest from their mentors and dissertation directors, or it could be that newly minted medievalists are simply not yet ready to review the profession's own history.

Obviously, these tables cannot tell us everything we would like to know about the state of Chaucer studies. They do not tell us how many applicants got jobs or, if they were successful, what kind of jobs. They do not tell us if the successful applicants will ever get a chance to teach their interests at their new institutions or how their interests will change during their careers. They do not tell us how many already with jobs were seeking to make lateral moves because of the parlous state of Chaucer or medieval studies at their home institutions. They do not tell us what kinds of resistance to Chaucer or other medieval subjects exist at any institutions or how resistance operates or what we can do to overcome it. They do not tell us which administrations, which departments, or which colleagues support medieval studies and which place little value on such work. And they do not tell us why some topics suddenly seem so powerful and others so old-fashioned and extraneous.

Most importantly, perhaps, this sample does not, can not, tell us which of these applicants will become the leaders of the field, making the future from this healthy, if sometimes embattled, present. It does

---

[7] Colleagues inform me that in other academic fields "love is back"—and, indeed, a formal discipline is already being codified; see, for instance, the review article by Virginia L. Blum, "Love Studies: Or, Liberating Love," *American Literary History* 17.2 (2005):335–48. I look forward to its manifestation in Chaucer studies.

not tell us who will bring new and unexpected topics and approaches to bear on these, and still other, authors and texts, thereby enlightening us all. But precisely because of what it cannot reveal, it also lets us know this: that despite the many resistances and drawbacks, the study of medieval literature is not only alive but kicking. A vigorous, though only partially foreseeable, next stage in the discipline is contained in the work of these applicants. And from what I see, from the perhaps somewhat skewed perspective of the chairship of a poor, large, public, North American and rather special English department, the future of Chaucer studies is in very good hands.

Chaucer and Medieval Studies in Canterbury

Peter Brown
University of Kent

CANTERBURY IS a natural home for Chaucer studies. Ever since the Board (now School) of English was founded at the University of Kent in 1965, undergraduates in their second and final years have had access both to a core, or survey, module that includes the *Canterbury Tales* (currently Medieval and Tudor Literature) and to a more specialized option focusing on particular aspects of Chaucer's works (e.g., *Troilus and Criseyde* and its cultural contexts). Chaucer has also featured in a first-year module, Explorations in Reading, which ran from *The Pardoner's Tale* to *Waiting for Godot* (or from Becket to Beckett). It follows that the department has always maintained a post for a medievalist (preferably one with broad sympathies), while other academic staff with different but related specialties have been prepared to make common cause. One example is a highly successful first-year module, Early Drama (from the liturgy to *Dr. Faustus*), which has run for many years Most of the texts have a Canterbury connection, and the module (current enrollment 118) is available to all students of English but is not compulsory. It challenges students' preconceptions about literature and dramatic representation, introduces them to key images and ideas in biblical mythography, and allows them to undertake a practical project. The end of the spring term sees a veritable mini-festival of medieval and early modern plays performed on campus and in the city. If students are at first discombobulated by the extent to which they are encountering a Christian culture (an early guided tour of the cathedral as theatrical space is a baptism of fire), the majority rise to the challenge and end as apologists for the literature of the period. Whatever their high school background (where the teaching of Chaucer, let alone of other medieval literature, is in decline), many students of English do come to the University of Kent at Canterbury with the reasonable expectation that Chaucer, and medieval literature more generally, will be on the agenda.

However, this contribution to the colloquium is not primarily about undergraduate studies as organized by individual departments, but about cross-departmental postgraduate studies; and not just about Chaucer, but about medieval (and adjacent) studies. Specifically, it is about a recent crisis that engulfed the Canterbury Centre for Medieval & Tudor Studies. Although the issues raised are not Chaucer-specific, they are relevant insofar as the teaching of Chaucer at the postgraduate level frequently takes place within the broader context of a medieval studies program. The issues concern interdisciplinarity, collegiality, the place of medieval (and Chaucer) studies in the curriculum, the impact of government and University funding policies, and the emphasis placed on departmental research ratings and teaching quality assessments as modes of evaluating the worth of staff.

Just as the enthusiasm generated in a first-year medieval module generates good recruitment into second- and final-year core and special modules in medieval literature, so well-received undergraduate modules in turn generate a thirst for postgraduate study in the same area. Colleagues in History at Kent, teaching a similar undergraduate program structure, and with the added benefit of more staff in the medieval and early modern periods, had experienced similar demands. So it seemed appropriate to join forces and mount an M.A. in Medieval and Tudor Studies, drawing on the resources of both disciplines, and with additional input from Drama and French. The M.A. enjoyed modest success throughout the 1980s and early 1990s, and was helped on its way by the loose interdisciplinary structure of the Faculty of Humanities and the collegiate structure of the University.

However, in the early 1990s, under pressure from the Thatcherite philosophies of accountability and line management, the University adopted more *dirigiste* policies toward both Faculties and colleges: "Boards of studies" became fully-fledged departments, located in a single place, and, as a consequence, colleges ceased to be sites of interdisciplinary interchange. The formation of the Canterbury Centre for Medieval & Tudor Studies was a direct response to these developments. It became, in effect, a postgraduate department responsible directly to the Dean of the Faculty (though without the power to appoint its own staff). It was an occasion also for development and self-definition. The Centre acquired the right to award its own research degrees, and it promulgated certain distinguishing features: an interdisciplinary out-look and practice; an insistence on the continuities, as well as the disjunctions, between the medieval and "Tudor" periods; a commitment to the culture of Canterbury and its region within a European context; and an expansion of existing links with Canterbury Cathedral Archives and Library, and the Canterbury Archaeological Trust. Within this framework, CCMTS has gone from strength to strength. At a time of declining postgraduate enrollments in the humanities, both locally and nationally, it steadily increased its intake; became the best-recruiting postgraduate M.A. in the Faculty; and raised its international profile by taking more overseas students and by participating energetically in international conferences.

Thus, at the beginning of academic year 2003–4, CCMTS was flourishing, but it was vulnerable—as it had always been—to cross-currents affecting the main departments that support it by providing staff: English and History. The prosperity of a Humanities department at Kent, as elsewhere in the U.K., depends upon two funding streams: research and teaching. Research income is dispensed to the University by a governement agency, the Higher Education Funding Council of England (HEFCE), and is directly related to the grade awarded to a department in the previous Research Assessment Exercise (RAE). The RAE is a national peer review, managed by HEFCE, which takes place once every five or six years. "Research active" members of the department submit items for evaluation (typically four), and although other criteria come into play (such as success in winning research grants), it is research output that carries the day. The results are calibrated on a scale of 1 to 5*. A department in the latter category is one where research output is predominantly of international standing.

A top RAE award is not enough. For a department to be financially viable, student recruitment also needs to be buoyant. To some extent, the two are linked: a department with a high RAE grade is likely to prove more popular with high-quality applicants. Applicants also take account of teaching quality, and there is another government regimen targeted at just that. Formerly, as with the RAE, teaching-quality grades were awarded to individual departments, but recently the process has changed to become that of an audit (again, by means of peer review) of the institution's internal mechanisms for ensuring that teaching quality is satisfactory. The outcome of an institutional audit is not reduced to numbers (the highest accolade is an assertion of "confidence" on the part of the auditors), and it is not directly tied to funding, but it is of crucial importance. The result, as with the RAE, is made public and, like the RAE grade, it is factored into the league tables beloved of quality newspapers. The league tables are required reading for applicants and their parents. Consumerism, quality control, the audit and review culture, a premium on research productivity, and a close regard for the bottom line are thus facts of life for a Humanities department. Somehow, in spite of it all, colleagues retain their enthusiasm for teaching and research, and students their enthusiasm for learning.

The results of the latest RAE were published in December 2002. English at Kent advanced from 3a to 5, while History stayed at 4. The latter grade might not have mattered so much but for a national tendency for departments to improve. HEFCE found that it could maintain full levels of funding only for top-rated departments. In real terms, History's level of research funding dropped significantly, while English's increased. Generally, departments at Kent did well, but because the University is keen to improve its research standing yet further, it launched its own reviews, involving external assessors, into the strategies that might be adopted to improve the research ratings of underperforming departments. One recommendation in the case of History was that it should take advantage of its distinctive location and strengthen research-active staff in the medieval period. At the time, History was facing a serious budget deficit exacerbated by its RAE result, and it saw matters differently. The then existing medievalists were not among the most research active of their staff. Here was an opportunity to reduce the budget deficit and improve research productivity by restructuring the department—with University support—precisely by shedding staff in the medieval and early modern periods.

All History staff received a letter offering generous terms for early retirement, but the letter also made clear that the target audience lay at the earlier end of the curriculum. Unfortunately, the policy had not been aired with representatives of CCMTS, who saw it as a direct threat to the Centre's continued existence. A person or persons unknown contacted the press, and both *The Times Higher Education Supplement* and *The Guardian* published lengthy reports. Ironically, *The Guardian* headline (September 26, 2003) used the same words from Chaucer's description of his Clerk, which, in earlier times, the University had used to promote itself. The headline ran "And gladly wolde he lerne—but not in Canterbury." The articles appeared at a time when BBC television was broad-

264

casting modernized versions of several Canterbury tales, and *The Guardian* was quick to point out that a department worth its salt should have been capitalizing on the sudden upsurge in interest in things medieval associated with Canterbury, not negating it. It also juxtaposed a glamorous picture of the singer and actress Billy Piper, who played Alisoun in the BBC's *Miller's Tale*, with solemn reportage about CCMTS—surely, in other contexts, a publicist's dream. The crisis deepened with the resignation of the Centre's director; e-mail inboxes filled up with protests from medievalists worldwide; and the postgraduate students in CCMTS began to express concern about the viability of their M.A.

The University authorities were taken by surprise. They had no intention of closing CCMTS, and said so publicly. At the same time, they were left in no doubt about the Centre's prestigious nature: the vice-chancellor received a carefully drafted latter from some eminent medievalists pointing out the international significance of its work and reputation. It was a moment of institutional embarrassment: two aspects of the University's policy were unintentionally in conflict, and the School of History was getting a bad press. An acting director of CCMTS was appointed to bring some stability to the situation.

There was also a somewhat more wide-ranging risk on the horizon. In mid-December, the university was due to enter into its first Institutional Audit. It is the nature of such audits that, if one part of the institution's provision is deemed unsatisfactory, then the whole of its provision is tarred with the same brush. The impact on recruitment of a substandard assessment could be severe. Now, institutional auditors, in assessing the teaching-quality regime of a particular university, focus in particular on the quality of the student experience, and are eager to talk to students to ensure that their educational experience is all their elders and betters claim it to be. In CCMTS, the quality of the student experience was being dramatically—and very publicly—affected by policies that the university had itself endorsed. So the first task of the acting director was to determine the perceived quality of CCMTS, the extent to which— especially in the student experience—that quality was being adversely affected, and how the situation might be remedied.

It was not difficult to establish the perceived quality of the Centre. There was the evidence of recent e-mails and letters in its support, written by people of some weight; and, more substantively, there was a recent, adulatory, official monitoring report by a panel (including a distinguished medievalist from another institution) commissioned by the University as part of its routine cycle of periodic review of programs. Neither was it difficult to determine the impact of the crisis on the students then enrolled in M.A. and Ph.D. programs: either through their representatives, or individually, they reported a loss of confidence in the University's and Faculty's commitment to CCMTS, a lowering of morale, and an uncertainty about the immediate viability of the curriculum. Some expressed their intention to leave, or to transfer to another university. International students felt the crisis with particular force, since their personal and financial investments tend to be greater than those of home students. Nor was the remedy far to seek: that the threat of staff redundancy be removed. (For one member of the staff, it was due to come into effect at Christmas, that is, in mid-program.)

The evidence was collected, submissions received, recommendations made, and the whole dossier, together with a "quality report," sent to appropriate senior members of the administration. To their credit, and perhaps with minds focused by the imminence of the institutional audit, they recognized the force of the evidence and key recommendation and removed any immediate threat of redundancy. Students were thereby relieved of much anxiety and were able to continue their studies into the spring term in a calmer atmosphere, and with confidence that they would be able to complete the program. As it happened, the institutional auditors did not focus their attention on CCTMS (although they indicated that they were aware of the press reports), and the University emerged from the audit with the highest level of approbation.

The next step was to secure the medium- and long-term future of the Canterbury Centre. To some extent, that meant revisiting familiar issues, and especially those to do with resources. The program-monitoring report had pointed out that the Centre's provision tended to depend on too few staff; that it lacked a single physical location with which students could identify; and that the Faculty's budgetary provision was inadequate. These and other topics were featured in a paper written by the acting director and at present are under discussion. Among its recommendations are that the participating departments should make formal staffing commitments to the Centre; that the staff involved should be credited with the hours they work as part of their regular work allocation, and not as extra to it; and that the job of director should be shared between an academic director and one responsible for the quality-assurance aspects of the program. The paper cleared a meeting of CCMTS itself, attended by members of all the participating Schools, and by student representatives, and it is now before departmental chairs and the Dean of the Faculty. The signs for its eventual acceptance are reasonably promising: members of the faculty not previously involved in the Centre have expressed interest in teaching; proposals for new modules have come forward (including one on Chaucer and Gower); and there has been some exploration of ways in which the M.A. program might be extended to include art history and more archaeology.

History's restructuring plan has now run its course. It has resulted in two voluntary redundancies within earlier periods (one in medieval history, one in Tudor) with effect from the beginning of 2004–5. So the provision of teaching in History for the Centre is somewhat depleted, but not disastrously so because it is to some extent compensated for by offers of help from new quarters. There is even talk of a new History appointment at the earlier end of the curriculum. English, meanwhile, has made a new permanent appointment in medieval literature. And, after a period of inactivity, teams of staff and research students are once again appearing at international gatherings (currently at Belfast and Leeds). Recruitment for the 2004 intake of coursework and research students was strong.

What are the *moralitees* of this cautionary tale? That extensive consultation is a prerequisite of effective consensual action. That the press is a powerful but unpredictable outlet for academic grievances. That university administrators can on occasion offer enlightened leadership. That too narrow a focus on departmental self-interest can be counterproductive. Perhaps, above all, that Canterbury not only is, but is seen to be, a natural home both for Chaucer studies and for medieval and Tudor studies.

Our "crafty science":

Institutional Support and Humanist Discipline

Mary Carruthers
New York University

I JUST PASSED a New York City bus with an advertisement on its side for a television docu-drama (horrid genre) about King Arthur: "Did the most famous king who ever lived, ever live?" It struck me as a fine example of a totally misconceived question, its nonevident premises rendering it unanswerable. With all respect to the editor of *SAC*, asking about "the future of Chaucer studies" strikes me as the same sort of question. One might even start similarly: Did "Chaucer studies" ever actually live—outside the purview of The New Chaucer Society, where, like some apparition, Chaucer studies manifest themselves in a hefty annual volume and a biennial conference? Can something with so evanescent a past have a future? And—crucial question—should it?

I've been asked to think about this subject as both a scholar and as a dean. Thinking as a scholar and thinking as a dean, I have found, are two different intellectual disciplines, each with its considerable professional pleasures and personal satisfactions, but with near-polar approaches to solving problems. A few years ago I thought about the issue as a scholar, in my 1998 presidential address.[1] In this essay, I will be thinking as a dean.

I cannot answer, any better than anyone else, the scholarly question, "Do Chaucer studies have a future?" except to observe that the study of Chaucer has one, though of what sort I can only speculate. But this is a

---

[1] Mary Carruthers, "'Micrological Aggregates': Is The New Chaucer Society Speaking in Tongues?" *SAC* 21 (1999): 1–26. Further notably fruitful thoughts on "new" philology and the possibilities for and limitations of "cultural criticism" in Chaucer studies are in the "Colloquium" on language study and Chaucer published in *SAC* 24 (2002): 299–354, perhaps particularly the essays by Christopher Cannon, "What Chaucer's Language Is" (pp. 301–8), and Stephanie Trigg, "The New Medievalization of Chaucer" (pp. 347–54).

different matter from "Chaucer studies." Lurking in the latter construction, from a dean's standpoint, are matters of organization and institutional support that are not really the same as those involved in "the study of Chaucer." We must try not to conflate the two in our own analysis, or we will cease to think clearly about either one. And institutional clarity is desperately needed. Also goodwill, but I will come to that a bit later.

The practical future of Chaucer studies cannot be addressed globally, certainly not by musing to other Chaucerians in the pages of the annual publication of The New Chaucer Society. Academics do rather too much preaching to their own choirs already. Rather, whatever the future may be, it will result from the aggregate of specific, local decisions made one institution at a time by the faculty, including the deans and chairs, of those institutions. I make my observations from my experience as Humanities dean at New York University; my office is to oversee faculty hiring and retention and the budgets for programmatic development of all units in the division of the Humanities in the Faculty of Arts and Science.

Institutionally, the future of Chaucer studies should not be considered except within the future of the humanities as a whole. It is time to stop thinking of each of the particular things we are doing as a separate "field" or "discipline," and to begin planning cooperatively with like-minded colleagues across the humanities departments. The dismay and discouragement motivating the *SAC* editor to commission this forum is shared across all faculties of the humanities—"we don't none of us get no respect." (Notice the deft use of the Middle English triple negative: we deans take our intellectual pleasures quietly and inoffensively. Like good courtiers, irony is our essential trope.)

One of the first things I noticed when I took office was that, although each of the three academic divisions of arts and science had roughly the same number of faculty (a bit more than two hundred apiece), the sciences were allotted among five major departments, the social sciences among six, and the humanities among sixteen departments and over a dozen more independent interdisciplinary degree programs staffed by faculty with joint appointments in other units, among which they "divided" their time. While my two divisional colleagues dealt with the plans and aspirations of half a dozen chairs and institute directors, I dealt with around thirty, each of whom saw his or her own unit as a separate territory and was of course out to get as much as possible for it. The principle of direct competition at all levels is so ingrained as an inherent good in the American academy that few ever consider its costs. But they have become stultifying. The predictable result of having so many separate entities in the humanities has been constant warring over smaller and smaller shares of resources, the virtual paralysis of small, weak programs (all of them "interdisciplinary") totally dependent on the collective mercy of their bigger colleagues, and a faculty that, to external eyes, looks academically incoherent and intellectually merely fractious. I used to defend our multiplicity to nonhumanists as a sign of liveliness and creativity. I don't any more, because I realize the institutional issues are not scholarly; they are political and economic, with consequences that do not favor the future of the humanities in their present state.

Unlike a great many other people, I don't think that the root of our problem is irreconcilable differences between the humanities and the quantitative sciences.[2] I think rather that the problem is a major intellectual crisis within the humanities themselves, as the project of cultural criticism has become the dominant focus of attention within a majority of departments. The majority of my colleagues in literature define themselves now as critics, not as historians, and believe that their task is criticism—"What do I do? I criticize," as one job candidate recently said to me. Unfortunately, the established disciplines of the humanities, oriented as they are toward recovering and contextualizing past particularities, are not especially well suited to this project. This strong divergence within the humanities over the definition of what—if anything—constitutes our science and its crafts is an essential component of "the future of Chaucer studies," one that I am not confident medievalists have yet fully appreciated.

Instead of bemoaning this situation, we can try to exploit it. Easier said than done, I realize after several years of trying. Yet when humanists—including especially medievalists—have brought to the university's research table things from which the projects of scientists and

[2] That the divergence between science and humanities is fostered and fueled by public policy is a sad reality, but we will really be devastated when it comes to academic policy if we merely continue to quarrel. NYU was the scene of the infamous *Social Text*/ Alan Sokal scam, and the intellectual dishonesty, on all sides, that fomented it into a national, even international, *querelle* accomplished very little that was positive in the end. See John Guillory, "The Sokal Affair and the History of Criticism," *Critical Inquiry* 28 (2002): 470–508 (with extensive bibliography), and the subsequent response by Christopher Newfield and reply by Guillory in *Critical Inquiry* 29 (2003): 508–46.

administrators can benefit, they have not been turned away. The rapid development of sophisticated programming that has made possible the digitizing of huge searchable libraries of images and texts has come into being in large part through the needs of military planners, to be sure, but also through the particular accessibility of complex medieval archives. As we all know, and many of us have helped to realize, late nineteenth- and twentieth-century scholarship and late twentieth-century technology have produced a stunning, massive archive for twenty-first-century scholarship and digital science to continue to explore together. On much smaller scales, individual humanists and scientists have found some common ground, and it is no longer unheard of for historians and scientists to give joint seminars and papers in fields like neuropsychology and sensory perception (optics and acoustics in particular).

Yet we need to do more than just join them. We need to articulate clearly what is our own discipline, the methods of learning that are unique in the humanities. What is our knowledge? In trying to find method for their project of cultural criticism, many humanities programs in the past three decades have borrowed extensively from social sciences, but at the risk of losing touch altogether with those disciplines developed in the humanities themselves. I think it's time to acknowledge this. Just what do scholars in humanities do that the social theorists, the neurobiologists, the psychologists, the linguists, do not do? What are the disciplines of the humanities? Are they coherent with the present set of departments and programs?

No, they are not. Indeed, the present institutional organization of humanities often conceals its particular disciplines.

As modern historians work increasingly with questions of the social valence of languages, and with literary materials in which matters like genre and audience are critical, and scholars in various literature departments work with archival materials, and with intersections of literature and music, visual art, and performance, the long experience of medievalists with just such multidisciplinary study is particularly appropriate. But our institutional structures lag far behind our multidisciplined inquiries. We in the humanities need to become organizationally far more flexible and imaginatively engaged with institutional change than we have been before.

Our analysis might start with a mental game: "If we did not have the present structure of academic departments, what would we design now?" Would it be at all like what we have—an organization in which a narrowly conceived departmental model governs interdisciplinary study itself, engendering department-like programs in area studies, ethnic studies, cultural studies, each aspiring to operate as independently as it can, each with separate curricula and degrees? Or would we perhaps design a much simpler, more encompassing, more permeable and flexible set of a few units, better adapted structurally to accommodate the frequent reconfigurations essential to nurture intellectual vitality within the humanities? This is how the other divisions are presently organized, with many curricula, labs, and interdisciplinary institutes contained within larger units (departments), which in their intellectual diversity can resemble small colleges. In principle, they are thus able to manage flexibility without simply fracturing.

I have been present, and have participated in, serious discussions about "the interdisciplinary disciplines," during which not one person at the table commented on the logically fatal contradiction of that phrase. The word "discipline" has come to be conflated with "department" to such a degree that all distinction between them has been lost. The *OED* helpfully distinguishes between "doctrine" and "discipline,"[3] between what content the master knows and teaches and what the disciple must learn to do in order to know. "Discipline" is craft practice, "doctrine" is content. The multiple departments and programs in humanities tend to be organized now into many units of doctrine but not of discipline. "Chaucer studies," like "medieval studies," is *doctrina*, the science (as *scientia*, human knowledge) taught by the faculty about a particular body of material. Learning to read scripts is *disciplina*, a craft practice that is equally useful for students to master in connection with many materials, for medievalists but also for modernists.

Among humanist disciplines, philology in its many aspects—the knowledge of several languages and their histories, codicology, and comparative textual analysis—is basic, not only in literature but in art history, philosophy, history, and musicology. Another discipline is archival research, and a third the analysis of propositions and their relationships, including the propositions of genre, in architecture and music as well as in literature and history. Another of our disciplines is rhetoric, essential to comprehending both narrative arrangement and performance. Broadly

---

[3] *OED*, s.v. *discipline*. The phrase I have used in my title, "crafty science," comes from *The Canon's Yeoman's Tale* (VIII.1253), where it is used in apposition to discipline.

considered, in its disciplines every humanities department is interdisciplinary, for these days all have faculty members who practice one or more of these methods of investigation on the matters with which they work. These are also the disciplines that are unique to the humanities, things we can bring to the table that are singularly useful to other disciplines of study and to many professional studies as well. But these disciplines are not the intellectual property of one department or another, indeed there is an evident disconnection between these basic disciplines and the departments into which an American humanities faculty is now typically organized.

The future of Chaucer studies cannot be solved solely by institutional reorganizing. Only superior "doctrine" (content and teaching) and "discipline" (learning methods of investigation) will maintain the health of our inquiries. But it would be better if institutions did not constantly place outdated, inflexible organizational structures in the way. The principle of entropy is well established, even promoted, in academic institutions: a smug history lesson and a collective shoulder shrug are all too frequently the faculty's response to a proposal to do things differently. Changing even a tiny item takes active cooperation, imagination, institutional knowledge, goodwill, stubbornness, patience, and hard work on the part of many individuals. And there is no gain if one inflexibility is simply replaced with yet another.

Here is a case in point, one of those quick half-victories that occasionally brighten a dean's life. A year ago this past spring, I had the experience of working out staffing and funding for an essential course for graduate students hoping to do meaningful research in medieval subjects, a summer double-course in elementary through intermediate Latin. At the heart of my tale is the budgeting and staffing maze of a very large yet very underendowed private research university.

During the regular academic year, beginning language classes are offered for undergraduates, at levels for which graduate students cannot get credit, a reasonable regulation of the Graduate School. An existing Classics course in medieval Latin, offered at a level for which graduate credit could be given, requires at least intermediate preparation in the basic language. Limited by staffing constraints, the Classics department has put its resources into undergraduate language instruction, enrollment-generating lecture courses, and advanced courses for its own majors and graduate students. Because of this combination of factors, each benign enough in itself, graduate students are essentially closed out of basic Latin during the year. But the summer was equally impossible. The university's instructional budget is composed of two distinct entities—the academic year budget and the summer budget. The summer budget is entirely tuition-based. So if graduate students take credit hours in the summer, someone needs to pay real money for them.

In this context of professional need and institutional stalemate, a few deans and faculty together addressed the problem of inadequate Latin preparation among the doctoral students.[4] I stress "together," because no one of us—no matter how well informed or well connected or well intentioned—had the institutional knowledge or resources to solve it alone. We were determined to have something that we could immediately implement for our students. It took about a week.

Instructors were found by the Classics department from their own graduate students, who were delighted to get extra money, and so for this summer at least several doctoral students are able to get some adequate preparation in Latin at their home university without paying an expensive tuition. Yet the underlying budget problem has not been solved. The course was "paid for" entirely as an unrecoverable loss from the Graduate School's summer budget. Given the reality that summer teachers must be paid from summer dollars, it cannot forever be carried along "for free" on the backs of other summer courses that must account for their dollars. It is an expensive addition in a system that has very little remaining tolerance for such things, and its future will depend on continuing imagination, goodwill, and cooperation.

So why do I do this job? Because I actually believe in a future for multidisciplinary humanistic study of the sort medievalists must do in order to work at all. As a dean, I can shape faculty policy directly in ways that an individual scholar, even a department chair, cannot. And my sense of what an institution should do for scholar-teachers seeking to do their very best work has been immeasurably sharpened and made practical by my present position. NYU has moved its planning for interdisciplinary study away from narrowly conceived, separately organized units toward simpler, more flexible structures. I believe this direction will secure the future study of Chaucer (and of the humanities more broadly) even if it does not result in a unit called "Chaucer Studies."

---

[4] They will forgive me for publicly thanking them: Professors Phillip Brian Harper (cultural criticism), Michael Peachin (ancient history), and Deans Catharine Stimpson (modernism/feminism) and James Matthews (experimental psychology) of the Graduate School of Arts and Science.

The figure of the humanist scholar-administrator is essential in this future, as necessary as is rigorous training and continuous practice in all the disciplines of our crafty science. If engaged faculty do not regularly take on positions in which they participate in the difficult and compromised policy-making process of academic institutions, the university will ever more rapidly succumb to a mode in which administration and faculty are completely separated. This will not strengthen the faculty. One of my fellow deans—not in arts and science—already has proposed to our university deans' council an institutional model of the president as CEO, the deans as management, the faculty as employees, the students as consumers, and "the public" (represented by parents and trustees) as stockholders. Goodness! Many of my fellows emailed him to congratulate him on what a great idea he had. I emailed him, taking his metaphor apart (inoffensively, of course), giving him a bit of history, suggesting other ways to think about the faculty's position in the university, reminding him that deans *are* faculty.

As a working dean, I find myself often teaching my fellow administrators about what the humanities are, what a typical career path is for a faculty member in the humanities, how we do our work, how young scholars publish, why humanists need continuing access to their archives (which are often in distant places), that there is research in the humanities, what it is and why humanists need to do it just as much as biologists do. What humanistic knowledge is. Why working humanists need regular sabbaticals when lab scientists never take theirs. How humanists use their libraries, especially that of their home institution. The list goes on, at a level sometimes so elementary that it still astounds me.

I conclude with a plea to all medievalists who are concerned about the future of Chaucer studies: when and if your colleagues approach you to take on a major administrative role such as chair or dean, do not simply turn them away, and do not proclaim with self-satisfaction that "My research takes all my time," or "I could never be a dean." Sure you could. Just don't succumb to the temptation to stay in office too long. When your colleagues want you to sign on for "just another term," tell them you can't because you have a new book to write, and it's somebody else's turn.

Response: Chaucerian Values

Elaine Tuttle Hansen
Bates College

RANK GRADY URGED participants in this colloquium to speak to our concerns about the future of Chaucer studies in light of our "practical administrative experience" and to reflect on our "dual role" as scholars and administrators. Each of the preceding four essays has taken the first part of this charge especially seriously, as each contributor tells a story rooted specifically in local institutional circumstances. Sylvia Tomasch writes from the point of view of a department chair searching for a medievalist at a large urban public university; Mary Carruthers as Dean of Arts and Sciences, interested in the "future of humanities as a whole," at a private research university; Martin Camargo from his comparative experience moving from one large Midwestern university to another; Peter Brown from across the Atlantic, focusing on one moment of crisis at an institution with a special, "natural" reason for studying Chaucer—its location in Canterbury. From each perspective, we see a cautiously, partially, and contingently sunny view of the landscape of Chaucer studies. Clouds on the horizon are acknowledged, but the good news is that crisis either has not materialized or has been averted—often through collaboration—and the forecast is not as bad as we might hear or suspect.

Contributors give far less explicit attention to their status as scholar/administrators. They note that in some cases the cooperation of deans, chancellors, and other senior administrators has been essential; as Brown observes, administrators can be "enlightened," and Camargo reiterates that the good things he has experienced could not have happened without the dean's support. Nonetheless, on the few occasions when they

I am grateful to several colleagues who took the time to share some of their thoughts about the future of Chaucer studies, including Susan Crane, Columbia University; Jennifer Summit, Stanford University; Anne Thompson, Bates College; and Craig Williamson, Swarthmore College.

speak directly about their dual role, our participants remain skeptical of administration and valorize the scholarly side. Wry parting comments are a vehicle for expressing this attitude, without overly dwelling on it. Carruthers says she is "thinking as a dean" and, in closing, calls for historians to be deans, but instructs them not to do so for "too long." And Camargo ends with a (perhaps tongue in cheek) warning to readers—pragmatic, heads-up advocacy and administrative savvy are essential, but watch out; if you are too good at it, "you just might end up an administrator yourself."

In closing, I will take some brief issue with this mildly negative attitude toward administration, but first let me focus in more depth on my worries about the future of Chaucer studies from the perspective of my particular institutional past and present, which is different enough that a quick personal preface may be in order. I was not originally trained as a Chaucerian. In my dissertation, first book, and a few early articles, I wrote about Old English poetry, but I have never had the opportunity to teach my graduate-school specialty. The job market being what it was when I completed my dissertation in 1975, I was grateful to find immediate employment at the Middle English Dictionary in the first year of its mid-1970s Mellon grant, when seven young medievalists were hired to ratchet up production. After three years (from approximately M-4 to P-6), this postdoc immersion in Middle English sufficiently enhanced my credentials for Chaucer jobs, which were a little less scarce than the Anglo-Saxon jobs, and my best first teaching offer just happened to come from a small liberal arts college. Two years later, I moved to a tenure-track position at another small liberal arts college, where I remained for the next twenty-two years. Like most faculty at such institutions, I probably taught more courses outside my field than inside, and my writing, as an outgrowth of my teaching, has been focused on other areas of interest as well as on Chaucer.

Moreover, I may already have been an administrator way "too long." My first foray into administrative matters involved collaborating on the creation of an interdisciplinary, inter-institutional program in feminist and gender studies in the mid-1980s. I then chaired my department for a term, served as the college's chief academic officer for seven years, and only recently moved on to become president of another liberal arts college in the Northeast. My dual career has thus been comfortably nestled in an increasingly small and in many ways atypical segment of the higher-education community—the highly selective private liberal arts college—not otherwise represented by the voices speaking here or in most other conversations about higher education today. With these caveats about my biases and limitations in mind, I reflect on four broader issues and trends in which my own worries about the future of Chaucer studies are at this point embedded.

What Can You Do with a Major in Classical and Medieval Studies?

Three years ago, when I arrived on this campus, the Bates Program in Classical and Medieval Studies (a successful interdisciplinary program of which our senior Chaucerian was a founder) ran a visible and popular ad campaign featuring posters entitled "What can you do with a major in CMS?" and displaying the pictures, degrees, and careers of several "celebrities"—Toni Morrison, J. K. Rowling, Steven Cohen, Ted Turner, James Baker, and me, the new president of Bates.

The Bates CMS poster campaign responds to a familiar fact of life: when Chaucerians seek to cultivate student interest in the literature and culture to which we have dedicated our professional lives, the practical value of doing so is almost always an issue. As an administrator advancing the cause of liberal education in a residential community, I deal with the same reality. We offer a four-year undergraduate program dedicated to the liberal arts and sciences, where the humanist disciplines are still strong, where humanities courses are still required and popular, and where a few students who never thought of doing so before they came to college will end up studying Chaucer or other ancient or medieval texts. To attract many students (and their parents) to this kind of education, we have to pitch relevance. Fortunately, it's possible to marshal a strong case for the practical value of both studying premodern literature and pursuing a liberal arts degree. As we often say, a CMS degree, an English major, or indeed any major in the liberal arts and sciences trains you for nothing and prepares you for everything. It is increasingly evident that the analytical, critical, and interpersonal skills fostered in the liberal arts college environment in general and in the humanities in particular are essential for people who will change jobs many times in their lives, pursuing careers in fields and disciplines that we cannot even name now. While it's a point we have to keep making, massaging, and marketing (even as we also understand the privilege and luxury of a four-year degree that doesn't guarantee immediate employment, and work hard to make our education available to those who can't afford it), it remains a valid, resilient, often persuasive argument.

At the same time, one of my worries is that something can be lost in pushing the relevance argument too far—namely, the idea of learning for its own sake, for the fun and joy and wonder of it. Even as we can, should, and do tout the practical, instrumental value of studying Chaucer or attending a liberal arts college, we may ask ourselves what we could also do to tackle a more daunting challenge—to preserve and widen the space for appreciating the intrinsic merit of our enterprise, or its worth to culture and the common good, apart from its value to individuals seeking top careers and high earnings.

Premature Specialization and Selective Admissions

Let me push this concern about the potential downside of the "relevance" issue a little further in order to raise a second worry. My younger daughter is a high school senior in the middle of her college search. Having spent the first fifteen years of her life living on the campus of a small liberal arts college and having been transplanted recently, against her will, to another one located at what she considers the frozen edge of civilization, she has been wondering whether she might prefer to attend a large university, as far from New England as possible. So in June of 2004, we visited the campus of an elite private university on the West Coast. Our attractive, articulate tour guide began by asking all the prospective students in the group to state their names, where they were from, and what they were interested in studying. One by one, these young teenagers (later we found out that the group consisted mostly of fourteen-, fifteen-, and sixteen-year-olds) from all over the country spoke confidently about their highly certain and specific plans: "I'm Jane Smith, I'm from Omaha, Nebraska, and I want to major in molecular biology with a focus on bioinfomatics," "My major will be international relations, and I have a special interest in Southeast Asia, but I also plan to minor in Spanish," "I plan on a double major in econ and computer science, and I'm really interested in applied mathematical models," and so on. With the exception of my child, every young person identified a definite and specific major—none of which were in the humanities—as well as one or two even more specific subfields or minors—one or two of which were in the humanities, although none in English or medieval studies. When my daughter's turn came, I listened with some suspense, as she visibly straightened her spine and spoke clearly and with a familiar edge of defiance: "My name is Isla, I'm from Maine, and I have no idea what I want to do." (After our tour, she asked me an interesting question: "So, Mom, what is the biggest small liberal arts college?")

The drive to specialize early—and thereby to distinguish, disambiguate, and promote oneself as a committed specialist in something—is part of the strategy for winning the elite admissions race, and as such it trickles down to far more students than will actually enroll in selective colleges and universities. Witnessing this spectacle of precocious or premature career-building must heighten the anxieties of both Chaucer scholars and small-college administrators. Those top students who know (or think they know, or think they ought to know) what they want to be at fourteen, fifteen, or sixteen, and so commit themselves to a narrow, pre-professional educational path, rarely identify themselves early on as interested in literary studies, since that is not a strategic, high-status choice. For similar reasons, they are somewhat less likely to choose liberal arts colleges.

But if undergraduates are pursuing a major in the social sciences or natural sciences at a large research university, where and how will they learn to care about humanist issues, ideas, and approaches? By taking one or two large lecture classes to fulfill a distribution requirement (assuming there is one) in the humanities, will students just happen to come to love books and appreciate the work of philosophers, artists, and writers? Busily fulfilling the requirements of their double majors or multiple secondary concentrations, will they get a chance to meet Chaucer in Middle English, and maybe other writers and periods and genres (not to mention theories and disciplines) that they haven't studied in high school? Who will care whether or not that happens? From my perspective, college is a time to find out who you are and what you love. To foster the love of literature and the reading of Chaucer, we need more, not fewer, liberally educated students who are permitted the luxury of exploring, sampling, finding, and following their passions. Early specialization, increasingly perceived as providing competitive advantage in admissions to our most prestigious universities, seems to me to stand starkly in contrast to the conditions that will over the long haul best preserve and enhance the study of Chaucer.

"And after wyn on Venus moste I thynke . . ."

My third worry entails the issue of relevance yet again but in a different way, as it touches on matters far from the normal purview of Chaucerians, extraneous to the academic curriculum and faculty concerns, and all too familiar to administrators. Apart from the demands of encouraging philanthropy and managing people (two activities faculty are not normally trained or temperamentally inclined to do), what often distresses me the most in my administrative position are issues of student residential life. Among these, arguably the most intransigent problems arise from cases of student misconduct in which young women, admittedly drunk (and mostly underage), report that they have been raped or sexually assaulted by male students. The men involved, who have almost always been "feeling the effects" to some degree themselves, normally acknowledge that sexual activity took place but insist that they asked for and received—sometimes directly and sometimes indirectly, sometimes once and sometimes repeatedly—the young women's consent. The women involved say that that they did not give consent, and/or that they were too drunk to remember the events, and/or were so impaired by their use of alcohol that it is impossible for any alleged consent to have been meaningful consent. The evidence of witnesses—fellow students who often testify as to "how drunk" one or both parties were or weren't—is partial, subjective, clouded, and contradictory.

College administrators must and do take these charges very seriously; we are morally concerned and legally constrained to do so. We construct, publish, and discuss widely our detailed definitions of terms like "sexual harassment," "sexual assault," "rape," "consent," and "force." We have elaborate, quasi-judicial procedures for investigating, bringing charges, and holding disciplinary hearings and appeals, often in cases where the police would be unlikely to take a charge forward. There are high stakes here. If an accused student is found guilty, that student's career will be fundamentally disrupted; if there is a finding of innocence, the effect on the accusing student and on the campus climate for women can be equally life-altering. The students, staff, and faculty charged with adjudicating these cases are sincere, well meaning, strongly opposed to violence against women, and eager to construct a community in which young men and women can live and learn together. A decision about whether consent was or wasn't given must be reached, but it is almost impossible for reasonable people to determine with certainty what took place.

To Chaucerians, however, at least one thing appears perfectly certain. More than six hundred years after the Wife of Bath's *Prologue* was written, female sexual desire seems to be just as hard to understand, and in some cases to de-couple from the effects of alcohol, as it is in the Wife of Bath's musings on her relationship with her fourth husband, a "revelour":

> And after wyn on Venus moste I thynke,
> For al so siker as cold engendreth hayl,
> A likerous mouth moste han a likerous tayl.
> In wommen vinolent is no defence—
> This knowen lecchours by experience."
> (Riverside, III.464–68)

In difficult cases, moreover, we appear to be no more capable of answering the question today, "What do women want?" than was the young knight-rapist in the Wife's *Tale*.

But how is this observation relevant to the future of Chaucer studies? At first glance it seems that Chaucer scholars are turning their back on the difficult questions about sexual politics that the Wife's *Prologue* and *Tale* pose. In her essay, Tomasch observes that feminist work on Chaucer has been "supplemented—if not yet entirely supplanted" by work on gender and sexuality and queer studies. This point was echoed in my recent conversation with a medievalist of a generation younger than my own, Jennifer Summit. Writing a chapter on recent feminist studies of Chaucer, Summit discovered that there has been far less work in the last five years than she expected to find. She expected to find it, in part, because she believes as I do that feminist or "women's issues" in Chaucer are not imposed or anachronistic but intrinsic, and so should be somewhat resistant to critical fashion. As Summit says, "Whenever I'm teaching Chaucer, I feel I'm teaching feminism," because that's what comes up in the classroom, that's what today's students want to know: was he sympathetic or hostile to women, pro- or anti-feminist, in our terms? If we look more closely, however, we see that what feminist work there is on Chaucer is increasingly about the very issues that most trouble student life: rape and consent.

I am not about to suggest that a course in *The Canterbury Tales*, or *The Legend of Good Women* or *Troilus and Criseyde* taught from a feminist perspective (whatever that might be) ought to be required of all undergraduates as a way of discouraging sexual misconduct. I've talked to too many young men and women and seen how they can know things in theory and ignore them in practice, as we all can. But one of the concerns that we focus on at residential colleges in particular is how to integrate academics and student life. We profess to teach, and to a large extent really do teach, "the whole student," with the understanding that learning goes on inside and outside the classroom, and that as a highly intentional learning community we will do a better job when the oversimplified and undertheorized boundaries between work and play are blurred and crossed. And because I remain interested in bridging the divide between reading/theory and living/practice, I am perhaps naive enough to believe that in this instance the relevance of Chaucer is not just a hook but a reality that we need to explore more fully. While Chaucerians have no panacea for late adolescent Americans' problems of binge drinking and date rape, what might we be able to do to educate students about issues of uneven power and violence if we yoked the reading of Chaucer and our preventive education around issues of alcohol and consent? Here the issue may be not so much what is threatening Chaucer studies, but the opportunities we may be missing.

One final word of caution on this point. My worry that we fail to consider how and where we can explore the relevance of Chaucerian texts to our students' lives is deepened and complicated by Sylvia Tomasch's comment on the health of Chaucer studies at Hunter College. Tomasch suggests that student interest in Chaucer at her institution has something to do with the fact that "remediation" programs have been removed from the senior colleges like Hunter to the community colleges. Are Chaucer studies/reading Chaucer then only surviving, even thriving, by moving up in the educational hierarchy—away from the lower-division curriculum to English majors and graduate students only? If so, this means we are reaching not only smaller numbers but also more sophisticated readers, hardly likely to be paying much attention to the value of reading great literary texts to the personal, social, and psychic development of young people.

Reading at Risk

In early July of 2004, the NEA released a study entitled "Reading at Risk: A Survey of Literary Reading in America." Based on interviews conducted by the Survey on Public Participation in the Arts over the course of three decades (1982, 1992, and 2002), polls show that the percentage of Americans who read at least one book of any kind has declined from 60.9 percent to 56.6 percent. The percentage who have read a work of literature declined even more, from 54 percent to less than half, or 46.7 percent. The report goes on to examine many intriguing demographic differences: women read more literature than men, self-identified white people read more literature than self-identified Hispanics and African Americans, people with higher incomes read more literature than people with lower incomes, and the sharpest decline in literary reading rates has occurred among people between the ages of eighteen and thirty-four. Identifying this as a crisis situation, chair of the NEA Dana Gioia says, "If literary intellectuals—writers, scholars, librarians, book people in general—don't take charge of the situation, our culture will be impoverished."

My experience confirms the results of the NEA report and suggests to me that we ought to be talking more about why we need readers and how to develop them. By "we" I mean at least three different groups. First, "we," not just as "book people" but as human beings "in general," need readers, and we especially need literary readers, because even as other sources of information may supplant books in terms of the widespread circulation of certain kinds of data and even knowledge, books remain a singularly important source of literary values, perspectives, and approaches. And literary values include things like what Martha Nussbaum writes about as the narrative imagination, the cultivation of empathy, understanding how others very unlike ourselves see, feel, and know, and the safe exploration of alternative identities and perspectives. Now more than ever, our world needs people who care about how other people see things, who can imagine things otherwise, who can reflect and discuss and change their minds.

Second, "we" as educators and administrators need readers for related reasons. Much of our professed mission and perceived value lies not only in preparing individuals for private lives that are rich, satisfying, textured, full of healthy, supportive, enriching relationships but also—although some may mistrust this claim, and it is not unrelated to my concern about student misconduct—in preparing citizens for civic life. We need readers quite literally to make both parts of this mission viable, to keep our doors open and to bear witness to the impact of our programs and policies.

Third, "we" as medievalists need readers because if you do not read much to begin with, you probably aren't going to find your way to Chaucer, and so you can't fall in love with Chaucer and understand or support or share our passion for studying Chaucer and passing Chaucer on to subsequent generations. In expressing this concern, I return to the anxiety I expressed above, that Chaucer studies may be thriving, but chiefly at higher levels in the educational system, with more mature and sophisticated readers rather than with the large numbers of more underprepared, more difficult-to-teach college students who are less interested in reading. The division of labor among postsecondary institutions may make pragmatic and pedagogical sense, but what does it say about our ability as educators to reach poorly prepared, less-privileged students and thus expand the shrinking population of readers? Perhaps this is not something that Chaucerians can worry about, but someone needs to wonder whether students who attend community colleges for "remediation" will have the opportunity to read any literary texts, let alone any medieval texts, taught by passionate teachers, and to become readers themselves.

Not asked to speak of solutions to the challenges I have reflected on here—ranging from prevailing careerism to the overall decline in literary reading—I propose none beyond what this forum in itself represents: the rare chance for Chaucerians to think together about a few of the broader issues in which our future is embedded. Returning briefly now to the issue of the "dual role" of the scholar/administrator, I close by suggesting that there are reasons why in fact Chaucerians are particularly well suited to think and act like administrators, and why we might encourage them to do so.

Successful administrators, for example, need to bring intellectual energy to the task of welcoming or at least dealing patiently with intractable problems and finding common ground for differing factions, and Chaucerians are scholars who have chosen difficulty and complexity, who relish irony and ambiguity, and who have experience in unifying the creativity of criticism with the discipline of history. Effective administrators today also need to think about the meaning and possibility of institutional stability during a time of economic, demographic, and technological transition—an issue that Chaucerian texts constantly examine. And as fellow medievalist and experienced college administrator Craig Williamson also reminded me, good administrators need to combine "a hard eye" with "an embracing heart," *auctoritee* with *gentilesse*. Like Chaucer the poet, administrators need to be ready to listen to everyone's story, keeping their judgments in the background, and keeping themselves in the background, always present yet never appearing, enabling the fabric to weave itself. For the sake of many worthy causes, then—Chaucer studies, the humanities in general, and the goals of an undergraduate education in the liberal arts and sciences, to name a few that are dear to my heart—I hope we can bring more Chaucerians, and more of what we might call Chaucerian values, to the administrative table.

REVIEWS

Dorsey Armstrong. *Gender and the Chivalric Community in Malory's "Morte d'Arthur."* Gainesville: University Press of Florida, 2003. Pp. viii, 272. $59.95.

This spirited and engaged account of Malory's *Morte* highlights the importance of the Pentecostal Oath as a chivalric code, one that Malory produces in reaction to "the trouble of his day" and that "unintention-al(ly)" institutionalizes "a particular ideal of gender relations," only for its fulfillment to hasten Arthurian society's downfall (p. 7). Armstrong offers a vigorous reading of how gender, community, and chivalric identity interact in the *Morte*, and traces how such concerns shape and give coherence to the narrative as a whole. Crucial to the argument is how the Arthurian knight both defines himself against and depends on a particular construction of the female as passive in complement to his own aggressive behavior. In successive chapters, Armstrong draws adroitly on literary theory to outline the effect of masculine and feminine as mutually defining and sustaining positions in the *Morte*, from the episode of Arthur's campaign against Lucius, through assessments of knighthood as performative, to the *Sankgreal* as a "critique" of chivalric values, and the final catastrophe (although one might want to modify the argument that the exercise of gender relations per se is "progressively degenerative" [p. 24] in the *Morte*).

In discussion, the Pentecostal Oath takes on a double function; it clearly reveals the failings of the society that produced it and that it produces, for the "stability of identity" it promises in codifying female and male roles is exposed as fictive in its disregard for the crucial role the feminine plays in masculine identity (p. 37), and while an inflexible gender model is imperative to maintaining the Arthurian order, adherence to it ultimately spells disaster for the community. At the same time, the Oath offers a guide to chivalric behavior, and the actions of women deemed to transgress its rule are also said to ruin the chivalric community while simultaneously exposing its inherent weakness as a social model. The tension in interpretation here seems to arise from the contradictions of Malory's narrative, which continually demonstrates an apparent lack of self-awareness coupled with a knowing anxiety over, and constant revision of, its own procedures. Armstrong is highly sensitive to the inadequacies of a restrictive binarism in considering gender in Malory, and yet local readings risk presenting women's autonomy primarily in the terms of a masculine anxiety traditional to chivalric romance, as though the thinking behind the Oath's prescriptions has sometimes leached into the act of critical reading.

The suggestion that it is Morgause's unruly volition that produces Mordred as monstrous (p. 54) is a somewhat disturbing case in point; the text itself does not condemn Morgause in these terms, and while the narrative may, of course, generally displace onto women problems that male chivalric behavior has generated, this reading homogenizes constructions of gender at a point where causation is most ambiguous and contested. If the Pentecostal Oath is the *Morte*'s "master signifier" (p. 28), it might be more productive to consider Mordred's career in the light of the Oath's astonishing conceptualization of, and inadequate provision for, "treson." Similarly, the assertion that Guinevere "should be held responsible" for Lancelot's actions at the end of the *Morte*, because "What Arthur seems to understand at long last is that the masculine project of chivalry is really nothing more than knights acting in accordance with the wishes of ladies" (p. 191), registers a specific power for the feminine as regards the action, but fails to address how the not-uncommon knightly disavowing (and anti-Oath) defense of killing on the grounds of obedience to women demands, by this point, consideration within the general breakdown in the rule of law and of social relations. And richly comic as is the idea that Morgan and her fellow queens engage in sexual mischief in the absence of a handbook to instruct them in proper behavior (p. 98), it does not explain why and how Morgan is so much more complex a character in Malory than in the French sources (where, more prominently villainous, she is also subject to stricter regulation).

Armstrong tends to repeat key sentences from critical positions, as when she quotes Gravdal on rape in Arthurian literature (pp. 11, 36, 241), or Shichtman and Finke on violence (pp. 37, 196). This certainly helps maintain the clarity of the argument, but it also intimates that there is room to engage with and refine, further than she does, the critical terms thus established as foundational. An occasional shift in a term's associations leaves some points undeveloped (for example, the contradictions in the relation of "the feminine" to virginity in Perceval's Sister's case [p. 238] and in Galahad's [p. 171]). Sometimes, discussion concentrates on one aspect of gender in a particular episode, where one would welcome broader contextualization and a concomitantly sharper focus on (say) masculine accountability, or the interaction of both masculine and feminine agency. For example, it would be interesting to look at the role of the Arthurian court as closely as at the role of marriage in the comparative histories of Fair Unknowns, or to compare Perceval's self-mutilation with Lyonet's control over Gareth's thigh wound.

Malory's work appears sometimes more relaxed toward gender than are his sources, and sometimes anxious to maintain a tighter control of gender—it is telling that Malory omits the eponymous hero's experience of the fractured shield in the Prose *Lancelot*. At the same time, the *Morte* textually inscribes the problems inherent in the attempt to invoke and deploy gender as reading strategy and as control mechanism, and in consequence gender accrues an epistemological function, its investigation integral to an understanding of the *Morte*'s literary strategies. Armstrong's analysis could perhaps go further in its project to uncover the complexities and ramifications of Malory's work, but in its acknowledgment of the text's dense ambiguities, its concern to find a critical vocabulary appropriate to the subject, and its provocative lines of inquiry, this book forms a thought-provoking contribution to the continuing debate about gender in Malory.

CATHERINE BATT
University of Leeds

C. DAVID BENSON. *Public "Piers Plowman": Modern Scholarship and Late Medieval English Culture.* University Park: The Pennsylvania State University Press, 2003. Pp. xix, 283. $45.00.

Most readers find *Piers Plowman* a difficult poem, and its difficulty has long been considered part of its greatness. Unlike the *Canterbury Tales*, whose greatness, for modern readers, lies in its near-mythic accessibility, the greatness of *Piers Plowman* lies in its difference, the feeling that its difficulty might be overcome by careful study of its particular past.

One of the most perplexing differences about *Piers Plowman*, however, is that it was so much a part of its own literary present. Not only does the poem address topical issues, and not only does it insist on its own currency, but also, for all its difficulties—some of which *must* have struck medieval audiences as such—the poem seems to have interested a variety of readers. We tend to think that a diverse readership indicates an accessible text, a text commonly understood in its moment, because we assume that ease of use is the same thing as ease of understanding. Likewise, we assume that time organizes a shared sense of culture. Yet the discrepancy between *Piers Plowman*'s style and reception continually invites us to re-historicize concepts such as "current," "shared," "accessible," or "public."

In his gracefully written new book, *Public "Piers Plowman"*, David Benson challenges us to find a critical approach that will make "this great poem more accessible, exciting and necessary to modern readers" (p. xix). For Benson, an ideal literary criticism would accomplish this objective by situating the poem "in the broad cultural environment of its time and place" (p. 111), by which he means a nonelite, nonscholarly medieval culture. Benson argues, in other words, that the poem's greatness—its difficulty—has to do, in part, with the way it participates in those cultural forms that were available to most medieval people. He argues further that what we now perceive to be the poem's difficulty was, in its own time, a kind of catholicity, an appeal to a wide range of audiences, the acceptance of which is evidenced by the poem's transmission. For Benson, such an appeal approaches democracy when read against a "public culture" comprised of those artworks, institutions, and spaces, which were not only accessible, but which also "blurred modern distinctions between secular and ecclesiastical use," and which "permitted interaction and cooperation between different groups" (pp. 157–58). As the title of the book suggests, "public" is the term with which Benson links the culture in which the poem participated to its disorderly composition and reception.

To make these arguments, Benson divides his book into two sections: the first presents a history of *Piers Plowman* criticism, biographical criticism in particular, and the second offers a corrective to this kind of criticism by reading the poem in light of late medieval literary texts, wall painting, and urban spaces. The idea is that previous scholarship, by focusing on composition rather than reception, has located the difficulty—and greatness—of the poem in the person of the poet. In the first section, divided into three chapters, Benson charts a genealogy of criticism indebted to the personal history of the author. In chapter 1, "The History of the Langland Myth," he argues that Skeat produced two interdependent myths, the myth of the poet and the myth of the poem, and he demonstrates convincingly that subsequent scholars have continually reinvented an author through which order might be imposed on a disorderly text. In chapter 2, "Beyond the Myth of the Poem," Benson observes that proponents of the A-B-C order have dogmatically insisted on the poet's desire for aesthetic perfection or ideological resolution while admitting, at the same time, that neither intention nor style can be definitively identified. He argues further that author-centered criticism has prevented scholars from realizing the implications of reception-oriented studies (pp. 60–62). In chapter 3, "Beyond the Myth of the Poet," Benson lucidly reviews alternatives to biographical criticism, arguing that even these tend to focus on the poem's author, at the expense of the poet's audience.

Ultimately, however, Benson is less interested in shifting focus from author to audience as he is in using the idea of audience to link *Piers Plowman* to medieval public culture. For him, the diverse reception *of* the poem helps us reconsider the diversity of opinions *in* the poem as evidence that the poem "looks outward as much as it looks inward" (p. 106). For Benson, moreover, a poem that "looks" outward looks not to a world "of elite learning that was available only to a few," but rather to "the more general, common culture of contemporary England: the public world" (p. 107). The trouble is that Benson, by identifying ideological complexity with public culture, romanticizes disorder as much as he romanticizes the idea of public culture. He also, peculiarly, identifies complexity with inclusiveness or accessibility: the poem entertains different opinions and voices, to be sure, but that is not the same thing as saying that it models conflict resolution or that it lends itself to learned and nonlearned, secular and ecclesiastic alike. Finally, it is problematic to distinguish between elite and nonelite medieval culture in the way that Benson does here. We might be able to figure out which institutions or individuals generated ideas represented in *Piers Plowman*. We may even be able to figure out why a specialized readership found the poem compelling. But I believe it is impossible for us to generalize from these discoveries a realm of learning and privilege opposed to a universally shared culture, not least because what is principally shared is not what one sees but how one chooses to interpret it.

Although I disagreed with the book's methodology, I found that the second section contained all sorts of wonderful local insights about *Piers Plowman*. In chapter 4, "Public Writing," Benson enumerates the shared features of *Piers Plowman*, *Mandeville's Travels*, and *The Book of Margery Kempe*. Among these, he notes "a looseness and ability to accommodate diverse materials and genres" (p. 115), an abiding interest in public venues and spectacles, and the tendency to publicize interior life or elite thought. In chapter 5, "Public Art: Parish Wall Paintings," the book's strongest chapter, he shows how wall paintings inform Langland's "artistic grammar"; especially illuminating are the parallels he draws between paintings of the Day of Judgment and Truth's Pardon (pp. 174–76). As he demonstrates in this chapter, the similarities between the two artistic mediums have to do with the ways that they translate theology into aesthetic practice. In chapter 6, "Public Life: London Civic Practices," he argues that London practices are central to *Piers Plowman*, and especially those religious, commercial, and judicial practices that characterize Cornhill. Benson focuses on Cornhill not simply because it is mentioned in *Piers Plowman,* but rather because it embodied those urban characteristics that inform the values of the poem, including love of neighbor and strict justice.

In sum, *Public Piers Plowman* is a thought-provoking study of a difficult poem and its scholarly traditions. Readers new to the poem will appreciate the book's reviews of Langland scholarship, and more experienced readers of the poem will enjoy arguing with its local readings and critical methods.

EMILY STEINER
University of Pennsylvania

GLENN BURGER. *Chaucer's Queer Nation*. Medieval Cultures 34. Minneapolis: University of Minnesota Press, 2003. Pp. xxv, 264. $49.95 cloth, $19.95 paper.

Queer medieval studies up to this point has been largely concerned with mapping sodomy as an abjected medieval cultural formation and as the historically specific site of the queer for the Middle Ages. In literary, religious, and historical studies of medieval sexuality, sodomy has provided the main location for Foucauldian revisions of medieval culture as well as more traditional scholarship. As a result of this focus, along with a curious tendency of medieval scholarship to transport modern heteronormativity to the past, the current map of medieval sexuality is oddly polarized between sodomitic vices and normative heterosexuality— oddly, given Foucault's clear assumption of the "normal implantation" alongside the "perverse implantation" in his first volume of *The History of Sexuality*. This is where the theoretical framing and structural design of Burger's book makes a critical entry into queer medieval studies: Burger contests the assumption of medieval heteronormativity for Chaucer's *Canterbury Tales* (and by implication, for medieval culture generally) and argues instead for dislodging the queer in medieval texts from the heterosexual or the implied identities associated with the binary oppositions of normal and deviant. Burger draws on Homi Bhabha's work to insist on a "middle" position in queer medieval studies that resists modern cultural formations, such as heterosexuality, nation, and canons. This then allows him to intervene in such traditionally "heteronormative" sites as the so-called Marriage Group of the *Canterbury Tales* to queer conjugality even as it is being used "to identify and ground a community of new 'gentils'" (p. xxii). What this means is that the Wife of Bath, that notorious figure of heteronormativity, ends up being queer (*contra* Carolyn Dinshaw in *Getting Medieval: Sexualities and Communities, Pre- and Postmodern*) in Burger's analysis. This is just one example of how utterly, well, queer, Burger's work is and how challenging to Chaucer studies it promises to be.

The other crucial move that Burger makes in the book is to pose his discussion of Chaucer's "queer nation" as a challenge to modern identity categories and discourses of empire and nation. Identity categories, medieval as well as modern, come under Burger's scrutiny from a number of angles. Like Jeffrey Jeremy Cohen in *Medieval Identity Machines* (University of Minnesota Press, 2003), Burger follows the theoretical lead of Gilles Deleuze and Félix Guattari by treating the category of identity itself as a "machinic assemblage." Rather than a unified finished product, identity is unfinished and multiple, and, in this sense, also queer. *The Miller's Tale* provides Burger with a starting point for his queer project of "seeing[ing] and claim[ing] previously disallowed medieval sexual positions (disallowed both by our modern blindnesses and by the workings of medieval hegemonies as both powerful and meaningful)" (p. xviii). Forging a hermeneutic link between John Preston's contemporary gay fiction and *The Miller's Tale*, Burger argues that Chaucer's work intervenes in a medieval masculinity that is construed through sadism, opening up a space for new and shifting masculine identities organized around shame, masochism, the feminine, and the bodily. The disorganizing power and the indelible pleasure of *The Miller's Tale* poses a provocative challenge to Fragment 1 of the *Canterbury Tales* that reverberates through the rest of the work.

The second and third chapters present a radical critique of our ways of viewing heteronormativity in the Middle Ages by insisting on conjugality as something different from modern heterosexuality and, at the same time, potentially disruptive. In fact, far from simply inscribing subjects in a heteronormative world order, conjugality provides the "gentils," a "modernizing elite" in Burger's formulation, a means of "asserting its agency and self-definition" (p. 59). Locating his argument in the radical redefinition of marriage of the twelfth and thirteenth centuries, Burger traces how "conjugality within the lay married estate, itself a new representational mode arising out of the Gregorian Reform, provides precisely that complex nexus of sex, gender, sexuality, class, and community identifications needed to map this more inclusive, yet still privileging, masculine 'gentil' identity" (p. 76). In the third chapter Burger offers a marvelous reading of the Wife of Bath, not as poster child for heterosexuality, as she is often read, but as a representative of the hybrid position of wife and "gentil," with all the claims to masculinity that such a position entails. Burger pursues the dislodging of gender and social categories in the Wife's *Prologue* and *Tale* through representations of conjugality in the Merchant's and Franklin's tales.

The fourth chapter takes up some of the issue of male sodomitical panic in the Physician's and Pardoner's tales. Instead of reading the Pardoner as a figure of the modern queer, Burger insists on the Pardoner's perverse gender and sexuality as a figure of the crisis of representation itself in the new bourgeois identity that is the Canterbury project.

The notoriously disorganized Fragment VII suggests, in Burger's analysis, a space where "the usual patterns of differentiation dissolve" and, with them, the usual structures of identity. In their place, from Melibee to *The Shipman's Tale*, is hybridity, multiplicity, and mobility. The final chapter meditates on the ways in which the concluding tales, especially *The Parson's Tale* and Chaucer's Retractions, gesture toward a kind of universal history and Christian subject as the endpoints of the tales. Instead, Burger argues passionately that this transcendentalizing move is actually complicitous with "another, newer, lay-authorizing historicism that has been at work throughout the *Tales*" (p. 190).

Burger's book offers medieval studies a newly queered landscape, one that is not so perdurably poised between the heteronormative and the perverse or same-sex desire and different-sex desire. Instead, Burger's queer is much more complexly situated and more complexly implicated in the modern landscape than we might have thought. How this newly queer medieval subject position that crisscrosses modern categories of desire founds a national self-concept—as the title promises—remains somewhat under-elaborated in the book, but Burger provides avenues aplenty for further considerations of the medieval national in terms of the medieval queer.

KARMA LOCHRIE
Indiana University

JEFFREY J. COHEN. *Medieval Identity Machines.* Medieval Cultures 35. Minneapolis: University of Minnesota Press, 2003. Pp. xxix, 336. $63.95 cloth, $22.95 paper.

Medieval Identity Machines is made up of six loosely related chapters. The first, "Time's Machines," argues for a nonlinear conception of time that enables reading medieval texts through contemporary theoretical lenses, and that unites the book's six hundred years of texts by rejecting linear time in favor of an "unbounded middle" time where ideological constructions from different historical moments can interact (p. 21). The second chapter, "Chevalerie," argues that the mounted and armed knight should be reconceived as a composite organism rather than a set of discrete entities. "Masoch / Lancelotism" takes on courtly ideology through psychoanalytic theory, arguing that masochism is crucial to the sexuality of literary heroes of adulterous love. In "The Solitude of Guthlac," Cohen proposes that religious discipline constrains Guthlac to disperse his personal history in confrontations with torturing demons, unmaking his secular identity and preparing him for solitary eremeticism. "The Becoming-Liquid of Margery Kempe" considers how Margery's adopted attributes, such as her white clothing and her roaring tearfulness, supplement her language and contribute to her effect on others, an effect importantly visceral as well as rational. The last chapter, "On Saracen Enjoyment," is a subtle assessment of how racial discourse accrues staying power from the pleasure it induces, propelling its circulation beyond any practical and ideological usefulness.

The "identity machine" of Cohen's title draws on the works of Gilles Deleuze and Félix Guattari, which conceive an escape from bourgeois modernity and stifling social constraint. Especially through fantasy and creativity, Deleuze and Guattari argue, identities can emerge that commingle and hybridize the human with the surrounding nonhuman environment. Cohen adapts their "desiring-machines" and "becoming-animals" in his term "identity machine" to characterize fusions of human and nonhuman that create unprecedented subjectivities with expanded or specialized capacities. The "identity machine" is a provocative frame for opening discussion on the diverse medieval sources gathered here. Its disadvantages are perhaps the price of its attractions. It appealingly shifts the terms of analysis from the familiar dichotomies of human versus animal, human versus environment, and human versus artifact, to focus on the inextricability of humanness from what is deemed nonhuman. But Deleuze and Guattari's specific theoretical purchase must go protean, morphing and even contradicting itself in the task of accounting for the medieval material; at the same time, the medieval material must be pressed out of shape in order to adjust it to this theoretical paradigm.

For example, the relationship of man and horse in chivalry is altogether worth analysis, but "becoming-animal" must be de-fanged to encompass chivalry. Deleuze and Guattari imagine a radical resistance to normality and social constraint—not just anti-Oedipal but anti-logical, anti-humanist, anti-systematic. Exceptional artists, seers, psychotics, children, and other marginals embrace aberrance in subversions and destabilizations of conventional social identities. This paradigm has little purchase on knights and horses in chivalry, even the chivalry of romance. Knighthood is not an oppressed or alienated status; a knight's commitment to authoritative and normative codes disqualifies him from the system-subverting becoming-animal of *A Thousand Plateaus*. Thus Cohen's general assessments of historical chivalry are not convincing: that the mounted knight "was in fact a creature composed of flux rather than essence, a centaur sustained through malleable alliance, a fantastic becoming-horse" (p. 47); or that "the supposedly inanimate stirrup is 'neither object nor subject' but a 'thing that possesses body and soul indissolubly'" (p. 49, quoting Bruno Latour). However necessary stirrups were to chivalry, and however richly symbolic a knight's accoutrements, nothing in Cohen's argument convinces me that medieval knights understood their stirrups to be animate, nor that it would be illuminating for scholars to accept that stirrups were animate. Donna Haraway's concept of the cyborg, not fully organic and not so grounded in subversion and marginality as the becoming-animal, might better account for chivalric self-expansion: the cyborg masters bodily prostheses such as sword, horse, and stirrup as empowering enhancements to identity. So fully can a pacemaker, a pair of eyeglasses, or a knight's sword be incorporated into physical identity that it could become less than relevant where body leaves off and prosthesis begins, and more relevant that the expanded organic and inorganic body functions as a coherent entity.

Literary works recruited to illustrate the becoming-animal of knights fare better than the historical data. *Sir Gawain and the Green Knight*, a text remarkably engaged in consideration of animals, has little to say about Gawain's horse beyond the companionship of their questing weeks and the good feed they both get at Bertilak's castle. Cohen over-reads the evidence in arguing that "Gringolet is in a way Gawain" and that "he is as well Gawain's only immutable love" (p. 75). On the other hand, the poet puts such narrative emphasis on the relation between humans and animals in hunting, and such structural pressure on the relation between the hunts and temptations, that Cohen's argument for "an affective alliance between the knight and the desperate animals" rings true. Exemplifying the entire book's energetic, compelling prose, Cohen points out that the third fitt's ominous atmosphere would be dissipated "if chivalric subjectivity did not spread out from the small space of the curtained bed and cling in uneven pieces to the deer, boar, and fox as they rush anxiously through an inimical world" (p. 74).

Much of the pleasure of this study resides in its counterintuitive suggestions about medieval culture. Books that engage their readers' imagination can begin two-way conversations with their readers' doubts. On the familiar figure of the "zodiac man," the human figure pictured in the cosmic place of the earth and surrounded by the spheres of the planets and signs of the zodiac, Cohen reverses the conventional medieval understanding that the zodiac man is microcosmic, that he focuses and expresses the coherence of all creation and of his own creation in God's image. Instead, Cohen understands the "zodiac man" as a creature "dispersed across the cosmos," pulled apart and upward along the connecting lines of cosmic influence, such that "human desire, human sexuality, become inextricable from sidereal desire, celestial sexuality" (pp. xv–xvi). Ahistorical misreading or stimulating postmodern counter-reading? Cohen does not mention that he is reversing the medieval conception of the "zodiac man": with regard to student readers, his omission is unfortunate, but it does clear a ground zero for rethinking the figure. Readers may then recall for themselves the standard meanings for a given medieval exemplar, try out the disorientation of Cohen's contrary reading, and assess the deconstructive possibility that the conventional interpretation invites its own inversion. The lines of influence from cosmos to human body, centrifugal as they look to medieval science, do trace potentially centripetal tracks of dispersion. Presenting the reader with such possibilities to ponder is the consistent strategy of Cohen's study.

SUSAN CRANE
Columbia University

CAROLYN DINSHAW and DAVID WALLACE, eds. *The Cambridge Companion to Medieval Women's Writing.* Cambridge: Cambridge University Press, 2003. Pp. xx, 289. $60.00 cloth, $22.00 paper.

This addition to the Cambridge Companion series broadly construes medieval women's relationship to writing. In so doing, it follows the lead of a number of recent studies that have emphasized historical and textual circumstances attending the emergence of the woman writer and women's writings in the Middle Ages, and have investigated the cultural systems and institutions that were enabling sites of textual production by and for women. Hence, this book's conception of medieval women's writing not only addresses the individual females, celebrated and anonymous, who were directly engaged in the making of texts but also examines the social and spiritual conditions and gendered states that necessarily framed medieval women's intersections with textual culture—as authors and readers, patrons and collaborators, agents and subjects of representation.

The book is divided into three parts. Part One, "Estates of Women," surveys familiar categories of medieval women's social/sexual identity, with Ruth Evans's essay on "Virginities," Dyan Elliott's on "Marriage," and Barbara A. Hanawalt's on "Widows." "Female Childhoods" by Daniel T. Kline and "Between Women" by Karma Lochrie fill in details of that picture less frequently limned in studies of medieval women's writing. Part Two examines "Texts and other spaces" in which medieval female literate practices occurred. Jennifer Summit's "Women and Authorship" proposes a broadened understanding of the term "author" that does not associate the concept with individual, originary acts, and then surveys social, material, and ideological conditions under which medieval women contributed to textual culture. Subsequent essays in Part Two implicitly expand on Summit's formulation. Christopher Cannon explores the construction of the female anchoritic subject through the literature of "Enclosure," a process that provides a paradigm for the "making of any self" (p. 119). Aptly characterizing the medieval women's life "At home; out of the house" as the life that Margery Kempe "refused" (p. 124), Sarah Salih analyzes the space of the household fashioned by women's conduct texts, letters, and Kempe's own testament to domestic resistance. Alcuin Blamires moves discussion of women's intersections with textual culture from these private spaces to more public arenas "Beneath the pulpit," where women could encounter suppression as well as opportunities for expression of their spiritual agency. Part Three, "Medieval Women," rounds out the collection with more detailed portraits of specific writers and genres: Christopher Baswell on Heloise; Roberta Krueger on Marie de France; David Hult on "The *Roman de la Rose*, Christine de Pizan, and the *querelle des femmes*"; Sarah McNamer on "Lyrics and Romances"; Nicholas Watson on Julian of Norwich; Carolyn Dinshaw on Margery Kempe, Alexandra Barratt on "Continental women mystics and English readers"; and Nadia Margolis on Joan of Arc.

By the editors' description, the focus of this collection is "England, viewed as part of a greater medieval Europe" (p. 1). Virtually all the evidence adduced to analyze the "estates" and "spaces" of medieval women's involvement with textual and literate culture is from English sources. To cite just one example, Ruth Evans's wide-ranging discussion employs exclusively English witnesses—in drama, devotional writing, autobiography, lyric, hagiography, romance, and letters—to document the multiplicity of virginities that were textually available to late medieval culture. Chaucer is a frequent touchstone in these essays (the index records more citations [72] of the poet and his works than of any other writer, including the women whose textual activities are featured here.

Christine de Pizan is second with 42 indexed citations). Most of these invocations of the English poet appear in parts one and two, where they underscore his preoccupation with women's literate practices and the extent to which the terms and conditions of medieval women's lives and texts reverberate throughout his fictions. But this frequency of citation also enhances the emphasis on English-language texts and sources in these parts. This emphasis shifts in Part Three; four of its eight essays focus on French language subjects. Such a shift is entirely in keeping with the recent tendency for historians and scholars of medieval women's writing to highlight the probable insular provenance of the works of Marie de France and to elaborate Christine de Pizan's many connections to late medieval English readers, translators, and printers. Yet the excellent essays on these writers in this collection are not framed in these terms by the editors in their introduction; neither are the contributions on the more notorious Heloise and Joan of Arc brought into any larger framework that might elaborate on the linguistic and cultural implications of the book's declared focus on "England, viewed as a part of a greater medieval Europe." Hence the opportunity to foreground what Roberta Krueger recognizes as the multilingual, multicultural dimensions of medieval women's writing in England (p. 182) goes largely unrealized. A related omission involves the absence of any sustained discussion of the Anglo-Norman women's literary culture whose breadth and importance for insular textual traditions, through the efforts of Jocelyn Wogan-Browne and others, we are just now beginning to comprehend.

Such limitations notwithstanding, these essays, contributed by a roster of distinguished scholars, are uniformly engaging as well as impressively concise in their treatment of potentially unwieldy topics. The effective balance of information, analysis, and helpful generalization of the essays fulfills the mission of the Cambridge series, making this book an excellent companion for the new as well as the more experienced student of medieval women's writing and thus also an excellent prospect for use in the classroom. Chris Africa's one-thousand-year chronology of Continental and insular textual activities and a bibliography of "Further Reading," including a brief, annotated list of electronic resources devoted to the study of medieval women, are additional features that make this collection even more attractive for classroom adoption.

THERESA COLETTI
University of Maryland

SYLVIA FEDERICO. *New Troy: Fantasies of Empire in the Late Middle Ages.*
Medieval Cultures 36. Minneapolis: University of Minnesota Press,
2003. Pp. xxiv, 207. $60.95 cloth, $21.95 paper.

Sylvia Federico's *New Troy: Fantasies of Empire in the Late Middle Ages*
joins a spate of recent critical works analyzing English fantasies of nation
and empire in the fourteenth and fifteenth centuries, in this case mining
the identifications and conflicts embedded in England's literary obsession with Troy. Engaging psychoanalytic accounts of fantasy and desire
and theories of utopianism with close textual and archival work, Federico's study advances the argument that late-middle English claims on
Troy positioned political and literary culture within a prestigious (if ambivalent) historical imaginary, one capable of advancing England toward
a national future. Her study awards national primacy of place to London—it here signifies "mainstream English culture" (p. 61)—thus helping us think about the medieval city as future metropole.

Chapter 1 inaugurates the focus on London in texts produced during
the period immediately following the Rising of 1381. London emerges
as a contentious and vibrant commercial space, linked to Trojan structures of meaning in both John Gower's *Vox Clamantis* and in Richard
Maidstone's *Concordia facta inter regem Riccardum II et civitatem Londonie*
(1393). Both texts figure Troy ambivalently as a means of coping with
the benefits and liabilities of such civic volatility and promise. Gower's
Book I, for example, casts London's rulers—unable to protect the city
from the rising—as Troy's traitors, positioning Gower himself as the
moral leader London (and by extension England) needs, a "type of Aeneas" (p. 17). The pageant, an attempt to convince an implacable Richard II to restore the freedoms and privileges recently taken from the
city, links Richard's "intervention in London's autonomy . . . to the
Greeks' invasion of Troy," thus placing Richard "on the wrong side of
the Trojan War" (p. 26). In each case, New Troy is feminized and eroti-
cized: for Gower, a London overrun with rebels appears as a widow too
free with her favors; in Maidstone's poem, Richard unites with the city
as sovereign and spouse, imaging the relation of ruler and ruled as a
display of the consent of wife for husband, subject for sovereign. Each
construes London as a space of possibility poised toward futurity: Gower's conservative fantasy idealizes the Trojan past in the utopian hope of
heralding a revivified future for postrevolt London; Maidstone's poem

likewise surfaces utopian civic hopes, exerting "symbolic pressure" on Richard to restore liberties denied.

Chapter 2 reads the Trojan references in Chaucer's *House of Fame* and *Sir Gawain and the Green Knight* as crises of interpretation. History and interpretation move toward the geographic consolidation that accompanies national community. Federico reads London's centrality in the regionalism of *Gawain,* specifically in the text's "delight" in the "wild terrain of Wales and the oddities found therein," as emblematic of the historical process whereby the region of the Gawain-poet is "drawn more into the national mainstream" (p. 61). Chaucer's *House of Fame,* written during the poet's London period, alludes to the hurly-burly of London (in the figure of the wicker house as a "marketplace of tidings"), where history and fame are made by the circulation of story and reputation. Federico smartly argues that each poem refigures the ambivalent meaning of Aeneas's journey so as to address ideologies of history, authenticity, and fable—finally coming to the "frustrating realization that the perversion of truth is the necessary concomitant to fame" (p. 31). *Gawain and the Green Knight* addresses the transmission of narrative—both the story of Trojan genealogy and that of Gawain's reputation—in the midst of the poet's awareness of the unpredictability of any text's reception. Chaucer's *House of Fame,* beginning in a way where *Gawain* leaves off, imagines New Troy as a "home for English letters" (p. 56).

Chapter 3, in many ways the historiographic heart of the book, analyzes the historical imagination legible in *Troilus and Criseyde.* Elaborating the "utopian" moves implicit in the first three books, Federico argues that in linking future, present, and past the poem raises, if tentatively, alternatives to the determinative Trojan narrative, pointing to the possibility that "Criseyde perhaps will not be false and . . . Troy perhaps will not fall" (p. 73). Criseyde here figures possibility, a space suspended in time, ripe with the promise of fulfillment, completion, consummation. This utopian fantasy, however, collapses when "history" reenters. In tracing the web of future, present, and past, Federico helps us see that part of the popularity of the Troy story involves (paradoxically) the wish for a different ending, the desire to resist history's determinative march. Yet in opposing history's determinism to fantasy's possibility (if not entirely, at least most urgently here), Federico tends to undercut what seems to me one of the strengths of a study like hers: that fantasies of loss, failure, and impossibility, fantasies whose pleasures lie "beyond the pleasure principle," collude with (perhaps even help produce) history *as* necessity. They help produce, that is, the view of history as the only possible outcome precisely as the outcome beyond possibility. History's claim on fantasy has its drive toward necessity via the historical subject's longing for impossibility and dissatisfaction, for an excess that can neither be managed nor fully directed.

Chapter 4 returns us to London, this time during the period of transition from Ricardian to Lancastrian rule, and to two narratives written between 1389 and 1422, Gower's *Confessio Amantis* and Lydgate's *Troy Book*. Investigating the contestatory claims and identities embedded in "Ricardian" and "Lancastrian"—their competing appropriations of Trojanness and concomitant claims to exemplary rule and history—Federico contrasts a Ricardian British otherness (identified here via Richard's links to the so-called celtic fringe but also to France) with Lancastrian Englishness. This opposition, she argues, is the means whereby the Lancanstrians (abetted, though not always straightforwardly, by Gower and Lydgate) define themselves as proper inheritors of an English nation centered on London. Yet this is an uncanny identity, a doubled and divided "self of Englishness" (p. 101). Richard's era haunts even as it is overthrown, just as Richard the patron haunts Gower's revisions of his text. In light of Lydgate's *Troy Book*, Chaucer emerges as a poet not for London, but for an English literary empire. Here, too, much depends upon Chaucer's links to Richard: "Chaucer confirms the empire of English letters precisely because of his Ricardian traces" (p. 142).

Federico is an agile reader of politics, and she builds strong connections to particular political events. We know a great deal more about the public uses of England's literary obsession with a Trojan past than we did when we started, and many of her connections are astute and convincing. And she forcefully and insightfully concludes that " 'history' is created through a loss of interpretive control," figured both by the productive nature of textual contestations and by the absence at the heart of history's claim on truth. Yet in a book concerned with the fictions of empire, this reader wished for a bit more sustained attention to the differential effects of that control and the slippage possible in the political effects of those fantasies. In its emphasis upon London's centrality, its concern with regional politics, and with the vernacular as the linguistic mode of "nation," for instance, *New Troy* at times duplicates certain fantasies of empire despite its clear interest in their analysis. If one of the attractions of Troy's story involves its delectation of loss, and if indeed Troy marks England's move toward nation as ambivalent, more might be made of the fractious fantasies of dissolution, dismay, and disunity embedded in the Trojan inheritance.

PATRICIA CLARE INGHAM
Indiana University

L. O. ARANYE FRADENBURG. *Sacrifice Your Love: Psychoanalysis, Historicism, Chaucer*. Medieval Cultures 31. Minneapolis: University of Minnesota Press, 2002. Pp. viii, 327. $19.95 paper, $59.95 cloth.

While psychoanalysis has a long and distinguished history in medieval studies, no medievalist has advocated as passionately for its indispensability to historicist literary study as L. O. Aranye (formerly Louise) Fradenburg. *Sacrifice Your Love* takes as its premise Lacan's ethical dictum from the seventh seminar (itself preoccupied with the medieval): "The only thing of which one can be truly guilty is of giving ground relative to one's desire." Humanity's moral sense, Lacan avows, derives from the dialectic of sacrifice and enjoyment at the center of Western ethical thought, from Aristotle to Kant, from Abelard to Nietzsche: "restraint, sacrifice, duty, 'containment,' *are* forms taken by desire" (p. 7), as are compensation, self-denying charity toward others, the act of giving in, or indeed the art of almost getting what one (thinks one) wants. *Jouissance* in this worldview is less pleasure or fulfillment and more a kind of "dirty immanence," in Georges Bataille's phrase, that never resolves the ethical confusion of desire and abnegation.

Sacrifice Your Love is a deductive book, and those predisposed against psychoanalytic approaches to literary study may resist Fradenburg's forthright enlistment of their psychologies and desires. The book's guiding thesis—"what we think we ought to do—even the very idea that we ought to do certain things—is always intimately related to our desire" (p. 2)—suggests that Fradenburg's central object of scrutiny will be not simply the desire of medieval subjects; rather, *we* are the subject of this book: *our* obligations, *our* modes of sacrifice and enjoyment. This *we*, though, does not exclude Chaucer and his contemporaries, and despite the strategically essentializing risk it takes, the untroubled use of the first-person plural throughout the book should not be read as ahistorical. To the contrary: *Sacrifice Your Love* is intended as a contribution to the writing of "the history of our sensibilities" (p. 2), a history that demands a disinvestment in what Fradenburg calls "alteritism." The notion that the Middle Ages is inexorably "other" to modernity has led to a fair measure of intellectual dishonesty: "What respect do we show the Middle Ages when we say that responsibility involves understanding the Middle Ages exclusively on its own terms, and then insist . . . that only postmedieval alteritist views of time and methods of knowledge production are capable of the attempt?" (p. 65).

In order to appreciate what this book is trying to do, we must first understand its rhetorical and critical style. Fradenburg's many paraphrases of psychoanalytic thought are most often presented as gnomic proclamations of psychic quiddity; the book's most riveting pages are also those in which psychoanalysis is made to speak with an analytic veracity few others would allow it. Indeed, Fradenburg inhabits her psychoanalytic idiom so forthrightly, so unapologetically, that the book has the effect of subsuming even a resistant reader into its Lacanian *habitus.* It is in this sense that we must comprehend the caliginous pleasures of Fradenburg's prose as integrally related to the relationship she outlines between desire and sacrifice: as she points out more than once, enjoyment is emphatically not synonymous with "ease," a sentiment illustrated through an abundance of neologism and syntactical ingenuity that, in her unrelentingly Lacanian argot, comes to feel almost intrinsic to the subjects at hand. For these and other reasons, Fradenburg emerges in this book as in many ways a more profound Lacanian than Lacan himself. She is certainly a more profound and subtle Lacanian *reader,* and as a psychoanalytic explicator of Chaucer she is without peer.

While *Sacrifice Your Love* presents itself as simultaneously a psychoanalytic intervention into medieval historicism and a study of Chaucer, Fradenburg could have done more to clarify the relationship between its two aims. The meta-theoretical conversations take up nearly a third of the book, and while the author wonderfully illuminates the diverse role of sacrifice in Chaucer's poetry, it is difficult to discern how her prescriptive arguments concerning method and critical self-consciousness relate to the conventionally Chaucerian readings that make up chapters 2 through 6. As a result, the Chaucer chapters have a strangely isolated feel, and Fradenburg's larger disciplinary arguments concerning popular medievalism, alteritism, and the ethics of historicism have no immediately apparent bearing on her discrete treatments of Chaucer.

This does nothing to detract from the interest of these chapters themselves, which a review of this length risks simplifying. Chapter 2 unfolds an intricate account of medieval and modern theory of tragedy not so much as genre, but as a mode of ethical practice that demands "prosthesis" in the face of tragic situations such as courtly love. The "rendering of courtly love as tragedy" gave medieval aristocratic culture "powerful . . . ways of defining subjectivity, sociality, and their interdependence." Chaucer's retelling of the story of Ceyx and Alcyon is thus "structured as a series of survivals" precedent to modern theories of tragedy, with all the sentimentality and "power of miniaturization" that accrues to them by the eighteenth century. Chapter 3, "The Ninety-Six Tears of Chaucer's Monk," takes a very different approach to tragedy, suggesting that the often "sadomasochistic" spectacle of the tragic as well as the "association of tragedy with critical moments in the history of responsibility" can do much to explain the construction of historical events such as the Peasants' Revolt of 1381 as "tragedies" by their chroniclers. *The Monk's Tale*'s "empty but exigent formality" speaks the dark truth both of the tragic itself and of Chaucer's larger project of collection and collocation: "The borderline between heterogeneous association and mass groupification haunts not only the Monk's performance but *The Canterbury Tales* as well" (p. 150).

The three subsequent chapters scrutinize chivalry, sacrifice, and desire in *The Knight's Tale*; charity, ethics, and the role of the neighbor or *Nebenmensch* within the "ethical structure of courtly love" (p. 186) informing *The Legend of Good Women*; and *Troilus and Criseyde* and the "failure" of tragedy to effect final resolution. The book's epilogue reads the movie *Babe* in light of "the tropes of antiutilitarian medievalism in the nineteenth century" (p. 239), taking the film as an allegory for the susceptibility of contemporary medieval studies to the utilitarian demands of the market university. As Fradenburg asks near the end of the book, "We need to decipher in medieval studies' *self*-marginalization both the destructivity within us and the enjoyment produced by our management of it, by the rarefaction of our phantasmatic modes of triumph over deadliness: medievalism's gift of death" (p. 252).

That Fradenburg is capable of discerning the death drive of our discipline in a movie about a pig's wish to avoid butchery points to the indisputable originality of *Sacrifice Your Love*, an originality that might have been enhanced had Fradenburg taken on more directly the many alternatives to the models of sacrifice, ethics, and desire proffered in this book. Her extensive engagement with the ethics of the *Nebenmensch*, for example, makes no mention of the far-reaching challenges Emmanuel Lévinas has posed to Lacan's ethics of neighborliness. The book also resists placing its findings on the ethics of sacrifice and desire in dialogue with the long scholarly tradition on psychoanalytic ethics, from L. S. Feuer to Ernest Wallwork to John Rajchman, whose influential work on Lacanian ethics and the historical logic of sacrifice tells a very different story from the one Fradenburg relates here.

These quibbles take nothing away from Fradenburg's accomplishments in this book. Psychoanalytic medievalism has reached its apogee in *Sacrifice Your Love*, which will set the course for work in this Chaucerian subfield for many years to come.

BRUCE HOLSINGER
University of Colorado

DOUGLAS GRAY, ed. *The Oxford Companion to Chaucer*. New York: Oxford University Press, 2004. Pp. xxvii, 526. $95.00.

The Oxford Companion to Chaucer is a remarkable and henceforth indispensable book for all interested in Chaucer. It is written in a direct, plain style free from jargon and fads, available to the nonspecialist and useful to the specialist alike. It is pleasant to be able to add a fact that was not available until July 2004, namely, Professor Linne Mooney's virtually certain identification of Adam Scriveyn, previously unknown, as the recorded scrivener Adam Pinkhurst. This was announced in a splendid lecture at the New Chaucer Society meeting in Glasgow in July 2004, soon to appear in *Speculum*.

For anyone wishing to annotate a Chaucerian text, most of the work is done here. The basis is a splendidly empirical Oxford emphasis on the meaning of names, but it extends to eighty-seven admirable brief essays each of up to a couple of thousand words on such general topics as The Ages of Man, Estates Satire, Folk Tale, Friendship, Penance, Rhetoric, Romance, along to Wine, Women, Youth: all concise, witty, and well balanced. The only serious omission is Honor, clearly a slip because in the entry to *The Knight's Tale* there is an asterisk as pointer to Honor as a general topic (p. 272). There are even two sections amounting to some three thousand words picking a path through the minefields of Chaucer Criticism old and new, paying appropriate justice to, for example, Muscatine, author of "the masterpiece of the New Criticism," to Donaldson and Robertson, along with the recent wave of feminist and "queer" (in every sense) criticism such as that by Dinshaw. Gray cautiously names and labels many other critics/scholars (he politely describes Brewer as "prolific"—meaning that he publishes a lot that you do not need to read). Besides all this there are special entries on all of Chaucer's works and on each Canterbury pilgrim and tale. Science is usually authoritatively dealt with by J. D. North, though much here remains arcane to me. The critic most often cited in the entries seems to be J. Norton Smith (1974). Versification is extensively and authoritatively discussed by E. G. Stanley. While rightly emphasizing the essential regularity of Chaucer's meter, he makes ample room for the great variety of rhythm.

Gray's work is in that general expository tradition that goes back to the eighteenth century and before, in what one may call (he does not) the "old" historicism, trying to judge "each work of wit / In the same spirit that the author writ." It used to be summed up in the phrase "understanding and appreciation," which of course implies its own theory of literature. On the other hand, much modern criticism tries deliberately to distort or undermine what it may be argued on historical grounds was the primary original meaning, in the name of (post)modernism, political correctness, etc., Gray does indeed pay some benign attention to such (for the moment) contemporary criticism.

The omission of an entry on Honor is regrettable. Honor is the underlying immensely influential ethos that underlies European medieval culture as it does other cultures. Honor sense is not quite dead in the West, for it is at bottom a classic example of a complex "trans-cultural value," too intrinsic to all human nature to disappear, but it is much modified in the West and so to say submerged, like the very notion of "transcultural values," which may make some people feel sick. There is a gulf in understanding between the value attached to Honor in different cultural mentalities that accounts for the incomprehension with which not only ancient and medieval European culture but some more modern cultures, notably Islamic, are met by the West. Honor is rooted in Prowess for men and Chastity for women. It is as well a fundamental demand for absolute personal loyalty (an aspect of *trouthe*) between men and women, or, rather, ladies and gentlemen. It is thus part of the ethos of the family and of the related honor-group. In Chaucer, Honor in all its primitive complexity is the basis of *The Physician's Tale* (essentially about an "honor-killing," of which there are plenty of modern instances even today). That *Tale* is primarily about patriarchal Honor, which is intimately linked with family Honor and the Honor of ladies. The Honor of ladies (a concept that has virtually disappeared in the West) is the basis of the sacrifice of the significantly named Virginia, as well as being essential to the attractiveness of the Duchess, to Criseyde's paradoxical wavering, as well as Troilus's unshakeable devotion, not to speak of the "sanctity" of the ladies of *The Legend of Good Women* and the wickedness of the men who betray them. Honor is part of the tension between Palamon and Arcite, and plays a very complex role in its relation to *trouthe* in *The Franklin's Tale*. Honor makes absolute demands on both sexes for integrity and revenge, which last makes its relation to Christianity always uneasy ("Forgive us our trespasses as we forgive . . ."), especially since the clergy are, or ought to be, outside the honor system.

These few remarks are not intended as a substitute for the brilliant essay that we may hope Gray will provide for us in that second edition of this admirable *Companion,* which will surely soon be called for. It is to be hoped that he will also add the topic of Virginity, classify the difference between Sex and Gender as concepts and critical terms (the essential difference being that while one can "have sex," one cannot "have gender," at least in that sense), expand the remarks on Rhetoric to include Translation; Orality and Literacy; add also Metaphor and Metonymy (Chaucer's poetry being notably short on Metaphor, said by some critics to be the heart of poetry). A little more on Editing would be welcome, touching on such concepts as *lectio difficilior,* the recognition of which is so crucial to detecting scribal mishandling. Gray accepts rather too easily in the *Canterbury Tales* the notion that the character of the Narrator as that person who is said for the moment to be telling the story can be deduced in retrospect from the tale itself, a notion that has occasionally led some (not Gray) to such absurd judgments, as, for example, that when *The Physician's Tale* is regarded (because of the emphasis on Honor) as bad poetry, the Physician himself must be a bad medical doctor. On other topics it is also possible to ask for a little more, as on Law, Lollardy, Arithmetic. Although all have entries written by notable special contributors, one might look for more references to cultural mentality or to actual persons or ideas. In Law, there should be references to Natural and Positive Law; in Lollardy, more information on Chaucer's friends, or at least colleagues, the Lollard Knights, and their doctrines; in Arithmetic, on its fundamental difference from Numerology (the practice of which is sometimes claimed, not without justice, for some of Chaucer's poems but which is not discussed). Chaucer's range and richness are not of course to be caught in a reference book even as good as this and such omissions are not to be taken as serious adverse criticism, or, I hope, as a captious desire to paint the lily by gilding it with refined gold.

There is only one error that I noticed (nine minor misprints are insignificant in so large and magisterial a work). The error is the entry on Artoys. The Knight is said to have fought there, that is, in Flaundres and in Picardie, whereas a major point in his portrayal, as somewhat less clearly emerges in the entry on the Knight himself, is precisely that he has never fought in France (like so many of Chaucer's fellow courtiers and Chaucer himself), but only on the borders of or beyond Christendom. In the entry on Artoys, he has become confused with the Squire. One might also query the entries on the identification of Ruce and Pruce in the formal description of the Knight (see Derek Brewer, "Chaucer's Knight as Hero and Machaut's *Prise d'Alexandrie*." in *Heroes and Heroines in Medieval English Literature*, ed. L. Carruthers [Cambridge, 1994]). The full entry on the Knight rightly dismisses recent nonsense about him being presented as a mercenary thug. The comments on the Squire have a similar polite robustness.

Gray's work includes sketch maps, some tables, and a useful, if inevitably incomplete, bibliography. It is beautifully produced, yet another instance of OUP's outstanding contribution to Chaucerian studies over many years. There are other excellent Companions to Chaucer studies already available, *by aventure yfalle/ In felaweshipe*, like the Canterbury pilgrims, like them with their own differences, being based on different principles of compilation (and perhaps I ought to confess an interest in one). Chaucer may be said to have a genial relationship to each. They do not cancel each other out, but Gray's work will always be a monument of learned and civilized literary Companionship.

DEREK BREWER
Cambridge University

SUZANNE C. HAGEDORN. *Abandoned Women: Rewriting the Classics in Dante, Boccaccio, and Chaucer.* Ann Arbor: University of Michigan Press, 2004. Pp. ix, 220. $60.00.

Suzanne Hagedorn constructs a compelling case for the richly complex medieval reception of Ovid's theme of abandoned women, as well as for the comparative thinness of our knowledge of that reception. In a series of detailed, witty, and insightful readings, she demonstrates the pervasive and often unsuspected lines of influence, echo, and transmission that link the authors of her title to one another and to their common classical past. Not the least of her achievements in this book is to delineate a Chaucer who is very much a European writer. This Chaucer, rather than writing under the tutelary influence of Italian sources, emerges as an author fully their companion in the project of late medieval adaptation of classical sources. All wrote within a received tradition that they altered to suit their present and various literary purposes.

Such writers in turn imply an audience not only literate but also familiar with the particular literary traditions they appropriate, an audience sensitive to the potential significance of ellipses, shifts, and lacunae. Audience and reception are central in this work. At the beginning of the book, Hagedorn lays out the theoretical context in which she has read the works she discusses. Given the essential project of the book, to argue the presence of literary tradition in the most elliptical and apparently skewed medieval narratives of classical stories, her invocation of Eco, Iser, and Jauss signals her interest in reception as well as in creation. Her argument depends upon a critical aesthetic of reader response and semiotic dynamics that in turn assumes a degree of uniformity in the referents, interpretants, and signifieds that late medieval audiences would have called forth as, for example, they heard echoes of Penelope's *timor* in Criseyde's fear.

The project of this book, to recover the "powerful and sympathetic views of women" to be found in the worlds of the medieval authors, is closely linked to a secondary and more provocative thesis, that stories of abandoned women expose the darker side of the heroic tradition and these authors' "disapproval of heroic forgetfulness" (p. 18). "[F]igures of abandoned women," Hagedorn contends, "challenge the centrality of the heroic code of the epic by calling attention to the private aspects of human experience that this masculine ethos tends to ignore" (p. 188).

To reach this end, she begins with an overview of the afterlife of Ovid's *Heroides* in the Latin Middle Ages, limning a variety of creative interpretive responses to and receptions of Ovid's text beyond what she terms the "flat-footed didactic schema set forth in the schoolmasters' commentaries" (p. 45). Chapter 2 reads Dante's *Inferno* 26 against Statius's *Achilleid*, in which Achilles abandons Deidamia at Ulysses' urging. The discussion of Statius's poem is particularly informative both for the deepened perspective it opens on the theme of the book—through what

313

Hagedorn terms the "back story" of Ulysses' duplicitous evocation of the heroic code and its disastrous results for both Deidamia and Penelope—and for its reminder of how much literature familiar to late medieval authors is comparatively unread today. In chapter 3, Hagedorn focuses on the story of Ariadne and Theseus and discusses how both Boccaccio and Chaucer handle the history of Theseus's betrayal of women. In close readings that persuasively recenter the Theseus of Chaucer's work against the partially suppressed tradition of his betrayals and manipulations of women, Hagedorn provides a fresh context in which to read both *The Legend of Good Women* and *The Knight's Tale*, where she sees a "doubled, potentially duplicitous Theseus" in Chaucer's evocation of this classical hero. Chapter 4, "Abandoned Women and the Dynamics of Reader Response: Boccaccio's *Amorosa Visione* and *Elegia di Madonna Fiametta*," follows Boccaccio's interest in the topos of the abandoned woman in his works after the *Teseida*. This chapter introduces Boccaccio's intertwined moralizing and affective responses to the trope of the abandoned woman in these two comparatively overlooked works, and, not coincidentally, provides a potentially fresh perspective from which to read Chaucer's *Legend of Good Women*. Thus it is a matter of some regret that the last two chapters of the book do not fully explore potential connections between the *Amorosa Visione* and the *Legend*. Chapter 5 is a sensitive reading of the "background presence" of abandoned women in the narrative and discourse of the *Troilus*, and of how Troilus himself exemplifies many of the markers of the abandoned lover. Chapter 6 turns to *The Legend of Good Women*, reading it as an ironic text, which "incorporates a play of stylistic registers and modes of discourse" that challenge the "narrow conventions of the courtly aesthetic imposed on the narrator by his inscribed reader, the God of Love" (p. 20). Much of the discussion of *The Legend of Good Women* focuses on the figure of Dido, closing the circle begun in the introduction. In this last chapter, Hagedorn uses Bakhtin to argue the presence of a variety of discourses—Virgilian, Ovidian, epic, romance, and liturgical—that work against "portraits of abandoned women in the literary tradition" (p. 191). The argument works well in respect to the polysemous quality of Chaucer's Dido narrative, but less so in constructing an opposition between the stylistic complexity of Chaucer's telling of the legend and courtly discourse, since it is debatable whether courtly narratives of abandoned women can truly be termed "monologic" in contrast to Chaucer's "dialogic" narratives (p. 20).

The great strength of this book is its expansive reading across the vernacular literary tradition of the late Middle Ages. This reading is accomplished in clear, articulate prose, with humor and complete authority. At the same time, this breadth of reading requires extensive and frequent citation of various texts essential to the argument. While the forest is never lost for the trees, it is sometimes obscured. Clear introductions and a retrospective Afterword consolidate and sharpen the complex argument, recalling the larger, overarching purposes of the book. This study is provocative in its theses and impressive in its learning. If one may quarrel with some of the interpretations and readings, one closes the volume full of ideas and questions about a freshly delineated field of reception and transmission of the topos of the abandoned woman in late medieval literature.

CAROLYN P. COLLETTE
Mount Holyoke College

CAROL F. HEFFERNAN. *The Orient in Chaucer and Medieval Romance.* Cambridge: D. S. Brewer, 2003. Pp. x, 160. $70.00.

Carol F. Heffernan's *The Orient in Chaucer and Medieval Romance* is a collection of essays on how the "orient" appears in Chaucer and a selection of medieval English romances. The book does not attempt to offer a coherent argument about medieval "orientalism," as Heffernan explains in her introduction: "This study focuses on a genre and a place— 'romance' and the 'Orient'—as they are exemplified in late medieval English literature, especially in Chaucer" (p. 1). Furthermore, Heffernan explains, "This study does not press anything like a continuous argument for medieval orientalism of a Postcolonial stamp, though a connecting purpose of the six chapters of this book is to show how the Orient and the people in it are presented in late medieval romance" (p. 1).

Arguing that one can discern an "oriental influence" in medieval romances, Heffernan argues that romance appeared in Europe following the Second Crusade and that this aristocratic genre makes "love," "courtship," and "marriage" central issues (p. 4). After a brief overview of crusade history, also covered in the introduction, five discussions of

315

romances follows. The first (chapter 2), "Mercantilism and Faith in the Eastern Mediterranean: Chaucer's *Man of Law's Tale*, Boccaccio's *Decameron* 5.2, and Gower's *Tale of Constance*," examines Chaucer's tale in light of its analogues. The issue of the "orient" slips into the background, as happens in a number of the book's discussions, as the author delves into her analysis of the differences and similarities between Chaucer and his sources. The result is that we get neither a solid philological study nor a thematic and theoretical discussion. Philology, as nineteenth-century scholars understood the term, has much to offer medieval scholars. This book reminds us that interdisciplinary knowledge applied to the entire written record of the past, including runic inscriptions, law codes, folktales, and high poetry or literature, and used systematically opens up themes and topics in the literature often overlooked by more theoretical approaches.

Chapter 3, "Two Oriental Queens from Chaucer's *Legend of Good Women*: Cleopatra and Dido," declares its subject, "another side of the Orient . . . the locale of secret pleasures and sexual excess" (p. 45), in the first sentence. This is fair enough, and virtually a commonplace of Western literature from Virgil to Chaucer. But here too I began to wonder why these two had been singled out. One of the more interesting aspects of *The Legend of Good Women* is that the women Chaucer chooses are from many different regions of the ancient world, and that Chaucer appears to challenge some of the received views of "oriental" women, as indeed with Dido, Cleopatra, and Medea. Unfortunately, this nuance, which is precisely what singles Chaucer out on this topic and makes his discussion of these famous women interesting, is lacking in the discussion.

Chapter 4, "*The Squire's Tale*," argues that although the tale represents a cornucopia of Eastern elements (motifs, themes, setting), its structure is European, even though it also exhibits traits of the framed narrative, a genre we know originated in the East. Arguing that "interlace" is European (pp. 68–81), Heffernan cites examples in Anglo-Saxon poetry and art. With an argument based on secondary sources discussing the *Thousand and One Nights*, *The Panchatantra*, and *The Thousand and One Days*, which are heavily contested as far as dating and origins, she posits that *The Squire's Tale* adopts the "interlaced structure of medieval French romances," which Chaucer has combined with "whatever oriental tales he read or heard" (p. 81).

The last two chapters discuss "Floris and Blauncheflur" and "Le Bone

Florence of Rome," respectively, each chapter addressing Eastern mate-rial in the two romances. Making an argument from absence, always tricky when source-seeking, Heffernan posits from the fact that all the extant English manuscripts of the Middle English versions of *Floris and Blauncheflur* lack "the part of the tale relevant to the birth of the hero-ine" (p. 83) that Blauncheflur's birth was a result of an incestuous rela-tionship between her Christian mother and the Saracen King of Spain, her mother's master and Floris's father. Given the sibling relationship of Islam and Christianity, "incest" is clearly a provocative metaphor for discussing the relationships between the two cultural worlds that are locked in an internecine struggle yet are members of the same family. The story of the three rings made by the same father (*Decameron* 1.3) demonstrates how commonplace the idea of the family relationship among the three religions was in medieval Mediterranean culture. In-deed, the romance offers us a textual route into such a discussion when "Floris and Blauncheflur are described as if spiritual brother and sister" (p. 92). Yet, Heffernan does not pursue this line of inquiry. Rather, she takes us far afield, hypothesizing whether Blauncheflur's mother was raped and using ancient Greek literature to support this notion (pp. 88–89).

Heffernan's discussion demonstrates solid knowledge of languages and sources, and in general the book is clearly and carefully written as far as style and expression are concerned, a considerable accomplish-ment. My overall concern is with the logic of the book because the essays do not build an argument; rather, they hover around a subject, the East as a topic in the romance genre. The author hypothesizes about sources but then retreats from such discussions. She refers to theoretical discussions of "orientalism" but seems uncomfortable pursuing these arguments too far.

The problem here, it seems to me, is that if we want to deal with *Quellenforschungen* in Eastern material, we need to start by recognizing how secular narratives, like merchants, have circulated across the an-cient roads for millennia. Interest in the East is not a uniquely nine-teenth-century European project. Attraction to the East has not been limited to the financial transactions of merchants, the goals of adventur-ers, governments, and armies, the ambitions of missionaries, or the in-terests of scholars, as expounded by the late great Edward Said in *Orientalism*. When we take into account both the philological work of the nineteenth and twentieth centuries that was entranced with finding sources together with the postcolonial discourse about "orientalism," what is surprising is how little attention is paid to the circulation and exchange of secular narratives and secular ethics and the entrepreneurial creativity of storytellers.

BRENDA DEEN SCHILDGEN
University of California, Davis

GERALDINE HENG. *Empire of Magic: Medieval Romance and the Politics of Cultural Fantasy*. New York: Columbia University Press, 2003. Pp. xii, 521. $45.00.

In this provocative study, Geraldine Heng defines romance capaciously as a genre that stages the collision of history with cultural fantasy. In her view, romance is a kind of performative cannibal that "coalesces from the extant cultural matrix at hand, poaching and cannibalizing from a hybridity of all and any available resources, to transact a magical relationship with history, of which it is in fact a consuming part" (p. 9). In Heng's view, historical trauma, tension, travail, and transition all leave their mark and seek amelioration within the desirous stagings of romance; in one of her metaphors, history is the irritant pearled and rendered pleasurable within romance's oyster, in a "graduated mutating of exigency into opportunity" (p. 3).

Heng seeks to correct previous scholarship's overidentification of romance with chivalric romance and instead proposes a five-headed typology of romances: historical, popular, chivalric, family, and travel. This widening of the social sphere of romance is both provocative and strategic, serving Heng's need to treat romance as a barometer for the desires of whole cultural moments rather than as indices of the situated interests of particular groups, notably the gentry or the clergy. To buttress the idea of romance as legible and performative zeitgeist, Heng sidelines the traditional romance-studies focus on authorship and authority in order to treat romance as a sedimentation of culture, enterprised and consumed by many in burgeoning textual traditions, disseminated in a variety of manuscript (and eventually print) cultures, and consumed by a diversity of audiences. Although she offsets her chosen texts with a formidable array of primary sources, she focuses on five central works or textual clusters: Geoffrey of Monmouth's *Historia*; the century-spanningly popular *Richard Coeur de Lion*; the Alliterative *Morte Arthure*; the Constance romance exemplified by Trevet's *Cronicles*, Gower's exemplum from the *Confessio Amantis*, and Chaucer's *Man of Law's Tale* (with a side excursion to *The Clerk's Tale*); and finally Mandeville's *Travels*.

What joins together this far-flung constellation of texts is Heng's consistent focus on crusade as romance's origin and ongoing obsession; she traces the haunting of romance by the crusading hunger for empire over four centuries. Crusade allows Heng to connect issues of nation and empire, race and religion, family and gender, and place and travel in provocative and original ways, and, throughout, she maintains a Foucauldian attention to the entwining of power, knowledge, and desire within these cultural projects. In her view, romance processes the ongoing trauma of crusade, from the threat of Islamic difference and the originary cannibalism at Ma'arra, through the conquest and loss of Jerusalem, Acre, and the other crusader kingdoms, to the exhilaration and disgrace of the Latin sack of Constantinople, to the depredations of the Genoese and Venetian profit-mongers, to the fourteenth-century efflorescence of crusade propaganda, and the debacle at Nicopolis. Within crusade, Heng returns to two concerns: the first is cannibalism, which she treats as both originary trauma and textual pleasure. Cannibalism works across chapters as an entry point into the texts and an orientation for Heng's readings. The second concern is Constantinople as a continuing locus of desire and cultural negotiation. Heng traces the shadows of Byzantium where I had never seen them before, and, in so doing, suggestively reconfigures the textual topographies she treats.

Chapter 1, "Cannibalism, the First Crusade, and the Genesis of Medieval Romance," argues that Geoffrey of Monmouth inaugurates medieval romance in his *Historia Regem Britanniae* by powerfully modeling how the trauma and sense of cultural pollution resulting from reports of crusader cannibalism at Ma'arra can be processed and turned toward more desirable fantasies of empire. The *Historia* transforms cannibalism in two ways: first, by projecting it onto a monster that can be killed, and, second, by reimagining it within the context of a self-sacrificing, exemplary loyalty in the story of Brian and Cadwallo. By transmuting the specter of crusader cannibalism, Geoffrey's *Historia* reflects its cultural moments and invents a fertile strategy for the processing of unpalatable history through cultural fantasy.

Chapter 2, "The Romance of England: *Richard Coeur de Lion* and the

Politics of Race, Religion, Sexuality, and Nation," notes another, bolder transmutation of cannibalism in the service of popular English nationalism: the joking aggression of Richard Coeur de Lion, whose monstrous cannibalistic performances foreground his crusading victories and gather his faltering compatriots into an imagined community.

Chapter 3, "Warring Against Modernity: Masculinity and Chivalry in Crisis; or, The Alliterative *Morte Arthure*'s Romance Anatomy of the Crusades," is a chapter of deft historical indexing in which Heng shows how the poem recapitulates crucial moments through the history of crusade, from the disaster at Nicopolis, to the pillage and loss of Byzantium, to developments within battle technology that destabilized conservative definitions of chivalric masculinity, whose crisis the poem demonstrates. Here the giant cannibal is revealingly indexed to Genoese venture capitalists who exploited the crusaders and their enemies and trafficked in slaves, enriching themselves from the bodies and ideals of European knighthood. Heng finds no conceptualization of nationalism here; the poem serves the interests of a single, chivalric class to the exclusion of any wider concerns.

By contrast, chapter 4, "Beauty and the East, a Modern Love Story: Women, Children, and Imagined Communities in *The Man of Law's Tale* and Its Others," shows how a national imaginary can be produced through consent rather than coercion, through the sentimental image of mother and child, whose need for protection and right-guidance can awake a communal consciousness of social justice. The family romances in this textual cluster take the wandering female cipher of hagiographic romance and powerfully sentimentalize her motherhood in the service of nation-building. At the same time, they transmute the frustrated dream of territorial conquest to a fantasy of religious and cultural (but not racial) conversion.

Chapter 5, "Eye on the World: *Mandeville*'s Pleasure Zones; or, Cartography, Anthropology, and Medieval Travel Romance," returns to the dream of territorial conquest in an epistemological vein by re-creating the world as a cabinet of curiosities, seeded with familiarity even at its nethermost reaches, and pleasurably consumed by readers at home. At the same time, however, Heng notes that very security of this consumption of difference fosters its toleration to an unusual degree, even as it whets the appetite for new expansions and conquests, preparing for Renaissance projects of empire.

Heng's interests are predominantly cultural rather than literary and one of the book's strengths is its depth of historical/cultural research. Her methodology is extensive and connective to the point of headiness, informed by Foucault and psychoanalytic, postcolonial, and gender theories. Her methodology resists the literary encapsulation of an organized reading, chosing rather to disperse the text as she constellates its historical and cultural indexes. One of Heng's most suggestive claims concerns medieval concepts of race, which she extrapolates from a reading of *The King of Tars*, and which she sees as a concept with cultural power in its own right. It is not simply a secondary function of religion; she argues that it deploys morally valenced physical attributes based in whiteness and blackness, but it also demonstrates lability and cultural performativity across different contexts.

Geraldine Heng's study of romance mingles conceptual acrobatics and deep research: fearless and provocative, a gestural display in an area of medieval studies that tends to the minute and insular. Whether or not you agree with her methodology or are convinced by all of her arguments, Heng's scholarship and sweep are admirable. This is a must-read for scholars interested in new ways of thinking about the diversity and cultural reach of medieval romance.

CHRISTINE CHISM
Rutgers University

SIMON HOROBIN. *The Language of the Chaucer Tradition*. Cambridge: D. S. Brewer, 2003. Pp. vi, 179. $75.00.

Simon Horobin's study of the language of the manuscripts of the *Canterbury Tales* is characterized principally by its deliberate diminution of the part played by Chancery in standardizing English at the beginning of the fifteenth century. He follows M. L. Samuels's 1963 identification of four written standards that distinguish between the language of Chaucer and other literary manuscripts (Type III) and government and commercial documents (Type IV), which after 1430 Samuels calls "Chancery Standard." Horobin's treatment is deliberate because the books and articles in which I have advanced the influence of Chancery are cited in his bibliography but never referred to in his text. Anent bibliography, it may be noted that the *Linguistic Atlas of Late Medieval English (LALME)*.

to which Horobin frequently refers, is not included in his bibliography or in any note that provides bibliographical information. It is edited in four volumes by Angus McIntosh, M. L. Samuels, and Michael Benskin (Aberdeen University Press, 1986).

The problem with Samuels's classification is that we know that at least one of the scribes that he and Horobin included in Class III, Thomas Hoccleve, was, like Chaucer himself, a government clerk. It is hard to believe that the other scribes who wrote literary manuscripts were not also writers of government and business documents. The few manuscripts that Horobin chooses to focus on would not have been enough to support a scribe. Literary scribes must have done commercial work as well and, if so, the dozen or so words on which Samuels and Horobin base their distinction of Types III and IV are less convincing. Henry IV and especially Henry V shifted Chancery and Privy Seal from Latin and French toward English. The stationers and guilds followed suite, and a tradition of writing in English, both commercial and literary, came into being.

Assisted by the continuing progress of P. M. W. Robinson's *Canterbury Tales* Project, which is producing computer transcripts of all the Chaucer manuscripts, looking forward to computer collation to produce a history of the texts, Horobin has made exhaustive counts of the spellings and grammatical forms of some twelve to fifteen words, especially in the Hengwrt and Ellesmere manuscripts. On pages 74–75, where he lists the presence or absence of Type IV (Chancery) forms of five words in Chaucer manuscripts between 1400 and 1500, Horobin concludes that chronology was the most significant factor in determining the presence of Type IV forms. Actually, it was the growing influence of Chancery models and training that helped to regularize writing. The forms that Horobin has cited with reasonable accuracy should be viewed against the background of Chancery practice. At the end of Fisher and Richardson's *An Anthology of Chancery English*, which Horobin cites but does not use, we have a glossary of the forms in the manuscripts. It lists the number of times each spelling appears in each government office and in the other writs in the PRO collections (we too composed by computer, which made the statistics available). It is interesting to see how often the favorite forms for the words in the glossary are the forms that have come down to us in Modern English. Chancery established the favorite forms early on. Against some sort of background like this,

Horobin's comparisons would have a context. They should not be treated as scribal idiosyncrasies but as aspects of a developing tradition.

Horobin's study represents careful work, but I have noted a few differences. On page 51, *MI* I.3654 should be *GP*. On page 53, GP I.77, Hg *come* should be *comen;* GP I. 651, Hg *excuse* should be *excusen* and El *excusen* should be *excuse*. On page 103, El I.67 and El I. 1016, *his* should be *hise*. On page 110, WB 268, *some* should be *som*. On page 116, *ender* of my lyf should be *endere*. The final e's are flourishes in the manuscripts, but transcribed as *e* in the *Variorum Wife of Bath*. Also on page 116, in the *And neer* quotation, line 805 is lacking. Horobin page 30 has only *th* (*þ them*) forms for the obj. 3rd pl. The Anthology glossary has 121 *th* (*them*) forms, but 150 *h* (*hem*) forms. Horobin page 32 gives *though* as the IV form; the glossary has *though* two times, *þow* two times, *thowe* once, *thof* three times. Horobin page 44–46 discusses *ayein* as a Chaucerian form; the Anthology has *ay* 67 times, *aȝ* 22 times, *ag* 23 times.

Horobin's study was very interesting to me for comparison with the Chancery material. But it offers little real information about Chaucer's language because it treats the forms in isolation, as if they sprang spontaneously from the inclination of the scribe. Against a broader background these, comparisons would be more meaningful.

JOHN H. FISHER
University of Tennessee

JACQUELINE JENKINS and KATHERINE J. LEWIS, eds. *St. Katherine of Alexandria: Texts and Contexts in Western Medieval Europe.* Medieval Women: Texts and Contexts 8. Turnhout: Brepols, 2003. Pp. xi, 257. $84.00.

This collection of essays, which is focused on medieval devotion to Saint Katherine, continues an important line of inquiry that has developed in the study of medieval hagiography: the ways in which saints' cults were constituted not just by medieval hagiographers but also by devotees of all social classes and educational backgrounds. One significant result of this approach is that researchers are demonstrating that there was no simple transmission of clerical text to lay audience in the medieval period. Indeed, the relationship between those who read and wrote hagiographical texts and those whose knowledge of the saints came through other means is complicated, and as recent studies have shown, the specificities of a given audience and their ritual practices change the way a cult is understood or celebrated. *St. Katherine of Alexandria: Texts and Contexts in Western Medieval Europe* is a collection that illustrates this point well. The volume includes essays from various disciplines that investigate the production and reception of Katherine's cult among various groups—women and men, aristocratic and lower-class families, clergy and laity. The ideology that underpins this work is supported by the range of geographical areas covered, for the essays address devotion to Katherine in France, Italy, Spain, Sweden, Wales, and England. As editors Jacqueline Jenkins and Katherine J. Lewis acknowledge, the book follows a pattern established by Kathleen Ashley and Pamela Sheingorn in their groundbreaking collection *Interpreting Cultural Symbols: Saint Anne in Late Medieval Society* (Georgia, 1990). Thus, in addition to the interdisciplinarity and the geographical diversity of topics, Jenkins and Lewis have gathered a rich set of essays that analyze a variety of medieval texts, including seals, *vitae*, manuscript illumination, breviaries, and devotional sites. The result is a book that illustrates that there was not one single medieval cult of Saint Katherine, but many.

That medieval saints were polysemous symbols is becoming a standard assertion in scholarship, and the essays included in *St. Katherine of Alexandria* demonstrate the multivalency of the Katherine image between the eleventh and fifteenth centuries. The ten essays include Christine Walsh's historical study of the Norman role in the early development of the cult; Katherine J. Lewis's discussion of rituals in which girls developed symbolic pilgrimages and prayed in English Katherine chapels for husbands; Jane Cartwright's account of the sites of Welsh devotion to Katherine, as well as her literary study of a Middle Welsh life of the saint; Tracey R. Sands's examination of aristocratic devotion to Katherine in medieval Sweden, evident in family names and women's seals; Anke Bernau's demonstration that Katherine's body became a symbol for the ideal Christian community where violence, faith, and knowledge converge; Emily C. Francomano's presentation of how Spanish romance heroines imitated Katherine's constancy in marriage; Jacqueline Jenkins's edition and analysis of a prohemium added to an English life in which Katherine enacts lay piety for women readers; Karen Winstead's assessment of the iconography of Katherine's short hair in French and English books of hours as a means for male readers to identify with the saint's masculine pursuits of preaching and teaching; Sherry L. Reames's examination of lessons in English breviaries, in which she illustrates that clerical readers were principally focused on Katherine's ability to preach, not her symbolism as a virgin martyr or *sponsa christi*; and finally, Alison Frazier's study of an Italian collection of saints' lives in which the Katherine text shows the author's anxiety about presenting medieval saints to humanist audiences.

The strengths here, in addition to the geographical diversity and richness of texts considered, are the essays that contest prevailing scholarship about female saints. The best of these are by Bernau, who shows how virginity is not a state of being but an action that Katherine's body must perform, and by Reames, who challenges the traditional view that clerical texts always eroticize the virginal body and reduce the virgin martyr legend to an exemplum modeled for women. However, a few read as the conference presentations from which this book was generated. A more difficult issue is that while several of the essays utilize material evidence, none of the contributions is written by an art historian. This is not to say that visual evidence of devotion to Katherine is not analyzed, for Winstead reads illuminated miniatures well and Sands uses medieval seals to document Swedish women's affinity with the saint. Instead, my critique is more about the contention of the book's interdisciplinarity when all the contributors are either literary scholars or historians. This problem is exacerbated by a dearth of art-historical projects on medieval hagiography listed in the bibliography. Individual essayists have noted the work of art historians in their footnotes (Jenkins and Winstead, for example), but the bibliography itself is highly focused on literary and historical scholarship, as well as being heavily weighted with scholarship on English devotion to Katherine. This lacuna prompted a consideration of other disciplinary areas, such as theology, which might fruitfully contribute to discussions of this saint's preaching and teaching. This concern is not to detract overmuch from a book that offers a great deal to those interested in Katherine and has value for others who work on female saints more generally. I offer it instead as evidence that, as the editors insist, there is still much work to be done on the medieval cults of Katherine, who was one of the most popular saints in Western Christendom.

VIRGINIA BLANTON
University of Missouri–Kansas City

TERRY JONES, ROBERT YEAGER, TERRY DOLAN, ALAN FLETCHER, and
JULIETTE DOR. *Who Murdered Chaucer? A Medieval Mystery.* London: Methuen, 2003. Pp. x, 408. $29.95.

Chaucerians everywhere will welcome a new book by Terry Jones, in
this case a book organized by him for publication with unspecified contributions from four fellow conspirators. He is a gleeful renegade, an
upsetter of applecarts, who relishes controversy, and is a breath of fresh
air, or perhaps a dose of salts, to our discipline. His book on *Chaucer's
Knight,* when it came out in 1980, provoked both delight (from students) and irritation (from some established scholars). The former took
great pleasure in seeing the sinister secrets of the mercenary Knight
exposed; the latter were annoyed by the lack of attention to the normal
rules of historical evidence. It was an episode in the history of criticism
with a happy ending for Chaucer studies. Serious scholars were obliged
to reexamine and restate more thoroughly and carefully the arguments
on which their views of the Knight and his *Tale* were based, and, as a
result, in some respects there were indeed modifications to established
critical opinion.

Terry Jones is a great lover of conspiracy. His books, like his informa-
tional programs about the Middle Ages on television, are based on the
idea that the academic authorities are in a plot to keep the real facts of
history from us. These facts, once revealed, tend always to the discredit
of established figures of authority. It is a recipe for readability, and not
far from the position taken by many recent Chaucer scholars. The new
book follows in this iconoclastic tradition. The argument begins with
the mysterious circumstances surrounding Chaucer's death: the lack of
contemporary record of the event, the lack of attention to the death of
such an important public figure, the omission of any mention of a funeral ceremony, the absence of a will. It develops the idea that Chaucer
during his life showed sympathy for Lollardy, as well as being closely
identified with Richard II, and, when Thomas Arundel resumed office as
archbishop of Canterbury after the deposition, came increasingly under
suspicion. He hastened to take up quarters in the Westminster Abbey
precinct where he might find sanctuary, his works were suppressed, and
in the end he was done away with at Arundel's instigation. The accumu-
lation of evidence, so enthusiastically marshaled by Jones and his cohort,
is often wildly compelling.

Yet the argument often employs deductions based on the absence of kinds of evidence that we are only occasionally and accidentally likely to have. It would be nice to have Chaucer's will, but it is no surprise that it does not survive, and its absence (though Nigel Saul, in conciliatory mood, calls it "a bit puzzling," p. 277) no base on which to build speculation. The lack of report of a funeral, "another odd thing" (p. 305), is actually much less odd than the presence of such a report would be. Chaucer's contemporary reputation is throughout vastly exaggerated—"one of the most prominent members of his society . . . the intellectual superstar of his time" (p. 3), "the literary spokesman of Richard's court" (p. 291). The use of evidence throughout is highly selective: one familiar method is to give the maximum prominence to any piece of evidence that supports or does not actually contradict the argument while ignoring evidence to the contrary. More often, the authors cite the opinions of scholars who have put forward views opposed to those being promulgated, and then, instead of answering them or refuting them or negotiating a position that takes them into account, take no further notice of them at all, but simply leave the opinions lying intact as inert witnesses to a kind of fair-mindedness while the main argument goes blithely forward as if its suppositions had been supported: "this playful allusion—if it is indeed that—demonstrates . . ." (p. 52); "We may not know the precise extent—if any—of Burley's involvement in the revolt of 1381, but one thing seems certain . . ." (p. 74); "Whether or not Chaucer was actually involved in the conspiring [of January 1400] . . ." (p. 159); "Of course, we are not suggesting that the Peasants' Revolt was necessarily instigated by the court party. But . . ." (p. 73); "Of course, it's not necessary to take the remark in the *Legend* as the literal truth, but . . ." (p. 278); "Of course, untimeliness is one of the 'great themes' in eulogies. . . . But . . ." (p.280); "As an isolated passage this could, of course, be passed off as totally conventional, but . . ." (p. 284); "Of course, we should bear in mind that Caxton was Chaucer's publisher . . . but . . ." (p. 285); "Of course, we don't know, and it may be none of these reasons, but . . ." (p. 326). In matters where what is needed is a scrupulous attempt at objectivity in weighing up conflicting and enigmatic evidence on crucial matters, we get instead a predetermined decision to interpret all the evidence in one way.

Yet, hidden away behind the conspiracy-to-murder story, the fantastical exposition of the contents of the lost "Book of the Lion" (confessedly "supposition heaped on supposition", p. 335, as if the admission conferred respect on the suppositions), the wild speculations about a 1402 date of death based on the evidence of MS Add.5141, there is a worth-while revisitation here of some familiar Chaucerian themes—Richard's role as a literary patron, Chaucer's closeness to him, Chaucer's reformist tendencies and vulnerability to anti-Lollard attack, the question of the Parson's *Tale* and the Retractions. We are reminded of how little we positively *know* about Chaucer's life. On some matters there is fresh and persuasive argument—the closeness of Richard and the young prince Henry, the role of Arundel as arch-persecutor during the reign of Henry IV, the occasion of Scogan's "Moral Envoy" in 1407, the influence of Prince Henry in encouraging the recognition of Chaucer and the circula-tion of his works. There are the makings here of a good popular survey of English politics and culture during exciting times, unfortunately ob-scured by the determination to have everything "inextricably bound up with the fate of Geoffrey Chaucer" (p. 128).

It is a broadbrush approach, but not unrespectable. The various au-thors avail themselves (I presume) of the umbrella provided by Terry Jones to write in a lively and companionably light-fingered way, not too worried about using vernacular asides and popular clichés. Some of the phrasing echoes the kind of comically exaggerated comparative allusion for which Jones is well known on television: "To offer men like Glouces-ter and Arundel tournaments with blunted weapons instead of real-life *chevauchées* into France was like asking Attila the Hun to settle down to a nice game of draughts and a cup of tea" (p. 15); in Oxford, in 1382, "the knives were out—literally. If they'd had machine guns, they'd have been ready in the violin cases" (p. 79).

The evidential basis for the murder-conspiracy argument is flimsy, and one's view of its likelihood is that it must lie somewhere in the gray area between the wildly implausible and the wholly preposterous. But nevertheless, the book is much to be welcomed. It will give pleasure to all, some extra employment for those scholars who feel obliged to dis-mantle the edifice of its argument, and may provoke some fresh and useful thinking about subjects that have grown stale. Instead of dismiss-ing it in an ungrateful way as simply all very unlikely, or as a work of historical fiction, or as a new experiment in the use of historical evi-dence, perhaps we could look upon the book as an attempt at a popular and provocative history of some exciting times.

DEREK PEARSALL
Harvard University

LISA LAMPERT. *Gender and Jewish Difference from Paul to Shakespeare.* Philadelphia: University of Pennsylvania Press, 2004. Pp. 277. $55.00.

There are elusive qualities in the phrases and sentences of this book. This represents both a virtue and a vice. Elusiveness is often the greatest gift of great poets. I have always been particularly drawn to the sentence, "Teach us to care and not to care," in T. S. Eliot's "Ash Wednesday." I do not know, or, if deep inside my mind I do know, I cannot clearly express what these words mean, but ever since I first read them I was seized with an absolutely unshakable conviction that they must mean something and, given the power of paradox, it must be profound. It might be possible to take cover behind an equally baffling assertion, namely, Gunther Stent's in his "Paradoxes of Free Will," that it is a tragic "failure of philosophers to find an acceptable resolution of the contradictory nature of such paradoxical pairs of deep truths" (*Proceedings of the American Philosophical Society* 148 [2004]: 207). Where philosophers fail, mere mortals can be forgiven. If the virtue of the prose of this book is that it convinces one that something genuinely important is being asserted and discussed, the vice is that one cannot easily describe to another person or perhaps even to oneself precisely what it is. What follows is my best attempt.

In an introduction, four chapters, and a brief conclusion, the author traces two intermeshed, mutually informed—"intersectional"—types, the "hermeneutical Jew" and the "hermeneutical Woman." The hermeneutical Jew is the Jew of Christian construction, changing over two millennia, but having a remarkable stability from the time of Saint Paul until the dawn of modernity. The traditional and conventional, indeed arbitrary, division of the medieval from the modern, the author dismisses, following the lead of a number of what might be called postmodern scholars of periodization. This allows her to emphasize continuities between the medieval and the modern, although she still takes seriously the warning of other scholars to avoid an easy narrative line from traditional anti-Judaism to modern anti-Semitism, let alone to the Holocaust.

The consistency the hermeneutical Jew enjoys is rooted in the overwhelmingly dominant and stable perception of Christianity, by nearly all its interpreters for two millennia, as a universal and universalizing faith, one having superseded Judaism. Only recently have learned apologists of Christianity disavowed or, perhaps better, tried to soften the supersessional and even universalist theology of Christianity. My own feeling is that these apologists still constitute only a vocal few among Christian theologians and popular interpreters and that they do not really command much support from the rank and file of Christian believers, who are quite comfortable with the traditional theology.

The hermeneutical Woman is a more subtle and variable concept over time. Yet, though unstable or less stable than that of the hermeneutical Jew, it has a certain consistency about it. Therefore, the author seems confident that it is permissible to draw on much late twentieth-century feminist writing that has explicitly or implicitly invoked the hermeneutical Woman as she navigates the texts she has chosen to analyze. Indeed, Lampert argues that any proper understanding of the literary and artistic relics of the past must take into consideration a kind of super-organizing principle, implied by the existence of but not entirely defined by the hermeneutical Woman, one that often goes or has gone unremarked. She uses Toni Morrison's image of the fishbowl to make the point. The fishbowl, transparent glass, is what makes the world within the fishbowl possible. Without it there would be chaos and rapid death and putrefaction. There is a bundle of myths, stereotypes, and imaginative landscapes, all rarely interrogated, that constitute the ever-changing but always present fishbowls of the past. Our job as scholars, at least our job in part, is to make our readers and listeners aware of these easily missed glass bowls that order or permit certain kinds of ordering in the worlds of the past.

Hermeneutical Jew and hermeneutical Woman are two constituent elements of the ancient, medieval, and early modern conceptual fishbowls that need to be implicated in fathoming the texts we study. Chapters 3, 4, and 5 of the book, therefore, offer exemplary inquiries—case studies—of three texts or sets of texts: Chaucer's *Prioress's Tale*, East Anglian drama (N-Town and *Croxton*), and Shakespeare's *Merchant of Venice*. The reader should note that none of these works was produced in an England that actually had any Jews living in it, a few exceptions aside, but then one does not need to have real Jews around to have a powerful and corrosive notion of the hermeneutical Jew. Nor should the reader understand the culmination of the study with Shakespeare as a silent acceptance of Shakespeare as literary god, unsurpassed and unsurpassable.

The author's readings of the texts she has selected tease out some of the actions and sentiments portrayed in them, particularly those rather troubling to a modern liberal understanding of the social good, and she usefully shows how and why they might be misread without taking account of the two hermeneutical types she has invoked. She also shows, again usefully, how much richer the thinking and writing about these texts become when one keeps always in the front of one's mind the ordering principle (the glass bowl) that gives and constrains the meanings of the texts. For example, she makes a good point that the hermeneutical Jew, as revealed in certain personal and relational traits of the Jewish characters in the texts, shows a far greater resistance to the totalizing image of transformation that was, in the high theology of the period, supposed to accompany baptism/conversion. This point owes a great deal to an analogy or parallel between the hermeneutical Jew and what I think the author might be willing to call the hermeneutical Alien (stranger to the community) and hermeneutical Racial (the dark-skinned "presence" or otherwise racialized presence defined, following recent medieval historiography, according to less somatically obvious distinctions). Finally, to see the past and past texts through these newly aware eyes of the hermeneutical Other is not to condemn the past for its mistakes ("to seek moral reckonings," p. 171), but to "seek ethical understandings" of it.

This is a book that one must return to from time to time to elicit its nuggets of insight. It is sometimes a beautiful read, but almost never an easy one. Returning to it, however, can be a genuinely rewarding experience.

WILLIAM CHESTER JORDAN
Princeton University

KATHY LAVEZZO, ed. *Imagining a Medieval English Nation.* Medieval Cultures 37. Minneapolis: University of Minnesota Press, 2004. Pp. xxxiv, 356. $68.95 cloth, $24.95 paper.

Emphasis must fall on the "imaginary" part of Kathy Lavezzo's title, since concepts of "nation" and "nationhood" are a good deal less present in this volume than the title would seem to imply. Actually, the commendably headstrong contributors are at their best when they jettison the doubtfully applicable concept of medieval nationhood altogether and strike out on their own. "Nation" is really only gesturally present, as Aranye Fradenburg pursues her recent interest in the underpinnings of sacrifice (with *patria* hailed as one of its justifications); when Andrew Galloway considers the contributions of Higden and Walsingham to monastic historiography; when Jill Havens reflects on the Lollards as an imagined community within the realm; when Peggy Knapp asks what "imagination" actually meant in the later Middle Ages—to think only of the first four contributions. Although this collection's blurb declares it to be "unusually coherent," I would tend to argue otherwise, in favor of the unruliness of its talented contributors, and their commendably centrifugal offerings, as its greater asset.

For all its inner diversity, this collection nevertheless does have a recurrent topic, preliminary or incidental to its stated one, and somewhat more agreeably indigenous to the Middle Ages. This is the subject of "community," in all its ramifications, and most of the contributors turn to it with evident relief. After pondering the possibility that Higden's interest in English *varietas* is itself a form of alienated national consciousness, Galloway turns to Walsingham, whose "most powerful sections access into his notions of English community" (p. 75). Havens observes that the polemic of Lollard texts "sets up an ideal of an imagined community, united by a belief in the ability of the English language to convey sacred truth" (p. 100). Kathleen Davis concerns herself with spatial and temporal disjunctions in Chaucer's *Parliament of Fowls*, as they create an "alogical" zone in which various impossibilities can be imagined—a completed poem, a consummated marriage, and a harmonious community. Larry Scanlon's restorative reassertion of Langland's political radicalism grounds itself on ideals of community and the "true commons." In his assertion of parallels between Edward III's and Langland's views of the problems and potentialities of monetary exchange, Vance Smith gesturally invokes the concept of a "national economy," but is more actively concerned with the contribution of the merchants as a group "whose own intrinsic, communal value helped to define . . . the very idea of English *communitas*" (p. 236). In a confident and revealing essay on Richard II's indebtedness to French ideas of sacral kingship, Lynn Staley interests herself in the extent to which even contentious engagements with Richard's emergent ideal of sacrality could also create occasions for new understandings of political community.

If "community" is this collection's manifest concern, it boasts a very powerful latent concern as well. Recurrent in many—in fact, most—of its essays is a painful sense of affront that people like Benedict Anderson (in his *Imagined Communities,* 1983) seem so intent on promulgating rules of engagement that have the effect of excluding us and our subject matter from some of the most exciting areas of contemporary inquiry and discussion. Or, to put it even more broadly, that *nobody* seems to want us involved: the early modernists with their disinclination to learn anything about our subject; Marxists and assorted modernists who think that the most cherished categories of analysis (class, heteroglossia, nationhood) did not exist prior to the industrial revolution; the postmodernists, who accept the canard that medieval culture was too static and hierarchical to entertain any alternate or contentious models. Among these last, preeminent is Anderson, whose ideas about imagined community are so pertinent to medieval studies, but who dismisses the entirety of our period as an object of analysis with the absurdly oversimplified claim that the presence of a universal language and a universal Church and the absence of a print culture automatically prohibit any medieval involvement in the imaginary self-delusions to which subsequent cultures have had such influential recourse. Despite, and because of, his categorical maneuver, Anderson haunts the pages of this collection to such an extent that one might almost declare him its absent cause. To her credit, Peggy Knapp addresses this issue frontally, locating Anderson's importance in the fact that his analysis reconciles "imaginative constructs" on the one hand and "social practices" on the other—a mediation of obvious importance for literary scholars who want to talk about texts and also about larger cultural and political enclosures. We want his style of thinking—when "nation" and "community" are at stake, we even *need* his style of thinking—and perhaps Knapp and Galloway and others are on the right track when they simply go ahead and use him in spite of it all!

Scanlon adds one more vital twist to this discussion, with an argumentatively ingenious but highly persuasive move. He demonstrates that, despite Anderson's attempt to banish medieval and premodern formations from the "modern" national consciousness, traces of these excluded materials resurface constantly as presuppositions of Anderson's own analyses, and as preconditions of the materials he takes in hand. As Scanlon wryly observes, Anderson's treatment of temporality was deeply influenced by the views of medievalist Erich Auerbach, and his key modernist categories of community and sovereignty were deeply implicated in medieval modes of apprehension.

To return to the rather occluded subject of "nation": actually, the essay that might have the most to say about it is the one most insistent on its impossibility, or at any rate its emergence only under the most threatened conditions. This is Claire Sponsler's concluding analysis of Froissart's reported story of Anglo-Irishman Henry Chrystede, a most arresting example of "the confusions of ethnic identity and national affiliation that shaped English life in the late fourteenth century" (p. 307). Fittingly, Thorlac Turville-Petre, who wrote a pioneering study, *England the Nation: Language, Literature, and National Identity, 1290–1340* (Oxford, 1996), provides a short afterword. He demonstrates a good deal of reserve about the "national" part of it, though, suggesting that the circumstances of 1290–1340 were peculiar ones, and that for Chaucer and the *Gawain*-poet issues of European culture trump questions of national identity.

Kathy Lavezzo is to be congratulated for assembling a provocative collection, by a number of our most stimulating practitioners, working at top form on issues of political consciousness and the state of polity in late medieval England. Incidentally, this volume is evidently among the last to be issued by the influential Minnesota "Medieval Cultures" series, a considerable disappointment, given the success of its thirty-four published volumes in raising questions of vital contemporary importance to members of our profession.

PAUL STROHM
Columbia University

TIM WILLIAM MACHAN. *English in the Middle Ages.* Oxford: Oxford University Press, 2003. Pp. x, 205. $65.00.

In the opening chapter of this book, Tim William Machan sets out the theoretical framework that underpins the subsequent chapters. His principal thesis is that an understanding of the status of a language and its use must be based on an integrated study of its sociolinguistic context, what Einar Haugen terms its "ecology," rather than relying on the work of independent and isolated disciplines. This commitment to an interdisciplinary method, and an ability to apply the theoretical insights of modern linguistics to Middle English, is the key strength of Machan's approach.

In chapter 2, Machan applies this methodology to a detailed study of the Proclamation of Henry III, placing it within its historical and political contexts. This document is a key text in histories of the language, frequently cited as evidence for the emergence of English as an official language, the development of the London dialect, and ultimately of standard written English. Rejecting the traditional scholarly assumption that identifies the document's use of English as a nationalistic appeal, Machan argues that the English of the Proclamation was a rhetorical strategy by Henry to manipulate the hostility to foreigners fostered by his Baronial opponents. Building on his earlier discussion of the ecology of English, Machan argues that connections between language and national identity that have become naturalized and accepted in many modern societies are anachronistic when applied to medieval society.

While the chapter's focus on this single document is justified by the depth of analysis and the lack of previous discussions of this kind, other contemporary uses of the vernacular are dismissed rather too briefly. Other examples of early Middle English writing are mentioned but are quickly rejected as contributing little to the status of the language or its speakers. There is also little attempt to engage with the opposing arguments of Thorlac Turville-Petre's *England the Nation* (Oxford, 1996), which identified these texts as responsible for fostering an identification between the English language and national identity.

In the following chapter, Machan discusses ME dialects, arguing that the ecology of ME prohibits any correlation between regional variation and social stratification. While it is apparent that speakers of ME were aware of the differences between regional varieties, and it is likely that these differences had sociolinguistic significance, we should not assume that this is identical to that of present-day English. Machan also tackles the question of the emergence of standardized varieties in ME, arguing sensibly that the institutional structures through which a standard language is codified and maintained were lacking in the ME period. Surprisingly, however, Machan accepts without question the identification of a Central Midland Standard, cultivated by the Lollards for the dissemination of their texts.

In chapter 4, Machan explores the social significance of regional variation within the ecology of ME, focusing on the use of Northern and Norfolk dialect in Chaucer's *Reeve's Tale*. Machan draws on social network theory to argue that Chaucer's Reeve was weakly tied to the social networks to which he was connected, and thus likely to accommodate his own variety to that of the other pilgrims. While Chaucer's use of dialect in *The Reeve's Tale* is an understandable object of study, its literary and fictional nature complicates Machan's interpretation of its significance. It is disappointing that Machan ignores the huge amount of primary, nonliterary evidence for ME dialect variation provided by the *Linguistic Atlas of Late Mediaeval English* (Aberdeen, 1986), and its associated studies, where issues such as the sociolinguistic implications of translation between dialects might have been pursued.

This chapter also considers register variation and its social significance, demonstrating how Middle English associated particular varieties with social and moral qualities, through an extended analysis of the bedroom scenes in *Sir Gawain and the Green Knight*. In both cases the texts chosen, *The Reeve's Tale* and *Sir Gawain*, are well known and much studied. The importance of Machan's contribution is his ability to apply modern sociolinguistic models, such as pragmatics, discourse analysis, and politeness theory, to find new meanings in familiar texts, while also situating such discussions within a broader theoretical framework.

In the final chapter, "After Middle English," Machan charts the changing status of English from the fifteenth century to the present day. Here he takes up again the vexed question of standardization, locating the beginnings of this process in the emergence of Chancery English. Machan is disappointingly uncritical of John H. Fisher's arguments, providing only a vague qualification to the view of Chancery English as a standard language. I would have liked to see Machan extend this analysis, drawing on current linguistic theories of standardization, such as those of Einar Haugen, and recent work on Chancery English by Michael Benskin, to apply the same mixture of skepticism and theoretical insight that characterize his earlier discussions to the issue of standardization.

This is an important book that breaks new ground in providing an account of the status of English in the Middle Ages informed by modern sociolinguistic theory. Machan's considerable expertise and knowledge of the literature and social and political history of the Middle Ages, and of contemporary linguistics, make this a book rich in detail and convincing in its arguments. Machan's book has much to offer scholars interested in English historical linguistics and medieval literature, and will be essential reading for students of these disciplines.

SIMON HOROBIN
University of Glasgow

PEGGY MCCRACKEN. *The Curse of Eve, the Wound of the Hero: Blood, Gender, and Medieval Literature.* Philadelphia: University of Pennsylvania Press, 2003. Pp. xii, 178. $38.95.

"Blood seems to be everywhere in medieval culture." So begins the preface of *The Curse of Eve, the Wound of the Hero.* From this simple observation, Peggy McCracken spins out her argument that medieval culture mapped gendered values onto blood as it manifested itself in menstruation, parturition, battlefield gore, martyrdom, and genealogy. In particular, the romances that described these phenomena did so in ways that naturalized ideologies of gender for medieval audiences. As the book's title suggests, women's blood—the blood of menstruation and parturition—is generally, but not exclusively, represented as polluting (the curse of Eve), while men's blood—whether shed on the battlefield or figured in genealogy—is associated with power and agency (the wound of the hero). Thus, according to McCracken, the negative and private values attributed to women's blood (which must remain unseen) are essential to figuring the positive and public values associated with male blood, these opposing values providing a template for the medieval gender system.

The book's premise seems simple enough; it is suggested by the cover, which depicts a scene of bloodletting from an historiated initial entirely in black and white except for a single stream of red blood issuing from the incision, a motif that is picked up by the words "curse" and "wound" in the title in blood-red letters. Working out the textual elaborations of this hierarchical gender system, however, proves more complex. The sexual economies—particularly the exchanges of women—depicted in romances depend on blood to create a nexus of beliefs, values, and practices connecting ideas about virginity, martyrdom, adultery, and juridical combat. If, as the first chapter argues, the symbolic potential of women's blood expressed in such texts remains tied to the body, while the significance of men's blood is tied to public contests between men, then what anxieties result when women's blood threatens to invade the public space of male combat in the figure of the woman warrior? McCracken explores fears about the feminization of warfare—specifically about the threat of "contamination" from menstrual blood—in medieval figures from Medb in the *Tain Bo Cúalnge* to Joan of Arc. And, if the female soldier is a threatening figure within medieval culture, how much more so is the homicidal mother? Medieval romances abound in tales of parents sacrificing their children, but these texts ascribe different meanings to maternal and paternal sacrifice based on the differential meanings of paternal and maternal blood—the blood of lineage and the blood of parturition. While the metonymic figure of shared blood establishes paternal authority over the child through lineage, the contributions of maternal blood are often debated in stories of monstrous birth and point to the significance of postpartum purity rituals, in particular the mother's ritual isolation after childbirth, called in Old French the *gesine*, in establishing the meaning of the blood of parturition. Ultimately what these practices and the romances that incorporate them suggest is that the mother's very visible, very material contribution of blood (the blood of parturition) during childbirth reinforces the link between women and body, while the symbolic relationship between father and child (figured by the father's blood) provides the child access to the "higher goods of lineage, covenant, honor, and worth" (p. 89). In the final chapter, the public and private, literal and figurative meanings of blood come together in the eucharistic ritual, when the eucharistic wine literally becomes the blood of Christ. The grail romances provide McCracken with an opportunity to explore the meaning of the blood sacrifice that is the central mystery of Christianity. The strange excesses of these romances not only bring together many of the themes explored in earlier chapters, but they also trouble these "essentializing representations of gendered blood" (p. 109), highlighting the occasional inadequacy of the medieval gender system to describe both bodies and their social interactions.

McCracken's sweep is ambitiously large as befits her ambitious claim. Her exploration of the meanings of blood in medieval texts ranges from the twelfth to the fifteenth centuries and, while her focus is primarily on French and English romances of this period, she also includes examples from Norse, Irish, Latin, Italian, and German literature in a broadly comparative study. She draws not only on literary texts but on historical, religious, and medical as well. She employs not only the methods of literary criticism but also the comparative methods of anthropology and religious studies. McCracken's ambition, however, is not limited simply to showing the ways in which quaint medieval ideas about blood grounded antiquated cultural beliefs about gender. Rather, she shows how persistent these ideas have been over time, even as the science and theology that underwrote them have been exploded. The story of Perceval's sister in the thirteenth-century *Queste del saint graal* provides a means of reading Alice Cooper's "Only Women Bleed." Joan of Arc and Ridley Scott's *G.I. Jane* provide remarkably similar commentaries on the anxieties that surround the woman warrior, anxieties as deeply embedded in our cultural consciousness in the wake of the first Gulf War as they were during the Hundred Years' War, when Joan was burned at the stake. (One can hardly resist invoking as further evidence of such anxiety Newt Gingrich's 1995 comment that women are unfit for combat because of their "monthly infections.") The brief analysis of Hans-Jürgen Syberberg's 1982 film of Wagner's *Parsifal* might be considered emblematic of McCracken's method: a late "twentieth-century interpretation of a nineteenth-century opera based on a thirteenth-century German romance" (p. 108). However, McCracken never allows her comparative method to become monolithic or essentialist; rather, each text is carefully located in its particular historical time and space; each elucidates the values embedded in the gender system of its own time. But such histories are not viewed as a series of discrete, isolated moments of time. Instead, the earlier texts and the hierarchies for which they are vehicles are shown to be sedimented in later ones, part of the European cultural imaginary that, despite its overvaluation of classical and Enlightenment values, is still surprisingly medieval.

LAURIE FINKE
Kenyon College

RICHARD J. MOLL. *Before Malory: Reading Arthur in Later Medieval England.* Toronto: University of Toronto Press, 2003. Pp. ix, 368. $60.00.

With this wide-ranging study of medieval Arthurian narratives, Richard Moll challenges the "modern supremacy of Malory's narrative," arguing that it is "less like the inevitable culmination of medieval Arthurian traditions" than a sharp divergence from the Brut tradition, especially in Malory's willingness to "accept a wide variety of material as authentic" (p. 228). Moll's main thesis is that chronicle writers before Malory were far more discriminating; they consistently sought to distinguish between the romance character and the historical figure, and were eager to defend the historicity of the Galfredian narrative. Moll excavates chronicles, both well known and obscure, and discovers a sharp awareness of competing narrative traditions and a critical, sophisticated historiographical consciousness that guided these chroniclers through the complexities of disparate textual traditions.

In chapter 1, "The Years of Romance," Moll surveys chronicles containing Arthurian matter, from universal chronicles such as Jacob van Maerlant's *Spiegal Historiael* to Wace's *Roman de Brut* and Mannyng's *Chronicle*. The thirteenth-century Flemish chronicler, Maerlant, provides the most explicit discussion of competing narrative traditions, criticizing "the silly fictions" of the Grail legend popularized in the French prose Vulgate cycle and casting aspersions on writers who included characters not found "in the Latin." Chroniclers such as Wace and Mannyng offered less extensive commentary, but they were more influential, and their handling of competing narrative traditions shaped the strategies of subsequent writers. Wace's particular contribution was twofold. He questioned the veracity of those adventures ascribed to the first period of peace by post-Galfredian storytellers, and this, in turn, encouraged writers to view that peaceful interlude as a potential repository for romance material. In this way, Wace created "a narrative space within the chronicle tradition in which dubious narratives could exist, albeit without any claim to historical veracity" (p. 16). Mannyng followed Wace's lead but added a further distinction: he located untrustworthy material culled from verse romance in the first period of peace, and he relegated episodes derived from the prose romances to the second period of peace. Subsequent translators and scribes thus inherited a strategy for handling conflicting narrative traditions, and Moll finds in a remarkable range of thirteenth-century chronicles the influence of their conjointure of narrative episode (the periods of peace) and theme (the difficulty of separating fable from truth).

Central to Moll's thesis is the assertion that chronicle writers before the fifteenth century perceived the French prose Vulgate cycle as an untrustworthy body of fabulous "romance" material. As Moll himself acknowledges, few writers offer the kind of explicitly disparaging commentary found in Maerlant. This poses a challenge: faced with tantalizing allusions to "magel" tales, how do we ascertain the chronicler's attitude toward the romance materials he interpolates? Moll often handles the difficulties deftly, as when he examines the Arundel redactor of Robert of Gloucester's *Metrical Chronicle*. The redactor turns to the Vulgate cycle as his source for the tale of Arthur pulling the sword from the stone. Moll argues provocatively that both the redactor's aside to his audience at this moment and his act of framing the interpolation with the rubric "Coronacio Arthuri, secundum sent Graal. Nota de historia Galfridus Monemouthe" (p. 204) were intended to set the story off from his historical narrative and mark it as the unreliable "stuff of romance" (p. 205). At other moments, Moll's method of working by implication is more strained, as when he argues that Mannyng's "refusal to translate French romance is a tacit rejection of it" (p. 28). Here one might legitimately question the confident assertion that absence implies a strategic rejection of romance material (p. 27).

In addition to treating chronicle accounts of the Arthurian past, Moll devotes several chapters to literary works, discussing the Alliterative *Morte Arthure* in chapter 4 and the romances, *Sir Gawain and the Green Knight* and the *Awntyrs off Arthure*, in chapter 5. As his title for chapter 5, "Adventures in History," emphasizes, Moll believes that all three poems should be contextualized in relation to the Brut tradition. Moll traces the indebtedness of these poems to the Galfredian model, examining their use of the historical pattern of rise and fall, their thematization of mutability, and, in the Alliterative *Morte Arthure*, the characterization of Arthur as "a king whose primary concern is political expansion and military conquest" (p. 104). The chapters offer insightful and detailed discussions of the imprint of Galfredian themes on each work. One might have hoped for a more careful discussion of the ways in which these texts negotiate the tensions between an assertively secular historiography (pace Hanning's now-classic treatment of the *Historia*) and the homiletic and penitential strains that critics have long discerned in these works. The problem is not that Moll challenges those who have read the poems as religious in theme, but rather that he never explains how the thematization of the Arthurian court's sinfulness (as emphasized in his reading of the *Awntyrs*) is consistent with a putative commitment to Geoffrey's secular, amoral view of history.

Throughout the study, readers will appreciate Moll's command of the source texts that medieval chroniclers blended and his ability to build dense readings that do much to explain how writers could both borrow from the romance tradition and maintain their claim to be discriminating historians committed to preserving the integrity of the Galfredian account. The conceptual apparatus is less rich, as in the treatment of the study's key definitional terms, history and romance. Moll begins by remarking, sensibly enough, that we need not impose rigid generic labels on Arthurian narratives, but his alternative conception of distinct traditions defined by their narrative content fails to address or resolve some of the real challenges that have been posed by scholars such as Gabriel Spiegel. Thus when Moll acknowledges that writers such as Wace introduced non-Galfredian material into their narrative (for example, the creation of the Round Table), his original criteria for distinguishing the chronicle tradition has to be jettisoned. What remains uncertain is precisely why the creation of the Round Table was, or should be, perceived as "historical," whereas other extra-Galfredian events are relegated to the status of fable. An implicit sense of what separates the historical from the fabulous is certainly at work here, but it remains inadequately theorized.

Despite some problems in the subsidiary arguments, this study presents a strong and convincing case for rethinking the relationship of chronicle writers and redactors to their sources. Moll's book will certainly enrich our sense of how communities of readers navigated a complex and multifaceted textual tradition. In so doing he offers a valuable contribution to both Malory studies and the increasingly exciting reevaluation of the chronicle tradition now under way.

PATRICIA DeMARCO
Ohio Wesleyan University

THOMAS A. PRENDERGAST. *Chaucer's Dead Body: From Corpse to Corpus.* New York: Routledge, 2004. Pp. vii, 180. $90.95 cloth, $24.95 paper.

Thomas Prendergast's book is both a study and a product of what he describes as "an ongoing historical obsession" with the interlinking of "body, death, corpus, money" in relation to Chaucer and his tomb—

"Chaucer" here signifying the physical body of the poet, his works, and the concepts he came to symbolize, in particular a concept of English-ness. "Money" was one of the earliest elements in his list, Prendergast tells us on the first page, on account of a series of references between 1566 and 1577 that debtors were to pay money "at the tombe of Jeffrey Chawcer," and he wondered why. He never does come up with an an-swer, but the search leads him through various byways of how the me-morialization of Chaucer has been thought about over the years, most especially in the nineteenth century, through a focus on what he calls the "preternatural leftover" of the physical body of the poet.

The book is organized as a chronological study. It starts with the fif-teenth century and proceeds by way of the 1556 erection of the tomb and Dryden's burial at the same site (Dryden, incidentally, being described throughout as an eighteenth-century poet), through nineteenth-century concerns about the state of the tomb, whether it actually contained Chaucer's body, and how big Chaucer was, to the twentieth-century "disembodiment" of Chaucer. Within that framework, Prendergast fol-lows a number of consistent themes. The double memorialization of Chaucer both in the *Works* and in the Westminster Abbey tomb and the widespread medieval troping of the body as book form the bedrock of his analysis—the equivalence, as the subtitle puts it, between corpse and corpus. He returns from various angles to the nexus between sym-bolic and financial capital. He worries not about whether the Father of English poetry is in a tomb that no longer memorializes him adequately through decay, or that he might not be in the tomb at all, but what it meant that such things worried other people. All attempts to memorial-ize Chaucer, in art or editions or a monument, are therefore subjected to a psychoanalytic or psychosexual analysis of motivation (except of course his own).

On the burial itself, and related questions such as whether Chaucer's remains were actually moved into the tomb and what the original in-scription might have been, he draws on the recent work by Joseph Dane and Derek Pearsall, to leave space for his own more theoretical analysis. He has interesting and provocative things to say about the portrayals of Chaucer, contrasting Hoccleve's concern to keep the physical image of Chaucer alive with our modern, "almost Lollard-like distrust of images" for their capacity to communicate a "false" Middle Ages. He notes the Victorian tendency to regard Chaucer's genius as peculiarly childlike, and links it with the contemporary debate over the correct height for a genius—either very tall or very short, a pair of alternatives that were confused by the claim that Chaucer's bones had been measured as 5'6" when Browning's tomb was being constructed (Prendergast, like others before him, doubts that they can have been Chaucer's). He argues that Chaucer's loss plunged Lydgate into a "perpetual melancholia" or an "intense guilt" that made him symbolically do away with him (the famous absence of Chaucer-pilgrim from the narrative frame of *The Siege of Thebes*, as interpreted by A. C. Spearing), though he later exonerates Lydgate from such a charge on the rather overliteral grounds that Chaucer would have been dead anyway by the time he was writing the poem. He suggests that Henry Poole, master mason of Westminster Abbey in the mid-nineteenth century, was motivated to paint in the near-illegible or illegible letters on the tomb, before the whole lot disappeared entirely, in order to disavow "the threat engendered in such absence or lack," which he reads (in an endnote) as castration anxiety; and since Poole chose gold for the painting, he also accuses him of fetishizing the text. The various Victorian attempts to raise money for a more comprehensive restoration of the tomb are read as deep anxieties about self-identity, a "fear of sepulchral instability," which means that "the ability of Chaucer's body to limn out the boundaries of Englishness is suspect." Prendergast has assembled some fascinating material in his Victorian chapters, and the relentlessness of its terminology about fatherhood and childlikeness and manliness and Englishness is excellently documented; but the norms of cultural discourse that inspired those forms of expression—not so much the political correctness of the moment, but the need to speak in the vocabulary that carried cultural weight—are overlooked, so that Chaucer comes out as inspiring unique psychological anxieties in the national unconscious. One feels that any conceivable attitude they might have taken to the tomb would have been read as neurosis rather than health.

Prendergast notes the widespread reluctance to engage with the actual decaying body of the poet rather than the transcendent corpus, but he is not really concerned with either. He focuses rather on the gap between the material and transcendent bodies of Chaucer, a gap that can appear stretched rather thin over the length of the book, and especially as repetition too often stands in for textual analysis. He quotes, for instance, Swinburne's lines on the contrast between the present understanding of an absent Chaucer, with how he once spoke

> With all men, sage and churl and monk and mime,
> Who knew not as we know the soul sublime,

and comments, "He further imparts that if 'we' cannot speak to Chaucer as did 'sage and churl and monk and mime,' we know (as they did not) Chaucer's soul sublime." Prendergast's larger context implies that the Victorians did not understand Chaucer's sublime soul either, whereas we understand both them and Chaucer; but they did at least evidently love and value the poet in ways that we have largely lost. "Sublime" is not a word in our own academic vocabulary. Stephanie Trigg's recent study of the reception of Chaucer conveys much more sympathetically that urge to identify, to recover, to restore.

At the start of his coda, Prendergast asks, "Why have printers, poets, antiquarians and academics kept returning to Chaucer's body?" Trigg's work would suggest it is due to something unique about Chaucer. Prendergast explains his own return, "If this book has been about anything, it has been about how the corpse of the author and the corpus of his works are vitalized by a mortuary imaginary that is not limited to an academic understanding of fidelity and infidelity." It is a covert recognition that an unfettered response can have more vitality than an academic one, and that the academic discourse of the book precludes any celebration of that vitality.

HELEN COOPER
Cambridge University

SARAH REES-JONES, ed. *Learning and Literacy in Medieval England and Abroad*. Utrecht Studies in Medieval Literacy 3. Turnhout: Brepols, 2003. Pp. 222. $70.00.

The essays in this volume chronicle the slow expansion of literacy from a craft skill embedded in an imported language of power and prestige to a common capacity exercised across the multilingual landscape of medieval English society. Or so the chronological arrangement of the articles implies; the editorial intention is unclear since, oddly, the book contains not a word from Sarah Rees Jones. An anonymous three-paragraph preface explains that the volume was assembled "in celebration of the thirtieth anniversary of the foundation of the Centre for Medieval Studies at the University of York," and that most of its contributors "completed their post-graduate work at the University of York" (p. vii). (This is all we are told about them; there is no information on the current status or affiliation of the contributors.) The preface is followed by a short (four-page) introduction, written not by the editor but by an illustrious ringer, Derek Pearsall. Celebrating the Centre for its pioneering interdisciplinarity, Professor Pearsall identifies this volume's focus on literacy—the question "How did people know what they knew and learn what they learnt?" (p. 2)—as a core issue for modern medieval studies.

It is ironic that a book apparently designed to trace the widening channels of medieval knowledge has so much the feeling of a coterie publication itself. Of course one can, and I did, read the articles and learn from them without knowing what the editor was thinking or who all the authors are. The lack of editorial care is visible in more crucial ways, however. Several papers could have used stronger copy-editing, and the proofreading has been similarly lax. Still more important, a few articles would have been considerably improved by tightening, trimming, and/or focusing—the sort of changes a good editor should suggest.

Only a few of the assembled articles address themselves explicitly to a wider context of theories about literacy. Katherine Zieman's "Reading, Singing, and Understanding: Constructions of the Literacy of Women Religious in Late Medieval England" is, to my mind, the article that most satisfactorily combines theoretical sophistication with a broadly important discussion of a particular area of research. Zieman eschews any essentializing characterizations, offering her analysis of how nuns understood the liturgy they sang as a deep description of one particular form of literacy. Most of these nuns could read, memorize, and sing Latin, without understanding what it meant—a condition Zieman labels "liturgical literacy" (p. 106). The more educated male clerics, by contrast, possessed "grammatical literacy"; that is, they understood the literal and sometimes even the spiritual meaning of the Latin they were reading. Zieman traces the gradual encroachment of female religious into the male preserve of "understanding"—though for most, the best-case scenario was access to a book such as the *Myroure of Oure Ladye*, which explicated the liturgy in English.

Debbie Cannon's "London Pride: Citizenship and the Fourteenth-

Century Custumals of the City of London" offers a similarly stimulating combination of theoretical framework and detailed observation. Cannon uses her discussion of the custumals compiled and donated to the Guildhall by the fishmonger Andrew Horn to challenge modern oppositions between public and private sphere, pragmatic and recreational reading, and custumal and commonplace book. Cannon's discussion of Horn's wide-ranging compilations illuminates the role of literacy in the constitution of individual and civic identity.

What surprises me about John H. Arnold's " 'A Man Takes an Ox by the Horn and a Peasant by the Tongue': Literacy, Orality, and Inquisition in Medieval Languedoc" is less its inclusion in this otherwise England-focused anthology than the author's apparent assumption that his call for a reconceptualization of "what 'orality' and 'literacy' mean in any given situation" (p. 39) is a new departure in medieval literacy studies. Arnold's random collection of literary and anthropological citations overlooks Brian Street's and Ruth Finnegan's foundational ethnographies of the complexities and coexistences of literacy and orality—as well as this reviewer's application of their insights to later medieval literary culture and D. H. Green's extensive work on earlier periods (only one of Green's articles is cited, in passing). Arnold uses the proverb of his title to demonstrate the "performative subjectivity" (p. 41) of the role of the (stupid, illiterate) peasant in the Albigensian Inquisition, illustrated via the story of a weaver who escaped with a relatively light punishment by playing off the inquisitor's assumption that he was a foolish *rusticus*. We cheer for the weaver of course, but I am not sure the episode pivots on literacy. The weaver escaped because of his intelligence and his acting skills; the essentialism his story challenges is more his examiner's reductive classism than our modern theories of modality. The actress Judy Holiday reportedly escaped the clutches of the House Un-American Activities Committee by playing the dumb blonde on the stand. Yet both Ms. Holiday and (one assumes) the members of HUAC were literate. This said, Arnold's exposition of inquisitorial intricacies is itself a valuable ethnography of heresy.

The other articles in the anthology bypass any general theoretical discussion, offering instead illustrations of literacy in action in a particular time and context. In "Learning Latin in Anglo-Saxon England: Traditions, Texts, and Techniques," Joyce Hill traces the antecedents and afterlife of Aelfric's *Grammar*, the first surviving English-language guide to Latin, and of his *Colloquy*, a Latin text with an Anglo-Saxon gloss added later. The last third of the article is devoted to a learned analysis of the manuscript tradition that will be most meaningful to fellow specialists. Janet Burton's "Selby Abbey and Its Twelfth-Century Historian" is enlivened by the story of the abbey's founder, a monk of Auxerre, who fled his monastery with a finger of Saint Germanus concealed, miraculously, in his arm. Burton's history of the *Historia Selebiensis Monasterii* certainly involves and displays much learning, but it does not link that learning to literacy as the following contributions do.

In her investigation of advice written by Goscelin of St. Bertin, Aelred of Rievaulx, and Anselm for their spiritual or real sisters, Linda Olson refutes the easy assumption that clerical authors who appealed to "affection" when writing for women were talking down to them. Instead, her "Did Medieval English Women Read Augustine's *Confessiones*? Constructing Feminine Interiority and Literacy in the Eleventh and Twelfth Centuries" demonstrates that these authors were passing on an emotionality that Augustine himself championed, and that was embraced as a model for male religious as well. Only near its end does the article swerve toward its titular question. The awkward transition contributes to the impression that Olson was trying to cram a dissertation into these twenty-eight pages. The footnotes threaten at times to engulf the text; the sentences can run on for over a hundred words. Here is one place an editor's friendly intrusion could have helped considerably.

P. H. Cullum's title, "Learning to Be a Man, Learning to Be a Priest in Late Medieval England," and her introductory comments claim her article explores how literacy plays into the construction of priestly masculinity. Under that trendy camouflage lurks a more objective account, derived from probate registers of the archdiocese of York, of how married clerics and lay literates gradually displaced the higher orders of clergy from secular administration. Cullum does not need to glamorize or camouflage archival work of this quality—but she does need to work on her grammar. The article is littered with comma faults and other small errors that detract from an otherwise good essay. Another article drawing on York diocesan and other records is Stacey Gee's "Parochial Libraries in Pre-Reformation England." Gee finds that these libraries possessed more nonliturgical books than had previously been supposed. Gee's detailed data give interesting insight into the gifting of books to churches and their status and usage *in situ*.

Finally, a small number of the contributions fail to deliver much on their promises; their articles seem more skimmed than dipped from the authors' well of learning. Pamela King's "The York Cycle and Instruction on the Sacraments" sets out to demonstrate the importance of the liturgy as an underlying structure of the York cycle plays. This turns into a checklist of sacraments and corresponding elements of plays. It is no surprise that the Baptism play concerns baptism, but the definitions get increasingly stretchy until any appearance of Christ on stage registers as an invocation of the Eucharist. The argument wavers and the connection to literacy is not that clear. Another formidable scholar not appearing at her best is Kathryn Kerby-Fulton, whose "The Women Readers in Langland's Earliest Audience: Some Codicological Evidence" jumps from premise to premise in an attempt to argue for female readership of Langland. Kerby-Fulton begins with the information that six manuscripts have women's names in them. This of course does not prove the women read the text. Next she remarks on the parallels between nuns' libraries and Langland's sources, disavows any suggestion that he used such a resource, declares (problematically) that his avoidance of classical sources suggests he was aiming at a mixed audience, and celebrates his concern for "single-parent heads of households"—an anachronism inappropriately equated to "poor women cottagers" (p. 126). When the article finally produces some solid evidence about female readership, it is from a manuscript created in 1532, which has five identifiable annotations by the copyist's wife. A reader from the eve of the Reformation can hardly be held to represent the "earliest audience" invoked in the article's title.

The cover illustration of this book shows Saint Anne teaching Mary to read, from a window in All Saints' Church in York. The Virgin's primer-text is a psalm, a written text meant to be read aloud (the words "exaudi" and "auribus" stand out clearly). Except for some passing comments in Cannon's article, however, none of the authors considers this practice of aurality—though it was one of the commonest means of experiencing every sort of literature throughout the Middle Ages. Nor does any article concern Anglo-Norman or French material, or come to grips with the interplay of England's three languages. If most of the articles in this volume stay with more traditional approaches to learning and literacy, however, they demonstrate that those traditions are still producing work of high value. The graceful image of Anne and Mary can also be seen to epitomize the combination of classic scholarly skills with a search for broader meaning that characterizes this book's best work.

JOYCE COLEMAN
University of North Dakota

JESÚS L. SERRANO REYES and ANTONIO R. LEÓN SENDRA, trans. *Geoffrey Chaucer: Cuentos de Canterbury*. Biblioteca Universal 24. Madrid: Gredos, 2004. Pp. 646. $46.50.

Recent years have witnessed a revival of interest in the works of Geoffrey Chaucer in Spain that is best exemplified by the publication both of Sáez Hidalgo's annotated translation of *Troilus and Criseyde* (Madrid, 2001; reviewed in *SAC* 25) and of the first Catalan translation of the *Canterbury Tales* by Victòria Gual (Barcelona, 1998). With their collaborative translation of *The House of Fame* (Córdoba, 1999) and with several studies that explore the relation of Chaucer and of his texts with contemporary medieval Spain, the translators of the book reviewed here have in part contributed to this renewed attention to Chaucer. Their collaboration has now resulted in the addition of Chaucer's masterpiece to the prestigious series Biblioteca Universal Gredos, which aims at presenting the classics in careful versions and making them available to a wide reading public.

This handsomely produced volume opens with an introduction that, first, describes Chaucer's historical, social, and literary contexts; next, it contains an outline of his biography and literary career, and continues with a discussion of the textual, thematic, linguistic, metrical, and narrative aspects of *The Canterbury Tales*. It ends with a detailed and helpful chronology covering the period 1340–1400 and with an adequate selected bibliography. Especially relevant is the authors' consideration of the link—both historical and literary—between Chaucer and Spain: they hypothesize that Chaucer might have learned Castilian during his visit of 1366 (p. 18) and refer to Petrus Alphonsus, Ramon Llull, and Juan Manuel as possible influences (p. 19). Apropos of Juan Ruiz's *Libro del Buen Amor*, however, the authors state that "se han buscado semejanzas . . . sin resultados significativos" [p. 19; similarities have been sought without significant results], although a recent essay sheds new light on this issue (Eugenio M. Olivares Merino, "Juan Ruiz's Influence on Chaucer Revisited: A Survey," *Neophilologus* 88 [2004], 145–61). With the Spanish approach of the introduction, Serrano and León demand greater scholarly attention to Chaucer's Iberian dimension, while making his oeuvre more accessible to Spanish readers, who, however, would have welcomed bibliographical references to the Spanish versions of the texts by Chaucer and by his contemporaries mentioned in the introductory section. The introduction contains one historical error in dating the Norman Conquest of 1066 "en la primera década del siglo XI" [p. 37; in the first decade of the eleventh century].

Like all previous Spanish translators of Chaucer, Serrano and León sensibly choose to render the original poetry in prose. Taking the *Riverside Chaucer* edition as their source, they aim at a faithful translation, and claim "haber conseguido una correspondencia bastante exacta entre los textos" [p. 49; to have achieved a sufficiently exact correspondence between the texts]. Written in an agile and fresh style following the original, the Spanish version is for the most part idiomatically successful. The translation, however, fails on a number of occasions to deliver the semantic and textual correspondence announced. Some proper names are mistranslated. For example, "Boloigne" (I.465) is rendered as "Bolonia" (p. 76) for "Boulogne-sur-Mer"; "Mount Vesulus" (IV.47, 58) as "Monte Vesubio" (pp. 260, 261) for "Monte Viso"; "Ladomya" (II.71) as "Ladomea" (p. 171) for "Laodamía" (cf. V.1445, p. 347). Other words and short phrases have been misread: "salueth" (I.1492) is rendered as "había *salido*" (p. 98) for "saludado"; "bores" (I.1699) as "osos" (p. 103) for "jabalíes"; "what myster men" (I.1710) as "qué misteriosos hombres" (p. 103) for "qué clase de hombres"; "on thyn auter" (I.2252) as "fuera de él" (p. 114). In addition, numerals are occasionally mistranslated. Since there is not space to discuss all the words and phrases that seem inaccurate to me, I must limit myself to representative examples and leave it to the reader to form his or her own judgment.

The sense of some sentences has also been altered, as in the following examples: "Ful ofte / Have I upon this bench faren ful weel" (III.1772–73) is rendered as "¡Cuántas veces *he estado pensando sólo* en este camastro!" (p. 244) for ". . . lo he pasado bien . . ."; "Telle where he is or thou shalt it abye" (VI.756) as "Di dónde está *o dónde vive*" (p. 374) for ". . . o pagarás por ello"; "it is nat pertinent to norice werre ne parties to supporte" (VII.1014) as "no es pertinente nutrir guerras *ni partes que soportar*" (p. 410) for ". . . ni secundar a ningún bando"; "Nothyng ne

351

liste hym thanne for to crowe" (VII.3276) is rendered as "Se le conge-laron entonces las ganas de cantar" (p. 493) for "Nada le apetecía más que cantar"; "God help me so, for he shal nevere thee!" (VIII.641) as "¡Que Dios me ayude! *¡Nunca se hará rico!"* (p. 517): "¡ . . . pues a ti nunca te ayudará!" See also III.87, p. 202; VI.364, p. 365; VII.568, p. 396; VII.1018–19, p. 411. Particularly significant to me seems the misinterpretation of the following words uttered by the narrator toward the end of the General Prologue: "Ne thogh I speke hir wordes pro-prely" (I.729) as "aunque *no* repita sus palabras con exactitud" (p. 83), when just the opposite is meant, as the narrator apologizes for reproduc-ing the graphic language and subject matter of certain tales.

This reviewer has been puzzled by the absence in the translation of some thirty lines from the original that must have been skipped: for example, I.1798 (p. 105), I.1913 (p. 107), I.1965 (p. 108), IV.1288–89 (p. 289), IV.1746, 1760–61 (p. 298), VIII.1013, 1019 (p. 525). More-over, direct discourse is not always properly indicated: for example, I.3874–98 (pp. 151–52), III.1109–218 (pp. 225–28), VIII.1133–39 (p. 527); in addition, VIII.426–27 are Almachius's words, not Cecile's, as in the translation (p. 511). Although some readers might have wel-comed slightly fuller notes, here the translators have encountered the constraints set by the collection, and thus they offer light annotation with special regard for biblical allusions. Yet, some of the attributions in the notes are inexact: line VII.987 refers not to John 11.36 (408 n. 259) but 11.35; lines VII.3123–24 allude not to Cicero's *De amicitia* (489 n. 438) but to his *De republica;* there is also a misplaced footnote reference on page 420 for line VII.1158: note 291 should appear after "alma." Finally, the text contains a few typographical errors: "Aberryst-wyth" (p. 32) for "Aberystwyth," "consideraros" (p. 106) for "consider-aos," "fijo" (p. 129) for "fijó," "sentimos reconciliamos" (p. 217; the first should be canceled), "el por qué" (pp. 289, 471) for "el porqué," "corrieran" (p. 292, line IV.1438) for "comieran," "demasiados" (p. 409) for "demasiado," "Gawer" (540 n. 466) for "Gower".

In sum, the collaboration between Serrano and León has resulted in an aptly fresh translation whose merits, however, have been undermined by the kind and extent of the inaccuracies reported. A second revised edition would be desirable.

JORDI SÁNCHEZ-MARTÍ
University of Alicante

JOEL T. ROSENTHAL. *Telling Tales: Sources and Narration in Late Medieval England.* University Park: The Pennsylvania State University Press, 2003. Pp. 217. $49.95.

The project of *Telling Tales* is to provide "a close reading of familiar historical texts from late medieval England" in order "to impose narrativity" upon them, the ultimate goal being "to impose social or sociological (if not literary) unity" upon the world from which they derive. What this somewhat rebarbative description means in practice is the analysis of three different archives—testimonies delivered in Proof of Age proceedings, depositions given in the course of the Scrope-Grosvenor dispute, and the letters of Margaret Paston—in order to elicit a sense of the world they directly or inadvertently describe. This is a bold and imaginative enterprise: the individual testimonies and depositions from the two judicial proceedings are brief and formulaic, and by limiting himself to Margaret Paston's 104 letters from the family total of 306 Rosenthal deliberately excludes relevant evidence. These limitations are part of the book's methodological point. Even the most unpromising materials, Rosenthal wishes to demonstrate, can be made to yield insights about late medieval English culture—specifically ways of understanding "the idea of community and the nature of memory"—that are otherwise unavailable. The results, unfortunately, suggest otherwise.

Proofs-of-age proceedings were held when an heir claimed to have reached the age of majority (twenty-one for men, sixteen for unmarried women, fourteen for married women) and wished to enter into property that had previously been held in wardship. As Rosenthal points out, these proceedings were not merely uncontested but were largely ceremonial. Twelve jurors with special knowledge testified to their knowledge that the heir was of age, usually by correlating the date of birth or baptism with some contemporaneous event in their own lives. Naturally this "proof" was entirely circular: that a birth or baptism occurred at the same time as some other event was hardly evidence that both took place the requisite number of years ago. But evidence was less important than testimony: if twelve men of substance were prepared to say that such-and-such was true, then—judicially if not ontologically—it was true. Rosenthal subjects some two thousand of these individual testimonies to a variety of analyses, some statistical, some thematic. He is interested in the distribution of ages among the jurors, the kinds of cognitive claims they made (did they see the baptism? did they hear about the birth?), and the sorts of events they remembered. Fairly soon, however, the analysis declines into what Rosenthal frankly admits is "a choice of impressions and anecdotes." Despite the claim that we will gain insight into "a world of feeling and evocative expression," we actually get a series of occasionally amusing or suggestive incidents that do not finally add up to much. The author tends to render this material more evocative with a glaze of sentimentality—"such memories (and their elaboration through retelling) were the centerpiece of many an evening's talk over ale or the spinning wheel"—although he is well aware of the dangers of "a 'Merry England' perspective." He also knows that questions of status are crucial here, since the jurors are far from ordinary villagers and are testifying to the fitness of someone who more often than not will exercise some form of power over them. Nonetheless, the harsher realities of medieval social life are kept well out of sight. It is doubtless true that "the whole dynamic of the recollections emphasizes the cooperative and harmonious aspects of village life," but of course that hardly means either that village life *was* cooperative and harmonious or that it was thought to be. It is also true, however, as Rosenthal disarmingly acknowledges, that neither this material nor his analysis is "going to open new vistas into behavior, life experience, or family relations."

The depositions from the well-known Scrope-Grosvenor dispute over the coat of arms Azure, a bend Or are not much more promising: "The depositions' repetitiveness is striking." For Rosenthal, however, here is the chivalric world as seen from the inside. He describes these brief and formulaic accounts of battle sites where the deponent saw the Scrope arms (for some reason he excludes the pro-Grosvenor depositions) as "heroic tales about families and their deeds," tales comparable to the *Iliad* and *Beowulf*—a comparison all the more charming for its extravagance. The brief lists the deponents provide should not even be compared to Gaston Febus whiling away a dull winter in his castle at Foix by dazzling the ever dutiful Froissart. They are simply lists, telling us little about the tellers. Rosenthal is of the Maurice Keen school of medieval chivalry, and he speaks in somewhat hushed tones of "men of high birth and valiant feats of arms," men "who could look on a long and vigorous career, graced with military and civilian distinctions," an "old fellowship" whose memories "were now covered with the rime of legend and nostalgia." The greatest generation, indeed. Rosenthal knows that this kind of account is sentimental bunkum, and he knows too that Scrope was especially anxious about his arms because he came from a family of lawyers. But this knowledge fades before the desire to make more of these texts than they can provide. Unable to offer new insights into the chivalric way of thinking, the depositions serve instead as the kind of complacent self-advertisements that have always appealed to the military mind.

Margaret Paston's letters are subjected to a detailed external analysis. The use of scribes, the structure of the letter, the form of salutation and farewell, the address, even the messengers who transported them are all queried—but to little effect. The following is an all-too-typical sentence: "The unknown hands pose a number of questions, none of which we can answer." Thematically, Rosenthal provides a sensible if familiar account of the strong-willed and often unpleasant Margaret, and of the intensely competitive world in which she lived. Much of this chapter is paraphrase, but it avoids any hint of either bathos or exaggeration. In that sense it is the best chapter in the book.

This review has turned out to be less generous than it was meant to be. Rosenthal has attempted a difficult task, and if he has succeeded less well than one might have wished he should nonetheless be applauded for the effort. Perhaps the effort will inspire others, who will follow his path and find richer rewards. Or perhaps the pot of interpretive gold is just not there at all. In either case, the book should not be damned with faint praise, or given false praise, but admired for its ambition, its seriousness, and its intellectual honesty.

LEE PATTERSON
Yale University

D. VANCE SMITH. *Arts of Possession: The Middle English Household Imaginary.* Medieval Cultures 33. Minneapolis: University of Minnesota Press, 2003. Pp. xviii, 318. $22.95 paper.

Vance Smith offers a dense and complex study of the medieval household, understood as central to both economic life and cultural practice in late fourteenth-century England. Drawing on a wide range of theorists from fields as diverse as economic anthropology, philosophy, and psychoanalysis, and incorporating extensive archival and historical research, Smith reads a handful of Middle English texts ranging from well to lesser known—*Winner and Waster, Piers Plowman, Sir Orfeo, Sir Launfal*, and the *Alliterative Morte Arthure*—in an attempt to trace the "household imaginary" that shapes them. Although the book moves well beyond its stated scope, particularly in its choice of literary texts to examine, its aim is to examine the household "as the trope that organizes the writing of romances in Middle English" (p. xiv).

The title of the book, which derives from Aristotle's description of the household as the location of the "possessive arts," signals Smith's particular interest in the economic significance of the household. Following the lead of social historians such as D. A. Starkey, Smith views the years after 1350 as the "age of the household," during which the household functioned as the most important institution in society. As historians have shown, the household had many guises: it was simultaneously a location, a social collectivity, and, most important for Smith's arguments, an "ideational place" in which "the commodities that allowed the very work of thinking to take place were kept" (p. 2). For Smith, the household is a crucial site that involves the self, the family, the realm, indeed, all life, and given this importance, it is no surprise that, as Smith notes, techniques for managing the household developed "in richly metaphorical and philosophical ways" (p. xiv).

The book's claim that Middle English romances take as their chief subject the exploration of an ethics of possession shaped by the household is boldly original. As Smith notes, the later fourteenth century was a period when ownership and dominion were matters of fascination and anxiety, and it thus makes sense that literary texts would frequently explore these subjects. Smith argues that the technical language of household management invades romances, perhaps because in his view their most likely authors were clerks responsible for household record-keeping. In English romances, we can see the working out of "a particular set of problems having to do with the household" (p. 6), particularly the problem of how to deal with surplus and excess, which Smith (following Bataille) views as an overriding concern in the period. Smith also considers the related problems of lack and scarcity, which he explores via psychoanalytic and economic theories. The role of gift-giving, anxieties about gentility in a monetary economy, and social mobility—including the apparent refusal to pursue it in some cases—all receive attention.

The range of reference is impressive. Bourdieu, Derrida, and Zizek all make appearances, as do Aristotle, Marx, and Freud, as well as Mary

Douglas, Félix Guattari, Melanie Klein, and many others. Government documents and legal records provide one source of historical evidence; objects from material culture, another—including heraldic insignia, merchants' marks, and coins. Smith moves with assurance across all this material, as comfortable discussing Freud's notion of the *unheimlich* as describing scholastic economic theory. One paragraph on page 48, for instance, segues from Isidore of Seville to Heidegger, and meshes Chaucer's *House of Fame* with the labor legislation of 1388, before ending in discussion of *communitas* and homelessness, all in the service of describing the way the imaginary household opened out to the larger world. This capaciousness enriches the book even if it at times risks obscuring the central arguments.

Smith's readings of literary texts are often brilliant and always provocative. He interprets the underworld in *Sir Orfeo*, for instance, as suggesting "the horror of a world whose inhabitants seem dead but are not, the horror of quiescent plenitude, of the remainder that is accumulated in the household" (p. 59), and describes Mont St. Michel in the *Alliterative Morte Arthure* as a place of accumulated death whose surplus threatens the economy of the surrounding lands. *Winner and Waster*, the subject of chapter 3, is read alongside heraldic devices and merchants' marks as a poem that is "intensely interested in the discursive limits of possession" (p. 75), while *Piers Plowman*, in chapter 4, is treated from the perspective of its engagement with mercantile culture. Chapters 5 and 6 consider, respectively, *Sir Launfal*'s intersection with the sumptuary world, and patrimonial claims in the *Alliterative Morte Arthure*.

Arts of Possession takes its place within the ever-growing body of work devoted to reading medieval literary texts through the twin lenses of modern theory and the social and economic history of the Middle Ages. The book contains a wealth of suggestive ideas and thought-provoking analyses, and is obviously based on exhaustive reading and many hours of resourceful library work. Readers will find much to admire in its wide-ranging syntheses, its imaginative use of archival material, and its nimble textual readings, while also perhaps wishing for clearer organization and prose style, as well as more coherent and sustained arguments. In an interesting congruence, the book at times feels as if, like the subjects it examines, it too is grappling with the problems of surplus—of lines of inquiry, of variety of texts, of sheer number of ideas. If that surplus sometimes threatens to escape control, it also contains untold nuggets of insight and revelation. With its deep commitment to the intricate nesting of literary texts in their cultural contexts and to the theorizing of relations between materiality and imaginary structures, this book raises the bar for studies of the social-situatedness of medieval literature and challenges us to do what Vance himself has done—muster our resources to understand that literature's workings.

CLAIRE SPONSLER
University of Iowa

FIONA SOMERSET, JILL C. HAVENS, and DERRICK G. PITARD, eds. *Lollards and Their Influence in Late Medieval England*. Woodbridge, Suffolk; and Rochester, N.Y.: Boydell Press, 2003. Pp. x, 344. $85.00.

The editors of this collection are to be complimented on bringing together a fine set of essays from literary scholars and historians on various aspects of the study of Lollardy and Wycliffism. As Fiona Somerset notes in the introduction, there has been "nothing less than an explosion in scholarly activity" (p. 9) since the 1960s on lollard or Wycliffite issues and materials, and the essays gathered here represent new work on various fresh topics by both established and newer scholars. The twelve essays—divided into four sections ("Lollers in the Wind," "Lollard Thought," "Lollards and Their Books," and "Heresy, Dissidence, and Reform")—are prefaced by a thought-provoking piece by Anne Hudson, who raises interesting questions about the philosophical and legal points of view from which heresy might be examined. A brief but valuable survey of the history of Wyclif scholarship from 1384 to 1984 by Geoffrey Martin follows the essays and the volume ends with a "Select Bibliography for Lollard Studies."

The first two essays, those by Wendy Scase and Andrew Cole, take up the issue of naming lollards. As Somerset comments in the Introduction, the general practice in recent scholarship is to use the terms "Wycliffite" and "lollard" interchangeably despite having sometimes been used to distinguish between Wyclif's academic and lay followers (p. 9 n. 1). Both these essays take up the problems of who was calling whom a "lollard" when and whom we, as modern scholars, might discern as "lollards" during the last two decades of the fourteenth century. Scase's essay reads the "dense intertexualities" (p. 36) in the public, rhetorical texts surrounding the Earthquake Council of 1382 and makes the intriguing suggestion that the famous public suspension of Henry Crumpe from scholastic acts as recorded in the *Fasculi Zizaniorum* was "because he called the Lollards heretics" rather than "because he called the heretics Lollards" (*quia vocavit haereticos lollardos;* pp. 19–20). In her examination, "*Heu! quanta desolatio*" and other libels attest to a Wycliffite hegemony at Oxford that flexes its rhetorical and textual muscle, motivated not solely by concern for academic freedom, in response to allegations of heresy from London. Cole's essay is an extremely insightful piece which argues that lollard identity does not coalesce until at least the late 1380s and that its projection back on events and people of the early 1380s is polemical in origin. The forthright statement that "as late as 1386, there were no 'lollards' in England, only Wycliffites" is perhaps the most useful, original contribution in the volume, restoring a sense of distinction between these two terms, and relieving "Langland of the burden of having to know about 'lollardy' before it exist[ed]" (p. 43). Cole then offers a nuanced reading of the "lollers" in C9 against contemporary models of religious mendicancy and vagrancy. This first section of the volume also includes essays by Andrew Larsen, who argues that "lollards" need to be more strictly distinguished from other heretics on the basis of shared, identifiable doctrines rooted in the teachings of Wyclif, although this is not unproblematic, and Maureen Jurkowski, who presents a detailed case study of Thomas Compworth of Oxfordshire, the first layman to be convicted of heresy, and his son of the same name.

Margaret Aston's essay on lollard attitudes to the cross and crucifix adoration opens the second section on "Lollard Thought" and dovetails nicely with Larsen's concerns. She finds that the lollards' questioning of the "accepted presence" of the cross in late medieval liturgical and devotional practices—a challenge that resonates with continued consistency among heretical practices up to the early sixteenth century—can be discerned as one of the central intellectual concerns of early Wycliffism (p. 100). David Aers returns to the sacrament of the altar in his fine essay on the eucharistic theology of the layman Walter Brut, and, contrary to Larsen and Aston, vitiates readings of Lollardy as a homogenous heresy. In characteristically pleasurable prose, he provides an examination of the "extraordinarily rich testimony" from the heresy trial of this "latinate layman" (p. 115), and finds that Brut's views on the Eucharist, while heretical, arise from a radically inclusive understanding of the communal and participatory nature of the Sacrament of the Altar—an understanding that allows for "women's power and authority in the ministry of the sacrament" (p. 125)—rather than from scholastic debate over terminology or "scriptural fundamentalism" (p. 116). Somerset's contribution to the volume is a stimulating piece that extends the interest in eucharistic theology and finds evidence of interest in the "Wycliffite doctrine of copresence" (p. 130) in a number of Latin and vernacular texts, including Chaucer's. The key issue involves the words of consecration, *Hoc Est Corpus Meum,* and how the *hoc* of this performative saying should be understood either literally as "this" or more metaphorically as *hic* or here. Somerset usefully dismantles the binary of Wycliffite and anti-Wycliffite as a mode of engagement with theological ideas and argues against the prevailing myth of censorship in the 1380s and 1390s.

In the third section, Ralph Hanna turns his attention to mid-fourteenth-century London biblical translation and the fate of that community of scribes, writers, and readers after the advent of Lollardy. Hanna too ultimately evinces an anti-censorship position when he argues that the lollard scriptures became, despite Arundel's *Constitutions,* "a . . . substitute and drove out, destroyed the circulation of, competing biblical versions" (p. 151). Thus, *pace* Strohm and Bowers, he takes issue with the representations of the Lancastrian position as wholly anti-Wycliffite. The conclusions of this interesting essay are supported, as is customary for Hanna, by superb codicological evidence. The only other essay in this disappointingly short section on "Lollards and Their Books" is Emily Steiner's examination of Lollardy's relationship to legal documents. She engages in detail the fifteenth-century revisions of the *Charter of Christ* poem (Long Version), which return this lollard-appropriated pseudolegal text to a more orthodox position, and suggests that the complex motivations behind such revision include not only censorship and the desire for a return to orthodoxy but also a creative impulse and the competition for the ownership of the language and symbols of vernacular devotion.

In the final section, Lawrence Clopper's essay argues for the presence of "rigorist" Franciscan positions (as exemplified by Ubertino da Casale and others opposed to the Conventuals) in reformist literature usually ascribed to the Wycliffites, and suggests that the "Wycliffite" translation of the Rule and Testament, "Of the Leaven of Pharisees," and "Fifty

REVIEWS

Heresies and Errors of the Friars" are the result of "dissident Franciscan presence in England" and have been hitherto "misascribed to the Lollards" (p. 196). Helen Barr seeks to investigate the "Wycliffite Representation of the Third Estate" in an attempt to explain how the Wycliffites came to be associated with civil rebellion in the view of numerous, contemporary commentators, such as Adam Usk, despite the "declaredly orthodox, and even quietist" lollard views on social organization and obedience to secular authority (p. 197). She concludes that while lollard representations of the pious, simple peasant might be read as seditious, it is when Wycliffite texts "argue for the superfluity of the second [estate], or indeed its eradication" that they are closest to the insurgents' polemic that would refigure the political community by consigning clerics to "the family of Cain" (pp. 215–16, passim). Mishtooni Bose's essay sheds fresh light on the vernacular attempts of Bishop Reginald Pecock's to construct an orthodox reforming theology in response to Lollardy. Her readings recover Pecock's work as a worthy object of study and she draws attention to the multigeneric and experimental nature of engaging in vernacular theology, where "the literate practices . . . were not defined or controlled exclusively by the clergy" (p. 236).

Somerset, Havens, and Pitard have done us a remarkable service in bringing together this volume, which demonstrates the range of exciting interests currently occupying scholars of Wycliffism. The volume should very quickly come to be seen as bookending securely the nearly two decades of research since the publication of *The Premature Reformation* (1988), and Derrick Pitard deserves unstinting thanks from all those interested in the study of Wycliffism for his herculean efforts in compiling the copious bibliography.

KALPEN TRIVEDI
University of Georgia

EMILY STEINER. *Documentary Culture and the Making of Medieval English Literature.* Cambridge: Cambridge University Press, 2003. Pp. xvi, 266. $60.00.

Emily Steiner argues that the identity of medieval English literary writing was shaped by a "documentary poetics." There is brief discussion of

361

Bracton, Deguileville, Margery Kempe, and William Thorpe, but the book focuses chiefly on the Charters of Christ and *Piers Plowman* and its aftermath. Discussion of Bracton's legal theory underpins an examination of how the intriguing Charter of Christ lyrics exploit documentary relations of absence and presence to dramatize the continual availability of the Word made flesh. Writers and illustrators were fascinated with the material form of these charters, as evidenced by the manuscript illustrations reproduced in chapter 2, but Emily Steiner's claim that this materiality enabled medieval writers to come to a self-reflexive understanding of the intricacies of subjectivity, lyric form, and genre seemed to me to be an overreading of the function of legal metaphor.

In a later chapter, Steiner shows how orthodox writers policed these lyrics by inserting an intervening clerical voice in order to make sure that the salvific claims of the Charter were mediated through ecclesiastical authority. More heterodox appropriations of these charters used them both to show the inutility of ecclesiastical documents and to bypass ecclesiastical apparatus. Given this argument, I thought that the later analysis of William Thorpe's trial could be pushed further. To my mind, Thorpe does not simply wrest documentary culture away from the archbishop to preach a sermon, but cunningly demonstrates that material ink, parchment, and rolls stored in cupboards are vain (in both senses of the word) "mannys ordinances" compared to the true sentence that is inscribed in the true believer's heart.

With *Piers Plowman*, Steiner offers an intriguingly bold and original reading of the Pardon scene, arguing that the Pardon should be seen as a "chirographum dei," a charter that promises a new contract for the individual soul. Piers's tearing of the pardon—*in two*—stresses Steiner, is not a crisis point, but an affirmation of the document through the process of indenture. Piers tears the document in order to witness and confirm its terms. This argument is heavily influenced by Augustine's treatment of the "chirographum dei" in his commentary on Psalm 144.

There are serious problems with this. One of Steiner's foundational statements is that in a document, the symbolic and the functional are inseparable; there is a peculiar and distinctive relationship of textual form to material text. In the Pardon scene, however, the materiality of whatever is sent by Truth (or is it the pope?) is wanting. Steiner's discussion of the "longer" and "shorter" versions immediately shows that no singular document can be witnessed. Will can look over shoulders and see that the "shorter pardon" is composed strictly of two lines. Piers can tear what Will calls a "bull" and what the priest calls a "pardon," only then not to be able to find one. For a document truly to be witnessed, surely we need to see its form, as we do later with Moses' "patente," where the materiality of parchment, ink, gilt pen, gloss, and seal is stressed? Moreover, if Piers's tearing indents the document (and it seems a very elevated spiritual responsibility for Piers to hold at this stage in the poem), who keeps the other half? And why is the indenture omitted in C if a document is being ratified, not destroyed in a manner that might chime with the activities of the 1381 rebels?

Steiner's insistence on the "trenchant materiality" of the documents in *Piers* makes it hard to understand her later argument that Moses and Peace are describing the same document as Truth's pardon and Hawkyn's patent (p. 119), and that Truth's original pardon assumes different guises depending on the context in the poem (p. 120). Different documents are not interchangeable, and this, I think, is more to the point in the pardon scene. Rather than the certainty of reaffirming God's covenant with human beings, the proliferation of text, voice, and confusion over the material form of the "document," together with its only very partial visibility and problematic audibility (who is narrating the "longer version"—whose will is being codified?), makes it extraordinarily hard to witness a key document at all. Enigmatic crisis rather than material solution, it seems to me, is what is being dramatized by Langland's awareness at this moment in the poem, not only of documentary form but also of documentary procedure.

Steiner argues that Langland invented public poetry from the matter of documentary culture, and that the texts that follow on from *Piers* continue this preoccupation, though their practice is differently inflected from Langland's. The Harley Lyrics need to be factored into this claim and also perhaps *Wynnere and Wastoure*. And while the argument that the free broadcasting of documentary writing is an interesting take on the notion of public writing, I do not think that there was sufficient differentiation between this and bill casting. Moreover, while the 1381 rebel letters borrow some phrases from documents, they are not themselves documents in Steiner's earlier sense of the term. As with the rather underpowered discussion of the *Book of Margery Kempe*, which was, for reasons I did not understand, exempted from the practice of "documentary poetics," Steiner could have done much more with *Mum and the Sothsegger*. To read the bag of books sequence as a disclosure of the institutional archives of the realm is interesting, but there is huge variety in the bag. Are they all "documents"? Should we pay attention to the differences, say, between pamphlets and quittances and ragman rolls, and, if so, why? Also given that documents ought to be stored in official places, what is the significance of the bag's having been concealed by mitered Mum and his confederates for many years? These were all questions that, given the nature of Steiner's enterprise, I hoped to find addressed.

In sum, I felt that this book made some large claims that were difficult to sustain, and in other places did not push material as far as it ought to go. There is excessive recapitulation of material that bloats the trajectory of the argument. But while I am in disagreement with many of the arguments and the consistency of the methodology, this is a book that made me think, and indeed to reread in a new light the texts that it examines.

HELEN BARR
Lady Margaret Hall, Oxford

EMILY STEINER and CANDACE BARRINGTON, eds. *The Letter of the Law: Legal Practice and Literary Production in Medieval England.* Ithaca: Cornell University Press, 2002. Pp. viii, 257. $45.00 cloth, $19.95 paper.

The Letter of the Law is an unusual collection of essays by diverse hands in that it reads, with few exceptions, almost as if it were a single-authored book on its subject. That is a compliment both to the discipline of the contributors and the management skills of the editors. Indeed, the contributors follow the general theses of one of the editors, Emily Steiner, in her highly regarded book, *Documentary Culture*: vernacular literature calls upon legal discourse to validate its own production. At the same time, vernacular literature also explores the contradictions, interstices, and exceptions ignored in formal legal documents. Literature, that is, both critiques formal legal institutions and proposes its own alternative legal fictions. Such an approach differs from many Law and Literature studies, such as the largely Hegelian enterprise of Theodore Ziolkowski, who reads major shifts in legal practice into key works of literature throughout history, and of the anti-Hegelian enterprise of

Richard Posner, who argues that literature and law are entirely distinct discourses that bear a different relation to language and practice. Indeed, the volume as a whole, with few exceptions, owes its intellectual allegiance less to the subdiscipline of literature and law studies and more to the critical historicism of recent medieval English studies, especially the work of Paul Strohm and David Wallace, and to a relation between discourse and practice that has engaged French social theory, especially the work of Bourdieu and Foucault. That is, the themes of many of the chapters are political rather than exclusively legal concepts, such as power, authority, resistance, and affinity.

Steiner and Barrington begin the volume with a helpful introduction, clearly setting forth the argument of the book and summarizing the contribution of the various chapters, frankly necessary given their density and allusiveness. Those chapters cover a wide range of writings and authors. Christine Chism delinks the Robin Hood ballads from their folkloric and romantic contexts, and reads them as complex critiques of power relations as centralized authority displaces local baronial control. Depending on their context, the Robin Hood ballads create parodic or parallel legal and governmental systems within and between the greenwood and the official world, but rather than always valorizing Robin and his men, the various plots stress the proper exercise of power and judicial authority. Jana Mathews offers an understanding of the trial scene in Henryson's *Testament of Cresseid*, noting the association of the heroine (and the narrator) with descriptions of landscape, thereby metaphorizing the relation of the female subject to the land, raising the vexed questions of land and ownership (especially where females were involved) that obsessed fifteenth-century Scottish legal proceedings. By visiting leprosy upon the heroine, her very legal personhood is thereby obliterated, but she reasserts her agency by her "Testament," a legal document that reinscribes her subjectivity. Andrew Galloway's "The Literature of 1388 and the Politics of Pity in Gower's *Confessio Amantis*" is more traditional (and more readable) in its narrative exposition, but it is highly original in its conclusion concerning the complex notion of "pity" in fourteenth-century usage, or at least Gower's usage, in reflecting Richard's role in the three major state trials of his later reign. If the *Confessio* referred to Richard's response to the Merciless Parliament only obliquely, by underlining the role of *pietas* in just rule, by the time of the *Cronica tripertita* in 1400, "pity" turns out to have a set of ironic and extralegal implications of violent retribution and judicial coercion associated with it. Richard Firth Green, whose important book on late medieval law and literature looms large over all the contributors, turns to the dispute between Palamon and Arcite in *The Knight's Tale*, where Chaucer injects a legal coloring into his source. Chaucer was reflecting the revival of the Court of Chivalry in the Ricardian period, a disturbing trend that seemed to threaten the return of trial by combat for domestic civil matters and to call into question the rationality of common-law courts. Emma Lipton's "Performing the Law in the N-Town Trial Play" notes how the trial of Mary and Joseph, by being performed, uncovers the degree to which court procedures were themselves staged rituals, and the framing of performative language within the play distinguishes the characters (and the audience and producers of the play) from a discourse of gossip, slander, and false accusation. Maura Nolan reads the textual difficulties of the Man of Law's *Epilogue* and the confusing ambiguity of the Man of Law's *Introduction* as an imitative form reflecting Chaucer's critique of the double-edged quality of legal discourse. At the same time, the particularity of the irresolvable manuscript evidence itself offers as a challenge to any abstract mode of thought, legal or theoretical. Borrowing Nicholas Watson's useful term "Vernacular Theology," Bruce Holsinger's "Vernacular Legality: The English Jurisdictions of *The Owl and the Nightingale*" suggests that the poem, and especially the Nightingale's responses, propose a "vernacular legality" that runs alongside official legal discourse and calls it into question at various points, uncovering the paradoxes of overlapping jurisdictions. Emily Steiner's "Inventing Legality: Documentary Culture and Lollard Preaching" describes the emerging fourteenth-century subgenre of the Charter of Christ, an imitation of a legal document. This genre is symptomatic of the interplay of legal document and literary text in the fourteenth century, both appropriating legal language and documentary power and emphasizing its fictionality. In the records of the Lollard trials, Steiner finds such documentary poetics turned against the legal process itself by the defendants, thereby questioning the authority of the evidentiary record. In *Richard the Redeless*, *Mum and the Sothsegger*, and Gower's *Cronica tripertita*, Frank Grady sees the abandonment of the visionary claims of the dream-vision format so dominant a few decades earlier in deference to a discourse of legal authority, instead modeling literary form on the language of legal documents and parliamentary debate, a change typical of the Lancastrian transition. An appendix offers Andrew Galloway's excellent translation into English with annotations of the "History or Narration Concerning the Manner and Form of the Miraculous Parliament at Westminster in the Year 1386, in the Tenth Year of the Reign of Richard the Second after the Conquest, Declared by Thomas Favent, Clerk."

A disappointment of the volume is the lack of either a bibliography or at least an indexing of footnotes. By doing justice to the particularity and complexity of the texts they examine, many of the chapters end up replicating the density and difficulty of legal debate, resulting in an extremely difficult reading experience even for those of us who know the (literary, at least) texts well. Whether or not intentionally, the hidden thesis of the volume is that what recent literary interpretation has identified as the totalitarian nature of the Lancastrian usurpation now seems to color what used to be previously regarded as the authoritarian nature of the Edwardian and Ricardian reigns, to borrow Hannah Arendt's terms. In addition to the importance of its subject matter, the book is also an introduction to the work of some of the leading figures among the next generation of scholars of Middle English literature, as well as collecting important contributions by such established figures as Galloway, Holsinger, and Green, making it essential reading for all readers of this journal.

JOHN M. GANIM
University of California, Riverside

CLAIRE M. WATERS. *Angels and Earthly Creatures: Preaching, Performance, and Gender in the Later Middle Ages.* Philadelphia: University of Pennsylvania, 2004. Pp. xi, 282. $55.00.

Recent studies of translation, Chaucer's appropriations, vernacular theology, and the Wycliffite heresy have drawn attention to the complicated relationship between the laity and the clergy and between lay and clerical interests and knowledge in the later Middle Ages. Waters's rich and engaging study offers a new perspective on this relationship, from the clerical side as it were, by reading the preacher himself (and his body) as marking the boundary: the preacher is a "hybrid," bridging the divide between church and laity and the body and the word (p. 2). And her close examination of preaching handbooks (the first part of the

367

study) reveals debates on how to theorize the preacher's authority in light of the humanity (and language) he shares with the laity. Such theories of course depend on understanding the preacher as male, and the attention to gender in discussions of preaching leads Waters to argue that women were essential to the construction of preaching as a male, clerical activity. For the second part of her study, she turns to women's preaching (both fictional and real) in two saints' lives from Voragine's *Legenda Aurea*, the writings of Hildegard of Bingen, Catherine of Siena, and Birgitta of Sweden, and Chaucer's Wife of Bath. In this way, she recuperates the marginal as central to the enterprise.

The first two chapters take up Waters's argument about the preacher's authority and his body. Chapter 1, "The Golden Chains of Citation," explores the ways in which church authorities, such as Gregory the Great and Bernard of Clairvaux, established the preacher's authority over the laity through citation—"of both authoritative words and authoritative individuals" (p. 14). Citation allowed male preachers to establish a lineage, through earlier models and Christ himself, from which women could be (and were) excluded. Here Waters uses speech-act theory to explain the way in which theorists set up a dichotomy between preaching (as the realm of the male clergy) and prophecy (open to both men and women): the former is "citable" and the second is extraordinary and noncitable (p. 23). With chapter 2, "Holy Duplicity: The Preacher's Two Faces," Waters examines the way in which embodiment complicates the preacher's authority, both the body's capacity to illustrate the preacher's message (by being a virtuous example) and to call it into question (by being a sinful example). Waters argues that in attempting to minimize the person of the preacher, the *artes* reveal an understanding of preaching as performance: both in the preachers' duplicity (those divisions between person and message) and the way in which "holy simplicity" (the congruity of words and persona) is constructed. And she locates the *artes'* concerns about the body in performance in Chaucer's contrasting preachers—the Parson and the Pardoner.

In chapters 3 and 4, Waters addresses two of the debates over the language of preaching. The first is the vernacular, and in "A Manner of Speaking: Access and the Vernacular," she argues for a common ground between preachers and laity in vernacular preaching and exempla. Yet, she does so not by examining the common ground itself (such as vernacular sermons) but by examining preaching handbooks (in Latin). The second is rhetoric, and in "'Mere Words': Gendered Eloquence and

Christian Preaching," Waters traces the history of the relationship between preaching and rhetoric from early Christianity, in the works of Tertullian and Augustine, which navigate the division between pagan, feminine rhetoric and Christian asceticism. As the medieval period progresses (and, one assumes, as the threat of paganism retreats), this anxiety about the seductive power of rhetoric recedes. But, with the growing interest in medieval preaching in the later medieval period, the anxieties reappear in another form—the effects of eloquence on the audience instead of the eloquence itself. This is a fascinating discussion of the way in which early theories of preaching shaped later conflicts, that is, the ways in which the gendered allegorical language of early preaching theorists, such as Augustine, was reappropriated and reinterpreted to refer to "real" women preaching.

With chapters 5 through 7, Waters shifts her attention to the female speaker: saint, visionary, Wife of Bath. Here she is less interested in women preaching than in women characters as vehicles for ideas about men preaching. For example, in her discussion of the lives of Katherine of Alexandria and Mary Magdalene from Voragine's *Legenda Aurea* in chapter 5, "Transparent Bodies and the Redemption of Rhetoric," she argues that the female saint offers a "less threatening context" for exploring "the preacher's embodied, persuasive appeals to his audience" (p. 96). For Waters, these stories acknowledge the power of feminine allure when it is put to a holy use. Similarly, the Wife, in chapter 7, is Chaucer's response to men (not women) preaching. This chapter, "*Sermones ad Status* and Old Wives' Tales; or The Audience Talks Back," presents a complicated argument that *sermones ad status* and estates satire undermined "the exceptional and unchallenged privilege of priestly speech" (p. 143) and that they demonstrate "how the association between clerical and female bodies begins to infect clerical speech" (p. 144). Thus Chaucer's Wife of Bath should be read in the context of estates satire about clerical concubines, as such demonstrating his "inheritances from and challenge to the preaching tradition," particularly around the preacher's debt to the body (p. 159). Only chapter 6, "The Alibi of Female Authority," takes up three "actual" women who addressed the church: Hildegard of Bingen, Birgitta of Sweden, and Catherine of Siena. For Waters, these women created a space, an "*alibi*," outside the clergy from which they addressed the failures of the clergy. What links these women is their alternative authority—their visionary experience.

As should be clear from this summary, Waters's understanding of preaching is based almost exclusively on texts in Latin. Such a focus is certainly illuminating (in her discussions of the preacher's embodiment), but in setting aside vernacular sermons and treatises, Waters sets aside much of the contentiousness surrounding preaching (and clerical knowledge more generally) in late medieval England (see H. Leith Spencer's study, *English Preaching in the Late Middle Ages* [Oxford, 1993]). Despite brief references to the Lollards and Margery Kempe, Chaucer is the only example of a vernacular challenge to preaching traditions in this study. Yet Chaucer's contemporaries, both Lollards and reformists, wrote vociferously and at times extensively about the very concerns of this book: authority, exemplarity, and women preachers/teachers. What happens to the authority of citation, for example, when authoritative texts are translated? To be sure, Waters never claims to be offering a comprehensive history of preaching. And, as a history of ideas about preachers in the Latin tradition, this study is a welcome addition to our understanding of late medieval devotion. Perhaps more important, it is an eloquent argument for including gender in the study of preaching.

KATHERINE LITTLE
Fordham University

DIANE WATT. *Amoral Gower: Language, Sex, and Politics.* Medieval Cultures 38. Minneapolis: University of Minnesota Press, 2003. Pp. xviii, 206. $60.95 cloth, $21.95 paper.

Amoral Gower is a provocative title, but Diane Watt's book is thought-provoking rather than shock-provoking. The phrase "amoral Gower" of course is a direct challenge to Chaucer's characterization of his literary counterpart as "moral Gower" in the dedication of *Troilus and Criseyde*. It is also a challenge to the many critics who, following Chaucer's lead and for other reasons, see Gower as a moralistic author. Watt's main focus is Gower's *Confessio Amantis*, but she also incorporates insightful discussions on the *Vox Clamantis* and *Mirour de l'Omme*. Her thesis addresses a question that has puzzled critics of the *Confessio* for a long time: Why are there inconsistencies and ambiguities in Genius's teachings? To Watt, these inconsistencies are not evidence of Gower's shortcomings

370

as a writer, as some critics have suggested. Quite to the contrary, they prove that Gower's *Confessio Amantis* is a daring project. In the preface she notes that Gower is not moral but amoral "because, insofar as he leaves the reader to make her or his own decisions . . . he does step outside of his own ethical system" (pp. xii–xiii). Gower's poem has us grapple with moral and ethical questions and experience the inevitable conflicts and contradictions that characterize "the sinful condition of humanity" (p. xiii). It does not aim at giving final and ultimate answers to these contradictions: "[Gower opens] up his text to multiple interpretations" (p. xii). To Watt, Gower's questions center on the relationship between language, sex, and politics, "interrelated concerns" in the *Confessio* (p. xv), which she examines by seamlessly combining contemporary theories, including feminist, psychoanalytic, and queer theory, along with textual criticism and linguistic and narrative theory.

In the introduction, Watt explains her main working assumptions. The book is then divided into three parts—"Language," "Sex," and "Politics"—each comprising two chapters. In the first chapter in "Part I: Language," Watt analyzes how certain Latin and vernacular passages in the *Confessio* suggest the indeterminacy of gender and sexuality, arguing that "a rich vein of linguistic gender play . . . involves its readers and . . . destabilizes its moral arrangement" (p. 34). This leads her to consider Gower's use of three languages in his overall work, Latin, Anglo-Norman, and Middle English. She suggests a connection between the story of the Tower of Babel, recounted in the *Confessio*, and the Fall, calling attention to the parallels between language and sexuality. The second chapter explores the links between rhetoric, genealogy, and gender. Watt argues that in the *Confessio* honest eloquence is "a masculine rather than a feminine quality" (p. 43), and she examines the ways in which deceptive rhetoric is associated with feminine qualities and adornments. This argument is compelling, although it underplays the role of eloquent women such as Peronelle in the "Tale of the Three Questions" or Thaise in the "Tale of Apollonius." This chapter also explores Gower's anxiety of influence by looking at the work of Brunetto Latini and Dante. Watt argues that Gower is ambivalent about rhetoric in ways that "forced him to question his own role as rhetorician and poet" (p. 54).

"Part II: Sex" starts by exploring the "homosocial and potentially homoerotic" (p. 65) implications of the relationship between Amans and Cupid and Amans and Genius. It also examines two tales about male cross-dressing and one about female cross-dressing and female-female sex. To Watt, sexual transgression in the *Confessio* "underlies all other forms of division (linguistic, ethical, even political), and division itself is at the heart of humankind's postlapsarian experience" (p. 89). Noticing that one form of "sexual transgression," male sodomy, is absent in the poem, Watt argues that this points to Gower's anxiety about the relationship between author and reader, about his own use of rhetoric, and about his relationship with his patron and his literary fathers. The second chapter in this part, titled "Sexual Chaos and Sexual Sin," considers first Venus's sexual ambiguity in the *Confessio*. Watt ties this ambiguity to the question of male and female accountability in stories of rape. The "Tale of Tereus," she argues, "constitutes a damning critique of aggressive masculinity" (p. 83). More significant, in this story "rape results in the dissolution rather than assertion of a stable masculine identity" (ibid.). It appears to make men effeminate rather than more masculine. Turning to the "Tale of Mundus and Paulina" and the "Tale of Nectanabus," Watt considers why these stories, even though they do not point to female culpability, depict rape somewhat positively and the rapists somewhat sympathetically. Watt's reading of these two tales is greatly nuanced but needs a clarification of terms—she refers to them sometimes as stories of rape and other times as stories of seduction. Drawing a line between rape and seduction, especially in the case of deceitful seduction, is a vexed issue, evident in contemporary discussions of rape, and addressing whether or not Genius distinguishes between the two and why he does or does not do so seems necessary, especially after a discussion of the story of Tereus's rape of Philomela.

In "Part III: Politics," Watt examines stories that appear to comment on monarchical rule generally and Richard II in particular. The first chapter starts by analyzing Nebuchadnezzar and Alexander. While in the story about Nebuchadnezzar's dream Gower is interested in apocalyptic motifs, in the story about his transformation, Watt argues, there is "a promise of restoration and recovery, of the reintegration of the monarch's divine and human aspects" (p. 114). The stories about Alexander, however, are more ambiguous, thus serving to articulate Gower's "anxieties concerning Richard as king and man" (p. 118). Watt then analyzes the tales about Lucrece and Virginia in Book VII and argues that through these tales Gower makes "comments about the current political situation, but does so only with considerable caution and some ambivalence" (p. 126). The final chapter, "Oedipus, Apollonius, and

Richard II," examines the "Tale of Apollonius" and links Oedipus, Apollonius, and Richard II with Amans/Gower in interesting ways. Watt argues that Apollonius shares in the sins of Antiochus and thus that Gower's depiction of Apollonius is deeply ambivalent. He, like Amans, does not learn from experience. These characters are meant to be warnings for the king and ultimately take us back to Gower: "Gower's decision, not only to sign his own narrative, but to identify himself with Amans, and thus implicitly with Richard himself, may indicate his personal frustration with and sense of failure about his role, not as poet of love, but as political advisor" (p. 148).

In the epilogue, "Ethical Gower," Watt returns to her main thesis and takes on very persuasively those who see the *Confessio* as unambiguous and moralistic. Gower's *Confessio*, she argues, does not present straightforward moral teachings. It is a skeptical work and shows some disillusionment at the possibility of reform: "Even at its closure, *Confessio Amantis* is characterized not by success but by failure, not by reconciliation but by division" (p. 160). *Amoral Gower* is a sophisticated book. Different readers might disagree with some of Watt's points, but all will find insightful readings and, overall, a highly compelling argument about the relationship between language, sex, and politics in the *Confessio*. In the preface Watt states: "I do not attempt to offer a final interpretation. My principal aim is to engage more readers, and thus to stimulate more interpretations" (p. xv). I have no doubt that Watt's main aim will be accomplished. This book is an excellent contribution to Gower scholarship and, more generally, to the study of fourteenth-century literature.

María Bullón-Fernández
Seattle University

RICHARD E. ZEIKOWITZ. *Homoeroticism and Chivalry: Discourses of Male Same-Sex Desire in the Fourteenth Century.* New York: Palgrave Macmillan, 2003. Pp. 216. $59.95.

In case anyone still doubts the relevance of queer theory to the Middle Ages, he or she should read the first chapter of this book. There Zeikowitz lays out the theoretical grounding of his argument and marshals an overwhelming (if a bit defensive) justification for this study and many more like it. Concentrating in the first chapter on pedagogical treatises on knighthood and their call for younger males to study their more experienced elders, he argues that the fixation, admiration, and transference that such intense mimesis and figuration involve is always at least potentially homoerotic. It follows that such intense absorption in the body of another, whether a knight, a saint, or sexual beloved, is already a step toward the imaginary figuration of the self that underlies identity formation and, concomitantly, sexual orientation. Although this might sound like standard medieval queer theory at work, Zeikowitz is quite clear from the start that his project is not one of unveiling proscribed queer desires within medieval texts. Rather, he chooses to focus on late medieval normative desire, which only today might be considered "queer." The difference between these two positions is striking and very well illustrated in the case studies that follow. How bodies react within normative discourse, and specifically within the norms of chivalric culture, is what interests him, whether or not such behavior ever approaches anything that might today be thought of as homoerotic. This insistence on same-sex relations as embedded within heteronormative discourse marks this book as a strikingly original way to approach a queer middle ages, that is, a middle ages that might have built upon inherent same-sex bonding (or attraction) as a way of strengthening what seem today to be ideologically constrictive domains such as chivalric or sainthood. Thus even the bonds between counselor and counseled (Pandarus and Troilus, Gaveston and Edward II), model and initiate, are scrutinized within the broadest and least constrictive senses of the homosocial.

After this long introductory chapter, the book is divided into two sections: the first part discusses homoerotic desire as integrated almost seamlessly into normative discourse, and the second part takes up critiques and condemnations of homoeroticism as falling outside political and social norms. In the first section, one encounters some of the usual suspects, *Sir Gawain and the Green Knight*, for example, but also the less expected, *Troilus and Criseyde.* Cleverly using Geoffroi de Charny's *Book of Chivalry* as a model of the sort of double messages that sustain chivalric discourse (make your fellow knight your model and love him as yourself, yet love a lady as the badge of your excellence and your pretext for further adventure), he examines chivalry as a discourse that bonds men in ways that adumbrate Sedgwick's notion of homosocial masculinity.

Although the argument is convincing, it is also quite speculative, as might be expected when one seeks evidence from a discourse whose integrity depends upon secrecy and exclusion. Chapter 2 extends the argument into the arena of treatises on friendship. Cicero and Aristotle give way to Aelred of Rievaulx and the *Romance of the Rose* before introducing an impressive discussion of *Amy and Amylion* and the *Prose Lancelot* as texts that blur the boundaries between devotion and love, duty and devotion. Although Zeikowitz is still careful to admit no actual sexual activity with the texts, this is as close as it comes to love and his discussion is impassioned and convincing. Chapter 3 is the longest, the most closely argued, and in some ways the least consequential. A long discussion of Troilus and Pandarus, through the lens of triangular desire, is so convincing that it does not really need this much discussion. His conclusion is, however, spot on: the scenarios in which "heterosexual desire is somehow infused with homoeroticism alert us to the limited usefulness of modern categories of desire" (p. 66). The final chapters of this section are brilliant and probably the most useful to others working in this area. Augustine's discussions of how emotions infuse visuality, phantasy, and memory leads us to a consideration of identification in film theory, which then segues into Freud's articulation of sadism and masochism. The final chapter puts this theory to work in considering male-male gazing, both from a religious perspective in which such gazing is crucial and undertheorized and a scientific/philosophical discussion of medieval models of vision involving, once again, *Sir Gawain and the Green Knight* and Charny's *Book of Chivalry*.

The second section, "Denigrations of Male Same-Sex Desire," concentrates largely on politically motivated denunciations of what could be called homosocial relations that veer into the homoerotic. The trial of the Templars provides a useful example of a case in which the charge of sodomy serves a pragmatic purpose. It is explicitly mentioned as part of Templar rituals and even the initiation ritual is said in some documents to include sexual, often nonconsentual elements (kissing the anus, for example). But what Zeikowitz brings out is that the homoerotic in such discussions is always linked with aggression and victimization. The testimony elicited in the Templar trials should not be taken as truth but as political fodder, specifically elicited to prove a point. This is even truer of the next cases discussed, the relationship of Edward II and Gaveston and that of Richard II and his court favorites. The implications of how a discourse of the homoerotic, framed as violent and exploitative, underpins even "innocent" relations (for example, Troilus and Pandarus) extend his argument to those normative texts that fall within heterosexualized boundaries. Finally, in a cogent conclusion, Zeikowitz calls into question the use of term such as "queer." Queer is not the marginal; it thrives within the normative and homosocial and becomes worthy of note only when these socially sanctioned relations are looked at from a different perspective. I have only the most minor of quibbles with this book. The final chapter of Troilus and Pandarus could probably have been incorporated into an earlier chapter so as not to overwhelm the extremely interesting material in chapters 4 and 5; and Zeikowitz does at times overargue a point, when less could be much more. Nonetheless, this is a very clever and enlightening study, the implications of which are broad and worth extending. This is not a book for a special-interest audience or one of marginal importance. It should be taken as a model for future studies that locate vestiges of the queer at the heart of the canonical.

WILLIAM BURGWINKLE
King's College, Cambridge

Books Received

Akbari, Suzanne Conklin. *Seeing Through the Veil: Optical Theory and Medieval Allegory*. Toronto: University of Toronto Press, 2004. Pp. x, 354. $65.00.

Beach, Alison I. *Women as Scribes: Book Production and Monastic Reform in Twelfth-Century Bavaria*. New York: Cambridge University Press, 2004. Pp. xiv, 198. $70.00.

Boitani, Piero and Jill Mann. *The Cambridge Companion to Chaucer*. New York: Cambridge University Press, 2003. Second edition. Pp. xiv, 317. $60.00 cloth, $23.00 paper.

Bowing, Richard. *Murasaki Shikibu: The Tale of Genji*. New York: Cambridge University Press, 2004. Second edition. Pp.xiii, 106. $43.00 cloth, $15.00 paper.

Burgwinkle, William. *Sodomy, Masculinity and Law in Medieval Literature*. New York: Cambridge University Press, 2004. Pp. ix, 298. $75.00.

Cooper, Helen. *The English Romance in Time: Transforming Motifs from Geoffrey of Monmouth to the Death of Shakespeare*. New York: Oxford University Press, 2004. Pp. xiii, 542. $125.00.

D'Arcens, Louise and Juanita Feros Ruys, eds. *Maistresse of My Wit: Medieval Women, Modern Scholars*. Turnhout, Belgium: Brepols Publishers, 2004. Pp. x, 384. $94.00.

Driver, Martha W. and Sid Ray, eds. *The Medieval Hero on Screen: Representations from Beowulf to Buffy*. Jefferson, N.C.: McFarland & Company, 2004. Pp.viii, 268. $35.00 paper.

Echard, Sian. *A Companion to Gower*. Woodbridge, Suffolk and Rochester, NY: D.S. Brewer, 2004. Pp. x, 286. $110.00.

Echard, Sian and Stephen Partridge, eds. *The Book Unbound: Editing and Reading Medieval Manuscripts and Texts*. Toronto: University of Toronto Press, 2004. Pp. xx, 236. $50.00.

Finke, Laurie A. and Martin B. Shichtman. *King Arthur and the Myth of History*. Gainesville: University Press of Florida, 2004. Pp.xiii, 262. $59.95.

Green, Richard Firth and Linne R. Mooney. *Interstices: Studies in Middle English in Honour of A. G. Rigg*. Toronto: University of Toronto Press, 2004. Pp. xxii, 219. $50.00.

Havely, Nick. *Dante and the Franciscans: Poverty and the Papacy in the Commedia*. New York: Cambridge University Press, 2004. Pp. xvi, 212. $75.00.

Hiatt, Alfred. *The Making of Medieval Forgeries: False Documents in Fifteenth-Century England*. Toronto: University of Toronto Press, 2004. Pp. xiv, 226. $60.00.

Hogg, Richard. *An Introduction to Old English*. New York: Oxford University Press, 2002. Pp. ix, 163. $19.95, paper.

Horobin, Simon and Jeremy Smith. *An Introduction to Middle English*. New York: Oxford University Press, 2002. Pp. viii, 182. $19.95, paper.

Huot, Sylvia. *Madness in Medieval French Literature: Identities Found and Lost*. New York: Oxford University Press, 2003. Pp. 224. $65.00.

Kelly, Henry Ansgar. *Love and Marriage in the Age of Chaucer*. Eugene: Wipf and Stock Publishers, 2004. Previously published by Cornell University Press, 1975. $29.60, paper.

Kelly, Henry Ansgar. *Tragedy and Comedy from Dante to Pseudo-Dante*. Eugene: Wipf and Stock Publishers, 2004. Previously published by University of California Press, 1989. $14.40. paper.

Kennedy, Ruth, ed.. *Three Alliterative Saints' Hymns: Late Middle English Stanzaic Poems*. EETS o.s. 321. New York: Oxford University Press, 2003. Pp. xcvii, 120. $74.00.

Kirkpatrick, Robin. *Dante: The Divine Comedy*. New York: Cambridge University Press, 2004. Second edition. Pp. xii, 118. $43.00 cloth, $15.00 paper.

Lawton, David, Rita Copeland and Wendy Scase, eds.. *New Medieval Literatures*. vol. 6. New York: Oxford University Press, 2003. Pp. vii, 317. $125.00.

Lee, Peter H. *A History of Korean Literature*. New York: Cambridge University Press, 2003. Pp. lxxvi, 580. $95.00.

McSheffrey, Shannon and Norman Tanner, eds. and trans. *Lollards of Coventry, 1486–1522*. Camden Fifth Series, vol. 23. New York: Cambridge University Press, 2003. Pp.x, 361. $70.00.

Meyer, Ann R. *Medieval Allegory and the Building of the New Jerusalem*. Cambridge: D. S. Brewer, 2003. Pp. x, 214. $70.00.

Minkova, Donka and Theresa Tinkle, eds. *Chaucer and the Challenges of Medievalism: Studies in Honor of H.A. Kelly*. Studies in English Medieval Language and Literature, 5. New York: Peter Lang, 2003. Pp. xxii, 403. $66.95 paper.

Scheil, Andrew P. *The Footsteps of Israel: Understanding Jews in Anglo-Saxon England*. Ann Arbor: University of Michigan Press, 2004. Pp. xii, 372. $65.00.

Scott, Anne M. *Piers Plowman and the Poor*. Portland: Four Courts Press, 2004. Pp. 263. $65.00.

Summers, Joanna. *Late-Medieval Prison Writing and the Politics of Autobiography*. Oxford: Oxford University Press, 2004. Pp. x, 229. $85.00.

Wetherbee, Winthrop. *Geoffrey Chaucer: The Canterbury Tales*. New York: Cambridge University Press, 2004. Second edition. Pp. x, 125. $43.00 cloth, $15.00 paper.

An Annotated Chaucer Bibliography, 2003

Compiled and edited by Mark Allen and Bege K. Bowers

Regular contributors:

Bruce W. Hozeski, *Ball State University* (Indiana)
George Nicholas, *Benedictine College* (Kansas)
Marilyn Sutton, *California State University at Dominguez Hills*
David Sprunger, *Concordia College* (Minnesota)
Winthrop Wetherbee III, *Cornell University* (New York)
Elizabeth Dobbs, *Grinnell College* (Iowa)
Teresa P. Reed, *Jacksonville State University* (Alabama)
William Snell, *Keio University* (Japan)
Denise Stodola, *Kettering University* (Michigan)
Brian A. Shaw, *London, Ontario*
William Schipper, *Memorial University* (Newfoundland, Canada)
Larry L. Bronson, *Mount Pleasant, Michigan*
Martha Rust, *New York University*
Warren S. Moore, III, *Newberry College* (South Carolina)
Amy Goodwin, *Randolph-Macon College* (Virginia)
Erik Kooper, *Rijksuniversiteit te Utrecht*
Cindy L. Vitto, *Rowan College of New Jersey*
Anne Thornton, *San Antonio College* (Texas)
Richard H. Osberg, *Santa Clara University* (California)
Brother Anthony (Sonjae An), *Sogang University* (South Korea)
Margaret Connolly, *University College, Cork* (Ireland)
Juliette Dor, *Université de Liège* (Belgium)
Mary Flowers Braswell and Elaine Whitaker, *University of Alabama at Birmingham*
Stefania D'Agata D'Ottavi, *University of Macerata* (Italy)
Gregory M. Sadlek, *University of Nebraska at Omaha*
Cynthia Ho, *University of North Carolina, Asheville*
Richard J. Utz, *University of Northern Iowa*

Rebecca Beal, *University of Scranton* (Pennsylvania)
Mark Allen and R. L. Smith, *University of Texas at San Antonio*
Andrew Lynch, *University of Western Australia*
Joerg O. Fichte, *Universität Tübingen* (Tübingen, Germany)
John M. Crafton, *West Georgia College*
Robert Correale, *Wright State University* (Ohio)
Bege K. Bowers, *Youngstown State University* (Ohio)

Ad hoc contributions were made by the following: Eileen Krueger (*Concordia, North Carolina*). The bibliographers acknowledge with gratitude the MLA type simulation provided by the Center for Bibliographical Services of the Modern Language Association; postage from the University of Texas at San Antonio Department of English, Classics, and Philosophy; and assistance from the library staff, especially Susan McCray, at the University of Texas at San Antonio.

This bibliography continues the bibliographies published since 1975 in previous volumes of *Studies in the Age of Chaucer*. Bibliographic information up to 1975 can be found in Eleanor P. Hammond, *Chaucer: A Bibliographic Manual* (1908; reprint, New York: Peter Smith, 1933); D. D. Griffith, *Bibliography of Chaucer, 1908–1953* (Seattle: University of Washington Press, 1955); William R. Crawford, *Bibliography of Chaucer, 1954–63* (Seattle: University of Washington Press, 1967); and Lorrayne Y. Baird, *Bibliography of Chaucer, 1964–1973* (Boston: G. K. Hall, 1977). See also Lorrayne Y. Baird-Lange and Hildegard Schnuttgen, *Bibliography of Chaucer, 1974–1985* (Hamden, Conn.: Shoe String Press, 1988); and Bege K. Bowers and Mark Allen, eds., *Annotated Chaucer Bibliography, 1986–1996* (Notre Dame, Ind.: University of Notre Dame, 2002).

Additions and corrections to this bibliography should be sent to Mark Allen, Bibliographic Division, New Chaucer Society, Department of English, Classics, and Philosophy, University of Texas at San Antonio 78249-0643 (Fax: 210-458-5366; E-mail: MALLEN@UTSA.EDU). An electronic version of this bibliography (1975–2003) is available via the New Chaucer Society Web page <http://artsci.wustl.edu/~chaucer/> or at <http://uchaucer.utsa.edu>. Authors are urged to send annotations for articles, reviews, and books that have been or might be overlooked.

Classifications

Abbreviations of Chaucer's Works

ABC	*An ABC*
Adam	*Adam Scriveyn*
Anel	*Anelida and Arcite*
Astr	*A Treatise on the Astrolabe*
Bal Compl	*A Balade of Complaint*
BD	*The Book of the Duchess*
Bo	*Boece*
Buk	*The Envoy to Bukton*
CkT, CkP, Rv–CkL	*The Cook's Tale, The Cook's Prologue, Reeve–Cook Link*
ClT, ClP, Cl–MerL	*The Clerk's Tale, The Clerk's Prologue, Clerk–Merchant Link*
Compl d'Am	*Complaynt d'Amours*
CT	*The Canterbury Tales*
CYT, CYP	*The Canon's Yeoman's Tale, The Canon's Yeoman's Prologue*
Equat	*The Equatorie of the Planetis*
For	*Fortune*
Form Age	*The Former Age*
FranT, FranP	*The Franklin's Tale, The Franklin's Prologue*
FrT, FrP, Fr–SumL	*The Friar's Tale, The Friar's Prologue, Friar–Summoner Link*
Gent	*Gentilesse*
GP	*The General Prologue*
HF	*The House of Fame*
KnT, Kn–MilL	*The Knight's Tale, Knight–Miller Link*
Lady	*A Complaint to His Lady*
LGW, LGWP	*The Legend of Good Women, The Legend of Good Women Prologue*
ManT, ManP	*The Manciple's Tale, The Manciple's Prologue*
Mars	*The Complaint of Mars*
Mel, Mel–MkL	*The Tale of Melibee, Melibee–Monk Link*
MercB	*Merciles Beaute*
MerT, MerE–SqH	*The Merchant's Tale, Merchant Endlink–Squire Headlink*

MilT, MilP, Mil–RvL	*The Miller's Tale, The Miller's Prologue, Miller–Reeve Link*
MkT, MkP, Mk–NPL	*The Monk's Tale, The Monk's Prologue, Monk–Nun's Priest Link*
MLT, MLH, MLP, MLE	*The Man of Law's Tale, Man of Law Headlink, The Man of Law's Prologue, Man of Law Endlink*
NPT, NPP, NPE	*The Nun's Priest's Tale, The Nun's Priest's Prologue, Nun's Priest's Endlink*
PardT, PardP	*The Pardoner's Tale, The Pardoner's Prologue*
ParsT, ParsP	*The Parson's Tale, The Parson's Prologue*
PF	*The Parliament of Fowls*
PhyT, Phy–PardL	*The Physician's Tale, Physician–Pardoner Link*
Pity	*The Complaint unto Pity*
Prov	*Proverbs*
PrT, PrP, Pr–ThL	*The Prioress's Tale, The Prioress's Prologue, Prioress–Thopas Link*
Purse	*The Complaint of Chaucer to His Purse*
Ret	*Chaucer's Retraction {Retractation}*
Rom	*The Romaunt of the Rose*
Ros	*To Rosemounde*
RvT, RvP	*The Reeve's Tale, The Reeve's Prologue*
Scog	*The Envoy to Scogan*
ShT, Sh–PrL	*The Shipman's Tale, Shipman–Prioress Link*
SNT, SNP, SN–CYL	*The Second Nun's Tale, The Second Nun's Prologue, Second Nun–Canon's Yeoman Link*
SqT, SqH, Sq–FranL	*The Squire's Tale, Squire Headlink, Squire–Franklin Link*
Sted	*Lak of Stedfastnesse*
SumT, SumP	*The Summoner's Tale, The Summoner's Prologue*
TC	*Troilus and Criseyde*
Th, Th–MelL	*The Tale of Sir Thopas, Sir Thopas–Melibee Link*
Truth	*Truth*
Ven	*The Complaint of Venus*

386

WBT, WBP, WB–FrL	*The Wife of Bath's Tale, The Wife of Bath's Prologue, Wife of Bath–Friar Link*
Wom Nob	*Womanly Noblesse*
Wom Unc	*Against Women Unconstant*

Periodical Abbreviations

AdI	*Annali d'Italianistica*
Anglia	*Anglia: Zeitschrift für Englische Philologie*
Anglistik	*Anglistik: Mitteilungen des Verbandes deutscher Anglisten*
AnLM	*Anuario de Letras Modernas*
ANQ	*ANQ: A Quarterly Journal of Short Articles, Notes, and Reviews*
ArAA	*Arbeiten aus Anglistik und Amerikanistik*
Archiv	*Archiv für das Studium der Neueren Sprachen und Literaturen*
Arthuriana	*Arthuriana*
BAM	*Bulletin des Anglicistes Médiévistes*
BJRL	*Bulletin of the John Rylands University Library of Manchester*
C&L	*Christianity and Literature*
CarmP	*Carmina Philosophiae: Journal of the International Boethius Society*
CE	*College English*
Chaucer Yearbook	*Chaucer Yearbook: A Journal of Late Medieval Studies*
ChauNewsl	*Chaucer Newsletter*
ChauR	*Chaucer Review*
CL	*Comparative Literature* (Eugene, Ore.)
CLS	*Comparative Literature Studies*
CML	*Classical and Modern Literature: A Quarterly* (Columbia, Mo.)
CollL	*College Literature*
Comitatus	*Comitatus: A Journal of Medieval and Renaissance Studies*
Comparatist	*The Comparatist: Journal of the Southern Comparative Literature Association*
CRCL	*Canadian Review of Comparative Literature/Revue Canadienne de Littérature Comparée*
Crossings	*Crossings: A Counter-Disciplinary Journal* (Binghamton, N.Y.)

DAI	*Dissertation Abstracts International*
Disputatio	*Disputatio: An International Transdisciplinary Journal of the Late Middle Ages*
DR	*Dalhousie Review*
ÉA	*Études Anglaises: Grand-Bretagne, États-Unis*
ÉC	*Études Celtiques*
EHR	*English Historical Review*
EIC	*Essays in Criticism: A Quarterly Journal of Literary Criticism*
ELH	*ELH*
ELN	*English Language Notes*
ELR	*English Literary Renaissance*
EMS	*English Manuscript Studies, 1100–1700*
Encomia	*Encomia: Bibliographical Bulletin of the International Courtly Literature Society*
English	*English: The Journal of the English Association*
Envoi	*Envoi: A Review Journal of Medieval Literature*
ES	*English Studies*
ESC	*English Studies in Canada*
Exemplaria	*Exemplaria: A Journal of Theory in Medieval and Renaissance Studies*
Expl	*Explicator*
Fabula	*Fabula: Zeitschrift für Erzählforschung/Journal of Folktale Studies*
FCS	*Fifteenth-Century Studies*
Florilegium	*Florilegium: Carleton University Papers on Late Antiquity and the Middle Ages*
FMLS	*Forum for Modern Language Studies*
Genre	*Genre: Forms of Discourse and Culture*
GRM	*Germanisch-Romanische Monatsschrift*
HLQ	*Huntington Library Quarterly: Studies in English and American History and Literature* (San Marino, Calif.)
InG	*In Geardagum: Essays on Old and Middle English Language and Literature*
Italica	*Italica: Bulletin of the American Association of Teachers of Italian*
JAIS	*Journal of Anglo-Italian Studies*
JEBS	*Journal of the Early Book Society*

JEGP	*Journal of English and Germanic Philology*
JELL	*Journal of English Language and Literature* (Korea)
JEngL	*Journal of English Linguistics*
JEP	*Journal of Evolutionary Psychology*
JMEMSt	*Journal of Medieval and Early Modern Studies*
JML	*Journal of Modern Literature*
JNT	*Journal of Narrative Theory*
JournalX	*Journal x: A Journal in Culture and Criticism*
JRMMRA	*Quidditas: Journal of the Rocky Mountain Medieval and Renaissance Association*
L&LC	*Literary and Linguistic Computing: Journal of the Association for Literary and Linguistic Computing*
L&P	*Literature and Psychology*
L&T	*Literature and Theology: An International Journal of Religion, Theory, and Culture*
Lang&Lit	*Language and Literature: Journal of the Poetics and Linguistics Association*
Lang&S	*Language and Style: An International Journal*
LeedsSE	*Leeds Studies in English*
Library	*The Library: The Transactions of the Bibliographical Society*
LRB	*The London Review of Books*
MA	*Le Moyen Age: Revue d'Histoire et de Philologie* (Brussels, Belgium)
MÆ	*Medium Ævum*
M&H	*Medievalia et Humanistica: Studies in Medieval and Renaissance Culture*
Manuscripta	*Manuscripta* (St. Louis, Mo.)
Mediaevalia	*Mediaevalia: An Interdisciplinary Journal of Medieval Studies Worldwide*
Mediaevistik	*Mediaevistik: Internationale Zeitschrift für Interdisziplinäre Mittelalterforschung*
MedPers	*Medieval Perspectives*
MES	*Medieval English Studies*
MFN	*Medieval Feminist Newsletter*
MichA	*Michigan Academician* (Ann Arbor, Mich.)
MLQ	*Modern Language Quarterly: A Journal of Literary History*

MLR	*The Modern Language Review*
ModA	*Modern Age: A Quarterly Review*
MP	*Modern Philology: A Journal Devoted to Research in Medieval and Modern Literature*
N&Q	*Notes and Queries*
Neophil	*Neophilologus* (Dordrecht, Netherlands)
NFS	*Nottingham French Studies*
NLH	*New Literary History: A Journal of Theory and Interpretation*
NM	*Neuphilologische Mitteilungen: Bulletin of the Modern Language Society*
NMS	*Nottingham Medieval Studies*
NOWELE	*NOWELE: North-Western European Language Evolution*
OT	*Oral Tradition*
PAPA	*Publications of the Arkansas Philological Association*
Parergon	*Parergon: Bulletin of the Australian and New Zealand Association for Medieval and Early Modern Studies*
PBA	*Proceedings of the British Academy*
PBSA	*Papers of the Bibliographical Society of America*
PLL	*Papers on Language and Literature: A Journal for Scholars and Critics of Language and Literature*
PMAM	*Publications of the Medieval Association of the Midwest*
PMLA	*Publications of the Modern Language Association of America*
PoeticaT	*Poetica: An International Journal of Linguistic Literary Studies*
PQ	*Philological Quarterly*
Prolepsis	*Prolepsis: The Tübingen Review of English Studies*
ProverbiumY	*Proverbium: Yearbook of International Proverb Scholarship*
RCEI	*Revista Canaria de Estudios Ingleses*
RenD	*Renaissance Drama*
RenQ	*Renaissance Quarterly*
RES	*Review of English Studies*
RMSt	*Reading Medieval Studies* (Reading, England)
Romania	*Romania: Revue Consacrée à l'Étude des Langues et des Littératures Romanes*

RSQ	*Rhetoric Society Quarterly* (University Park, Pa.)
SAC	*Studies in the Age of Chaucer*
SAF	*Studies in American Fiction* (Boston, Mass.)
SAP	*Studia Anglica Posnaniensia: An International Review of English*
SAQ	*South Atlantic Quarterly*
SB	*Studies in Bibliography: Papers of the Bibliographical Society of the University of Virginia*
SCJ	*The Sixteenth-Century Journal: Journal of Early Modern Studies* (Kirksville, Mo.)
SEL	*SEL: Studies in English Literature, 1500–1900*
SELIM	*SELIM: Journal of the Spanish Society for Medieval English Language and Literature*
ShakS	*Shakespeare Studies* (Baltimore, Md.)
ShY	*The Shakespeare Yearbook*
SIcon	*Studies in Iconography*
SiM	*Studies in Medievalism*
SIMELL	*Studies in Medieval English Language and Literature*
SMART	*Studies in Medieval and Renaissance Teaching*
SN	*Studia Neophilologica: A Journal of Germanic and Romance Languages and Literatures*
SoAR	*South Atlantic Review*
SP	*Studies in Philology*
Speculum	*Speculum: A Journal of Medieval Studies*
SQ	*Shakespeare Quarterly*
SSF	*Studies in Short Fiction*
SSt	*Spenser Studies: A Renaissance Poetry Annual*
TCBS	*Transactions of the Cambridge Bibliographical Society*
Text	*Text: Transactions of the Society for Textual Scholarship*
TLS	*Times Literary Supplement* (London, England)
TMR	*The Medieval Review* <http://www.hti.umich.edu/b/ bmr/tmr.html>
Tr&Lit	*Translation and Literature*
TSLL	*Texas Studies in Literature and Language*
UCrow	*The Upstart Crow: A Shakespeare Journal*
UTQ	*University of Toronto Quarterly: A Canadian Journal of the Humanities* (Toronto, Canada)

Viator	*Viator: Medieval and Renaissance Studies*
WS	*Women's Studies: An Interdisciplinary Journal*
YER	*Yeats Eliot Review: A Journal of Criticism and Scholarship*
YES	*Yearbook of English Studies*
YULG	*Yale University Library Gazette*
YWES	*Year's Work in English Studies*
YLS	*The Yearbook of Langland Studies*
ZAA	*Zeitschrift für Anglistik und Amerikanistik: A Quarterly of Language, Literature and Culture*

Bibliographical Citations and Annotations

Bibliographies, Reports, and Reference

1. Allen, Mark, and Bege K. Bowers. "An Annotated Chaucer Bibliography, 2001." *SAC* 25 (2003): 459–546. Continuation of *SAC* annual annotated bibliography (since 1975); based on contributions from an international bibliographic team, independent research, and *MLA Bibliography* listings. 295 items, plus listing of reviews for 85 books. Includes an author index.

2. Allen, Valerie, and Margaret Connolly. "Middle English: Chaucer." *YWES* 82 (2003): 190–224. A discursive bibliography of Chaucer studies for 2001, divided into four subcategories: general, *CT*, *TC*, and other works.

3. Blake, Norman F., David Burnley, Masatsugu Matsuo, and Yoshiyuki Nakao, eds. *A New Concordance to "The Canterbury Tales" Based on Blake's Text Edited from the Hengwrt Manuscript*. Okayama: University Education Press, 1994. viii, 1,008 pp. A comprehensive concordance to *CT* based on Blake's text from the Hengwrt manuscript. Includes an alphabetical and frequency word list; describes spellings, words, syntax, and metrics.

4. ————, eds. *A New Rime Concordance to "The Canterbury Tales" Based on Blake's Text Edited from the Hengwrt Manuscript*. Okayama: University Education Press, 1995. v, 520 pp. A comprehensive rhyming dictionary showing a full line for each rhyme word (showing seven lines for rhyme royal), based on Blake's text from the Hengwrt manuscript.

5. Gray, Douglas, ed. *The Oxford Companion to Chaucer*. Oxford: Oxford University Press, 2003. 526 pp.; 15 b&w illus.; 4 maps. A single-volume encyclopedia with more than 2,000 entries, composed by a team of thirteen contributors and the editor. Alphabetized entries include each of Chaucer's works, important sources and analogues, character and place names, select contemporaries and critics of Chaucer, and a variety of general literary and cultural topics (e.g., "allusion," "London," "versification"). Longer entries include brief bibliographies keyed to a reference bibliography, and the entries are cross-listed.

See also no. 92.

Recordings and Films

6. Blandeau, Agnès. "De l'écrit au filmique: Métamorphoses. Des *Canterbury Tales* à *I racconti di Canterbury*." In Adrian Papahagi, ed. *Méta-morphoses* (*SAC* 27 [2005], no. 130), pp. 229–43. There is more to Pier Paolo Pasolini's film version of *CT* than mere adaptation, for the shift from one semiotic system to another implies some puzzling metamorphoses. Yet, paradoxically, the spirit of the original is cleverly restored on the screen.

7. ———. "Narrative Play and the Display of Artistry in Chaucer's *Canterbury Tales* and Pasolini's *I racconti di Canterbury*." In Wendy Harding, ed. *Drama, Narrative and Poetry in* The Canterbury Tales (*SAC* 27 [2005], no. 114), pp. 35–50. Although Pasolini's visualization of *CT* chooses to emphasize "solaas" rather than "sentence," both the film-maker and the poet offer metafictional reflections on their art and the "discourse of the narrative."

8. Burton, Tom, dir. *The Manciple's Tale*. Occasional Readings, no. 32. [Provo, Ut.]: Chaucer Studio, 2003. 1 CD-ROM. 25 min. Read by Philip Thiel; edited by Troy Sales and Paul Thomas. Recorded by Ewart Shaw at Radio Adelaide. Includes *ManPT*.

9. ———, dir. *The Second Nun's Tale*. Occasional Readings, no. 33. [Provo, Ut.]: Chaucer Studio, 2003. 1 CD-ROM. 38 min. Read by Katherine Davis; edited by Troy Sales and Paul Thomas. Recorded by Ewart Shaw at Radio Adelaide. Includes *SNPT*.

10. Forni, Kathleen. "Reinventing Chaucer: Helgeland's *A Knight's Tale*." *ChauR* 37 (2003): 253–64. Despite inaccuracies and major differences from Chaucer's *KnT*, Helgeland's film *A Knight's Tale* does maintain a "Chaucer effect" that has secured the poet's "iconic status" since the Renaissance. Yet anachronisms abound; rock music replaces chant; and the central premise of the plot—that patents of nobility are necessary to compete—is inaccurate.

11. Myerson, Joel, dir. *The Canterbury Tales III*. [Cardiff]: S4C and Christmas Films, 2000. 1 VHS videorecording; VHS M6616. 30 min. Distributed by Schlessinger Media (Wynnewood, Pa.). Animated versions of *SqT* (with a completed plot), *CYPT*, and *MilT* and *RvT* (with plots interpolated), presented as tales told on each of three days as the pilgrims return from Canterbury to London. Includes a teacher's guide (pamphlet).

12. Reed, Teresa P. "Overcoming Performance Anxiety: Chaucer

Studio Products Reviewed." *Exemplaria* 15 (2003): 245–61. Argues that spoken recordings of Chaucer's works (and other Middle English writings) are useful in the classroom. Surveys critical attitudes toward such recordings and comments on the products produced by the Chaucer Studio.

Chaucer's Life

13. Ganim, John. "Mary Shelley, Godwin's *Chaucer*, and the Middle Ages." In Donka Minkova and Theresa Tinkle, eds. *Chaucer and the Challenges of Medievalism: Studies in Honor of H. A. Kelly* (*SAC* 27 [2005], no. 125), pp. 175–89. Ganim argues that Mary Shelley was influenced by her father, William Godwin, who wrote *Life of Chaucer* and from whom she learned a dual attitude toward the Middle Ages: people are shaped by historical circumstances, and they must seek to rise above these circumstances through reason and individual discovery.

14. Jones, Terry, Robert Yeager, Terry Dolan, Alan Fletcher, and Juliette Dor. *Who Murdered Chaucer? A Medieval Mystery*. London: Methuen, 2003; New York: St. Martin's Press, 2004. x, 408 pp.; 130 illus. A biography and social history of Chaucer's final years, focusing on Henry Bolingbroke's Lancastrian overthrow of Richard II and the political and social turmoil from which the usurpation resulted and to which it contributed. The book presents Thomas Arundel, Archbishop of Canterbury, as a key figure, both in the political arena and in efforts to suppress *CT* for its scandalous depictions of the Church. Obscurities surrounding Chaucer's death may indicate that Arundel's suppression was effective, perhaps deadly to Chaucer himself. The study assesses "censorship" of the illustrations to the Ellesmere manuscript and reads *ABC*, *ParsT*, and *Ret* as Chaucer's responses to suppression. Reprises suggestions by early biographers that Chaucer may not have died until 1402, perhaps finding temporary refuge in Holland.

15. Rosenthal, Joel T. *Telling Tales: Sources and Narration in Late Medieval England*. University Park: Pennsylvania State University Press, 2003. xxvi, 217 pp. Provides close historical analysis of three groups of archives: proofs of age from the reigns of Richard II and Henry IV, depositions from the Scrope-Grosvenor controversy, and Margaret Paston's letters. Discussion of the depositions includes commentary on Chaucer's testimony.

See also nos. 131, 145, 146, 151.

Facsimiles, Editions, and Translations

16. Ajiro, Atsushi. "On Two Editions of Chaucer's Works—(I) *The Parliament of Fowls* (1)." *Daito Bunka Review* (Daito Bunka University) 22 (1991): 1–13 (in Japanese). Ajiro investigates editorial differences in manuscript readings between Robinson's second edition of *PF* and the text in Benson's *The Riverside Chaucer*; considers what manuscripts were used in their editing.

17. ———. "On Two Editions of Chaucer's Works—(I) *The Parliament of Fowls* (2)." *Daito Bunka Review* (Daito Bunka University) 23 (1992): 65–86 (in Japanese). Examines differences in punctuation between Robinson's second edition of *PF* and the text in Benson's *The Riverside Chaucer*. Concludes that modern punctuation might sometimes distort Middle English style, especially in colloquial speech.

18. Benton, Megan L. "Typography and Gender: Remasculating the Modern Book." In Paul C. Gutjahr and Megan L. Benton, eds. *Illuminating Letters: Typography and Literary Interpretation.* Studies in Print Culture and the History of the Book. Amherst: University of Massachusetts Press, 2001, pp. 71–93. Exploring the relationship between gender identity and book production at the turn of the twentieth century, Benton assesses the format and typography of the Kelmscott Chaucer (1896) and Eric Gill's illustrations to *The Canterbury Tales* (1930). Also considers editions of Whitman's *Leaves of Grass*.

19. Bordalejo, Barbara. *Caxton's* Canterbury Tales*: The British Library Copies.* The Canterbury Tales Project. Leicester: Scholarly Digital Editions-Boydell and Brewer, 2003. 1 CD-ROM. Includes full-color facsimiles of the first and second editions of *CT*: the Royal copy of the first edition and the Grenville copy of the second, i.e., British Library 167.c.26 and C.21.d.

20. ———. "The Collational Formula of Caxton's Second Edition of the *Canterbury Tales*." *ANQ* 16.4 (2003): 8–9. Bordalejo corrects the bibliographic description of Caxton's second edition of *The Canterbury Tales* (Cx²), held at St. John's College Library, Oxford.

21. Carlson, David R. "The Woodcut Illustrations in Early Printed Editions of Chaucer's *Canterbury Tales*." In William K. Finley and Joseph Rosenblum, eds. *Chaucer Illustrated: Five Hundred Years of the* Canterbury Tales *in Pictures* (*SAC* 27 [2005], no. 105), pp. 73–119. Revised version of 1997 essay "Woodcut Illustrations of the *Canterbury Tales*, 1483–

1602" (*SAC* 21 [1999], no. 10). Includes a descriptive catalog of wood-cuts in editions of *CT*, 1483–1602.

22. Edwards, Robert R. "Translating Thebes: Lydgate's *Siege of Thebes* and Stow's Chaucer." *ELH* 70 (2003): 319–41. Discusses John Stow's 1561 edition of Chaucer's works, in which Stow includes Lydgate's "Siege of Thebes" to expand Chaucer's canon. The inclusion helped shape the idea of Chaucer in the Renaissance, with far-reaching consequences for subsequent editions and understandings of Chaucer's canon.

23. Holliday, Peter. "The Golden Cockerel Press, *The Canterbury Tales* and Eric Gill: Decoration and the *Mise en Page*." In William K. Finley and Joseph Rosenblum, eds. *Chaucer Illustrated: Five Hundred Years of the* Canterbury Tales *in Pictures* (*SAC* 27 [2005], no. 105), pp. 326–67. Holliday considers Eric Gill's wood-engraving illustrations to *The Canterbury Tales* (4 vols., Golden Cockerel Press, 1929–31) in light of Gill's collaboration with Robert Gibbings (owner of the press), the legacy of Edward Johnston (Gill's teacher of lettering), and the Arts and Crafts movement, which can be traced to William Morris. Gill's breaks with tradition are evident in his greater concern with typographical design than with historical atmosphere.

24. Jimura, Akiyuki, Yoshiyuki Nakao, and Masatsugu Matsuo, eds. *A Comprehensive Textual Comparison of Chaucer's Dream Poetry*. Okayama: University Education Press, 2002. v, 173 pp. A computer-assisted comparison of editions of *BD, HF,* and *PF*. Clarifies spellings, lexis, syntax, and metrics, analyzing versions by Benson, Robinson, Root, Brewer, and Havely.

25. Kelen, Sarah A. "Climbing up the Family Tree: Chaucer's Tudor Progeny." *JEBS* 6 (2003): 109–23. Demonstrates that "Tudor editions of Chaucer imagined Chaucer himself as a Tudor poet" (109); concludes with three illustrations from Houghton Library copies of STC 5075 and 5077.

26. Lerer, Seth. "Unpublished Sixteenth-Century Arguments to *The Canterbury Tales*." *N&Q* 248 (2003): 13–17. Prints handwritten summaries from a copy of the 1550 edition of Chaucer's works (Cambridge University Library Peterborough B.6.13) and discusses their usefulness for a history of the literary argument, documenting one reader's response to *CT* and providing a record of the changing English lexicon.

27. Robinson, Duncan. "The Kelmscott Chaucer." In William K. Finley and Joseph Rosenblum, eds. *Chaucer Illustrated: Five Hundred Years*

of the Canterbury Tales *in Pictures* (*SAC* 27 [2005], no. 105), pp. 274–310. The essay describes the personal and social conditions that led to the 1896 production of the Kelmscott Chaucer by William Morris and Edward Burne-Jones. Robinson compares preliminary sketches and final woodcut illustrations. Adapted from Robinson's *Companion Volume to the Kelmscott Chaucer* (1975).

28. Sasamoto, Hisayuki, trans. *A Complete Translation of* The Canterbury Tales. Tokyo: Eihosha, 2002. 677 pp. A complete Japanese translation of *CT* based on the text in *The Riverside Chaucer*.

29. Wein, Jake Milgram. "Rockwell Kent's Canterbury Pilgrims." In William K. Finley and Joseph Rosenblum, eds. *Chaucer Illustrated: Five Hundred Years of the* Canterbury Tales *in Pictures* (*SAC* 27 [2005], no. 105), pp. 311–25. Wein examines and appreciates the ways Kent's illustrations of the Canterbury pilgrims broke with formal and interpretive traditions. The essay focuses on the aesthetic impact of the lavish 1930 limited edition (published by Covici-Friede), later frequently reprinted.

See also nos. 33, 41, 60, 95, 105, 126, 137.

Manuscripts and Textual Studies

30. Bordalejo, Barbara. "The Phylogeny of the Order in the *Canterbury Tales*." *DAI* 64 (2003): 1669A. Bordalejo uses traditional and electronic methods to explore the various orders of the tales in manuscripts of *CT*, concluding that the order was affected by accident in some cases but by scribal intervention in others.

31. Caie, Graham. "'Glosyinge is a glorious thyng': Chaucer's Rhetoric, Manuscripts and Readers." *Hiroshima Studies in English Language and Literature* 46 (2002): 1–12. Caie comments on the presence of glosses in English literary manuscripts, arguing that glosses to *WBP*, *MerT*, and *MLT* can be read as attempts by Chaucer (or his scribes) to contain the subversive potential of texts that the glosses accompany.

32. Da Rold, Orietta. "The Quiring System in Cambridge University Library MS Dd.4.24 of Chaucer's *Canterbury Tales*." *Library*, ser. 7, 4 (2003): 107–28. The arrangement of quires in this early fifteenth-century manuscript indicates that the scribe was working from an unrubricated text, the order of *CT* was not yet stable, and the scribe may have helped create the Ellesmere ordering.

33. Dane, Joseph A. *The Myth of Print Culture: Essays on Evidence, Textuality, and Bibliographical Method.* Studies in Book and Print Culture. Buffalo and Toronto: University of Toronto Press, 2003. viii, 242 pp. Wide-ranging discussion of the opposition between evidence (physical materials) and discourse (abstractions covered by the word "text") in bibliographical and literary study, with sustained attention to editions of Chaucer and their methods and assumptions. Dane demonstrates the methodology of collation with several versions of the epitaph on Chaucer's tomb. He interrogates the usefulness and consistency of the concept "basis of collation" as used in the service of predilections that underlie Skeat's edition, Manly and Rickert's edition, the *Variorum* edition, and *Caxton's* Canterbury Tales on CD-ROM (*SAC* 27 [2005], no. 19).

34. Eagleton, Catherine. "A Previously Unnoticed Fragment of Chaucer's Treatise on the Astrolabe." *JEBS* 6 (2003): 161–73. Eagleton identifies a fragment of *Astr* washed from MS 358 in the Royal College of Physicians, London. Reproduces the explicit that names Chaucer as author; six photographs; and two tables.

35. Hardman, Phillipa. "Presenting the Text: Pictorial Tradition in Fifteenth-Century Manuscripts of the *Canterbury Tales*." In William K. Finley and Joseph Rosenblum, eds. *Chaucer Illustrated: Five Hundred Years of the* Canterbury Tales *in Pictures* (*SAC* 27 [2005], no. 105), pp. 37–72. Focuses on the ordinatio and implications of illustrations to *CT* (apart from those in the Ellesmere MS): the "generic 'author' image" found in MS Lansdowne 851, MS Bodley 686, and the "Devonshire" MS; the portrait of the Friar in MS Rawlinson poet. 223; the "possibly Ellesmere-derived" pilgrims in Cambridge University Library Gg.4.27 and the "Oxford" MS; and the sins and virtues in CUL Gg.4.27. Generally, these illustrations convey to the reader a sense of oral delivery.

36. Jimura, Akiyuki, Yoshiyuki Nakao, and Masatsugu Matsuo. *A Comprehensive Collation of the Hengwrt and Ellesmere Manuscripts of* The Canterbury Tales: *General Prologue.* Hiroshima: Hiroshima University Studies, Graduate School of Letters, 2002. iv, 100 pp. A computer-assisted comparison of the Hengwrt and Ellesmere manuscripts of *GP*. Clarifies differences and similarities in spellings, lexis, syntax, and metrics in the two manuscripts.

37. Mooney, Linne R., and Lister M. Matheson. "The Beryn Scribe and His Texts: Evidence for Multiple-Copy Production of Manuscripts in Fifteenth-Century England." *Library*, ser. 7, 4 (2003): 347–70. The

Northumberland manuscript of *CT* (Alnwick Castle 455) shows evidence that the scribe had access to a manuscript of *CT* that included the *Prologue* and *Tale of Beryn* and that he worked in a scriptorium that produced multiple copies of popular texts.

38. Olson, Mary C. *Fair and Varied Forms: Visual Textuality in Medieval Illuminated Manuscripts*. Studies in Medieval History and Culture. New York and London: Routledge, 2003. xxviii, 232 pp.; 51 b&w illus. Proposes and applies several "reading strategies" for understanding the relationships between word and image in several Old English manuscripts and the Ellesmere manuscript of *CT*. The discussion of Ellesmere is a version of the author's "Marginal Portraits and the Fiction of Orality: The Ellesmere Manuscript"; see no. 39.

39. ———. "Marginal Portraits and the Fiction of Orality: The Ellesmere Manuscript." In William K. Finley and Joseph Rosenblum, eds. *Chaucer Illustrated: Five Hundred Years of the* Canterbury Tales *in Pictures* (*SAC* 27 [2005], no. 105), pp. 1–35. Olson describes the visual features of the Ellesmere manuscript and assesses its illustrations as schematic, metonymic, and stereotypic—representations of character types rather than realizations of fictional individuals. The juxtaposition of *Th* and *Mel* produces a tension analogous to the oral/literate tension of the manuscript.

40. Robinson, Peter. "The History, Discoveries, and Aims of the *Canterbury Tales* Project." *ChauR* 38 (2003): 126–39. *The Canterbury Tales* Project takes up where Rickert and Manly left off, presenting extant texts in ways that are accessible to and useful for all readers. Since the manuscripts derive from those copied by a select group of scribes a few years after Chaucer's death, attention has focused on these as a means of determining Chaucer's methods of revision. The use of technology for showcasing this project must be carefully thought out to avoid confusion.

41. Russell, Raegan Leigh. "Non-Professional Readers and the Professional Bookmaker: The Ellesmere Manuscript and Kelmscott *Chaucer* as Guides to Chaucer." *DAI* 63 (2003): 2537A. Examines illustrations as cues to engage nonprofessional readers of the Ellesmere manuscript and the Kelmscott Chaucer. These techniques may suggest ways of engaging present-day nonprofessional readers of Chaucer as well.

42. Spencer, Matthew, Barbara Bordalejo, Li-San Wang, Adrian C. Barbrook, Linne R. Mooney, Peter Robinson, Tandy Warnow, and Christopher J. Howe. "Analyzing the Order of Items in Manuscripts of

The Canterbury Tales." *Computers and the Humanities* 37 (2003): 97–109. Construction of a stemma for *CT* based on gene-order analysis supports the idea that there was no established order when the first manuscripts were written. The resulting stemma shows relationships predicted by earlier scholars, reveals new relationships, and shares features with a word-variation stemma.

43. Spencer, Matthew, Barbara Bordalejo, Peter Robinson, and Christopher J. Howe. "How Reliable Is a Stemma? An Analysis of Chaucer's *Miller's Tale." L&LC* 18 (2003): 407–22. Drawing techniques from biology, the authors gauge the reliability of several aspects of textual stemmata: whether separate sections of a given text have separate histories, the quantity of text necessary for a reliable stemma, the levels of agreement between individual variants and the best stemma, and which features of a given stemma are most reliable. Examines e-texts of *MilT*.

See also nos. 14, 61, 74, 176, 177, 275, 295.

Sources, Analogues, and Literary Relations

44. Alexander, Michael. "Poets in Paradise: Chaucer, Pound, Eliot." *P N Review* 29.4 (2003): 6–7. Comments on Chaucer's, Pound's, and Eliot's indebtedness to Dante.

45. Archibald, Elizabeth. "Sex and Power in Thebes and Babylon: Oedipus and Semiramis in Classical and Medieval Texts." *Journal of Medieval Latin* 11 (2003): 27–49. Archibald surveys accounts of Oedipus and of Semiramis in classical and medieval texts, focusing on their concern or lack of concern with incest. Recurrent mention of Dante, Boccaccio, Christine de Pizan, and Chaucer—in particular *TC, MLT, PF,* and *LGW*.

46. Bloomfield, Josephine. " 'The Doctrine of These Olde Wyse': Commentary on the Commentary Tradition in Chaucer's Dream Visions." *Essays in Medieval Studies* 20 (2003): 125–33. In *LGWP, PF,* and *HF,* Chaucer absorbs several conventions and concerns from the commentaries that he used as sources, thereby suggesting that his audience was familiar not only with traditional texts but also with the commentaries on them.

47. Butterfield, Ardis. "Chaucer's French Inheritance." In Piero Boitani and Jill Mann, eds. *The Cambridge Companion to Chaucer,* 2nd ed.

(*SAC* 27 [2005], no. 92), pp. 20–36. Butterfield surveys the French literature available to Chaucer and argues that French language and literature pervade Chaucer's entire career. The French influence is a fundamental "habit of mind" that resides in the deep and surface structures of his works.

48. Cooper, Helen. "Chaucerian Poetics." In Robert G. Benson and Susan J. Ridyard, eds. *New Readings of Chaucer's Poetry* (*SAC* 27 [2005], no. 90), pp. 31–50. The Anglo-French duality of Chaucer's literary roots underlies the complexity of his representations of the self and others. In this light, *HF* should likely be dated later than it traditionally is.

49. Edwards, Robert R. "Medieval Literary Careers: The Theban Track." In Patrick Cheney and Frederick A. de Armas, eds. *European Literary Careers: The Author from Antiquity to the Renaissance*. Toronto: University of Toronto Press, 2002, pp. 104–28. The twin rubrics of succession and invention guide Statius's response to Virgil and, in turn, Boccaccio's response to Statius, Chaucer's responses to Boccaccio, and Lydgate's response to Chaucer. By exploiting the silences of their predecessors, the medieval authors of Thebes create dynamic rather than teleological careers for themselves. In *Anel* and *KnT*, Chaucer suppresses Boccaccio's eroticism and reclaims Statian political concerns; in *Siege of Thebes*, Lydgate advocates abandoning the heroic enterprise.

50. Lindeboom, B. W. "Chaucer's Testament of Love: The Impact of the *Confessio Amantis* on the *Canterbury Tales*." Ph.D. diss., Free University, Amsterdam. 469 pp. In response to Gower's words to Chaucer at the end of *Confessio Amantis* (8.2941–57), Chaucer first revised *LGWP* and then completely restructured the plan for *CT* (e.g., taking *Mel* away from the Man of Law and giving him a "Gower" tale instead).

51. Watt, Diane. *Amoral Gower: Language, Sex, and Politics*. Medieval Cultures, no. 38. Minneapolis and London: University of Minnesota Press, 2003. xviii, 219 pp. Reads John Gower's *Confessio Amantis* as a work that "encourages its audience to take risks in interpretation, to experiment with meaning, and to offer individualistic readings." The work pursues a "negative critique of ethical poetry" and enables important engagements with complexities of language, sex, and politics. Recurrent references to Chaucer indicate that the two poets shared a common audience, competed with each other, and explored "ethical ambiguities" in different ways.

52. Wong, Jennifer. "Public Chaucer: Translation and the Uses of Prose." *DAI* 64 (2003): 896A. To understand Chaucer as a political

court poet and a philosophical poet, we must read his prose as well as his poetry. Wong considers variations between *Bo* and its Boethian source, *Mel* as a model for how Chaucer treats his sources, *Astr* as a source of information, and the roles of the lost translation of Innocent's *De miseria condicionis humanae.*

See also nos. 55, 100, 115, 180, 182, 185, 189, 190, 194, 196, 199, 200, 209, 212–14, 218, 228, 229, 233, 240, 243, 250, 254, 264, 265, 270–72, 277, 281.

Chaucer's Influence and Later Allusion

53. Baldwin, Elizabeth. "Chaucer, Medieval Drama, and a Newly Discovered Seventeenth-Century Play: The Survival of Medieval Stereotypes?" In Wim Hüsken and Konrad Schoell, eds. *Farce and Farcical Elements.* Ludus: Medieval and Early Renaissance Theatre and Drama, no. 6. Amsterdam and New York: Rodopi, 2002, pp. 85–105. Argues that a seventeenth-century play, *The Wisest Have Their Fools About Them,* may reflect the influence of Chaucerian fabliau and some late medieval stage traditions. Baldwin's analysis focuses on stereotypical characters.

54. Coldiron, A. E. B. "Paratextual Chaucerianism: Naturalizing French Texts in Early Printed Verse." *ChauR* 38 (2003): 1–15. In the course of "Englishing" certain foreign texts, some early printers used Chaucerian "paratexts," evoking Chaucer's works, allusions, or style in efforts to bridge the gap between one literary period and the next and to express nostalgia for a late medieval mode. Such paratexts served as advertising "book jackets," authorizing the work and creating the impression of "literary continuity across time and across the boundaries and nation."

55. Cooper, Helen. "After Chaucer." *SAC* 25 (2003): 3–24. Presidential Address, The New Chaucer Society, Thirteenth International Congress, 18–21 July 2002, University of Colorado at Boulder. Comments on Chaucer as a translator (especially his adaptations of Dante in *HF* and *MkT*) and on the reception of his works over time as a legacy of translating and adapting him. Cooper details Chaucer's influence and adaptations of his works in the 1590s. Includes a text of the ballad *The Wanton Wife of Bath.*

56. Kinney, Clare R. "Marginal Presence, Lyric Resonance, Epic Absence: *Troilus and Criseyde* and/in *The Shepheardes Calender.*" *SSt* 18

(2003): 25–39. Using numerous small allusions to *TC*, Spenser situates himself within the English literary canon through a strategy of association with an "uncouthe, unkiste" Chaucer.

57. Lightsey, Scott. "Lydgate's Steede of Brass: A Chaucerian Analogue in *Troy Book* IV." *ELN* 38.3 (2001): 33–40. Suggests that the mechanical aspects of the Trojan Horse in Lydgate's poem were influenced by the steed of brass in *SqT*.

58. Postmus, Bouwe. "The Woe That Is in Marriage." In Tony Bex, Michael Burke, and Peter Stockwell, eds. *Contextualized Stylistics: In Honour of Peter Verdonk*. Amsterdam: Rodopi, 2000, pp. 103–11. Comments on *WBPT* as a source of Robert Lowell's "To Speak of Woe That Is in Marriage" and Seamus Heaney's "The Wife's Tale," offering "a reading" of the latter as a critique of rural suppression of married women.

59. Sepherd, Robert K. "Criseyde/Cresseid/Cressida: What's in a Name?" *Sederi: Journal of the Spanish Society for English Renaissance Studies* 4 (1993): 229–36. Considers Shakespeare's Cressida to be a "delicate literary graft" of the ambiguous aloofness of Chaucer's Criseyde and the "frankness personified" of Henryson's Cresseid.

60. Simpson, James. "Chaucer's Presence and Absence, 1400–1550." In Piero Boitani and Jill Mann, eds. *The Cambridge Companion to Chaucer*, 2nd ed. (*SAC* 27 [2005], no. 92), pp. 251–69. Changes in literary practice in the late fifteenth century helped modify reception of Chaucer's works. Remembered as a personal figure to be reckoned with by Hoccleve and Lydgate, Chaucer—like his works—was later objectified in the "philological" practices of early print culture, reaching a kind of humanist apotheosis in the 1532 edition of William Thynne.

See also nos. 10, 13, 99, 288.

Style and Versification

61. Brown, Emerson, Jr. "The Joy of Chaucer's Lydgate Lines." In Alan T. Gaylord, ed. *Essays on the Art of Chaucer's Verse* (*SAC* 25 [2003], no. 64), pp. 267–79. Brown discourages emendation ("dreary refinements") of Chaucer's meter, arguing that "broken-backed" or "Lydgatian" lines recorded in good manuscripts are likely to be Chaucer's own. Metrical variation within Chaucer's dominant patterns can have powerful poetic effects.

62. Cable, Thomas. "Clashing Stress in the Metres of Old, Middle,

and Renaissance English." In C. B. McCully and J. J. Anderson, eds. *English Historical Metrics* (*SAC* 21 [1999], no. 126), pp. 7–29. Cable traces a pattern of development in English stress "clashing," affected by stress subordination and stress spacing. Chaucer's "alternating metre has frequent stress subordination, but it is less clear that it makes systematic use of stress spacing," found more frequently in alliterative and Shakespearean meters.

63. Cannon, Christopher. "Chaucer's Style." In Piero Boitani and Jill Mann, eds. *The Cambridge Companion to Chaucer*, 2nd ed. (*SAC* 27 [2005], no. 92), pp. 233–50. Though traditional at root, Chaucer's diction, syntax, and rhetoric are made fresh by the poet's careful combination and articulation of traditional features. Doubleness (as in mixed styles, ambiguity, and irony) is characteristic of his style and a means to "generate dynamism in language."

64. Minkova, Donka, and Robert Stockwell. "Emendation and the Chaucerian Metrical Template." In Donka Minkova and Theresa Tinkle, eds. *Chaucer and the Challenges of Medievalism: Studies in Honor of H. A. Kelly* (*SAC* 27 [2005], no. 125), pp. 129–39. Of roughly 30,000 lines of Chaucer's iambic pentameter, only a tiny subset is variant. The majority of his lines follow a template of ten syllables, each foot beginning with a weak syllable. The essay refers specifically to *FranT*.

65. Osberg, Richard H. " 'I kan nat geeste': Chaucer's Artful Alliteration." In Alan T. Gaylord, ed. *Essays on the Art of Chaucer's Verse* (*SAC* 25 [2003], no. 64), pp. 195–227. Assesses Chaucer's uses of alliteration as recurrent adornment despite the poet's distance from the so-called alliterative tradition. Focuses on the role of alliteration in various kinds of rhetorical situations (high style, courtliness, prayer, and satire), drawing examples from *CT* and *LGW*.

66. Pearsall, Derek. "Towards a Poetics of Chaucerian Narrative." In Wendy Harding, ed. *Drama, Narrative, and Poetry in* The Canterbury Tales (*SAC* 27 [2005], no. 114), 99–112. Although much medieval English writing is verse rather than poetry, Chaucer's poetic skill is an important and distinctive part of his narrative. Pearsall examines a number of passages (*KnT*, *MilT*, *RvT*, *WBP*, and *PardT*) to show how poetic adornment (e.g., diction, metaphor, symbol, rhythm and meter, nonprose syntax, and allusion) contributes to the understanding of the movement and dramatic significance of the narrative.

67. Redford, Michael. "Middle English Stress Doubles: New Evidence from Chaucer's Meter." In Paula Fikkert and Haike Jacobs, eds.

Development in Prosodic Systems. Studies in Generative Grammar, no. 58. Berlin and New York: Mouton de Gruyter, 2003, pp. 159–95. Redford analyzes Chaucerian evidence pertaining to Middle English words that "appear to have initial stress" in certain contexts and "final stress in others." Examines several prominent theories and explanations, arguing that meter can be useful in determining normal language patterns, that scribal diacritics can be useful, and that in metrical contexts Middle English word stress was "initial, except at the end of phrases, where both syllables were prominent."

See also nos. 175, 226, 267.

Language and Word Studies

68. Blake, N. F. "Standardisation of English and the Wife of Bath's Prologue." In Masahiko Kanno, Gregory K. Jember, and Yoshiyuki Nakao, eds. *A Love of Words: English Philological Studies in Honour of Akira Wada* (*SAC* 27 [2005], no. 118), pp. 3–24. Blake examines the spelling variants of terminal *–n* and *–m* in a variety of words in *WBP* to show that *fro/from* was relatively erratic. Similar analysis indicates that final *–e* was obsolescent as a plural marker and in weak adjectives. Blake suggests several implications for meter.

69. Davidson, Mary Catherine. "Code-Switching and Authority in Late Medieval England." *Neophil* 87 (2003): 473–86. Examples from *The Chronicle of Peter Langtoft*, *Piers Plowman*, and *CT* (*WBP* and *PardP*) indicate how patterns of mixed-language speech reflect the social motivations of the speakers, especially their efforts to construct authority and restrict social membership.

70. Eaton, R. D. "Gender, Class, and Conscience in Chaucer." *ES* 84 (2003): 205–18. Eaton connects various uses of the word *conscience* in Chaucer's works with the social classes of the characters with whom the word is associated and with gender differences such as the structuring of physical space.

71. Green, Richard Firth. "Changing Chaucer." *SAC* 25 (2003): 27–52. Biennial Chaucer Lecture, The New Chaucer Society, Thirteenth International Congress, 18–21 July 2002, University of Colorado at Boulder. Explores the semantic and cultural background of the word *elvysshe* as applied to alchemy in *CYT* (8.751, 8.842). Like elves, alchemists were secretive, elusive, liminal figures, distrusted and associated

with transformation. Though modern editors gloss *elvysshe* metaphorically, its literal sense is applicable, indicating Chaucer's disillusionment with the scientific potential of alchemy.

72. Honegger, Thomas. "'And if ye wol nat so, my lady sweete, thane preye I thee, [. . .]': Forms of Address in Chaucer's *Knight's Tale*." *Pragmatics and Beyond*, n.s., 107 (2003): 61–84. Honegger argues that analyses of international forms of address would gain depth if critics considered "situational" factors and even "competing interactional" factors along with traditional considerations of *ye/thou* pronouns. Focuses on addresses to the gods in *KnT* to demonstrate such complicating factors.

73. Horobin, S. C. P. "Pennies, Pence, and Pans: Some Chaucerian Misreadings." *ES* 84 (2003): 426–30. In *RvT* 3944 and *FrT* 1614, *panne* can be read as the plural of *penny* instead of *pan* or *dish*. In early fourteenth-century Type II London dialect, *panne* is a common variant of *peni*. In this light, Chaucer's authorship of fragments B and C of *Rom* ought to be reconsidered.

74. Horobin, Simon. *The Language of the Chaucer Tradition*. Chaucer Studies, no. 32. Cambridge: D. S. Brewer, 2003. x, 179 pp. Horobin explores how linguistic issues affect questions of attribution, reception, and manuscript authority, focusing not only on lexicon but also on orthography, phonology, and grammar. The language of the Hengwrt manuscript of *CT* (perhaps produced as a text for oral presentation) is closer to Chaucer's original language than has previously been thought; the language of Ellesmere (perhaps produced for silent reading) is much more regularized. Linguistic evidence in *Equat* does not support Chaucerian authorship, while new evidence about the London dialect suggests reconsideration of Chaucer's authorship of the B and C fragments of *Rom*. Fifteenth-century scribes were careful to preserve details of Chaucer's language, even archaic or dialectal features, resisting fifteenth-century movement toward a standardized English language.

75. Jimura, Akiyuki. "Metathesis in Chaucer's English." In Masahiko Kanno, Gregory K. Jember, and Yoshiyuki Nakao, eds. *A Love of Words: English Philological Studies in Honour of Akira Wada* (*SAC* 27 [2005], no. 118), pp. 103–14. Some examples of metathesis in *CT* and *TC* (e.g., *ax/ask*, *thurgh/thrugh*, *open/opne*) may result from modern editorial selection; others (e.g., *lisped/lipsed* in *GP* 1.264–65) may indicate Chaucer's creative indication of individual speech patterns.

76. Kanno, Masahiko. "Chaucer's View of 'Mesure.'" In Masahiko

Kanno, Gregory K. Jember, and Yoshiyuki Nakao, eds. *A Love of Words: English Philological Studies in Honour of Akira Wada* (*SAC* 27 [2005], no. 118), pp. 115–31. Kanno examines instances of *mesure* and its synonyms in Chaucer's works, comparing those meanings with the virtue of moderation in Confucianism. The meanings range from "calculation" to "moderation." Generally, Chaucer's distinction between good and evil is based on a practical point of view.

77. Machan, Tim William. *English in the Middle Ages*. Oxford: Oxford University Press, 2003. x, 205 pp. Machan studies the "social meanings, functions, and status of the English language in the late-medieval period," i.e., its "sociolinguistic contextualization." He explores Henry III's letters of 1258; the relationships between language, dialects, and nationhood; *RvT* and *Sir Gawain and the Green Knight*; and the early afterlife of Middle English. Chaucer uses aberrant dialectical forms in *RvT* not to record a northern dialect, but to represent the dynamics of social ambition through linguistic form—a technique he also uses in *PF* and in the reference to the Revolt of 1381 in *NPT*.

78. Matsuo, Masatsugu. "A Multivariate Analysis of English Poems: Examples of Blake and Chaucer." In Michio Kawai, ed. *Language and Style in English Literature: Essays in Honour of Michio Masui*. Tokyo: Kenkyusha Shuppan, 1983, pp. 83–92 (in Japanese). Using Hayashi's Quantification Method Type III (a multivariate analysis), Matsuo describes distinctive features of several linguistic structures and clarifies clusters of similarities and dissimilarities. Cites examples from poetry by Chaucer and Blake.

79. Nakao, Yoshiyuki. "Ambiguity in the Language of Chaucer's Romances, with Special Regard to *Troilus and Criseyde* and *The Merchant's Tale*" (in Japanese). *Faculty of Education Bulletin* (Yamaguchi University) 44.1 (1994): 45–66. Discusses Chaucer's suggestive use of courtly language, with illustrations from *TC* and *MerT*.

80. ———. "Chaucer's *Moot/Moste*: A Case Study of Grammaticalization and Subjectification." *English and English-American Literature* (Yamaguchi University) 31 (1996): 69–122 (in Japanese). Discusses Chaucer's *moot/moste* from a cognitive-linguistic point of view.

81. ———. "Chaucer's Use of Ambiguity: The Case of *Sely*." *Essays on English and American Language and Literature in Honour of Hiroshi Matsumoto*. Tokyo: Eihosha, 1988, pp. 401–7 (in Japanese). Discusses ambiguity arising from the polysemy of *sely* in Middle English.

82. ———. "Movement Towards the Semantic Unity of the Modal

Auxiliaries in Chaucer's *Troilus and Criseyde*: The Fusion of Their Root and Epistemic Senses." In Masahiko Kanno et al., eds. *Medieval Heritage: Essays in Honour of Tadahiro Ikegami* (*SAC* 21 [1999], no. 118), pp. 441–54 (in Japanese). Discusses the fusion of the root and epistemic senses of modal auxiliaries such as *mot/moste, may/myghte, shal/sholde,* and *wol/wolde* in *TC*.

83. ———. "A Semantic Note on the Middle English Phrase *As He/She That.*" *NOWELE* 25 (1995): 25–48. Discusses the semantic possibility of the Middle English phrase "as he/she that" in comparison with its Old French original "com cil/cele qui."

84. ———. "The Semantics of Chaucer's *Moot/Moste*: A Focus on Its External Causals." In Yukio Oba et al., eds. *Currents in Linguistic Research: A Festschrift for Professor Kazuyuki Yamamoto on the Occasion of His Retirement from Yamaguchi University.* Tokyo: Kaitakusha, 1999, pp. 231–46. Discusses external causals, one of the pragmatic features in the use of Chaucer's *moot/moste.* Clarifies the fusion of fate, divine intervention, and the speaker's subjective factors.

85. ———. "The Semantics of *Shal/Sholde* in *Troilus and Criseyde*: An Aspect of the Semantic Unity of Chaucer's Modal Auxiliaries." In *English and English Teaching, Vol. 2: A Festschrift in Honour of Kiichiro Nakatani.* Hiroshima: Department of English Faculty of School Education, Hiroshima University, 1997, pp. 23–42. Discusses the semantic unity of *shal/sholde* in *TC*, focusing on degrees of subjectivity on the part of the speaker.

86. ———. "Social-Linguistic Tension as Evidenced by *Moot/Moste* in Chaucer's *Troilus and Criseyde.*" In Masahiko Kanno, Masahiko Agari, and Gregory K. Jember, eds. *Essays on English Literature and Language in Honour of Shun'ichi Noguchi.* Tokyo: Eihosha, 1997, pp. 17–34. Discusses Chaucer's uses of *moot/moste,* focusing on the fusion of social objective factors and the speaker's subjective implications.

87. ———. "The Syntax of Chaucer's *of*-Phrase: Its Variability." *English and English-American Literature* (Yamaguchi University) 20 (1985): 35–60. Explores the syntactic variability of Chaucer's *of*-phrase, focusing on its capability of being transposed and separated from its modifying head.

See also nos. 67, 118, 150, 186, 192, 210, 227, 248, 266, 273, 290–94.

Background and General Criticism

88. Ackroyd, Peter. *Albion: The Origins of the English Imagination*. London: Chatto & Windus, 2002. xxii, 516 pp. Ackroyd discusses Chaucer within the larger context of describing and defining the distinctive qualities of English imagination, focusing on Chaucer's themes of remembrance, science, and truth as part of the process of becoming English. Considers *HF, LGW, PF, TC, BD, CT*, and *RvT*. Includes a bibliography and index.

89. Baughn, Gary. "Avoid the Edifice Complex and Enjoy Teaching Chaucer." *EJ* 93 (Sept. 2002): 60–65. Pedagogical approach to *CT* for an eleventh-grade honors survey of British literature, combining popular twentieth-century music with activities related to *CT*: analysis of *GP* descriptions, storytelling, and writing assignments.

90. Benson, Robert G., and Susan J. Ridyard, eds. *New Readings of Chaucer's Poetry*. Chaucer Studies, no. 31. Rochester, N.Y., and Cambridge: D. S. Brewer, 2003. vii, 200 pp. Ten essays by various authors and a descriptive introduction by Derek Brewer. The papers were originally delivered at the Sewanee Medieval Colloquium at the University of the South in April 2000; the colloquium was devoted to Chaucer's work on the 600th anniversary of his death. The volume includes an index. See nos. 48, 99, 131, 158, 199, 215, 234, 241, 274, and 283.

91. Bezella-Bond, Karen Jean. "Florescence and Defloration: Maytime in Chaucer and Malory." *DAI* 63 (2003): 3952A. Focusing on literary depictions of maying activities in medieval records and *Le Roman de la Rose*, Bezella-Bond assesses their depiction in Malory and in Chaucer's *BD, PF, LGWP, KnT, MerT*, and *WBPT*.

92. Boitani, Piero, and Jill Mann, eds. *The Cambridge Companion to Chaucer*. 2nd ed. Cambridge: Cambridge University Press, 2003. xiv, 317 pp. Revised version of the 1986 original, now with seventeen essays, five of which are new. Revised pieces are "The Social and Literary Scene in England" (Paul Strohm); "Chaucer's Italian Inheritance" (David Wallace); "Old Books Brought to New Life in Dreams: The *Book of the Duchess*, the *House of Fame*, the *Parliament of Birds*" (Piero Boitani); "Telling the Story in *Troilus and Criseyde*" (Mark Lambert); "Chance and Destiny in *Troilus and Criseyde* and the *Knight's Tale*" (Jill Mann); "The *Canterbury Tales*: Personal Drama or Experiments in Poetic Variety?" (C. David Benson); essays on romance, comedy, pathos, and exemplum and fable in *CT* by J. A. Burrow, Derek Pearsall, Robert Worth Frank Jr.,

and A. C. Spearing, respectively; and a bibliography of further reading by Joerg O. Fichte. For the five new essays, see nos. 47, 60, 63, 102, and 270.

93. Børch, Marianne Novrup. *Chaucer's Poetics: Seeing and Asking.* 2 vols. Odense: Odense University, 1993. 715 pp. Børch derives a poetics of reading Chaucer from Chaucer's own poetry, arguing that he frustrates "intertextual" approaches by being consistently evasive. Attention to style and content clarifies how the poetry shapes readers' responses. *BD* and *HF* challenge traditional notions of literary authority; *TC* depicts the narrator-as-reader suspended between emotional response and hoped-for objectivity. In *CT*—particularly in *FranT, KnT, ManT, SNT,* and *ClT*—Chaucer "dramatizes his conviction that authority is contingent upon the individual." A printing of the author's dissertation; includes Danish summary.

94. Borroff, Marie. *Traditions and Renewals: Chaucer, The* Gawain-*Poet, and Beyond.* New Haven, Conn., and London: Yale University Press, 2003. xii, 275 pp. Ten essays by the author, three of them published here for the first time. Topics include *CT, Pearl, Sir Gawain and the Green Knight,* and Shakespeare's *Hamlet.* For two new essays that pertain to Chaucer, see nos. 140 and 141.

95. Bowden, Betsy. "Tales Told and Tellers of Tales: Illustrations of the *Canterbury Tales* in the Course of the Eighteenth Century." In William K. Finley and Joseph Rosenblum, eds. *Chaucer Illustrated: Five Hundred Years of the* Canterbury Tales *in Pictures* (*SAC* 27 [2005], no. 105), pp. 121–90. Reproduces and assesses various eighteenth-century depictions of *CT* or the Canterbury pilgrims, including Thomas Stothard's illustrations for Bell's British Poets (1782–83), the set of pilgrim portraits (here associated with John Vanderbank) in John Urry's 1721 edition, and works drawn or executed by John H. Mortimer, James Jeffreys, Edward Francesco Burney, George Vertue, Lady Diana Beauclerk, Angelica Kauffman, John Francis Rigaud, Richard Westfall, and Henry Fuseli.

96. Carruthers, Leo, and Adrian Papahagi, eds. *Paroles et silences dans la littérature anglaise au Moyen Âge.* AMAES, no. 10. Paris: Association des Médiévistes Anglicistes de l'Enseignement Supérieur, 2003. Includes two essays that pertain to Chaucer; see nos. 149 and 269.

97. Clark, Glenn Jeffrey. "Drama and the Culture of Commercial Hospitality in Early Modern England." *DAI* 63 (2003): 2550A. Clark

mentions Chaucer in the context of conceptions of "drinking-house culture."

98. Clarke, Catherine A. M. "Overhearing Complaint and the Dialectic of Consolation in Chaucer's Verse." *RMSt* 29 (2003): 19–30. Clarke discusses the motif of eavesdropping in *TC, KnT*, and *BD*. Overhearing (both deliberate and accidental) places speaker and listener in a dialectic relationship.

99. Cooper, Helen. "Chaucerian Representation." In Robert G. Benson and Susan J. Ridyard, eds. *New Readings of Chaucer's Poetry* (*SAC* 27 [2005], no. 90), pp. 7–30. Surveys the evolution of critical appropriations and pictorial representations of Chaucer from the fifteenth to the twenty-first centuries, suggesting that oversimplifications of Chaucer recur because he is so deeply concerned with the generative processes of literature. Cooper confronts the question, "What is it that Chaucer imitates or represents?" Recurrent attention to *PF, Th,* and imitations of Chaucer.

100. Dauby, Hélène. "Du vivant à l'image et inversement." In Adrian Papahagi, ed. *Métamorphoses* (*SAC* 27 [2005], no. 130), pp. 183–95. Dauby examines the transformations from living characters to artifacts and vice versa, the interplay between life and art. A comparative study of *Sir Degrevant*, Lancelot, the Tristan legend, and poems by Chaucer leads to a typology of the metamorphoses into art: ornamental though relevant scenery, animated works of art, the retrieval of past experience, the intrusion of the future.

101. Di Rocco, Emilia. *Letteratura e Legge nel Trecento Inglese*. Rome: Bulzoni Editore, 2003. 318 pp. Examines law and literature in the works of Chaucer, Gower, and Langland, focusing on three major topics: marriage, crime, and covenants. An introductory chapter explores the relations between law and literature. Throughout, there is comparison of canon law and civil law, as well as separation from Latin tradition.

102. Dinshaw, Carolyn. "New Approaches to Chaucer." In Piero Boitani and Jill Mann, eds. *The Cambridge Companion to Chaucer*, 2nd ed. (*SAC* 27 [2005], no. 92), pp. 270–89. Dinshaw contemplates recent critical trends in medieval studies in light of the events of September 11, 2001, tracing the developments of feminist, queer, and postcolonial approaches to Chaucer's works by focusing on *MLT*.

103. Driver, Martha W. "Reading Images of Reading." *The Ricardian* 13 (2003): 186–202; 14 illus. In the context of a broader discussion

of late medieval depictions of people reading, Driver mentions illustrations that depict Chaucer reading.

104. Finley, William K. "Chaucer at Home: The Canterbury Pilgrims at Georgian Court." Appendix 3 in William K. Finley and Joseph Rosenblum, eds. *Chaucer Illustrated: Five Hundred Years of the* Canterbury Tales *in Pictures* (*SAC* 27 [2005], no. 105), pp. 423–37. Introduces and reprints Robert van Vorst Sewell's *The Canterbury Pilgrimage: A Decorative Frieze* (New York: American Art Galleries, n.d.), which Sewell wrote to accompany the mural frieze he painted in George Gould's Georgian Court mansion, now part of Georgian Court College, Lakeside, N.J. The introduction comments on other interior decorations in the United States that use *CT* as subject matter.

105. ———, and Joseph Rosenblum, eds. *Chaucer Illustrated: Five Hundred Years of the* Canterbury Tales *in Pictures*. New Castle, Del.: Oak Knoll; London: British Library, 2003. xxxiii, 445 pp.; 42 color plates and 149 b&w illus. Includes an introduction by the editors and ten essays and three appendices by various authors, who describe and discuss visual depictions of the Canterbury pilgrims and their tales in books and paintings, from the Ellesmere manuscript into the twentieth century. Appendix 1 reprints the Chaucer portion of *A Descriptive Catalogue of Pictures, Poetical and Historical Inventions, Painted by William Blake . . .* (1809). The volume includes an index. See nos. 21, 23, 27, 29, 35, 39, 95, 104, 106, 124, 132, and 137.

106. Fisher, Judith L., and Mark Allen. "Victorian Illustrations to Chaucer's *Canterbury Tales*." In William K. Finley and Joseph Rosenblum, eds. *Chaucer Illustrated: Five Hundred Years of the* Canterbury Tales *in Pictures* (*SAC* 27 [2005], no. 105), pp. 233–73. The authors explore two kinds of Victorian medievalism (antiquarian detail and moral didacticism) in visual tradition, surveying Victorian depictions of *CT* in painting and book illustration and focusing on various illustrations of *ClT*. Includes a descriptive catalog of illustrations to *CT*, 1809–96.

107. Fleming, John V. "Muses of the Monastery." *Speculum* 78 (2003): 1071–1106. Discusses hostility toward fiction within ascetic cultures of the Middle Ages; brief references to *ParsT*, *NPT*, and *MilT*.

108. Fletcher, Alan J. "Chaucer the Heretic." *SAC* 25 (2003): 53–121. Chaucer deploys his "appropriations of the culture of heresy with versatility" in *ABC*, *LGWP*, and *CT* (Pardoner, Friar, Summoner, Monk, and Parson). Fletcher measures these appropriations against the

shifting political fortunes of Lollardy in Chaucer's lifetime to reflect upon the difficulties of reading biography through literature.

109. Fumo, Jamie Claire. "The Road to Delphi: Chaucerian Poetics and the Legacy of Apollo." *DAI* 64 (2003): 891A. A mythographic history of the figure of Apollo from Augustan Rome to Chaucer. Fumo focuses on the importance of Apollo to Chaucer's poetic self-conception and on Chaucer's representations of the deity in *TC*, in *SqT* and *FranT*, and in *ManT*.

110. Godsall-Myers, Jean E., ed. *Speaking in the Medieval World*. Boston: Brill, 2003. xii, 194 pp. Eight essays by various authors suggest that looking carefully at the ways characters speak in medieval texts gives information about the social networks extant in medieval society and reveals artistic skills of writers who considered speech significant. For three essays that pertain to Chaucer, see nos. 180, 210, and 224.

111. Goldie, Matthew Boyd. *Middle English Literature: A Historical Sourcebook*. Oxford: Blackwell, 2003. xxxviii, 301 pp.; 13 b&w illus. Collects forty-five documents and images as backgrounds to fourteenth- and fifteenth-century English literature; arranged under seven headings and keyed (by chart) to a variety of canonical Middle English literary texts. All of the selected texts are Middle English or Middle English translations from Latin or French; most are excerpted. Topics include social institutions, conflict, sexuality, labor, spectacle, etc. An introduction accompanies each selection, and the volume includes a Middle English glossary, table of dates, bibliography, and index. Designed for classroom use.

112. Guha, Arnab. "Weaving the Word: A Textual Consideration of User-Disorientation in Hypertextual Space." *DAI* 63 (2003): 4133A. Considers the work of Chaucer, among others, as an example of nonhypertextual writing that nonetheless creates the user disorientation often associated with negotiations of hypertext.

113. Haas, Renate. "Caroline Spurgeon—English Studies, the United States, and Internationalism." *SAP* 38 (2002): 215–28. Considers Spurgeon's work on the history of Chaucer criticism in the context of Spurgeon's career as a teacher and her role as a leader in seeking full standing for women in the academy.

114. Harding, Wendy, ed. *Drama, Narrative, and Poetry in the* Canterbury Tales. Collection Interlangues: Littératures. Toulouse: Presses Universitaires du Mirail, 2003. 246 pp. Fifteen essays by various authors examine ways of reading tales in *CT* in terms of relationships to a partic-

ular literary mode, whether theater, narrative, or poetry. The collection includes an introduction by the editor. See nos. 7, 66, 139, 144a, 144b, 148, 153, 160, 179, 198, 203, 221, 226, 252, and 253.

115. Heffernan, Carol F. *The Orient in Chaucer and Medieval Romance*. Studies in Medieval Romance. Woodbridge, Suffolk; and Rochester, N.Y.: Boydell and Brewer, 2003. x, 160 pp. A series of studies focusing on depictions of the Orient and people from the Orient in medieval romances: *MLT*, Dido and Cleopatra from *LGW*, *SqT*, *Floris and Blaun-cheflur*, and *Le Bone Florence*. The introduction concentrates on how contact with the East during the Crusades encouraged the development of romance in the West. Heffernan compares *MLT* with analogous tales in Gower and Boccaccio to show how Chaucer emphasizes the role of merchants in contact with the East. The orientalism of Dido and Cleopatra is expressed in terms of pleasure and sexual excess. In *SqT*, Chaucer experiments with combining oriental plot and Western "interlace" technique.

116. Herold, Christine. *Chaucer's Tragic Muse: The Paganization of Christian Tragedy*. Studies in Mediaeval Literature, no. 23. Lewiston, N.Y.: Mellen, 2003. iv, 319 pp. The medieval conceptualization of tragedy has its roots in classical tradition, especially Seneca as mediated by Boethius. Herold surveys classical, patristic, and medieval ideas of tragedy and the tragic, exploring how Chaucer, among others, "displays deep understanding of the Senecan tragedic conventions and the Boethian-Platonic innovations." Treats tragedy and the tragic in *BD*, the short poems, *HF*, *PF*, *LGW*, *TC*, and *CT*—especially *SNPT*, *ClT*, *NPT*, *MkT*, *KnT*, and *MilT*.

117. Jenkins, Charles M. *The Paradox of the Mystical Text in Medieval English Literature*. Studies in Mediaeval Literature, no. 25. Lewiston, N.Y.: Mellen, 2003. [viii], 268 pp. Jenkins surveys scriptural, Latin patristic, Anglo-Saxon, and late medieval English representations and appropriations of mysticism, arguing that "medieval indeterminacy" is in many ways epistemologically and theologically grounded in mysticism. Includes discussion of *Pearl* in comparison with *BD* as, respectively, failed mysticism and mockery of mysticism. Also reads *TC* as a "satirical parody" of motifs drawn from mysticism that leads its audience to "true spiritual desire."

118. Kanno, Masahiko, Gregory K. Jember, and Yoshiyuki Nakao, eds. *A Love of Words: English Philological Studies in Honour of Akira Wada*. Tokyo: Eihosha, 1998. xii, 303 pp. Sixteen essays on topics ranging

417

from Old English semantics to Joyce's *Portrait of the Artist as a Young Man*, commemorating the 65th birthday of Akira Wada. Four essays pertain to Chaucer; see nos. 68, 75, 76, and 290.

119. Karras, Ruth Mazo. "Sex, Money, and Prostitution in Medieval English Culture." In Jacqueline Murray and Konrad Eisenbichler, eds. *Desire and Discipline: Sex and Sexuality in the Premodern West*. Toronto: University of Toronto Press, 1996, pp. 201–16. Karras surveys depictions of female commercialized sex in the English late Middle Ages. It is difficult, she suggests, to separate kinds and degrees of prostitution, because prostitution was regarded as an "extreme case" of the general sinfulness of female sexuality. Chaucerian examples include the Wife of Bath and the wives in *ShT*, *CkT*, and *ManT*.

120. Kuczynski, Michael. "Don't Blame Me: The Metaethics of a Chaucerian Apology." *ChauR* 37 (2003): 315–28. Scriptural injunctions underlie Chaucer's apology in *MilP* 1.3172–81 and his encouraging the audience to be cautious when judging his poetic enterprise.

121. Leech, Mary Elizabeth. "The Rhetoric of the Body: A Study of Body Imagery and Rhetorical Structure in Medieval Literature." *DAI* 63 (2003): 2536A. Leech attempts to formulate a context for understanding medieval body images, using Rolle, Hilton, Julian of Norwich, and Kempe along with Chaucer. Chapter 5 considers *KnT*, *GP*, *WBT*, and *ParsT*.

122. Lerer, Seth. "Medieval English Literature and the Idea of the Anthology." *PMLA* 118 (2003): 1251–65. Discusses the idea of the anthology as a fundamental characteristic of medieval literature, using *CT* as an example because individual tales were often copied into other anthologies.

123. McCracken, Peggy. *The Curse of Eve, the Wound of the Hero: Blood, Gender, and Medieval Literature*. Philadelphia: University of Pennsylvania Press, 2003. xii, 178 pp. Mentions *MLT*, *PrT*, and *ClT* in the larger context of gender and blood in medieval culture. McCracken argues that gendered cultural values are "mapped onto blood and that cultural values are inscribed into a natural order." Compares Chaucer's *MLT* with *Le roman du comte d'Anjou*, which makes an implicit connection between the "polluting blood of parturition and the supposedly nonnoble blood of the mother," suggesting that Chaucer's reference to monstrous birth refers to the "contested lineage and rituals that define the impurity of childbirth." Bibliography and index.

124. McGarrity, Maria, ed. and introd. "William Paulet Carey, *Criti*-

cal Description of the Procession of Chaucer's Pilgrims to Canterbury, Painted by Thomas Stothard, Esq., R.A. 2nd ed. (London: W. Glindon, 1818)." Appendix 2 in William K. Finley and Joseph Rosenblum, eds. *Chaucer Illustrated: Five Hundred Years of the* Canterbury Tales *in Pictures* (*SAC* 27 [2005], no. 105), pp. 379–422. Edition (with notes) and brief introduction to Carey's "assessment and portrait of Stothard's visual interpretation" of *CT*.

125. Minkova, Donka, and Theresa Tinkle, eds. *Chaucer and the Challenges of Medievalism: Studies in Honor of H. A. Kelly.* Studies in English Medieval Language and Literature, no. 5. Frankfurt and New York: Peter Lang, 2003. xxii, 403 pp. Twenty-three essays by various authors examine intellectual currents in medievalism, arranged in six categories: Text, Image, and Script; Text and Meter; Reception; Chaucer; Hagiography; and Lay Piety and Christian Diversity. For the nine essays that pertain to Chaucer, see nos. 13, 64, 229, 239, 243, 246, 275, 279, and 284.

126. Morse, Charlotte C. "Popularizing Chaucer in the Nineteenth Century." *ChauR* 38 (2003): 99–125. Charles Cowden Clarke, Charles Knight, and John Saunders were the most effective popularizers of Chaucer for the common reader in nineteenth-century England. These individuals translated Chaucer into modern English and bowdlerized his language in order not to offend their audiences. The works of these writers probably kept Chaucer alive in school and university curricula, leading the way for twentieth-century editors, readers, and translators.

127. Mulligan, Anne. "Rhetorical Portraiture: Finding the Subject Image and Memory in the Middle Ages." *DAI* 64 (2003): 1645A. A range of medieval literary portraits derive techniques from rhetorical memory devices and, in turn, shape notions of subjectivity. Mulligan considers Langland's Lady Meed, the Green Knight, Henryson's Cresseid, and various Chaucerian characters, from *BD* through *CT*, including some of the Ellesmere portraits.

128. Neufeld, Christine Marie. "Xanthippe's Sisters: Orality and Femininity in the Later Middle Ages." *DAI* 64 (2003): 1248A. Examines how women are presented in medieval satire as gossips, scolds, and cursing witches, all manifestations of women with orality. Assesses works by Chaucer, Dunbar, and Kempe, and material from cycle plays.

129. Okuda, Hiroko. *A Journey to Chaucer's Medieval Italy.* Tokyo: Ochanomizu Shobo, 2003. 121 pp. An intercultural comparative study

of medieval Italy and Italians and Chaucer's connection with the country and its people.

130. Papahagi, Adrian, ed. *Métamorphoses*. Actes du XIe Colloque de l'AMAES, Cluj [Roumanie]. AMAES, no. 26. Paris: Association des Médiévistes Anglicistes de l'Enseignement Supérieur, 2003. Includes four essays that pertain to Chaucer; see nos. 6, 100, 264, and 271.

131. Provost, William. "Chaucer's Endings." In Robert G. Benson and Susan J. Ridyard, eds. *New Readings of Chaucer's Poetry* (*SAC* 27 [2005], no. 90), pp. 91–106. Since the Black Death framed Chaucer's life, he was set on thinking about last things. The end of *PF* shows a flagging of spirits; the end of *TC* is complex and self-reflexive. Although several early poems indicate that Chaucer could not think of an ending or that he lost interest, *ABC* is notable as a return to the beginnings.

132. Read, Dennis M. "Thomas Stothard's *The Pilgrimage to Canterbury* (1806): A Study in Promotion and Popular Taste." In William K. Finley and Joseph Rosenblum, eds. *Chaucer Illustrated: Five Hundred Years of the* Canterbury Tales *in Pictures* (*SAC* 27 [2005], no. 105), pp. 211–31. Read discusses the conditions of production and marketing of Stothard's *Pilgrimage to Canterbury*, arguing that the success of the painting and its engravings was due in good part to promotion by Robert Hartley Cromek, an antagonist of William Blake.

133. Sauer, Michelle M., ed. *Proceedings of the 11th Annual Northern Plains Conference on Early British Literature*. Minot, N.D.: Minot State University, 2003. xxvi, 247 pp. Twenty essays by various authors on topics in British literature before 1800: five essays on Shakespeare; three on medieval uses of Christ's death (in *Beowulf, Song of Roland*, and *El Cid*). Other topics include Julian of Norwich and Margery Kempe, Richard Hooker, Thomas Heywood, Aphra Behn, protestant preaching in the Renaissance, More's *Utopia*, Montaigne and Bacon, Quaker women writers from 1650 to1800, eighteenth-century smuggling in Rio de Janeiro, Jonathan Swift's puns, eighteenth-century popular music, and Mary Wollstonecraft. For two essays that pertain to Chaucer, see nos. 195 and 297.

134. Somerset, Fiona, Jill C. Havens, and Derrick G. Pitard, eds. *Lollards and Their Influence in Late Medieval England*. Woodbridge, Suffolk; and Rochester, N.Y.: Boydell Press, 2003. x, 344 pp. Thirteen essays by various authors on topics such as the conceptualization of Lollardy as a movement, its underlying thought, its book culture, and its relationships with other movements. Includes an extensive bibliography

of Lollard study, with a section on "Langland and Chaucer," and one article that pertains directly to Chaucer; see no. 211.

135. Spivack, Charlotte, and Christine Herold, eds. *Archetypal Readings of Medieval Literature*. Studies in Mediaeval Literature, no. 22. Lewiston, N.Y.: Mellen, 2002. iv, 202 pp.; 6 illus. Nine readings by various authors of archetypal patterns in medieval works. Topics include Marie de France, Christine de Pizan, Julian of Norwich, Joan of Arc, Gottfried von Strassburg, Chrétien de Troyes, the Spanish *Shriek of the Sage Merlin*, *Sir Gawain and the Green Knight*, and Chaucer. For two essays that pertain to Chaucer, see nos. 167 and 201.

136. Stévanovitch, Colette, and René Tixier, eds. *Surface et profondeur: Mélanges offerts à Guy Bourquin à l'occasion de son 75ᵉ anniversaire*. Grendel, no. 7. Nancy: Association des Médiévistes Anglicistes de l'Enseignement Supérieur, 2003. Includes two essays that pertain to Chaucer; see nos. 233 and 244.

137. Stevenson, Warren. "From Canterbury to Jerusalem: Interpreting Blake's *Canterbury Pilgrims*." In William K. Finley and Joseph Rosenblum, eds. *Chaucer Illustrated: Five Hundred Years of the* Canterbury Tales *in Pictures* (*SAC* 27 [2005], no. 105), pp. 191–209. Stevenson interprets William Blake's depiction of the Canterbury pilgrims (rendered in several manifestations) in light of contemporaneous works and Blake's *Descriptive Catalogue* (1809). Visual symbols, juxtapositions, and contrasts indicate that Blake "invites the viewer to consider the classes of men in the light of eternity and to participate in the human and divine vision of forgiveness."

The Canterbury Tales—General

138. Allman, W. W., and D. Thomas Hanks Jr. "Rough Love: Notes Toward an Erotics of *The Canterbury Tales*." *ChauR* 38 (2003): 36–65. A "bodily economy of piercing men and pierced women" can be found throughout *CT*. Lovemaking is associated with cutting, stabbing, bleeding, and dying. The only accounts of lovemaking not connected to stabbing or bloodletting occur in the musical interlude of *MilT* and at the end of *WBT*.

139. Benson, C. David. "Trust the Tale, Not the Teller." In Wendy Harding, ed. *Drama, Narrative, and Poetry in* The Canterbury Tales (*SAC* 27 [2005], no. 114), pp. 22–33. Benson argues against interpreting *CT* in terms of dramatic theory: the pilgrims are not fully developed human

characters, nor are their tales expressions of their individual psychologies. The most developed pilgrims—the Pardoner and the Wife of
Bath—are far from naturalistic, and the art that underlies them is more
interesting than their lives are. Although the Nun's Priest is indistinct
as a character, his *Tale* is one of the richest and most challenging works.

140. Borroff, Marie. "Dimensions of Judgment in the *Canterbury
Tales*: Friar, Summoner, Pardoner, Wife of Bath." In *Traditions and Renewals: Chaucer, The* Gawain-*Poet, and Beyond* (*SAC* 27 [2005], no. 94),
pp. 3–49. Wycliffite elements of *SumT* and of the *GP* description of the
Friar are submerged, but Chaucer sympathized with Wycliffite thought
and believed that the Summoner's friar was damned. Borroff surveys
anti-fraternal tradition, comments on Fals-Semblant of *Le Roman de la
Rose* as a source of Chaucer's Friar Hubert and Friar John (and of Chaucer's Pardoner), and notes Wycliffite elements both in *WBP* (helping to
unify Part 3 of *CT*) and in the *GP* description of the Parson.

141. ———. "Silent Retribution in Chaucer: The *Merchant's Tale*,
the *Reeve's Tale*, and the *Pardoner's Tale*." In *Traditions and Renewals:
Chaucer, The* Gawain-*Poet, and Beyond* (*SAC* 27 [2005], no. 94), pp. 50–
70. Clearly implied but not stated, May's pregnancy in *MerT* results
from having sex with Damian and helps to punish January's foolishness.
In similarly covert ways, the parson of *RvT* is punished by the pregnancy
of Malyne, and all pardoners are criticized through the Host's response
at the end of *PardT*. Such covert meanings indicate Chaucer's sympathies with Wycliffite thought.

142. Bourgne, Florence. *The Canterbury Tales. Geoffrey Chaucer*. Paris:
Armand Colin; [Poitiers]: CNED, 2003. vi, 168 pp. After a short discussion of the genesis of *CT*, Bourgne successively explores its structure
(collection of tales, importance of commerce and exchanges, prologues,
labyrinth); shifts between oral and written literatures, or audiences and
readerships; spaces of the narrative (pilgrimage, movement, places, cosmology, literary and social orders); rhetoric (traditional medieval rhetoric and Chaucer's own), with a brief account of major figures; sentence/
solace, knowledge and carnival; various forms of time; language and
versification.

143. Burger, Glenn. *Chaucer's Queer Nation*. Medieval Cultures, no.
34. Minneapolis and London: University of Minnesota Press, 2003. xxvi,
264 pp. *CT* can destabilize essentialist categories of sexuality, subjectivity, and nationality. From a queer and postcolonial perspective, *CT* enables or compels neither a symbolically simple London originary nor an

allegorically closed ending, but rather an ongoing "middle" that reflects a late medieval social context useful in deconstructing reductionist historicisms and traditional criticism. Burger focuses on shame, pleasure, masochism, and subjectivity in *MilPT*; conjugality and the new *gentil* elite in *WBT*, *MerT*, and *FranT*; effacement of the feminine and touching the queer in *PhyT* and *PardT*; dismantling hierarchies in Fragment 7 (especially *Mel*); and the process of denying ending in Fragments 8, 9, and 10.

144a. Carruthers, Leo. "Narrative Voice, Narrative Framework: The Host as 'Author' of *The Canterbury Tales*." In Wendy Harding, ed. *Drama, Narrative and Poetry in* The Canterbury Tales (*SAC* 27 [2005], no. 114), pp. 51–67. Carruthers examines the framing structure and links of *CT*, with particular attention to the Host's role. Harry Bailey is both a unifying instrument in the poet's hands and an extension of Chaucer's identity, an alter ego who will ultimately be silenced in *Ret*.

144b. Dauby, Hélène. "The Generation Gap in *The Canterbury Tales*." In Wendy Harding, ed. *Drama, Narrative, and Poetry in* The Canterbury Tales (*SAC* 27 [2005], no. 114), pp. 237–41. Most of the pilgrims seem to be about the same age, but the problem of age is not ignored: e.g., old and young husbands (*WBPT*); the relationship between father and son (Knight and Squire, Franklin, Chauntecleer) or daughter (*RvT*); and the relationship between parents and children (*CIT*, *MLT*). Comparisons with Molière set off Chaucer's attitude.

145. Di Rocco, Emilia. *Chaucer: Guida ai* Canterbury Tales. Rome: Carocci Editore, 2003. 126 pp. An introduction to *CT*, including discussion of Chaucer's life, the structure of *CT*, plots and themes of the tales, analyses of the pilgrims and major characters in their tales, and Chaucer's language and meter. Includes bibliographies for each chapter and a list of further readings.

146. Engel, Elliot. *A Dab of Dickens and a Touch of Twain: Literary Lives from Shakespeare's Old England to Frost's New England*. New York: Pocket, 2002. xvii, 349 pp. Summary information about the lives and works of English authors; includes Chaucer's biography and introductory presentation of *CT*.

147. Flake, Timothy Harve. "Experience and Repentance in Three 'Canterbury Tales.'" *DAI* 64 (2003): 1645A. Chaucer attempts to represent simultaneously three levels of reality in his three "confessional" characters (the Wife of Bath, the Pardoner, and the Canon's Yeoman): actual life, idealized fiction, and higher truth.

148. Ganim, John M. "Drama, Theatricality, and Performance: Radicals of Presentation in *The Canterbury Tales.*" In Wendy Harding, ed. *Drama, Narrative, and Poetry in* The Canterbury Tales (*SAC* 27 [2005], no. 114), pp. 70–82. *CT* accommodates apparently conflicting forms of address and confusions of narrative, dramatic, and expository genres. Chaucer manipulates a number of Northrop Frye's "radicals of presentation," allowing perpetual reinterpretation through the overlay of what had usually been considered quite distinct radicals of presentation.

149. Greenwood, Maria Katarzyna. "Tell It All or Not At All: Tact, Tactlessness, and Good Advice in *The Manciple's Tale, The Tale of Melibee, and The Parson's Tale.*" In Leo Carruthers and Adrian Papahagi, eds. *Paroles et silences dans la littérature anglaise au Moyen Âge* (*SAC* 27 [2005], no. 96), pp. 135–54. *ManT, Mel,* and *ParsT* are hardly tales at all, but rather a joke, an allegory, and a sermon. Yet they provide interesting comparisons between speakers and listeners, ways of speaking and ways of holding back. Reading between the lines is needed before the wisdom of the works emerges.

150. Harding, Wendy. "Gendering Discourse in the *Canterbury Tales.*" *BAM* 64 (2003): 1–11. By representing the narrator of *CT* first as a disembodied authority and then as a storyteller in the pilgrimage game, Chaucer explores the parameters of voice, gender, and authority. The perception of gender in speech is shown to be a social construct, rather than grammatical or linguistic. Associating discourse with gender, either masculine or feminine, diminishes its validity by exposing it to the criticism of the addressee or the reader.

151. Hirsh, John C. *Chaucer and the* Canterbury Tales: *A Short Introduction.* Blackwell Introductions to Literature. Oxford: Blackwell, 2003. x, 175 pp.; 7 b&w illus. Introduces students to Chaucer's life (opening chapter), comments on critical approaches to Chaucer, and presents several groups of recurring topics in *CT*: gender, religion, race, and class; love, sex, and marriage; God and spirituality; adaptations of dream-vision literature in *CT*; and representations of fate and death. The volume includes a selected bibliography and brief indexes of subjects and critics' names. A separate chapter includes plot summaries of each of the *Tales.*

152. Hughes, Alan. *Signs and Circumstances: A Study of Allegory in Chaucer's* Canterbury Tales. Pentrefoelas, Wales: AlaNia, 2003. x, 160 pp. Hughes reads *CT* as an allegorical political critique of the reign of Richard II. The *GP* descriptions allegorically represent aspects of Rich-

ard's personality or persons in his court. Each of the individual tales comments on specific political events and/or pervasive social conditions. The book also discusses political allegory in *Scog* and *Buk*.

153. Kendrick, Laura. "Linking the *Canterbury Tales*: Monkey-business in the Margins." In Wendy Harding, ed. *Drama, Narrative, and Poetry in* The Canterbury Tales (*SAC* 27 [2005], no. 114), pp. 83–98. Kendrick compares the jocular action and imagery of the links in *CT* to the marginal imagery of Gothic psalters and Books of Hours.

154. Knight, Stephen. "The Voice of Labour in Fourteenth-Century English Literature." In James Bothwell, P. J. P. Goldberg, and W. M. Ormrod, eds. *The Problem of Labour in Fourteenth-Century England*. Wood-bridge, Suffolk; and Rochester, N.Y.: York Medieval Press, 2000, pp. 101–22. Knight considers Chaucer's Plowman (among other figures) in an effort to construct a "structure of feeling" pertinent to late medieval English labor. As in the mystery plays and in *Piers Plowman*, the depiction of labor in *CT* is first idealized, then undercut.

155. Melnarik, Tim George. "'And for pleye as he was wont to do': Chaucer's Games in *The Canterbury Tales*." *DAI* 63 (2003): 2537A. Examines *CT* structurally in the context of the fourteenth-century popular view of games and gaming. Also deals with the rules of *CT*, its game in action, violations of the rules, and Chaucer himself as the game's most important piece.

156. Nardo, Don, ed. *Readings on* The Canterbury Tales. Greenhaven Press Literary Companion Series. San Diego, Calif.: Greenhaven, 1997. 192 pp. Seventeen previously published essays and excerpts, accompanied by an introduction, a biography, a chronology, and a brief bibliography intended for student use. Contributors include Donald Howard (on structure and on social rank), Glending Olson (on game), Dieter Mehl (on the narrator), Sigmund Eisner (on symbolic time), M. W. Grose (on language and verse), Esther C. Quinn (on pilgrimage), George L. Kittredge (on marriage), Joyce T. Lionarons (on magic and technology), J. A. Burrow (on romance), Marchette Chute (on characterization), Michael Stevens (*KnT*), Eileen Power (the Prioress), Margaret Hallissy (*MilT*), Saul N. Brody (*NPT*), Trevor Whittock (*Mel*), and Michael Hoy (*PardT*).

157. Phillips, Kim M. *Medieval Maidens: Young Women and Gender in England, 1270–1540*. Manchester Medieval Studies. Manchester and New York: Manchester University Press, 2003. xvi, 246 pp. Examines how the "experiences and voices" of young, unmarried women in late

medieval England reflect ideals of femininity and the social processes of becoming adult women. Focuses on social history and literature, with recurrent mention of *CT*, *TC*, and *LGW*.

158. Plummer, John F. " 'Beth fructuous and that in litel space': The Engendering of Harry Bailly." In Robert G. Benson and Susan J. Ridyard, eds. *New Readings of Chaucer's Poetry* (*SAC* 27 [2005], no. 90), pp. 107–18. Plummer explores sexual references and innuendoes in the speeches of the Host, arguing that sexual and textual power are inseparable for the Host. The Parson's concern with spiritual productivity balances the Host's concern with physical generation, reflecting two different understandings of pilgrimage.

159. Reed, Teresa P. *Shadows of Mary: Reading the Virgin Mary in Medieval Texts*. Religion and Culture in the Middle Ages. Cardiff: University of Wales Press, 2003. 171 pp. Examines allusions to the Virgin Mary in connection to five literary characters: Chaucer's Constance and Wife of Bath, the medical woman of the English *Trotula*, Saint Margaret of Antioch, and the *Pearl* maiden. Chapter 1 focuses on parallels between Constance and Mary in relation to law and to death that is not realized. Chapter 2 argues that the Wife of Bath and Mary reflect each other in an inverse relationship through narrative techniques and motifs. Chaucerian works discussed include *MLT*, *WBPT*, and *ABC*. Bibliography and index.

160. Robertson, Elizabeth. "Marriage, Mutual Consent, and the Affirmation of the Female Subject in the *Knight's Tale*, the *Wife of Bath's Tale*, and the *Franklin's Tale*." In Wendy Harding, ed. *Drama, Narrative, and Poetry in* The Canterbury Tales (*SAC* 27 [2005], no. 114), pp. 175–93. Robertson considers *KnT*, *WBT*, and *FranT* in the light of contemporary marital law, Christian doctrine, and the question of mutual consent to marriage. Chaucer's profound interest in the legitimacy of the female subject is a subset of his larger interest in the nature of free will, choice, and autonomy.

161. Rubin, Miri. "The Languages of Late-Medieval Feminism." In Tjitske Akkerman and Siep Stuurman, eds. *Perspectives on Feminist Political Thought in European History: From the Middle Ages to the Present*. London and New York: Routledge, 1998, pp. 34–49. Mentions *NPT* and *Rom* in a survey of late medieval "pervasive understandings" of women and femininity. Finds places within this survey for instances of "feminist moments" and the "dialects within which they were set."

162. Rutter, Russell. "Malvolio the Fowler: A Note on *Twelfth Night*

3.4.74–75." *ELN* 36.3 (1999): 23–33. Traces the history of the metaphor of Satan as a "fowler" who seeks to trap souls as he would trap
birds. Discusses examples from the time of the Church fathers to Shakespeare, including three instances in which Chaucer employs related metaphors: *WBT* 3.932–34, *LGWP* F134–39, and *TC* 1.353.

163. Saul, Nigel. "A Farewell to Arms? Criticism of Warfare in Late
Fourteenth-Century England." *Fourteenth Century England* 2 (2002):
131–45. Criticism of warfare at the end of the fourteenth century focused on greed and pride as "evils of the times," rather than on burdens
of taxation, an earlier preoccupation. In *Sted, Form Age, Mel,* and *Th,*
Chaucer's dislike of war is evident, and his concerns are similar to those
of his contemporaries—John Gower, Sir John Clanvowe, and others—
perhaps as a result of the way warfare was financed.

164. Scala, Elizabeth. "Historicists and Their Discontents: Reading
Psychoanalytically in Medieval Studies." *TSLL* 44 (2002): 108–31. Assesses the debate between psychoanalytic and historicist critics, arguing
that psychoanalytic assumptions and interpretations are embedded in
historicist analysis, despite historicist claims of rejecting psychoanalysis.
Considers works by major Chaucerians: Louise Fradenburg, Anne Middleton, David Aers, and Lee Patterson.

165. Stemmler, Theo. "Der Bauernaufstand von 1381 in der Zeit-
genössischen Literatur Englands." In Fritz Peter Knapp and Manuela
Niesner, eds. *Historisches und Fiktionales Erzählen im Mittelalter.* Berlin:
Duncker & Humblot, 2002, pp. 45–62. Stemmler assesses representa-
tions of the Uprising of 1381 in several contexts: the *Anonimalle Chroni-
cle,* Henry Knighton's *Chronicon,* Thomas Walsingham's *Historia
Anglicana,* Jean Froissart's *Chroniques,* John Gower's *Vox Clamantis,*
Chaucer's *NPT,* and various references to John Ball.

166. Turco, Lewis. "Our Friend, Dan Chaucer." *English Record* 53.3
(2003): 47–54. A personal memoir recording a childhood experience of
reading about "Dan" Chaucer in *The Book of Knowledge,* leading to an
early understanding of the unchanging drives and characteristics of
human nature. A childhood neighbor was like the Wife of Bath.

167. Wolfe, Matthew C. "Jung and Chaucer: Synchronicity in *The
Canterbury Tales.*" In Charlotte Spivack and Christine Herold, eds. *Archetypal Readings of Medieval Literature* (*SAC* 27 [2005], no. 135), pp. 181–
202. The Jungian notion of synchronicity—the significant coincidence
of psychological and physical states—helps one understand medieval
notions of astrology, mysticism, and the supernatural. Wolfe comments

on the meeting of Palamon and Arcite in *KnT*, John's gullibility in *MilT*, the demise of the elves in *WBT*, January's regaining his eyesight in *MerT*, dream elements in *Th* and *NPT*, and the Parson's decision to eschew fable.

168. Woods, William F. "The Chaucer Foundation: Composition, Social History, and *The Canterbury Tales*." *SMART* 10.2 (2003): 51–85. Describes a freshman writing course that focuses on late medieval social history, structured by means of *GP* and eight of the tales in *CT*. Includes a complete syllabus, writing exercise, and supplemental information.

169. Yiavis, Kostas. "Chaucer and the Death of the Father as a Figure of Authority." *Gramma/Γράμμα: Journal of Theory and Criticism* 9 (2001): 13–29 (with Greek abstract). Chaucer's depreciation of the father figure (biological, theological, literary predecessor) enables him to conceive of poetry separate from the needs for stable interpretation and didactic meaning. Throughout his corpus, his "polyvocal open-endedness" compels readers to be active in their interpretations.

See also nos. 7, 19–21, 23, 26–30, 32, 35, 40, 42, 50, 65, 88, 89, 93, 105, 106, 108, 114, 116, 122, 124, 180, 224, 232.

CT—The General Prologue

170. Chickering, Howell D. "Ironic Tones of Voice in the *General Prologue*." In Nicolay Yakovlev, ed. *Lecture Series*. St. Petersburg: Linguistic Society of St. Petersburg, 2003, pp. 20–37. Rpt. from *Yazyk i rechevaya deyatet'nost'* (*Language and Language Behavior*) 4 (2001): Supplement. Close reading of several *GP* descriptions (including the Knight, Monk, Clerk, Sergeant at Law, and Summoner) shows how Chaucer's shifting tones produce ironic implications.

171. Cohen, Jeffrey J., ed. *Medieval Identity Machines*. Medieval Cultures, no. 35. Minneapolis and London: University of Minnesota Press, 2003. xxix, 323 pp. Bodies in medieval literature are depicted as rhizomatic, unfinished identity machines invented by texts, such as *TC*, *CT*, and others. Commentary draws on theories of Gilles Deleuze, Félix Guattari, and others. Particular references to *SqT*, *WBP*, *PardT*, *MLT*, and especially *GP*, with a close comparison to the opening of *The Sultan of Babylon*.

172. Kane, George. *The Liberating Truth: The Concept of Integrity in Chaucer's Writing*. London: Athlone, 1980. 34 pp. John Coffin Memorial

Lecture, 11 May 1979, University of London. Chaucer's uses of the term *trouthe* (truth, integrity) indicate that he is a serious moralist, though sometimes ironic. Kane focuses on *GP* but also draws examples from *FranT*, *CYT*, *Anel*, and Langland's *Piers Plowman*.

173. Morgan, Gerald. "Moral and Social Identity and the Idea of Pilgrimage in the *General Prologue*." *ChauR* 37 (2003): 285–314. Morgan critiques modern claims for Chaucer's innovation in *GP*, arguing that Chaucer's methods resulted from the moral and artistic training of his time. We should read the pilgrim Chaucer both as earnest and as effective in displaying the sins of his fellow travelers.

174. Nakao, Yoshiyuki. "Chaucer's Use of Similes and Metaphors in the General Prologue to *The Canterbury Tales*—In Relation to Characterization." *Phoenix* (Graduate School of English Philology and Literature, Faculty of Letters, Hiroshima University) 16 (1980): 3–23 (in Japanese). Discusses disharmony between the characters' words and deeds in *GP* by examining Chaucer's similes and metaphors.

175. Owen, Charles A., Jr. "Chaucer's Witty Prosody in the General Prologue." In Alan T. Gaylord, ed. *Essays on the Art of Chaucer's Verse* (*SAC* 25 [2003], no. 64), pp. 339–78. Sustained close reading of *GP* demonstrates Chaucer's virtuosity, especially his dexterity with varieties of rhyme and stress. Owen focuses on lines 1–42 of *GP* and then offers observations on the individual descriptions, Chaucer's apology, and the words of the Host.

176. Rosenblum, Joseph, with William K. Finley. "Chaucer Gentrified: The Nexus of Art and Politics in the Ellesmere Miniatures." *ChauR* 38 (2003): 140–57. The artists of the Ellesmere manuscript carefully deviated from Chaucer's descriptions of the pilgrims to deflect the satire from the upper and upper-middle classes to the lower orders. When Chaucer's own descriptions were ambiguous, the artists removed from the illustrations those things that might make them seem so.

177. Shuffelton, George Gordon. "The Miscellany and the Monument: Collecting in Chaucer, Gower, and Langland." *DAI* 63 (2003): 3547A. As part of larger argument that miscellanies were an "essential material condition of vernacular literature before the introduction of printing," Shuffelton considers *CT* as a booklet miscellany.

178. Vermeule, Blakey. "Satirical Mind Blindness." *CML* 22.2 (2002): 85–101. Describes the cognitive condition of "mind blindness," often associated with autism, and argues that a literary version of the condition recurs in satire, where authors use the blind spots of characters

to ironically convey unstated information. Uses examples from modern political discourse, classical and eighteenth-century satires, and Chaucer's descriptive technique in *GP*.

See also nos. 36, 89, 140, 152, 230, 251.

CT—The Knight and His Tale

179. Brewer, Derek. "Knight and Miller: Similarity and Difference." In Wendy Harding, ed. *Drama, Narrative, and Poetry in* The Canterbury Tales (*SAC* 27 [2005], no. 114), pp. 127–38. Although written for the same fourteenth-century courtly audience/readership, *KnT* and *MilT* are two very different types of narrative. One of the features of Chaucer's Gothic aesthetic was to shift between high and low styles. These two *Tales* represent extreme limits of his verse, and there are variations of style and attitude even within the *Tales*.

180. Broughton, Laurel. " 'He Conquered Al the Regne of Femenye': What Chaucer's Knight Doesn't Tell About Theseus." In Jean E. God-sall-Myers, ed. *Speaking in the Medieval World* (*SAC* 27 [2005], no. 110), pp. 43–63. By adjusting his source, Chaucer allows the Knight to construct a Theseus who appears noble and positively inclined toward women. Chaucer also reminds us, however, that Theseus is not always the champion of women and the exemplar of chivalry. A number of possible, conflicting readings shape the larger conversation of *CT* on the nature of truly noble behavior.

181. Chance, Jane. "Representing Rebellion: The Ending of Chaucer's *Knight's Tale* and the Castration of Saturn." *SAP* 38 (2002): 75–92. The Knight, in representing the gods, omits any reference to the castration of Saturn in order to justify the ascendancy of Jupiter, the authority of Theseus, and the political situation of the later fourteenth century, "a dark time in which Jupiter's lechery, doubleness, and treason substitute for the Golden Age of Saturn."

182. Hazell, Dinah. "Empedocles, Boethius, and Chaucer: Love Binds All." *CarmP* 11 (2002): 43–74. Explores how the character Theseus in *KnT* does and does not embody principles of political philosophy found in Boethius's *Consolation of Philosophy*. Combining "idealism and political exigency," Theseus fulfills the "composite model of an ideal" late medieval ruler, but not that of a Boethian philosopher. His closing

speech aligns with the "Empedoclean model" or worldview, in which strife and love vie in a mechanistic way.

183. Johnston, Andrew James. "The Keyhole Politics of Chaucerian Theatricality: Voyeurism in the *Knight's Tale.*" *Poetica* 34 (2002): 73–97. Focuses on the *occupatio* that addresses Emelye's ritual ablutions in the temple of Diana. Discusses the way Chaucer identifies different modes of seeing—all-inclusive panoramic vision vs. the privileged view of the voyeur—with the Knight's staging of his own narratorial power and the specific politics of chivalric culture.

184. Murtaugh, Daniel M. "The Education of Theseus in *The Knight's Tale.*" *SELIM* 10 (2000): 141–65. Reads Theseus as a uniquely dynamic character in *KnT* and in *CT* more generally—able to "change over time in response to experience." In the course of the *Tale*, Theseus achieves some of the detachment and insight that characterize the Knight.

185. Stretter, Robert. "Rewriting Perfect Friendship in Chaucer's *Knight's Tale* and Lydgate's *Fabula Duorum Mercatorum.*" *ChauR* 37 (2003): 234–52. In *KnT*, Chaucer uses conventions of the friendship tradition to explore the power of erotic desire; Lydgate rewrites the fatal rivalry to emphasize male friendship over male-female attraction.

See also nos. 10, 49, 72, 91, 93, 98, 116, 156, 160, 167, 215, 230.

CT—The Miller and His Tale

186. Ortego, James. "Gerveys Joins the Fun: A Note on *Viritoot* in the *Miller's Tale.*" *ChauR* 37 (2003): 275–79. In *MilT*, *viritoot* can best be deciphered as a slang pun on *virtutis*, ridiculing Absolon's manhood.

187. Schlaeger, Jürgen. "Chaucer läßt lachen." In Werner Röcke and Helga Neumann, eds. *Komische Gegenwelten: Lachen und Literatur im Mittelalter und Früher Neuzeit.* Paderborn: Schöningh, 1999, pp. 123–31. Short introduction to various theories of laughter, followed by a brief analysis of laughter in *MilT* and *TC*.

188. Semenza, Gregory M. Colón. "Historicizing 'Wrastlynge' in *The Miller's Tale.*" *ChauR* 38 (2003): 66–82. Members of the aristocracy and the middle class engaged in wrestling. Thus, Chaucer's reference to the Miller as a wrestler cannot be dismissed as a reference to the lower class.

See also nos. 43, 107, 116, 120, 138, 143, 156, 167, 179.

CT—The Reeve and His Tale

189. Shomura, Tetsuji. *Chaucer's* Reeve's Tale*: Traditional Reception and Interpretation*. Kumamoto: Kumamoto Gakuen University Foreign Affairs Research Institute, 2003. 178 pp. Examines *RvT*, considering such matters as its construction and function as a *Tale*, its moral, and its sources.

See also nos. 73, 77, 88, 141.

CT—The Cook and His Tale

See no. 119.

CT—The Man of Law and His Tale

190. Black, Nancy B. *Medieval Narratives of Accused Queens*. Gainesville: University Press of Florida, 2003. xviii, 261 pp. In narratives of falsely accused queens, the queens frequently undergo periods of exile that refine their souls through poverty and suffering. Black compares the Constance narratives by Nicholas Trevet, Gower, and Chaucer, examining each version in light of its writer's generic and thematic aims: Trevet's interest in history and his association of an active, learned Custance with Mary of Woodstock; Gower's focus on didactic themes; and Chaucer's development of Constance (from her initial youthful simplicity to her deepening spirituality), the pathos of the *Tale*, the narrator's untrustworthiness, and innovative allusions to Pope Innocent III's *De miseria condicionis humanae*.

191. Lee, Brian S. "Christian Adornment in *The Man of Law's Tale*." *PMAM* 10 (2003): 31–48. The absence of details of physical dress or adornment applied to Custance in *MLT* coincides with the presentation of her as a virtuous, Christian heroine. Though descriptive details are conventional in romances, their relative absence here is consistent with exemplary religious narratives.

192. McCarthy, Conor. "Injustice and Chaucer's Man of Law." *Parergon*, n.s., 20 (2003): 1–18. Chancery highlighted problems posed in the medieval common-law courts by failures in jurisprudence. *MLT* raises questions about injustice that reflect critically on the Sergeant of Law. Though he is shown to be an expert in jurisprudence, he is satirized by

language—specifically the word *termes*, used elsewhere in Chaucer to suggest technical or deceptive language.

193. Robertson, Elizabeth. "Nonviolent Christianity and the Strangeness of Female Power in Geoffrey Chaucer's *Man of Law's Tale*." In Sharon Farmer and Carol Braun Pasternack, eds. *Gender and Difference in the Middle Ages*. Medieval Cultures, no. 32. Minneapolis and London: University of Minnesota Press, 2003, pp. 322–51. A revised version of the author's essay, "The 'Elvyssh' Power of Constance: Christian Feminism in Geoffrey Chaucer's *The Man of Law's Tale*" (*SAC* 25 [2003], no. 189).

See also nos. 31, 45, 52, 102, 115, 123, 159, 171, 222, 229.

CT—The Wife of Bath and Her Tale

194. Besamusca, Bart. "In Quest of What's on a Woman's Mind: Gauvain as Dwarf in the Middle Dutch *Wrake van Ragisel*." *Neophil* 87 (2003): 589–96. In the Middle Dutch *Wrake van Ragisel* (adapted from the Old French *Vengeance Raguisel*), "Walewein, who is transformed into a dwarf, learns that women are exclusively led by their sexual desire," a different answer to the life question than is found in analogous versions of the tale, including *WBT*.

195. Brown, Muriel. "'Gentilesse' in Chaucer's *Wife of Bath's Tale*." In Michelle Sauer, ed. *Proceedings of the 11th Annual Northern Plains Conference on Early British Literature* (*SAC* 27 [2005], no. 133), pp. 82–89. Brown approaches the loathly lady's sermon on "gentilesse" as political allegory, emphasizing "the transforming power of relinquishing control over those who work, the third estate."

196. Carter, Susan. "Coupling the Beastly Bride and the Hunter Hunted: What Lies Behind Chaucer's *Wife of Bath's Tale*?" *ChauR* 37 (2003): 329–45. Chaucer's *WBT* destabilizes gender roles rather than focusing on the issues of kingship at the core of most of the loathly-lady tales. *WBT* engages issues of personal power politics as it creates a lively, garrulous character, but the moral lies in the collapse of gender roles and the acceptance of ambivalence.

197. Dor, Juliette. "The Sheela-na-Gig: An Incongruous Sign of Sexual Purity?" In Anke Bernau, Ruth Evans, and Sarah Salih, eds. *Medieval Virginities*. Cardiff: University of Wales Press, 2003, pp. 33–55. Dor links the exhibitionist sheela-na-gig with the widespread Celtic

mythological motif of Lady Sovereignty that has been identified with the transformation motif in *WBT*.

198. ———. "The Wife of Bath's 'Wandrynge by the Weye' and Conduct Literature for Women." In Wendy Harding, ed. *Drama, Narrative, and Poetry in* The Canterbury Tales (*SAC* 27 [2005], no. 114), pp. 139–55. The Wife of Bath's "wanderings" reflect the multivalent meanings of the word. She contravenes the codes governing female behavior, including the standards for governing noble women and the values involved in "What the Good Wife Taught Her Daughter." In *WBP*, she travesties deportment literature, and she holds up unruliness as a model in her revised mini–conduct book.

199. Fleming, John V. "The Best Line in Ovid and the Worst." In Robert G. Benson and Susan J. Ridyard, eds. *New Readings of Chaucer's Poetry* (*SAC* 27 [2005], no. 90), pp. 51–74. Fleming examines Chaucer's mixture of sacred and secular texts and illustrates how Chaucer's idea of the Wife of Bath grew from an amalgamation of *Le Roman de la Rose*, Ovid, and Saint Jerome, particularly in *WBP*.

200. Hernández Pérez, Mᵃ Beatriz. "Alice de Bath o el Poder de la Palabra." *Atlantis* 24 (2002): 117–32. Feminist narratological analysis of *WBPT* reveals that the Wife's arguments, based in traditional misogyny, overwhelm this misogyny through dynamic engagement of it.

201. Herold, Christine. "Archetypal Chaucer: The Case of the Disappearing Hag in *The Wife of Bath's Tale*." In Charlotte Spivack and Christine Herold, eds. *Archetypal Readings of Medieval Literature* (*SAC* 27 [2005], no. 135), pp. 47–65. Herold reads *WBT* as an "individuation myth" in which the knight gains "wisdom and self-empowerment" in his encounters with the anima, manifested in the "triple-aspect of the Great Mother Archetype": maiden, queen, and loathly lady.

202. Kim, Jae-Whan. "M/W: A Deconstructive Reading of the Wife of Bath." *JELL* (Seoul) 44 (1998): 255–74 (in Korean, with English abstract). Chaucer prompts his readers to recognize that the Wife of Bath misreads and adapts the authorities she confronts, reminding us that multiple meanings are everywhere possible. This deconstruction of meaning prompts deconstruction of the male/female dichotomy and echoes throughout *WBPT*, *ClT*, *MerT*, and even *Ret*.

203. Lawton, Lesley. "'Glose Whoso Wole': Voice, Text, and Authority in *The Wife of Bath's Prologue*." In Wendy Harding, ed. *Drama, Narrative, and Poetry in* The Canterbury Tales (*SAC* 27 [2005], no. 114), pp. 157–74. The Wife's discourse is on the cusp between the clerkly

and the carnivalesque. She is the unstable product of the interplay of various intertexts, creating the illusion of a complex personality. Though sometimes championed by feminists, she at once challenges and is subordinated to official discourse.

204. McCarthy, Conor. "The Position of Widows in the Later Fourteenth-Century English Community and the *Wife of Bath's Prologue.*" In Donald Mowbray, Rhiannon Purdie, and Ian P. Wei, eds. *Authority and Community in the Middle Ages.* Phoenix Mill, Gloucestershire: Sutton, 1999, pp. 101–15. Because they were not subject to fathers or husbands, widows posed a challenge to dominant views of women in late fourteenth-century England. Chaucer's Wife of Bath is portrayed as lecherous, yet she may also embody broader concerns about widowhood.

205. Passmore, S. Elizabeth. "Painting Lions, Drawing Lines, Writing Lives: Male Authorship in the Lives of Christina Markyate, Margery Kempe, and Margaret Paston." *Medieval Feminist Forum* 36 (2003): 36–40. Passmore discusses three examples of "written women," whose stories are "filtered through the impressions and words of a male writer." The Wife of Bath's question about who painted the lion (*WBP* 3.692) indicates that women's writings, if unmediated by men, would be "more accurate in their self-depictions."

206. Perfetti, Lisa Renée. *Women and Laughter in Medieval Comic Literature.* Ann Arbor: University of Michigan Press, 2003. ix, 286 pp. Explores literary representations of women's laughter from the thirteenth to the sixteenth centuries and examines the contexts that shaped how women told jokes. The Wife of Bath's use of play coincides with Chaucer's own, dramatizing antifeminism as a game; blurring lines between masculine and feminine, authority and experience; and attacking the premise beneath her discourse. Chaucer's presentation invites women to respond with laughter and join the game. Perfetti assesses *WBPT* and *BD.*

207. Pugh, Tison. "Queering Genres, Battering Males: The Wife of Bath's Narrative Violence." *JNT* 33 (2003): 115–42. Reading the Wife of Bath's romance through her fabliau spirit reveals Chaucer's distaste for the Arthurian romance tradition (elsewhere seen in *SqT, NPT*) and (as seen in *SqT, Th,* and *FranT*) his ironic attitude toward male narrative authority, his "queering of heteronormative masculine identity" (135).

208. Webb, Diana. "Freedom of Movement? Women Travellers in the Middle Ages." In Christine Meek and Catherine Lawless, eds. *Studies on Medieval and Early Modern Women: Pawns or Players?* Dublin and Port-

land, Ore.: Four Courts, 2003, pp. 75–89. Webb briefly cites two *CT* characters: the Prioress is an unusual, but not impossible, instance of a nun on a local (as opposed to a foreign) pilgrimage; the Wife of Bath parallels several historical women who capitalized on their peripatetic adventures.

See also nos. 31, 55, 58, 68, 69, 91, 119, 138–40, 143, 147, 159, 160, 162, 166, 167, 171, 230.

CT—The Friar and His Tale

See nos. 73, 140.

CT—The Summoner and His Tale

209. Kabir, Ananya Jahanara. "From Twelve Devouring Dragons to the *Develes Ers*: The Medieval History of an Apocryphal Punitive Motif." *Archiv* 238 (2001): 280–98. Traces the history of the motif of infernal punishment in the devil's anus, suggesting that the earliest evidence of the motif is found in the "Seven Heavens Apocryphon" of Irish visionary tradition and that Chaucer's use of the motif in *SumP* derives from this tradition, perhaps inflected by the *Visio sancti Pauli*.

210. Shippey, Tom. "Bilingualism and Betrayal in Chaucer's *Summoner's Tale*." In Jean E. Godsall-Myers, ed. *Speaking in the Medieval World* (*SAC* 27 [2005], no. 110), pp. 125–44. Just as in *RvT* Chaucer plays on his audience's awareness of dialect geography, in *SumT* he exploits strong contemporary awareness of linguistic class markers. If Chaucer was in some sense a philologist, he was also an efficient and deliberate sociolinguist.

211. Somerset, Fiona. "Here, There, and Everywhere? Wycliffite Conceptions of the Eucharist and Chaucer's 'Other' Lollard Joke." In Fiona Somerset, Jill C. Havens, and Derrick G. Pitard, eds. *Lollards and Their Influence in Late Medieval England* (*SAC* 27 [2005], no. 134), pp. 127–38. Argues that details of *SumT* gain dimension in light of the contemporary debate concerning the Eucharist and transubstantiation as recorded in the *Upland Series*. Division of the indivisible fart is a blasphemous joke on questions of divisibility in the Eucharistic debate.

See also no. 140.

CT—The Clerk and His Tale

212. Campbell, Emma. "Sexual Poetics and the Politics of Translation in the Tale of Griselda." *CL* 55 (2003): 191–216. Campbell applies Judith Butler's theories of performative gender identity and "cultural translation" to *ClT* and its sources in Petrarch and Boccaccio. In Chaucer's version, authority is translated to the vernacular and to oral discourse, challenging to Petrarch's version but nevertheless asserting masculine authority over feminine texts and bodies.

213. Evans, Deanna Delmar. "Introducing Christine de Pizan into the Chaucer Course: Tales of Griselda as Textual Context." *PMAM* 9 (2002): 116–33. Describes a pedagogy for teaching *ClT* in comparison to the Griselda story in Christine de Pizan's *The Book of the City of Ladies*—as part of a course that treats "Chaucer in context" as a means to encourage students to engage actively in their reading.

214. Farrell, Thomas J. "Source or Hard Analogue? *Decameron* X, 10 and the *Clerk's Tale.*" *ChauR* 37 (2003): 346–64. Farrell argues that clear differentiation among types of analogues may enable us to analyze Chaucer's works with more subtlety. A "source" is a work we are certain Chaucer knew; a "hard analogue" is a work that was available to him; a "soft source" has only remote parallels. Although the *Decameron* is a hard source for *ClT*, Chaucer did not necessarily draw from it.

215. Lawler, Traugott. "Delicacy vs. Truth: Defining Moral Heroism in the *Canterbury Tales.*" In Robert G. Benson and Susan J. Ridyard, eds. *New Readings of Chaucer's Poetry* (*SAC* 27 [2005], no. 90), pp. 75–90. Lawler argues that Chaucer privileged simplicity and disapproved of decadence and over-refinement. Lexical examination demonstrates Chaucer's preference for "delicacy," evident most clearly in Griselda of *ClT* and supported by evidence from *KnT* and *ParsT*.

See also nos. 93, 106, 116, 123, 202, 227.

CT—The Merchant and His Tale

216. Crocker, Holly A. "Performative Passivity and Fantasies of Masculinity in the *Merchant's Tale.*" *ChauR* 38 (2003): 178–98. The comedy in *MerT* is produced by May herself, whose "conduct demonstrates that the feminine passivity upon which the masculine performance of agency depends is *of course* an act." May exposes the ridiculous

nature of all claims to masculine authority, and hence Chaucer demonstrates the collaboration of men and women to make fictions of gender convincing.

217. Finlayson, John. "*The Merchant's Tale*: Literary Contents, the Play of Genres, and Institutionalized Sexual Relations." *Anglia* 121 (2003): 557–80. The combination of genres in *MerT* (fabliau, encomium, moral allegory, mock-heroic, and parody) satirizes the social institutions and literary genres within which sex and love are contained and represented. The encomium fuses reality and idealization; the allegorical debate mocks January and parodies the literary elevation of sex. The garden scene parodies courtly love, the Edenic fall, and the authority of the gods.

218. Heffernan, Carol Falvo. "Three Unnoticed Links Between Matthew of Vendôme's *Comedia Lidie* and Chaucer's *Merchant's Tale*." *N&Q* 248 (2003): 158–62. Argues that Chaucer had direct knowledge of Vendôme's text and suggests a possible manuscript source of it: Florence, Biblioteca Medicea-Laurenziana, Pluteus 33.31.

219. Hertog, Erik. "The Mapping Structure of Metaphor: An Analysis of Chaucer's *Merchant's Tale*." *Linguistica Antverpiensia* 23 (1989): 101–37. Structuralist analysis of how metaphors develop into themes in *MerT* and, in turn, "steer the plot."

See also nos. 31, 79, 91, 141, 143, 167, 202, 289.

CT—The Squire and His Tale

220. Ambrisco, Alan S. "Teaching the *Squire's Tale* as an Exercise in Literary History." *SMART* 10.1 (2003): 5–18. Ambrisco describes teaching *SqT* as an "unsolved problem in Chaucerian reception"—*SqT* is a work favored by the Franklin and early readers such as Spenser and Milton, but it is decried or ignored by formalist critics. Opening class discussion to the orientalism of *SqT*, this approach empowers students to develop their own understanding of the *Tale* and of other works of medieval literature.

See also nos. 57, 109, 115, 171.

CT—The Franklin and His Tale

221. Fein, Susanna. "Boethian Boundaries: Compassion and Constraint in the *Franklin's Tale*." In Wendy Harding, ed. *Drama, Narrative,*

and Poetry in The Canterbury Tales (*SAC* 27 [2005], no. 114), pp. 195–212. *FranT* describes a true-love marriage in Boethian terms and impossible contradictions, in a language that strains for comprehensibility amid paradox and conditions that tend to undo prior terms. Stability and union replace oppositions, dualities, verbal ambiguities, and dilemmas after two opposed natures (male and female) almost reach the breaking point. The couple's metaphorical child, Aurelius, withdraws as a result of Arveragus's masculine *gentilesse* and Dorigen's feminine compassion (which places her at the center of the *Tale*).

222. Nachtwey, Gerald R. "Geoffroi de Charny's *Book of Chivalry* and Violence in *The Man of Law's Tale* and *The Franklin's Tale*." *Essays in Medieval Studies* 20 (2003): 107–20. Nachtwey applies the "vertical" social relations of chivalry as understood by Geoffroi de Charny to *MLT* and *FranT*. As a perfect Christian, Constance "muddles" the chivalric ideal of a wife, and Dorigen's rashness makes her somewhat inconsistent with the ideal as well. The male figures are more consistent with chivalric standards.

223. Pitcher, John A. " 'Word and Werk' in Chaucer's *Franklin's Tale*." *L&P* 49 (2003): 77–109. Lacanian psychoanalysis of how words used to describe the objects of desire in *FranT* do not accord with the work of desire actually performed.

224. Schutz, Andrea. "Negotiating the Present: Language and Trouthe in the *Franklin's Tale*." In Jean E. Godsall-Myers, ed. *Speaking in the Medieval World* (*SAC* 27 [2005], no. 110), pp. 105–24. Language itself is important in *FranT*, but so is the intention of the speaker. Moreover, authorial intention in *CT* as a whole affects how we use language for our own ends, because we learn from everything we read. Authors must consider the consequences of the words they write.

225. Smith, D. Vance. *Arts of Possession: The Middle English Household Imaginary*. Medieval Cultures, no. 33. Minneapolis and London: University of Minnesota Press, 2003. xviii, 318 pp. Considers the household as a complex image central to understanding late medieval England, exploring literary, historical, and economic representations for what they disclose about the "ethics of possession." Analyzes aspects of *Winner and Waster*, *Piers Plowman*, and other narratives. Reads *FranT* as the teller's "fantasy" of gentle behavior and the Franklin as Chaucer's exploration of the "interplay between display and reticence."

226. Stévanovitch, Colette. "Polysyllabic Words in End-of-Line Position in the *Franklin's Tale*." In Wendy Harding, ed. *Drama, Narrative,*

and Poetry in The Canterbury Tales (*SAC* 27 [2005], no. 114), pp. 113–24. The author explores some of the effects arising from polysyllables (i.e., here words with more than one stressed syllable), concentrating on those in rhyming position, especially words referring to *worthynesse* and *gentilesse*, the virtues credited to Arveragus in *FranT*.

227. Wilcockson, Colin. "Thou and Tears: The Advice of Arveragus to Dorigen in Chaucer's *Franklin's Tale*." *RES* 54 (2003): 308–12. The subtlety of Arveragus's use of the second-person singular pronoun (*FranT* 5.1479–86) invites readers' sympathy. Here and in *ClT*, Chaucer adapts his source by varying the register between the formal (plural) and familiar (singular) forms of the pronoun.

See also nos. 64, 93, 109, 143, 160, 172.

CT—The Physician and His Tale

228. Pitcher, John A. "Chaucer's Wolf: Exemplary Violence in *The Physician's Tale*." *Genre* 36 (2003): 1–27. Examines allegorical, typological, eschatological, and pathetic registers and wordplay in *PhyT*, showing how Chaucer thematizes violence and cultural forms that would valorize it. Pitcher compares Chaucer's rendering with that in *Le Roman de la Rose* and argues that the image of the wolf (lines 101–2) applies to Virginius. Within the framework of *CT*, the *Tale* indicts the family as an institution of violence.

See also nos. 143, 234.

CT—The Pardoner and His Tale

229. Brosamer, Matthew. "The Cook, the Miller, and Alimentary Hell." In Donka Minkova and Theresa Tinkle, eds. *Chaucer and the Challenges of Medievalism: Studies in Honor of H. A. Kelly* (*SAC* 27 [2005], no. 125), pp. 235–51. Brosamer investigates hell-mouth imagery in *PardT*, *MLT*, and *LGWP*, drawing upon a number of sources, especially *De miseria condicionis humanae* by Pope Innocent III. The corruption of sin has an alimentary dimension, from ingestion to defecation.

230. Fowler, Elizabeth. *Literary Character: The Human Figure in Early English Writing*. Ithaca: Cornell University Press, 2003. xiv, 263 pp. Fowler explores literary character and characterization as processes of

the reader's engagement with "social persons" posited by a given text through various habituated devices and understood in light of various historical contexts—psychological, political, economic, and philosophical. She focuses on Chaucer's Pardoner (particularly in light of three constructions of intentionality—confessional, ministerial, and poetic), Langland's Lady Meed, Skelton's Elynour Rummynge, and figures from Spenser's *Faerie Queene*. Includes commentary on *ParsT* and *Ret*, *ShT*, *WBP*, and the *GP* descriptions of the Knight and Prioress.

231. Gellrich, Jesse M. "Allegory and Materiality: Medieval Foundations of the Modern Debate." *Germanic Review* 77 (2002): 146–59. Modern notions of the "key role of materiality in allegory," as theorized by Walter Benjamin and echoed by Paul de Man, have clear precedents in patristic and medieval commentaries on allegory and supposition, although the sense of "material" is more broadly construed in medieval thought. In *PardPT*, Chaucer explores the materiality of allegory, the random contingency of reference, and the self-referential nature of the allegorical mode.

232. Jeffrey, Chris. "Registers in Chaucer's *Pardoner's Prologue* and *Tale*." In Katja Lenz and Ruth Möhlig, eds. *Of dyuersitie & chaunge of langage: Essays Presented to Manfred Görlach on the Occasion of His 65th Birthday*. Heidelberg: Winter, 2002, pp. 319–38. Applies "register-theory" to *PardPT* to demonstrate Chaucer's "Gothic" juxtapositioning of various kinds of discourse. Jeffrey examines the mode, domain, topic, and tenor of the discursive units in *PardPT* and suggests that the characteristic variety of *CT* can be laid clear through such analysis.

233. Kendrick, Laura. "Chaucer's Pardoner and the Figure of the Charlatan in Medieval French and Occitan Poetry." In Colette Stévanovitch and René Tixier, eds. *Surface et profondeur: Mélanges offerts à Guy Bourquin à l'occasion de son 75ᵉ anniversaire* (*SAC* 27 [2005], no. 136), pp. 165–78. Kendrick considers a portion of *PardP* (lines 352–88) in light of two thirteenth-century charlatans' spiels invented for performance by jongleurs: Rutebeuf's "Dit de l'herberie" and Peire Cardenal's "Dit de l'onguent."

234. Lewis, Celia. "Framing Fiction with Death: Chaucer's *Canterbury Tales* and the Plague." In Robert G. Benson and Susan J. Ridyard, eds. *New Readings of Chaucer's Poetry* (*SAC* 27 [2005], no. 90), pp. 139–64. Late medieval preoccupation with mortality defies the solace of fiction. *PhyT* and *PardT* offer no hope of physical or spiritual life, and *ParsT* kills storytelling.

235. Low, Anthony. *Aspects of Subjectivity: Society and Individuality from the Middle Ages to Shakespeare and Milton*. Medieval & Renaissance Literary Studies. Pittsburgh: Duquesne University Press, 2003. xxi, 242 pp. Subjectivity and a sense of the importance of the inner self and the individual developed gradually from the early Middle Ages to the seventeenth century. Nothing is altogether new in the stunning early-modernist sense of a vast, inner world of the self. What is new is the sense that the world within is more real than the world outside. Chaucer's Pardoner displays little awareness of his inner self. His despicable character and behavior make him a negative exemplar, whom Chaucer holds up for his audience's blame and execration.

236. Minnis, Alastair. "Reclaiming the Pardoner." *JMEMSt* 33 (2003): 311–34. Noting the heritage of critical commentary about the Pardoner's sexuality, Minnis calls for refocusing attention on the central issue: the Pardoner's immorality. The Pardoner, probably a lay person, is placed within the context of medieval indulgence theory and practice to show his egocentric manipulation of complexities and confusions within the system.

237. Osborn, Marijane. "Transgressive Word and Image in Chaucer's Enshrined *Coillons* Passage." *ChauR* 37 (2003): 365–84. The "coillons" interchange between the Pardoner and the Host at the end of *PardT* goes much deeper than previously noticed. Echoing a passage from *Le Roman de la Rose* found in some manuscripts, the lines evoke a transgressive inversion of the "nut in the shell" imagery.

238. Richardson, Gudrun. "The Old Man in Chaucer's *Pardoner's Tale*: An Interpretative Study of His Identity and Meaning." *Neophil* 87 (2003): 323–37. Richardson surveys various interpretations of the Old Man in *PardT*. Concentrates on the imagery of Mother Earth and of suicide, arguing that the Old Man can be seen as the Pardoner's undying soul.

See also nos. 52, 69, 139, 141, 143, 147, 156, 171, 253.

CT—The Shipman and His Tale

239. Jager, Eric. "The Shipman's Tale: Merchant's Time and Church's Time, Secular and Sacred Space." In Donka Minkova and Theresa Tinkle, eds. *Chaucer and the Challenges of Medievalism: Studies in Honor of H. A. Kelly* (*SAC* 27 [2005], no. 125), pp. 253–60. Jager draws upon

commentary by Jacques Le Goff and Gerhard Dohrn-van Rossum regarding how time was measured in the late Middle Ages. He argues that *ShT* indicates how merchant time, space, and values triumph over those of the Church because of an expanding middle class and a growing awareness of the value of time.

240. Reiff, Raychel Haugrud. "The Legendary Don Juan: A Possible Source for Chaucer's 'The Shipman's Tale.'" *Journal of the Short Story in English/Les Cahiers de la Nouvelle* 39.2 (2002): 11–21. Suggests that Daun John and aspects of *ShT* may have been inspired by a popular legend (perhaps oral) of Don Juan.

241. Rogers, William, and Paul Dower. "Thinking About Money in Chaucer's *Shipman's Tale*." In Robert G. Benson and Susan J. Ridyard, eds. *New Readings of Chaucer's Poetry* (*SAC* 27 [2005], no. 90), pp. 119–38. Rogers and Dower review considerations of money and its circulation in *ShT*, questioning whether Chaucer praises or blames money or whether the topic was as mixed for him as it is today.

See also nos. 119, 230, 251.

CT—The Prioress and Her Tale

242. Dutton, Marsha L. "Chaucer's Two Nuns." In Benjamin Thompson, ed. *Monasteries and Society in Medieval Britain: Proceedings of the 1994 Harlaxton Symposium*. Harlaxton Medieval Studies, no. 6. Stamford: Watkins, 1999, pp. 296–311. Dutton reads the Prioress and the Second Nun as paired opposites: one childish, the other adult. In *PrPT*, the Creator is subordinated to his creatures, who seem "unaware of the effects of the Incarnation." *SNPT* reasserts the proper order, in which Christians exercise chastity and charity while rejecting wrath and vengeance.

243. Fleming, John V. "Madame Eglentyne: The Telling of the Beads." In Donka Minkova and Theresa Tinkle, eds. *Chaucer and the Challenges of Medievalism: Studies in Honor of H. A. Kelly* (*SAC* 27 [2005], no. 125), pp. 205–33. The description of the Prioress's rosary exemplifies Chaucer's wordplay and his literary engagement with other writers, particularly Jean de Meun and Ovid. Fleming compares the Prioress's rosary with rosaries in medieval art and assesses the significance of her name, Madame Eglentyne, in romance and sacred romance alike.

244. Greenwood, Maria Katarzyna. "Pointless Piety and Pathos in

Chaucer's *Prioress's Tale*." In Colette Stévanovitch and René Tixier, eds. *Surface et profondeur: Mélanges offerts à Guy Bourquin à l'occasion de son 75ᵉ anniversaire* (*SAC* 27 [2005], no. 136), pp. 179–98. Piety and pathos heighten the impact of *PrT* and promote the narrator's reputation for religious correctness, yet all aspects of her *Tale* are undermined by pointlessness. Greenwood argues that the *Tale* is dialogistic and Menippean; a satirical subtext emerges out of the contrast between polysemia and aporia of expressions of feelings, on the one hand, and clarity and factual exposition, on the other.

245. McGowan, Joseph P. "Chaucer's Prioress: *Et Nos Cedamus Amori*." *ChauR* 38 (2003): 199–202. The Prioress's ambiguous motto—"love conquers all"—is only half of a quotation from Virgil. The remainder—"and we must give in to it"—does not lessen the equivocal nature of the portrait.

246. Olson, Glending. "A Franciscan Reads the *Facetus*." In Donka Minkova and Theresa Tinkle, eds. *Chaucer and the Challenges of Medievalism: Studies in Honor of H. A. Kelly* (*SAC* 27 [2005], no. 125), pp. 143–55. Olson examines Gerard of Odo's *Facetus, multa documenta*, a commentary on Aristotle's *Nichomachean Ethics*, as background to the Prioress's description in *GP*. The Franciscan commentary may indicate that the courtliness of the description is more than just satire.

See also nos. 123, 156, 208, 230.

CT—The Tale of Sir Thopas

247. Hernández Pérez, Mª Beatriz. "Geoffrey Chaucer's Antagonistic Personalities: 'Sir Thopas' and 'Melibee' Face to Face." In I. Moskowich-Spiegel Fandiño, ed. *Re-Interpretations {sic} of English: Essays on Literature, Culture, and Film (I)*. [La Coruña]: Universidade da Coruña, 2001, pp. 85–101. Explores issues of persona, authorship, and reception in *Th* and *Mel*, focusing on the links between *Tales*, the Host's role, and the "evolution" of the pilgrim Chaucer.

248. Nakao, Yoshiyuki. "A Computer-Assisted Approach to the Language of Sir Thopas." In Toshio Saito, ed. *Studies of English Language and Literature with a Computer*. Tokyo: Eihosha, 1992, pp. 177–94 (in Japanese). Describes Chaucer's uses of rare and unique words in *Th*

through comparison with the language of other romances by Chaucer and other writers.

See also nos. 39, 71, 99, 163, 167.

CT—The Tale of Melibee

249. Moore, Stephen G. "Apply Yourself: Learning While Reading the *Tale of Melibee.*" *ChauR* 38 (2003): 83–97. The narrative structure of *Mel* compels the reader to read backward and forward between scenes and episodes, encouraging affective involvement in the universal sentential wisdom of the *Tale.* The purpose is not that Melibee learn, but that the reader learn.

250. Serrano Reyes, Jesús L. "Las 'Sententiae' en Juan Manuel y Chaucer." *Lemir: Revista Electrónica sobre Literatura Española Medieval y del Renacimiento* 3 (1999): n.p. Compares verbal and conceptual parallels among *sententiae* in Juan Manuel's *El Conde Lucanor* and in Chaucer's *Mel.*

See also nos. 39, 50, 52, 143, 149, 156, 163, 247.

CT—The Monk and His Tale

251. Pearsall, Derek. "'If heaven be on this earth, it is in cloister or in school': The Monastic Ideal in Later Medieval English Literature." In Rosemary Horrox and Sarah Rees Jones, eds. *Pragmatic Utopias: Ideals and Communities, 1200–1630.* Cambridge: Cambridge University Press, 2001, pp. 11–25. Late medieval changes in monastic life affected the presentation of monks in secular English literature, including works by Langland, Chaucer, and Lydgate. Chaucer's presentation of monks in *GP*, *MkT*, and *ShT* reflects the "new monk," who uses practical abilities for spiritual good.

See also nos. 55, 116.

CT—The Nun's Priest and His Tale

252. Crépin, André. "The Cock, the Priest, and the Poet." In Wendy Harding, ed. *Drama, Narrative, and Poetry in* The Canterbury Tales *(SAC*

27 [2005], no. 114), pp. 227–36. In *NPT*, the Nuns' Priest (*Nonnes* is plural) confesses his own temptations of lust and pride, under the guise of Chauntecleer. The priest is another persona of Chaucer the poet, interested in the same topics (dreams, astronomy, free will, the biter bit) and apprehensive about the effects of rhetoric.

253. Raybin, David. "Poetry and Play in the *Nun's Priest's Tale* and the *Pardoner's Tale*." In Wendy Harding, ed. *Drama, Narrative, and Poetry in* The Canterbury Tales (*SAC* 27 [2005], no. 114), pp. 213–26. Raybin interrogates challenges to the dramatic approach to *CT*, concentrating on the personalities of the narrators of *NPT* and *PardT*. The Pardoner and Chauntecleer share a number of characteristics and artfully mix sentence and solace. Their voices articulate an aspect of Chaucer and convey a coherent message about the purposes of pilgrimage.

254. Thomas, Paul R. "Chaucer Transforming His Source: From Chantecler and Pinte to Chauntecleer and Pertelote." *Journal of the Utah Academy of Sciences, Arts, and Letters* 75 (1998): 82–90. Contrasts aspects of *NPT* with *Roman de Renart* Branch IIIa to show that Chaucer makes his rooster more masculine and his hen more feminine than in the source. Includes a translation of Branch IIIa, 4175–4315.

See also nos. 77, 107, 116, 139, 156, 161, 165, 167.

CT—The Second Nun and Her Tale

255. Ashton, Gail. "Bridging the Difference: Reconceptualising the Angel in Medieval Hagiography." *L&T* 16 (2002): 235–47. Uses Luce Irigaray's notion of the "ethics of alterity" to explore the fusion of masculine and feminine in the depiction of angels in several medieval narratives, including Marian accounts and Chaucer's and Bokenham's stories of Saint Cecilia. In *SNT* and elsewhere, angels are masculine constructs, associated with sight, but they are also feminized symbols associated with smell, sound, and touch.

256. Hirsh, John C. "Feminism and Spirituality in Chaucer: *The Second Nun's Tale*." In John C. Hirsh. *The Boundaries of Faith: The Development and Transmission of Medieval Spirituality*. Studies in the History of Christian Thought, no. 67. Leiden: Brill, 1996, pp. 78–90. Revised version of "The Second Nun's Tale," first published in C. David Benson

and Elizabeth Robertson, eds. *Chaucer's Religious Tales* (*SAC* 14 [1992], no. 231).

See also nos. 9, 93, 116, 242.

CT—The Canon's Yeoman and His Tale

257. Brawer, Robert A. "Chaucer in Cyberspace." *Changing Times* 39.6 (2002): 11–12. Brawer compares infatuation with "dot.com start-ups" with aspects of *CYPT*, arguing caution in such ventures, given the number of repeated failures.

See nos. 71, 147, 172.

CT—The Manciple and His Tale

258. Børch, Marianne. "Chaucer's Poetics and the *Manciple's Tale*." *SAC* 25 (2003): 287–97. *ManT* asserts a "repressive poetics" that challenges fiction-making in *CT*—especially in *KnT*—and at the same time rejects the validity of penitential self-examination offered by the Parson.

259. Ginsberg, Warren. "The Manciple's Tale: Response." *SAC* 25 (2003): 331–37. Comments on the five contributions to *SAC* 25's "Colloquium: *The Manciple's Tale*," reading them as a "snapshot of some of the ways . . . Chaucerians read today" and exploring how the interruptions and reversals in *ManT* efface moral distinctions. See nos. 258 and 260–63.

260. Hines, John. "'For sorwe of which he brak his minstralcye': The Demise of the 'Sweete Noyse' of Verse in the *Canterbury Tales*." *SAC* 25 (2003): 299–308. *ManT* and the depiction of the Manciple reflect Chaucer's effort to undermine bourgeois threats to court culture, his critique of practical "wit," and, simultaneously, his affirmation of the destructive power of adultery.

261. Salisbury, Eve. "Murdering Fiction: The Case of *The Manciple's Tale*." *SAC* 25 (2003): 309–16. Considers the acceptance of "spousal homicide" in *ManT* and the "perfunctory dismissal" of the *Tale* in *ParsP*, arguing that the shift from legal to penitential concerns eludes indictment for the murder.

262. Travis, Peter W. "The Manciple's Phallic Matrix." *SAC* 25 (2003): 317–24. Psychoanalytic analysis of *ManT* as "an example of a

narrator's strenuously repressing the maternal yet subliminally negotiating its inevitable return." Various features of the *Tale* are projections of infantile "primal" relations with the mother: "sensorimotor disorder, oral consumption, human aggression, language, and the demonized feminine."

263. Trigg, Stephanie. "Friendship, Association, and Service in *The Manciple's Tale*." *SAC* 25 (2003): 325–30. *ManPT* set in opposition two kinds of homosociability: friendship and service. The irresolution of the opposition reflects Chaucer's anxieties about his status as servant and poet.

See also nos. 8, 93, 109, 119, 149.

CT—The Parson and His Tale

See nos. 14, 107, 140, 149, 158, 167, 215, 230, 234, 258.

CT—Chaucer's Retraction

See nos. 14, 144, 202, 230.

Anelida and Arcite

See nos. 49, 172.

A Treatise on the Astrolabe

See no. 34.

Boece

See no. 52.

The Book of the Duchess

264. Bourquin, Guy. "La non-métamorphose de Céyx et Alcyone dans le *Livre de la Duchesse* de Chaucer." In Adrian Papahagi, ed. *Métamorphoses* (*SAC* 27 [2005], no. 130), pp. 218–29. In *BD*, the omission of the transformation of Ceyx and Alcyone—included in other versions

of the narrative—runs counter to the expectation of readers, thus exacerbating the anticonsolatory element in the adjacent narrator's dream.

265. McDonald, Rick. "The Christianization of Classical Myth: Chaucer's Use of Ovid in *The Book of the Duchess*." *Journal of the Utah Academy of Sciences, Arts, and Letters* 75 (1998): 76–81. Chaucer's version of the Seys-Alcyone story differs from its predecessors in ways that emphasize how love can transcend death, helping to make the consolation of the poem particularly Christian.

266. Rašovic, Tiffany. "Chaucer's *Book of the Duchess* and the Limits of Narrative." *Year's Work in Medievalism* 14 (1999): 67–79. Explores in *BD* Chaucer's attitudes toward language and its (in)ability to communicate successfully. The skepticism or nominalism of *BD* is modified by indications of the power of "extra-linguistic" symbols and signs, providing some "rescue from despair."

267. Wetherbee, Winthrop. "Theme, Prosody, and Mimesis in the *Book of the Duchess*." In Alan T. Gaylord, ed. *Essays on the Art of Chaucer's Verse* (*SAC* 25 [2003], no. 64), pp. 283–95. The "seeming eccentricities" in the verse of *BD* are an index to the poem's "complex intention." Close reading demonstrates how variations in verse communicate "the delicate psychological process the poem describes."

See also nos. 24, 88, 91, 93, 98, 116, 117, 206.

The Equatorie of the Planetis

See no. 74.

The House of Fame

268. Prescott, Anne Worthington. *Imagining Fame: An Introduction to Geoffrey Chaucer's* The House of Fame. Santa Barbara, Calif.: Fithian, 2003. 126 pp. Prescott introduces *HF* to the general reader as simple to read, yet full of Chaucer's mischievous fun. In *HF*, Chaucer reveals the way fame was viewed by his contemporaries, plus the way he thinks they and we should see it. He gives readers much to laugh about as he travels through the universe poking fun at pomposity and disclosing unfairness in the world of celebrity.

See also nos. 24, 46, 48, 55, 88, 91, 93, 116, 280.

The Legend of Good Women

269. Aloni, Gila. "What Chaucer's 'Good Women' Dared Not Say." In Leo Carruthers and Adrian Papahagi, eds. *Paroles et silences dans la littérature anglaise au Moyen Âge* (*SAC* 27 [2005], no. 96), pp. 119–34. Three concerns in *LGW*—space in "Thisbe," rhetoric in "Lucrece," and the exchange of women in "Hypsipyle and Medea"—demonstrate that the power of apparently passive women lies in their moral superiority over men.

270. Boffey, Julia, and A. S. G. Edwards. "The *Legend of Good Women*." In Piero Boitani and Jill Mann, eds. *The Cambridge Companion to Chaucer*, 2nd ed. (*SAC* 27 [2005], no. 92), pp. 112–26. Boffey and Edwards confront several scholarly and critical issues that pertain to *LGW*: date, occasion, sources and models, patronage, and the relation of the F and G versions of *LGWP*. The authors emphasize the variety in the legends themselves and suggest that the narrator grows impatient as the legends accumulate.

271. Dor, Juliette. "Virgile et Ovide métamorphosés: Didon sanctifiée par Chaucer." In Adrian Papahagi, ed. *Métamorphoses* (*SAC* 27 [2005], no. 130), pp. 197–218. In *LGW*, Chaucer questions his two major sources—Virgil's *Aeneid* and Ovid's *Heroides*—to express the naked text of the myth and, simultaneously, to assert his own authority. Aeneas is selfish and irresponsible in *LGW* (Chaucer's third treatment after *BD* and *HF*); Dido is a saint of love who combines the attributes of the heroine of a medieval romance with those of a martyr.

272. Hamaguchi, Keiko. "'For Thorgh Yow Is My Name Lorn': Does Dido Accuse Virgil and Aeneas in the *House of Fame?*" *Doshisha Literature* 46 (2003): 1–17. Postcolonial analysis of the Dido account in *LGW* reveals that when Dido accuses Aeneas of ruining her reputation, Chaucer simultaneously accuses Virgil of "epistemic imperialism," a function of the "unreliability of representation." Hamaguchi compares Chaucer's Dido with Bertha Mason of Jean Rhys's *Wide Sargasso Sea*.

273. Nakao, Yoshiyuki. "Chaucer's Ambiguity in *The Legend of Good Women*." *ERA* [English Research Association of Hiroshima] 6.1 (1988): 14–49. Discusses Chaucer's ambiguous use of words such as *sely*, *gentil*, and *pite* in *LGW*, clarifying the gap between efforts to define "good women" and their human weaknesses.

274. Palmer, R. Barton. "Chaucer's *Legend of Good Women*: The Narrator's Tale." In Robert G. Benson and Susan J. Ridyard, eds. *New Read-*

ings of Chaucer's Poetry (*SAC* 27 [2005], no. 90), pp. 183–94. Palmer argues that *LGW* is not merely a collection of tales retold from Ovid; it is also the story of the narrator's problematic relationship to the God of Love.

275. Tinkle, Theresa. "The Imagined Chaucerian Community of Bodleian MS Fairfax 16." In Donka Minkova and Theresa Tinkle, eds. *Chaucer and the Challenges of Medievalism: Studies in Honor of H. A. Kelly* (*SAC* 27 [2005], no. 125), pp. 157–74. The treatment of Cupid in the various works of Bodleian MS Fairfax 16 reveals a cultural transition from the Gallic tradition of the supremacy of love—and from the Latinate tradition of the supremacy of religion—to a new English poetic tradition. This new tradition appeals specifically to a community of men, both educated and uneducated, as sufferers in the tradition and writers of the genre. Tinkle includes discussion of *LGW*.

See also nos. 45, 46, 50, 65, 88, 91, 108, 115, 116, 157, 162, 229.

The Parliament of Fowls

276. Krier, Theresa M. *Birth Passages: Maternity and Nostalgia, Antiquity to Shakespeare.* Ithaca: Cornell University Press, 2001. xvii, 266 pp. Treats Chaucer's topoi of bird song, maternal goddess Nature, voice, mother tongue, and biblical gardens in *PF*. Argues that the movement from aggressive plot to lyric in the poem and its male protagonist's oblique approach to the maternal draw the reader into an ethical stance of welcoming natality, the mother's otherness, and the pleasures of maternal sound. Compares Chaucer's treatment to works by Spenser and Shakespeare.

277. Newman, Barbara. "Did Goddesses Empower Women? The Case of Dame Nature." In Mary C. Erler and Maryanne Kowaleski, eds. *Gendering the Master Narrative: Women and Power in the Middle Ages.* Ithaca: Cornell University Press, 2003, pp. 135–55. Traces two medieval constructions of Nature as goddess: the antifeminist tradition that runs from Alan de Lille through Jean de Meun to Chaucer's *PF*, and the relatively profeminist legacy of Heldris of Cornwall (*Roman de Silence*) and Christine de Pizan.

See also nos. 16, 17, 24, 45, 46, 77, 88, 99, 116, 131.

The Romaunt of the Rose

See nos. 73, 74, 161.

Troilus and Criseyde

278. Bankert, Dabney Anderson. "Secularizing the Word: Conversion Models in Chaucer's *Troilus and Criseyde*." *ChauR* 37 (2003): 196–218. Conversions in *TC* are modeled ironically on those of Saint Paul and Saint Augustine. Like Paul, Troilus cannot escape his fate; he can only accept and serve. Like Augustine, Criseyde vainly tries to master the narrative that is out of her control.

279. Condren, Edward I. "The Disappointments of Criseyde." In Donka Minkova and Theresa Tinkle, eds. *Chaucer and the Challenges of Medievalism: Studies in Honor of H. A. Kelly* (*SAC* 27 [2005], no. 125), pp. 195–204. In *TC*, Criseyde's appeals to Hector for clarification of her status in Troy suggest that Criseyde seeks a romantic response from Hector rather than the official response she receives. This disappointment acts as a catalyst for future behavior in the narrative.

280. Federico, Sylvia. *New Troy: Fantasies of Empire in the Late Middle Ages*. Medieval Cultures, no. 36. Minneapolis and London: University of Minnesota Press, 2003. xxiv, 207 pp. Federico combines historicism and psychoanalysis to explore the "fascination with Troy" in late medieval England as a "symbolic appropriation" and a means of establishing English identity. Examines the gendered representations of Troy in Gower's *Vox Clamantis* and in Richard Maidstone's *Concordia facta inter regem Riccardum II et civitatem Londoniae*; assesses how the protagonists of *Sir Gawain and the Green Knight* and *HF* reflect the notion of a flawed Aeneas. In *TC*, Criseyde's innocence "figures the contemporary cultural nostalgia" for a "new Troy made clean." In Gower's *Confessio Amantis* and Lydgate's *Troy Book*, the "Lancastrian empire" rethinks its Ricardian past. Throughout, the female characters of Troy are used to create the masculinist illusion that some versions of history are true and others false.

281. Fumo, Jamie C. "'Little *Troilus*': *Heroides* 5 and Its Ovidian Contexts in Chaucer's *Troilus and Criseyde*." *SP* 100 (2003): 278–314. Fumo analyzes Chaucer's use of Ovid's *Heroides* 5 (Oenone's letter to Paris) in *TC*, discussing Chaucer's sustained and allusive use of this text and its "metanarrative function" in the structure of *TC*.

282. Gilles, Sealy. "Love and Disease in Chaucer's *Troilus and Criseyde.*" *SAC* 25 (2003): 157–97. Reads the depiction of Troilus's love-sickness against "new theories of contagion" that resulted from the devastations of the plague. Criseyde internalizes the antifeminist "logic of disease" and names herself the "infective other." Troilus's "love-sickness mimics the progress of a viral infection" and leads—in his "apotheosis"—to a cure only when his body leaves the "earthbound cycle of contagion."

283. Hill, John. "Aristocratic Friendship in *Troilus and Criseyde:* Pandarus, Courtly Love, and Ciceronian Brotherhood in Troy." In Robert G. Benson and Susan J. Ridyard, eds. *New Readings of Chaucer's Poetry* (*SAC* 27 [2005], no. 90), pp. 165–82. In light of Cicero's *De amicitia,* the noble friendship between Troilus and Pandarus helps to elevate *TC* to a great tragedy.

284. Kolve, V. A. "Looking at the Sun in Chaucer's *Troilus and Criseyde.*" In Donka Minkova and Theresa Tinkle, eds. *Chaucer and the Challenges of Medievalism: Studies in Honor of H. A. Kelly* (*SAC* 27 [2005], no. 125), pp. 31–71. Kolve investigates the iconic importance of Criseyde's dream of the eagle and Troilus's dream of the boar and their embedded affiliations with the sun. In *TC*, these images illustrate the gap in the worth of two men and underscore the poor choice Criseyde makes.

285. Martin, Carl Grey. " 'Bitraised Thorugh False Folk': Criseyde, the Siege, and the Threat of Treason." *ChauR* 37 (2003): 219–33. The romance "The Siege of Thebes" being read by Criseyde at the beginning of the poem prepares us for her preoccupation with "siege" throughout the work. Pandarus persuades her to conceptualize Troilus as an antidote for the siege's danger, while Troy depends on the expense of the war effort. Traded to the Greeks, Criseyde becomes an outsider, joining the ranks of expatriates and exiles incessantly shifting around her.

286. Massey, Jeff. " 'The *Double Bind* of Troilus to Tellen': The Time of the Gift in Chaucer's *Troilus and Criseyde.*" *ChauR* 38 (2003): 16–35. *TC* exhibits a notable conflict between gift and not-gift economics—between ideal giving and practical commodity exchange. The rules of courtly love, ostensibly designed to ennoble the lover and enable "true" love, in practice disallow unconditional giving and reduce true love to commodity. The theories of Mauss and Derrida can profitably be applied to this text.

287. McAlpine, Monica E. "Criseyde's Prudence." *SAC* 25 (2003): 199–224. In her "active suffering," Criseyde reflects a Boethian notion

of agency. In her prudential counseling of Troilus, she properly dissuades him from "treasonable elopement in time of war." The article explores how Criseyde's advice to Troilus and her later commentary on Prudence (*TC* 5.744–49) reflect her fundamental *trouthe*. McAlpine contrasts Criseyde's perspectives with those of Troilus, Calkas, and Cassandra to disclose Chaucer's anxieties about how knowledge of the future can distort ethical judgment.

288. Mehl, Dieter. "A Note on *Troilus and Criseyde*: Shakespeare Reading Chaucer." In Boika Sokolova and Evgenia Pancheva, eds. *Renaissance Refractions: Essays in Honour of Alexander Shurbanov*. Sofia: St. Kliment Ohridski University Press, 2001, pp. 47–54. Compares how Chaucer's Criseyde and Shakespeare's Cressida reflect each respective author's concerns with literary and historical authority.

289. Nakao, Yoshiyuki. "Allegory and Realism in Chaucer." *Hiroshima Studies in English Language and Literature* 29 (1985): 15–26 (in Japanese). Discusses Chaucer's organic use of allegory in *TC* and *MerT*, focusing on personified abstractions.

290. ———. "Causality in Chaucer's *Troilus and Criseyde*: Semantic Tension Between the Pragmatic and Narrative Domains." In Masahiko Kanno, Gregory K. Jember, and Yoshiyuki Nakao, eds. *A Love of Words: English Philological Studies in Honour of Akira Wada* (*SAC* 27 [2005], no. 118), pp. 79–102. Explores the "ambiguity of causality as a measure of the moral status" of the narrator and characters of *TC*, particularly Criseyde. Nakao tabulates and examines causal phrases beginning with *because*, *since*, and *for* in light of their contexts and intentions.

291. ———. "Chaucer's Ambiguity in *Troilus and Criseyde*: Degrees of the Relation Between Verbal Elements from the Reader's Viewpoint." In Yoshiyuki Nakao and Akiyuki Jimura, eds. *Originality and Adventure: Essays on English Language and Literature in Honour of Masahiko Kanno*. Tokyo: Eihosha, 2001, pp. 225–59 (in Japanese). Discusses how and why ambiguity is likely in *TC*, focusing on the relations between verbal elements such as contiguous structure.

292. ———. "Lexis and Context in Chaucer: *Slydynge* and Its Related Words in *Troilus and Criseyde*." In *English and English Teaching: A Festschrift in Honour of Prof. Hisashi Takahashi and Prof. Jiro Igarashi*. Hiroshima: Department of English, Faculty of School Education, Hiroshima University, 1993, pp. 177–85 (in Japanese). Discusses *slydynge* and related words (such as *kynde* and *pite*) with regard to Criseyde's

characterization. Examines also the syntactic structures containing those words.

293. ————. "The Structure of Chaucer's Ambiguity: A Focus on 'God loveth . . .' in *Troilus and Criseyde* 3.12–14." In Masahiko Kanno, ed. *Ful of Hy Sentence: Lexical Studies in English.* Tokyo: Eihosha, 2003, pp. 21–33 (in Japanese). Explores ambiguity arising from the polysemy of *love* in *TC*, with a comparative note on *charite* and *amor/ous*.

294. ————. "Syntactic Ambiguity in Chaucer's *Troilus and Criseyde.*" *English and English-American Literature* (Yamaguchi University) 28 (1993): 53–76. Examines the syntactic fluidity that parallels Criseyde's shifting psychology.

295. ————. "The Textual Variants of Chaucer's *Troilus and Criseyde* and the Question of Readings." *English and English-American Literature* (Yamaguchi University) 29 (1994): 51–94 (in Japanese). Textual variants in Chaucer's *TC* can indicate ambiguous interpretations.

296. Pearcy, Roy J. "Chaucer's *Troilus and Criseyde.*" *Expl* 61.2 (2003): 69–70. When Troilus kisses only Criseyde's eyes in *TC* 3.1352–55, the gesture marks a departure from Boccaccio, whose lovers kiss eyes, lips, and breasts. Following thirteenth-century French literary convention, the behavior may illustrate Chaucer's attempt to communicate the "alterity" of the antique culture.

297. Ruud, Jay. "Blinded by the Light: *Troilus'* Dawn Song and Christian Tradition." In Michelle Sauer, ed. *Proceedings of the 11th Annual Northern Plains Conference on Early British Literature* (*SAC* 27 [2005], no. 133), pp. 43–55. The dawn song in *TC* (3.1415–1526) stresses "contrast between the mundane love of the two lovers and the heavenly love associated with the dawn and the light in a Christian context."

298. Turner, Marion. "*Troilus and Criseyde* and the 'Treasonous Aldermen' of 1382: Tales of the City in Late Fourteenth-Century London." *SAC* 25 (2003): 225–57. Examines how records of the Uprising of 1381 reflect contemporary attitudes toward treason, truth, and social fragmentation. This background helps to clarify how *TC* undermines social idealism through its depictions of civil division and betrayal—Troilus's, Criseyde's, Pandarus's, and that of Helen and Deiphoebus. Troy is destroyed from the inside.

299. Zeitoun, Franck. "The Eagle, the Boar, and the Self: Dreams, Daydreams, and Violence in *Troilus and Criseyde.*" *Cercles* 6 (2003): 45–53. Zeitoun studies dreams and daydreams in *TC*, especially daydreaming in Book 1, Criseyde's dream of the eagle, and Troilus's dream of the

boar. Violence in the poem has less to do with war than with the internal states of the characters; these states are allegories of love and symbols of the characters' lack of free will.

See also nos. 45, 59, 79, 82, 85, 86, 88, 93, 98, 109, 116, 117, 131, 157, 162, 187.

Lyrics and Short Poems

300. Kendrick, Laura. "Chaucer's 'Many a Leccherous Lay' and the Bawdy Balades in Paris, Arsenal MS Fr. 5203." *BAM* 63 (2003): 35–56. Kendrick explores the transgressive use of the balade for noncourtly discourse on sex and women in the period just before Chaucer and Deschamps.

301. Wong, Jennifer. "Chaucer's 'Boethian' Lyrics." *CarmP* 11 (2002): 93–116. In mood and details, *Form Age* and *For* enable us to see Chaucer's pessimistic attitudes toward "Boethian concerns." *Truth*, *Gent*, and *Sted* also emphasize the wretchedness of the present world rather than recognition of divine order and the consolation of detachment from the world.

See also no. 116.

An ABC

See nos. 14, 108, 131, 159.

The Envoy to Bukton

See no. 152.

The Envoy to Scogan

See no. 152.

The Former Age

302. Gwiazda, Piotr. "Reading the Commonplace: Boethius, Chaucer, and the Myth of the Golden Age." *CarmP* 11 (2002): 75–91. Reads

Form Age as a "document of hope"; its lamentation of present ills recalls the Golden Age of the past but does so to provide a blueprint for a perfect and enduring future.

See also nos. 163, 301.

Fortune

See no. 301.

Gentilesse

See no. 301.

Lak of Stedfastnesse

303. Edwards, A. S. G. "A New Version of Part of Chaucer's 'Lak of Stedfastnesse.'" *Archiv* 240 (2003): 106–8. British Library MS Additional 37049 contains a variant of the third stanza of *Sted*. The most striking feature is the translation from rhyme royal into couplets. The stanza suggests memorial transmission.

See also nos. 163, 301.

Truth

See no. 301.

Chaucerian Apocrypha

See nos. 22, 37.

Book Reviews

304. Aers, David, ed. *Medieval Literature and Historical Inquiry: Essays in Honor of Derek Pearsall* (*SAC* 25 [2003], no. 87). Rev. John M. Ganim, *SAC* 25 (2003): 339–44; Wendy Scase, *Speculum* 78 (2003): 1239–40.

305. Archibald, Elizabeth. *Incest and the Medieval Imagination* (*SAC* 25 [2003], no. 88). Rev. Georgiana Donavin, *SAC* 25 (2003): 344–48.

306. Baker, Denise N., ed. *Inscribing the Hundred Years' War in French and English Cultures* (*SAC* 24 [2002], no. 133). Rev. Peter Brown, *Speculum* 78 (2003): 132–34.

307. Barr, Helen. *Socioliterary Practice in Late Medieval England* (*SAC* 25 [2003], no. 89). Rev. Andrew Galloway, *Speculum* 78 (2003): 456–58; Roger Ladd, *SCJ* 34 (2003): 1214–15; Veronica O'Mara, *Anglia*, 121 (2003): 476–77; Lee Patterson, *N&Q* 248 (2003): 99–100.

308. Braswell, Mary Flowers. *Chaucer's "Legal Fiction": Reading the Records* (*SAC* 25 [2003], no. 93). Rev. Candace Barrington, *SAC* 25 (2003): 353–56; Thomas J. Farrell, *Speculum* 78 (2003): 1256–58.

309. Brown, Peter, ed. *A Companion to Chaucer* (*SAC* 24 [2002], no. 140). Rev. Fritz Kemmler, *Anglia* 121 (2003): 308–13; Yoshiyuki Nakao, *SIMELL* 18 (2003): 64–70 (in Japanese); Nigel Saul, *EHR* 118 (2003): 765–66.

310. Bullón-Fernández, María. *Fathers and Daughters in Gower's* Confessio Amantis*: Authority, Family, State, and Writing* (*SAC* 25 [2003], no. 95). Rev. Richard W. Fehrenbacher, *SAC* 25 (2003): 356–59.

311. Burger, Glenn, and Steven Kruger, eds. *Queering the Middle Ages* (*SAC* 25 [2003], no. 97). Rev. Valerie Allen, *SAC* 25 (2003): 359–62; Katherine Crawford, *SCJ* 34 (2003): 274–75; Greg J. Wilsbacher, *CollL* 30 (2003): 195–203.

312. Burrow, J. A. *Gestures and Looks in Medieval Narrative* (*SAC* 26 [2004], no. 120). Rev. Mary Theresa Hall, *SCJ* 34 (2003): 1155–57; Victoria Simmons, *Comitatus* 34 (2003): 214–17.

313. Collette, Carolyn P. *Species, Phantasms, and Images: Vision and Medieval Psychology in "The Canterbury Tales"* (*SAC* 25 [2003], no. 154). Rev. Andreea [*sic*] D. Boboc, *Rev* 25 (2003): 261–68; Warren Ginsberg, *Speculum* 78 (2003): 149–52.

314. Correale, Robert M., and Mary Hamel, eds. *Sources and Analogues of "The Canterbury Tales."* Vol. 1 (*SAC* 26 [2004], no. 47). Rev. Charlotte C. Morse, *N&Q* 248 (2003): 228–29; Daniel Wekelin, *RES* 54 (2003): 516–17.

315. Crane, Susan. *The Performance of Self: Ritual, Clothing, and Identity During the Hundred Years' War* (*SAC* 26 [2004], no. 126). Rev. Lynn T. Ramey, *Arthuriana* 13 (2003): 104–7.

316. Cullen, Dolores L. *Chaucer's Pilgrims: The Allegory* (*SAC* 24 [2002], no. 202). Rev. Norman Klassen, *MÆ* 72 (2003): 327–29.

317. Delany, Sheila, ed. *Chaucer and the Jews: Sources, Contexts, Mean-

ings (*SAC* 26 [2004], no. 129). Rev. John Micheal Crafton, *C&L* 52 (2003): 569–72.

318. Dyas, Dee. *Pilgrimage in Medieval English Literature, 700–1500* (*SAC* 25 [2003], no. 155). Rev. Allen J. Frantzen, *Speculum* 78 (2003): 1283–84; Anne Hudson, *RES* 54 (2003): 402–4.

319. Edwards, Robert R. *Chaucer and Boccaccio: Antiquity and Modernity* (*SAC* 26 [2004], no. 49). Rev. Karla Taylor, *MÆ* 72 (2003): 326–27.

320. Ellis, Steve. *Chaucer at Large: The Poet in the Modern Imagination* (*SAC* 24 [2002], no. 75). Rev. Derek Brewer, *JEGP* 102 (2003): 426; R. Radulescu, *Parergon* 19 (2002): 192–93.

321. Fenster, Thelma S., and Clare A. Lees, eds. *Gender in Debate from the Early Middle Ages to the Renaissance* (*SAC* 26 [2004], no. 212). Rev. Merry Wiesner-Hanks, *SCJ* 34 (2003): 555–56.

322. Forni, Kathleen. *The Chaucerian Apocrypha: A Counterfeit Canon* (*SAC* 25 [2003], no. 292). Rev. John M. Bowers, *SAC* 25 (2003): 369–71; A. S. G. Edwards, *N&Q* 248 (2003): 96; Mary Theresa Hall, *SCJ* 34 (2003): 607–8; H. L. Spencer, *RES* 54 (2003): 109–10.

323. Foster, Edward E., and David H. Carey. *Chaucer's Church: A Dictionary of Religious Terms in Chaucer* (*SAC* 26 [2004], no. 4). Rev. Fritz Kemmler, *Anglia* 121 (2003): 308–13.

324. Gaylord, Alan T., ed. *Essays on the Art of Chaucer's Verse* (*SAC* 25 [2003], no. 64). Rev. T. L. Burton, *SAC* 25 (2003): 372–74.

325. Ginsberg, Warren. *Chaucer's Italian Tradition* (*SAC* 26 [2004], no. 50). Rev. Helen Cooper, *MLR* 98 (2002): 808–9; Daniel Pinti, *MÆ* 72 (2003): 329–30; Sherry Roush, *RenQ* 56 (2003): 543–44.

326. Goodall, John A. *God's House at Ewelme: Life, Devotion, and Architecture in a Fifteenth-Century Almshouse* (*SAC* 26 [2004], no. 14). Rev. Susan Powell, *JEBS* 6 (2003): 192–93.

327. Green, Richard Firth. *A Crisis of Truth: Literature and Law in Ricardian England* (*SAC* 23 [2001], no. 92). Rev. Elizabeth Fowler, *Speculum* 78 (2003): 179–82.

328. Hildalgo, Ana Sáez. *Geoffrey Chaucer: Troilo y Criseida* (*SAC* 25 [2003], no. 17). Rev. María Bullón-Fernández, *SAC* 25 (2003): 374–77.

329. Hodges, Laura F. *Chaucer and Costume: The Secular Pilgrims in the General Prologue* (*SAC* 24 [2002], no. 229). Rev. Alan T. Gaylord, *JEGP* 102 (2003): 149–52.

330. Holsinger, Bruce W. *Music, Body, and Desire in Medieval Culture: Hildegard of Bingen to Chaucer* (*SAC* 26 [2004], no. 136). Rev. James

Borders, *Speculum* 78 (2003): 518–20; Warren Ginsberg, *CL* 55 (2003): 78–81; Seth Lerer, *MLQ* 64 (2003): 380–83.

331. Jacobs, Kathryn. *Marriage Contracts from Chaucer to the Renaissance Stage* (*SAC* 25 [2003], no. 157). Rev. Mary Flowers Braswell, *SAC* 25 (2003): 386–89; Nancy Gutierrez, *RenQ* 56 (2003): 544–45; Henry Ansgar Kelly, *Speculum* 78 (2003): 1321–32; Shannon McSheffrey, *SCJ* 34 (2003): 608–10; Greg J. Wilsbacher, *CollL* 30 (2003): 195–203.

332. Johnston, Andrew James. *Clerks and Courtiers: Chaucer, Late Middle English Literature, and the State Formation Process* (*SAC* 25 [2003], no. 111). Rev. John M. Bowers, *MÆ* 72 (2003): 326–27; Fritz Kemmler, *Anglia* 121 (2003): 308–13; Maura B. Nolan, *SAC* 25 (2003): 389–91; Emily Steiner, *JEGP* 102 (2003): 134–38.

333. Jones, Timothy S., and David A. Sprunger, eds. *Marvels, Monsters, and Miracles: Studies in the Medieval and Early Modern Imaginations* (*SAC* 26 [2004], no. 139). Rev. Norbert A. Wethington, *PMAM* 9 (2002): 134–36.

334. Kawasaki, Masatoshi. *Chaucer's Literary World: "Game" and Its Topography* (*SAC* 19 [1997], no. 102). Rev. Noriko Matsui, *SIMELL* 15 (2000): 93–103 (in Japanese).

335. Kerby-Fulton, Kathryn, and Maidie Hilmo, eds. *The Medieval Reader: Reception and Cultural History in the Late Medieval Manuscript.* New York: AMS Press, 2001. xviii, 256 pp. Rev. Jessica Brantley, *SAC* 25 (2003): 393–96.

336. Knapp, Peggy A. *Time-Bound Words: Semantic and Social Economies from Chaucer's England to Shakespeare's* (*SAC* 24 [2002], no. 107). Rev. Albrecht Classen, *FCS* 28 (2003): 263–64.

337. Krier, Theresa M., ed. *Refiguring Chaucer in the Renaissance* (*SAC* 22 [2000], no. 73). Rev. Isamu Saito, *SIMELL* 16 (2001): 93–101.

338. Lynch, Kathryn L. *Chaucer's Philosophical Visions* (*SAC* 24 [2002], no. 171). Rev. Mark Miller, *SAC* 25 (2003): 399–402; James Simpson, *MLR* 98 (2203): 426–27.

339. Matthews, David, ed. *The Invention of Middle English: An Anthology of Primary Sources* (*SAC* 24 [2002], no. 173). Rev. John H. Fisher, *SAC* 25 (2003): 402–5.

340. Mehl, Dieter. *English Literature in the Age of Chaucer* (*SAC* 25 [2003], no. 120). Rev. J. A. Burrow, *Archiv* 240 (2003): 182–83.

341. Minnis, A. J., ed. *Middle English Poetry: Texts and Traditions. Essays in Honour of Derek Pearsall* (*SAC* 25 [2003], no. 121). Rev. John M. Ganim, *SAC* 25 (2003): 339–44; Simon Horobin, *JEBS* 6 (2003):

200–203; Dieter Mehl, *Archiv* 240 (2003): 175–76; Ronald Waldron, *N&Q* 248 (2003): 93–94.

342. Morey, James H. *Book and Verse: A Guide to Middle English Biblical Literature* (*SAC* 24 [2002], no. 175). Rev. Michael G. Sargent, *SAC* 25 (2003): 408–11.

343. *New Medieval Literatures.* Volumes 3 and 4 (*SAC* 24 [2002], no. 354; *SAC* 25 [2003], nos. 47, 56, and 294). Rev. Joerg O. Fichte, *Archiv* 240 (2003): 176–79.

344. Ogilvie-Thomson, S. J., ed. *The Index of Middle English Prose: Handlist XVI. Manuscripts in the Laudian Collection, Bodleian Library, Oxford* (*SAC* 24 [2002], no. 57). Rev. Veronica O'Mara, *Archiv* 240 (2003): 179–81.

345. Percival, Florence. *Chaucer's Legendary Good Women* (*SAC* 22 [2000], no. 301). Rev. Laura L. Howes, *Speculum* 78 (2003): 244–46.

346. Pratt, John H. *Chaucer and War* (*SAC* 24 [2002], no. 183). Rev. John M. Hill, *MLR* 98 (2003): 161–62.

347. Prendergast, Thomas A., and Barbara Kline, eds. *Rewriting Chaucer: Culture, Authority, and the Idea of the Authentic Text, 1400–1602* (*SAC* 23 [2001], no. 112). Rev. Kate Gartner Frost, *Libraries and Culture* 38 (2003): 407–8.

348. Quinn, William A., ed. *Chaucer's Dream Visions and Shorter Poems* (*SAC* 23 [2001], no. 113). Rev. P. Whiteford, *Parergon* 19 (2002): 221–23.

349. Rhodes, Jim. *Poetry Does Theology: Chaucer, Grosseteste, and the Pearl-Poet* (*SAC* 25 [2003], no. 129). Rev. Lawrence Besserman, *SAC* 25 (2003): 413–16.

350. Robertson, Elizabeth, and Christine M. Rose, eds. *Representing Rape in Medieval and Early Modern Literature* (*SAC* 25 [2003], no. 130). Rev. Michael Calabrese, *SAC* 25 (2003): 416–20; Daniel Kline, *Medieval Feminist Forum* 36 (2003): 62–64.

351. Russell, J. Stephen. *Chaucer and the Trivium: The Mindsong of the Canterbury Tales* (*SAC* 22 [2000], no. 184). Rev. Zacharias P. Thundy, *CarmP* 11 (2002): 117–20.

352. Saito, Isamu. *Chaucer: Ambiguity, Mischief, Piety* (*SAC* 24 [2002], no. 186). Rev. Masatoshi Kawasaki, *SIMELL* 15 (2000): 93–103 (in Japanese).

353. Salih, Sarah. *Versions of Virginity in Late Medieval England* (*SAC* 25 [2003], no. 134). Rev. Kathleen Ashley, *SAC* 25 (2003): 420–23.

354. Saunders, Corinne. *Chaucer* (*SAC* 25 [2003], no. 136). Rev.

Roger Dalrymple, *RMSt* 29 (2003): 82–83; Fritz Kemmler, *Anglia* 121 (2003): 308–13.

355. ⸻. *Rape and Ravishment in the Literature of Medieval England* (*SAC* 25 [2003], no. 137). Rev. Dieter Mehl, *Archiv* 240 (2003): 187–88.

356. Schildgen, Brenda Deen. *Pagans, Tartars, Moslems, and Jews in Chaucer's* Canterbury Tales (*SAC* 25 [2003], no. 165). Rev. Lois Bragg, *SAC* 25 (2003): 426–29; Jennifer R. Goodman, *Speculum* 78 (2003): 1398–1400; John C. Hirsh, *MÆ* 72 (2003): 136–37; H. L. Spencer, *RES* 54 (2003): 517–19; Theresa Tinkle, *Rev* 25 (2003): 77–79.

357. Shoaf, R. Allen. *Chaucer's Body: The Anxiety of Circulation in the* Canterbury Tales (*SAC* 25 [2003], no. 166). Rev. Alcuin Blamires, *MÆ* 72 (2003): 135–36; Carolyn P. Collette, *SAC* 25 (2003): 429–31; John M. Ganim, *JEGP* 102 (2003): 146–49; Stephen Knight, *Speculum* 78 (2003): 1405–7.

358. Simpson, James. *Reform and Cultural Revolution, 1350–1547* (*SAC* 26 [2004], no. 152). Rev. Greg Walker, *EHR* 118 (2003): 766–67.

359. St. John, Michael. *Chaucer's Dream Visions: Courtliness and Individual Identity* (*SAC* 25 [2003], no. 140). Rev. P. Whiteford, *Parergon* 19 (2002): 231–34.

360. Steiner, Emily, and Candace Barrington, eds. *The Letter of the Law: Legal Practice and Literary Production in Medieval England* (*SAC* 26 [2004], no. 154). Rev. Wenxi Liu, *SCJ* 34 (2003): 510–11; Wendy J. Turner, *Comitatus* 34 (2003): 253–54.

361. Strohm, Paul. *Theory and the Premodern Text* (*SAC* 24 [2002], no. 191). Rev. John M. Bowers, *Speculum* 78 (2003): 1003–5.

362. Stubbs, Estelle, ed. *The Hengwrt Chaucer Digital Facsimile* (*SAC* 25 [2003], no. 19). Rev. Diane Watt, *SAC* 25 (2003): 436–38.

363. Sweeney, Michelle. *Magic in Medieval Romance from Chrétien de Troyes to Geoffrey Chaucer* (*SAC* 24 [2002], no. 285). Rev. Malcolm Jones, *MLR* 98 (2003): 948–49.

364. Taavitsainen, Irma, et al., eds. *Placing Middle English in Context* (*SAC* 24 [2002], no. 122). Rev. Thomas Honegger, *Anglia* 121 (2003): 108–10.

365. Trigg, Stephanie. *Congenial Souls: Reading Chaucer from Medieval to Postmodern* (*SAC* 26 [2004], no. 157). Rev. Helen Cooper, *SAC* 25 (2003): 438–41; John M. Ganim, *Parergon* 19 (2002): 239–40.

366. Wallace, David, ed. *The Cambridge History of Medieval English*

Literature (*SAC* 23 [2001], no. 124). Rev. D. S. Ortig, *SCJ* 34 (2003): 1160–61.

367. Webb, Diana. *Pilgrimage in Medieval England* (*SAC* 25 [2003], no. 168). Rev. Gary Dickson, *Speculum* 78 (2003): 627–29.

368. West, Richard. *Chaucer, 1340–1400: The Life and Times of the First English Poet* (*SAC* 24 [2002], no. 13). Rev. Peter G. Beidler, *SI-MELL* 17 (2002):101–5.

369. Wheatley, Edward. *Mastering Aesop: Medieval Education, Chaucer, and His Followers* (*SAC* 24 [2002], no. 319). Rev. A. E. Wright, *JEGP* 102 (2003): 586–89.

370. White, Hugh. *Nature, Sex, and Goodness in a Medieval Literary Tradition* (*SAC* 25 [2003], no. 144). Rev. Henry Ansgar Kelly, *SAC* 25 (2003): 450–53.

371. Wogan-Browne, Jocelyn; Rosalynn Voaden; Arlyn Diamond; Ann Hutchison; Carol M. Meale; and Lesley Johnson, eds. *Medieval Women: Texts and Contexts in Late Medieval Britain* (*SAC* 24 [2002], no. 194). Rev. Karen A. Winstead, *SAC* 25 (2003): 453–56.

Author Index—Bibliography

The New Chaucer Society
Fourteenth International Congress
July 15th–19th, 2004
University of Glasgow

"Regions, Nations, Empires"

THURSDAY 15TH JULY

14.00   **Trustees' Meeting**

15.00–16.30   **Special Sessions** with opportunities for discussion of collaborative and other work.

SS 'A': Scribes of Chaucer's Works
Organizer and Chair: Linne R. Mooney, University of Maine
- "The Scribe of British Library MSS Egerton 2864 and Additional 5140," Daniel Mosser, Virginia Tech
- "The Significance of Scribal Quirks," Orietta DaRold, Leeds University
- "An Augustinian Canon at Thurgarton and a Copy of Chaucer's *Treatise on the Astrolabe*," Catherine Eagleton, University of Maine
- "Scribes of Chaucer's *Troilus*," Simon Horobin, Glasgow University

17.00   **University Reception and Opening of Manuscript Exhibition, Hunterian Museum**

20.30   **Reception at home of Ruth Evans and Jonathan Sawday**

FRIDAY 16TH JULY

9.30–11.00   **Opening Meeting and Presidential Address**
- **Welcome from University of Glasgow hosts; Introductory remarks by Alcuin Blamires, Chair of the Programme Committee; Executive Director's Report by David Lawton.**
- **Presidential Address**
Chair: David Wallace, University of Pennsylvania
"Chaucer and the European Tradition," Winthrop Wetherbee III, Cornell University

11.00   **Coffee**

11.30–13.00   **Plenary Session: "Maps, Mapping, and the World of Chaucer"**
Chair: Julia Boffey, Queen Mary's University of London
- "Comparative Cartographies: Opicinus de Canistris and the Remapping of Europe," Diane O. Hughes, University of Michigan

- "Revolutionary Space and the Pain of Martyrs," James Simpson, Harvard University

13.00   **Lunch**

14.00–15.30   **Concurrent session (A): papers**

PR 1: Home
Organiser and Chair: Matthew Boyd Goldie, Rider University
- "The Falcon's Mew," Elizabeth Allen, University of California, Irvine
- "Chaucer's Household Economies," Brian Gastle, Western Carolina University
- "Her is non hoom," Priscilla Martin, St. Edmund Hall, Oxford University
- "Trading Spaces in the 'Reeve's Tale,'" Jo Koster, Winthrop University

PR 2: Cultural Translation in the Age of Chaucer
Organiser and Chair: Warren Ginsberg, University of Oregon
- "'And with this swerd shall I sleen envie': Images of Aggression in Chaucer's Theory of Translation," Brendan O'Connell, Trinity College, Dublin
- "Gilbert Banester and the Motives of Translation," Karla Taylor, University of Michigan, Ann Arbor
- "From Summa to Summary: Chaucer the Translator as Homely Scholar," Krista Twu, University of Minnesota, Duluth
- "Chaucer Translates the Matter of Spain," Robert F. Yeager, University of West Florida

PR 3: Middle Scots Poetry and the Reception of English Writing
Organiser: Michael Sharp, Binghamton University
Chair: Nicola Royan, University of Nottingham
- "The Origins and Significance of the Term 'Scottish Chaucerians,'" Priscilla Bawcutt, University of Liverpool
- "The Reception of John Gower's *Confessio Amantis* in Late Medieval and Early Modern
- Scotland," Joanna Martin, Lincoln College, Oxford
- "'My maisteris dere': The Acknowledgment of Authority in *The Kingis Quair*," Alessandra Petrina, Università degli Studi di Padova
- "The Transmission of Womanhood: Chaucer, Gower, and Henryson," Tara N. Williams, Rutgers University

PR 4: Chaucer and Folktale
Organiser and Chair: Richard Firth Green, The Ohio State University
- "The Franklin's Fairy Tale," Marianne Børch, University of Southern Denmark
- "Animal Captor Persuaded to Talk," Susan Crane, Columbia University
- "The Living Dead in Chaucer's Folk Legends: The Hag in the 'Wife of Bath's Tale,'"" Kathryn McKinley, Florida International University
- "Touching St Margaret's Foot," Andrew Taylor, University of Ottawa

PR 5: Generation Conflict in Chaucer and His Contemporaries
Organisers and co-Chairs: Christa Jansohn, Centre for British Studies, Bamberg, and Dieter Mehl, University of Bonn
- "Revel and Youth in the 'Cook's Tale' and the 'Tale of Gamelyn,'" Donna Crawford, Virginia State University
- "Age, Consciousness, and Despair: Saint Paul's 'Vetus Homo' in the *Canterbury Tales*," Shearle Furnish, West Texas A&M University
- "The Consolation of Old Age: 'Deeth is an ende of every worldly sore,'" Velma Bourgeois Richmond, Holy Names College
- "On 'Ressoning betuix Aige and Yowth' in Robert Henryson's Poetry," Anna Torti, University of Perugia

15.30   Tea / Coffee

16.00–17.30   Concurrent session (B): papers (90 minutes)

PR 6: Writing History, North and South
Organiser and Chair: Tom Goodman, University of Miami
- "Chaucer and the Serious Game of Battle," Valerie Allen, John Jay College of Criminal Justice, CUNY
- "Imagining England: Laurence Minot and Nationalism," David Matthews, University of Newcastle, Australia
- "The Historiography of the Absent Sovereign: Or, What Happens When the King Gets Captured?" Nicola Royan, University of Nottingham

PR 7: Chaucer the Clerk
Organiser and Chair: Neil Cartlidge, University College Dublin
- "Narrative Authority in the 'Clerk's Tale,'" Laura Ashe, Gonville and Caius College, Cambridge

- "The Relationship between the Clerk and Nun's Priest," Carol F. Heffernan, Rutgers University
- "Chaucer and the 'Consolatio Pandari': Ennodius, Maximian, Boethius," Allan Mitchell, University of Kent at Canterbury
- "Chaucer's 'eyryssh bestes,'" Daniel J. Ransom, University of Oklahoma

PR 8: *Troilus and Criseyde*: Poem of Empire, Nation or Region?
Organiser, NCS Programme Committee
Chair: Lawrence Besserman, Hebrew University, Jerusalem
- "One Flew over the Trojan Wall," Setsuko Haruta, Shirayuri College, Tokyo
- "New Troy and the Greek Camp," John Hines, Cardiff University
- "And ay the peple cryde, 'Here cometh oure joye'"; Violence, Nation, and Desire in *Troilus*," John Plummer, Vanderbilt University
- "On Holding Peoples Joined: Nationalism and Postmedievalism in the *Troilus*," Carolynn Van Dyke, Lafayette College

PR 9: Chaucer's Language and the *Middle English Compendium*
Organiser and Chair: Simon Horobin, University of Glasgow
- "Chaucer and the Auchinleck Manuscript," Christopher Cannon, Pembroke College, Cambridge
- "*The Middle English Dictionary* and the Reader of Chaucer: A Cognitive View," Louise Sylvester, University of Manchester
- "Macaronic Writing and Borrowing," Judith Tschann, University of Redlands
Response: Frances McSparran, Editor, *Middle English Compendium*, University of Michigan

PR 10: English Chaucer / British Chaucer
Organiser and Chair: Sylvia Tomasch, Hunter College, New York
- "English Chaucer, British Chaucer, Southern Chaucer: Locating the Father of English Poesy in His Regional Context," Robert Barrett, University of Illinois at Urbana-Champaign
- "On Petrarch's Misplaced Skull," Patricia Clare Ingham, Indiana University
- "Englyssh Gaufride, British Chaucer?" Simon Meecham-Jones, University of Cambridge.

18.00 **Civic Reception, City Chambers**

SATURDAY 17TH JULY

9.30–11.00   Concurrent session (C): papers

PR 11: Chaucerian Topography
Organisers, Alfred Hiatt, University of Leeds, and Scott D. Westrem, City University of New York.
Chair: Alfred Hiatt.
- "Saracens, Surrye, and the Tartars of Sarray and Sicily," Henry Ansgar Kelly, University of California at Los Angeles
- "Just Looking: Ironic Reporting in *The Canterbury Tales* and *Mandeville's Travels*," George Shuffelton, Carleton College
- "Toponyms and the Construction of Difference in Late Medieval English Literature," Emily Steiner, University of Pennsylvania

PR 12: Chaucer and the Ballad
Organiser, Richard Firth Green
Chair: Derek Brewer, Emmanuel College Cambridge
- "Did Chaucer know 'Glenkindie?'" Richard Firth Green, The Ohio State University
- "Pilgrim's Progress and the Scottish Variant of The Wanton Wife of Bath," Betsy Bowden, Rutgers University, Camden
- "How Medieval Are American Ballads?" John Hirsh, Georgetown University
- "Chaucer and Outlaw Ballads," Matthew Holford, University of Durham

PR 13: Hagiography and Historiography in Chaucer
Organiser and Chair: Mark Sherman, Rhode Island School of Design
- "Chaucer's Saints and the Uses of Hagiographic Discourse," Karen D. Youmans, Oklahoma Baptist University
- "Hagiography and Historiography in Chaucer's *Legend of Good Women*," Fiona Tolhurst, Alfred University
- "Clerical Voices and the Historicizing of English Kings in Chaucer's S. Cecilia," Donna Alfano Bussell, Columbia University
- "Chaucerian Legends: History, Exemplarity, and England in Fifteenth-Century Saints' Lives," Catherine Sanok, University of Michigan

PR 14: Chaucer and East Anglia

Organiser: Nancy Bradley Warren, Florida State University
Chair: Beverly Boyd, University of Kansas

- "Chaucer's Women Pilgrims and Margery Kempe," Denise Baker, University of North Carolina, Greensboro
- "Bringing Canterbury to East Anglia: Emulation and Insubordination in Lydgate's *Siege of Thebes*," Disa Gambera, University of Utah
- "John Capgrave and the 'East-Anglicization' of Chaucer's Lombardy," Joseph Grossi, Canisius College
- "Monks' Tales: Bury and Canterbury in an Account of Chaucerian Pilgrimage," Stella Singer, University of Pennsylvania

PR 20: Chaucerian Theologies

Organiser, Alastair Minnis, The Ohio State University
Chair: Alcuin Blamires, Goldsmiths' University of London

- "Chaucer's Parson and the Theology of Penance," Karen Winstead, The Ohio State University
- "The Ends of Love: Criseyde, Chaucer, and Belief," Jamie C. Fumo, Mount Holyoke College

Response: Alastair Minnis

11.00   **Coffee**

11.30–13.00   **PLENARY SESSION: "Medieval Scottish Literature"**

Chair: Priscilla Bawcutt, University of Liverpool

- "Letter and Spirit in the Chaucerian Humanism of James I of Scotland," Rod Lyall, University of Amsterdam
- "Henryson, Chaucer, and Troy," Sally Mapstone, St. Hilda's College Oxford

13.00   **Lunch**

14.00–16.00   **Concurrent session (D): seminar panels**

SR I: Colonial Chaucer
Organisers, Candace Barrington, Central Connecticut State University, and Sarah A. Kelen, Nebraska Wesleyan University
Chair: Sarah Kelen

- Eileen Bach, Ithaca High School, Ithaca, New York, "Teaching Chaucer in American Schools"

- Candace Barrington, Central Connecticut State University, "Chaucer in an American Seaport"
- Laurel Broughton, University of Vermont, "The Chaucer Coloring Book"
- Geoffrey Gust, Glendale Community College, Phoenix, "Worlds Apart? Chauceriam (Re)Constructions in Britain and America"
- Erik Mortenson, King and Low-Heywood Thomas School, Stamford, Connecticut, "Fragmenting Chaucer and His Tales"
- Kellie Robertson, University of Pittsburgh, "Chaucer Behind Glass"

SR II: Sex and Wishful Thinking in Chaucer's Writings
Organiser, NCS Programme Committee
Chair: Eve Salisbury, Western Michigan University
- Kristin Bovaird-Abbo, University of Kansas, "Wearing Your Heart on Your Sleeve: Gender and the Heart in Chaucer's *The Canterbury Tales*"
- Holly A. Crocker, University of Cincinnati, "Between the Men and the Boys: Local Knowledge and Clerical Masculinity in the 'Reeve's Tale'"
- Shayne Legassie, Columbia University, "'Your maistresse is not here': Politics and Sexual Deviance in *Troilus and Criseyde* and in *Il Filostrato*"
- William A. Quinn, University of Arkansas, "The Squire's Young Imagination"

SR III: Medieval Gossip
Organiser and Chair: Tom Prendergast, College of Wooster, Ohio
- Ed Craun, Washington and Lee University, "Gossip and Deviant Speech"
- Mary Erler, Fordham University, "Gossip About Ghosts"
- Tom Goodman, University of Miami, "The Name of the Game: Gossip, Rumor, Fame"
- Emma Lipton, University of Missouri–Columbia, "Gossip and the Politics of Complaint"
- Susan Phillips, Northwestern University, "Transforming Talk: The Problem with Gossip in Late Medieval England"
- Stephanie Trigg, University of Melbourne, "The Countess of Salisbury's Garter: Shame, Honour, and Gossip in Chivalric Culture"

SR IV: Early Women Scholars and the History of Reading Chaucer
Organiser and Chair: Richard Utz, University of Northern Iowa
- Tom Bestul, University of Illinois at Chicago (on Ramona Bressie)

- Margaret Connolly, University College, Cork (on Mary Haweis)
- Louise D'Arcens, University of Wollongong, Australia (on Hermiene Ulrich)
- Juliette Dor, University of Liège, Belgium (on Caroline Spurgeon)
- Joerg Fichte, University of Tübingen, Germany (on Hedwig Korsch)
- Hannah Johnson, Princeton University (on Elizabeth Cooper)
- William Snell, Keio University (on Edith Rickert)
- Sylvia Tomasch, Hunter College, CUNY (on Edith Rickert)

SR V: Re-reading and Re-thinking the *General Prologue*
Organiser and Chair: Jim Rhodes, University of Southern Connecticut
- Howell Chickering, Amherst College
- Rosalind Field, Royal Holloway University of London
- Alan Gaylord, Dartmouth College
- Anne Middleton, University of California, Berkeley
- Lee Patterson, Yale University
- R. N. Swanson, Birmingham University

16.00   **Tea / Coffee**

16.30–18.00   **Special Session (collaborative and other work)**

SS 'C' The Digitisation of Manuscripts
Organiser and Chair: Paul R. Thomas, Brigham Young University
- "Digitisation of Caxton's Chaucer and the Winchester MS: Updates of the HUMI Project," Toshi Takamiya, Keio University
- "The Cotton Nero A.x. Project: A Progress Report," Murray McGillivray and Kenna Olsen, University of Calgary
- "Reading Damaged Manuscripts Using Multi-Spectral Imaging Technology," Steve Booras, Brigham Young University
- "Multi-Spectral Imaging of Chaucer: The Wet-Damaged Folios of BL MS Sloane 1686," Paul R. Thomas

Special Session, SS 'D':"The Hengwrt/Ellemere Scribe"
Organiser: The New Chaucer Society Programme Committee on behalf of the project team Linne Mooney, University of Maine; Simon Horobin, University of Glasgow; and Jane Roberts, King's College London
Chair: Derek Pearsall, Harvard University and University of York
- "New Evidence on the Hengwrt/Ellemere Scribe and the City," Linne Mooney, University of Maine

18.30   **GCMRS Reception in Cloisters**

19.00   **Conference Dinner in Bute Hall**

20.30   **Ceilidh, Bute Hall**

SUNDAY 18TH JULY

9.30–11.30   Concurrent session (E): seminar panels

SR VI: Empires Out of Time
Organisers: Kellie Robertson, University of Pittsburgh, and Andrew Cole, University of Georgia, Athens
Chair: Paul Strohm, Columbia University
- Kathleen Davis, Princeton University, "The Constitution of the 'Middle Ages' and Reframings of 'Empire'"
- John Ganim, University of California, Riverside, "Orientalizing the Middle Ages"
- Elliot Kendall, University College London, "Gower's Arion, Regionalism, and the Disruption of *Translatio imperii*"
- Ruth Nissé, University of Nebraska, "Empire and the End of History"
- Kellie Robertson, University of Pittsburgh, "Imperialism, a Medieval Cargo Cult?"

SR VII: Spaces and Boundaries in Chaucer's Writings
Organiser: NCS Programme Committee
Chair, Corinne Saunders, University of Durham
- María Bullón-Fernández, Seattle University, "Breaking Boundaries in Chaucer's 'Miller's Tale'"
- Seeta Chaganti, University of California, Davis, "The Margin of the Sea: A Medieval Poetics of Landscape in the 'Franklin's Tale'"
- Yoshiko Kobayashi, University of Tokyo, "Female Subjectivity and Space in the Criseyde Story"
- Andrew James Johnston, Freie Universität, Berlin, "Non-existing Topographies in Chaucer's *House of Fame*"
- Tom Liszka, The Pennsylvania State University, "Oswald the Reeve

and St. Oswald: A Perverse Superimposition of Space, Character, and Genre"
- Karen Smyth, Queen's University Belfast, "The Changing Space of Troilus's Sphere"

SR VIII: Chaucerian Piety: The Case of *The Clerk's Tale*
Organisers and Co-Chairs; Lynn Staley, Colgate University, and Larry Scanlon, Rutgers University
- Glenn Burger, Queen's College, CUNY
- Mark Miller, University of Chicago
- Charlotte Morse, Virginia Commonwealth University
- Nicole Nolan, East Carolina University
- Christine Rose, Portland State University

SR IX: Chaucer in the Classroom
Organiser, Gail Ashton, University of Manchester
Chair: Louise Sylvester, University of Manchester
- Gail Ashton, University of Manchester, "Group Project for the *Canterbury Tales*"
- Deanna Evans, Bemidji State University, Minnesota, "Using Sources and Analogues"
- Moira Fitzgibbons, Marist College, "Cross-voiced Assignments"
- Peggy Knapp, Carnegie Mellon University, "Addressing Language and the Pilgrims in the *Canterbury Tales*"
- Steve Kruger, Queen's College and Graduate Center CUNY, "Individual / Group Assignments"
- Greg Roper, University of Dallas, "Chaucer as an Introduction to Literary Study"
- Richard Utz, University of Northern Iowa, "Textual Work in the Classroom"
- Susan Yager, Iowa State University, "Expert Teachers and Novice Learners"

SR X: The Afterlife of Origins: Chaucer and His Sources
Organisers, Arlyn Diamond, University of Massachusetts, and Nancy M. Bradbury, Smith College
Chair: Arlyn Diamond
- Peter G. Beidler, Lehigh University, "The One 'Hard' Analogue to *The Miller's Tale*: Heile van Beersele"

- Kenneth Bleeth, Connecticut College, "*The Physician's Tale* and 'Remembered Texts'"
- Nancy Mason Bradbury, Smith College, "'Soft' Sources for the *Canterbury Tales*"
- Carolyn Collette, Mount Holyoke College, "*The Canon's Yeoman's Tale* and 'Sources' Study
- Dolores W. Frese, University of Notre Dame, "Chaucerian 'Traces' of Dante's *De Vulgari Eloquentia*"
- Amy Goodwin, Randolph-Macon College, "Chaucer's *Clerk's Tale*: Sources, Influences, and Allusions"
- Betsy McCormick, University of North Carolina, Asheville, "Chaucerian 'Makying' and the Debate About Woman"

11.30   **Coffee**

12.00   **Plenary Session: Biennial Chaucer Lecture**
Chair: Winthrop Wetherbee, Cornell University
- "'I speke of folk in seculer estaat': Vernacularity and Secularity in the Age of Chaucer," Alastair Minnis, The Ohio State University

13.00   **Picnic Lunch**

14.00   **Excursions: Mackintosh Tour; Distillery and Loch Lomond; Stirling Castle and Trossachs**

MONDAY 19TH JULY

9.30–11.00   **Concurrent session (F): papers**

PR 16: Deschamps and Chaucer
Organiser and Chair: Laura Kendrick, Université de Versailles
- "Chaucer, Deschamps, and the City," Florence Bourgne, Université de Tours
- "'A droit jugier je me tien a la flour': The Flower and Leaf Cult in Chaucer and Deschamps," Joyce Coleman, University of North Dakota
- "Deschamps and England," James Laidlaw, University of Edinburgh

- "Chaucer and Deschamps: Some Examples of Differing Views of Women," Christine Scollen-Jimack, University of Glasgow

PR 17: Chaucer's Neighbours
Organiser and Chair: Aranye Fradenburg, University of California at Santa Barbara
- "Extimacy in *The Miller's Tale*," Gila Aloni, Visiting Professor, Florida International University
- "Fremde and Neighbor: On Chaucer's Encounter with *Il Filostrato*," George Edmondson, University of California at Los Angeles
- "Charity and *The Squire's Tale*," Ruth Evans, University of Stirling
- "Mary's Neighbourhood," Miri Rubin, Queen Mary's University of London

PR 18: *The Reeve's Tale*
Organiser and Chair: David Raybin, Eastern Illinois University
- "Estates Theory into Poetics: *The Reeve's Tale* and Fragment A of the *Canterbury Tales*," Wendy Allman, Baylor University
- "Chaucer's Southern Accent: Strategies of Condescension in *The Reeve's Tale*," Robert Epstein, Fairfield University
- " 'Men may dyen of ymaginacioun': Chaucer's Poetic Theory and the Quarrel Between the Miller and the Reeve," Sherron Knopp, Williams College
- "Class Warfare and *The Reeve's Tale*," Helen Phillips, University of Liverpool

PR 19: Chaucer and Diplomacy
Organiser and Chair: Michael Hanly, Washington State University
- "Chaucer, the Shipman, and the Language of Diplomacy," Willliam R. Askins, Community College of Philadelphia
- "Thomas Hoccleve: A Model of International Exchange," Helen Maree Hickey, University of Melbourne
- "Diplomacy and Pragmatic Language in Froissart's *Chronicles* and Chaucer's *Troilus and Criseyde*," Gerald Nachtwey, Loyola University of Chicago
- "Peace in Our Time? Diplomacy, 'Melibee,' and Philippe de Mézières," Marion Turner, King's College, London

PR 20: Chaucer and the Auchinleck Manuscript
Organiser and Chair: Elizabeth Scala, University of Texas, Austin
- "The Shapes of Tail-Rhyme," Jessica Brantley, Yale University
- "'Sir Thopas,' Auchinleck, and Authorship," Stephen Partridge, University of British Columbia
- "Before Chaucer," Derek Pearsall, Harvard University and University of York
- "Chaucer and the Auchinleck MS: Canterbury Fragments and Manuscript Booklets," Míceál F. Vaughan University of Washington, Seattle

11.00   Coffee

11.30–13.00   Concurrent session (G): papers (90 minutes)

PR 21: Boccaccio and Chaucer: Comparative Sociopoetics
Organiser and Chair: Bob Hanning, Columbia University
- "Dorigen's Flirtations and Chaucer's Boccaccian Description of Women's Language," Michael Calabrese, California State University, Los Angeles
- "Displacement and the Ethical Life in Chaucer and Boccaccio," Leonard Koff, Associate, UCLA Center for Medieval and Renaissance Studies
- "Trauma Management: Boccaccio's Plague and Chaucer's Rebellion," Jon Williams, Columbia University

PR 22: Chaucerian Texts and MSS: Issues and Problems of Cultural Mapping
Organiser and Chair: John Thompson, Queen's University Belfast
- "Chaucer's Texts and London Books," Alexandra Gillespie, Balliol College, University of Oxford
- "John Nuton's Books: Reading and Copying Chaucer in Fifteenth-Century Kent," Jason O'Rourke, Queen's University, Belfast
- "MSS Oxford, Bodleian Library, Lat. misc. c. 66, and Laud misc. 416, and Problems of Congruence in the Definition of Some 'Commonplace Books,'" Jean-Pascal Pouzet, Paris IV–Sorbonne and University of Limoges
Respondent: Stephen Kelly, Queen's University, Belfast

PR 23: Henryson Reconsidered

Organiser: New Chaucer Society Programme Committee
Chair: Ruth Kennedy, Royal Holloway University of London

- "The Multiple Etiologies of Robert Henryson," Sealy Gilles, Long Island University
- " 'Venus, luifis quene': Humanism and Historical Distance in Henryson's *Testament of Cresseid*," Ann Higgins, University of Massachusetts, Amherst
- "Henryson's Tragedy of Love: Creative Inversion of Romance," Jean E. Jost, Bradley University
- "The Prophetic Body of Henryson's Cresseid as Response to Chaucer's Emily," Stephen Yandell, Xavier University

PR 24: Inside Chaucer

Organiser and Chair: Kathryn Lynch, Wellesley College

- " 'Hir hertes gost withinne': Inside Criseyde," James Goldstein, Auburn University
- "The Prague Jewry and *The Prioress's Tale*: City, Body, and the Eucharistic Host," Sarah Stanbury, College of the Holy Cross
- "Inside, Outside, and In Between: *The Legend of Good Women* as Penitential Performance," Cathryn Meyer, University of Texas at Austin

PR 25: A Europe of Nations

Organiser and Chair: Ardis Butterfield, University College, London

- "One Nation Under God: Charles the Bold, Religion, and Burgundian Nationhood," Nancy Bradley Warren, Florida State University
- " 'The Foreign Europe of Medieval England," Barry Windeatt, Emmanuel College, Cambridge
- "France, Italy, England," Kevin Brownlee and David Wallace, University of Pennsylvania

13.00   Lunch

14.00–15.00   **Closing Session:** "Reflections on the Congress, and on Its Implications for Current and Future Directions of Chaucer Studies"
- Rita Copeland, University of Pennsylvania
- Henry Ansgar Kelly, University of California at Los Angeles
- Jeremy Smith, University of Glasgow
- Stephanie Trigg, University of Melbourne

INDEX

Abulafia, David 149n

Adler, Michael 130n, 131, 131n, 132n, 133n, 134, 134n, 135n, 136, 136n, 137, 137n, 138n, 139n, 140n, 141, 147, 147n

Aelfric 244

Aers, David 121n

Alegi, Nicoletta 4n

Alfred 253

Allen, Elizabeth 66n

Aloni, Gila 129n

Andreas Capellanus 40, 40n, 41n

Aquinas, Thomas 53n, 66, 224n

Archibald, Elizabeth 64n, 66, 66n, 67n

Aristotle 25, 26n, 28, 29, 32–38, 38n, 39n, 41n, 47n, 51–53, 56, 57; *Economics*, 38, 39, 41n, 51n; *Ethics*, 38n, 39n, 52, 53n, 56; *Politics*, 25, 27n, 28, 29, 29n, 34, 35n, 37n, 41n, 56

Armitage-Smith, Sydney 151n

Armstrong, C. Cyril 38n

Armstrong, Dorsey *Gender and the Chivalric Community in Malory's "Mort d'Arthur"* 289–91

Arnold, Morris S. 5n

Arundel, Thomas 31n, 253; *Constitutions*, 31n

Aston, Margaret 159n, 173n

Atchley, Clinton 213n, 217n, 218, 218n, 219, 219n, 221, 221n

Augustine 57, 66, 66n, 201–03, 202n

Babington, Churchill 219n

Badel, P.-Y. 45n

Baird, Joseph L. 45n

Baker, Derek 27n

Baldwin, John W. 26, 26n

Baldwin, Spurgeon 33n, 36n, 37n, 53n

Ball, R.M. 234n

Banks, Mary MacLeod 218n

Barnum, Priscilla Heath 215n

Barrette, Paul 33n, 36n, 37n, 53n

Barrington, Candace, ed., *The Letter of the Law: Legal Practice and Literary Production in Medieval England* 365–69

Barron, Caroline M. 165n, 166n

Bartholomaeus Anglicus 28, 182

Beardwood, Alice 159n

Becket, Thomas 194, 205, 205n, 209n, 210

Beckett, Samuel 261; *Waiting for Godot*, 261

Bede 253

Bennett, Judith 102n

Bennett, Michael 32, 32n

Benson, C. David *Public "Piers Plowman":Modern Scholarship and Late Medieval English Culture* 291–94

Benson, Larry D. 7n, 71n, 97n, 129n ; *Riverside Chaucer*, 7n, 71n, 98n, 153n

Beowulf 246, 254

Bergen, Henry 63n

Berkeley, Elizabeth 32

Berkeley, Sir Thomas 30, 32, 175, 181

Bersuire, Pierre 36

Besserman, Lawrence 129n, 151n

Bestul, Thomas 9n, 20n

Bettridge,William E. 104n

Bible *Exodus* 254; *Genesis* 56, 254; *Isaiah* 223

Biller, Peter 26, 26n, 219n

Blake, Norman 95n

Blamires, Alcuin 123n

Block, Edward A. 73n

Blum, Virginia L. 258n

Boccaccio, Giovanni 3, 6, 9, 10, 12, 13, 21, 54, 59–62, 60n, 61n, 79, 84, 89, 90n, 104, 104n, 106, 108, 108n, 109, 253; *De casibus virorum illusratium* 6, 9, 59, 60, 60n; *Decameron* 12, 104, 104n, 108, 108n; *Il Filostrato* 12; *Teseida* 106

Boethius 13, 29, 32n, 44–46, 48, 50n, 51, 54n, 59, 88, 89; *De consolatione philosophia* 29, 32, 32n, 44–46, 48–51, 54n

Raymo, Robert 213n
Reames, Sherry L. 202n
Reddan, M. 130–132, 130n, 131n, 132n, 135n
Rees-Jones, Sarah, ed., *Learning and Literacy in Medieval England and Abroad* 346–50
Remley, Paul G. 30n, 35n, 36n, 42n, 52n, 56n
Reynolds, Susan 205n
Ricci, P.G. 6n
Richardson, H.G. 166n, 167n
Richmond, Colin 159n
Rivière, J. 29n
Robert, Ulysse 160n
Robertson, D.W. 49, 49n
Rosenthal, Joel T. *Telling Tales: Sources and Narration in Late Medieval England* 353–56
Roth, Cecil 143n, 144n, 146, 146n
Rowling, J.K. 279
Roy, Bruno 37n, 41n, 44n
Rubinstein, W.D., 156, 157n
Russell, P.E. 143n, 150n, 151n
Rymer, Thomas 136n, 143n, 144n, 159n

Salesbury, Paul 156n
Sanok, Catherine 202n
Sargent, Michael 219n
Saul, Nigel 156n
Sayle, Charles 179n
Scala, Elizabeth 61n
Scanlon, Larry 64n, 88, 88n, 93n, 229n
Scase, Wendy 96n, 97n, 181n
Scattergood, V.J. 32n
Schildgen, Brenda Deen 129n
Schlauch, Maragret 153n
Schoeck, R.J. 49n
Serrano Reyes, Jesús L., trans., *Geoffrey Chaucer: Cuentos de Canterbury* 350–53
Severs, J. Burke 103n. 104n, 123n, 176n
Shakespeare, William 253; *King Lear*, 5
Shanley, J.L. 49n
Sharon-Zisser, Shirley 129n
Sharpe, Richard R. 165n, 166n
Shaw, Judith 68n

Shawver, Gary W. 177n
Sherborne, J.W. 32n
Sherman, C.R. 28n, 38n
Shoaf, R.A. 88n
Showerman, Grant 63n
Shumway, David R. 251n
Simonsohn, Shlomo 147n
Simpson, James 59n, 77n, 78, 78n, 91n, 172n, 193n, 199n, 221n, 227n
Skandera, Laura 18n
Skinner, Patricia 130n
Smeltz, John W. 217n, 224n
Smith, D. Vance *Arts of Possession: The Middle English Household Imaginary* 356–58
Smith, Lucy Toulmin 152n, 153n, 155, 155n
Sokal, Alan 271n
Somerset, Fiona 182, 182n, 192n, 195n, 223n, 227n, 237n; ed., *Lollards and Their Influence in Late Medieval England* 358–62
Spearing, A.C. 63n
Spector, Stephen 95n
Speed, Diane 152n, 202n
Spencer, H. Leith 214, 214n, 215n, 216n, 217, 217n, 221n
Spenser, Edmund 253
Spiazzi, R.M. 53n
Sprung, Andrew 94n, 115, 115n
Stacey, Robert 132n, 138, 157n
Staley, Lynn 120n, 121n
Stein, Robert M. 251n
Steiner, Emily *Documentary Culture and the Making of Medieval English Literature* 362–64; ed., *The Letter of the Law: Legal Practice and Literary Production in Medieval England* 365–68
Stewart, H.F. 46n
Stimpson, Catharine 275n
Stokes, H.P. 140
Stoudt, D.L. 215n
Stover, Edna 217n
Stow, John 166n
Strassburg, Gottfried von 50
Strohm, Paul 27n, 59n, 60n, 73n, 91n
Stroud, Theodore 49n
Summit, Jennifer 277n, 283